LAWYER'S DESK BOOK

TENTH EDITION

by Dana Shilling

1999
SUPPLEMENT

PRENTICE HALL
Paramus, New Jersey 07652

Library of Congress Cataloging-in-Publication Data

Lawyer's desk book / by Dana Shilling. — 10th ed., 1999 Supplement
    p.   cm.
    Includes bibliographical references and index.
    ISBN 0-13-266248-5
    ISBN 0-13-880270-X
    1. Law—United States.   2. Practice of Law—United States.
I. Shilling, Dana.
KF386.L39   1999
349.73—dc20   95-13736
[347.3]   CIP

This publication is designed to provide accurate and authoritative information in
regard to the subject matter covered. It is sold with the understanding that the
publisher is not engaged in rendering legal, accounting, or other professional service.
If legal advice or other expert assistance is required, the services of a competent
professional person should be sought.

—From a Declaration of Principles jointly adopted by a Committee of the American
Bar Association and a Committee of Publishers and Associations.

Printed in the United States of America

10 9 8 7 6 5 4 3 2 1

ISBN 0-13-918350-7

ATTENTION: CORPORATIONS AND SCHOOLS

Prentice Hall books are available at quantity discounts with bulk purchase for educational,
business, or sales promotional use. For information, please write to: Prentice Hall Career &
Personal Development Special Sales, 240 Frisch Court, Paramus, NJ 07652. Please supply:
title of book, ISBN number, quantity, how the book will be used, date needed.

PRENTICE HALL
Career & Personal Development
Paramus, New Jersey 07652
A Simon & Schuster Company

On the World Wide Web at http://www.phdirect.com

Prentice-Hall International (UK) Limited, *London*
Prentice-Hall of Australia Pty. Limited, *Sydney*
Prentice-Hall Canada, Inc., *Toronto*
Prentice-Hall Hispanoamericana, S.A., *Mexico*
Prentice-Hall of India Private Limited, *New Delhi*
Prentice-Hall of Japan, Inc., *Tokyo*
Simon & Schuster Asia Pte. Ltd., *Singapore*
Editora Prentice-Hall do Brasil, Ltda., *Rio de Janeiro*

INTRODUCTION

This supplement covers the legal events of 1997. Probably the most dramatic of these events is the passage of the Tax Reform Act of 1997, which completely changes the taxation of capital gains (both on securities and home sales), phases in a much larger unified credit to shelter gifts and estates from taxation, and makes other changes.

1997 was also, although not "the" year of the computer, certainly "a" year of the computer as Internet usage became a more common tool in law firms, and the World Wide Web dominated all other parts of the Internet. Many cases had to be decided on the status of trademarks on the Web, and there is an emerging, very significant issue of when and how maintenance of a Web site provides jurisdiction. The Supreme Court struck down the major portions of the Communications Decency Act, those dealing with allegedly obscene communications on-line.

In 1997, cases involving arbitration-securities arbitration, and arbitration of employment discrimination claims (especially in situations where employers wanted to mandate arbitration, but employees wanted to litigate)—were numerous and prominent.

This will be the last Supplement for the Tenth Edition of the Lawyer's Desk Book. Look for a completely revised and restructured Eleventh Edition just after the turn of the century (...and just when "Year 2000" computer problems take a major role in the court system....)

Dana Shilling

HOW TO USE THIS SUPPLEMENT

This Supplement provides additional information on important developments that have occurred since publication of the Tenth Edition.

The section titles and paragraph numbers used in the Tenth Edition are retained in the Supplement to facilitate its use. To illustrate: the subject Arbitration is Paragraph 401 in the Tenth Edition; it is updated concerning Labor Arbitration by the inclusion of Paragraph 401.2 in this Supplement. In addition, part of this Supplement is a cumulative index, including entries for the Tenth Edition as well as the Supplement entries. The latter entries are preceded by the prefix "**S**." The cumulative index should be used in place of the index in the Tenth Edition. To look up a topic, the reader need only check the cumulative index to find the major topic and any recent additions to it.

TABLE OF CONTENTS

ANTITRUST PROBLEMS: PRICES AND UNFAIR COMPETITION

[¶201] Antitrust consent decrees can be modified or terminated—provided that the defendant can show that the basic purposes of the decree (e.g., safeguarding competition within the market; preventing market power) have been achieved.[1]

The statute of limitations in an antitrust case can be tolled for fraudulent concealment. The defendant must commit affirmative acts of concealment, but they need not be identifiable separate and apart from the underlying antitrust conspiracy.[2]

In 1995, the Eleventh Circuit ruled that international antitrust disputes are arbitrable, and that domestic ones are not; however, when it reconsidered the same case in 1996, the Eleventh Circuit joined four other Circuits in upholding an agreement to arbitrate a domestic antitrust dispute, on the grounds that the distinction between domestic and international arbitration is diminishing.[3] The Tenth Circuit takes the view that antitrust claims are arbitrable provided that they have a reasonable factual connection with a contract containing an arbitration clause. Thus, antitrust claims of a conspiracy to divide the U.S. beer market were properly litigated rather than arbitrated, since the claims are not covered by an arbitration clause in the brewery licensing agreement predating the allegedly anticompetitive deal between the defendant and a third brewer.[4]

An obvious trend in the health care system is increasing care management, and increasing consolidation of ownership of health care facilities. The Federal Trade Commission and the Department of Justice have issued several statements, the most recent being the "Statements of Antitrust Enforcement Policy in Health Care," of August 28, 1996.[5] The August 1996 statement authorizes more types of provider networks, and views sharing of financial and other risks within a network as a positive sign of efficiency that can justify integration of facilities. Indeed, multiprovider networks that include competing providers can have a joint pricing schedule, as long as they share substantial financial risks (e.g., through capitation plans or a global fee schedule).

Institutional investors can be included as class members and even class representatives in a class action charging leading NASDAQ market makers with conspiring to increase their own earnings by refusing to quote stock prices in "odd eighths" (i.e., insisting on raising the price quote to 24 1/2 instead of 24 3/8). The Southern District of New York found the trading patterns of institutional investors to be similar enough to those of individual investors to justify including them in the class. Because institutional investors trade much more actively, they have an even greater incentive to pursue the class claims.[6]

Two successive Congresses have granted relief to charities from antitrust liability, if they set up pooled income funds, to agree to use uniform rates, or to offer charitable remainder trusts or charitable gift annuities. The relevant legislation is P.L. 104-62, the Philanthropy Protection Act of 1995, P.L. 104-63, the Charitable Gift Annuity Antitrust Relief Act of 1995, and P.L. 105-26, the Charitable Donor Antitrust Immunity Act of 1997.

[¶201.1]　Antitrust Aspects of Mergers

On April 8, 1997, the Department of Justice and the FTC announced a revision of the 1992 Horizontal Merger guidelines.[7] The revised guidelines focus on analysis of efficiencies. The new guidelines probably won't change the outcome of merger analysis very often; only a few close cases will be affected. Under the revised guidelines, a merger might be deemed anticompetitive when it reduces competition in the relevant market, even if the efficiencies of the combined firm make it possible to offer lower prices, better service, higher quality, or new products. The point of the guidelines is to determine which efficiencies derive from the proposed merger, and whether equal efficiencies could be achieved with less damage to competition.

The buyer of a manufacturing company is not liable for the seller's retail price maintenance activities. However, summary judgment is unavailable, and the buyer does have to defend against a terminated dealer's antitrust allegations relating to perpetuation of the price maintenance agreement and the dealer's termination for failure to maintain the prices.[8] Although a "substantial continuity" test would probably be applied in a labor-law case, this court refused to apply it in the antitrust context. As a result, the successor corporation did not have liability based on the predecessor's price maintenance activities.

[¶202]　MONOPOLIZATION

Early in 1995, the District Court for the District of Columbia rejected a proposed consent decree involving the Department of Justice's allegation that Microsoft had monopolized the market for computer operating systems. The applicable statute, the Tunney Act (15 U.S.C. §16[e]), requires that the court certify that a proposed decree is in the public interest. The District Court felt unable to do so because the government did not provide enough information for the court to assess the public interest impact. Furthermore, the decree was characterized as too narrow in scope and lacking adequate compliance mechanisms.[9]

When the case next appeared in court mid-year, the D.C. Circuit held that the District Court's rejection was improper. The court considered the possibility of anticompetitive use of "vaporware" (announcement of fictitious products in an attempt to dissuade purchasers from buying competitive products that already existed or that might be developed), even though the Department of Justice did not make this allegation. The D.C. Circuit interprets that the court's job under the Tunney Act is to determine whether the proposed consent decree is in the public interest—not to raise new issues or possible areas of contention.[10]

The case against Microsoft was back in late 1997, this time raising the question of whether Microsoft violated its consent decree with the Department of Justice by requiring PC manufacturers to license Microsoft's Web browser, Internet Explorer (IE). The crux of the matter is that the consent decree permits Microsoft to "integrate" software products, although the company is forbidden to condition a licensing agreement for an operating system (e.g., Windows '95 or '98) on licensing of another product.

In December, the D.D.C. ordered a six-month discovery period, and appointed a special master to review the Sherman Act implications of tying licensing of Windows '95 to the computer manufacturer's agreement to install IE. In October, the Department of Justice went to the D.D.C. to request that Microsoft be fined $1 million per day as a contempt fine for violation of the consent decree [11]

The Sixth Circuit will not permit a supplier to sue for illegal tying on the basis of a franchisor's requirement that franchisees must buy all supplies from approved suppliers, on the grounds that would-be suppliers assert only an economic injury, not an antitrust injury.[12]

A similar Third Circuit case upholds a franchise agreement that requires the franchisee to purchase all supplies from the franchisor itself. In this analysis, the obligation derives from the contract, and not the franchisor's power in the market for commodity supplies. Therefore, there is no Sherman Act violation.[13]

The First Circuit found that Sherman Act §1 forbids conduct outside the United States, if it is intended to have substantial effects within the United States. Thus, allegations that a Japanese company held meetings in Japan to fix the price of fax paper in the United States should not have been dismissed by the District Court.[14]

[¶203]   THE RELEVANT MARKET

In a recent Seventh Circuit case,[15] one HMO charged another with signing up so many doctors that the plaintiff HMO could not enlist enough doctors to furnish a competing service. However, the court denied that HMOs are a separate market where competition can be analyzed. Instead, all HMOs compete with other methods of delivering health care services (especially Preferred Provider Organizations). Furthermore, doctors have high mobility between HMOs, or between HMOs and the fee-for-service sector.

[¶206]   HORIZONTAL RESTRAINTS

The partners of a law firm in the course of dissolution signed an agreement not to advertise in one another's territories. Because the lawyers were personal injury attorneys heavily dependent on advertising, the Seventh Circuit treated the action as a horizontal allocation of markets among competitors and a *per se* violation of Sherman Act §1.[16] However, the plaintiffs in the action were co-signatories who were equally responsible for the restraint and had no antitrust injury, so Clayton Act treble damages were not available to them.

Unless a horizontal conspiracy can be proved, there is no Sherman Act §1 violation in a newspaper's exclusive contracts with news services or features syndicates. According to the Seventh Circuit,[17] the arrangement is an exclusive distributorship (which does not restrict entry into the market) and not an exclusive dealing contract that rules out sales to competitors.

[¶210]   REFUSALS TO DEAL

A company in the business of issuing "junk e-mail" launched several attacks against America Online in 1996. As discussed at ¶1305, all were unsuccessful. The Eastern District of Pennsylvania refused to grant a temporary restraining order in a Sherman Act §2 case, finding it extremely unlikely that the claim could succeed. The e-mailer said that America Online refused to deal in an essential facility (reaching AOL subscribers through Internet e-mail). However, the Eastern District said[18] that AOL could properly refuse to deal with any advertiser who breaks its rules. Furthermore, no essential facility was involved, because there were other potential methods of communicating with the subscribers.

[¶211]   CONSCIOUS PARALLELISM

In mid-1996, the Supreme Court decided an antitrust case that is not likely to have wide repercussions—but then, there are sports fans on the High Court as well as everywhere else. The ruling[19] was that, after a bargaining impasse, employers can group together to implement their last good-faith wage offer. Specifically, National Football League substitute players on "developmental squads" could legitimately be paid a uniform $1,000 per week without violating Sherman Act §1; there was no necessity to give each squad member the chance to negotiate individual compensation.

[¶214]   VERTICAL RESTRAINT AGREEMENTS BETWEEN SELLER AND BUYER

According to the Seventh Circuit,[20] there is a *per se* Sherman Act §1 violation when a gasoline wholesaler/lessor requires its retailers to rebate all the profits the retailers earn by charging more than the wholesaler's suggested retail price. In this analysis, fixing a maximum price is just as illegal as fixing a minimum price. In 1997, however, the Supreme Court ruled[21] that the rule of reason, and not a *per se* illegality analysis, is appropriate to vertical fixing of maximum retail prices, because there is too little injury to consumers or competition to apply *per se* analysis. The Supreme Court directed trial courts to look for anticompetitive conduct and effect.

A distributor that went out of business sued Sylvania, alleging business injury because it couldn't get the discounts offered to larger companies. The Ninth Circuit decided in April, 1997[22] that in a secondary-line Robinson Patman Act price discrimination case, a showing of injury to an individual company creates an inference of competitive injury. The defendant cannot overcome this inference by showing the health of competition within the relevant market.

According to the Seventh Circuit, an umbrella business liability insurance policy that covers "discrimination" claims is broad enough to cover antitrust claims of price discrimination; the policy language is not narrowly tailored to cover only employment discrimination claims.[23]

[¶216]   PATENTS AND THE ANTITRUST LAWS

An antitrust claim that a patent was obtained fraudulently and used to destroy competition is not a compulsory counterclaim in an infringement suit involving that patent.[24]

The Federal Circuit ruled that antitrust liability cannot be asserted on the basis that a patent applicant failed to cite a known prior art reference, with the result that the assignee filed an infringement suit. The contrary result would, as the court pointed out, transform most patent disputes into antitrust cases.[25]

— ENDNOTES —

1. *U.S. v. Eastman Kodak,* 63 F.3d 95 (2nd Cir. 8/4/95).
2. *Supermarket of Marlinton, Inc. v. Meadow Gold Dairies Inc.,* 71 F.3d 119 (4th Cir. 12/1/95).
3. *Kotam Electronics Inc. v. JBL Consumer Products Inc.,* 59 F.3d 1155 (11th Cir. 7/28/95) and 93 F.3d 724 (11th Cir. 8/19/96). For arbitrability of international matters, see *Mitsubishi Motors Corp. v. Soler Chrysler-Plymouth,* 473 U.S. 614 (1985).
4. *Coors Brewing Co. v. Molson Breweries,* 51 F.3d 1511 (10th Cir. 3/30/95), on remand, 889 F.Supp. 1394.
5. See 65 LW 2157.
6. *In re NASDAQ Market-Makers Antitrust Litigation,* 65 LW 2697 (S.D.N.Y. 4/14/97).
7. See 65 LW 2678.
8. *Baker's Carpet Gallery Inc. v. Mohawk Industries Inc.,* 942 F.Supp. 1464 (N.D. Ga. 9/23/96).
9. *U.S. v. Microsoft Corp.,* 159 F.R.D. 318 (D.D.C. 2/14/95).
10. *U.S. v. Microsoft Corp.,* 56 F.3d 1448 (D.C. Cir. 6/16/95).
11. *DOJ v. Microsoft,* 66 LW 2246, petition filed, (D.D.C. 10/20/97).
12. *Valley Products Co., Inc. v. Landmark,* 66 LW 1276 (6th Cir. 10/22/97).
13. *Queen City Pizza Inc. v. Domino's Pizza Inc.,* 66 LW 1163 (3rd Cir. 8/27/97).
14. *U.S. v. Nippon Paper Industries Co.,* 65 LW 2617 (1st Cir. 3/17/97).
15. *Blue Cross and Blue Shield of Wisconsin v. Marshfield Clinic,* 63 F.3d 1406 (7th Cir. 9/18/95).
16. *Blackburn v. Sweeney,* 53 F.3d 825 (7th Cir. 5/3/95).

17. *Paddock Publications Inc. v. Chicago Tribune Co.,* 103 F.3d 42 (7th Cir. 12/16/96).

18. *Cyber Promotions Inc. v. America Online,* 948 F. Supp. 436 (E.D. Pa. 11/26/96).

19. *Brown v. Pro Football Inc.,* #95-388, 116 S.Ct. 2116 (6/20/96).

20. *Khan v. State Oil Co.,* 93 F.3d 1358 (7th Cir. 8/29/96).

21. *State Oil Co. v. Khan,* #96-871, 66 LW 4001 (Sup.Ct. 11/4/97).

22. *Chroma Lighting v. GTE Products Corp.,* 111 F.3d 653 (9th Cir. 4/10/97); the Third Circuit agrees with this position, but the D.D.C. disagrees.

23. *Federal Insurance Co. v. Stroh Brewing,* 66 LW 1184 (7th Cir. 9/19/97).

24. *Hydranautics v. FilmTec Corp.,* 70 F.3d 533 (9th Cir. 11/15/95).

25. *Nobelpharma AB v. Implant Innovations Inc.,* 66 LW 1384 (Fed.Cir. 11/18/97).

— FOR FURTHER REFERENCE —

Atkins, Raymond A., "An Economic Model of Tying: Obtaining a First-Mover Advantage," 5 *George Mason L.Rev.* 525 (Spring '97).

Baker, Jonathan B., "Product Differentiation Through Space and Time: Some Antitrust Policy Issues," 42 *Antitrust Bulletin* 177 (Spring '97).

Chin, Andrew, "Antitrust by Chance: A Unified Theory of Horizontal Merger Doctrine," 106 *Yale L.J.* 1165 (January '97).

Conrad, Keith, "Media Mergers: First Step in a New Shift of Antitrust Analysis," 49 *Federal Communications Law J.* 675 (April '97).

Floyd, Douglas C., "Antitrust Victims Without Antitrust Remedies: The Narrowing of Standing in Private Antitrust Actions," 82 *Minnesota L.Rev.* 1 (November '97).

Klein, Joel I., "Cross-Licenses, Patent and Copyright Pools and the U.S. Antitrust Laws," *Copyright World* (no volume number) 44 (September '97).

Kobak, James B. Jr., "Running the Gauntlet: Antitrust and Intellectual Property Pitfalls on the Two Sides of the Atlantic," 64 *Antitrust Law J.* 341 (Winter '96).

McFadden, Douglas B., "Antitrust and Communications: Changes After the Telecommunications Act of 1996," 49 *Federal Communications L.J.* 457 (February '97).

Paredes, Troy, "Turning the Failing Firm Defense Into a Success," 13 *Yale J. on Regulation* 347 (Winter '96).

Piraino, Thomas A. Jr., "A Proposed Antitrust Analysis of Telecommunications Joint Ventures," 1997 *Wisconsin L.Rev.* 639 (July–August '97).

Reynolds, Steven P., "Guide From the Trenches: Using Training as a Tool for Antitrust Compliance," 13 *Corporate Counsel's Quarterly* 124 (October '97).

Yancey, Jay P., "Is the Quick Look Too Quick? Potential Problems with the Quick Look Analysis of Antitrust Litigation," 44 *U. of Kansas L. Rev.* 671 (May '96).

APPEALS

[¶302] It is interesting to note that in both 1995 and 1996, the Supreme Court devoted a significant proportion of its very small caseload to cases dealing with the appeals process (in addition to cases dealing with habeas and other criminal issues, especially death-penalty appeals).

At the end of 1996, the Supreme Court decided *M.L.B. v. S.L.J.*,[1] requiring that if a state maintains an appellate procedure for terminations of parental rights, the procedure must be made available to indigent parents whose rights have been terminated, even if they cannot afford the fees usually imposed for printing the transcript of the hearing.

A mid-year Supreme Court decision[2] upheld a New York statute that allows a state appellate court to review jury verdicts and grant new trials where verdicts deviate materially from providing reasonable compensation to the injured party. The statute was applied in a diversity case using New York law. According to the Supreme Court, the New York law does not violate the Seventh Amendment guarantee of a jury trial, provided that the federal trial judge applies the review standard. Federal appellate review of the trial judge's determination is limited to whether or not the trial judge abused his or her discretion.

[¶302.1]   Timing of Appeals

Attorney negligence may constitute "excusable neglect" under the Federal Rules of Appellate Procedure, sufficient to justify a late filing.[3]

When a motion to stay federal District Court proceedings pending arbitration is filed, then the motion is denied and the denial is appealed, the District Court is required to suspend consideration of the matters, provided that the appeal is non-frivolous.[4]

Once an administrative agency issues a final order on the merits, the time for appeal starts to run, even if attorneys' fee issues have not been resolved.[5]

Although a court-appointed bankruptcy trustee is considered an officer of the court having the power to remove cases under 28 U.S.C. §1442, he or she does not fit the definition of an "officer of the United States" under Federal Rules of Appellate Procedure 4(a). Therefore, the time to appeal a trustee's ruling is 30 days, not the 60-day period available with respect to decisions by an officer of the United States.[6]

Under the Federal Rules of Bankruptcy Procedure 8002, filing a motion to reconsider tolls the time for filing a notice of appeal. The Seventh Circuit has ruled that this is true even if the motion is filed in bad faith; if there have been improprieties, they should be addressed by sanctions rather than by altering the timing of the motion.[7]

[¶302.2] Interlocutory and Immediate Appeals

In early 1996, the Supreme Court ruled that if a claim of qualified immunity is raised in a civil rights suit, denial of the claim is a final decision and therefore is immediately appealable. If the basis for a summary judgment motion is qualified immunity, denial of that motion is a final decision that is entitled to immediate appeal under 28 U.S.C. §1291. The immediate appeal is available even if the defendant has already lost an interlocutory appeal on denial of his motion to dismiss based on the same grounds.[8]

Another Supreme Court case a few months later said that a federal court's remand order (using abstention grounds to send a case back to state court) is also immediately appealable as a final order, because it has the effect of ending the litigation.[9]

The Supreme Court returned to the question of denial of immunity in §1983 cases in mid-1997, holding that defendants in state 1983-type actions do not have a federal right to interlocutory appeal when their claim of qualified immunity is denied.[10]

The order of a federal District Court, denying protection from discovery, is a collateral order, and therefore is immediately appealable.[11]

In an antitrust case dealing with a contract for performance of dialysis at a hospital, the defendants moved for summary judgment based on state action immunity. The District Court's denial of the motion is immediately appealable under the collateral order doctrine. Even though the denial is not a final judgment, it does have the effect of determining important claims of right that are separate from the main action (i.e., whether the hospital, as a subdivision of the state, acted under a clear state policy).[12]

An automobile manufacturer's informal, non-binding Alternative Dispute Resolution mechanism, set up under the Magnuson-Moss Act and the state Lemon Law, is not "arbitration" as defined by the FAA. FAA arbitration requires an agreement to submit to the final and binding decision of a third party. Therefore, FAA §16 cannot be used to obtain an interlocutory appeal of the District Court's denial of a motion to compel arbitration.[13]

Once an attorney is no longer involved with a case for which he or she has been sanctioned, the attorney can appeal the sanctions immediately, without waiting for the case to be completed. This is true even if no monetary penalty was imposed on the attorney; the Fifth Circuit says that the value of professional reputation is sufficient to support an immediate appeal.[14]

[¶303] SCOPE OF APPELLATE REVIEW

When an appellate court reviews a trial court's determination of the reasonableness of a stop or the existence of probable cause for a search, the standard of review is *de novo*—but findings of "historical fact" are reviewed for clear error. However, the Supreme Court told appellate courts to bear in mind the local conditions as assessed by local police and judges.[15]

Another mid-1996 Supreme Court ruling stated that *de novo* appellate review is inappropriate when the issue is departures from the sentencing guidelines. In that context, the proper standard of review is abuse of discretion.[16]

The Second Circuit issued five opinions taking up 140 pages in mid-1997 to rule that, after an employment discrimination plaintiff makes out a prima facie case and the finder of facts then rules for the plaintiff based on a finding that the employer's explanation is pretextual, an appellate court can nevertheless review the pretextuality finding for clear error. The majority opinion in this case treats a finding of pretextuality as proving only that the employer is concealing something; therefore, the underlying finding of discrimination is reviewable by an appellate court.[17]

In a late-1995 Supreme Court case, a creditor sued a debtor in state court to collect rent and enforce a guaranty of performance. A successor in interest to the guarantor used 28 U.S.C. §1452(a), and the general removal statute, §1441(a), to bring the action into federal court. The holding is that if there is a timely objection to the removal procedure or to the court's subject-matter jurisdiction, and the case is remanded to a state court, that remand is not reviewable. The Court of Appeals has no jurisdiction under §1447(d) in that situation.[18]

Turning to another removal provision, 28 U.S.C. §1452(b), the District Court can remand removed claims that are not related to bankruptcy "on equitable grounds." (The remand order is not appealable.) In this context, "equitable" means "fair and reasonable" grounds, not those derived from a Chancery (equitable) cause of action.[19]

Under the Rules of Bankruptcy Procedure, every "judgment" (i.e., every appealable order") must be set out in a separate document. An order granting summary judgment is separate from the order denying a motion for reconsideration, so separate documents are required.[20]

The U.S. Trustee's decision to remove a member of the Chapter 7 trustee panel from the active roster is not appealable. According to the Sixth Circuit,[21] panel membership is not a "license" that can only be canceled by following the procedures of the Administrative Procedures Act. Merely being placed on the panel does not create a property interest in future assignments. Furthermore, the statute is so broad that a reviewing court wouldn't have any standard for reviewing the U.S. Trustee's decision to deny future assignments to a panel member.

The 1996 Anti-Terrorism and Effective Death Penalty Bill makes a final order of deportation premised on certain crimes unappealable to any court. However, the Seventh Circuit held in 1996[22] that the ban on appeals does not apply where deportability was conceded before the effective date of the statute, and if the applicant can assert at least a colorable defense to deportation.

The AEDPA also restricts repeated habeas petitions from prisoners condemned to death. Naturally, the AEDPA has been challenged on Constitutional grounds, but the Supreme Court has upheld the validity of the statute. Since the Supreme Court can still consider initial habeas petitions, it is not deprived of jurisdiction.[23]

When a District Court confirms or does not vacate an arbitration award, that order is subject to ordinary standards of review. In other words, questions of law are reviewed *de novo,* not merely to see if an abuse of discretion has occurred. Questions of fact are reviewed to see if the court's determination was clearly erroneous.[24]

If an arbitration agreement states that "errors of law are subject to appeal," the Fifth Circuit says that the appellate court is supposed to review questions of law in the arbitration award *de novo,* even though the FAA does not allow an award to be vacated unless there was fraud, partiality, corruption, or action by the arbitrators exceeding their appropriate powers.[25] (Parties to an arbitration award can voluntarily agree to accept standards for judicial review of the award that are stricter than the FAA standards.[26])

If a case is settled after an appeal was filed or certiorari applied for (and thus becomes moot), the federal appellate court is not justified in vacating the underlying judgment unless exceptional circumstances are present.[27]

A bankruptcy court's denial of a motion to disqualify counsel cannot be challenged; it is neither a collateral order nor a final order appealable under 28 U.S.C. §158(d).[28]

— ENDNOTES —

1. #95-853, 117 S.Ct. 555 (Sup.Ct. 12/16/96).

2. *Gasperini v. Center for Humanities Inc.,* #95-719, 116 S.Ct. 2211 (Sup.Ct. 6/24/96).

3. *Reynolds v. Wagner,* 55 F.3d 1426 (9th Cir. 5/26/95). See *Pioneer Investment Services Co. v. Brunswick Assoc. LP,* 113 S.Ct. 1489, 123 L.Ed.2d 74 (Sup.Ct. 1993) treating attorney negligence as excusing a late filing of an appeal under Bankruptcy Rule 9006(b)(1).

4. *Bradford-Scott Data Corp. v. Physician Computer Network Inc.,* 128 F.3d 503 (7th Cir. 10/14/97).

5. *Fluor Constructors Inc. v. Reich,* 111 F.3d 94 (11th Cir. 4/15/97).

6. *Newman v. Boehm, Pearlstein & Bright Ltd.,* 119 F.3d 477 (7th Cir. 7/2/97).

7. *Law Offices of Peter Francis Geraci v. Bryson,* 131 F.3d 601 (7th Cir. 10/28/97).

8. *Behrens v. Pelletier,* #94-1244, 116 S.Ct. 834 (Sup.Ct. 2/21/96).

9. *Quackenbush v. Allstate Insurance Co.,* #95-244, 116 S. Ct. 1712 (Sup.Ct. 6/3/96).

10. *Johnson v. Fankell,* #96-292, 117 S.Ct. 1800 (Sup.Ct. 6/9/97).

11. *Kelly v. Ford Motor Co.,* 110 F.3d 954 (3rd Cir. 4/9/97).

12. *Martin v. Memorial Hospital at Gulfport,* 86 F.3d 1391 (5th Cir. 7/10/96).

13. *Harrison v. Nissan Motor Corp.,* 111 F.3d 343 (3rd Cir. 4/15/97).

14. *Walker v. Mesquite, Texas,* 66 LW 1373 (5th Cir. 12/10/97).

15. *Ornelas v. U.S.,* #95-5257, 116 S.Ct. 1657 (Sup.Ct. 5/28/96).

16. *Koon v. U.S.,* #94-1664, -8842, 116 S.Ct. 2035 (Sup.Ct. 6/13/96).

17. *Fisher v. Vassar College,* 114 F.3d 1332 (2nd Cir. 6/5/97).

18. *Things Remembered Inc. v. Petrarca*, #94-1530, 116 S.Ct. 494 (Sup.Ct. 12/5/95).

19. *In re Cathedral of the Incarnation v. Garden City Co.*, 99 F.3d 66 (2nd Cir. 10/29/96).

20. *U.S. v. Schimmels (In re Schimmels)*, 85 F.3d 416 (9th Cir. 5/30/96).

21. *Joelson v. U.S.*, 86 F.3d 1413 (6th Cir. 6/24/96).

22. *Reyes-Hernandez v. INS*, 89 F.3d 490 (7th Cir. 7/17/96).

23. *Felker v. Turpin*, #95-8836(A-890), 116 S.Ct. 2333 (Sup.Ct. 6/28/96). Also see *Lindh v. Murphy*, #96-6298, 117 S.Ct. 2059 (Sup.Ct. 6/23/97), 28 U.S.C. §2254(d), as amended by AEDPA, re grant of habeas corpus as to claims adjudicated in state court, does not apply to cases filed before AEDPA's effective date; and *Burris v. Parke*, 95 F.3d 465 (also 7th Cir. 9/12/96), AEDPA does not apply retroactively to prisoners whose first habeas petition was filed pre-AEDPA, but review is limited to issues at the guilt phase, not the death sentence itself.

24. *First Options of Chicago Inc. v. Kaplan*, #94-560, 115 S.Ct. 1920 (Sup.Ct. 5/22/95).

25. *Gateway Technologies Inc. v. MCI Telecommunications Corp.*, 64 F.3d 993 (5th Cir. 9/27/95).

26. *LaPine Technology Corp. v. Kyocera Corp.*, 66 LW 1372 (9th Cir. 12/9/97).

27. *U.S. Bancorp Mortgage Co. v. Bonner Mall Partnership*, #93-714, 115 S.Ct. 386 (Sup.Ct. 11/8/94).

28. *Brouwer v. Ancel & Dunlap*, 46 F.3d 653 (7th Cir. 1/31/95).

— FOR FURTHER REFERENCE —

Barclay, Scott, "Posner's Economic Model and the Decision to Appeal," 19 *Justice Systems J.* 77 (Spring '97).

Boskey, Bennett and Eugene Gressman, "The 1997 Restatement and Revisions of the Supreme Court's 1995 Rules," 170 *West's Federal Rules Decisions* 30 (March '97).

Elligett, Robert T. Jr. and John M. Scheb, "Appellate Standards of Review—How Important Are They?" 70 *Florida Bar J.* 33 (February '96).

Evans, James, "Legal Sites: Appellate Law," 17 *California Lawyer* 52 (December '97).

Hanes, Connie, "The Riddle of the Early, Late Notice of Appeal," 43 *The Federal Lawyer* 34 (February '96).

Hennigan, John P., "Toward Regularizing Appealability in Bankruptcy," 12 *Bankruptcy Developments J.* 583 (Fall '96).

Sisk, Gregory, "The Balkanization of Appellate Justice: The Proliferation of Local Rules in the Federal Circuits," 68 *U. of Colorado L.Rev.* 1 (Winter '97).

Strazzella, James A., "The Relationship of Double Jeopardy to Prosecution Appeals," 73 *Notre Dame L.Rev.* 1 (November '97).

Ulrich, Paul G., "Creating Appellate Handbooks for Fun and Profit," 36 *Law Office Economics & Management* 455 (Winter '96).

Wood, Diane P., "Judicious Advice for the Occasional Appellate Lawyer," 11 *CBA Record* 16 (April '97).

ARBITRATION

[¶401] The traditional role of arbitration is an accessory of collective bargaining agreements between union and employer. However, in recent years, this traditional role has been eclipsed by two new roles: arbitration of securities claims, including the employment-related claims of brokerage employees, and arbitration of employment discrimination claims of employees in various industries. To an increasing extent, employers are seeking to substitute arbitration for litigation of claims of discrimination and sexual harassment. The courts face the challenge of deciding which of these arbitration agreements should be enforced. An emerging, related issue is the extent to which HMOs and other managed care organizations can require disaffected patients to arbitrate rather than litigate their health-related claims.

Issues also arise as to who are the proper parties. A guarantor cannot be forced to arbitrate disputes about his liability on the guarantee, unless the guarantor expressed consent to the arbitration clause contained in the underlying agreement.[1] Although several courts have ruled to the contrary, a mid-1997 decision finds that a surety that issues a performance bond lacks the right to enforce an arbitration clause in the contract between the obligee and the principal, even if the contract is incorporated by reference into the bond.[2]

Individuals who are subject to an agency shop requirement and pay representation fees to a union, but are not union members, are not parties to the CBA. Therefore, their disputes about the amount of the representation fee can be brought directly to court, without exhausting administrative remedies.[3]

[¶401.1] Securities Arbitration

The U.S. Supreme Court permits an award of punitive damages if the arbitration agreement incorporates a Self-Regulatory Organization's rules by reference, and those rules permit punitive damages. This is true even if the arbitration agreement also has a choice of law provision calling for interpretation under the laws of a state in which punitive damages can only be ordered by a court.[4]

A securities customer can demand arbitration of a claim that one firm made misrepresentations about a stock in which it was a market maker, resulting in overvaluation—even if the customer purchased the stock from a different firm.[5]

The standard customer agreement compels a doctor who purchased limited partnership interests for a pension plan to arbitrate ERISA claims relating to those securities.[6]

The statute of limitations under §15 of the NASD arbitration code is six years; it begins to run at the occurrence of the last event that would permit the claim to survive a FRCP 12(b)(6) motion. Therefore, the same claimant might have multiple claims based on multiple occurrences; some of the claims could be tenable and some time-barred.[7] It's up to the arbitrator, and not a court, to determine if a claim falls within that six-year statute of limitations.[8]

If the underlying agreement (here, one dealing with commodities trading) does not specifically provide for class arbitration, the court cannot order it, because Federal Arbitration Act §4 requires enforcement of arbitration agreements in accordance with their terms.[9] Nor can a court compel expedition unless the arbitration agreement specified expedited arbitration.[10]

Even where the underlying claims stem from the '34 Securities Exchange Act, federal courts do not have federal question jurisdiction over an action to stay arbitration.[11]

A dissatisfied claimant cannot sue NASD for appointing an arbitrator who was partial (even if the result was that the award was vacated for partiality), because NASD is entitled to "arbitral immunity" similar to judicial immunity.[12]

It constitutes unauthorized practice of law for non-lawyers to get paid to represent investors at securities arbitrations—even though the manual jointly published by the Securities Industry Association and the self-regulatory organizations allows representation by non-attorneys. According to the Florida Supreme Court, the SEC would have the power to preempt this field; but in the meantime, representation by non-attorneys is potentially harmful because non-attorneys are not regulated and are not subject to sanctions for misconduct or negligence.[13]

[¶40L.2]   Labor Arbitration

If a commercial arbitration agreement is silent on the arbitrability of an issue, arbitrability of that issue must be decided by the court system;[14] however, the Ninth Circuit ruled that this principle does not apply to arbitration clauses in a collective bargaining agreement[15] because the parties agree to let the arbitrator determine arbitrability. In a labor case, unlike a commercial case, it is known and accepted that disputes will be arbitrated—including disputes about arbitrability itself.

According to the Third Circuit, an arbitrator was justified in suspending rather than discharging a bus driver who caused a rear-end collision. The underlying contract merely permitted discharge for "proper cause," so the arbitrator could appropriately interpret this to mean that a system of progressive discipline was intended.[16]

According to the D.C. Circuit, the arbitrator's authority is only over issues raised by the parties, not the broader interests of the entire bargaining unit. After a hotel laid off all its busboys and ordered waiters to bus the tables (allegedly in violation of the collective bargaining agreement), the arbitrator ordered the hotel to reinstate the busboy jobs. The Court of Appeals held that the arbitrator should have confined the award to the position of the employees who brought the grievance.[17]

[¶40L.3]   Arbitration of Employment Discrimination Claims

Employees who wish to litigate may find that they have signed arbitration agreements in several contexts. For instance, if they are union members, they may be bound by a collective bargaining agreement that compels arbitration of grievances involving charges of discrimination. They may be securities industry employees who have signed the U-4. They may have entered into individual employment contracts containing arbitration provisions. The courts have to strike a balance. On the one hand, arbitration is favored as a comparatively speedy, inexpensive way to resolve disputes. On the other hand, employees may be compelled to surrender valuable rights even though they have no negotiating power and may be unaware of the surrender.

It is the position of the EEOC that employees should not be compelled to arbitrate federal statutory discrimination claims if they prefer to litigate them (although the EEOC is in favor of voluntary ADR efforts). A July 10, 1997 policy statement announces that the EEOC will continue to bring suits in cases where arbitration agreements appear to have been obtained by coercion. The EEOC opposes compelled arbitration because court cases can set precedents, advancing enforcement of civil rights laws; arbitration awards do not serve this function. Furthermore, the employer has much greater experience with arbitration and can overpower the employee.[18]

The EEOC got a preliminary injunction preventing an employer from requiring its employees to sign and abide by an "ADR policy" instead of suing for alleged violations of Title VII. The employer was further enjoined from forcing employees to agree to pay ADR costs, and from interfering with the EEOC charge or any ensuing Title VII action.[19] Yet, in a similar case, a pre-dispute arbitration agreement was upheld by the D.C. Circuit, as long as the agreement provided for neutral arbitrators; discovery was reasonably available; the plan provided remedies comparable to litigation remedies; and the employer agreed to pay all the fees involved in the arbitration process.[20] Also apropros of fees, a late-1997 Southern District of New York case[21] upholds enforcement of an employment agreement mandating arbitration, but strikes down a provision in that agreement that the employee must waive attorneys' fees when arbitrating a claim. That clause was deemed invalid because of the public policy of promoting the advancement of meritorious claims.

The U-4—the standard employment agreement within the securities industry—requires arbitration of whatever disputes are made arbitrable by a Self-Regulatory Organization. The NASD manual says that any dispute arising out of members' business is arbitrable. The Ninth Circuit found that, although employees can certainly agree to submit their ADEA and Title VII claims to arbitration, they cannot be compelled to arbitrate unless they knowingly waive the right to litigate such claims. The U-4 does not explicitly deny the possibility of a Title VII suit, so U-4 signatories retain the right to sue when they allege discrimination.[22]

The converse situation arose in the Second Circuit: a broker signed both a U-4 (calling for arbitration of employment disputes) and an employment agreement with the firm, waiving all right to arbitration. The Second Circuit found the imposed waiver of the right to arbitrate to be void, as contrary to public policy, citing a 1987 NASD resolution forbidding the organization's members to require their employees to waive arbitration.[23]

In a mid-1997 Ninth Circuit case, a newly hired securities-industry employee signed the U-4 "as may be amended." After she signed, the NASD code was amended to make employment-related claims mandatory subjects of arbitration. The Ninth Circuit declined to enforce the arbitration requirement against the employee, ruling that employees cannot waive Title VII litigation rights in the abstract; they must have specific awareness of the claims that cannot be litigated.[24]

Typically, collective bargaining agreements (CBAs) will contain arbitration clauses. Yet, the individual employees have not negotiated on this issue, and may even be unaware of it. Courts have reached various conclusions as to whether the CBA clause will prevent employees from taking their discrimination claims to court.

To the Third Circuit, a CBA clause that specifically refers to federal statutory discrimination claims, and which permits either the employer or the employee to compel arbitration, is valid and enforceable and will prevent litigation of Title VII claims.[25] To the District Court for the District of Connecticut, a CBA that expressly provides for arbitration of federal statutory discrimination claims requires arbitration of 42 U.S.C. §1981 race discrimination claims.[26]

However, to the Eleventh Circuit, a CBA probably will not preclude litigation of discrimination claims, unless the CBA meets high standards: the employee individually agreed to the contract; the employee has the right to compel arbitration if he or she is dissatisfied with the outcome of the grievance procedure; and the arbitrator is given the power to resolve federal statutory discrimination claims.[27] At the furthest point on the spectrum, the Seventh Circuit has ruled that a CBA cannot force an unwilling employee to arbitrate federal statutory discrimination claims, given that arbitral remedies might be lesser than the statutory remedies; the union might be dilatory or even practice discrimination itself; and union officials might be insensitive to the needs of minority employees.[28]

Probably the highest degree of negotiating power belongs to the executive, manager, professional or other person who negotiates an individual employment contract rather than working at the will of the employer or being subject to a CBA. According to the Third Circuit, New Jersey public policy does not forbid enforcement of the arbitration clause contained in an individual employment contract. Therefore, the person signing the contract was not permitted to bring sex discrimination claims under the state anti-discrimination law.[29]

The employee's negotiating power is somewhat less with respect to arbitration clauses contained in employee handbooks which are published by the employer and distributed to new hires and employees. In the view of the Eighth Circuit, an arbitration provision printed on the last page of the employee handbook, highlighted as important information, and separately signed by the employee, is enforceable under the FAA even if the rest of the handbook does not have the status of an employment contract.[30] Employers usually take the position that employee handbooks do not create enforceable contracts or remove the employer's power to fire at will. In contrast, the Ninth Circuit permitted an employee to litigate an ADA claim even after signing a form indicating that the employee handbook containing the arbitration clause had been read and understood. To the Ninth Circuit, understanding a document is not the same as agreeing to its contents, so there had been no knowing waiver of the right to sue. Furthermore, the arbitration clause had been unilaterally imposed by the employer.[31]

An arbitration clause contained in a job application has been held to be unenforceable, because the employer doesn't promise anything, even that it will consider hiring the candidate. Therefore, the clause fails for want of consideration.[32]

An employee can bring a Fair Labor Standards Act suit in federal court without first arbitrating the wage claim under his or her collective bargaining agreement.[33]

An employee who signed an arbitration agreement with the former owner of a hospital cannot bring an Americans with Disabilities Act suit against the hospital's current owner. In the view of the Eastern District of Louisiana, the successor owner inherits the arbitration clause as well as various forms of successor liability.[34]

Although an age discrimination plaintiff who sued in federal court and prevailed would be entitled to a mandatory attorneys' fee award, an NASD arbitration panel's failure to make a fee award cannot be overturned by the court system, because the arbitrators did not show "manifest disregard" of the law.[35]

Charges that a supervisor committed sexual assault and false imprisonment against a subordinate employee during a business trip were definitely outside the supervisor's scope of employment, so the claims did not arise in connection with employment and therefore were not subject to the U-4's arbitration clause. However, claims of sexual harassment and pay discrimination against the supervisor and the employer were arbitrable, because they related to the employer's response to the harassment charges (as distinct from the supervisor's acts themselves).[36]

An employer's internal grievance procedure is not equivalent to arbitration (because arbitration requires a third-party decision maker, a final and binding decision, and a mechanism to insure the impartiality of the decision). Thus, an employee's agreement to use the grievance procedure is not equivalent to an agreement to arbitrate, and does not bar the employee from suing for race- and sex-based wrongful termination.[37]

Once a statutory employment claim is arbitrated, the standard for judicial review of the arbitrators' decision is the same as for any other issue: whether the arbitrator was guilty of manifest disregard of the law.[38]

[¶404]   HOW TO PROVIDE FOR ARBITRATION

In July of 1996, the Department of Justice's civil litigating components announced ADR policies covering arbitration, mediation, mini-trials, summary jury trials, early neutral evaluation, and other methods. The policies cover the selection of cases suitable for ADR and how to choose among ADR techniques. Under the Guidelines (published at 61 *Federal Register* 36895 (7/15/96), ADR is not suitable in a case where a judicial decision would be needed to secure compliance, or where there has been improper conduct that merits public sanction.

Federal agencies, unlike private citizens, used to have the right unilaterally to vacate unfavorable arbitration rulings, but Congress removed this power in 1996 via the Administrative Dispute Resolution Act, P.L. 104-320.

The Court of Federal Claims decided in late 1995 that there is no Constitutional barrier preventing federal agencies from forming agreements that contain binding arbitration clauses.[39]

The parties to an arbitration agreement can agree to standards for judicial review of the award that are stricter than those provided by the FAA itself.[40]

Some state cases tackled the question of doctor-patient arbitration in 1996. The Tennessee case[41] finds that the Uniform Arbitration Act permits a doctor-patient agreement to arbitrate malpractice claims—provided that the agreement is clear, does not yield an unfair advantage to the doctor, and does not diminish the doctor's underlying duty of care in treating the patient. The Utah case[42] finds it unconscionable to present a surgical patient with the arbitration agreement less than one hour before surgery. However, it permits the unconscionability to be cured via a clause that gives the patient 14 days after signing to revoke the agreement, and as long as the patient is aware of any injury that occurred during the surgery.

In 1997, two cases in California afforded new insights. A federal case permits enforcement of the HMO's arbitration clause in a dispute over whether the HMO must pay for surgery on a plan participant's wife performed at a non-HMO hospital.[43] The state Supreme Court case rules that, if an HMO deliberately delays arbitration of malpractice claims, that policy could be fraud sufficient to defeat the right to compel arbitration—either on a waiver theory, or because of fraud in the inducement of the contract containing the arbitration clause. (In this case, the HMO took an average of 674 days to appoint a neutral arbitrator, and the average time to hearing was 863 days from the claim, so the conclusion that arbitration was deliberately delayed is a compelling one.)[44]

A Vermont law allows an arbitration agreement "contained in a contract of insurance" to be revoked at any time before an arbitration award is published. The law was struck down by the Vermont Supreme Court in late 1997, on the grounds that it is preempted by the FAA provisions that, in effect, make arbitration contracts irrevocable. Because the state law was invalid, a coverage dispute about uninsured motorist coverage had to be arbitrated and not litigated.[45]

[¶405] ARBITRABLE ISSUES

Early in 1995 the U.S. Supreme Court applied Federal Arbitration Act §2 (arbitration provisions are enforceable in contracts "evidencing a transaction involving commerce") to any contract that in fact involves interstate commerce—whether or not the contracting parties contemplated substantial interstate activity. Therefore, state anti-arbitration laws were preempted by the FAA.[46]

Later that year, the Supreme Court held that the arbitrator decides whether the dispute is arbitrable under the FAA if the parties have agreed to submit this threshold issue to arbitration.[47] Otherwise, the judge must make an independent determination of the issue. The usual standards of review apply to a District Court's order confirming or not vacating an arbitration award—i.e., questions of law are reviewed *de novo* and not merely to test abuse of discretion. Questions of fact are reviewed to see if the District Court's decision was clearly erroneous.

FAA §1 excludes the contracts of "seamen, railroad employees, or any other class of workers engaged in foreign or interstate commerce" from arbitrability, but the Sixth Circuit read this narrowly to include only workers who actively move goods between states, not all employment affecting commerce.[48]

Even though, in general, the FAA assigns questions of timeliness to the arbitrator, the FAA does not preempt a New York arbitration law that places statute of limitations questions within the domain of the judge.[49] However, the FAA does pre-empt a Montana state law requiring notice of arbitrability to appear, in capital letters and underlined, on page one of the contract. FAA §2 can be used to void inappropriate arbitration clauses (such as one buried on page 9 of the contract) using general contract theories.[50]

Where the securities arbitration agreement says that all controversies over construction of the agreement are arbitrable, then questions of arbitrability and timeliness under New York law are of necessity arbitrable.[51] Nevertheless, the majority rule is that it is for courts, not arbitrators, to decide the timeliness of arbitration under NASD's Arbitration Code §15 (substantive jurisdiction).[52]

A joint venture agreement between two clothing companies contained an arbitration clause, and also assigned trademarks. A dispute arose as to the validity of the assignment, and one disputant wanted arbitration and the other wanted to litigate, resulting in a petition to compel arbitration. The Fourth Circuit found that the FAA requires subject matter jurisdiction, which was lacking in this instance because the Lanham Act does not furnish grounds for jurisdiction. It was inherently an ordinary contract dispute, even though the nominal subject was intellectual property.[53]

According to the Fifth Circuit, the arbitrator and not the federal court is responsible for determining the timeliness of an investor's claims against a securities brokerage. This is a question of "procedural arbitrability," and not a substantive eligibility requirement to be established by a federal court prior to the brokerage's obligation to submit to arbitration. The Eighth Circuit agrees.[54]

FAA §4, allowing a petition to compel arbitration in any district (with the arbitration to be held there), does not override the forum selection clause of the underlying agreement. Nor can the District Court in which the petition was filed enjoin arbitration in the location that is proper under the forum selection clause.[55]

The statute of limitations for an FAA action does not begin until there has been an unequivocal refusal to arbitrate. Noncompliance with an arbitration demand, or other unambiguous manifestation of unwillingness to arbitrate, would qualify.[56]

The Coors and Molson brewing companies entered into a licensing agreement. Later, Molson entered into an allegedly anticompetitive deal with the Miller brewery. Coors brought suit, charging a conspiracy to divide the United States beer market. The Tenth Circuit held[57] that Coors was entitled to litigate the antitrust claims instead of arbitrating them, because the claims fell outside the licensing agreement's arbitration clause. Antitrust claims are arbitrable,[58] but only if they have a reasonable factual connection to the contract that contains the arbitration clause.

In 1996, the Eleventh Circuit changed its position, and now agrees with four other Circuits, holding even domestic antitrust disputes to be arbitrable.[59]

Alleged misappropriation of trade secrets is a separate tort and does not "arise out of" breach of a licensing agreement, and thus is not covered by the arbitration clause within the licensing agreement.[60]

Because there is the potential for contracts of adhesion in the consumer context, issues have arisen about the enforceability of consumer arbitration agreements. The Seventh Circuit upheld the provisions (including the arbitration clause) of a contract shipped in the box with a computer ordered by telephone. The contract specified that its terms applied unless the computer was returned within 30 days. A consumer who did not read the contract, but who also didn't return the computer, was held to be subject to the arbitration requirement.[61]

In contrast, the Middle District of Alabama held that a mobile home manufacturer cannot enforce the arbitration clause in an installment sales and financing contract between the dealer and the purchaser of the mobile home. In this reading, the purpose of the Magnuson-Moss Act is to give angry consumers a day in court, and permitting binding arbitration clauses would conflict with this objective.[62] In another automotive context, the Third Circuit said that auto manufacturers' "first resort" procedures (informal, non-binding ADR mechanisms required by Magnuson-Moss and state Lemon Laws) are not arbitration as defined by the FAA. Therefore, FAA §16 cannot be used to obtain interlocutory appeal of a District Court's denial of a motion to compel arbitration.[63]

In a late-1997 Southern District of New York case, the owner of a company entered into an agreement (which contained an arbitration clause) with a sales representative. The company owner in effect made the agreement worthless by selling company assets, including worldwide marketing rights, to someone else. The court permitted the sales representative to pierce the corporate veil and arbitrate fraud claims against the company owner, on the grounds that the owner had used his control to perpetrate fraud or economic injury.[64]

When a non-frivolous appeal is filed after a motion to stay federal District Court proceedings pending arbitration has been denied, the District Court must suspend its consideration of the matter until the appeal is resolved.[65]

[¶413]   ENFORCEMENT OF THE ARBITRATION AWARD

In mid-1996, the Alaska Supreme Court upheld the constitutionality of the state's mandatory arbitration program for legal fees. Although the awards are more or less final (appealability is quite limited), the state's power to police the practice of law was held to justify a higher standard of review than the one imposed in other compulsory arbitration cases. Although limitations on judicial review can be a disadvantage for lawyers involved in the process, this detriment is outweighed by the general benefit of making the process more efficient.[66]

Florida's statute, requiring 35% of the punitive damages in any "civil action" to be paid to the state, applies only to litigation, not to arbitration proceedings.[67]

Under FAA §§9 and 10, the District Court in the district in which an arbitration award was made can enforce (or vacate) the award. However, according to the Fifth Circuit, this is only a permissive venue provision, and not a mandatory one. Therefore, the District Court where the initial filing was done has jurisdiction to enforce or vacate the award.[68]

[¶414]   VACATING ARBITRATION AWARD

If the arbitration agreement provides that "errors of law are subject to appeal," the appellate court is supposed to provide *de novo* review of questions of law in the arbitration award—even though the FAA does not allow an award to be vacated absent fraud, partiality, corruption, or action by the arbitrators exceeding their powers.[69]

Even if the arbitrator acted with factual support (and did not listen to the urgings of the lawyer who urged the arbitrator to "do the right thing" rather than following legal standards), an arbitration award must be vacated for manifest disregard of the law where such urgings were given.[70]

A lawyer who serves as arbitrator does not have an obligation to investigate and discover if his or her former law firm has a connection with a party to the arbitration.[71]

— ENDNOTES —

1. *Grundstad v. Ritt,* 106 F.3d 201 (7th Cir. 2/4/97).

2. *Hartford Accident & Indemnity Co. v. Scarlett Harbor Associates,* 346 Md. 122, 695 A.2d 153 (Md.App. 6/18/97).

3. *Miller v. Air Line Pilots Ass'n,* 108 F.3d 1415 (D.C. Cir. 3/14/97).

4. *Mastrobuono v. Shearson Lehman Hutton Inc.,* #94-18, 115 S.Ct. 1212 (Sup.Ct. 3/6/95), *reversing* 20 F.3d 713; on remand, 54 F.3d 779. Also see *Roubek v. Merrill Lynch,* 28 Sec.Reg.L.Rep. 640 (Ill.App. 5/1/96) permitting the arbitration panel to award punitive damages in a case whose choice of law provisions called for interpretation under New York law.

5. *Lehman Brothers Inc. v. Certified Reporting Co.,* 939 F.Supp. 1333 (N.D. Ill. 9/5/96).

6. *Kramer v. Smith Barney,* 80 F.3d 1080 (5th Cir. 4/23/96).

7. *Kidder, Peabody & Co. v. Brandt,* 66 LW 1412 (11th Cir. 12/22/97).

8. *Smith Barney Shearson Inc. v. Sacharow,* 66 LW 1381 (N.Y. App. 12/4/97).

9. *Champ v. Siegel Trading Co.,* 55 F.3d 269 (7th Cir. 5/18/95).

10. *Salvano v. Merrill Lynch,* 647 N.E.2d 1298 (N.Y.App. 2/21/95).

11. *Westmoreland Capital Corp. v. Findlay,* 100 F.3d 263 (2nd Cir. 11/7/96).

12. *Olson v. NASD,* 85 F.3d 381 (8th Cir. 6/27/96).

13. *Florida Bar Re: Advisory Opinion on Nonlawyer Representation in Securities Arbitration,* 696 So.2d 1178 (Fla.Sup. 7/3/97).

14. *First Options of Chicago v. Kaplan,* 115 S.Ct. 1920 (Sup.Ct. 1995).

15. *United Brotherhood of Carpenters v. Desert Palace Inc.,* 94 F.3d 1308 (9th Cir. 9/4/96).

16. *Transportation Union Local 1589 v. Suburban Transit Corp.,* 51 F.3d 376 (3d Cir. 3/16/95).

17. *Madison Hotel v. Hotel & Restaurant Employees Local 23,* 66 LW 1300 (D.C. Cir. 11/7/97).

18. See 66 LW 2055. The text of EEOC Chairman Gilbert Casellas' statement is available on-line at http://www.eeoc.gov/docs/mandarb.txt. Also see *EEOC v. Kidder, Peabody & Co.,* 65 LW 1252 (S.D.N.Y. 10/6/97): if the EEOC brings a pattern-or-practice discrimination suit against an employer in the securities industry, whose employees are covered by the U-4, the EEOC's suit can proceed (despite the arbitration provision in the U-4), because of the public interest in relief for individuals beyond the immediate litigants, but the EEOC will not have authority to seek monetary relief for individual securities industry employees.

19. *EEOC v. River Oaks Imaging and Diagnostic,* 63 LW 2733 (S.D.Tex. 4/19/95).

20. *Cole v. Burns International Security Services,* 105 F.3d 1465 (D.C.Cir. 2/11/97).

21. *DeGaetano v. Smith Barney,* 66 LW 1315 (S.D.N.Y. 11/6/97).

22. *Prudential Insurance Co. v. Lai,* 42 F.3d 1299 (9th Cir. 12/20/94). But see *Austin v. Owens-Brockway Glass Container Inc.,* 78 F.3d 875 (4th Cir. 3/12/96): CBA mandating arbitration of sex and disability claims can be enforced against a union member who wants to bring Title VII and ADA claims in the court system.

23. *Thomas James Associates Inc. v. Jameson,* 102 F.3d 60 (2nd Cir. 12/12/96). Also see *Ahing v. Lehman Brothers Inc.,* 66 LW 1336 (S.D.N.Y. 10/15/97): if an individual subject to the U-4 goes through mediation of a Title VII race discrimination claim, and mediation fails, participation in mediation does not prevent the employer from compelling arbitration of the Title VII claim.

24. *Renteria v. Prudential Insurance Co.,* 113 F.3d 1104 (9th Cir. 5/20/97).

25. *Martin v. Dana Corp.,* 65 LW 2824 (3rd Cir. 6/12/97).

26. *Almonte v. Coca-Cola Bottling Co. of New York,* 959 F.Supp. 569 (D.Conn. 3/11/97).

27. *Brisentine v. Stone & Webster Engineering Corp.,* 117 F.3d 519 (11th Cir. 7/21/97).

28. *Pryner v. Tractor Supply Co.,* 109 F.3d 354 (7th Cir. 3/20/97).

29. *Great Western Mortgage Corp. v. Peacock,* 110 F.3d 222 (3rd Cir. 4/3/97).

30. *Patterson v. Tenet Healthcare Inc.,* 113 F.3d 832 (8th Cir. 5/12/97).

31. *Nelson v. Cyprus Bagdad Copper Corp.,* 119 F.3d 756 (9th Cir. 7/10/97).

32. *Brooks v. Circuit City Stores Inc.,* 65 LW 2823 (D.Md. 5/30/97).

33. *Tran v. Tran,* 54 F.3d 115 (2nd Cir. 5/5/95).

34. *Jones v. Tenet Health Network Inc.,* 65 LW 2815 (E.D. La. 4/7/97).

35. *Di Russa v. Dean Witter Reynolds,* 936 F.Supp. 104 (S.D.N.Y. 7/29/96).

36. *Hill v. J.J.B. Hilliard, W.L. Lyons Inc.,* 65 LW 2060 (Ky.App. 6/21/96).

37. *Cheng-Canindin v. Renaissance Hotel Associates,* 50 Cal.App.4th 676, 57 Cal.Rptr.2d 867 (Cal.App. 10/30/96).

38. *Chisholm v. Kidder, Peabody,* 65 LW 2805 (S.D.N.Y. 5/29/97).

39. *Tenaska Washington Partners II LP v. U.S.,* 34 Fed.Cl. 434 (Ct.Fed.Cl. 11/9/95).

40. *LaPine Technology Corp. v. Kyocera Corp.,* 66 LW 1372 (9th Cir. 12/9/97).

41. *Buraczynski v. Eyring,* 919 S.W.2d 314 (Tenn.Sup. 4/1/96).

42. *Sosa v. Paulos,* 924 P.2d 357 (Utah Sup. 9/20/96).

43. *Toledo v. Kaiser Permanente Medical Group,* 65 LW 2664 (N.D. Cal. 2/12/97). This case also finds that ERISA preempts all claims against the HMO, because the plan was provided by the claimant's employer.

44. *Engalla v. Permanente Medical Group,* 15 Cal.4th 951, 64 Cal.Rptr.2d 843, 938 P.2d 903 (Cal.Sup. 6/30/97).

45. *Little v. Allstate Insurance Co.,* 66 LW 1243 (Vt.Sup. 10/10/97).

46. *Allied-Bruce Terminix Cos. v. Dobson,* #93-1001, 115 S.Ct. 834 (Sup.Ct. 1/18/95).

47. *First Options of Chicago Inc. v. Kaplan,* #94-560, 115 S.Ct. 1920 (Sup.Ct. 5/22/95). Also see *U.S. Fire Insurance Co. v. National Gypsum Co.,* 101 F.3d 813 (2nd Cir. 11/4/96): if any facet of a dispute calls for interpretation of an arbitration agreement, then a question of the issue-preclusive effect of the prior judgment is also arbitrable.

48. *Asplundh Tree Expert Co. v. Bates,* 57 F.3d 592 (6th Cir. 12/14/95).

49. *Smith Barney v. Luckie,* 647 N.E.2d 1308 (N.Y.App. 2/21/95).

50. *Doctor's Associates Inc. v. Casarotto,* #95-559, 116 S.Ct. 1652 (Sup.Ct. 5/20/96).

51. *Paine Webber Inc. v. Bybyk,* 81 F.3d 1193 (2nd Cir. 4/19/96).

52. *Cogswell v. Merrill Lynch,* 78 F.3d 474 (10th Cir. 2/26/96). The 10th joins four other Circuits: *Paine Webber v. Hoffmann,* 984 F.2d 1372 (3rd Cir. 1993); *Dean Witter Reynolds v. McCoy,* 995 F.2d 649 (6th Cir. 1993); *Smith Barney v. Schell,* 53 F.3d 807 (7th Cir. 1995); *Merrill Lynch v. Cohen,* 62 F.3d 381 (11th Cir. 1995).

53. *Gibraltar PR Inc. v. Otoki Group Inc.,* 104 F.3d 616 (4th Cir. 1/13/97).

54. *Smith Barney v. Boone,* 47 F.3d 750 (5th Cir. 3/20/95); *FSC Securities Corp. v. Freel,* 14 F.3d 1310 (8th Cir. 1994).

55. *Merrill Lynch v. Lauer,* 49 F.3d 323 (7th Cir. 3/1/95).

56. *PaineWebber Inc. v. Faragalli,* 61 F.3d 1063 (3rd Cir. 8/4/95).

57. *Coors Brewing Co. v. Molson Breweries,* 51 F.3d 1511 (10th Cir. 3/30/95); *on remand,* 889 F.Supp. 1394.

58. See *Mitsubishi Motors v. Soler Chrysler-Plymouth,* 473 U.S. 614 (1985).

59. *Kotam Electronics Inc. v. JBL Consumer Products Inc.,* 59 F.3d 1155 (11th Cir. 7/28/95) and 93 F.3d 724 (11th Cir. 8/19/96).

60. *Tracer Research Corp. v. National Env. Services Co.,* 42 F.3d 1292 (9th Cir. 12/19/94).

61. *Hill v. Gateway 2000 Inc.*, 105 F.3d 1147 (7th Cir. 1/6/97).

62. *Wilson v. Waverlee Homes Inc.*, 954 F.Supp. 1530 (M.D.Ala. 2/4/97).

63. *Harrison v. Nissan Motor Corp.*, 111 F.3d 343 (3rd Cir. 4/15/97).

64. *Freeman v. Complex Computing Co.*, 931 F.Supp. 1115 (S.D.N.Y. 10/14/97).

65. *Bradford-Scott Data Corp. v. Physician Computer Network Inc.*, 128 F.3d 503 (7th Cir. 10/14/97).

66. *A. Fred Miller P.C. v. Purvis*, 921 P.2d 610 (Alaska Sup. 7/26/96).

67. *Miele v. Prudential-Bache Securities Inc.*, 656 So.2d 470 (Fla.Sup. 6/8/95).

68. *Sutter Corp. v. P&P Industries Inc.*, 66 LW 1277 (5th Cir. 10/27/97).

69. *Gateway Technologies Inc. v. MCI Telecommunications Corp.*, 64 F.3d 993 (5th Cir. 9/27/95).

70. *Montes v. Shearson Lehman Brothers Inc.*, 66 LW 1339 (11th Cir. 11/24/97).

71. *Al-Harbi v. Citibank*, 85 F.3d 680, (D.C.Cir. 6/11/96) cert. denied 117 S.Ct. 432.

— FOR FURTHER REFERENCE —

Bingham, Lisa B., "Emerging Due Process Concerns in Employment Arbitration," 47 *Labor Law J.* 108 (February '96).

Byars, Linda S., "Limiting an Arbitrator's Remedial Powers," 48 *Labor Law J.* 29 (January '97).

Cole, Sarah Rudolph, "Incentives and Arbitration: The Case Against Enforcement of Executory Arbitration Agreements," 64 *U.M.K.C. L. Rev.* 449 (Spring '96).

Giovannucci, Marilou T., "Understanding the Role of the Mediator in Child Protection Proceedings," 35 *Family and Conciliation Courts Rev.* 143 (April '97).

Hogler, Raymond, "Mental Disabilities, the EEOC and Labor Arbitration," 48 *Labor Law J.* 544 (September '97).

Icenogle, Marjorie L. and Robert A. Shearer, "Emerging Due Process Standards in Arbitration of Employment Discrimination Disputes," 48 *Labor Law J.* 81 (February '97).

Louthan, Thomas Carter and Steven C. Wrappe, "Building a Better Resolution: Adapting IRS Procedures to Fit the Dispute," 13 *Tax Notes International* 1473 (October 28 '96).

Moberly, Robert B., "Mediator Gag Rules: Is it Ethical for Mediators to Evaluate or Advise?" 38 *South Texas L.Rev.* 669 (May '97).

Pacia, Raymond, "Arbitrating the Uninsured Motorist Case," 33 *Trial* 26 (February '97).

Pickens, Andrew, "Appraisement: An Old But Effective Form of ADR for Contract Liabilities," 60 *Texas Bar J.* 18 (January '97).

Post, David G., "Virtual Magistrates Virtual Law: On-Line Arbitration Has Finally Arrived," 18 *American Lawyer* 104 (July-August '96).

Sansing, Richard, "Voluntary Binding Arbitration as an Alternative to Tax Court Litigation," 50 *National Tax J.* 279 (June '97).

Silverman, Stuart I., "Punitive Damage Awards in Commercial Arbitration," 102 *Commercial L.J.* 306 (Fall '97).

Strong, Elizabeth S., "The Nuts and Bolts of ADR for Business Disputes," *N.Y.L.J.* 3/6/97 p. 1.

Terrell, Thomas E., "The Americans With Disabilities Act and Labor Arbitration: Recent Awards," 48 *Labor Law J.* 3 (January '97).

ATTORNEYS' FEES

[¶501] Attorneys' fees are not only an expense that litigants must pay, but also are property belonging to attorneys. According to the West Virginia Supreme Court, an attorney who is in the process of getting a divorce has separate property in the part of a contingent fee that relates to work done on a case after separation. It is not necessary to construct a legal fiction that the attorney resigned from his law firm on the date of the separation.[1]

The defendant in a personal injury case agreed to a structured settlement and also bought annuities to cover the required future payments to the plaintiff's attorneys. The Eleventh Circuit ruled[2] that the attorneys did not have income in the year of the annuity purchase: the agreement was unfunded and unsecured, and they did not have "property" as defined by Code §83. The attorneys did not constructively receive the money paid for the annuity because they did not have an immediate right to receive any funds.

Attorneys can be compelled to testify about fee arrangements when the federal government tries to seize assets from convicted money launderers. The District Court for the District of Rhode Island said that in this situation, the lawyers are not being compelled to incriminate themselves; nor are discussions about fees legal advice qualifying for attorney-client privilege.[3]

Unpaid attorneys' fees left over from earlier unsuccessful attempts at Chapter 11 and 12 reorganizations do not get administrative expense priority when the debtor tries again in Chapter 7—only the expenses of the current proceeding qualify.[4]

A Chapter 7 debtor's pre-petition agreement to pay attorney's fees in installments after the petition, has been held[5] to be dischargeable. The court acknowledged that this might impair debtors' ability to secure legal counsel, but believed the solution to be a legislative rather than a judicial matter. In the view of the First Circuit, attorneys' fees for enforcing family support obligations are nondischargeable, as are the underlying obligations themselves.[6]

A bankruptcy court can only order payment of special counsel fees under Bankruptcy Code §330 from the estate if the services benefit the estate itself. This inquiry is separate from authorization under Bankruptcy Code §325(e) to employ such counsel. Appointees should be warned that there is a risk of nonpayment if the appointment is deemed to be proper but the services are not deemed to benefit the estate.[7]

Alaska's mandatory program for arbitration of legal fees has been upheld as constitutional, despite severe limitations on the appealability of the arbitration awards.[8] The Alaska Supreme Court's rationale was that the state power to regulate the practice of law justifies imposing a higher standard of review in the arbitration of legal fees than in other compulsory arbitration cases. Furthermore, the benefit of an efficient process outweighs the detriment of limitations on judicial review.

According to the Eleventh Circuit, once an administrative agency issues a final order on the merits of a case, the time to appeal starts to run, even if attorneys' fee issues have not yet been resolved.[9]

[¶502]   FEDERAL STATUTES RE ATTORNEYS' FEES

P.L. 104-308, the Just Compensation: Patents Used by the U.S. Act, permits attorneys' fees and costs to be awarded against the U.S. when a patentee prevails in a suit against the federal government for unlicensed use of a patent.

The Prison Litigation Reform Act, 42 U.S.C. §1997e, denies attorneys' fee awards other than those incurred in proving an actual violation of prisoners' rights. The hourly rate for any fee awarded cannot exceed 150% of the rate for appointed counsel. In the view of the Fourth Circuit, a juvenile facility is a prison for purposes of this statute. The limitation on fees applies to fee awards made after the effective date of the PLRA, even for work done before that date, because there is no "award" until and unless the court issues a fee order.[10]

According to the District Court for the Central District of California, ERISA preempts a state domestic relations law that requires pension plans to pay attorneys' fees incurred in connection with Qualified Domestic Relations Orders (QDROs).[11]

In ERISA cases, the prevailing parties are not presumed entitled to a fee award. Entitlement depends on factors such as the loser's culpability and ability to pay fees; whether a fee award would serve to deter improper conduct; the value of the victory to plan participants; and the relative strength of the arguments adduced by each side.[12]

In a Clean Water Act citizen suit, all plaintiffs who want a fee award must satisfy the pre-suit notice requirement; it is not permitted for one plaintiff to provide notice for the plaintiffs as a group.[13]

Another federal environmental statute, the Clean Air Act, does not preempt the EAJA. A defendant who was required to pay a CAA judgment, but in an amount lower than its pretrial offer, is a "prevailing party" who can get an EAJA award, even if the government did not act unreasonably. However, unless unreasonable government action can be proved, attorneys' fees are not a "cost" recoverable under Fed.Rul.Civ.Pro. 68. This result follows because a defendant cannot recover attorneys' fees as "costs" under F.R.C.P. 68 unless the government acted unreasonably. However, EAJA costs can be recovered whether or not the government's action was reasonable.[14]

A creditor of a forfeiture defendant who brings a claim under 21 U.S.C. §853(n), as a third party with a legal interest in the forfeited property, is deemed to have brought a "civil action" for EAJA purposes (even though the forfeiture is based on criminal charges). Thus, a fee award can be made to a creditor who prevails in the challenge.[15] On another issue involving creditors, the Seventh Circuit has found that although a prevailing creditor can enforce a contractual provision awarding costs or fees in a dischargeability action, a prevailing debtor cannot get a fee award after defending the dischargeability of a particular debt in bankruptcy.[16]

If a successful *qui tam* relator under the False Claims Act seeks attorneys' fees, the fees are paid straight to the attorney—not to the relator.[17]

Although the Age Discrimination in Employment Act mandates a fee award to a successful plaintiff, nevertheless an arbitration panel's failure to make a fee award cannot be disturbed, because the panel did not show "manifest disregard" of the law.[18] An arbitration award that requires a person subject to mandatory arbitration of employment discrimination claims to waive attorneys' fees is void because it violates the public policy favoring pursuit of meritorious claims.[19]

Plaintiffs who win a §1983 suit on the basis of a state-law issue can still get a fee award under §1988, as long as the federal and state issues are closely interconnected.[20]

If an FRCP 68 offer of judgment is made, and the offer (and the underlying statute) fail to include attorneys' fees as a cost of litigation, the defendant making the offer is stuck with the fees over and above its offer. Rule 68 shifts costs rather than fees, except in situations where the statute awards fees to the prevailing party.[21]

NLRA §10(c) does not give the NLRB the authority to order an employer to pay the litigation costs of a union (or the NLRB's general counsel) in unfair labor practices proceedings. The statute is not clear enough to support shifting the burden.[22]

[¶503]   DEFINITION OF PREVAILING PARTIES

A plaintiff who was not awarded damages in her civil rights case because of her failure to mitigate damages (but who received a large judgment on associated state-law claims) was nevertheless a prevailing party entitled to fees and costs, because of her achievement of some of her litigation objectives.[23]

The Southern District of New York tackled EAJA issues in early 1995,[24] finding that determination of the substantial justification of the government position need not be made at each procedural stage of a case. However, once the case is concluded, it is appropriate to examine each distinct claim to test the justification of the government position, and to see whether an EAJA fee is appropriate with respect to that claim. In 1997, the Eleventh Circuit took another viewpoint: that EAJA fees can be awarded if the government's position as a whole is not substantially justified, even if an individual claim is justified.[25]

In late 1997, the Eighth Circuit found that plaintiffs retained their character as prevailing parties, in a civil rights action involving school desegregation, who could receive attorneys' fees under §1988 to defend the remedial orders before the Supreme Court, even though the Supreme Court reversed some of the remedial orders (such as those requiring higher salaries for teachers until standardized test results improved) as overbroad.[26]

In a copyright infringement suit, a prevailing defendant can get a fee award; the plaintiff need merely be unsuccessful, not necessarily culpable in the sense of having brought the action in bad faith.[27] Lanham Act §35(a) permits attorneys' fee awards in "exceptional cases," so either a losing plaintiff or defendant might be forced to pay fees, based on bad faith or malicious conduct. However, in September, 1997, the Ninth Circuit declined to impose a fee award against a losing plaintiff, because the plaintiff had a legitimate purpose for bringing suit and raised colorable (albeit not successful) issues of fact and law.[28]

Cumulative refunds due to retired federal employees who prevailed in a challenge to state taxation of retiree benefits do not constitute a common fund from which an attorney's fee can be paid. The funds are not considered a pool of money created by attorney efforts, but are individual amounts owed to individual retirees based on their incomes.[29]

In contrast, a common fund was found to exist when refunds were granted after a challenge to Florida's motor vehicle impact fee—but nevertheless, the attorney's fee was based on the lodestar rather than a percentage of the fund.[30]

In the view of the Second Circuit, shareholders have created a common benefit (and thus can be awarded attorneys' fees) if they win an action under securities law Rule 14a-8 and the action results in the inclusion of a shareholder proposal in a corporate proxy statement.[31] This is true even if the proposal is soundly defeated when the vote is held. To the Second Circuit, corporate voters at least got to consider the proposal, so they were benefited by the ability to exercise a broader corporate franchise.

The mere fact that a hospital has a lien on a patient's settlement with respect to the injury that necessitated hospitalization does not mean that a common fund has been created that would obligate the hospital to pay a proportionate share of the attorneys' fees. In this situation, the hospital is merely a creditor. Its position is not the same as that of a subrogated insurer, because the hospital has no rights against the tortfeasor and is unable to sue the tortfeasor.[32]

An employee covered by a group health plan was injured in a car accident. The health plan had subrogation rights. Under the state's (Illinois') common-fund doctrine, the health plan was entitled to receive attorneys' fees and costs out of the tort settlement; ERISA did not preempt the issue.[33] An insured who prevails against the insurance company as to the insurer's duty to defend is entitled to a fee award, because insured persons should be able to enforce the insurance contract without having out-of-pocket legal expenses.[34]

Code §7430 permits the award of fees against the IRS and to a prevailing party, subject to the EAJA's net-worth limits ($2 million for an individual, $7 million and 500 employees for a corporation) at the time the civil action was filed. However, the Seventh Circuit points out that the net worth of an estate always declines over time and vanishes when the distribution is complete. Thus, an estate's ability to litigate without help from the EAJA depends on the net value of the entire estate, adding in assets that were already distributed when the suit was filed.[35]

The Ninth Circuit has ruled on the perhaps obvious point that a bankruptcy court is a "court of the United States" able to award §7430 fees to a prevailing party and against the IRS.[36] On another bankruptcy question, the same court ruled that the contempt power does not authorize a bankruptcy court to sanction the state for violating the automatic stay by forcing it to pay the debtor's legal fees for the appeal. (If a party is forced into a frivolous appeal, the appellate court can make the fee award—but the bankruptcy court cannot.[37])

A defendant who is awarded attorneys' fees after defending against a frivolous civil rights suit is also entitled to be reimbursed for the necessary expenses of collecting the award.[38]

[¶504]   COMPUTATION OF FEES

An agreement among the lawyers in a common-fund class action as to allocation of the fees is not binding on the court, even if the agreement does not violate any ethical rules, and does not provide windfalls and is not unfair to the class. The court makes its own determination as to the relative efforts of the various attorneys and the relative values of those efforts.[39]

A corporate or organizational prevailing plaintiff represented by staff attorneys is entitled to a fee award based on the open-market cost of acquiring comparable legal services.[40]

In a civil rights case, the lodestar is used to calculate the fees except in cases where the "prevailing" party gets only nominal damages and fails to achieve any significant non-monetary results. In a recent Ninth Circuit case, a $139,000 fee was held justified where the plaintiff's $17,500 award was accompanied by significant non-monetary results.[41]

In Social Security Act §406(b) SSI disability cases, the lodestar remains the primary determinant of the fee—although the lodestar may be adjusted in accordance with the contingent fee agreement.[42]

Where an attorney prevails on one of multiple claims, the fee should be based on the hours reasonably expended to secure the result; there should not be an automatic reduction based on the lack of success of the other claims.[43]

An attorney was awarded $150/hour in a complex bankruptcy case, because it was below her prevailing rates, and her special expertise justified an increase from the ordinary $75 rate. However, she was awarded only $100 for each hour spent on the fee application, because there was no complex legal analysis involved in pursuing the award.[44]

In a case that continues over several years, the D.C. Circuit ruled in favor of a "historic" fee award (calculated on the basis of $75/hour plus the CPI for each year in which services were rendered) rather than a "current" inflation adjustment (involving the CPI from 1981, the effective date of the EAJA.[45]

In a Florida case, it was held that the true value of services rendered to the client before the discharge, not the lodestar, should be used to set the quantum meruit fee of a contingent-fee attorney who was discharged without cause before the contingency occurred.[46]

Retainers and fixed fees have also given rise to complex questions. In a late 1997 Pennsylvania case, an asbestos company demanded a non-negotiable $1 million fixed fee agreement as a condition of employing a law firm. (The company's aim was controlling litigation costs.) After ten weeks, the company demanded that its lawyers file complaints against other attorneys; the firm refused to do so without investigating first, and was fired. The asbestos company then brought suit for rescission of the fee contract and breach of fiduciary duty (claiming that the law firm was unethically attempting to collect an excessive fee). The Eastern District of Pennsylvania found for the law firm, stating that the fee was fair and fully earned. The client, not the lawyer, had insisted on the fee arrangement, which was the creation of a sophisticated business firm and not a law firm's imposition.[47]

The conservator of a failed credit union does not have an automatic right to get a refund of the non-refundable retainer paid by a credit union customer to the law firm representing the customer in bank proceedings relating to the credit union failure. The law firm had no actual knowledge, and no reason to know, that the money was actually involved in the check kiting scheme that caused the credit union's demise. The Eighth Circuit remanded to see if the retainer was excessive or used to hide the assets of a bankrupt; except in such cases, the law firm would not be guilty of any impropriety.[48]

For the record, it should be noted that counsel for the investor class in the Prudential Securities class action received fees of close to $30 million in connection with a partial settlement dealing with sale of more than 700 limited partnerships.[49]

[¶505]   DEDUCTIBILITY OF LEGAL FEES

In law-firm "gross fee" contracts, firms get a percentage of settlement or judgment proceeds, but nothing—including expenses—if the case is lost. A law-firm partner has been permitted to deduct (under Code §162) litigation costs that the firm paid[50]—even though local ethical rules forbid the firm to do anything except advance costs for later repayment. The holding depends on the fact that there was no state statute making it unlawful for law firms to assume responsibility for expenses; "unethical" expenses can be deducted, although "unlawful" ones cannot.

At least in a continuing retainer relationship, the Court of Federal Claims permits deduction of a law firm's retainer fee as an ordinary and necessary business expense of the payor, even though the actual legal work performed in a particular year involved a capital acquisition.[51]

— ENDNOTES —

1. *White v. Williamson,* 453 S.E.2d 666 (W.Va.Sup. 12/21/94).

2. *Childs v. Comm'r,* 96-2 USTC ¶50,504 (11th Cir. 6/11/96).

3. *U.S. v. Saccoccia,* 898 F.Supp. 53 (D.R.I. 8/28/95).

4. *Stuart v. Carter (In re Larsen),* 59 F.3d 783 (8th Cir. 7/14/95).

5. *Hessinger & Associates v. Voglio,* 191 B.R. 420 (D.Ariz. 12/12/95).

6. *Macy v. Macy,* 114 F.3d 1 (1st Cir. 5/23/97).

7. *Ferrara & Hantman v. Alvarez,* 66 LW 1149 (3rd Cir. 9/3/97). Also see *Stroock & Stroock & Lavan v. Hillsborough Holdings Corp.,* 66 LW 1323 (11th Cir. 11/18/97), finding that a bankruptcy court awarding attorneys' fees should not decide that certain categories of law firm expenses are "overhead" not subject to reimbursement. Items such as postage or on-line research should be considered client-specific and not part of the firm's overhead already reflected in the fee.

8. *A.Fred Miller P.C. v. Purvis*, 921 P.2d 610 (Alaska Sup. 7/26/96).

9. *Fluor Constructors Inc. v. Reich*, 111 F.3d 94 (11th Cir. 4/15/97).

10. *Alexander S. v. Boyd*, 113 F.3d 1373 (4th Cir. 5/28/97).

11. *AT&T Management Pension Plan v. Tucker*, 902 F.Supp. 1168 (C.D.Cal. 8/17/95).

12. *Eddy v. Colonial Life Co.*, 59 F.3d 201 (D.C.Cir. 7/7/95).

13. *New Mexico Citizens for Clean Air and Water v. Espanola Mercantile Co.*, 72 F.3d 830 (10th Cir. 1/2/96).

14. *U.S. v. Trident Seafoods Corp.*, 92 F.3d 855 (9th Cir. 8/7/96).

15. *U.S. v. Douglas (Lussier)*, 55 F.3d 584 (11th Cir. 6/21/95); *U.S. v. Bachner*, 877 F.Supp. 625 (S.D.Fla. 1/20/95).

16. *In re Sheridan*, 105 F.3d 1164 (7th Cir. 1/29/97).

17. *U.S. ex rel. Virani v. Lewis Truck Parts*, 89 F.3d 574 (9th Cir. 7/10/96).

18. *Di Russa v. Dean Witter Reynolds*, 936 F.Supp. 104 (S.D.N.Y. 7/29/96).

19. *DeGaetano v. Smith Barney*, 66 LW 1315 (S.D.N.Y. 11/6/97).

20. *Williams v. Hanover Housing Authority*, 65 LW 113 F.3d 1294 (1st Cir. 5/22/97).

21. *Nusom v. COMH Woodburn Inc.*, 66 LW 1134 (9th Cir. 8/26/97).

22. *Unbelievable Inc. v. NLRB*, 118 F.3d 795 (D.C. Cir. 7/18/97).

23. *Bridges v. Eastman Kodak Co.*, 102 F.3d 56 (2nd Cir. 12/10/96).

24. *SEC v. Morelli*, 143 F.R.D. 42 (S.D.N.Y. 1/11/95).

25. *U.S. v. Jones*, 66 LW 1285 (11th Cir. 10/29/97).

26. *Jenkins v. Missouri*, 66 LW 1259 (8th Cir. 10/14/97).

27. *Fantasy Inc. v. Fogerty*, 94 F.3d 553 (9th Cir. 8/26/96).

28. *Stephen W. Boney Inc. v. Boney Services Inc.*, 127 F.3d 821 (9th Cir. 9/30/97).

29. *Hagge v. Iowa Department of Revenue*, 539 N.W.2d 148 (Ia.Sup. 10/25/95).

30. *Kuhnlein v. Department of Revenue*, 662 So.2d 309 (Fla.Sup. 10/12/95).

31. *Amalgamated Clothing and Textile Workers Union v. Wal-Mart Stores*, 54 F.3d 69 (2nd Cir. 4/20/95).

32. *Trevino v. HHL Financial Services Inc.*, 66 LW 1183 (Colo.Sup. 9/15/97).

33. *Scholtens v. Schneider*, 671 N.E.2d 657 (Ill.Sup. 9/19/96).

34. *Preferred Mutual Insurance Co. v. Gamache*, 66 LW 1312 (Mass.Sup. Jud.Ct. 11/7/97).

35. *Estate of Woll v. U.S.*, 44 F.3d 464 (7th Cir. 12/30/94).

36. *U.S. v. Yochum*, 89 F.3d 661 (9th Cir. 7/16/96).

37. *California Employment Development Dept. v. Taxel*, 98 F.3d 1147 (9th Cir. 10/23/96).

38. *Vukadinovich v. McCarthy,* 59 F.3d 58 (7th Cir. 7/5/95).

39. *Hayes v. Haushalter,* 105 F.3d 469 (9th Cir. 1/17/97).

40. *Central States Pension Fund v. Central Cartage Co.,* 84 F.3d 998 (7th Cir. 1/22/96).

41. *Morales v. San Rafael, California,* 96 F.3d 359 (9th Cir. 9/6/96).

42. *Allen v. Shalala,* 48 F.3d 456 (9th Cir. 2/24/95).

43. *Goos v. National Association of Realtors,* 68 F.3d 1380 (D.C.Cir. 10/31/95).

44. *In re Brickell Investment Corp.,* 75 AFTR2d 2032 (D.Fla. 1995). Also see the 42 U.S.C. §1988 civil rights case, *Thompson v. Gomez,* 45 F.3d 1365 (9th Cir. 1/25/95), which holds that if the attorneys' fee requested on the merits is reduced, it is not a judicial abuse of power for the "fees on fees" application for the cost of recovering the fees to be reduced proportionately.

45. *Masonry Masters Inc. v. Nelson,* 105 F.3d 708 (D.C.Cir. 2/7/97).

46. *Searcy, Denney et.al. v. Poletz,* 652 So.2d 366 (Fla.Sup. 3/16/95). Also see *Klein v. Eubank,* 663 N.E.2d 599 (N.Y.App. 1/9/96): the attorney maintains a charging lien if he or she voluntarily withdraws from representation for just cause; the lien is not limited to the counsel of record at the time of judgment or settlement of the case. The charging lien is lost only if the attorney refuses or neglects to pursue a case without just cause. *Carbonic Consultants Inc. v. Herzfeld & Rubin Inc.,* 699 So.2d 321 (Fla.App. 9/24/97) says that a firm that voluntarily terminated representation (after the departure of the only attorney in the firm who was well-versed in the subject area of the case) could not get a quantum meruit fee in a contingent case. The fee was denied because the client was not at fault and did not create any ethical problems for the firm.

47. *Raymark Industries Inc. v. Butera, Beausang, Cohen & Brennan,* 66 LW 1372 (E.D. Pa. 12/1/97).

48. *National Credit Union Administration Board v. Johnson,* 66 LW 1435 (8th Cir. 1/15/98).

49. *In re Prudential Securities Inc. Limited Partnerships Litigation,* 911 F.Supp. 135 (S.D.N.Y. 1/22/96).

50. *Boccardo v. C.I.R.,* 56 F.3d 1016 (9th Cir. 5/26/95).

51. *Dana Corp. v. U.S.,* 66 LW 1091 (Ct.Fedl.Claims 7/15/97).

— FOR FURTHER REFERENCE —

Amkraut, Robert N., "Taxing Contingency Fee Attorneys as Investors," 71 *Washington L. Rev.* 745 (July '96).

Baker, Cynthia A., "Fixing What's Broken: A Proposal for Reform of the Compensation System in Bankruptcy," 5 *J. of Bankruptcy Law and Practice* 435 (July-August '96).

Bernstein, Paul, "Cost Recovery and the Business of Law," 33 *Trial* 76 (February '97).

Chanen, Jill Schachner, "Getting Paid in Trade: Barter Can Be a Boon for Cash-Strapped Practitioners," 83 *A.B.A.J.* 82 (December '97).

Grace, Thomas P. and Peter J. Neeson, "Alternatives to Traditional Fee Arrangements," 38 *For the Defense* 31 (May '96).

Hay, Bruce L., "The Theory of Fee Regulation in Class Action Settlements," 46 *American U. L.Rev.* 1429 (June '97).

Makar, Scott D., "Post-Judgment Motions for Attorneys' Fees: Time for a Bright-Line Rule?" 71 *Florida Bar J.* 14 (February '97).

McLean, Jay, "Practical Suggestions to Avoid Problems with Fees," 51 *Washington State Bar News* 48 (February '97).

Pertnoy, Leonard D., "An Attorney's Right to Retain Fees Derived from a Fraudulent Law Suit," 8 *St. Thomas L. Rev.* 533 (Spring '96).

Pettit, D. Bradley, "Tax: Can an Attorney Defer Recognition of Fee Income in a Case Involving a Structured Settlement?" 70 *Florida Bar J.* 36 (November '96).

Poll, Edward, "Fixed Fees," 14 Compleat Lawyer 60 (Winter '97).

Proctor, Marcia L., "Privilege and Fee Agreements," 75 *Mich. Bar J.* 822 (August '96).

Ray, Bruce L., "Optimal Contingent Fees in a World of Settlement," 26 *J. of Legal Studies* 259 (January '97).

Ross, William C., "The Ethics of Time-Based Billing by Attorneys," 58 *Alabama Lawyer* 40 (January '97).

Schaer, Angela D., "The Standards for Awarding Attorney Fees Against a State Agency," 32 *Idaho L. Rev.* 437 (Summer '96).

Schratz, James P. and Susan R. Brown, "Recovering Legal Fees and Using Legal Fee Auditors in Fee-Shifting Cases," 20 *Trial Diplomacy J.* 299 (October '97).

Tamery, James E. and Linda L. Harrington, "California's Mandatory Fee Arbitration Program," 9 *The Professional Lawyer* 18 (November '97).

ATTORNEYS' RULES OF PROFESSIONAL CONDUCT

[¶601] An attorney who helps the police perform an unconstitutional search can be subject to liability under *Bivens v. Six Agents of the Federal Bureau of Narcotics,* 403 U.S. 388 (1971), because the attorney is deemed to be a federal agent under these circumstances. Also, the qualified *Bivens* immunity given to government employees is not available to the attorney—although a good-faith defense may be.[1]

A law firm can be held liable for participating in a RICO enterprise if the firm was involved in concealing kickbacks and aided and abetted the predicate acts of mail fraud, because the law firm has played an operational or management role in the criminal enterprise.[2]

If an attorney permits the statute of limitations to expire, thus depriving the client of the ability to be awarded a judgment, the uncollectability of the judgment must be used to adjust the malpractice damages.[3]

Jury trial is available in a legal malpractice suit—even if a jury trial was unavailable in the underlying case where the lawyer allegedly committed malpractice.[4]

Neither settlement of a shareholder derivative suit, nor a Savings & Loan institution's bankruptcy, collaterally estops the S&L's shareholders from suing the S&L holding company's lawyers for malpractice. In the Ninth Circuit's view,[5] the magistrate judge did not decide all the legal issues—for instance, the adequacy of the law firm's representation of the holding company, or whether the settlement was reasonable for malpractice purposes.

New Jersey's tort reform statute requires an "affidavit of merit" in a professional malpractice action: someone within the profession has to go on record that the claim is meritorious. The District Court for the District of New Jersey decided in late 1997 that in a diversity case, an affidavit of merit is not required if the defendant is an out-of-state attorney who does not have a New Jersey license.[6]

Under Tennessee law, a legal malpractice claim is a chose in action, but it is not assignable. Public policy forbids the assignment, because client confidentiality would be compromised. (Attorneys can defend themselves by disclosing confidential communications; the client can control this risk by choosing to sue or not to sue, but the risk is out of the client's hands once an assignee becomes involved.[7])

According to the D.C. Circuit,[8] a client who sues for breach of fiduciary duty in order to receive a return of legal fees (not compensatory damages) is not required to prove causation and damages. The value of legal representation declines, as a matter of law, whenever the duty of loyalty is violated, so at least a partial refund is justified. This case leaves unresolved the questions of whether the entire fee has to be returned, and whether a violation of an ethics rule on representation of multiple clients is necessarily a breach of fiduciary duty.

An attorney formerly employed as house counsel can sue for wrongful discharge if it is alleged that discharge was a penalty for complying with a statutory or ethical duty—provided that the attorney doesn't have to violate client confidences to prove the case.[9] Attorney-client privilege does not preclude a Title VII retaliation suit brought by an attorney formerly employed as in-house counsel by a company. However, the Third Circuit has ruled that, in appropriate circumstances, the court can use sealing and protective orders, or even hold in camera proceedings, to prevent confidential information from general release.[10]

Alcoholism, manic depression, and bipolar disorder have been held not to be mitigating factors that would prevent disbarment of an attorney who has misappropriated client funds or engaged in other very severe misconduct. The need to protect clients outweighs compassion for impaired attorneys. Although mental illnesses are disabilities as defined by the Americans with Disabilities Act, it is impossible to modify working conditions to prevent further attorney misconduct.[11]

Fortunately for clients, attorney negligence is sometimes treated as "excusable neglect" under the Federal Rules of Appellate Procedure that would justify late filing of a bankruptcy appeal.[12]

According to the Fifth Circuit, a mandatory IOLTA program is a "taking" that violates the Fifth Amendment unless the *clients* (rather than the attorneys) have consented to the IOLTA program's use of the clients' funds.[13]

The Florida Bar has set an "aspirational goal" of 20 hours' pro bono work, or payment of $350 to a legal aid organization, per year. The Eleventh Circuit found it permissible to make it a disciplinary offense not to report compliance with this requirement on the annual dues statement. A due process challenge failed, because the state has a clear interest in getting pro bono work done; reporting is a rational means of monitoring the success of the system.[14]

On December 1, 1997, the American Bankruptcy Board of Certification announced that it would change its name to the American Board of Certification, and would certify specialists in business and consumer bankruptcies and creditors' rights.[15]

It constitutes unauthorized practice of law for non-lawyers to be compensated for representing investors at securities arbitrations—even though the Securities Industry Association manual allows representation by non-attorneys.[16]

An attorney offered non-lawyer employee a share of the business she brought in. The attorney reneged on the agreement, and was sued by the by-now ex-employee. The Indiana Supreme Court held the agreement void as against public policy, because lawyers cannot split fees with non-lawyers. A law firm can maintain a profit-sharing plan that covers non-employee staff, but it must be based on the profits of the entire firm, not specific fees.[17]

[¶601.1] Sanctions Under FRCP 11

Sanctions cannot be imposed on an attorney for filing a grounded complaint in a proper forum—even if the forum is not the most convenient one for the defendant, and even if the plaintiff's lawyer tried to get the defendant to settle by threatening to create bad publicity for the State of Israel. In this reading,[18] if there is a valid legal grievance, the impropriety of the motives of those who pursue it does not support sanctions.

The First Amendment protected a variety of unflattering statements that a lawyer made about a judge to a reporter ("ignorant," "anti-Semitic," "drunk on the bench")—and thus the attorney could not properly be sanctioned by a suspension. Statements about a judge's integrity are protectable under the First Amendment unless they are susceptible of factual proof (e.g., alleging that a particular judge is a bigamist or did not pass the bar exam).[19]

As long as an attorney has exercised his or her best efforts to get the client to comply, the attorney should not be sanctioned for the client's failure to comply with a court order (in this case, ordering the client to appear at a settlement conference).[20] Similarly, the Third Circuit says that the lawyer can be sanctioned only if the court can show how the attorney (as distinct from the client) has violated the rule or statute cited to support the sanctions.[21]

One product of the 1995 securities reform legislation (see ¶3808) is sanctions against unsuccessful securities plaintiffs and their attorneys. Sanctions were properly imposed in a Seventh Circuit case in which neither of the two theories in the complaint was supported by specific factual allegations, and the theories lacked reasonable grounding in fact or law.[22]

The Seventh, Ninth, and Tenth Circuits have found that Bankruptcy Code §105 gives bankruptcy courts the power to sanction attorneys for unreasonable and vexatious multiplication of proceedings. The Seventh Circuit did not reach the issue of whether the bankruptcy court can impose sanctions under 28 U.S.C. §1927, but it said that bankruptcy courts do not fit the definition of "courts of the United States" under 28 U.S.C. §451.[23]

A sanctioned attorney who is no longer involved in a case (and therefore is not obligated to wait until the case is completed) can appeal the sanctions immediately. The Fifth Circuit permitted this result even when no monetary penalty was imposed, in light of the value of the sanctioned attorney's professional reputation.[24]

[¶602] CLIENT-LAWYER RELATIONSHIP

Sexual relations with a divorce client are not *per se* a breach of professional responsibility (in a jurisdiction with no explicit rule on this point). However, if other ethical rules, such as those involving conflict of interest, are violated, the West Virginia Supreme Court says that the attorney can be disqualified from further representation of that client.[25] In the view of the Illinois Court of Appeals, a client's claim that a lawyer initiated a coercive sexual relationship states a claim for battery but not for malpractice (because the quality of representation was not affected), negligence, or breach of fiduciary duty.[26]

A criminal defense attorney is required to complete the IRS Form 8300 currency transaction report, naming a client who has paid more than $10,000 in cash, even if this disclosure harms the client in the case the lawyer is defending (e.g., money laundering). Potential harm to the client does not constitute a "reasonable cause" that would rebut the IRS' contention that the lawyer is guilty of "willful neglect".[27]

Where the lawyer is the target of an IRS investigation, and his or her clients are not, the IRS can serve the lawyer with a summons requiring the disclosure of names of clients that were not reported on Form 8300. The IRS does not have to follow its John Doe summons procedure (which requires court authorization). In general, client identity and the nature of fee arrangements are not privileged—particularly when the IRS isn't investigating the clients anyway.[28]

A limited partnership is an entity and must act through its agents, so a bankruptcy trustee, acting for a debtor limited partnership, can waive the attorney-client privilege.[29]

Attorney-client privilege is not available for in-house counsel's work in negotiating contracts and reporting to management on negotiations. The Southern District of New York deemed this work to be business advice, not the traditional, confidential functions of an attorney.[30] A company's communications with its attorneys about amendments to pension and benefit plans are privileged, and cannot be discovered by employees challenging the plan amendments, even if the company received advice from the same attorney about non-fiduciary aspects of plan administration.[31]

Where a law firm's senior partner assigned associates to investigate another attorney's alleged misuse of client funds, a Grand Jury investigation of the target lawyer could not subpoena the associates with respect to their conversations with the partner. The Ninth Circuit found the internal investigation privileged, even though the firm was not paying the associates specifically for the investigation. Nevertheless, they were constructively acting as in-house counsel. Since the investigation of alleged improprieties was conducted by lawyers, there was a reasonable expectation of privilege as to investigative results.[32]

A District Court's order denying a motion for protection from discovery (based on asserted attorney-client and work product privileges) is a collateral order, and therefore is immediately appealable.[33]

Under the "crime-fraud" exception to the attorney-client privilege, discussions cease to be privileged if the government makes a prima facie showing that the communications furthered either present or intended illegality. The privilege protects the client rather than the lawyer, so it's the client's guilty knowledge that matters—the crime-fraud exemption can be invoked even if the lawyer takes no affirmative steps to further the crime (and, indeed, even if the lawyer is unaware of it).[34] The crime-fraud exception applies only in situations where the client sought the lawyer's help in actually committing the crime. Therefore, an attorney who warned the police that the client might be about to commit a crime does not have to testify as to what the client said.[35]

Attorney-client privilege protects preliminary drafts of documents even though the finalized documents were publicly filed. Therefore, the drafts were not discoverable by shareholders bringing a derivative suit charging waste and breach of fiduciary duty. In the analysis of the Delaware Chancery,[36] the changes between draft and final version reflect privileged discussions with the company's attorneys. However, documents prepared by the corporation's Vice President/Secretary were not privileged even though the corporate officer happened to be an attorney, because he was not performing legal work while preparing or reviewing the documents.

A trust beneficiary cannot discover confidential communications about trust administration between the trustee and an attorney hired to advise the trustee.

However, the trustee (and not the attorney) has a duty to disclose all material facts about their rights to beneficiaries, and a beneficiary can depose a trustee as to factual matters such as the trustee's handling of trust property. Even the attorney can testify on those factual matters—but not about confidential attorney-client matters.[37]

After the termination of an attorney-client relationship, the New York Court of Appeals ruled that the ex-client is entitled to inspect and copy the entire case file, including work product material, unless the work product documents were created for internal use within the law firm or unless disclosure would violate a duty to someone else.[38]

In the case of another type of termination of relationship—the client's death—attorney-client privilege might be lost as to information pertinent to a Grand Jury investigation and not otherwise available. The D.C. Circuit decided that, although the client still has a protectable post-mortem reputation, the client is no longer at risk of imprisonment or other practical negative consequences.[39]

Communications with a consulting expert who does not testify are protectable work product, but the privilege is lost if the expert also testifies in the case.[40]

Neither tort nor contract law (in California) makes lawyers liable if they violate a private agreement with opposing counsel not to disclose confidential documents that were uncovered during the discovery process.[41] This is true even if the agreement was incorporated into a protective order from the court.

Although the upshot of the disclosure of the documents was substantial litigation against the corporation that sought to keep the documents confidential, the California Court of Appeals ruled that it is not tortious to induce a third party to pursue a meritorious claim. Although sanctions are available for violation of the protective order, the underlying contract was extinguished by the protective order, so damages for breach of contract were not available.

If a client stubbornly refuses to follow an attorney's advice to settle a case, even the court's consent to the firm's withdrawal does not constitute "just cause" for withdrawal that will entitle the firm to get paid—if the stubborn client still wants the firm to remain on the case.[42]

An attorney can obtain dismissal from a tax case when, as soon as the attorney becomes aware of a lien on the client's property, the attorney brings an interpleader action and deposits money in the court's registry. The attorney does not have to turn over funds in the client trust account to the IRS.[43]

Under California law, an attorney has no duty to advise an ex-client to get a new lawyer before the statute of limitations runs out, where the lawyer must stop representing that client because of that client's potential claims against a current client of the lawyer. Giving such advice would violate the duty of loyalty to the current client, by making it easier to subject that client to liability.[44]

Under Idaho law, there is a continuing duty to ex-clients, so it constitutes malpractice to represent another party who is adverse to the ex-client, in a substantially related matter. This is true even if the former client's confidences are not violated during the subsequent representation.[45] A 1995 Arkansas case finds a conflict of interest if one of a firm's lawyers represents the plaintiff in a malpractice suit against a hospital where another lawyer from the same firm recently served on the hospital's Board of Governors.[46]

A firm representing a selling corporation and its sole shareholder in a merger cannot later represent the selling shareholder in a suit by the surviving corporation. The surviving corporation is carrying on the original business, so it has an attorney-client relationship with the lawyer. The buyer has the privilege as to communications about business operations before the sale, but not communications about the actual merger negotiations.[47] According to the California Court of Appeals, however, it is not a conflict of interest for a firm that has represented a subsidiary corporation to represent another party on an unrelated matter adverse to the subsidiary's parent corporation, unless the subsidiary and parent are alter egos, and do not merely possess a unity of interests.[48]

Clearly, however, not every contact between attorney and business will result in an attorney-client relationship. A 1996 Kansas case, for instance, finds that a lawyer who was hired by a corporation to do a general presentation on employment law, but who did not gain access to any confidential corporate communications, did not have a conflict preventing representation of a civil rights plaintiff against the corporation six years later. The past employment was not related to any issues occurring within the civil rights lawsuit.[49]

[¶603] COUNSELOR

A divorce lawyer can be sued for malpractice for failing to give proper advice about well-established legal principles (e.g., the substantive law governing termination of the alimony obligation upon remarriage of the former spouse).[50]

ERISA does not preempt a malpractice suit against a pension plan's lawyers.[51]

[¶604] ADVOCATE

Given the attorney's duty to be truthful and trustworthy, an adversary can sue a defendant's attorney for deliberate misrepresentation of the amount of the defendant's insurance, where the misrepresentation induced the plaintiff to settle the case.[52] Ohio has a rule imposing *per se* suspension in disciplinary cases where the attorney has misrepresented a material fact or point of law to a tribunal.[53]

Damages for malicious defense of a tort action (involving false evidence and testimony fabricated by the defense counsel) are available on the same terms as for malicious prosecution, on the theory that a litigant is not made whole by mere reimbursement of attorneys' fees.[54]

In mid-1996, the Seventh Circuit relieved two lawyers from criminal contempt penalties when they failed to arrive in court immediately after the jury reached its verdict (because of beeper failure, they didn't know about the verdict).

The Seventh Circuit left open the possibility of an "Order to Show Cause" why the lawyers should not have to reimburse the Treasury for the extra cost of reassembling the jury the next day. Not testing the beepers might constitute negligence, but was not tantamount to criminal contempt.[55]

[¶605] Transactions with Persons Other Than Clients

Preliminary injunction was granted against a Hawaii rule forbidding attorneys to contact jurors *ex parte*; the District Court for the District of Hawaii found the rule to be vague and overbroad, in that it violates attorneys' rights of free speech without really protecting jurors against harassment.[56]

An attorney can't be liable to a nonclient if recognizing a duty to the nonclient would require breaching a client's confidentiality. Therefore, the attorney for a mortgagee cannot be liable to the assignee of the mortgage for preparing an incomplete title certificate.[57]

A 1997 Oregon case[58] finds that a director/shareholder removed in an alleged corporate squeeze-out does not have standing to sue the corporation's lawyers for breach of fiduciary duty. The lawyer's fiduciary duty, if any, ran to the corporate client, and not to non-client directors.

The New Jersey Supreme Court found a duty of attorneys to third parties whom the attorney knows will rely on the attorney's representations (here, the condition of real estate vis-a-vis its septic system). No duty exists if the third party is too remote from the representation to be entitled to protection.[59]

In a Florida case, adoptive parents falsified Florida residence, with the result that a child was taken away from the grandmother who cared for the child, and then unlawfully adopted out-of-state. The child was held to have standing to sue the adoptive parents' lawyers (one of whom acted as intermediary with the birth mother). A limited exception was read into the privity requirement for attorney malpractice where the plaintiff was the intended beneficiary of the attorney's actions.

Furthermore, attorneys who act as adoption intermediaries have a duty to act in the best interests of the child. The child was also permitted to sue the attorneys for malicious prosecution, because the gravamen of that tort is the misuse of legal machinery for an unlawful purpose. However, the claim for intentional infliction of emotional distress was dismissed, because interstate transport of a child by a mother who had legal custody at that time did not constitute conduct that is "reckless and utterly outrageous in a civilized community."[60]

Attorneys have been held liable to nonclients for negligent misrepresentations in opinion letters, where the opinion letter either is addressed to the third party or expressly authorizes reliance by the third party (e.g., as here, where there was a material misstatement of fact as to a bank's purchase of bonds issued by a municipality represented by the attorney).[61] However, this case says that a malpractice claim requires privity.

In contrast, absolute judicial privilege has been deemed to protect allegedly defamatory statements about potential defendants made in solicitation letters sent (at a client's request) to fellow corporate shareholders at a time when litigation was contemplated in good faith.[62]

[¶606]   LAW FIRMS AND ASSOCIATIONS

A New York law firm can't enforce a fee agreement with a California client for services rendered in California, if no one in the firm was admitted in that state and the firm failed to associate local counsel.[63] On the other hand, the firm can recover on a quantum meruit basis for work done in New York.

According to the New Jersey Superior Court, it is inappropriate for a law firm employment agreement to restrict the amount a lawyer can earn from clients who move with him when the firm fires him. In this analysis, no matter how much a firm may invest in a contingent case, it's just one of the risks of doing business.[64]

In contrast, the New York Court of Appeals upheld an arbitrator who in turn upheld a provision in a law firm partnership agreement that limited compensation paid to withdrawing partners based on their income from other sources. The court viewed the provision as "competition neutral" because it did not single out partners who leave to join competing law firms.[65] Massachusetts has held that it is improper for a law firm to deprive departing partners who compete with the firm of payments that non-competing departing partners can receive. However, the departure payments can be limited if competition from the ex-partner poses a significant threat to the firm's financial integrity.[66]

New Jersey law permits retainer agreements to include reasonable limitations on a client's right to discharge the attorney. However, automatic renewal of the agreement and a requirement of six months' notice of termination is unreasonable. In a 1996 case, the court found that the client was also unreasonable in giving the attorney only 3 days' notice of termination when there had been no prior complaints about the quality of representation. The lawyer was awarded half the fee provided by the retainer agreement.[67]

Under certain circumstances, the principles of agency law permit a law firm to claim contribution from a negligent associate whose poor work caused the firm to encounter liability.[68] To succeed in such a claim, the firm must prove that its supervision of the attorney did not constitute authorization or ratification of the inappropriate conduct. Furthermore, in New Jersey, contribution theory requires proof that the associate acted for his or her personal gain—mere professional incompetence is not enough.

A lawyer who serves as arbitrator is not obligated to investigate to find out if his or her former law firm has a connection to a party to the arbitration.[69]

[¶607]   INFORMATION ABOUT LEGAL SERVICES

Both a Florida statute and a Texas bar rule that forbid direct-mail solicitation of accident victims within 30 days of an accident have survived First Amendment challenges brought by lawyers wishing to send such solicitations.[70] In both cases, the state was permitted to protect the privacy of victims and their families, even if perhaps the restriction on commercial speech could have been more narrowly tailored.

The issue arose again in 1997, in the Fourth and Tenth Circuits (with respect to Maryland and New Mexico laws). The Fourth Circuit struck down, on First Amendment grounds, a Maryland law forbidding direct-mail solicitation by attorneys within 30 days of an accident, disaster, or criminal charge. In the Fourth Circuit's analysis, a direct-mail ban would favor attorneys who are already well-known or who can afford television advertising. Furthermore, targeted direct mail does not invade privacy much more than a generalized brochure. The Fourth Circuit distinguished the Maryland from the Florida law discussed above because the Maryland law had a lesser connection with private grief (because the ban was broad enough to include solicitation of criminal defendants).[71]

The Tenth Circuit also held that a complete ban on direct mail solicitation of personal injury victims violates the First Amendment. The state disciplinary board disapproved direct mail because of its potential to convey a false message that the soliciting lawyer is uniquely qualified to handle the case. The Court of Appeals found that New Mexico did not choose the narrowest means to combat the real risk of attorney misrepresentation. For example, letters could be screened, or a 30-day blackout period could be imposed.[72]

Florida's state bar had the obligation of proving the validity of the limitations it imposed on the use of testimonials, illustrations, and dramatizations in attorney advertisements. The Eleventh Circuit ruled that lawyers did not have the burden of proof, because they were challenging the application of the rules, not their facial validity.[73]

Another Florida statute, forbidding the use of information from traffic citations in commercial solicitation was struck down by the Southern District of Florida in 1996,[74] on First Amendment grounds. The statute was deemed to violate the First Amendment because it regulated the use of public information. Lawyers' nondeceptive solicitations are protected as commercial speech. Furthermore, the privacy concerns were vitiated because driver safety training courses were granted access to the same information and were permitted to use the information for solicitation.

Louisiana's Supreme Court called it a "close question," but not quite an illegal solicitation, for a lawyer to telephone a widow with information about the manner of her husband's death. The bar disciplinary counsel failed to prove by clear and convincing evidence that the lawyer's motive for the call was soliciting business from the widow.[75]

The Michigan State Bar Committee on Professional and Judicial Ethics has weighed in with an informal opinion[76] permitting use of the Internet to distribute information about a firm's legal services, without complying with the solicitation rule—on condition that a generally accessible medium, such as the World Wide Web, is used. Solicitation by real-time electronic conversation (such as videoconferencing) is forbidden, and solicitation by e-mail is subject to the 30-day wait imposed by the solicitation rule.

[¶608]   ADMISSION TO THE BAR

The Third Circuit has upheld a challenge by a New York-resident lawyer to the New Jersey rules that require members of the New Jersey bar to maintain an office and attend CLE programs in that state. In this reading, the state has a legitimate interest in encouraging full-time practice of law and ensuring that attorneys maintain current knowledge. This state interest outweighs any burden imposed on interstate commerce. Furthermore, the requirements were found to be the same for residents and non-residents, and not unduly burdensome on the non-residents of New Jersey.[77]

A rule requiring sponsorship by a local lawyer who has an office and practices daily within the state as a condition of *pro haec vice* admission was upheld by the Fourth Circuit. The rule was deemed not to be a residency requirement, because the sponsoring attorney might live outside the state and still go to the in-state office on a daily basis. Furthermore, although practicing law is a fundamental right subject to the Privileges and Immunities clause, the Fourth Circuit does not deem sponsoring other attorneys for *pro haec vice* admission to be a fundamental part of the practice of law.[78]

The Eleventh Circuit takes a broader view of *pro haec vice* admissions: it ruled in mid-1997 that for a District Court to deny a petition for *pro haec vice* admission to the federal courts, it must demonstrate a degree of unethical conduct (as defined by the rules of professional conduct) that would justify disbarment.[79]

— ENDNOTES —

1. *Vector Research Inc. v. Howard & Howard,* 76 F.3d 692 (6th Cir. 2/14/96).

2. *In re American Honda Motor Co. Dealerships Relations Litigation,* 965 F.Supp. 716 (D.Md. 3/11/97).

3. *Klump v. Duffus,* 71 F.3d 1368 (7th Cir. 12/18/95).

4. *Ceriale v. L.A. Superior Court,* 22 Fam. Law Reporter 1518 (Cal.App. 8/29/96).

5. *Durkin v. Shea & Gould,* 92 F.3d 1510 (9th Cir. 8/19/96).

6. *RTC Mortgage Trust 1994 N-1 v. Fidelity National Title Insurance Co.,* 66 LW 1259 (D.N.J. 10/20/97).

7. *Can Do Inc. Pension & Profit Sharing Plan v. Manier, Herod, Hollabaugh & Smith PC,* 64 LW 2749 (Tenn.Sup. 5/6/96).

8. *Hendry v. Pelland,* 73 F.3d 397 (D.C.Cir. 1/19/96).

9. *GTE Products Corp. v. Stewart,* 653 N.E.2d 161 (Mass.Sup.Jud.Ct. 8/1/95).

10. *Kachmar v. SunGard Data Systems Inc.,* 109 F.3d 173 (3rd Cir. 3/26/97).

11. *Attorney Grievance Commission v. Kenney,* 339 Md. 578 (Md.App. 9/11/95) [alcoholism]; *Florida Bar v. Clement,* 662 So.2d 690 (Fla.Sup. 11/2/95): manic depression/bipolar disorder.

12. *Pioneer Investment Services Co. v. Brunswick Association LP,* 504 U.S. 956 (Sup.Ct. 1993); *Reynolds v. Wagner,* 55 F.3d 1426 (9th Cir. 5/26/95).

13. *Washington Legal Foundation v. Texas Equal Access to Justice Foundation,* 94 F.3d 996 (5th Cir. 9/12/96).

14. *Schwarz v. Cogan,* 66 LW 1435 (11th Cir. 1/12/98).

15. See 66 LW 2358; call (703) 739-1023 for information.

16. *Florida Bar Re: Advisory Opinion on Nonlawyer Representation in Securities Arbitration,* 696 So.2d 1178 (Fla.Sup. 7/3/97).

17. *Trotter v. Nelson,* 66 LW 1179 (Ind.Sup. 9/12/97).

18. *Sussman v. Bank of Israel,* 56 F.3d 450 (2d Cir. 6/2/95).

19. *Standing Committee on Discipline v. Yagman,* 55 F.3d 1430 (9th Cir. 5/30/95).

20. *Universal Cooperative Inc. v. Trial Cooperative Marketing Development Federation of India,* 45 F.3d 1194 (8th Cir. 1/23/95).

21. *Martin v. Brown,* 63 F.3d 1252 (3d Cir. 8/23/95).

22. *Katz v. Household International Inc.,* 91 F.3d 1036 (7th Cir. 8/9/96).

23. *In re Volpert,* 110 F.3d 494 (7th Cir. 4/1/97).

24. *Walker v. Mesquite, Texas,* 66 LW 1373 (5th Cir. 12/10/97).

25. *Musick v. Musick,* 453 S.E.2d 361 (W.Va.Sup. 1/25/95).

26. *Kling v. Landry,* 66 LW 1399 (Ill.App. 10/10/97).

27. *Gerald B. Lefcourt PC v. U.S.,* 66 LW 1167 (2nd Cir. 9/10/97).

28. *U.S. v. Blackman,* 72 F.3d 1418 (9th Cir. 12/29/95).

29. *U.S. v. Campbell,* 73 F.3d 44 (5th Cir. 1/3/96).

30. *Georgia-Pacific Corp. v. GAF Roofing Mfg. Corp.,* 64 LW 2497 (S.D.N.Y. 1/24/96).

31. *Becher v. LILCO,* 66 LW 1311 (2nd Cir. 11/12/97).

32. *U.S. v. Rowe,* 96 F.3d 1294 (9th Cir. 9/27/96).

33. *Kelly v. Ford Motor Co.,* 110 F.3d 954 (3rd Cir. 4/9/97).

34. *In re Grand Jury Proceedings (Appeal of the Corporation),* 87 F.3d 377 (9th Cir. 6/27/96).

35. *Purcell v. District Attorney for Suffolk District,* 424 Mass. 109 (Mass.Sup.Jud.Ct. 1/13/97).

36. *Lee v. Engle,* 64 LW 2479 (Del.Chancery 12/15/95).

37. *Huie v. DeShazo,* 64 LW 2540 (Tex.Sup. 2/9/96).

38. *Sage Realty Co. v. Proskauer, Rose, Goetz & Mendelssohn LLP,* 66 LW 1355 (N.Y.App. 12/2/97).

39. *In re Sealed Case,* 116 F.3d 550 (D.C. Cir. 6/17/97).

40. *Emergency Care Dynamics Ltd. v. Superior Court of Arizona,* 65 LW 2538

(Ariz.App. 2/4/97).

41. *Westinghouse Electric Corp. v. Newman & Holtzinger PC,* 39 Cal.App. 4th 1194, 46 Cal.Rptr.2d 151 (Cal.App. 10/30/95).

42. *Augustson v. Linea Aerea Nacional-Chile S.A.,* 76 F.3d 658 (5th Cir. 2/29/96).

43. *Kurland v. C.I.R.,* 919 F.Supp. 419 (M.D.Fla. 3/6/96).

44. *Flatt v. Superior Court (Daniel),* 885 P.2d 950 (Cal.Sup. 12/28/94).

45. *Damron v. Herzog,* 67 F.3d 211 (9th Cir. 9/26/95).

46. *Berry v. Saline Memorial Hospital,* 70 F.3d 981 (Ark.Sup. 10/23/95).

47. *Tekni-Plex Inc. v. Meyer and Landis,* 674 N.E.2d 663 (N.Y.App. 10/22/96).

48. *Brooklyn Navy Yard Cogeneration Partners LP v. Superior Court,* 66 LW 1430 (Cal.App. 12/19/97).

49. *Marten v. Yellow Freight System,* 65 LW 2319 (D.Kan. 9/5/96).

50. *McMahon v. Shea,* 657 A.2d 938 (Pa.Super. 2/23/95).

51. *Custer v. Sweeney,* 89 F.3d 1156 (4th Cir. 7/22/96).

52. *Fire Insurance Exchange v. Bell,* 643 N.E.2d 310 (Ind.Sup. 11/28/94).

53. *Office of Disciplinary Counsel v. Greene,* 655 N.E.2d 1299 (Ohio Sup. 11/1/95).

54. *Aranson v. Schroeder,* 671 A.2d 1023 (N.H.Sup. 10/31/95).

55. *U.S. v. Mottweiler,* 64 LW 2709 (7th Cir. 5/3/96).

56. *Rapp v. Hawaii Supreme Court Disciplinary Board,* 916 F.Supp. 1525 (D.Hawaii 2/2/96).

57. *One National Bank v. Antonellis,* 80 F.3d 606 (1st Cir. 4/3/96).

58. *Granewich v. Harding,* 945 P.2d 1067 (Ore.App. 9/17/97).

59. *Petrillo v. Bachenberg,* 655 A.2d 1354 (N.J.Sup. 3/29/95).

60. *Rushing v. Bosse,* 652 So.2d 869 (Fla.App. 3/8/95).

61. *Mehaffy, Rider, Windholz & Wilson v. Central Bank Denver N.A.,* 829 P.2d 230 (Colo.Sup. 1/30/95). But see *Rubin v. Schottenstein, Zox & Dunn,* 110 F.3d 1247 (6th Cir. 4/15/97), in which a corporation hired a lawyer to draft an opinion letter dealing with a private placement. The letter did not mention that engaging in the proposed financing would constitute default on certain bank loans. The attorney was sued by unhappy investors, but prevailed, on the grounds that he was not hired to prepare an offering circular or discuss the terms of the company's financing. An attorney's silence was deemed to constitute a securities violation only given a duty to disclose. Nor could the investors, who had their own attorneys and could ascertain the terms of the corporation's loans, claim justifiable reliance on what the attorney said.

62. *Kittler v. Eckberg, Lammers, Briggs, Wolff & Vierling,* 535 N.W.2d 653 (Minn.App. 8/8/95).

63. *Birbrower, Montalbano, Condon & Frank v. Superior Court,* 56 Cal.Rptr.2d 857 (Cal.App. 9/25/96). Also see later proceedings in the same case, 66 LW 1420 (Cal.Sup. 1/5/98) denying the New York firm compensation for representing California clients during private dispute resolution in California.

64. *Leonard & Butler PC v. Harris,* 653 A.2d 1193 (N.J.Super. 2/27/95).

65. *Hackett v. Milbank Tweed,* 654 N.E.2d 95 (N.Y.App. 7/5/95).

66. *Pettingell v. Morrison, Mahoney & Miller,* 66 LW 1430 (Mass.Sup.Jud.Ct. 12/10/97).

67. *Cohen v. Radio-Electronics Officers Union,* 679 A.2d 1188 (N.J.Sup. 8/14/96).

68. *Kramer v. Nowak,* 908 F.Supp. 1281 (E.D.Pa. 12/13/95).

69. *Al-Harbi v. Citibank,* 85 F.3d 680 (D.C. Cir. 6/11/96), *cert. denied* 117 S.Ct. 432.

70. *Florida Bar v. Went For It Inc.,* 115 S.Ct. 2371 (Sup.Ct.6/21/95); *Moore v. Morales,* 65 F.3d 358 (5th Cir. 8/23/95); *Moore* was remanded to test the effect of the solicitation statute on other professions, such as the medical profession.

71. *Ficker v. Curran,* 119 F.3d 1150 (4th Cir. 7/23/97).

72. *Revo v. New Mexico Supreme Court Disciplinary Board,* 106 F.3d 919 (10th Cir. 2/5/97). *cert.denied* 117 S.Ct. 2515.

73. *Jacobs v. Florida Bar,* 50 F.3d 901 (11th Cir. 4/10/95).

74. *Babkes v. Satz,* 944 F.Supp. 909 (S.D. Fla. 10/23/96).

75. *In re D'Amico,* 668 So.2d 730 (La.Sup. 2/28/96).

76. Informal Op. RI-276 (7/11/96); see 65 LW 2334.

77. *Tolchin v. New Jersey Supreme Court,* 111 F.3d 1099 (3rd Cir. 5/2/97).

78. *Parnell v. West Virginia Court of Appeals,* 110 F.3d 1077 (4th Cir. 4/14/97).

79. *Schlumberger Technologies, Inc. v. Wiley,* 113 F.3d 1553 (11th Cir. 6/5/97).

— FOR FURTHER REFERENCE —

Carr, Maureen, "The Effect of Prior Criminal Conduct on the Admission to Practice Law," 66 *The Bar Examiner* 10 (February '97).

Feldman, Henry A. Jr., "Attorneys as Professional Trustees: Another Way to Build Your Practice," 23 *Law Practice Management* 44 (January–February '97).

Ford, Michael J., "Survival Traits for Young Lawyers," 54 *Bench and Bar of Minnesota* 32 (February '97).

Golden, Christopher A., "Fair Debt Collection Practices Act: An Emerging Source of Liability for Attorneys," 69 *New York State Bar J.* 14 (February '97).

Harrington, Mona, "Is Time-Out for Family Unprofessional?" 33 *Trial* 70 (February '97).

Johnson, Robert J., "In-House Counsel Employed by Insurance Companies: A Difficult Dilemma Confronting the Model Code of Professional Responsibility," 57 *Ohio State Bar J.* 945 (June '96).

Justian, Charles F., "A Time for Change: Helping Attorneys Who Have Mental or Physical Illnesses that Precipitate Grievances," 75 *Michigan Bar J.* 1026 (October '96).

Martin, Robert W., "Affiliated Firm Arrangements Raise Ethical Issues," 39 *Advocate* 16 (January '96).

Needham, Carol A., "Splitting Bar Admission into Federal and State Components," 45 *U. of Kansas L.Rev.* 453 (March '97).

Pope, Daniel J. and Helen Whatley Pope, "Rule 1.6 and the Noisy Withdrawal," 63 *Defense Counsel J.* 543 (October '96).

Proctor, Marcia, "Leaving a Firm-Client Notices," 76 *Michigan Bar J.* 84 (January '97).

Rockas, George C., "Lawyers for Hire and Associations of Lawyers: Arrangements that are Changing the Way Law is Practiced," 40 *Boston Bar J.* 8 (November–December '96).

Summa, Jeffrey D., "Should You Convert Your Practice to a Limited Liability Company?" 22 *Law Practice Management* 26 (September '96).

Thar, Anne E., "The New Malpractice Time Bomb: Problem Associates and Partners," 85 *Illinois Bar J.* 85 (February '97).

Tollin, Howard M. and Tammy Feman, "Litigation Management: What Legal Defense Costs are Reasonable and Necessary?" 63 *Defense Counsel J.* 529 (October '96).

Wrona, James S. and Robert J. Tribeck, "Practice Tips for Litigating in Federal Court," 68 *Pennsylvania Bar Ass'n Quarterly* 1 (January '97).

BANKRUPTCY

[¶701] See the Bankruptcy Reform Act of 1994, P.L. 103-394 (10/22/94) for provisions designed to improve the administration of bankruptcy cases. In the commercial context, the procedures for electing trustees were changed; the trustee's avoiding power was subjected to new limits; and creditors' rights provisions for demanding return of goods were enhanced. Consumer bankruptcy fraud was criminalized; more exceptions to dischargeability were enacted; and child support and alimony were given additional protection from discharge.

False statements in unsworn papers filed in Bankruptcy Court cannot give rise to an indictment under 18 U.S.C. §1001 (false statements in any matter within the jurisdiction of any "department or agency of the United States,") because the U.S. Supreme Court says that a federal court is neither a department nor an agency.[1] But a bankruptcy court is a "court of the United States" with authority under Internal Revenue Code §7430 to order the IRS to pay a prevailing party's attorneys' fees.[2] A private bankruptcy trustee appointed by a court is an "officer of the court" who can remove cases under 28 U.S.C.§1442, but such a trustee is not an "officer of the United States" as defined by Federal Rules of Appellate Procedure 4(a). Therefore, the time to appeal is 30 days, not the 60 day period available to an officer of the United States.[3]

The mere fact that a personal injury defendant or co-defendant is bankrupt (utilizing the federal bankruptcy statute) will not justify removal of what is inherently a state personal injury action to the federal court system.[4] However, state tort claims alleging improper filing of an involuntary bankruptcy petition are impliedly preempted by the Bankruptcy Code's own §303(i) penalties for wrongful filing.[5]

The U.S. Trustee's decision to remove a member of the Chapter 7 trustee panel from the active roster cannot be appealed. Joining the panel does not create a property interest in future assignments; and panel membership is not a "license" whose cancellation requires adherence to administrative law procedures.[6]

On December 1, 1997, the American Bankruptcy Board of Certification announced that it would change its name to the American Board of Certification, and would offer certification in business bankruptcy, consumer bankruptcy, and creditors' rights.[7]

Note: In most legal contexts, it's clear that a reference to "the Code" means the Internal Revenue Code. However, there is also a Bankruptcy Code and, because of the relevance of tax issues to bankruptcy planning and practice, it's important to be sure which "Code" is being referenced in any given citation.

[¶704]   VOLUNTARY BANKRUPTCY

Joint bankruptcy filing is available only for legally married couples—not, e.g., for a same-sex couple who have undergone a religious marriage ceremony.[8]

The termination date for the right to cure a default is the date that the property was foreclosed and sold. Even if the debtor's time to exercise the right of redemption has not expired under state law, the debtor can't cure a pre-petition default by paying the arrears as part of a Chapter 13 plan, then continuing mortgage payments *outside* the plan.[9]

A partnership in the process of dissolution is not a "person" and therefore cannot make a Chapter 11 filing. Furthermore, according to the Second Circuit, the purpose of a Chapter 11 filing is business reorganization, and the relevant state law (New York's) does not permit a dissolving partnership to do anything other than wind up its affairs.[10]

[¶704.1]   Operation of the Automatic Stay

Imposing Code §6672 tax penalties that violate the automatic stay is merely voidable, not void. Thus, a taxpayer is not necessarily able to void the assessment in bankruptcy, as long as the assessment does not frustrate the purpose of the automatic stay.[11]

The automatic stay does not apply to benefit the partners, guarantors, sureties, or insurers of the bankruptcy debtor.[12] However, IRC §6503(h)—which suspends the tax statute of limitations during the taxpayer's bankruptcy—also suspends the running of the statute of limitations against derivatively liable parties such as partners of a bankrupt partnership.[13] The theory is that if derivatively liable parties can take advantage of the statute of limitations which time-bars a main suit, they are back on the hook if the main suit can be revived.

Bankruptcy courts have discretion to lift the automatic stay so that an equitable distribution action against the debtor can proceed in state court.[14]

In a matrimonial case, the Bankruptcy Court for the Eastern District of California ruled that a District Attorney's office, enforcing a wage assignment against a delinquent child support obligor, should either have filed for relief from the automatic stay or stopped accepting payments once it became aware of the obligor's Chapter 13 filing. However, the nondischargeable nature of the child support obligation means that the office had no obligation to return amounts already collected.[15]

In another matrimonial case, the automatic stay was held not to prevent distribution of 50% of a pension, based on a decree granted before the filing of the Chapter 13 petition. However, because spousal support payments come from current income, which becomes property of the estate, the trustee cannot make the payments without getting relief from the automatic stay.[16]

The automatic stay is not violated if the creditor sends a nonthreatening, noncoercive letter to the debtor's attorney (with a copy to the debtor), requesting reaffirmation of the debt. The Seventh Circuit said[17] that the stay protects the debtor against lawsuits, but not necessarily against communications that are not abusive.

Where a plaintiff does not have notice of the transfer of the Chapter 11 debtor's assets (including a disclaimer of liability for certain personal injury claims), the bankruptcy court cannot enjoin a personal injury suit against the purchaser of all the debtor's assets. In one such case, retailers and wholesalers of firearms produced by the debtor did not have notification and had no chance to comment on the reorganization plan, and so were not prevented from bringing suit against the purchaser of his assets.[18]

Although a bankruptcy court has contempt power, it cannot sanction a state for violating the automatic stay by ordering the state to pay the debtor's attorney's fees for a frivolous appeal made necessary by the violation. (However, the appellate court does have the power to sanction the state, according to the Ninth Circuit.[19])

Corporate debtors are not "individuals" who can get damages under Bankruptcy Code §362(h) for willful violation of the automatic stay.[20]

[¶705] PROCEDURAL STEPS IN BANKRUPTCY PROCEEDINGS

When a case is converted from Chapter 11 to Chapter 7, the two-year limitation period for bringing avoidance actions does not start over again; there is only one two-year period, running from the appointment of the *first* trustee.[21] In the case of such a conversion, if the estate can't pay both sets of administrative expenses and the U.S. Trustee's fee, the trustee fee has to be prorated, with the Chapter 7 expenses taking priority. Therefore, the trustee's fee has the same priority as the Chapter 7 expenses, above that of the Chapter 11 expenses.[22]

28 U.S.C. §1452(b) lets the District Court remand removed claims, not related to bankruptcy, "on equitable grounds." (The remand order is not appealable.) In this context, "equitable" has been interpreted by the Second Circuit to mean "fair and reasonable"—not descending from an equity action in a British Chancery court.[23]

State tort claims dealing with wrongful filing of an involuntary petition are preempted by the Bankruptcy Code §303(i) penalties for wrongful filing.[24]

The Rules of Bankruptcy Procedure call for setting out every "judgment" (in other words, every appealable order) in a separate document. The Ninth Circuit says that an order granting summary judgment is separate from an order denying a motion for reconsideration—therefore, separate documents are required.[25]

Under the Federal Rules of Bankruptcy Procedure 8002, filing a motion to reconsider tolls the period for filing notice of appeal, even if the motion is filed in bad faith. Any improprieties can be punished by sanctions, rather than by dismissing "untimely" appeals.[26] As for sanctions, a Seventh Circuit case from Spring, 1997 agrees with the Ninth and Tenth Circuits, that Bankruptcy Code §105(a) gives the bankruptcy court the power to sanction attorneys who unreasonably and vexatiously multiple the proceedings in a bankruptcy case. The Seventh Circuit did not reach the question of whether the bankruptcy court can impose 28 U.S.C.§1927 sanctions, but it opined that bankruptcy courts are not "courts of the United States" as defined by 28 U.S.C.§451.[27]

An examiner appointed by a bankruptcy court is absolutely immune from a negligence suit dealing with the findings and conclusions in the report. The examiner serves as a fiduciary who is answerable only to the court.[28]

[¶707]   PROPERTY OF THE ESTATE

A debtor received the former family home in connection with a divorce that occurred while her bankruptcy petition was pending. The Fourth Circuit held in early 1996[29] that the divorce severed tenancy by the entireties, so the marital exemption was lost, and the house became her sole property and therefore part of her bankruptcy estate. Even if a residence is in the bankruptcy estate, the trustee is not entitled to take advantage of the Tax Code's exclusion of capital gains on the sale of a personal residence. Only natural persons can use that provision. Furthermore, the bankruptcy estate is not entitled to a stepped-up basis for the residence.[30] A net operating loss carryover becomes part of the bankruptcy estate, and therefore cannot be used by the debtor to reduce individual income for the year of the bankruptcy filing.[31]

Despite the debtor's power to withdraw pension assets, the Ninth Circuit found that the pension assets did not become part of the bankruptcy estate because of Bankruptcy Code §541(c)(2).[32] In the Third Circuit's analysis, IRAs do not enter the bankruptcy estate because New Jersey's N.J.S.A. §25:2-1(b), an applicable non-bankruptcy law, keeps out property in a "qualifying trust," defined to include Internal Revenue Code §408 plans such as IRAs.[33] A 62-year-old Chapter 13 debtor's IRA funds were not "disposable income" as long as they remained in the IRA. The amount of such funds affects confirmation of the plan (by affecting whether the plan satisfies the best interests of the creditors), but state law makes these funds exempt as retirement plans.[34]

In a Ninth Circuit case from late 1997, a Chapter 7 debtor was awarded a judgment equaling her contribution to retirement for herself and her former domestic partner. But, because this was a property settlement and not employment-related, it was not a "retirement plan" and therefore was not exempt from execution.[35]

A debtor who receives payments after filing the petition, in exchange for compliance with a noncompete agreement that is part of a pre-petition sale of a business, must include the payments in the bankruptcy estate; the "earnings from services performed" exception is not available.[36]

A trustee cannot sell pending tort claims (e.g., a claim for misappropriation of confidential business information) if state law forbids prejudgment assignment of tort claims. The chose in action does pass into the bankruptcy estate, but Congress did not show clear intent to preempt such state laws.[37]

[¶709]   ATTORNEYS' FEES

Although a prevailing creditor can enforce a contract provision awarding costs and fees in a dischargeability action, the prevailing debtor is not entitled to a fee award when defending dischargeability.[38]

In making an attorneys' fee award, the bankruptcy court cannot decide that certain categories of expenses are non-reimbursable overhead, although items such as postage or on-line research can be analyzed as client-specific (but they cannot be treated as part of the overhead already built into the fee award).[39]

Special counsel fees cannot be ordered paid out of the estate (under Bankruptcy Code §330) unless they actually benefit the estate itself. This inquiry is separate from the §325(e) authorization to employ the counsel in the first place. Appointed counsel should be warned of the risk of non-payment.[40]

On the related subject of the services of paraprofessionals hired by the trustees to provide services to the estate (e.g., a bookkeeper), their fees are subject to the cap on trustee services unless the court's permission is obtained separately to hire the paraprofessionals.[41]

[¶710] THE TRUSTEE'S AVOIDING POWER

In early 1996, the Ninth Circuit became the first Court of Appeals to decide whether a bankruptcy court has the power to appoint a Chapter 11 trustee *sua sponte*. The Ninth Circuit decided that, although a party to the case can move for appointment of a trustee, the court can also make the appointment on its own motion.[42] Also, since a bankruptcy trustee is an appointed officer of the court—not an ordinary fiduciary—a bankruptcy trustee can't be held personally liable under CERCLA for the debtor's violations of environmental law.[43]

Bankruptcy Code §113, which limits the trustee's power to avoid a collective bargaining agreement, applies only to Chapter 11 and not to Chapter 7. The Ninth Circuit decided[44] that the statutory language reflects the Chapter 11 reorganization process rather than liquidation.

Only a pension plan administrator or the PBGC can terminate a pension plan—the trustee can't do it unilaterally, and can't be ordered to do so by the bankruptcy court.[45] However, emergency interim modifications of a collective bargaining agreement, ordered under Bankruptcy Code §1113(e), do not constitute "rejection" of the agreement under Bankruptcy Code §365(g).[46]

[¶712] AVOIDANCE OF PREFERENCES

The test of whether a transaction is ordinary or preferential is whether the transaction would be considered aberrant in the relevant industry, and not whether the transaction resembles the *majority* of transactions in the industry, or whether it fits the transactional pattern of a significant percentage of the industry's customers.[47]

[¶714] RIGHTS OF SECURED CREDITORS

In early 1998, the Supreme Court returned to the subject of bankruptcy in *Fidelity Financial Services Inc. v. Fink*.[48] The Court decided that a state relation-back statute that gives a creditor a certain number of days to perfect a lien, which will then relate back to the first day, cannot be used to extend the Bankruptcy Code §547(c)(3)(B) 20-day period for perfecting a security interest that will escape the trustee's avoidance as a preferential transfer.

A pre-petition creditor must assert the Bankruptcy Code §553 right of setoff before confirmation of the reorganization plan; otherwise, the right expires.[49]

Although the question of the value of a secured creditor's interest arises frequently, there is no simple uniform answer. One variable is the position taken by various courts; another is the fine detail of the situation.

According to the Ninth Circuit,[50] where a debt to the IRS is secured by a tax lien on a residence, and the debtors' Chapter 11 plan calls for them to continue living there, no foreclosure is contemplated. Therefore, the creditor's security interest is valued at the fair market value of the property and not its foreclosure value.

According to the Fourth Circuit, in Chapter 13 it is not permitted to split an undersecured home mortgage debt into secured and unsecured pieces, but it is permissible to pay the remaining debt over the period of the Chapter 13 plan.[51]

When cramdown occurs pursuant to Bankruptcy Code §1325(a)(5)(B), the value of the creditor's secured claim is the wholesale price of the collateral—not its retail price or replacement value.[52] Although other Circuits have opted for either the wholesale or retail value of the collateral, in 1996 the Seventh Circuit took an intermediate approach: in Chapter 13, the value of the creditor's security interest in an income-producing asset is halfway between the wholesale and retail values.[53]

[¶715]   MAKING CLAIMS AGAINST A BANKRUPT

A due process challenge to Bankruptcy Code §523(a)(3)(B), dealing with objections to dischargeability, was unsuccessful in the Second Circuit.[54] The provision requires creditors to take action to protect their claims when they have actual knowledge, but no formal notice, of a petition. According to the Second Circuit, mere knowledge that a petition has been filed does not inform creditors of the bar date—but creditors can make an estimate based on the petition's filing date.

It is not "reasonably ascertainable" who counts as a former resident of, or visitor to, an environmentally contaminated site; so, such persons cannot be considered "known creditors" entitled to notice of bankruptcy proceedings involving the site's owner.[55]

[¶717]   ALLOWANCE OF CLAIMS

The Tenth Circuit refused to apply *res judicata* to prevent the IRS from making additional claims for taxes in a year in which the bankruptcy court has already determined an amount of taxes—notwithstanding the argument that this prevents the debtor from achieving a fresh start.[56] Under this analysis, a reasonable debtor would expect the IRS to seek all nondischargeable taxes, so the IRS was not guilty of misconduct in failing to inform the debtor that further claims might be made. The IRS was not guilty of misrepresentation or concealment of material fact, so equitable *estoppel* was not available—assuming *arguendo* that the IRS can be estopped. The Tenth Circuit did not regard this as a settled issue.

IRS Form 872-A (extension of time to assess tax) operates as a waiver of the statute of limitations, not as a contract that automatically terminates 60 days after the taxpayer's bankruptcy filing.[57]

[¶719]   HOW ASSETS OF THE BANKRUPT ARE DISTRIBUTED: PRIORITIES OF CLAIMS

In 1996, the Supreme Court tackled two cases dealing with claims priorities. When a bankrupt company failed to make its annual funding contributions to its pension plans, the 10% tax imposed on the accumulated funding deficiency was punitive in nature (the federal government did not encounter a pecuniary loss because of the company's failure to make the contribution). Therefore, it was not an "excise tax" entitled to priority in bankruptcy; it was merely an ordinary unsecured claim. However, the Supreme Court found that the Tenth Circuit erred in equitably subordinating that claim to other unsecured claims.[58]

In the second case it was ruled that bankruptcy courts do have a power of equitable subordination (see Bankruptcy Code §510(c)), but they are not permitted to subordinate categories of claims in any way contrary to the Code's priority system. Therefore, a post-petition tax penalty must retain its first priority as an administrative expense—it cannot be downgraded.[59]

When the bankruptcy petition is filed in the middle of the debtor's tax year, tax on post-petition income is a first-priority administrative expense, but tax on the pre-petition portion of the income takes only seventh priority. The total tax liability remains the same, only the timing of payments is affected by splitting the claim.[60]

Federal taxes on the debtor's income earned or accrued before the bankruptcy petition, but payable after the petition, are not treated as first-priority administrative expenses. Instead, they are unsecured claims, entitled to seventh priority.[61]

The Third Circuit says that an IRS tax claim gets priority even in cases where the petition was filed more than three years after the tax returns were due, because the automatic stay tolls the three-year period during which unpaid taxes are nondischargeable. In essence, the federal government is entitled to an unimpaired three-year collection period.[62]

According to the Sixth Circuit, in Chapter 13 even IRS priority claims must be timely filed to be allowed.[63] The Second and Ninth Circuits have allowed untimely IRS claims in Chapter 7 cases,[64] but Chapter 7 is liquidating bankruptcy, unlike Chapter 13 where the debtor retains assets and makes periodic payments to creditors.

Future rent under leases assumed by the debtor-in-possession takes first priority as an administrative expense—even if the trustee rejects the leases. The future rent is not subject to the one-year cap on unpaid rent otherwise provided by Bankruptcy Code §502(b)(6).[65]

Unpaid Workers' Compensation premiums are not considered contributions to an employee benefit plan entitled to priority under Bankruptcy Code §507(a)(4), because that priority is limited to wage substitutes that employer and employees bargained for. In the view of the Tenth Circuit, the Workers' Compensation premiums are compulsory, and are paid more to keep the company out of trouble than to benefit the workers.[66]

Under a similar analysis, the Sixth Circuit permitted the PBGC to get only part of a corporation's post-petition obligation toward minimum funding of a pension plan classified as a first-priority administrative expense. Amounts allocable to plan benefits earned pre-petition could not achieve administrative expense priority.[67]

Unpaid attorneys' fees remaining from earlier, unsuccessful attempts at Chapter 11 and Chapter 12 reorganization do not get administrative expense priority when the debtor takes another swing at it in Chapter 7. Only the expenses of the current proceeding qualify for the administrative expense priority.[68]

[¶720]   DISCHARGE OF THE DEBTOR FROM HIS DEBTS

A prepetition agreement by a debtor to pay attorneys' fees in installments after the petition, is dischargeable in bankruptcy. The District Court for the District of Arizona noted that this result might make it difficult for debtors to secure representation, but felt that the problem had to be corrected by Congress, not by the courts.[69]

Unless a doctor actually wanted to injure the patient, or thought that injury was substantially certain to occur, judgment debt from a medical malpractice case is dischargeable in bankruptcy.[70]

In the Ninth Circuit's analysis, fees paid to health professionals in a custody case, as well as Guardian ad Litem fees in such a case, are not directly owed to the former spouse or child, and therefore are dischargeable.[71] Most courts, however, treat the GAL fees as child support.

In the First Circuit, actual damages for fraud were not dischargeable, but punitive damages for fraud were.[72] Similarly, tax liabilities stemming from fraud are not dischargeable, but liabilities stemming from negligence are dischargeable, and the bankruptcy court is bound by the Tax Court's allocation between the two types of liability.[73]

[¶721]   EXCEPTIONS TO DISCHARGE

Certain broad classes of transaction are often involved in litigation: e.g., fraudulent or allegedly fraudulent transactions; federal tax enforcement; and support of the ex-spouse or children of a dissolved marriage. After the supplement period, the Supreme Court decided (in the case of *Cohen v. De La Cruz*, 66LW 4209 (Sup.Ct. 3/24/98) that neither compensatory nor punitive damages for fraud can be discharged in bankruptcy.

The personal property of a Chapter 13 debtor is exempt from the IRC §6334 administrative levy. Nevertheless, the property is not exempt from a federal tax lien under §6321 (neglect or refusal to pay a tax after an IRS demand).[74]

The taxpayer's knowledge that taxes were not paid is not sufficient to prove a willful attempt to evade or defeat the tax (see Bankruptcy Code §523(a)(1)(C)) that would prevent discharge of the tax liabilities. Evasion has been deemed by the Eleventh Circuit to be worse than simple nonpayment.[75] However, hiding income or assets or failing to file returns is likely to be interpreted as a willful attempt to evade or defeat liability, notwithstanding the fact that simple nonpayment of taxes is not a felony.[76] Filing a sham bankruptcy petition, with the objective of releasing an IRS levy on wages, has been held by the Ninth Circuit, to constitute a willful attempt to evade the tax.[77]

A debtor's obligation to pay part of his military pension to his ex-wife, created by a decree entered nine days before filing of the bankruptcy petition, is not dischargeable. The wife's pension share becomes her separate property, and never enters the bankruptcy estate; the debtor becomes a constructive trustee of the separate share.[78]

Compare this with the Eighth Circuit's determination[79] that the obligation to pay a set amount to the former spouse to settle the pension interest, embodied in a pre-petition divorce decree, is dischargeable, even if installment payments were supposed to continue after the filing of the petition. The divorce decree was neither a Qualified Domestic Relations Order (QDRO) nor linked to amounts actually received by the employee spouse. The Eighth Circuit saw the obligation as an amount certain that the debtor had to pay from whatever assets he had. In other words, it was a pre-petition debt that was not for maintenance or support, and thus was dischargeable. A 1997 Ninth Circuit case, however, treats a pre-petition pension distribution in divorce as non-dischargeable.[80]

An "equalization" payment is a lump sum that a divorce court orders one spouse to pay the other to equalize the division of their property and debts. Whether or not this is dischargeable depends on which spouse is financially better off—and whether permitting discharge would benefit the potential payor more than it would create detriment to the potential payee.[81]

When the non-debtor spouse is the one who is financially better off, this factor may promote dischargeability. For instance, a divorce settlement required the husband to reimburse the wife for her loss in the post-divorce sale of the marital home. Finding that the benefit of discharge to the husband outweighed the detriment to the financially better-off wife, the bankruptcy court allowed discharge of the obligation to reimburse the loss.[82] However, given factors such as willful intent to deprive the payee spouse of amounts he or she is entitled to, discharge is more likely to be denied. For instance, discharge of a cash property settlement was not allowed where the ex-husband gave land to his parents and continued to farm it rent-free (showing intent to deprive).[83]

Even though a marital settlement agreement incorporated in a divorce decree, obligating the bankruptcy debtor to assume mortgage payments on his former wife's home, was described as dischargeable, the Eighth Circuit nonetheless treated the obligation as a non-dischargeable spousal maintenance obligation.[84] The court treated agreements affecting subsequent discharge as disfavored by public policy.

Homestead and other property exempt under Bankruptcy Code §522 can become subject to court orders for pre-bankruptcy matrimonial debts. Hence, a debtor who elected to use the state exemptions could be ordered to convey the homestead to his ex-wife so she could enforce debts under the divorce judgment and property settlement.[85]

Post-divorce obligations created by an antenuptial agreement are considered non-dischargeable property settlement agreements, on the theory that divorcing spouses should not lose agreed-upon support merely because the agreement was made before, rather than after, marriage.[86]

In an ongoing marriage, one spouse is reasonably entitled to rely on the other spouse's recordkeeping (if they have agreed that one of the spouses is responsible for family recordkeeping). Therefore, the Ninth Circuit determined that the trial court erred in refusing a discharge to the spouse who delegated the duties because of the other spouse's poor recordkeeping. The debtor spouse had no affirmative duty to question the recordkeeper unless there was reason to suspect some error or irregularity.[87]

The discharge exception for spousal and child support has been interpreted quite broadly. For instance, the fees that a divorce court orders one spouse to pay to the other spouse's lawyer in a divorce and custody provision have been denied discharge, even though they are paid to the attorney rather than to the spouse or child. In the Tenth Circuit's reading, coping with support issues is a higher priority of the legal system than giving the debtor a fresh start.[88] Nor can an ex-husband discharge child support *arrears* that his ex-wife assigned to a nongovernmental collection agency, on the grounds that the ex-wife did not make a true assignment (which would have been dischargeable), but only an assignment for collection.[89]

Even obtaining a discharge is not necessarily a panacea: discharge of an equitable distribution award may be treated as a change in circumstances that warrants an upward adjustment in the spousal support of the spouse who was supposed to receive the award.[90]

CERCLA and RCRA claims made by the buyer of environmentally contaminated property were not discharged by the seller's bankruptcy because, at the time of the sale, the buyer did not have enough information to make environmental claims against the seller before the bankruptcy filing. In the Seventh Circuit's interpretation, the dischargeability of a cleanup order depends on whether it can be converted into a right of payment (i.e., a monetary obligation).[91]

Although an obligation to make restitution in a criminal case is not dischargeable, the Sixth Circuit has ruled that criminal fines (and costs imposed in state criminal proceedings) are merely debts and therefore can be discharged.[92]

Promissory notes for the obligation to make installment payments to settle federal False Claims Act civil claims and common-law fraud claims are nondischargeable. The D.C. Circuit said[93] that these notes fall under the Bankruptcy Code §523(a)(2)(A) ban on discharge of debts involving money or property obtained by fraud.

If a debt was incurred because of fraud, false pretenses, or false representations by the debtor, the Eleventh Circuit says that the debt is nondischargeable as long as the creditor's reliance would have been justified. Neither actual nor reasonable reliance is required.[94] However, the mere fact that a debtor lacked the ability to repay credit card debts when they were incurred is not proof of intent not to repay. Therefore, the Ninth Circuit has held that discharge cannot be blocked by claiming actual fraud.[95]

A debtor fraudulently transferred property with actual intent to hinder creditors, within a year of the petition. The property was later re-conveyed to the debtor, but the First Circuit ruled that this did not cure the fraudulent transfer or allow the debtor to be discharged.[96] In other words, transferred property doesn't have to stay transferred to prevent the discharge.

[¶723] BANKRUPTCY APPEALS

The Seventh Circuit says that there is no way to get review of a bankruptcy court's denial of a motion to disqualify counsel—because this is neither a collateral order nor a final order that is appealable under 28 U.S.C. §158(d).[97]

[¶724] TAX PLANNING FOR BANKRUPTCY

Taxpayers can claim a capital loss for worthless, canceled shares in a bankrupt corporation, even if they make an unrelated capital investment to purchase shares in the reorganized corporation.[98]

Even though the bankruptcy trustee has the status of a hypothetical bona fide purchaser, the trustee is not entitled to exemption from a federal tax lien under Internal Revenue Code §6323; Congress places a high priority on enforcement of such liens.[99]

In a case where the IRS served notice of levy on a bankruptcy trustee, but the trustee nevertheless gave the proceeds of a property sale to the bankrupt taxpayer, the trustee became personally liable for the amount subject to the levy.[100]

— ENDNOTES —

1. *Hubbard v. U.S.*, #94-172, 115 S.Ct. 1754 (Sup.Ct. 5/15/95).

2. *U.S. v. Yochum*, 89 F.3d 661 (9th Cir. 7/16/96).

3. *Newman v. Boehm*, 119 F.3d 477 (7th Cir. 7/2/97).

4. *McCratic v. Bristol-Myers Squibb & Co.*, 183 B.R. 113 (N.D.Tex. 6/14/95).

5. *Mason v. Smith*, 672A.2d 705 (N.H.Sup. 3/7/96).

6. *Joelson v. U.S.*, 86 F.3d 1413 (6th Cir. 6/24/96). The later case of *Brooks v. U.S.*, 66 LW 1351 (9th Cir. 11/4/97) similarly finds that due process is not violated by removing someone from the Chapter 7 trustee panel. There is no privacy or liberty interest in continuing service on the panel. Even if a liberty interest were implicated, the removal process, though informal, provided due process.

7. See 66 LW 2358. The Board's telephone number is (703) 739-1023.

8. *Bone v. Allen,* 186 B.R. 769 (Bank. N.D.Ga. 10/3/95).

9. *Commercial Federal Mortgage Co. v. Smith,* 85 F.3d 1555 (11th Cir. 6/26/96).

10. *C-TC 9th Avenue Partnership v. Norton Co.,* 113 F.3d 1304 (2nd Cir. 5/30/97).

11. *Bronson v. U.S.,* 46 F.3d 1573 (Fed.Cir. 1/26/95). *Goldston v. U.S.,* 65 LW 2486 (10th Cir. 1/6/97) adds that the IRS can pursue its responsible person claim for trust fund taxes even after violating the automatic stay; a valid assessment of tax liability is not a prerequisite.

12. *National Tax Credit Partners v. Havlik,* 20 F.3d 705 (7th Cir. 1994).

13. *U.S. v. Wright,* 57 F.3d 561 (7th Cir. 6/14/95).

14. *Roberge v. Roberge,* 188 B.R. 366 (E.D.Va. 11/7/95).

15. *In re Price,* 179 B.R. 209 (Bank. E.D.Cal. 3/14/95).

16. *Debolt v. Comerica Bank,* 177 B.R. 31 (Bank. W.D.Pa. 12/23/94).

17. *In re Duke,* 79 F.3d 43 (7th Cir. 3/15/96).

18. *Western Auto Supply Co. v. Savage Arms Inc.,* 43 F.3d 714 (1st Cir. 12/14/94).

19. *California Employment Development Dep't v. Taxel,* 98 F.3d 1147 (9th Cir. 10/23/96).

20. *Sosne v. Reinert & Duree PC,* 65 LW 2647 (8th Cir. 3/13/97).

21. *Jobin v. Boryla,* 75 F.3d 586 (10th Cir. 1/24/96).

22. *U.S. Trustee v. Endy,* 65 LW 2475 (9th Cir. 1/14/97).

23. *In re Cathedral of the Incarnation v. Garden City Co.,* 99 F.3d 66 (2nd Cir. 10/29/96).

24. *Mason v. Smith,* 672 A.2d 705 (N.H.Sup. 3/7/96).

25. *U.S. v. Schimmels (In re Schimmels),* 85 F.3d 416 (9th Cir. 5/30/96).

26. *Law Offices of Peter Francis Geraci v. Bryson,* 66 LW 1334 (7th Cir. 10/28/97).

27. *In re Volpert,* 65 LW 2743 (7th Cir. 4/1/97).

28. *Kovalevsky v. Carpenter,* 66 LW 1246 (S.D.N.Y. 10/9/97).

29. *Cordova v. Mayer,* 73 F.3d 38 (4th Cir. 1/9/96). *Massie v. Yamrose,* 169 B.R. 585 (W.D.Va. 1994) and *In re Alderton,* 179 B.R. 63 (Bank. E.D. Mich. 1995) reach the same conclusion.

30. *In re Barden,* 97-1 USTC ¶50,244 (2nd Cir. 1/29/97).

31. *Kahle,* TC Memo 1997-91 (2/20/97).

32. *Barkley v. Conner,* 73 F.3d 258 (9th Cir. 1/11/96). Also see *McCafferty v. McCafferty,* 96 F.3d 192 (6th Cir. 9/18/96): pension benefits awarded to the ex-wife in a pre-bankruptcy divorce never entered the bankruptcy estate, and therefore are not dischargeable.

33. *Orr v. Yuhas*, 65 LW 2492 (3rd Cir. 1/22/97); the Eleventh Circuit reached a similar conclusion as to Georgia law: *Meehan v. Wallace*, 102 F.3d 1209 (11th Cir. 1/8/97).

34. *Solomon v. Cosby*, 67 F.3d 1128 (4th Cir. 10/23/95).

35. *Sticka v. Wilbur*, 126 F.3d 1218 (9th Cir. 10/6/97).

36. *Andrews v. Riggs National Bank of Washington*, 80 F.3d 906 (4th Cir. 4/1/96).

37. *Integrated Solutions Inc. v. Service Support Specialties Inc.*, 66 LW 1133 (3rd Cir. 8/22/97).

38. *In re Sheridan*, 65 LW 2567 (7th Cir. 1/29/97).

39. *Stroock & Stroock & Lavan v. Hillsborough Holdings Corp.*, 66 LW 1323 (11th Cir. 11/18/97).

40. *Ferrara & Hantman v. Alvarez*, 66 LW 1149 (3rd Cir. 9/3/97).

41. *Boldt v. U.S.*, 66 LW 1374 (9th Cir. 12/3/97).

42. *Fukutomi v. U.S. Trustee*, 76 F.3d 256 (9th Cir. 1/24/96).

43. *Tennsco Corp. v. Estey Metal Products Inc.*, 200 B.R. 542 (D.N.J. 9/17/96).

44. *Carpenters Health & Welfare Trust Funds v. Robertson*, 53 F.3d 1064 (9th Cir. 5/8/95).

45. *PBGC v. Pritchard*, 33 F.3d 509 (5th Cir. 4/5/95).

46. *United Food and Commercial Workers v. Almac's Inc.*, 90 F.3d 1 (1st Cir. 7/24/96).

47. *Luper v. Columbia Gas of Ohio Inc.*, 91 F.3d 811 (6th Cir. 8/2/96).

48. #96-1370, 66 LW 4057 (Sup.Ct. 1/13/98).

49. *U.S. v. Continental Airlines*, 66 LW 1451 (3rd Cir. 1/20/98).

50. *Taffi v. U.S.*, 96 F.3d 1190 (9th Cir. 9/17/96).

51. *Witt v. United Companies Lending Corp.*, 65 LW 2761 (4th Cir. 5/21/97). The inability to divide is a consequence of *Nobelman v. American Savings Bank*, 508 U.S. 324 (1993).

52. *Associates Commercial Corp. v. Rash*, 90 F.3d 1036 (5th Cir. 7/30/96).

53. *In re Hoskins*, 102 F.3d 311 (7th Cir. 12/12/96).

54. *GAC Enterprises Inc. v. Medaglia*, 52 F.3d 451 (2nd Cir. 4/14/95).

55. *Chemetron Corp. v. Jones*, 72 F.3d 341 (3rd Cir. 12/18/95).

56. *De Paolo v. U.S.*, 45 F.3d 373 (10th Cir. 1/9/95).

57. *Bilski v. C.I.R.*, 69 F.3d 64 (5th Cir. 11/20/95).

58. *Reorganized CF&I Fabricators of Utah, Inc.*, 116 S.Ct. 2106 (Sup.Ct. 6/20/96). But see *U.S. v. Juvenile Shoe Corp. of America*, 99 F.3d 898 (8th Cir. 11/7/96), holding that another excise tax, the 15% levy on overfunding that reverts to

the employer (Internal Revenue Code §4980) takes priority as an "excise tax," and is not an ordinary unsecured claim.

59. *U.S. v. Noland*, #95-323, 116 S.Ct. 1524 (Sup.Ct. 5/13/96).

60. *U.S. v. Hillsborough Holdings Corp.*, 116 F.3d 1391 (11th Cir. 7/10/97).

61. *Towers v. IRS*, 64 F.3d 1292 (9th Cir. 8/23/95). The same thing is true of state taxes: *Missouri Department of Revenue v. L.J. O'Neill Shoe Co.*, 64 F.3d 1146 (8th Cir. 8/30/95).

62. *In re Taylor*, 81 F.3d 20 (3rd Cir. 4/3/96).

63. *U.S. v. Chavis*, 47 F.3d 818 (6th Cir. 2/23/95).

64. *In re Vecchio*, 20 F.3d 555 (2nd Cir. 1994); *In re Pacific Atlantic Trading Co.*, 33 F.3d 1064 (9th Cir. 1994).

65. *Nostas Associates v. Costich*, 78 F.3d 18 (2nd Cir. 2/16/96).

66. *State Insurance Fund v. Mather*, 210 B.R. 838 (10th Cir. 7/28/97).

67. *PBGC v. Sunarhauserman Inc.*, 66 LW 1195 (6th Cir. 9/25/97).

68. *Stuart v. Carter (In re Larsen)*, 59 F.3d 783 (8th Cir. 7/14/95).

69. *Hessinger & Associates v. Voglio*, 191 B.R. 420 (D.Ariz. 12/12/95).

70. *Geiger v. Kawaauhu*, 93 F.3d 443 (8th Cir. 5/14/97).

71. *Chang v. Beaupied*, 66 LW 1127 (9th Cir. 7/18/97).

72. *Aetna v. Markarian*, 65 LW 2798 (1st Cir. 5/13/97), but see *Cohen v. DeLaCruz*.

73. *In re Palmer*, 97-1 U.S.T.C. ¶50,228 (D.Mont. 12/13/96).

74. *In re Voelker*, 42 F.3d 1050 (7th Cir. 12/12/94).

75. *Haas v. IRS*, 48 F.3d 1153 (11th Cir. 3/30/95). Also see *U.S. v. Fegeley*, 118 F.3d 979 (3rd Cir. 7/8/97).

76. *Bruner v. U.S.*, 55 F.3d 195 (5th Cir. 6/21/95).

77. *U.S. v. Huebner*, 48 F.3d 376 (9th Cir. 12/16/94).

78. *McGraw v. McGraw*, 176 B.R.149 (Bank. S.D. Ohio 12/23/94). However, *In re Omegas Group Inc.*, 16 F.3d 1443 (6th Cir. 1994) reaches the opposite conclusion. *Debolt v. Comerica Bank*, cited above, also takes the position that the divided pension interest immediately becomes separate property of the recipient spouse and does not enter the bankruptcy estate.

79. *In re Ellis*, 72 F.3d 628 (8th Cir. 2/18/95).

80. *Gendreau v. Gendreau*, 122 F.3d 815 (9th Cir. 8/15/97).

81. *Samayon (Jodoin) v. Jodoin*, 22 Fam.L.Rep. 1371 (Bank. E.D.Cal. 5/16/96) [discharge permitted; doctor-husband had higher resources and standard of living than nurse-wife]; *Bodily v. Morris* 193 B.R. 949 (Bank. S.D.Cal. 4/3/96) [discharge rejected].

82. *Taylor v. Taylor*, 191 B.R.760 (Bank. N.D.Ill. 1/23/96).

83. *Straub v. Straub,* 192 B.R.522 (Bank. D.N.D. 2/22/96).

84. *In re Tatge,* 66 LW 1286 (8th Cir. 10/8/97).

85. *In re Davis,* 65 LW 2540 (5th Cir. 2/5/97).

86. *Sparks v. Sparks,* 206 B.R. 481 (N.D. Ill. 3/24/97).

87. *Cox v. Lansdowne,* 41 F.3d 1294 (9th Cir. 12/2/94).

88. *Miller v. Gentry,* 55 F.3d 1487 (10th Cir. 5/19/95). Also see the similar cases of *Brown v. Brown,* 177 B.R. 116 (Bank. M.D. Fla. 11/22/94) and *Holliday v. Kline,* 65 F.3d 749 (8th Cir. 9/12/95) and *Macy v. Macy,* 114 F.3d1 (1st Cir. 5/23/97). However, *In re Perlin,* 30 F.3d 39 (6th Cir. 1994) does permit discharge of the fees.

89. *Smith v. Child Support Enforcement,* 21 Fam.L.Rep. 1287 (D.Utah 4/13/95).

90. *Dickson v. Dickson,* 22 Fam.L.Rep. 1475 (Va.App. 8/20/96).

91. *AM International Inc. v. Datacard Corp.,* 65 LW 2583 (7th Cir. 2/11/97).

92. *Hardenberg v. Virginia,* 42 F.3d 986 (6th Cir. 12/9/94).

93. *U.S. v. Spicer,* 57 F.3d 1152 (D.C.Cir. 6/30/95).

94. *City Bank & Trust Co. v. Vann,* 67 F.3d 277 (11th Cir. 10/19/95).

95. *Anastas v. American Savings Bank,* 94 F.3d 1280 (9th Cir. 9/3/96).

96. *Martin v. Bajgar,* 65 LW 2491 (1st Cir. 1/17/97).

97. *Brouwer v. Ancel & Dunlap,* 46 F.3d 653 (7th Cir. 1/31/95).

98. *Delk v. C.I.R.,* 65 LW 2757 (9th Cir. 5/7/97).

99. *Battley v. U.S.,* 121 F.3d 535 (9th Cir. 8/14/97).

100. *U.S. v. Ruff,* 99 F.3d 1559 (11th Cir. 11/21/97).

— For Further Reference —

Baker, Cynthia A., "Fixing What's Broken: A Proposal for Reform of the Compensation System in Bankruptcy," 5 *J. of Bankruptcy Law and Practice* 435 (July–August '96).

Batson, Neal, "Selected Issues in Single-Asset Real Estate Cases," 6 *J. of Bankruptcy Law and Practice* 3 (November–December '96).

Cohen, Melanie Rovner and Christopher Combert, "Bankruptcy and Limited Liability Entities," 42 *Practical Lawyer* 77 (June '96).

Felsenfeld, Carl, "A Comment About a Separate Bankruptcy System," 64 *Fordham L. Rev.* 2521 (May '96).

Hennigan, John P., "Toward Regularizing Appealability in Bankruptcy," 12 *B*

Johnson, Meredith, "At the Intersection of Bankruptcy and Divorce," 97 *Columbia L.Rev.* 91 (January '97).

Martin, Natalie D., "Fee Shifting in Bankruptcy: Deterring Frivolous, Fraud-Based Objections to Discharge," 76 *North Carolina L.Rev.* 97 (November '97).

McClain, Bruce W. and Donald C. Haley, "Should the Judgment Debtor File for Bankruptcy?" 42 *Practical Lawyer* 59 (January '96).

Mendales, Richard E., "Looking Under the Rock: Disclosure of Bankruptcy Issues Under the Securities Laws," 57 *Ohio State L. J.* 731 (June '96).

Ponoroff, Lawrence, "Vicarious Thrills: The Case for Application of Agency Rules in Bankruptcy Dischargeability Litigation," 70 *Tulane L. Rev.* 2515 (June '96).

Raby, Burgess J.W. and William L. Raby, "Do Contingent Liabilities Count for Section 108 Insolvency?" 78 *Tax Notes* 205 (1/12/98).

Reibman, Richard T., "Limited Liability Companies and the Bankruptcy Code," 74 *Taxes: The Tax Magazine* 617 (October '96).

Schmelzer, Nicolas M., "Taxation of Reconveyances During Insolvency," 41 *Res Gestae* 45 (November '97).

Schwarcz, Steven L. and Janet Malloy Link, "Protecting Rights, Preventing Windfalls: A Model for Harmonizing State and Federal Laws on Floating Liens," 75 *North Carolina L.Rev.* 403 (January '97).

Searles, David A., "Practice Tips in Handling Individual Bankruptcy Cases," 68 *Pennsylvania Bar Ass'n Quarterly* 41 (January '97).

Theuer, Jeffrey S., "Aligning Environmental Policy and Bankruptcy Protection," 13 *Thomas M. Cooley L. Rev.* 465 (May '96).

White, Michaela M., "Divorce After the Bankruptcy Reform Act of 1994," 29 *Creighton L. Rev.* 617 (March '96).

Zapata, Julio M., "Taming the Bankruptcy Code's Toothless Tiger, 11 U.S.C. 521(2)," 72 *Washington L.Rev.* 1195 (October '97).

COMPENSATION AND FRINGE BENEFITS

[¶1201] An early 1995 Supreme Court case clarifies ERISA §402(b)93, which requires plans to maintain a procedure for amending the plan, including the identity of the person(s) with authority to amend. According to the Supreme Court, this requirement is satisfied by reserving the right of "the company" to amend, without greater specificity.[1]

In the spring of 1996, the Supreme Court ruled that the employer acted as an ERISA fiduciary when, in its role as plan administrator, it informed employees that they would retain their benefits if they transferred employment and benefit plan participation to a reorganized corporate entity. In fact, the reorganized entity was insolvent, and the employees lost benefit entitlement. The employees were permitted to sue for breach of fiduciary duty based on the employer's deceptive scheme. Individual beneficiaries can sue for breach of fiduciary duty; the cause of action is not limited to relief for the plan as an entirety.[2]

The Pension Annuitants Protection Act of 1994, P.L. 103-401 (10/22/94), amends 29 U.S.C. §1132(a). The Department of Labor, a plan participant or beneficiary, or a plan fiduciary can sue to make sure that a participant or beneficiary actually receives the amounts that are supposed to be provided under an insurance contract or annuity purchased in connection with the termination of the beneficiary's status as a plan participant. In other words, if the insurer or annuity fails, the deprived beneficiary or persons acting on his or her behalf will have legal redress.

The State Income Taxation of Pension Income Act, P.L. 104-95 (1/10/96) amends 4 U.S.C. §114. A state is not permitted to impose income tax on retirement income paid to anyone who is neither a resident or domiciliary of the would-be taxing state. (Residency is determined by the would-be taxing state's own laws.) The ban applies to income from qualified plans, IRAs, SEPs, and 403(a) and (b) annuity plans, as long as the income is provided in substantially equal periodic payments, at least annually, for a period of at least 10 years, or for the life of the participant or the joint lives of participant and beneficiary.

Because of the high cost of providing benefits, employers often want to have tasks performed by independent contractors, leased employees, and others who are not full-time permanent employees. Thus, it becomes important to distinguish full-time employees from others. The Ninth Circuit decided a landmark case on this issue in October, 1996.[3] A group of Microsoft workers were described by the company as freelancers, independent contractors who submitted bills to Microsoft's accounts receivable department rather than being paid by the payroll department and who did not receive overtime. The IRS ruled that these persons were actually common-law employees, at which point the workers applied for benefits, including participation in the company's Savings Plan and ESOP. The Ninth Circuit determined that all Microsoft common-law employees, including the "freelancers," were eligible for participation, whether or not they were formally paid by the payroll department. In July, 1997, the three-judge panel's decision was upheld by the full court.[4]

The Fifth Circuit ruled in mid-1996 that a company did not violate the minimum participation and coverage rules by excluding leased employees from its pension plan. However, the leased employees did have a colorable claim to coverage, so they were "participants" for ERISA purposes and entitled to receive plan information from the administrator. The administrator's refusal to provide the information could give rise to statutory penalties.[5]

[¶1202] PENSION AND PROFIT-SHARING PLANS

One of the first questions that arises in the context of a pension plan is whether there is a "plan" at all. To the First Circuit, for instance, a series of four early retirement offers made in connection with reductions in force did not constitute an ERISA plan, because the offers were unrelated and did not impose a continuing obligation on the company.[6] A Chapter 7 bankruptcy debtor's award of a judgment equaling her contribution to the retirement of herself and her one-time domestic partner was held not to be a retirement plan (on the grounds that it was a property settlement that was not related to employment). Thus, it was not exempt from execution.[7]

The actuarial assumptions of a defined benefit plan are tested to see if they are reasonable in the aggregate—not whether they are "substantially unreasonable"; but they are not presumed to be reasonable. The plan's actuary must satisfy a procedural test of making the best estimate of the funds needed to satisfy the obligations. The actuary can properly make conservative assumptions, but the Sixth Circuit found that the actual assumptions behind one law firm's plan were unreasonable—e.g., assuming partners would retire at age 60, although enhanced benefits were not available unless they deferred retirement to age 63.[8]

Even where the employer has the option of reducing or terminating non-vested benefits (in this case, early retirement benefits), ERISA's anti-retaliation provision forbids firing employees as a means of avoiding making the payments.[9]

It is fairly common for employers to promise their workers that health benefits will be maintained at the existing level (often 100% paid for by the employer) for the lifetime of those who retire early—and then to attempt to terminate the benefits or increase the payments expected of the employees. An early 1996 Sixth Circuit case granted an injunction forcing the employer to reinstate the benefits to their original level, premised on the likelihood that the employees will prevail on their LMRA §301 claim.[10]

However, in this reading, the employees are not entitled to a jury trial because their claim for damages (health costs incurred because of the employer's inappropriate termination of benefits) is merely incidental to the equitable remedy of injunction. A little later, the Eleventh Circuit decided that employees do have a Seventh Amendment right to jury trial of their LMRA §301 claim that the employer breached its collective bargaining agreement obligations with respect to retirement benefits.[11] In this interpretation, the right to a jury trial is not lost by joining the LMRA claim and an ERISA claim for the same monetary relief.

Because of ERISA's anti-alienation clause, an employee's release given in connection with an early retirement agreement cannot bar a suit about pension plan entitlements, but it can preclude a suit about contested claims arising out of the retirement agreement itself.[12]

The IRS has ruled that defined benefit plans with 100 or more participants must maintain liquid plan assets approximately equal to three times the total disbursements made from the plan trust in the 12-month period preceding each quarter in which a quarterly contribution must be made to the plan.[13] However, according to the Second Circuit, a defined benefit plan that has a surplus when it merges with another plan is not required to modify its terms to increase the benefits in light of the surplus, as long as the plan is not liquidated.[14]

When a plan is terminated, the 1987 ERISA amendments affecting 29 U.S.C. §1362 (employer's liability to the PBGC for unfunded benefits) preempt LMRA §301, so neither employees nor the union can bring a claim to recover non-guaranteed pension benefits.[15]

The Circuits are split as to whether rights to a spouse's pension can be surrendered via a separation agreement that becomes incorporated into the divorce decree. Recently, the Fourth Circuit joined[16] the Seventh, Eighth, and Tenth Circuits in permitting the waiver, on the theory that a plan administrator can comply with a waiver just as easily as with a QDRO. The Second and Sixth Circuits hold that the plan administrator is bound by whatever beneficiary designation is on file, so the waiver is ineffective. According to the District Court for the District of Delaware,[17] ERISA doesn't define the waiver process. Therefore, federal common law applies, and a divorce-related waiver must specifically mention each plan whose benefits are waived; it is not adequate to make a generalized waiver.

Although in general ERISA will preempt domestic relations laws, divorce courts do have the power to issue Qualified Domestic Relations Orders (QDROs) that can bind plan administrators.

Acceptability is a key concept, because plan administrators have a duty to examine orders that purport to be QDROs to see if they are valid. Both state and federal courts have concurrent jurisdiction to determine whether an order counts as a QDRO. A mid-1997 California case finds that the order cannot be a QDRO if it is made before the employee spouse retires and orders payment of early retirement benefits that are not actuarially reduced. "Rule of 75" benefits (paid without reduction to people over 55 whose age plus years of service add up to 75 or more) are an employer subsidy, and therefore cannot be paid to a non-employee spouse without actuarial reduction.[18]

The QDRO exception to ERISA preemption applies to welfare benefit plans as well as pension plans, so a divorce judgment requiring naming of the couple's children as beneficiaries of a life insurance policy operated as a QDRO. This resulted in the death benefits going to the children and not to the ex-wife.[19]

An employee's ex-wife had a judgment for post-due alimony when the employee, now remarried, retired. The trial court granted a QDRO naming the ex-wife as payee of the death benefits. However, in the Fourth Circuit's view, survivorship benefits vest at the time of retirement, and so a QDRO can no longer be used to reallocate them.[20]

67

In a Tax Court case from mid-1995, a wife filed for divorce in February, 1985. In March of 1986, the husband's corporation voted to terminate its profit-sharing plan. He withdrew his balance (about $200,000 in community property and $100,000 in separate property) and gave it to his wife, who distributed the balance in accounts in her sole name designated as rollover IRAs.

The couple entered into a separation agreement in October, 1988. This agreement, later incorporated into the divorce decree, awarded the profit-sharing plan to the wife. The husband was in the unfortunate position of being held liable for early distribution of the lump sum (he was only 49 when the amount was distributed) and the tax on excess plan distributions. The wife was liable for the excise tax on excess contributions to a plan because the amount was far greater than one year's permissible IRA contribution. The deposit into her IRA could not qualify as a rollover because the Tax Court says it is impermissible for one person to roll over a balance to another person's IRA. The QDRO rules do not apply, because the transfer was made before the separation agreement and therefore could not have implemented the agreement.[21]

On a simpler QDRO question, the Central District of California has held that ERISA preempts a state domestic relations law that requires pension plans to pay attorneys' fees in connection with QDROs.[22] According to the Eighth Circuit, no QDRO was present in a case in which a bankruptcy debtor was obligated to pay a set amount to his spouse to settle her interest in his pension. The obligation was created by a pre-petition divorce decree. The Eighth Circuit permitted discharge of this obligation in bankruptcy. It considered the obligation as a simple pre-petition debt (even though installment payments were due after filing), and not liability for family support or maintenance that would be nondischargeable.[23] In the Ninth Circuit, a pre-petition divorce decree awarding half of the pension benefits to the non-employee ex-spouse is not dischargeable. The non-employee spouse's claim is against the pension plan, and is not a personal liability that the employee spouse can discharge in bankruptcy.[24]

In mid-1997, the Supreme Court ruled that ERISA preempts a state law that permits a non-employee spouse to dispose by will of a community property interest in undistributed pension benefits. (The Supreme Court reversed the Fifth Circuit on this matter.) The result was that an ex-wife's will provision, leaving her sons part of her community interest in her ex-husband's undistributed plan benefits, was ineffective. His current wife was entitled to those benefits, because a will obviously is not a QDRO (the sole effective method of disposing of not-yet-due pension benefits).[25]

Reference should also be made to recent IRS rulemaking on compensation issues, such as Notice 97-10, 1997-2 IRB 41 (approved language for spousal consent in waiving a Qualified Joint and Survivor Annuity or Qualified Preretirement Survivor Annuity), and Notice 97-11, 1997-2 IRB 49 (sample language for a QDRO that satisfies the requirements of 1996's Small Business Job Protection Act).

Also with respect to bankruptcy issues, the Ninth Circuit ruled that Bankruptcy Code §541(c)(2) kept the debtor's pension assets out of his bankruptcy estate, despite his power to withdraw them.[26] The Fifth Circuit held that only a plan administrator or the PBGC can terminate a pension plan—a bankruptcy trustee can neither do so on his own motion nor be ordered to do so by a bankruptcy court.[27]

Prevailing parties in ERISA cases (unlike those in civil rights cases) are not presumed entitled to attorneys' fees. It depends on factors such as the loser's degree of culpability, ability to pay fees, deterrent effect of fee awards, the relative strength of each side's arguments, and the value of the victory to plan participants.[28]

[¶1202.1] Small Business Job Protection Act

A 1996 statute, the Small Business Job Protection Act (SBJPA), P.L. 104-188, makes numerous changes in the treatment of pension plans and their participants:

➤ Internal Revenue Code §72 is amended to alter the taxation of employee pensions received as an annuity. The employee's calculation of the "exclusion ratio" (the portion of each payment that is not taxed because it is considered a return of the employee's own investment in the contract) is based on a simple schedule, based on the employee's age range, rather than on more complex actuarial calculations. The SBJPA also simplifies the definition of "highly compensated employee" used for many plan-related purposes. Basically, a Highly Compensated Employee is one earning over $80,000 a year. See Notice 97-45, 1997-33 IRB 7, for guidance on how to apply the altered definition.

➤ For a three-year period (1997, 1998, 1999), the excise tax on excess lump-sum withdrawals from a pension plan is suspended. However, the tax on excess accumulation within the estate remained in effect, so there was an incentive to make large enough withdrawals to reduce estate accumulation below the point at which an excise tax would be imposed. As noted below, TRA '97 permanently eliminated both excise taxes, thus making it possible to base the decision on how much to withdraw purely on financial factors.

➤ The SBJPA also eliminates the requirement that rank-and-file participants in a pension plan begin to receive their pensions no later than April 1 of the year in which they reach age $70^1/_2$. (The requirement remains in force for IRAs, and also for 5 percent owners of the company sponsoring the pension plan.) See IRS Announcement 97-24, 1997-11 IRB 24, for guidance in deferring that initial payment for employees who continue to work past 70 1/2 for companies whose plan has not yet been amended to comply with the SBJPA on this point.

➤ The SBJPA eliminates five-year averaging for pensions received as lump sums, although the elimination does not take effect until 2000. After 2000, 10-year averaging will still be permitted, but only for people born before 1936. Congress' rationale for eliminating five-year averaging is that plan participants who do not want to receive (or pay income tax on) a lump sum can avoid the problem via a rollover into an IRA or another qualified plan. Thus, averaging provisions that prevent severe tax impact are less necessary.

➤ The §415 "combined limit" for persons who participate in both a defined-benefit and defined-contribution plan has been eliminated.

    ➤ Defined-contribution plans are no longer subject to minimum participation requirements.

Also see IR-96-43 (10/24/96), effective January 1, 1997, which increases the maximum payable under a qualified defined benefit plan to $125,000 a year. (The maximum addition to a defined contribution plan remains $30,000 a year). The definition of "excess distribution" has been increased from $155,000 to $160,000 a year.

Small businesses (those with 100 or fewer employees) have the option of providing a SIMPLE pension plan: in essence, an enhanced IRA. IRS Notice 97-6, 1997-2 IRB 26 explains the requirements for SIMPLE plans in question-and-answer form. Rev.Proc. 97-29, 1997-24 IRB 9, gives sample forms and language for creating a SIMPLE plan.

The SBJPA also amends ERISA §401 to provide that, for lawsuits filed after 11/7/95, claims of fiduciary breach will not be heard with respect to pension moneys held in an insurer's general account. An early 1997 Florida case[29] thus requires dismissal of most of the claims by a plan's trustees against its insurance company for mismanagement and misappropriation of plan assets. However, the contract gives the trustees the right to direct funds to a separate investment account, so claims involving the separate account are tenable.

[¶1202.2] Tax Reform Act of 1997

TRA '97, as noted above, repeals Code §4980A and amends §691(c)(1), with the result that the 15% excise tax is permanently repealed as to both excess withdrawals from a qualified plan and excess accumulations of qualified plan benefits in the estate. This change gives taxpayers more planning freedom, because they can tailor withdrawals to planning needs, current income tax position, and estate objectives without having to structure withdrawals to avoid the excise tax.

However, another compensation-related excise tax is increased: the excise tax on a qualified plan's prohibited transactions under Code §4975(a) has been increased from 10% to 15%.

Under an amendment to ERISA §407(b), companies cannot require their employees to invest more than 10% of their 401(k) accounts in the company's own stock, although it is permissible for the employee to have a higher concentration of employer stock in the 401(k) if this is a voluntary choice.

The employer's failure to comply with the maternity and mental health parity requirements is now a violation of the Internal Revenue Code (at §4980D) as well as an ERISA violation, and can be penalized by up to $100 per day per plan participant affected by the failure to provide parity.

[¶1203] QUALIFICATION REQUIREMENTS

An early 1997 Ninth Circuit case was brought by retirees who claimed that the company used plan surplus (about half of which derived from employee contributions) to fund early retirement and a new non-contributory plan covering employees who were not covered by the contributory plan. The court ruled that the employees had a cognizable claim under ERISA §403(c)(1), which forbids private inurement of benefits from a plan (other than to participants and beneficiaries). Although an employer no longer has to contribute to a plan once it is in surplus status, the employer is not permitted to benefit from the surplus. It is irrelevant under ERISA §403 whether or not the employer was acting as a fiduciary. Furthermore, ERISA §203 requires employees to be paid the excess of employee contributions and their income over the scheduled defined benefit.[30]

A plan can be amended to raise the normal retirement age from 65 to 67 without violating ERISA's vesting or accrual requirements, as long as early retirement benefits (including employer subsidies) accrued before the date of the plan amendment are preserved.[31]

ERISA is not violated by denying a special early retirement program to especially valued employees of a plant that was about to be sold. The plant was more valuable as a going concern with an intact workforce, so denying early retirement was in the best interests of management.[32]

ERISA §510's ban on retaliation against participants and beneficiaries who engage in protected activity extends to any adverse action taken by the plan. There is no requirement that the activity be employment-related. Therefore, §510 covers action by an estate in terminating payments to a widow under an antenuptial contract after she received death benefits from the deceased's pension plan. For this purpose, the estate was a "person" subject to ERISA.[33]

[¶1205] INDIVIDUAL RETIREMENT ACCOUNTS (IRAs)

TRA '97 made many significant changes in the availability and tax status of IRAs. Clearly, Congress intends the IRA to be a significant basic tool of financial planning (perhaps because Social Security benefits may not be fully available, or available at all, to many Baby Boomers). TRA '97 increases the AGI levels at which individuals who are active plan participants can make deductible IRA contributions, with further increases scheduled to phase in until 2005. If one spouse is a qualified plan participant, the other spouse can take a full IRA deduction, because the other spouse's plan participation will no longer be attributed to him or her.

Certain early withdrawals can be made from an IRA without penalty. (The withdrawn amounts still constitute taxable income, but there is no excise tax.) The 10% excise tax is not imposed on amounts used to pay qualified higher education expenses of the taxpayer, the taxpayer's spouse, or their children or grandchildren. A first-time homebuyer can also withdraw up to $10,000 from the IRA without penalty, if the money is used to buy a principal residence for the taxpayer or a member of a defined class of relatives of the taxpayer.

TRA '97 creates two new kinds of IRA: the Education IRA and the Roth IRA. Contributions of up to $500 per child per year can be deposited in an Education IRA; the deduction is limited or eliminated as the parent/depositor's AGI increases. Once the child reaches college age, amounts up to the tuition bill can be taken from the education IRA tax-free.

The Roth, otherwise known as the back-loaded IRA, does not give rise to a current tax deduction. The maximum contribution is $2,000 per year. However, amounts left in the Roth IRA for at least five years can be withdrawn tax-free, and funds can also be rolled over from a conventional to a Roth IRA. A penalty is imposed if minimum distributions are not taken from a conventional IRA by the year after the year in which the account holder reaches age 70 1/2. This rule does not apply to Roth IRAs, so they can be used for estate planning purposes more conveniently than a conventional IRA can.

Also see *Henry v. C.I.R.*[34] finding that individuals earning over $35,000 a year cannot take an IRA deduction. In this case, the taxpayer was a plan participant for less than one month and didn't contribute to the plan, but was nevertheless precluded from making a deductible IRA contribution.

[¶1216]   GROUP HEALTH INSURANCE

Although ERISA does not provide for vesting of health insurance benefits, the Supreme Court has ruled that ERISA §510's ban on terminating employees to prevent their receipt of benefits applies to health and other non-vesting benefits. The statute forbids interference with rights under a plan, not just vested benefit rights under a pension plan.[35]

P.L. 104-204, the Veterans Affairs, Housing and Urban Development and Independent Agencies Appropriation Act of 1996, on its face, requires health plans to offer benefit parity between physical and mental illnesses. However, there are so many exceptions to the requirements that the measure of protection is somewhat illusory.

Under P.L. 104-204, a plan cannot impose a lifetime or annual limit on mental health benefits if it does not impose such limits on medical or surgical benefits for treatment of physical illness. If limits are imposed (as in most plans), they must be the same for mental and physical illnesses. However, the definition of mental illness does not include addiction/substance abuse treatment. If a plan does not have mental health coverage, it is not required to add it. Although there must be parity in annual or lifetime coverage limits, it remains permissible to have different deductibles, coinsurance requirements, number of visits covered, and days of coverage for mental and physical illnesses. Furthermore, employers with fewer than 50 employees are exempt from the parity requirement, and any plan can achieve exemption by demonstrating that parity raises its costs by 1 percent or more.[36]

By and large, employers draft their plans reserving the right to alter or even terminate the benefits, and such provisions are valid and enforceable. However, employers may subject themselves to liability if they make independent promises that benefits will be continued, especially if the employees surrender something (such as current compensation or continued employment) in return for the promise. An employer also may be liable if it misleads its employees and ex-employees, even though it would not be liable if it had communicated truthfully to them and informed them that benefits would not be available.

An employer was enjoined against violating its promise of lifetime retiree health benefits, at no cost to the employees, by the Sixth Circuit.[37] However, the plaintiff employees could not get a jury trial in their quest for damages (health care costs they encountered because the employer broke its promise), on the grounds that the damages are only incidental to the equitable remedy of the injunction.[38]

There is a line of cases dealing with employer falsehoods. In this reading, it is wrongful for an employer to give a vague or incorrect answer to a specific employee inquiry, particularly on a "repeated or pervasive basis."[39] However, given the equitable nature of the claim, employees cannot get money damages for the breach of fiduciary duty—only equitable, restitutionary measures such as back benefits and restoration of the status quo.

Although outright falsehoods are forbidden, plans are not required to disclose hypothetical future changes to the plan. The trigger is whether a new or amended retirement program is under "serious consideration," a definition fleshed out by 1997 cases. To the Tenth Circuit, the ERISA duty to disclose arises when senior managers who have the authority to implement a plan change begin to discuss a specific proposal for the purpose of implementing it. To the First Circuit, disclosure in response to a plan participant's inquiry was not required because serious consideration of an improved retirement program did not occur until a month after his retirement.[40]

Prudent employers retain the right to amend or modify plans, but at least two cases find that a unilateral change from fee-for-service health care to a managed care plan is not permitted, because it goes beyond the normal power of amendment.[41]

The Georgia Supreme Court upheld a city ordinance providing health and other benefits to the domestic partners of municipal employees, because the statute's definition of dependent was consistent with other statutes.[42] However, in the view of the New Jersey Court of Appeals, failure to offer spousal health coverage to the same-sex life partners of employees does not violate the state Constitution's guarantee of equal protection, and does not violate the state's anti-discrimination law, because a state can rationally draw a line between married and unmarried individuals.[43]

Two 1996 cases disagree about plan participants' remedies when the plan negotiates discounts from health care providers, but calculates employee copayments based on the full, unreduced cost of the services. This practice forces employees to undertake a larger share of the cost of the plan. According to the District Court for the Western District of Pennsylvania, participants are entitled to seek equitable relief under ERISA §501(a)(3), because the fiduciary (who was also the health insurer) misinterpreted the plan and failed to act solely in the interests of participants. However, the Eastern District of Michigan said that the insurer had already discontinued the controversial practice, so there was no equitable relief that could be awarded to the participants.[44]

An insurer denied a pregnancy-related claim on the grounds that the employee failed to disclose her history of heart trouble on the insurance application. Ohio law allows denial of claims when the policy would not have been issued but for misrepresentation. However, the Sixth Circuit found this state law to be preempted by ERISA. In effect, the insurer raised an affirmative defense to a claim for benefits under an ERISA plan. The state statute dealt with basic fraud principles rather than insurance, and it did not alter the spread of risk, and thus did not qualify for the insurance regulation exemption from ERISA preemption.[45]

Given the increasing prevalence of managed care in employment-related health plans, there is an understandable increase in the amount of litigation brought by patients dissatisfied by treatment received from an HMO or other managed care organization (MCO), or aggrieved by the plan's refusal to authorize or pay for treatment sought by a covered individual.

In the First Circuit, a survivor of a deceased cancer patient whose health plan refused to pay for a new treatment has no ERISA cause of action against the plan, and neither compensatory nor punitive damages are available for failure to provide benefits in accordance with the terms of the plan.[46] In contrast, on a related issue, the Eighth Circuit decided that ERISA imposes a fiduciary duty on an HMO to disclose to plan participants and beneficiaries any financial incentives that discourage gatekeeper doctors from making referrals to specialists.[47] In Wisconsin, subscribers have a right to sue their HMO for bad faith denial of coverage.[48]

HMO claims do not always involve employees. A 1997 Fifth Circuit case, for instance, involves a hospital that twice inquired about a patient's health coverage status, and was told twice that the patient was covered. The hospital treated the patient in reliance on these representations, which proved to be incorrect. The insurer tried to use an ERISA preemption defense to dismiss the hospital's suit for deceptive and unfair trade practices (negligent misrepresentation). The attempt was unsuccessful; the Fifth Circuit found the hospital to be an independent third party, so ERISA did not preempt the case.[49]

The Seventh Circuit had to interpret a health insurance plan which limited coverage to "unintentionally caused" events, although its SPD merely referred to "injuries." The SPD was deemed to control and because the common meaning of "injury" is not limited to unintentional events, coverage had to be provided to an employee who was shot by a police officer who was called to a scene of domestic violence.[50]

ERISA does not preempt the state common-fund doctrine, so a health plan is entitled to an award of attorneys' fees and costs out of a personal injury settlement when an employee is injured in a car accident and receives health care from the plan.[51]

An employer can sue its Third Party Administrator and excess insurer for failure to process and seek reimbursement on a claim. Such suits are not preempted by ERISA because they are ordinary state suits for breach of contract. The claim has only a tenuous connection with the plan, and contracts between insurer and employer are not related to ERISA's enforcement scheme.[52]

Nor does ERISA preempt a state tort action charging negligent misrepresentation as to whether the policy covered work-related injuries, because the employee seeks payments from the insurer, not the plan, and because allowing a state suit and recovery will not impair plan administration.[53]

An employer has the right to revoke gratuitous benefits, such as keeping an employee on the payroll and maintaining his health benefits after a heart attack, even though the heart attack was a preexisting condition that was not covered by the long-term disability plan. In a Fourth Circuit case, the employee demanded more benefits and threatened to sue the employer. The Fourth Circuit did not deem the revocation to violate the anti-retaliation provision of ERISA §510 (and did not want to impose a disincentive on employers to help disabled employees).[54]

The Ninth Circuit permitted a plan's fiduciaries to sue the fiduciaries of a predecessor plan for harm caused to the second plan by the errors of the earlier fiduciaries because mergers or spinoffs should not be used to protect fiduciaries against the consequences of their own mistakes.[55]

[¶1216.1]   Health Insurance Portability

The Health Insurance Portability and Accountability Act of 1996, P.L. 104-191 (HIPAA) adds new requirements of guaranteed availability of coverage, and portability of coverage, to all health plans that have two or more participants on the first day of the plan year. HIPAA adds a new concept, "creditable coverage," to the benefits lexicon. If an employee is a participant in a health plan, the employee's "creditable coverage" in the prior health plan must be used to reduce any preexisting condition limitation imposed by the current health plan. The objective, of course, is that the employee will be covered by the new plan.

Creditable coverage includes Medicare, Medicaid, and health insurance purchased by the individual in the past. However, creditable coverage becomes disqualified if there is ever a break in coverage that lasts for 63 days or more; and no coverage before July 1, 1996 can be considered creditable coverage.

HIPAA also limits the use of preexisting condition limitations by group health plans. A preexisting condition is one for which medical advice or treatment was either received or recommended during the six months before the enrollment date in the new health plan. (In other words, conditions that existed, but which were not treated, are not considered preexisting conditions.) The longest permissible limitation period is 12 months, or 18 months for a person who enrolls in a health plan after the first permissible date.

Another HIPAA objective is making health insurance more available. Group health plans (and insurers who issue policies to group plans) must not condition eligibility or continued eligibility on factors such as health status, physical or mental medical condition, claims experience, genetic information, or past history of receiving health care. However, plans are still permitted to exclude certain conditions from coverage, and they can impose a lifetime cap on a particular benefit or on benefits in general.

These HIPAA requirements are now part of the requirements for plan qualification, and thus come under the Internal Revenue Code and ERISA jurisdiction. The Department of Health and Human Services also has the power to impose civil money penalties for violations of the portability and availability requirements. However, no enforcement action can be taken before January 1, 1998 (or even later, if the necessary regulations are not drafted in time).

Effective January 1, 1997, HIPAA also extends COBRA continuation coverage: if a disabled individual provides the required notice, the continuation coverage period for both him or her and his or her family members is 29 months, not 18 months. Interim rules for applying HIPAA can be found at 62 FR 67687 (12/29/97). Also see T.D. 8716, 1997-19 IRB 5 for portability rules.

HIPAA also authorizes a pilot project for the administration of Medical Savings Accounts, a counterpart of the IRA for medical purposes, defined at newly added Internal Revenue Code §220.[56]

[¶1216.2]   Disability Coverage

The purpose of health insurance is to pay medical bills; the related but intellectually distinct purpose of disability coverage is to replace income lost when an employee is injured or too ill to work.

An individual fraudulently obtained disability benefits from one plan, went to work for another company, and legitimately obtained disability benefits from the second company's plan. Both plans purchased coverage from the same insurer. The Ninth Circuit refused to grant setoff against the second set of disability benefits that was sought by the insurer and the fiduciaries of the first plan. The two plans were completely separate (it was merely a coincidence that they shared an insurer) and setoff is a remedy limited to ERISA violations, not commonplace fraud.[57]

The Eighth Circuit required a disability plan participant to exhaust administrative remedies within the plan before litigating a claim for disability benefits, even though the plan did not explicitly require exhaustion of remedies. To the Circuit Court, it is common knowledge that administrative routines must be followed before seeking relief in court.[58]

Wisconsin has a "notice and prejudice" law—that is, a law that a claim cannot be denied based on late proof of loss unless the delay actually results in prejudice to the insurer. The law was applied in favor of an employee who didn't realize the company's long-term disability plan was an insurance plan, and therefore failed to file within the required 90-day period. The Eastern District of Wisconsin did not accept the insurer's ERISA preemption argument, finding it a simple matter of insurance regulation.[59]

[¶1218]   CAFETERIA PLANS

Temporary and Proposed Regulations at 62 FR 60195 and 60196 (11/7/97) give employers more leeway in changing cafeteria plan elections based on a change in employee status or an employee's family status.

[¶1220]   PLAN ADMINISTRATION AND FIDUCIARY ISSUES

As a general rule, a plan administrator's factual determinations and interpretations of the plan will be reviewed under a *de novo* standard unless the plan explicitly awards the administrator discretion to make those decisions, in which case the standard will be whether this discretion was abused.[60]

In an early 1996 Supreme Court case, an ERISA plaintiff was unable to collect his judgment against the corporation, allegedly because a corporate officer who was not a fiduciary misappropriated the money. The Supreme Court did not allow the corporate veil to be pierced, finding that there was not a close enough relation to the ERISA for federal jurisdiction to be present. Ancillary jurisdiction wouldn't work either, because a judgment cannot be enforced against someone who was not liable in the first place.[61]

In mid-1996, the Supreme Court ruled that plan sponsors are not acting as fiduciaries when they adopt, modify, or terminate plans. Clearly, then, they cannot be guilty of fiduciary violations in this context, and setting up an early retirement program that is conditioned on waiving employment claims is not a "prohibited transaction" for ERISA purposes.[62]

An insurance company hired to administer an ERISA plan can be a fiduciary even if the contract with the plan sponsor says that it is not a fiduciary. What controls is whether the insurance company has check-writing authority for the plan or can exercise discretion over the payment of benefits.[63]

When a participant requests, ERISA §104(b)(4) requires disclosure of "other instruments under which the plan is established or operated." However, that category does not include the plan's actuarial valuation reports, because the plan fiduciaries are not obligated to accept the assumptions of those reports, and are not bound by their conclusions.[64]

The right to vote ESOP shares does not involve plan assets, so directors who manipulated the voting of ESOP shares so that they stayed on the corporation's Board of Directors were not guilty of a breach of fiduciary duty.[65]

The fiduciary duties are the same for trustees of multiemployer as for single-employer plans. But, to the Third Circuit, amending a plan to increase payouts to the 85% of participants who participated in both pension and welfare plans did not violate fiduciary duty under ERISA §404, building on the *Spink* finding that when an employer amends a plan, it acts as a trust settlor and not as a fiduciary, because the amendment is a business decision rather than a plan administration decision.[66] The statute of limitations for a claim for withdrawal liability under the Multi-Employer Pension Plan Amendments is six years from the employer's default on any scheduled payment of withdrawal liability. It begins to run when liability arises, and mere withdrawal is not a violation as long as the mandated payments are made.[67]

Even if it receives advice from the same attorney on non-fiduciary issues of plan administration, a company's communications with the attorney about plan amendments are privileged, and cannot be discovered by employees challenging the adoption of the amendments.[68]

Under ERISA §404(c), fiduciaries are relieved of liability for losses due to a participant's exercise of control over assets in the participant's own account. In a case involving Guaranteed Investment Contract investments that held a high proportion of failed junk bonds, the Third Circuit ruled that §404(c) applies only if the exercise of control is permitted by a specific plan provision, and is a substantial factor that contributes to the loss.[69]

ERISA §502(a)(5) (availability of "appropriate equitable relief") gives the Secretary of Labor the power to bring a civil suit against a plan's party-in-interest who is accused of engaging in a prohibited transaction.[70]

The Federal District Court has independent subject matter jurisdiction under ERISA to hear a suit brought by a pension fund to enforce a settlement involving the employer's compliance with its contribution obligations. Jurisdiction exists because the suit requires construction of ERISA provisions.[71]

A company was not subject to ERISA liability based on its decision not to provide benefits to laid-off workers under the severance plan, because in this case the company acted in its role as employer rather than plan fiduciary, given that the plan was an unfunded plan payable from the employer's general operating funds.[72]

In the employer corporation's bankruptcy proceedings, the PBGC can only get part of the unpaid post-petition minimum funding obligation classified as an expense taking administrative priority as an actual necessary cost of preserving the estate. Any portion allocable to benefits earned before the bankruptcy filing cannot be classified as an administrative expense.[73]

An employer's suit for breach of contract against a third party administrator (a company that takes over back-office functions for ERISA plans) and an excess insurer who failed to process a claim and seek reimbursement under the claim, is not preempted by ERISA. In the view of the Ninth Circuit, the case is an ordinary state suit for breach of contract. The contracts between employer and TPA and insurer are not related to the ERISA enforcement scheme, and the connection between the suit and the plan is too tenuous for preemption to be viable.[74]

A plan combined ERISA benefits such as early retirement with a non-ERISA educational expense reimbursement plan for retirees. After the employer discontinued the education assistance, ex-employees sued, claiming that they were induced to retire early by their belief that education benefits would be available. The corporate defendant sought to remove the case to federal court, and then get it dismissed on the basis of ERISA preemption. The Eleventh Circuit refused, because the education assistance was not a welfare benefit as defined by ERISA, and preemption does not occur merely because a non-welfare benefit is included in a package with welfare benefits.[75]

[¶1225] TAX ISSUES IN PLAN MANAGEMENT

IRS Announcement 96-15, 1996-11 IRB 22 says that the IRS will *not* impose the §4975 excise tax on companies that take advantage of the Department of Labor's Pension Payback program to make corrective payments before September 7, 1996. The corrective payback payments are not treated as annual additions for the limitation year in which they are made. However, a payback that restores a delinquent contribution is an annual addition for the year in which the transfer to the plan was required.

The Code §4980 excise tax of 15 percent of any overfunding that reverts to the employer is treated as an excise tax for purposes of Bankruptcy Code §507(a)(7); it is not an ordinary unsecured claim.[76] However, the 10 percent of the accumulated funding deficiency assessed under IRC §4971 is a penalty, and thus an ordinary unsecured claim, not an excise tax entitled to seventh priority.[77]

Despite ERISA's anti-alienation provision, a taxpayer's vested interest in a qualified plan can be garnished to satisfy an IRS judgment for unpaid taxes. The regulations defining a qualified plan state specifically that tax enforcement by *levy* does not violate the anti-alienation rule.[78]

As ¶4201 shows, issues continue to arise as to what precisely is a "personal injury," compensation for which can be excluded from gross income for tax purposes. According to the Fifth Circuit, settlement proceeds for a wrongful termination case should not have been included in gross income, because the trial court should not have relied on cases subsequent to the settlement and limiting ERISA compensatory damages.[79] In this reading, the settlement proceeds were tort damages insofar as they represented emotional distress and other nonpecuniary losses. The back pay and future lost wage awards should not have been subjected to employment taxes, either.

In contrast, a settlement arising from an employer's scheme to violate ERISA by avoiding pension liabilities was held not to involve personal injury, so the settlement proceeds had to be included in gross income by the recipient employee, because it falls under an "expansive" definition of wages and does not resemble a traditional tort action.[80]

On another tax issue, the Ninth Circuit held that pass-through income from an S Corporation does not constitute net earnings from self-employment that can be used to calculate the Keogh plan deduction.[81]

— **ENDNOTES** —

1. *Curtiss-Wright Corp. v. Schoonejongen*, #93-1935, 115 S.Ct. 1223 (Sup.Ct. 3/6/95).

2. *Varity Corp. v. Howe*, #94-1471, 116 S.Ct. 1065 (Sup.Ct. 3/19/96), affirming 36 F.3d 746 and 41 F.3d 1263, both 8th Cir. 1994. In *Sprague v. General Motors*, 92 F.3d 1425 (6th Cir. 8/14/96), the Sixth Circuit instructed the District Court to follow *Varity* and examine ERISA claims that the employees were misled about the availability of lifetime benefits at no cost, bearing in mind that the SPD prevails if it conflicts with language in other documents. The result of the examination, however, was that the employer was permitted to amend the plan, based on the reservation, although the SPD called for lifetime benefits at no cost: *Sprague v. General Motors*, 66 LW 1423 (6th Cir. 1/7/98). Also see *Association of Machinists v. Masonite Corp.*, 122 F.3d 228 (5th Cir. 9/4/97), a case remanded for interpretation of a union contract calling for benefits "until death." The retirees interpreted this to mean benefits continuing throughout their lifetimes. The employer said the language was intended as a limitation on dependent benefits. The Fifth Circuit remanded because the language was ambiguous, so further evidence was needed for its interpretation.

Also see *Coyne & Delany Co. v. Selman*, 98 F.3d 1457 (4th Cir. 10/25/96): malpractice suit by employer, against the benefit design consulting firm that advised the employer to self-insure, is not preempted by ERISA, because ERISA's aim is to protect beneficiaries. A dispute between employer and consultant does not involve ERISA, and *Custer v. Sweeney*, 89 F.3d 1156: ERISA does not preempt a malpractice suit against the plan's attorneys. The Ninth Circuit held in *Jacobson v. Hughes Aircraft Co.*, 105 F.3d 1288 (9th Cir. 1/23/97) that summary judgment for the employer should not have been granted: employees have a viable ERISA claim when they assert that the employer has misappropriated pension plan surplus for its own benefit.

3. *Vizcaino v. Microsoft Corp.*, 97 F.3d 1187 (9th Cir. 10/3/96).

4. *Vizcaino v. Microsoft Corp.*, 97-2 U.S.T.C. ¶50,566 (9th Cir. 7/24/97).

5. *Abraham v. Exxon Corp.*, 85 F.3d 1126 (5th Cir. 6/10/96). Also see *Springfield v. Comm'r*, 88 F.3d 750 (9th Cir. 7/3/96), ruling that a used car dealer was entitled to safe harbor relief, and a refund of employment taxes and penalties, because he reasonably relied on industry practice and treated sales staff as independent contractors rather than employees.

6. *Belanger v. Wyman-Gordon Co.*, 71 F.3d 451 (1st Cir. 12/14/95).

7. *Sticka v. Wilbur*, 126 F.3d 1218 (9th Cir. 10/6/97).

8. *Rhoades, McKee & Baer v. U.S.*, 43 F.3d 1071 (6th Cir. 1/10/95). Compare with *Citrus Valley Estates Inc. v. C.I.R.*, 49 F.3d 1410 (9th Cir. 3/8/95) permitting conservative actuarial assumptions in a defined benefit plan (which have the effect of increasing both the employer's contributions to the plan and its tax deductions) because the actuary's responsibility includes prevention of underfunding in addition to preventing inappropriate contributions and tax deductions.

9. *Heath v. Varity Corp.*, 71 F.3d 256 (7th Cir. 11/30/95). Also see *Ahng v. Allsteel Inc.*, 96 F.3d 1033 (7th Cir. 9/25/96): the ERISA §204(g) ban on amending a pension plan to reduce accrued benefits also applies to early retirement benefit plans, and *Kowalski v. L&F Products*, 82 F.3d 1283 (3rd Cir. 5/2/96): §510 action is cognizable even if the alleged retaliatory discharge occurred after the employee got the benefits, not before.

10. *Golden v. Kelsey-Hayes Co.*, 73 F.3d 648 (6th Cir. 1/18/96). Also see *Diehl v. Twin Disk Inc.*, 102 F.3d 301 (7th Cir. 12/12/96): an unambiguous promise of lifetime retiree welfare benefits in a plant shutdown agreement must be followed, because the promise of lifetime benefits ended the employee's ability to modify retiree coverage.

11. *Steward v. KHD Deutz of America Corp.*, 73 F.3d 1522 (11th Cir. 2/28/96). But see *Sullivan v. LTV Aerospace & Defense Co.*, 82 F.3d 1251 (2nd Cir. 5/6/96); jury unavailable in ERISA case, because of the inherently equitable nature of the claims.

12. *Lynn v. CSX Transportation Inc.*, 84 F.3d 970 (7th Cir. 5/24/96).

13. Rev.Rul. 95-31, 1995-1 C.B. 76.

14. *Brillinger v. General Electric Co.*, 66 LW 1376 (2nd Cir. 12/3/97).]

15. *United Steelworkers of America v. United Engineering Inc.*, 52 F.3d 1386 (6th Cir. 5/2/95).

16. *Estate of Altobelli v. IBM*, 77 F.3d 78 (4th Cir. 2/28/96). But see *Hopkins v. AT&T Global Information Solutions Co.*, 105 F.3d 153 (4th Cir. 1/24/97): unless a QDRO is entered before the date of retirement, the benefits vest in the current spouse and not the former spouse.

17. *Trustees of Iron Workers Local 451 Annuity Fund v. O'Brien*, 22 Fam.L.Rep. 1515 (D.Del. 8/2/96).

18. *Oddino v. Oddino*, 16 Cal. 4th 67, 65 Cal. Rptr.2nd 566, 939 P.2d 1266 (Cal.Sup. 7/28/97).

19. *Metropolitan Life Ins. Co. v. Fowler*, 922 F.Supp. 8 (E.D. Mich. 4/15/96). Note that the SBJPA has eliminated the tax exemption for death benefits, so it is less likely that plans will offer such benefits if they do not provide tax benefits for the recipients.

20. *Hopkins v. AT&T Global Info. Solutions Co.*, 105 F.3d 153 (4th Cir. 1/24/97).

21. *Rodoni v. C.I.R.*, 105 T.C. No. 3 (7/24/95). Also see *Hawkins v. C.I.R.*, 86 F.3d 982 (10th Cir. 6/14/96): divorce decree's award of $1 million from husband's pension to wife operated as a QDRO, so the wife (and alternate payee) and not the husband was liable for taxes on the $1 million.

22. *AT&T Management Pension Plan v. Tucker*, 901 F.Supp. 1168 (C.D.Cal. 8/17/95).

23. *In re Ellis*, 72 F.3d 628 (8th Cir. 2/18/95).

24. *Gendreau v. Gendreau*, 122 F.3d 815 (9th Cir. 8/15/97).

25. *Boggs v. Boggs*, #96-79, 117 S.Ct. 1754 (Sup.Ct. 6/2/97).

26. *Barkley v. Conner*, 73 F.3d 258 (9th Cir. 1/11/96). Also see *McCafferty v. McCafferty*, 96 F.3d 192 (6th Cir. 9/18/96); husband's duty to make monthly payments to wife, equivalent to about half of the value of his pension at the time of the divorce, starting five years after the divorce, is not dischargeable in bankruptcy, because the ex-wife's interest in the pension never entered the bankruptcy estate.

27. *PBGC v. Pritchard*, 33 F.3d 509 (5th Cir. 4/5/95).

28. *Eddy v. Colonial Life Co.*, 59 F.3d 201 (D.C.Cir. 7/7/95).

29. *Adkins v. John Hancock Mutual Life Insurance Co.*, 957 F.Supp. 211 (M.D. Fla. 1/21/97).

30. *Jacobson v. Hughes Aircraft Co.*, 105 F.3d 1288 (9th Cir. 1/23/97).

31. *Lindsay v. Thiokol Corp.*, 112 F.3d 1068 (10th Cir. 4/18/97).

32. *McNab v. GM*, 66 LW 1432 (S.D. Ind. 12/5/97).

33. *Mattei v. Mattei*, 66 LW 1197 (6th Cir. 9/25/97).

34. 66 LW 1224 (Tax Court 9/22/97).

35. *Inter-Modal Rail Employees Ass'n v. Atchison, Topeka & Santa Fe Railroad*, #96-491, 65 LW 4319 (Sup.Ct. 5/12/97). But see *Stafford v. True-Temper*

Sports, 123 F.3d 291 (5th Cir. 9/25/97), holding that an ERISA §510 claim that the employee was fired to prevent vesting of his pension and because he filed an expensive health insurance claim was precluded by a state unemployment insurance board finding that the employee was fired for intentionally claiming that he worked more hours than he actually did.

36. On a related issue, see *EEOC v. CNA Insurance Co.,* 96 F.3d 1039 (7th Cir. 9/27/96): it does not violate the Americans with Disabilities Act to maintain a long-term disability plan that has no limit for physical disabilities but imposes a two-year limit on benefits for mental disabilities. The theory is that all employees are subject to the same limitations, whatever their health status. Furthermore, the court rejected the framing of the issue in ADA terms, finding that the case should have been brought as an ERISA claim for inartful plan drafting.

37. *Golden v. Kelsey-Hayes Co.,* 73 F.3d 648 (6th Cir. 1/18/96).

38. But see *Adams v. Cyprus Amax Mineral Co.,* 954 F.Supp. 1407 (D.Colo. 2/7/97) finding that the Seventh Amendment permits jury trial of an employee's ERISA §502(a)(1)(B) action to recover benefits under the terms of the plan. Although in general ERISA actions are equitable, a claim of this type is similar to a breach of contract claim. The employees seek money damages, a legal remedy that can be determined by a jury.

39. *In re UNISYS Corp. Retiree Medical Benefits ERISA Litigation,* 58 F.3d 896 (3rd Cir. 6/28/95); *Ballone v. Eastman Kodak,* 65 LW 2626 (2nd Cir. 3/21/97). On the duty to disclose in the pension context, see *Fischer v. Philadelphia Electric Co.,* 96 F.3d 1533 (3rd Cir. 10/1/96); Administrator is not permitted to lie to participants; the duty to disclose a contemplated change in the plan is triggered by senior management's consideration of a proposal that might really be implemented—as distinct from a mere feasibility study.

40. *Hockett v. Sun Company Inc.,* 109 F.3d 1515 (10th Cir. 3/24/97); and *Vartanian v. Monsanto Co.,* 66 LW 1391 (1st Cir. 12/15/97).

41. *UAW v. Alcoa,* 64 LW 2764 (N.D.Ohio 4/22/96) [retirees]; *Loral Defense Systems-Akron,* 320 NLRB No. 54 (1/31/96) [unionized active workers; collective bargaining required for the change]. According to *Grondorf, Field, Black & Co. v. NLRB,* 107 F.3d 882 (D.C.Cir. 3/7/97), after impasse occurs, the employer does not have the power to terminate union-sponsored health and retirement plans and replace them with employer-sponsored plans that were mentioned during negotiations, if there was no concrete proposal under discussion as to the replacement.

42. *Atlanta v. Morgan,* 66 LW 1320 (Ga.Sup. 11/3/97).

43. *Rutgers Council of AAUP Chapters v. Rutgers University,* 65 LW 2612 (N.J.App. 3/12/97).

44. *In re Blue Cross of Western Pennsylvania Litigation,* 942 F.Supp. 1061 (W.D. Pa. 9/5/96); *Brown v. Blue Cross/Blue Shield of Michigan,* 65 LW 2304 (E.D. Mich. 9/16/96).

45. *Davies v. Centennial Life Insurance Co.*, 128 F.3d 984 (6th Cir. 10/16/97).

46. *Turner v. Fallon Community Health Plan*, 66 LW 1288 (1st Cir. 10/20/97).

47. *Shea v. Esensten*, 107 F.3d 625 (8th Cir. 2/26/97).

48. *McEvoy v. Group Health Cooperative of Eau Claire*, 66 LW 1311 (Wis.Sup. 11/12/97).]

49. *Cypress Fairbanks Medical Center Inc. v. Pan-American Life Insurance Co.*, 110 F.3d 280 (5th Cir. 4/17/97).

50. *Williams v. Midwest Operating Engineers Welfare Fund*, 66 LW 1218 (7th Cir. 9/30/97).

51. *Scholtens v. Schneider*, 671 N.E.2d 657 (Ill.Sup. 9/19/96).

52. *Geweke Ford v. St. Joseph's Omni Preferred Care*, 66 LW 1415 (9th Cir. 12/10/97).

53. *Wilson v. Zoellner*, 114 F.3d 713 (8th Cir. 5/21/97).

54. *Stiltner v. Beretta USA Corp.*, 81 F.3d 490 (4th Cir. 2/2/96).

55. *Pilkington PLC v. Perelman*, 72 F.3d 1396 (9th Cir. 12/27/95).

56. IRS Notice 96-53, 1996-51 IRB 5 explains, in question-and-answer format, how to establish an MSA, contribute to an MSA, and other practical questions.

57. *Standard Insurance Co. v. Saklad*, 66 LW 1280 (9th Cir. 10/31/97).

58. *Kinkead v. Southwestern Bell*, 49 F.3d 454 (8th Cir. 4/9/97).

59. *Bogusewski v. Life Insurance Company of North America*, 66 LW 1250 (E.D. Wis. 10/10/97).

60. *Perez v. Aetna Life Ins. Co.*, 96 F.3d 813 (6th Cir. 9/23/96).

61. *Peacock v. Thomas*, #94-1453, 116 S.Ct. 862 (Sup.Ct. 2/21/96).

62. *Lockheed v. Spink*, #95-809, 116 S.Ct. 1783 (Sup.Ct. 6/10/96).

63. *IT Corp. v. General American Life Ins. Co.*, 107 F.3d 1415 (9th Cir. 3/3/97).

64. *Board of Trustees of the CWA/ITU Pension Plan v. Weinstein*, 65 LW 2579 (2nd Cir. 2/24/97).

65. *Grindstaff v. Green*, 66 LW 1424 (6th Cir. 1/8/98).

66. *Walling v. Brady*, 66 LW 1086 (3rd Cir. 7/30/97).

67. *Bay Area Laundry and Dry Cleaning Pension Trust Fund v. Ferbar Corporation of California Inc.*, #96-370, 118 S.Ct. 542 (Sup.Ct. 12/15/97).

68. *Becher v. LILCO*, 66 LW 1311 (2nd Cir. 11/12/97).

69. *Meinhardt v. Unisys Corp.*, 74 F.3d 420 (3rd Cir. 1/4/96). With respect to the consequences of GIC investments, see *Texas Life Accident Health & Hospital Service Insurance Guaranty Ass'n v. Gaylord Entertainment Co.*, 105 F.3d 210 (5th Cir. 1/24/97), *cert. dismissed* 117 S.Ct. 2501. The state guaranty association asserted that it has derivative claims against the plan administrators for breaching of fiduciary duty by investing in the GICs, thus requiring the bail-

out. The Fifth Circuit disagreed, because the administrator did not make a knowing, express assignment of the fiduciary breach claim, and such claims are important enough to plan participants that only express, not implied, assignments can be given effect.

70. *Reich v. Stangl,* 73 F.3d 1027 (10th Cir. 1/10/96).

71. *Board of Trustees of Hotel & Restaurant Employees v. Madison Hotel,* 97 F.3d 1479 (D.C.Cir. 10/15/96). Also see *PBGC v. Carter & Tillery Enterprises,* 66 LW 1464 (9th Cir. 1/9/98) holding that ERISA §4003 gives the PBGC authority to file suit dealing with unpaid premiums, unfunded liabilities, and accumulated funding deficiencies—even if the PBGC failed to follow the ERISA §4068 lien procedure.

72. *Aminoff v. Ally & Gargano,* 65 LW 2400 (S.D.N.Y. 11/21/96).

73. *PBGC v. Sunarhauserman,* 66 LW 1195 (6th Cir. 9/25/97).

74. *Geweke Ford v. St. Joseph's Omni Preferred Care,* 66 LW 1415 (9th Cir. 12/10/97).

75. *Kemp v. IBM,* 65 LW 2673 (11th Cir. 4/8/97).

76. *U.S. v. Juvenile Shoe Corp. of America,* 99 F.3d 898 (8th Cir. 11/7/96). Note that ERISA does not forbid *overfunding.* If a plan has more than enough money to provide the required plan benefits, the fiduciary is not obligated to use the extra money to enhance benefits available to participants.

77. *U.S. v. Reorganized CF&I Fabricators of Utah Inc.,* #95-325, 116 S.Ct. 2106 (Sup.Ct. 6/20/96).

78. *U.S. v. Sawaf,* 74 F.3d 119 (6th Cir. 1/26/96).

79. *Dotson v. C.I.R.,* 87 F.3d 682 (5th Cir. 6/27/96).

80. *Hemelt v. U.S.,* 65 LW 2400 (D.Md. 10/22/96). But see Code §104 as amended by by the SBJPA.

81. *Durando v. U.S.,* 70 F.3d 548 (9th Cir. 11/16/95).

— **FOR FURTHER REFERENCE** —

Bianchi, Alden J., "The ERISA Preemption Doctrine and the Assignment of Employee Welfare Plan Benefits," 25 *Tax Management Compensation Planning Journal* 231 (10/3/97).

Coleman, Dennis and Robin Hoesly, "Suspension of Benefits—Still Confusing After All These Years," 25 *Tax Management Compensation Planning Journal* 9 (January 3, 1997).

Coskey, Susan L., "Vizcaino v. Microsoft Corporation: A Labor and Employment Lawyer's Perspective," 48 *Labor Law J.* 91 (February '97).

Creech, Catherine L., "Worker Classification Issues: Consequences for Employee Benefit Plans," 21 *ALI-ABA Course Materials J.* 5 (August '97).

Davis, Victoria F., "Designing, Bidding Out, and Implementing a Managed Care Plan," 9 *Benefits Law J.* 63 (Fall '96).

Ellentuck, Albert B., "Retaining Key Executives by Using a Parachute Payment Agreement," 28 *Tax Adviser* 50 (January '97).

Ertz, Michael S., "Lock It Up: Ensuring the Payment of Nonqualified Pension Plan Benefits," 51 *J. American Society CLU/ChFC* 8 (January '97).

Fellows, James A. and Michael A. Yuhas, "Reasonable Compensation: The Search for a Defining Concept," 75 *Taxes: The Tax Magazine* 114 (February '97).

Frankel, George, "Planning Strategies for Inherited IRA Withdrawals," 24 *Taxation for Lawyers* 231 (January-February '96).

Gallagher, Robert F., William F. Hanrahan and Mary Ann Dominy Edgar, "The Expanding Universe of ERISA's Duty to Disclose," 22 J. of *Pension Planning & Compliance* 37 (Fall '96).

Golub, Ira M., "Multiemployer Group Health Plans and COBRA," 21 *J. Pension Planning and Compliance* 1 (Winter '96).

Harris, Jonathan W., "Post-Employment Health Coverage for Executives and Their Families," 24 *Estate Planning* 59 (February '97).

Lee, Stephanie, "Is Forfeited Vacation Money in the Bank?" 136 *Trusts and Estates* 8 (March '97).

Miller, Christopher S. and Brian D. Poe, "Attendance-Based Bonus Plans and the FMLA: Does Coming to Work Still Pay Off?" 48 *Labor Law J.* 59 (February '97).

Naegele, Richard A., "An Overview of Form 5500 Filing Requirements," 22 *J. of Pension Planning and Compliance* 50 (Fall '96).

Siegel, Jack B., "New Bottles, Same Wine: Using Interactive Media for Employee Benefit Communications," 10 *Benefits L.J.* 87 (Spring '97).

COMPUTER LAW

[¶1301] As the use of computers becomes ubiquitous in society, and the Internet becomes more popular and more broadly used, certain legal issues are emerging as significant. The extent to which maintaining a Web site or transmitting information on the Internet gives rise to personal jurisdiction has been litigated several times. Intellectual property issues, especially involving copyrights and trademarks, are commonly raised, especially in connection with designation of the "domain names" by which Web sites are identified. Soon, it will be necessary to adapt traditional commercial law concepts to accommodate electronic commerce. Many concerns have been raised about the prevalence of obscene materials on-line, and the potential harm caused by those materials (especially to minors).

The Telecommunications Act of 1996, P.L. 104-104 (enacted 2/8/96) includes §509, "Online Family Empowerment." This section, which adds a new section, 47 U.S.C. §230, is nicknamed the Communications Decency Act. The Congressional findings for the enactment are that although Internet and other interactive computer services have immense educational and information potential, families need control over what materials are transmitted to their homes.

To this end, on-line services and Internet service providers are encouraged to screen the materials appearing on their networks, and to eliminate offensive materials. (See ¶1305, below, for court cases that create the problem Congress was trying to eliminate.) Furthermore, a provider or user of an on-line or Internet service is not treated as the "publisher" or "speaker" of information that derives from another information content provider. There is a "good Samaritan" rule that absolves on-line and Internet services from liability if they undertake the burden of restricting access to obscene, violent, harassing, or other objectionable material.[1]

As the discussion below shows, court rulings discourage computer services from exercising editorial control; Congress wants to "remove disincentives for the development and utilization of blocking and filtering technologies that empower parents to restrict their children's access to objectionable or inappropriate on-line material."[2]

Another Congressional objective is "vigorous enforcement of Federal criminal laws to deter and punish trafficking in obscenity, stalking, and harassment by means of computer."[3]

A coalition of civil liberties and computer users' organizations successfully challenged the statute's conformity to the First Amendment. The District Courts for the District of Pennsylvania and the Southern District of New York both found the statute unconstitutional and overbroad, in that it not only regulated the display of obscene materials to children, but also impermissibly restricted protected speech between adults.

The Supreme Court found the ban on knowing transmission of obscene or indecent material to minors, or transmitting material patently offensive under community standards, invalid under the First Amendment. The provisions were invalid because they contained no provision for parental consent to the transmission of such material; because the ban was not limited to commercial transmissions; because there was no requirement that illegal material lack redeeming social value; and because blanket content-based restrictions on Internet speech are inappropriate. (The decision focuses on First Amendment issues and does not reach the question of whether the challenged provisions were impermissibly vague under the fifth Amendment.)[4]

On the issue of transmission of obscene material, the Sixth Circuit decided early in 1996 that 18 U.S.C. §1465, knowing transport in interstate commerce of obscene materials, applies to transmission of pornographic images on a BBS (computer bulletin board system).[5] The defendants said that the computer image files were intangible and therefore not covered by the legislation. However, the court found the means of transmission to be irrelevant if the illicit result occurs. To protect themselves, BBSs can limit downloading of images to areas where the images are not in violation of community standards.[6]

For a First Amendment issue not involving obscenity, see *Bernstein v. Department of State*,[7] prohibiting the prior restraint involved in the State Department requirement that cryptographic software be licensed before export. (The Department of State considers the software a "defense article.") According to the Northern District of California, the licensing system is fatally defective because it lacks procedural protections, such as time limits and an appeal procedure.

The Department of Justice engaged in a prolonged investigation as to whether Microsoft had monopolized the market for operating systems. A consent decree was agreed to. The District Court for the District of Columbia initially refused to grant the required approval of the consent decree, finding that the scope of the decree was too narrow; the government had not furnished enough information to test the impact on the public; and the decree did not have adequate enforcement mechanisms. The D.C. Circuit reversed the District Court, however, finding that the trial court improperly extended its inquiry to subjects that were outside the scope of the DOJ's investigation.[8]

The case against Microsoft was back in late 1997, this time raising the question of whether Microsoft violated its consent decree with the Department of Justice by requiring PC manufacturers to license Microsoft's Web browser, Internet Explorer (IE). The crux of the matter is that the consent decree permits Microsoft to "integrate" software products, although the company is forbidden to condition a licensing agreement for an operating system (e.g., Windows '95 or '98) to licensing of another product. In October, the Department of Justice went to the D.D.C. to request that Microsoft be fined $1 million per day as a contempt fine for violation of the consent decree.[9] The D.D.C. ordered a six-month discovery period and appointed a special master to research the Sherman Act status of tying Windows 95 licensing to the manufacturer's agreement to install the IE browser. In January, 1998, Microsoft agreed to permit computer manufacturers to install the latest version of Windows '95 without also being required to install the IE browser.[10]

Spare parts used to repair computers under service contracts have been held not to be inventory by the Federal Circuit. The parts are not held primarily for sale to customers, so they can be treated as a depreciable capital asset.[11] According to the Tax Court, software acquired for use in a company's business, under a non-exclusive license that did not transfer the underlying intellectual property rights in the software, is tangible personal property that qualifies for the investment tax credit.[12] For the latest rules on using computers to file taxes, see IR 97-5, CCH Federal Tax Reporter ¶46,280 and Rev.Proc. 97-34, 1997-30 IRB 14, giving the electronic and magnetic tape filing requirements for 1997 Form 1090s, 1099s, 5498s, and W-2Gs.

A defendant's skills as a computer hacker can properly be taken into account in enhancing his sentence under the federal Sentencing Guidelines provision that lengthens the sentence if a special skill was used to facilitate the commission of a crime.[13]

[¶1302] COMPUTERS AND THE COURT SYSTEM

"Cyberspace," where computer communications occur, is not a physical place. The court system is beginning to come to grips with the question of where (if at all) court jurisdiction can be obtained over cyberspace activities.

Several recent cases permit a state to exercise long-arm jurisdiction on the basis of frequent electronic communications delivered to the forum from outside, although the Southern District of New York disagrees and has been affirmed by the Second Circuit.[14]

The jurisdiction issue continued to be significant in 1997, with an emerging consensus that electronic communications in a forum furnish minimum contacts.[15]

Another group of cases draws a distinction between an "active" Web site, which is transactional or otherwise solicits business, and a "passive" Web site, which can merely be viewed.[16]

Although New York has been restrictive in its view of Internet-derived jurisdiction, two 1997 cases do find jurisdiction to be present in special circumstances. The state's Attorney General can sue in state court to punish consumer fraud and false advertising committed over the Internet by companies based in New York, where victims were found both inside and outside the state. Sufficient presence occurred because products were sold through an ISP in New York; the opinion notes that merely maintaining a site accessible to New Yorkers would not be sufficient.[17]

An August, 1997 case from the Southern District of New York found personal jurisdiction in a trademark infringement case against a Georgia-based consulting firm that got six New York subscribers from its Web advertisement. Jurisdiction was proper because activity was purposefully directed toward New York by mailing software packages to subscribers.[18]

Another 1997 case goes past the jurisdiction issue to deal with venue for a Lanham Act passing-off action in a case where the plaintiff alleges injury from misrepresentations contained on the defendant's Web site. The proper district for venue is the one in which people are likely to be confused as to the origin of the products. But the district from which the site originated was not the proper venue for a case against the company that drafted the prospectus containing the alleged misrepresentations.[19]

The Indian Gaming Regulatory Act completely preempts a claim that an on-reservation Internet gaming site violated state consumer protection law.[20]

It is permissible to charge under a computer crime statute, rather than a fraud statute carrying lesser penalties, when a computer has allegedly been used to alter insurance claim forms. The use of the computer introduces a new, and more serious, element of the crime.[21]

In an early 1997 case, an IRS employee accessed confidential file information on various people he knew or felt hostility toward. However, when there was no proof that he disclosed the information to a third party or intended to use it; he did his work effectively; and he did not receive anything of value for the information, he could not be convicted of wire fraud or computer fraud under federal law.[22]

It is now quite common (if not universal) for law firms to prepare litigation documents with the use of computers. Can they bypass the stage of creating paper printouts of electronically generated documents? A federal District Court has granted a motion for a "paperless trial," in which documents will be stored as images on a computer, which will then be displayed on monitors during the trial. One procedural adaptation was required: the defense had to be given witness statements earlier than usual, to give additional time for review and to prepare for cross-examination.[23]

To file a CD-ROM brief in the Federal Circuit, a party must obtain leave of the court and consent of the other party. The filer must disclose the hardware and software specifications required to view the brief and use its hyperlinks. The filer must move for leave to file a CD-ROM brief before, or at the same time as, submitting 12 copies of the CD-ROM to the court.[24]

[¶1303] E-COMMERCE

Traditional commercial transactions often involve face-to-face discussions, and are usually memorialized in written and signed documents. Although courts may have to interpret these documents, they do so against a background of legislation and court decisions. There is a great deal of interest in using e-mail and the Internet to place orders for goods and services, but there are very significant questions about what constitutes a "writing" or a "signature" in these media. An article 2B on electronic commerce has been drafted for the UCC, but it has not achieved widespread acceptance. The National Conference of Commissioners on Uniform State Laws issued a discussion draft of a Uniform Electronic Transactions Act in 1997.[25]

It contains six parts:

➤ General topics

➤ Electronic records and signatures

➤ Secure records and signatures

➤ Electronic contracts and communications

➤ Public records in electronic form

➤ Miscellaneous provisions

The issues to be resolved include whether it should be presumed that electronic signatures and unaltered records are valid; and when an electronic record becomes effective when it is transmitted by the sender's computer, received by the recipient's computer, or at some other time?

On July 1, 1997, the Clinton administration's policy statement on e-commerce was released. The administration is opposed to taxation of on-line products or services. In this view, market forces in the private sector should lead the development of e-commerce. The government's role is limited to prevention of fraud and protection of privacy. This "Framework for Global Electronic Commerce" can be found at http://www.whitehouse.gov/WH/New/Commerce.

[¶1304] COMPUTERS AND COPYRIGHT ISSUES

A major Copyright Office report was published on 8/21/97.[26] The Copyright Office raised issues about the copyrightability of databases, but did not issue formal recommendations. Perhaps the sweat equity involved in compiling a database should be recognized. There might be First Amendment issues implicated in granting protection, but perhaps these could be solved by noting that the underlying facts can be copied. The Copyright Office noted that the Berne Convention and the Agreement on Trade-Related Aspects of Intellectual Property Rights do accord copyright protection to databases, and the European Union has issued a database directive, effective January 1, 1998, making the structure of a database eligible for copyright.

The case of *Lotus Development Corp. v. Borland* has had an adventurous history in the courts. The case arose when Borland's *Quattro Pro* spreadsheet program copied Lotus' "menu tree" (the arrangement of about 500 computer commands into over 50 menus and submenus) in order to make *Quattro Pro* files compatible with Lotus files. The District Court deemed this to be an infringement of Lotus' copyright on its software. However, in early 1995, the First Circuit reversed the District Court, finding the menu tree to be a "method of operation" rather than copyrightable subject matter. Certiorari was granted. However, at the beginning of 1996, the Supreme Court merely affirmed the First Circuit, 4-4 (Justice Stevens did not participate) without opinion.[27]

Publishers scored a major victory in August, 1997, when the Southern District of New York ruled that newspaper and magazine publishers' copyrights in collective works allow them to control reproduction and revision. Therefore, the publishers can place the work of freelance writers who contributed to the newspapers and magazines on databases and CD-ROMs without the consent of the writers (or additional payments to them).[28]

A company that invested heavily in compiling a CD-ROM telephone directory was defeated in the Western District of Wisconsin when it sued for copyright infringement after a competitor put the contents of the proprietary CD-ROMs on the Internet.[29] In the court's judgment, the competitor proceeded by copying the CDs on the hard drive of its own computer, then adding its own search engine for Internet use. The copying to the competitor's hard drive was deemed "personal use," so there was no copyright infringement; furthermore, the telephone directories were not copyrightable subject matter because they were purely factual listings. The CD-ROM disks were sold with the conventional "shrink-wrap license" that forbids copying, but the District Court refused to enforce the shrink-wrap license, deeming it to be a contract of adhesion contrary to the Uniform Commercial Code.

However, the shrink-wrap license was enforced by the Seventh Circuit, finding the license to be an ordinary bilateral contract that can properly be regulated by states and is not preempted by the Copyright Act. In this analysis, it would be pointless to require the licensor to print out the lengthy license and display it on the cardboard box the software comes in, especially since purchases made by phone or over the Internet do not involve viewing any packaging at all.

The federal wire fraud statute cannot be used to pursue criminal copyright infringement charges under 17 U.S.C. §506(a) against the operator of a BBS who allowed users to download pirated copies of copyrighted software. This result was reached because the BBS operator did not profit financially from software piracy, and the criminal copyright infringement statute (unlike the wire fraud statute) requires proof of personal financial advantage to the infringer.[30]

This case was the impetus for passage of P.L. 105-147, the No Electronic Theft Act (enacted 12/16/97). P.L. 105-147 imposes penalties for willful copyright infringement even if there is no commercial gain from the act of infringement. Under this Act, reproducing or distributing one or more copies or phono-records of one or more copyright books, with a total retail value equal to or greater than $1,000, is a crime that can be penalized by fines and imprisonment of up to one year. If more than 10 copies and value of $2,500 or more are involved, the penalty can be up to three years' imprisonment, or six years' imprisonment for repeat violations.

The Southern District of California granted TROs, ordering Internet Service Providers (ISPs) to block access to "music archive" Web sites that were charged with unauthorized distribution of copyrighted music. The court viewed the risk of irreparable harm to be significant enough to grant the injunction.[31]

[¶1304.1]   Other Intellectual Property Issues

As noted below, "domains" in cyberspace that are used by particular businesses or organizations are identified by "domain names," which are subject to centralized registration. However, this registration process is separate from the trademark registration process, so procedures are evolving for linking the two. The agreement between the National Science Foundation and Network Solutions, Inc. expires in 1998, leading to serious confusion as to what will happen in registration after that time. On July 2, 1997, the Department of Commerce requested comment on current and possible future systems for registering domain names: see 62 FR 35896. (By 1997, 70,000 domain names were being registered per month, so the potential for chaos is immense.)[32]

It has been held[33] that an Internet domain name can infringe a trademark— so preliminary injunction was granted against the use of "juris.com" for a bulletin board system or Internet site, because of the likelihood of infringement of the registered trademark "Juris." Furthermore, the practice of "trademark greenmail" (registering a trademark belonging to someone else as a domain name, with the intention of collecting payment from the trademark holder) can be penalized as dilution under the 1995 Trademark Dilution Act.[34]

Although greenmail is usually commercially motivated, it can be ideological as well. In *Planned Parenthood Federation of America Inc. v. Bucci*[35] an anti-abortion activist registered the domain name plannedparenthood.com to display anti-abortion materials. (Planned Parenthood's site has the domain name ppfa.org.) A Lanham Act §32 and 43(a) injunction was granted, given the likelihood of confusion to Internet users and harm to Planned Parenthood's service mark. The court treated the use of interstate telephone lines to connect to the Web site as use of the mark in commerce. Commercial use was also present because the site was used to sell an anti-abortion book and to raise funds. Confusion was likely because it is common for individuals seeking a particular site to add .com to the name of the site's sponsor, even if (as in this case) it technically qualifies for an .org registration.

An emerging group of cases deals with the more difficult case, in which neither user of a potentially confusing domain name has any wrongful motivation: each is attempting to secure a Web presence for a name that it uses in good faith.

According to the Central District of California, registrar Network Solutions, Inc. is not liable to the owner of a federally registered trademark if it gives out a domain name that allegedly infringes that trademark. In this analysis, registering a domain name is not commercial use under the Trademark Dilution Act, and a domain name does not function as a trademark if it is merely used to identify an Internet site.[36] The Northern District of Illinois has also ruled that mere registration of a domain name is not a Lanham Act "use in commerce". Furthermore, it ruled that there is no independent cause of action for trademark misuse (misuse is a defense, not a separate cause of action), and trademark holders, unlike patent holders, do not have the potential to destroy competition.[37] In contrast, however, the Eastern District of Virginia did permit a Lanham Act action when a company registers a competitor's trademark as its own domain name, if consumer confusion is likely to result, and it did believe that unauthorized use of a trademark as a domain name is Lanham Act use in commerce.[38]

Suing for infringement of a trademark or service mark is essentially a tort case, making registrants of domain names that are similar or identical to a trademark joint tortfeasors. Thus, the plaintiff can sue less than all of the potential defendants, and the potential defendants are not FRCP 19(b) indispensable parties in the trademark infringement action.[39]

The District Court for the District of Massachusetts found that a patent issued for a data processing system that handles accounting calculations for mutual fund investments is invalid. In this reading, the system is either a business system or a collection of mathematical operations with no associated physical process steps— and neither one of those is patentable.[40]

Interestingly, recent cases probe not only the nature of knowledge—but the nature of sports. It has been held that the U.S. Golf Association's carefully and expensively developed formulas for generating golf handicaps are entitled to common-law protection. Embodying the formulas into computer software, without permission, misappropriates the USGA's property, even without proof of direct competition.[41]

The Southern District of New York ruled in September, 1996[42] that using an on-line computer network to transmit real-time information about basketball games over beepers misappropriates NBA property. Thus, both transmission of the games, and dissemination of information about ongoing games on America Online, were enjoined. The injunction was dissolved in January, 1997 by the Second Circuit, which drew a distinction between the broadcast of a sports event (protectable expression) and the game itself (not a work of authorship). The misappropriation theory was also rejected. The Second Circuit showed some willingness to permit a narrow "hot news" area in which misappropriation might be cognizable, but would not apply it to the case of sports scores, which are pure facts and not protectable.[43]

[¶1305] DEVELOPMENTS RELATING TO COMMERCIAL ON-LINE SERVICES

In mid-1995, the New York Supreme Court decided that the on-line service Prodigy was a "publisher" that could be sued for libel because the allegedly libelous communication appeared on a "forum" that had a moderator. Prodigy had claimed that it pre-screened posted material and exercised editorial control over material appearing on the service.[44]

A number of confidential, and copyrighted, Scientology documents were posted to the Internet by disaffected former Scientologists. Two District Courts reached opposite conclusions about the status of such activities. One court denied a preliminary injunction, finding the posting to be fair use because it was non-commercial, did not harm the church financially, and because it occurred in the context of discussion and criticism of the church.[45] Two months later, however, another court decided that a BBS or Internet Service Provider can be contributorily liable for copyright infringement if it is on actual notice—or should have known—that the posts were infringing yet failed to remove them once their copyright status became known.[46]

A company that sent "spam" (unsolicited e-mail advertisements to a broad list of recipients) annoyed America Online customers enough for AOL to block the unsolicited ads. The company challenged AOL in federal District Court using several theories—all unsuccessful.[47] The court refused to grant a temporary restraining order, finding it unlikely that a Sherman Act §2 claim based on refusal to deal in an essential facility could succeed at trial. In this analysis, refusal to deal is justified if one company refuses to abide by its potential trading partner's rules. Nor did AOL e-mail constitute an essential facility, because AOL subscribers could be reached by other means.

First Amendment arguments were also unsuccessful. The court did not believe that AOL, which is a private company, provides a "critical pathway of communication" that must be made available to everyone who wants to use it. The court did not accept the analogy between AOL and a "company town" where free speech must be permitted even contrary to the wishes of the owner. The significance of this series of cases extends far beyond the importance of the particular quarrel between two not particularly popular companies: it helps define the extent to which on-line speech is private or public.

At the beginning of 1998, AOL filed a complaint in the Eastern District of Virginia, charging bulk e-mailers with violating the Computer Fraud and Abuse Act, and with violating the Lanham Act by using a false aol.com return address. AOL charged trespass to chattel on the grounds that it had to spend a great deal of money to eliminate the spam, and that it suffered loss of reputation.[48] The common-law trespass to chattel action was recognized early in 1997 by the Southern District of Ohio[49] against a company that continued to send unsolicited e-mails after the on-line service told them to stop. In this analysis, computerized electronic signals are tangible enough to constitute trespass. The cause of action for trespass to chattel, unlike the conversion action, does not require substantial interference with the right to possession of the chattel.

Preliminary injunction was granted against enforcement of a Georgia law banning computer network transmission of data with a false sender ID or using a trademark without authorization. The Northern District of Georgia found the statute to be probably unconstitutional in that it imposed content restrictions on protected speech, and was vague and overbroad.[50]

An on-line service that encourages uploading of files and maintains a screening process for uploaded files can be held liable as a direct as well as a contributory infringer when copyrighted files are uploaded, in violation of the copyright holder's rights to control public display and distribution.[51]

[¶1305.1]   Regulation of E-Mail

Sending e-mail to co-workers, complaining about a company's new vacation policy, has been held by the NLRB to be protected concerted activity. Therefore, the employer was not justified in firing the worker for misconduct after he refused to apologize for the communications.[52]

Also apropos of searches and pornography, an undercover police officer bought two pornographic CD-ROMs from the plaintiff in *Davis v. Gracy*,[53] who mentioned that he had a BBS offering similar material. A judge issued a search warrant covering pornographic materials. The police seized computers containing many e-mail messages, not all of which had been delivered to their intended recipients. The plaintiff asserted that the seizure violated both the Fourth Amendment and the Electronic Communications Privacy Act, but the Tenth Circuit disagreed. The computer was an instrumentality of the crime, not a mere container for contraband. In the execution of a warrant, it is legitimate to seize an object with both licit and illicit purposes. The warrant permitted seizure of the entire computer, not merely its CD-ROM drives. The police were entitled to assert a good faith defense under the Electronic Communications Privacy Act, given their reasonable reliance on the warrant.

There is no reasonable expectation of privacy in chat room conversations or in e-mails sent to other chat participants. Consequently, there has been no search, much less an unlawful search, when federal agents collect chat-room messages about child pornography.[54]

Inadvertently viewing an e-mail message on someone else's computer screen is not an "interception" as defined by the Electronic Communications Privacy Act.[55]

[¶1306]   LEGAL IMPLICATIONS OF ON-LINE SECURITIES TRANSACTIONS

Prior to widespread use of networked computers, there was only one possible form of disclosure in the securities regulation context: giving or mailing printed prospectuses to potential investors. Actual purchases of the securities were handled by mail, telephone, or wire transfer. Given today's expanded use of computerized communications, it is inevitable that efforts would be made not only to buy and sell securities on-line, but to involve computers in the issue process.

The SEC has announced that it will not take enforcement action against two brokerage firms that maintain "screen-based" systems for qualified institutional buyers to trade in unregistered real estate securities.[56] No-action letters have also been issued with respect to a company's making a market in its own stock on the Internet.[57] The Commodity Futures Trading Commission has issued an interpretation requiring commodity pool operators and commodity trading advisors using the Internet to comply with all normal regulatory requirements. A six-month pilot project to test electronic filing of disclosure documents was launched in August, 1996.[58]

The SEC's Division of Corporate Finance granted relief under the '33 Act, thus permitting IPONET to offer private placement securities on an Internet site. The site, which includes red herrings and tombstones (complete with an electronic "coupon" for manifesting interest in making a purchase) is limited to accredited investors. Would-be investors register with the site; the site's proprietors perform an investigation to determine that the applicants really are accredited. If the test is passed, the investors can review data about Regulation D private offerings, posted by companies that agree to work with IPONET.[59]

Cyberspace, like any frontier town, attracts its share of outlaws, so the SEC has its own on-line Internet Enforcement Complaint Center, http://www.sec.gov/enforce/comctr.htm. This site connects the public with the Division of Enforcement for reports of possible securities fraud. In July 1996, the District Court for the Southern District of Florida issued a TRO against an individual and two associated entities who were allegedly using newsgroup postings and CompuServe advertisements to make fraudulent securities offerings.[60]

[¶1307]   LAW OFFICE COMPUTING

Once an exotic device found only in the largest, most prosperous, and most technologically daring firm, the computer is now a device that (in desktop or laptop form) is becoming universal in all kinds of law practice settings. Law office computing can perform many functions:

➤ Simple word processing

➤ Document assembly

➤ Time keeping, calendaring, scheduling

➤ Billing

➤ Litigation support

➤ Preparation of exhibits and presentation materials

➤ Document transmission (fax, e-mail, file transfers)

➤ Communications among lawyers, between lawyers and clients, etc. (groupware)

➤ Management of databases (such as names and addresses of clients, past clients, potential clients). There are also powerful databases of corporate information, patent applications, trademarks, and many other areas available as software or on-line.

➤ Legal research

➤ Law firm marketing

➤ Obtaining referrals; referring matters

➤ Training attorneys (e.g., in courtroom skills).

In order to use these powerful functions effectively, the attorney or law firm must choose the right balance of hardware and software. Depending on individual needs and technological sophistication, the choice might be made by practicing lawyers; delegated to Management Information Systems (MIS) personnel within a firm; or premised on advice from an outside consultant.

The equation is complicated by the rapid pace of change in computer technology. Many firms have confidently invested large sums of money in what was then advanced technology, only to find that their equipment is soon wildly outdated, incompatible with other firms' and court system equipment, and hard to use in the bargain.

A consensus has emerged: the vast majority of law office computing now uses IBM or IBM clone computers (PCs), and most of those use some version of the Windows operating system, with an increasing trend toward adopting Windows 95. Some lawyers still prefer Apple computers, a few prefer the more technically elaborate Unix system, but overall DOS and especially Windows on a PC "platform" are favored.

Computers are described in terms of their operating system (OS), such as Windows 95 or Unix; in terms of the kind of processor running the computer (the most common kinds on the market today are 486, Pentium, and Pentium Pro), how fast they operate (specified in megahertz, or mHz; speeds over 200 mHz are typical); how much Random Access Memory—RAM—they have available (4 MB is an absolute minimum for running Windows, and 8 MB or 16 MB is better); and how much storage space they have on their hard drives. Law office computers need at least 200 megabytes of hard disk storage for each machine; it's easy to buy computers that store more than 1 gigabyte (a gigabyte is 1,000 megabytes). Most law offices use laser printers to print their work. Two or more computers can share a single printer. Printer speed is measured in terms of pages per minute; an 8 ppm printer is conventional for law office use.

[¶1307.1] Law Office Hardware

At its most basic, a law office computing system requires at least a Central Processing Unit (CPU) for handling data, devices for inputting data (keyboard and mouse are the most common), a monitor for viewing data, and a printer for producing output on paper. A sole practitioner, or an individual lawyer within a firm, may choose to supplement (or even replace) a desktop computer unit with a laptop—a portable computer that has a flat screen in the lid instead of a separate monitor.

A laptop computer can be transported on a business trip, to a law library, to court, or to the location of a deposition. Functions such as word processing and data transmission can be carried out from these remote locations. Clearly, then, the laptop computer offers many advantages over the traditional yellow legal pad. However, it also has several disadvantages: the laptop weighs several pounds instead of several ounces; nothing too bad happens if you drop a yellow legal pad; and legal pads are not particularly attractive to thieves.

A more sophisticated law office system will include anywhere from a handful of computers to hundreds of them. Where there are multiple computers, it makes sense to connect them into a network so software, files, and printers can be shared. Two conventional ways of doing this are Ethernet and LAN (Local Area Networking). Networking requires additional hardware, software, and expertise. A LAN with more than two or three computers requires the firm to have a "server" (a special computer dedicated to directing information over the network).

Networking also has its own problems and risks: a problem on one computer could crash the whole system; data could inadvertently be made available to someone who isn't supposed to see it. Any information on any computer is at risk of being "hacked" by an inquisitive or hostile person, or by someone with an interest in industrial espionage. Networks are especially vulnerable because they are designed to share information.

Computers and computer systems can also include other options for capturing and transmitting information. For instance, scanners—which capture a drawing, photograph, or other image and transmit it into computer-usable form—can be used to add documents to a database or word processing system without having to retype text.

The traditional medium for storing data is either the hard disk (within the computer) or the floppy disk. Newer options include CD-ROM drives, which play small, silvery platters that look like music CDs. Originally, CDs were "read-only" mechanisms—that is, users could read them but could not make their own recordings. Today, it is fairly easy and fairly inexpensive to create CDs with desktop equipment, so this may become an option for backing up large amounts of data (e.g., litigation documents).

A research session may require the use of multiple CDs: for instance, one CD containing cases from your state's trial courts, another CD with state appellate cases, a third with federal cases, and a fourth containing a treatise on practice in your state. Storage devices called "towers" or "jukeboxes" are useful so you can access multiple CDs quickly. These devices are also useful for a law firm library, where many lawyers share single copies of CD publications.

There are other options for back-up, including tape drives, portable hard disks, and "floptical" drives and magnetic media that are something like a hybrid between a floppy disk and a hard drive. Backing up data is vitally important for all users, and especially so for law firms—a computer or system malfunction could easily wipe out thousands of hours of work. However, computer and back-up technology evolve continually, so a one-time perfect solution may become obsolete. It doesn't do much good to have years of data stored on 8″ floppy disks using proprietary software, if you don't own and can't buy any equipment that uses 8″ disks, and no one remembers how to use the software! Every law firm must have policies for backing up data, and it's a useful discipline for solo practitioners to develop personal routines for ensuring regular back-ups.

In addition to fax machines (which are really a specialized type of computer printer), law offices can have fax modems. A modem—which stands for MODulator/DEModulator—transmits computer signals over telephone lines. A modem is used to transmit information between two computers. They can be four feet apart, in the same office, or several continents apart. Modems are also used to connect to on-line services, the Internet, and the World Wide Web. Modems are measured by the speed at which they can transmit data. Standard modems are rated at 9600 kB (thousand bytes transmitted per second; a byte is a unit of data approximately equal to one character) or 14.4 kB (14,400 bytes per second). The fastest modems commonly used at this writing have a speed of 28.8 or 33.6 kB, but as technology improves, speed increases.

However, there are many factors that reduce the actual speed of a modem way below the maximum speed that its manufacturer advertises. A modem can't work any faster than the other modem it's communicating with, and problems with the telephone line over which the communication takes place can also slow things down considerably.

Law office computing also has implications for the firm's phone system. Voice mail is a useful service that complements electronic mail (e-mail) and written communications. Furthermore, if a law firm spends a lot of time connected to the Internet, it may make sense to replace its conventional telephone service with special ISDN or T-1 lines. These lines make it possible to speed up electronic communications significantly, but they also require heavy investment in nonstandard equipment.

E-mail is an extremely useful technology, and one which can be utilized by anyone with a computer (even an old computer with limited memory) and a modem. E-mail service is provided by on-line services and Internet service providers, or by purchasing specialized communications software.

Messages and computer files can be transmitted directly to anyone who has an e-mail address. Lawyers find it particularly useful because it avoids "telephone tag" (when one party attempts to return a phone call from someone who is now unavailable, and leaves a message which in turn is returned when the caller is unavailable). E-mail makes it possible to transmit factual information in writing without having to dictate the information to a clerical worker or leave a voice mail message. However, it must always be remembered that e-mail is not entirely private. Confidential matters should not be transmitted because there is a risk that unauthorized people will gain access to the e-mail message.

To date, ethics committees and other regulators have not really come to grips with the implications of electronic communications for lawyer-client contacts. However, the Michigan State Bar Committee on Professional and Judicial Ethics has taken an interesting first step by issuing an Informal Opinion.[61] Under this regulatory scheme, law firms are permitted to use the Internet to distribute information about their legal services without having to comply with the bar association solicitation rule—as long as the communication is made through a publicly available medium such as the World Wide Web. It is forbidden to solicit clients during real-time electronic "conversation" (such as an on-line discussion in a chat room), and the solicitation rule must be followed if individuals are specifically contacted by e-mail.

[¶1307.2]   Electronic Legal Research

Anyone with a modem can connect to distant computers. For more than a decade, huge repositories of legal information have been available on for-profit computer systems such as LEXIS and Westlaw. To use these research resources, the attorney gets an account with the service provider, learns how to search the databank, and agrees to pay fees for the time connected to the service. Each service (and sometimes, each part of a service) has its own methods for setting up "queries" (requests to the system to perform a computer search). Complaints from users have borne fruit—services are making it easier to do "natural language" searches that are closer to the ideal of just telling the computer what you want.

Electronic legal research can also be done by buying CD-ROMs from legal publishers. CD-ROMs can store the equivalent of dozens or even hundreds of books; CD technology makes it easy to search through the material on the CD for a particular case, or for information on a particular topic. "Hybrids" are common— i.e., the publisher sells a CD-ROM that contains an archive of cases, regulations, or other materials, and also gives the customer on-line access to the latest update material to supplement the disks.

[¶1308]   THE INTERNET

The much-hyped Internet began as a U.S. military project for devising a computer system that would survive a nuclear war so government operations could resume after the smoke cleared. A "protocol" (communications standard) was developed so computers at great distances could communicate over ordinary tele-phone lines. The Internet, then, consists of all the computers that can use this basic protocol or a related protocol.

Although the military is no longer involved in Internet operations, original-ly the Internet was very much a sophisticated scientific tool. Initially, there was no interest in making it "user-friendly." However, as more and more people became interested in Internet access, programmers designed "front ends" (interfaces that make it easier to connect to the Internet, and to communicate with other Internet users).

Sites on the Internet are identified by "domain names." A domain name in many ways resembles a trademark. A domain name is acquired by registration, but in this case, with a voluntary organization rather than with a government agency. Domains are divided into several types: .com, for commercial domains, .edu for educational organization domains (typically, universities), .gov for government agencies, and .org for organizations (usually nonprofit organizations). (It has been proposed that seven new "TLDs" (Top Level Domains) be added, including .firm and .store for commerce and .rec for recreational materials and .arts.) There are some significant intellectual property and antitrust issues in selecting a domain name—for instance, InterNic had to act to prevent "grabbing" of a competitor's domain name for the specific purpose of denying the competitor access to its own name.[62]

[¶1308.1]   On-Line Services

In addition to specialized legal on-line services, law firms may use more general on-line services such as America Online. These on-line services have data-banks of information (e.g., continually updated stock quotes). Subscribers to the service can also join "forums" or "chat rooms" where they can communicate with other subscribers by typing into their own computers and reading typed messages from others. In general, on-line services provide their subscribers with free soft-ware for connecting to the service. The users pay a monthly fee, and often have to pay an additional fee based on the amount of time they spend connected to the service. There may also be additional charges—e.g., for access to specialized forums or for copying documents from those forums.

On-line services offer several benefits to the law firm whose staff has little technical sophistication. It's easy to set up the account, use the software, and estab-lish communications. On-line service subscribers also get an e-mail (electronic mail) address. E-mail is the extremely useful ability to type a message into one's own desktop computer, have it conveyed to the on-line service's central computer, and have that computer convey the message in a form that can be accessed by the intended recipient or recipients of the message. (The same message can easily be sent to multiple parties—e.g., a request to reschedule a deposition.)

A few years ago, there was a clear distinction between the proprietary nature of on-line services, where fees were charged for access to a database, and the free materials available from the Internet. However, today the distinction is blurred.

Most on-line services make it possible for their users to connect to the Internet and the World Wide Web. Furthermore, there is an increasing trend to require subscriptions or other fees for access to materials on the Internet.

[¶1308.2] The World Wide Web

Originally, the Internet was designed by computer scientists for computer scientists, so the ability to find (or program) complex software, and use arcane Unix commands, was necessary to use the Internet. As more people became interested in Internet access, more "user-friendly" front-end programs were created to make it easier to use the Internet.

At the same time, the concepts of Graphical User Interface (GUI) and hyperlinks were evolving. Instead of communicating with the computer by typing commands or using menus, the GUI user communicates by using the computer mouse to point to and click on "icons"—pictures representing the desired item or computer function. Hyperlinks are highlighted items within a computer document. Pointing to one of these items and clicking on it results in a "jump" to that item. For instance, if a cite within a court opinion is highlighted, it is possible to retrieve the cited case by pointing and clicking on the cite. Originally, this mechanism was called hypertext, but today links can be made to images, sounds, even videos, so the broader term is used.

The World Wide Web is the portion of the Internet that uses GUIs and hyperlinks. To be usable by the Web, files have to be coded with HTML, the Hypertext Mark-Up Language, a simple system of identifying text, captions, headlines, and other features of a computer display.

An important—and fashionable—feature of the Web is the "home page." A person, agency, corporation, or organization that has a home page makes information available on the World Wide Web. Web users who reach the home page can learn about that person or institution, as well as linking to other information.

For example, a law firm can use a home page as an enhancement of its firm brochure and firm newsletter. The home page can give basic information about the firm; users can click on various areas in the home page to get more information about attorneys at the firm, their backgrounds and specialties, or about planning tips and new legal developments.

[¶1308.3] Internet and Web Connections

The first requisites for using the Internet and World Wide Web are a computer, a modem or other means of connection, and a mouse. The broadest opportunities are available for those using Windows or Unix; Internet access is moderately available for Apple computer users, and very limited for DOS users.

Next, the user must have a way to connect. As noted above, joining most on-line services provides some degree of Internet access, and the companies supply their own software for reaching and using the Internet and Web. It is also possible to contract with an Internet Service Provider (ISP)—the equivalent of a telephone company—that offers a more direct connection to the Internet. As a general rule, ISPs charge a monthly fee; the fee may be a flat fee for unlimited usage, or there may be a basic entitlement with charges for additional hours or for connection to certain files. Very heavy Internet users can install special telephone lines for direct Internet connection without an ISP.

For the individual practitioner or firm, the choice comes down to whether an on-line service offers useful material in addition to Internet access, and whether the convenience and ease of use of an on-line service makes up for its higher cost as compared to establishing an account with an Internet Service Provider.

Using the various Internet tools, or connecting with the Web, requires special software. You may be able to get the software free, as part of your deal with an ISP or on-line service. A great deal of software can be borrowed or downloaded electronically because it is "freeware." Freeware is created by programmers who are willing to make their work available without charge. Another possibility is "shareware," which can be downloaded (copied from an Internet site or an electronic bulletin board) without an explicit charge. However, shareware uses an honor system: if you like the software, you are expected to pay a fee. The fee, in turn, entitles you to manuals, technical support, updates, and other advantages.

Sometimes freeware or shareware is a limited version of a commercial program; to get all the features of the program, you have to buy it. Huge quantities of software are available in computer stores and by mail order. There is an increasing trend to sell software directly over the Internet: as soon as payment is arranged, the software is transferred directly to your computer.

To search the Web, you will require two kinds of special software: a "socket" program (called a Winsock) and a "browser," such as Internet Explorer™ or Netscape Navigator™, for actually looking at files and transferring their contents to your own computer.

[¶1308.4]   Internet/Web Tools

Immense quantities of information are available electronically, and more information is added each day. Of course, the mere fact that information comes from a computer does not make it any more reliable than information delivered verbally or in print. This obvious fact is often ignored, facilitating various kinds of errors and frauds.

The Internet isn't really run by anybody, and there are very few standards for placing material on the Internet (other than some standards relating to obscenity, and ordinary legal principles of intellectual property and libel). In effect, the Internet is the equivalent of the Library of Congress, if all the books were dumped on the floor, without call numbers and in no discernable order.

Materials on the Internet and World Wide Web don't have "call numbers," but they have Uniform Resource Locators, or URLs, which function as the equivalent of addresses or telephone numbers. The domain name (see above) is part of the URL; the rest of the URL identifies specific materials located within the domain.

URLs for Websites usually (though not inevitably) begin with "http://www." (HTTP is the hypertext transmission protocol, used for coding files so they can be displayed on the Web.) So the URL http://www.BigMovieStudio.com would take you to the home page of Big Movie Studio, a commercial organization.

There are many ways to search for information on the Internet. You might see a potentially interesting URL in a book or article. If it's a Web site, then viewing that site gives you the opportunity to link to other, related sites simply by clicking on the relevant hyperlink. For instance, a site about real estate law might have links to related subjects such as real estate taxation and environmental law. Software for using the Internet gives users the opportunity to create "bookmarks," so it's easy for them to return to favorite sites during later sessions of computer research.

There are several "search engines" (Yahoo!, Excite and Lycos are among the most famous). Search engines are powerful programs that look at vast amounts of information and then create indexes, informing you of sites where relevant information may be located.

If you have a specific question to research, and need to learn the URLs of, or get access to, Internet and Web sites that contain relevant information, a search engine may offer the help you need. Most federal agencies, and an increasing number of state governments, courts, and agencies have an Internet presence, so you may gain access to the relevant documents that way. There are also major research facilities maintained by universities and specialized organizations.

One of the earliest Internet tools still remaining in use is the gopher—a menu system that you consult when you want to "go for" information. You get gopher software (by purchase; from your on-line service or ISP; by downloading it) and then use it to make connections to files that are listed on the gopher system of a particular server (central Internet computer) or other gopher servers. Most legal information is found on large computers called "gopher servers," so expertise with the gopher tool is an important part of electronic legal research.

Another early Internet tool is "archie," the cumulative index of all the files on all Internet servers. There are variants and developments of archie called, of course, veronica and jughead. (No betty, though.)

Telnet is the process of "calling" a remote computer, so you need to know the relevant URL. You'll also need to know the passwords required to log-on to that computer and access its files.

Once you know where to find a file you want to see, you can view the file or you can transfer the file to your own computer. The most common way of doing this is "anonymous FTP" (using the File Transfer Protocol on an "anonymous" basis—you identify yourself as "anonymous" when you log in, and you use your e-mail address as a password). About half of all the traffic on the Internet consists of FTP. Using FTP requires mastering some UNIX commands. Many of the files are stored in compressed form, so you'll need decompression software to make them usable. Depending on the kind of Internet access you have, using FTP may transfer files to your server's computer instead of yours, so you'll need additional software and an extra step to get the files downloaded to your own computer. However, because the World Wide Web has achieved such predominance in the Internet world, it may be possible to have a very satisfactory on-line experience without ever doing anything other than "pointing and clicking" on the Web.

[¶1308.5] Mailing Lists and Newsgroups

The Internet is not just a repository of existing information which can be viewed passively; it is also an important communications tool. People with common interests can create mailing lists and newsgroups so they can stay current on their favorite topics, or exchange information and opinions.

Listserv is a very basic technology under which individuals who have a computer and modem (whether or not they have Internet access) exchange information via e-mail. If you subscribe to a Listserv (which is done by sending e-mail to the Listserv's central administration), messages from the Listserv will be listed with your other e-mail messages. You can "post" (send) your own messages to the Listserv, or reply to messages posted by other participants.

A newsgroup is an electronic mailing list that is restricted to a predefined subject area. For instance, a legal newsgroup might deal with a specialized area such as breast implant products liability litigation. Some newsgroups limit the number or types of users who can participate. Many of them have a moderator to keep the discussion on-track. A defined time period may be set for a particular discussion.

A "thread" is a series of e-mail messages relating to the same topic. For instance, a Kansas attorney may post a query about the use of a particular type of trust in estate planning. Responses may be posted by two other Kansas attorneys, as well as lawyers in Ohio, New Jersey, and Florida. One important feature in choosing e-mail software is whether it only displays messages in chronological order, or whether it can arrange all the messages of a "thread" together. The messages make much more sense displayed together than scattered through all your other mail.

You subscribe to a mailing list or newsgroup by sending an e-mail message to the central administration e-mail address. Your request is usually granted automatically, but for moderated groups, you may need to ask permission. A similar routine is followed to "unsubscribe" if you don't like a list or newsgroup, or have too much e-mail to read.

[¶1308.6] Law Firm Marketing on the Web

Several hundred law firms already have their own Web home pages. Some on-line services and ISPs provide the software for constructing simple home pages, and allow a simple home page to be displayed for free. At the high end of the market, it's possible to spend hundreds of thousands of dollars designing a site and thousands of dollars a month to display and maintain it. In between, it's easy to learn enough HTML (the Web language) to create a page that is somewhat more sophisticated than the basic model. It usually costs between $100 and $300 a month to display your page on a commercial Web server.

A law firm home page serves the same function as a firm brochure or client newsletter. However, merely putting those print materials into electronic form is not very appealing. It's better to offer clients and potential clients two-way interactive communication with the firm, and to make sure the information is constantly updated so clients will want to consult the home page (and think about your firm) frequently.

To give access to your home page to Web users, you can list it with the search engines. (So far, this is usually simple to do and free.) You can also contact law-related Web sites (such as Law Journal Extra) and see if they will list your firm's home page.

— ENDNOTES —

1. The Communications Decency Act preempts state-law causes of action against ISPs for negligently permitting on-line dissemination of defamatory statements: *Zeran v. America Online,* 958 F.Supp. 1124 (E.D. Va. 3/21/97). The affirming opinion, 66 LW 1317 (4th Cir. 11/12/97) clarifies that the ISP is immune for suits filed after the enactment of the CDA, even if the defamatory statement was posted earlier.

2. 47 U.S.C. §230(b)(4), as enacted by P.L. 104-104.

3. 47 U.S.C. §230(b)(5), as enacted by P.L. 104-104.

4. *Shea v. Reno,* 930 F.Supp. 916 (S.D.N.Y. 7/29/96); *Reno v. American Civil Liberties Union,* 96-511, 117 S.Ct 2329 (Sup. Ct 6/26/97). By the way, one of the amicus briefs was a "cyber-brief," filed in CD-ROM format. Also see *American Library Association v. Pataki,* 969 F.Supp. 160 (S.D.N.Y. 6/20/97), finding New York's statute barring on-line indecency to be invalid and enjoining its enforcement as an unconstitutional restraint on interstate commerce. In this reading, there must be a national enforcement scheme because of the nation-wide reach of the Internet. The law made it a felony to use a computer system to distribute materials to minors that are "harmful to minors." The Southern District deemed the statute invalid because it regulates conduct wholly outside the state, and the burden on interstate commerce outweighs the possible benefits that might be derived within the state. However, *New York v. Barrows,* 66 LW 1272 (N.Y.Sup. 9/26/97) upholds a related statute that penalizes transmission of sexual material to a minor, via computer, in order to induce the minor to engage in a sexual act. The court distinguishes *ALA v. Pataki* because this statute deals with conduct within the state of New York, rather than speech which might be wholly outside the state.

Bans are imposed on pornography that depicts children as well as pornography transmitted to children. Under *U.S. v. Carroll,* 105 F.3d 740 (1st Cir. 2/3/97) *cert. denied* 117 S.Ct. 2424, digitizing photographs depicting child pornography and posting the results on the Internet is transportation in interstate commerce, and hence a violation of 18 U.S.C. §2251(a). 18 U.S.C. §2256(8), which criminalizes depictions (including adapted or modified depictions) of what appears to be a minor engaging in sexually explicit conduct, has been upheld by the Northern District of California. (*Freedom of Speech Coalition v. Reno,* 66 LW 1125 (N.D.Cal. 8/12/97). In this reading, the intention is to regulate the effect of what appears to be child pornography, not to regulate ideas. The statute satisfies important state interests of protecting children from being harmed by pornography.

5. *U.S. v. Thomas,* 74 F.3d 701 (6th Cir. 1/29/96).

6. Pornographers aren't always the most scrupulous in other respects, either. *FTC v. Audiotex Connections Inc.,* 65 LW 2568 (E.D.N.Y. 2/13/97) grants an injunction against the deceptive trade practice of offering free adult images without disclosing that receiving the images entailed a $2-a-minute telephone call to Moldova that lasted until the hopeful smut-seeker turned off his computer. See 66 LW 2319 for a follow-up story on a settlement with seven people and firms who agreed to pay more than $2.74 million to settle charges involving Moldovan "hijacking". The consent orders can be viewed on the FTC Web site, http://www.ftc.gov/os/9711/Adtxprmford.htm and http://www.ftc.gov/os/9711/beylenagr.htm#31.

7. 945 F.Supp. 1279 (N.D.Cal. 12/16/96); 66 LW 1155 (N.D. Cal. 8/25/97).

8. *U.S. v. Microsoft Corp.,* 159 F.R.D. 318 (D.D.C. 2/14/95), *reversed* 56 F.2d 1448 (D.C.Cir. 6/16/95).

9. *DOJ v. Microsoft,* 66 LW 2246 [petition filed] (D.D.C. 10/20/97). Also see Don Clark, "Microsoft is Unlikely to Be Hurt by Ruling," *Wall Street Journal* 12/15/97 p. B8.

10. See David Bank and John R. Wilke, "Microsoft and Justice End a Skirmish, Yet War Could Escalate," *Wall Street Journal* 1/23/98 p. A1.

11. *Hewlett-Packard Co. v. U.S.,* 71 F.3d 398 (Fed.Cir. 12/7/95).

12. *Norwest Corp. v. C.I.R.,* 69 F.3d 1404 (Tax Court 4/30/97), *cert. denied* 116 S.Ct. 1704.

13. *U.S. v. Petersen,* 98 F.3d 502 (9th Cir. 10/22/96).

14. See, e.g., *Heroes Inc. v. Heroes Foundation,* 65 LW 2486 (D.D.C. 12/19/96); *CompuServe Inc. v. Patterson,* 89 F.3d 1257 (6th Cir. 7/22/96), *Inset Systems Inc. v. Instruction Set Inc.,* 937 F.Supp. 161 (D.Ct. 1996), *Maritz v. CyberGold Inc.,* 40 USPQ2nd 1729 (E.D. Mo. 1996); but contra *Bensusan Restaurant Corp. v. King,* 937 F.Supp. 295 (S.D.N.Y. 9/10/96), *aff'd* 66 LW 1181 (2nd Cir. 9/10/97); because the club that allegedly infringed the New York club's trademark did not derive "substantial" revenue in interstate commerce; it was a purely local business.

15. See, e.g., *SuperGuide Corp. v. Kegan,* 66 LW 1303 (W.D.N.C. 10/8/97); but finding of jurisdiction could be reversed on a showing that few North Carolina residents actually accessed the site; *State v. Interactive Gaming & Communications Corp.,* 66 LW 2054 (indictment filed by Missouri Attorney General 6/26/97), re state gambling-law violations alleged against an Internet casino; *Hall v. LaRonde,* 66 Cal.Rptr.2d 399 (Cal.App. 8/7/97); business e-mail and telephone calls constitute minimum contacts, semble *Cody v. Ward,* 954 F.Supp. 43 (D.Conn. 2/4/97) and *Resuscitation Technologies Inc. v. Continental Health Care Corp.,* 65 LW 2694 (S.D. Ind. 3/24/97); *Telco*

Communications Inc. v. An Apple a Day Inc., 66 LW 1212 (E.D. Va. 9/24/97); *Minnesota v. Granite Gate Resorts Inc.,* 66 LW 1208 (Minn.App. 9/5/97); *Digital Equipment Corp. v. Alta Vista Technology, Inc.,* 960 F.Supp. 456 (D.Mass. 3/12/97); personal jurisdiction derives from transacting business on the Internet and entering into a licensing agreement with a Massachusetts resident, governed by Massachusetts law; *Hasbro v. Clue Computing Inc.,* 66 LW 1287 (D.Mass. 9/30/97).

16. See, e.g., *Zippo Manufacturing Co. v. Zippo Dot Com Inc.,* 952 F.Supp. 1119 (W.D. Pa. 1/16/97); *SF Hotel Co. L.P. v. Energy Investments Inc.,* 66 LW 1399 (D.Kan. 11/19/97); *Cybersell Inc. v. Cybersell Inc.,* 66 LW 1357 (9th Cir. 12/2/97); *Weber v. Jolly Hotels,* 66 LW 1211 (D.N.J. 9/12/97); analogizing a passive site to a magazine, requiring active and repeated transmission of files for personal jurisdiction.

17. *New York v. Lipsitz,* 66 LW 1045 (N.Y.Sup. 6/23/97).

18. *American Network Inc. v. AccessAmerica/Connect Atlanta Inc.,* 66 LW 1175 (S.D.N.Y. 8/13/97).

19. *IA Inc. v. Thermacell Technologies Inc.,* 66 LW 1400 (E.D. Mich. 11/10/97).

20. *Missouri v. Coeur D'Alene Tribe,* 66 LW 1232 (W.D. Mo. 9/29/97).

21. *Utah v. Kent,* 66 LW 1223 (Utah App. 9/5/97).

22. *U.S. v. Czubinski,* 106 F.3d 1069 (1st Cir. 2/21/97).

23. *U.S. v. Labovitz,* 65 LW 2139 (D.Mass. 7/24/96). See Wendy R. Liebowitz, "When High-Tech is Over the Top: Is a CD-ROM Brief Fair or Foul?" *Nat'l L.J.* 3/3/97 p. B8.

24. *Yukiyo Ltd. v. Watanabe,* 111 F.3d 883 (Fed.Cir. 4/15/97). This case is cited in *In re Berg,* 66 LW 2074 (Fed. Cir. 7/11/97), the first instance in which counterpart CD-ROM briefs were permitted to be filed in an appeal from a Patent and Trademark Office decision. CD-ROM filing was permitted even though the PTO lacks the capacity to prepare CD-ROM briefs.

25. See 66 LW 2197.

26. The report is available at the Library of Congress site, http://lcweb.loc.gov/copyright/more.html#rpt. (The URL does not contain the customary www prefix.)

27. *Lotus Development Corp. v. Borland,* 831 F.Supp.223 (D.Mass. 1993), *reversed* 49 F.3d 807 (1st Cir. 3/9/95), affirmed #94-2003, 116 S.Ct. 1062 (Sup.Ct. 1/16/96). Also see *Softel Inc. v. Dragon Medical & Scientific Communications, Inc.,* 118 F.3d 955 (2nd Cir. 7/9/97), holding that when infringement of software structure is alleged, the structure of both programs must be compared, including unprotectable individual elements, because a compilation of non-copyrightable elements might be entitled to copyright protection.

28. *Tasini v. New York Times Corp.,* 972 F.Supp. 804 (S.D.N.Y. 8/13/97).

29. *Pro CD Inc. v. Zeidenberg,* 908 F.Supp. 640 (W.D.Wis. 1/4/96), rev'd in part 86 F.3d 1447 (7th Cir. 6/20/96).

30. *U.S. v. LaMacchia,* 871 F.Supp. 535 (D.Mass. 12/28/94). Also see *Ohio v. Perry,* 65 LW 2571 (Ohio App. 2/12/97), finding that the federal Copyright Act preempts a state prosecution for posting copyright software on a BBS without authorization, on the grounds that uploading material to a BBS is copying as defined by the federal statute.

31. *Sony Music Entertainment Inc. v. Internet Sites,* 66 LW 1016 (S.D. Cal. 6/10/97).

32. Also see 66 LW 2254, noting the complaint filed in the D.D.C. on 10/16/97 in the case of *Thomas v. Network Solutions Inc.,* alleging that the 1997 NSF/NSI contract was invalid because it exceeded the NSF's authority; is unconstitutional; and denies potential domain name registration organizations free access to the market. The complaint seeks to certify a class of everyone who paid a registration fee to NSI.

33. *Comp Examiner Agency v. Juris Inc.,* 64 LW 2724 (C.D.Cal. 4/26/96). Also see *TeleTech Customer Care Management v. Tele-Tech Co.,* 65 LW 2832 (C.D. Cal. 5/9/97), granting an injunction to prevent dilution of a federally registered trademark, TeleTech, against the domain name teletech.com registered by the user of the common law service mark TeleTech. It was not deemed a valid defense that the defendant did not know that a hyphen could be used in a domain name. One wonders, however, what the hyphen would have done to prevent confusion.

34. *Panavision Int'l L.P. v Toeppen,* 938 F.Supp. 616 (C.D. Cal. 11/1/96). See Barney D. Tumey's article, "'Cybersquatters' Find Little Gold Online," 66 LW 2387, noting that cybersquatters seldom receive large payments for the domain names they have hoarded, and that infringement and dilution causes of action are useful against them.

35. 65 LW 2662 (S.D.N.Y. 3/19/97).

36. *Lockheed Martin Corp. v. Network Solutions Inc.,* 66 LW 1350 (C.D. Cal. 11/17/97).

37. *Juno Online Services, LP v. Juno Lighting Inc.,* 65 LW 1253 (N.D. Ill. 9/29/97). In this case, the on-line service registered the domain name juno.com with the NSI. It tried to get federal trademark and service mark protection, but was blocked by Juno Lighting Co., which had two federal trademarks involving "Juno". The lighting company secured juno.online.com as a domain name, triggering the suit for misuse. The NSI's contract with the National Science Foundation, under which the NSI acted as registrar, was scheduled to expire in March, 1998. For a discussion of potential new means of registering domain names, including new types of domain names, see, e.g., Wendy R. Leibowitz, "New Domain Name Regimes May be Doomed by Disarray, Discord," *National Law Journal* 1/19/98 p. B9 and Paul M. Eng, "Get Your Hands Off My.Com," *Business Week* 7/28/97 p. 88.

38. *Cardservice Int'l Inc. v. McGee*, 950 F.Supp. 737 (E.D. Va. 1/16/97).

39. *Lockheed Martin Corp. v. Network Solutions Inc.*, 65 LW 2744 (C.D. Cal. 3/19/97).

40. *State Street Bank & Trust v. Signature Financial Group Inc.*, 927 F. Supp. 502 (D.Mass. 3/26/96).

41. *U.S. Golf Ass'n v. Arroyo Software Corp.*, 65 LW 2368 (Cal.Super. 10/25/96).

42. *NBA v. Sports Team Analysis and Tracking Systems Inc*, 931 F.Supp. 1124 (S.D.N.Y. 9/9/96), aff'd in part and vac. in part 103 F.3d. 841.

43. *NBA v. Motorola, Inc.*, 103 F.3d 841 (2nd Cir. 1/30/97).

44. *Stratton Oakmont v. Prodigy Services Co.*, 63 LW 2765 (N.Y.Sup. 5/30/95).

45. *Religious Technology Center v. FACTNET Inc.*, 901 F.Supp. 1519 (D.Colo. 9/15/95); also see *Religious Technology Center v. Lerma*, 908 F. Supp. 1362 (E.D. Va. 10/4/96); former Scientologist did not exercise fair use when uploading copyrighted Scientology texts onto the Internet. He was not engaging in newsgathering, scholarship, time-shifting, or other recognized form of fair use.

46. *Religious Technology Center v. Netcom*, 907 F.Supp. 1361 (N.D.Cal. 11/21/95).

47. *Cyber Promotions Inc. v. America Online*, 948 F. Supp. 436 456 (E.D.Pa. 11/4/96, 11/26/96, 12/19/96).

48. *AOL v. IMS*, Complaint No. 98-001-A filed in the E.D. Va. 1/6/98; see 66 LW 2432.

49. *CompuServe Inc. v. Cyber Promotions Inc.*, 962 F.Supp. 1015 (S.D. Ohio 2/3/97).

50. *ACLU of Georgia v. Miller*, 66 LW 1064 (N.D. Ga. 6/20/97).

51. *Playboy Enterprises Inc. v. Russen Hardenburgh Inc.*, 66 LW 1431 (N.D. Ohio 11/25/97); *Playboy Enterprises Inc. v. Webbworld Inc.*, 66 LW 1463 (N.D. Tex. 12/11/97).

52. *Timekeeping Systems Inc. v. Lawrence Leinweber*, 323 NLRB No. 30 (1997).

53. 111 F.3d 1472 (10th Cir. 4/21/97).

54. *U.S. v. Charbonneau*, 66 LW 1271 (S.D. Ohio 9/30/97). As for searches of computers without pornography, see *U.S. v. Norwest Corp.*, 116 F.3d 1227 (8th Cir. 6/26/97), holding that the IRS' investigative powers include ordering a corporation being audited to turn over the tax preparation software used to prepare returns.

55. *Wesley College v. Pitts*, 66 LW 1256 (D.Del. 8/11/97).

56. *Institutional Real Estate Clearinghouse*, Fed. Sec.L.Rep. ¶77,234 (SEC Division of Market Regulation 5/28/96).

57. *Real Goods Trading Corp.* 28 Sec.Reg.L.Rep. 850 (staff letter, 6/25/96).

58. *See* 28 Sec.Reg.L.Rep. 983 (8/8/96).

59. *See* 28 Fed.Sec.L.Rep. 990.

60. *SEC v. Sellin,* 28 Fed.Sec.L.Rep. 944 (S.D. Fla. 7/25/96).

61. Informal Opinion RI-276 (7/11/96); see 65 LW 2334.

62. See Ethan Horwitz and Robert S. Weisbein, "Claiming Internet Domain Names," *Nat L.J.* 3/18/96 p. S1.

— FOR FURTHER REFERENCE —

Articles

Ameen, Philip D. and Daniel J. Noll, "Internal-Use Computer Software: The Fixed Asset of the Information Age," 183 *J. of Accountancy* 14 (March '97).

Bauman, Lori Irish, "Personal Jurisdiction and Internet Advertising," 14 *The Computer Lawyer* 1 (January '97).

Crangle, Jan Steensen, "Record Retention Rules of the Electronic Highway," 28 *Tax Adviser* 43 (January '97).

De Carlo, Kean J., "Tilting at Windmills: Defamation and the Private Person in Cyberspace," 13 *Georgia State U.L.Rev.* 547 (February '97).

Fischer, John P., "Computers as Agents: A Proposed Approach to Revised UCC Article 2," 72 *Indiana L.J.* 545 (Spring '97).

Flaming, Todd H., "Windows and the Hand-Held Personal Computer," 85 *Illinois Bar J.* 81 (February '97).

Hrcik, David, "Confidentiality and Privilege in High-Tech Communications," 60 *Texas Bar J.* 104 (February '97).

Livermore, John and Krailerk Euarjai, "Electronic Bills of Lading: A Progress Report," 28 *J. of Maritime Law & Commerce* 55 (January '97).

Nash, Stephen, "Surf's Up! Legal Job Hunting Online," 40 *Advocate* 14 (January '97).

Pearlman, Alan, "The Road Warrior: Portable Computing for Lawyers on the Go," 19 *Family Advocate* 32 (Winter '97).

Pridgen, Dee, "How Will Consumers be Protected on the Information Superhighway?" 32 *Land & Water L.Rev.* 237 (Winter '97).

Quinn, Peter C., "Websurfing for Case Law on a Shoestring Budget," 33 *Trial* 74 (January '97).

Siegel, Howard and David J. Stein, "Music Performance Rights on the Net," *N.Y.L.J.* 11/3/97 p. 54.

Swerdloff, Nicholas and Juan J. Farach Jr., "Internet Domain Name-Grabbing, or Cyber-Squatting: An Analysis of Remedies Under Federal Law," 71 *Florida Bar J.* 30 (February '97).

Websites

ABA Law Links http://www.abanet.org/lawlink/home.html

ABA Tax section (includes a searchable version of the Internal Revenue Code)

http://www.abanet.org/tax/sites.html

American Association of Law Librarians Compleat Internet Researcher http://www.aallnet.org/products/crab/index.html

ALSO (American Law Sources Online)   http://www.lawsource.com/also/usa.htm

Federal Web Locator http://law.vill.edu/fed-agency/fedwebloc.html (no www)

FindLaw http://www.findlaw.com

Indiana University School of Law http://www.law.indiana.edu

Legal Information Institute (Cornell) http://www.law.cornell.edu

Center for Corporate Law (University of Cincinnatti School of Law): http://www.law.uc.edu

Criminal Justice (Vera Institute of Justice): http://broadway.vera.org

Meta-Indexes

(a meta-index is an index of other indexes; in fact, there's even an index meta-indexes, at http://www.kentlaw.edu/lawlinks/meta.html)

Hieros Gamos http://www.hg.org/hg1.html

University of Indiana Meta-Index http://www.cs.indiana-edu/meta-index.html

Search Engines

Alta Vista: http://www.altavista.com

Yahoo: http://www.yahoo.com

Lycos: http://lycos.cs.cmu.edu/

WebCrawler: http://webcrawler.com

Excite!: http://www/excite.com

Savvy Search: http://www.sc.colostate.edu/~dreiling/smartform.html

Music licensing information: www:ascap.com/newmedia/licensing.html

www.bmi.com/licensing/web.html

CORPORATE MERGERS, ACQUISITIONS, AND REORGANIZATIONS

[¶1702] MERGERS

1997 and especially 1998 saw gigantic mergers occurring and proposed. Yet, surprisingly little major law has emerged from this period: discussion of mega-mergers appears more on the business page than in the case reporters.

See 65 LW 2678 for a discussion of revised horizontal merger guidelines promulgated by the Department of Justice and the FTC on April 8, 1997. The guidelines might deem a merger anticompetitive if it results in lesser competition in the relevant market, even if efficiencies are present—if those efficiencies might be achieved in other ways that preserve competition. On March 11, 1998, the FTC, DOJ, and the National Association of Attorneys General agreed on a protocol for coordinating federal and state investigations of mergers: see http://www.ftc.gov/os/9803/mergerco.op.htm.

A Delaware corporation went through a short-form merger. Some of the shareholders did not tender their shares. The result was that they became creditors rather than stockholders, with a right to redeem their stock for cash. However, the merged corporation filed a Chapter 11 bankruptcy petition. According to the Seventh Circuit, the non-tendering shareholders were merely unsecured creditors of the corporation. Their claims could be subordinated equitably to the claims of other general unsecured creditors even if there is no proof that the shareholders acted wrongfully in any way.[1]

After a merger, the surviving corporation is responsible for all obligations of the merged constituent corporations, including stock purchase agreements between a merged entity and its shareholders.[2]

In a late-1997 Delaware case, a corporation's largest shareholder (another corporation) was preliminarily enjoined against starting a tender offer for the company's stock that was conditional on the corporation's pending merger with yet a third corporation being defeated. The merging company and its major shareholder had a contract obligating the shareholder to support acquisitions, and the tender offer was inconsistent with this obligation.[3]

A corporation whose attempt to merge with another corporation is unsuccessful can sue a competitor for tortious interference with contractual relationships and prospective business relations only if there was either an enforceable contract that could be breached; or violence, fraud, or other wrongful means involved.[4]

If a proxy statement includes a discussion of the history of the merger, the statement is incomplete if it fails to mention a rejected bid that was actually higher than the bid accepted by the merged company's Board of Directors.[5]

Later proceedings in that case say that corporations involved in a merger are not vicariously liable for one corporation's director's breach of the duty to make the required disclosures in the merger proxy statement.[6]

Once a bank merger is approved by the Federal Reserve Board, low- and middle-income neighborhood groups do not have standing to challenge the merger within either the Federal Reserve system or the Federal Deposit Insurance Corporation, even if they claim that the merger violates the Community Reinvestment Act.[7]

[¶1715] TAX ATTRIBUTES

In a mid-1996 case, the taxpayer had a stock purchase agreement covering all of the target company's stock. The Fourth Circuit ruled that money paid under this agreement to defer the transaction's closing date (and therefore the obligation to pay for the stock) can be deducted under Code §163(a) as interest.[8]

Amounts properly allocable to non-interest portions of acquisition debt (such as fees for raising capital to do a leveraged buy-out) and amortized over the term of the indebtedness are allowable corporate expenses for tax purposes.[9]

[¶1721] BUYER'S ASSUMPTIONS OF SELLER'S LIABILITIES

A law firm that represented both a seller corporation and its sole shareholder in a merger cannot represent the shareholder in a post-merger dispute with the purchaser corporation about the company's environmental compliance. The purchaser corporation inherits the attorney-client privilege with respect to business operations prior to the merger (although not as to the actual merger negotiations.)[10]

[¶1725] SEC REQUIREMENTS

In early 1995, the U.S. Supreme Court ruled that §12(2) of the Exchange Act, banning material misrepresentation or omission of fact in a prospectus or oral communication, is limited in its application to public offerings by an issuer or controlling shareholder. It does not apply to a private secondary sale of substantially all of the stock in a close corporation. Statements made in the contract of sale for such a transaction, whether true or not, do not constitute a prospectus.[11]

In early 1996, the Court ruled that federal courts must give full faith and credit to a state court release of class-action federal securities claims with respect to parties who failed to object or opt out,[12] even though the claims are subject to the exclusive jurisdiction of the federal court. The underlying Delaware suit involved a stockholder challenge to a takeover; the federal suit covered Exchange Act claims.

A lender who provides financing for a leveraged buy-out (LBO), but does not exercise control over the day-to-day management or policies of the borrower corporation, is not a "controlling person" as defined by Exchange Act §20(a), and therefore cannot be liable under Rule 10b-5 for fraud committed by the borrower in connection with the LBO.[13]

[¶1727.1] The Board's Duties and Adoption of Defensive Measures

In the fall of 1995, the Fourth Circuit upheld four Virginia anti-takeover statutes. The Court of Appeals did not find any Commerce Clause problems with the statutes, nor were they preempted by federal securities laws because of the state's role in regulating corporations within the state. In this reading, the Williams Act's investor protection function is not impaired by state statutes that give advantages to the retention of existing management.[14]

A "lockup," or termination fee of $550 million was included in a merger agreement as damages to be paid if the merger failed to go through. A stockholder sued, charging that the fee was unconscionably high. However, the Delaware Supreme Court applied the business judgment rule and upheld the arrangement as a reasonable estimate of potential future damages, and not large enough to coerce stockholders into voting for the merger.[15]

A hostile bidder was denied an injunction, because it is permissible for a defending company to cancel its annual meeting, then re-schedule the meeting on the same day as a special meeting called to vote on a white knight merger proposal.[16]

The Tax Court says that the costs of defending against a class action brought by minority shareholders who allege breach of fiduciary duty in a merger must be capitalized, not deducted currently.[17]

It also denied a current deduction for printing costs and investment banking fees incurred in response to a hostile takeover. (Eventually, the initial hostility was overcome and the target accepted the transaction.) In this analysis, such expenses are not "ordinary and necessary" because they do not relate to the production of current income or immediate corporate needs. The Tax Court theorized that a §165 loss deduction might have been available for the costs of an abandoned transaction (e.g., an unsuccessful attempt to find a white knight), but clearly this was unavailable in the case of a consummated transaction. The Seventh Circuit did not find these arguments persuasive, and permitted a §162 deduction for investment banking fees expended in an unsuccessful defense against a hostile takeover.[18]

[¶1729] SHAREHOLDER'S RIGHT OF APPRAISAL

When Delaware's Chancery Court values stock in an appraisal proceeding pursuant to a short-form merger, it is impermissible for the court to announce at the beginning of the case that it accepts one of the competing experts' opinion as the sole measure of value of the stock.[19] This case also rules that the going concern value of a corporation before a merger should not be adjusted to include the capitalized value of changes that new management might make after the merger.

— ENDNOTES —

1. *In re Envirodyne Industries Inc.,* 79 F.3d 579 (7th Cir. 3/15/96).

2. *ASA Architects Inc. v. Schlegel,* 28 Sec.Rep.L.Rep. 950 (Ohio Sup. 7/3/96).

3. *Publicis, S.A. v. True North Communications Inc.,* Del.Sup. #545 (12/12/97).

4. *NBT Bancorp Inc. v. Fleet/Norstar Financial Group Inc.,* 28 Sec.Reg.L.Rep. 504 (N.Y.App. 3/26/96).

5. *Arnold v. Society for Savings Bancorp Inc.,* 650 A.2d 1270 (Del.Sup. 12/28/94).

6. *Arnold v. Society for Savings Bancorp. Inc.,* 678 A.2d 533 (Del.Sup. 6/25/96).

7. *Lee v. Board of Governors of the Federal Reserve System,* 118 F.3d 905 (2nd Cir. 7/2/97); *Lee v. FDIC,* 923 F.Supp. 451 (S.D.N.Y. 9/15/97).

8. *Halle v. C.I.R.,* 83 F.3d 649 (4th Cir. 5/6/96).

9. *Fort Howard Corp. v. C.I.R.,* 107 T.C. No. 12 (10/22/96).

10. *Tekni-Plex Inc. v. Meyner & Landis,* 674 N.E.2d 663 (N.Y. App. 10/22/96).

11. *Gustafson v. Alloyd Co.,* #93-404, 115 S.Ct. 1061 (Sup.Ct. 2/28/95); on remand, 53 F.3d 333.

12. *Matsushita Electric Industrial Co. v. Epstein,* #94-1809, 116 S.Ct. 873 (Sup.Ct. 2/27/96).

13. *Paracor Finance Inc. v. G.E. Capital Corp.,* 79 F.3d 878 (9th Cir. 3/13/96).

14. *WLR Foods Inc. v. Tyson Foods Inc.,* 64 F.3d 1172 (4th Cir. 9/22/95).

15. *Brazen v. Bell Atlantic Corp.,* Del.Sup. #130 (5/27/97).

16. *H.F. Ahmanson Co. v. Great Western Financial Corp.,* 66 LW 1047 (Del.Chancery 6/3/97).

17. *Berry Petroleum Co.,* 104 T.C. No. 30 (5/22/95).

18. *A.E. Staley Mfg. Co.,* 105 T.C. No. 14 (9/11/95), *rev'd* 119 F.3d 482 (7th Cir. 7/2/97).

19. *Gonsalves v. Straight Arrow Publishers Inc.,* Del Sup. #17 (10/27/97).

— FOR FURTHER REFERENCE —

Bourtin, Jean-Pierre A., "United States Regulation of Foreign Takeovers," 70 *Tulane L. Rev.* 1609 (May '96).

Brown, Meredith M. and Paul Ford, "Takeover! A Power Play," 25 *International Business Lawyer* 52 (February '97).

Brownstein, Andrew R. and Steven A. Cohen, "Shareholder Rights Plans Are Under Board Review," *National L. J.* 4/15/96 p. C6.

Cryan, Thomas M. and Mary B. Doyle, "New Employment Tax Reporting Procedures in Business Acquisitions," 28 *Tax Adviser* 696 (November '97).

Henderson, Gordon D. and Stuart J. Goldring, "Berry Petroleum and Section 382," 70 *Tax Notes* 893 (February 12, 1996).

Fromm, Eva M., Edward C. Lewis and Heather M. Corken, "Allocating Environmental Liabilities in Acquisitions," 22 *J. of Corporate Law* 429 (Spring '97)

Hechler, Miriam P., "Towards a More Balanced Treatment of Bidder and Target Shareholders," 1997 *Columbia Business Review* 319 (Summer-Fall '97).

Hermalin, Benjamin and Alan Schwartz, "Buyouts in Large Companies," 27 *J. of Legal Studies* 351 (June '96).

Johnson, Calvin H., "Time to Get Out of the Pool: Pooling Methods for Acquisitions," 76 *Tax Notes* 810 (8/11/97).

Kattan, Joseph and William R. Vigdor, "Game Theory and the Analysis of Collusion in Conspiracy and Merger Cases," 5 *George Mason L.Rev.* 441 (Spring '97).

Lipton, Richard M., "Divided Tax Court Applies INDOPCO to Hostile Takeovers," 84 *J. of Taxation* 21 (January '96).

Malt, R. Bradford, "Some Acquisition Basics," 21 *ALI-ABA Course Materials J.* 17 (April '97)

Thompson, Samuel C. Jr., "A Lawyer's Guide to Valuation Techniques in Mergers and Acquisitions," 21 *J. of Corporation Law* 457 (Spring '96).

Waltonen, Andrea L., "Negotiating the Business Acquisition," 12 *Corporate Counsel's Q.* 116 (July '96).

Yde, Paul L. and Michael G. Vita, "Merger Efficiencies: Reconsidering the 'Passing-On' Requirement," 64 *Antitrust Law J.* 735 (Spring '96).

CREDIT AND COLLECTIONS, DISCLOSURE, AND CONSUMER PROTECTION

[¶1805] COLLECTION BY LAWSUIT

When extraordinary circumstances are present, a collection attorney is justified in using power of attorney agreements to endorse debtor drafts with the names of the attorney's creditor-clients. Furthermore, contingent fees can be deducted from the payments made by debtors; it is not necessary for the client to approve each fee deduction in advance.[1]

A creditor is permitted to send a nonthreatening, noncoercive letter to a debtor's attorney (with a copy to the debtor), suggesting a reaffirmation of the underlying debt, without violating the bankruptcy automatic stay. The Seventh Circuit read the purpose of the automatic stay as limited to protecting debtors from lawsuits, and not not preventing nonabusive communications during this time.[2]

In contrast, the Eighth Circuit disapproved a creditor's practice of sending Chapter 7 debtors a carbon copy of letters sent to their attorneys, suggesting that credit can be re-established if the debtors reaffirm their debts. The Court of Appeals ruled that this practice violates an Iowa law against direct debt collection communications with any debtor who is represented by counsel. It also ruled that the state law is not preempted by the Bankruptcy Code's provisions about negotiated reaffirmations of debt.[3]

[¶1813] APPLICABILITY OF CONSUMER PROTECTION LAWS

The Telemarketing and Consumer Fraud and Abuse Prevention Act, P.L. 103-297 (8/16/94) enacts a new 15 U.S.C. §6101. The FTC has the power to issue rules that prohibit deceptive or otherwise abusive telemarketing acts or practices. Unsolicited calls may not be made in a pattern that is coercive or violates recipients' privacy. Prompt disclosure must be made that the call is a sales call. States Attorneys General have the power to bring civil suits in federal District Court to enjoin or seek damages for abusive telemarketing.

According to the Third Circuit, the federal National Bank Act preempts state regulation of late fees and fees for exceeding the credit limit that national banks charge their credit customers—these fees are "interest" and therefore federally regulated.[4]

A customer is deemed to have received notice of a credit card change-of-terms agreement containing an arbitration clause when he or she has read the original agreement, which allows for later written amendments. The customer cannot deprive the amendment of effectiveness by neglecting or refusing to read it.[5]

[¶1814] TRUTH-IN-LENDING

During the supplement period, Congress passed two Truth-in-Lending measures. P.L. 104-12, the Truth in Lending Class Action Relief Act of 1995, was enacted on May 18, 1995. From that date until October 1, 1995, no court was permitted to certify any class action with respect to a closed-end transaction (a refinancing or consolidation secured by a first lien on a dwelling or other real property). Such cases were not allowed if the premise of the suit was a failure to disclose the finance charge or provide due notice of rescission rights, and if the lender attempted to provide notice but chose the wrong model form for the purpose. Class actions during that period were permitted if based on an Annual Percentage Rate higher than the permitted level.

The Truth in Lending Amendments of 1995, P.L. 104-29, were enacted on September 30, 1995. The amendments provide that the finance charge does not include the fees of third party closing agents (attorneys, title companies, escrow companies, settlement agents) if the creditor neither requires that the services be performed or charges imposed, nor retains the charge for the services. However, the finance charge does include mortgage broker fees paid by the borrower, and taxes on evidence of indebtedness (if payment of taxes is a condition of registering the mortgage). There is no right to rescind a transaction based on the form of notice if the creditor uses one of the official notices.

Revisions to the staff commentary on Regulation Z were proposed by the Federal Review Board at the end of 1997: see 62 FR 64769 (12/9/97). Under the proposal, issuers of open-end credit must disclose not only initial rates but higher penalty rates applied to late payments and extensions of credit over the set credit limit. The proposal also explains the disclosures that must be made for "same as cash" financing (where no interest is charged if payment in full is made by a certain date).

TILA applies to pawn transactions—whether or not the transaction constitutes an "extension of credit" under state law.[6] In the Eleventh Circuit's view, a bail bond transaction collateralized with a promissory note and mortgage is not subject to TILA (nor is the bondsman's enforcement subject to the FDCPA). This result was reached because the court deemed the transaction to resemble a letter of credit more than a consumer debt obligation.[7]

Where a borrower charges TILA violations, the defendant is not permitted to allege state-law defenses such as fraudulent statements in the loan applications; therefore, the plaintiff can retain damages and attorneys' fees awarded—notwithstanding the defendant's claim of fraud.[8]

[¶1825.6] Finance Charges

A charge of $400 for a debt cancellation agreement in an auto loan is really a form of insurance (it limits the borrower's liability to the lender when the car is lost or stolen). This amount is not paid "incident to" the loan, so it cannot be deemed a finance charge.[9]

Car dealers disclosed that $800 was paid to a third party for a warranty, but failed to disclose that they actually kept most of this amount. The Seventh Circuit found two TILA violations in the practice: failure to disclose the finance charge accurately (the real cost of credit was higher because the dealers kept more than disclosed) and incorrect itemization of the amount financed.[10]

[¶1830]   RIGHT OF RESCISSION

Where the lender misstated the expiration date of the right of rescission, and failed to provide TILA disclosures until after construction was completed, the homeowner was given three *years,* not three days, to rescind the home improvement loan under 15 U.S.C. §1635(f).[11]

[¶1837]   EQUAL CREDIT OPPORTUNITY

A spouse who is forced to sign a guarantee that violates the ECOA can use the ECOA defensively to defeat enforcement of the guarantee—even if the statute of limitations for recovering ECOA damages has expired.[12]

The ECOA statute of limitations is two years from the signing of the allegedly improper loan agreement, but the alleged violation can be raised as a defense against collection even after the statute of limitation has run.[13]

ECOA was not drafted with a federal immunity provision, so the federal government (e.g., the FHA) can be sued for rejecting an application on the basis of race.[14]

[¶1843]   FAIR CREDIT REPORTING

Major FCRA amendments took effect on September 30, 1997:

➤ Credit bureaus are obligated to resolve consumer complaints about disputed information faster, and must offer more options

➤ Employers are limited in their ability to obtain and use credit reports in the hiring process

➤ Credit bureaus are required to have toll-free numbers, disclosed in each credit offer so that consumers can have their names removed from the lists used to solicit credit cards and insurance. They must also provide written forms for permanent removal of a consumer's name from the solicitation list.

➤ When a consumer complains about information in the file, the credit bureau is obligated to investigate, review all relevant information, and report inaccuracies and omissions to all other national credit bureaus.[15]

The states have the power to take enforcement action on behalf of consumers in federal or state court, up to $1,000 per violation. The FTC is empowered to seek up to $2,500 per violation.

Pursuant to these amendments, the FTC drafted three new notices about consumer rights; the responsibilities of consumer reporting agencies; and the duties of users of consumer information. See 62 FR 35586, 7/1/97.

A mailing list generated by a consumer reporting agency, compiled from its database, which lists individuals that fall into stipulated marketing categories, is not a "consumer report" when it is sold to companies that want to do targeted marketing. This is because the marketing company uses the information to sell products, not to determine the customers' credit eligibility.[16]

A mid-1997 Colorado case[17] involved collection notices sent by a creditor. The alleged debtor's attorney responded, denying that the alleged debtor even had such a credit card. The creditor reported the amount as a bad debt. The debtor sued under a state law forbidding false and defamatory credit information that causes loss of reputation and access to credit. However, this law was deemed preempted by the FCRA, which bars defamation actions against anyone providing information to a credit bureau, unless the reporter acted with malice or intent to injure the consumer.

An FCRA plaintiff can resist summary judgment by producing facts from which the jury can infer that the credit reporting agency failed to follow reasonable procedures. Inaccuracies in the credit report (such as blaming an individual for his father's poor credit history) create a triable issue. It is not necessary for the plaintiff to produce affirmative proof of the reporting agency's failure to maintain reasonable procedures.[18]

[¶1848] THE FAIR DEBT COLLECTION PRACTICES ACT

In April, 1995, the U.S. Supreme Court held that attorneys are "debt collectors" for FDCPA purposes if they regularly engage in litigation to collect consumer debts.[19]

If a lawyer sends out form letters saying "I have authority to see suit is filed against you if payment is not received in five days," the FDCPA is violated provided that the lawyer lacks the actual intention to file suit. A form letter's reference to an attorney is a false threat of suit unless the attorney has been hired to collect a *particular* debt, and has not merely been hired by the creditor company for general collection duties.[20]

The FDCPA is violated when lawyers help write form dunning letters, which are sent out by paralegals using the firm's stationery with a facsimile of the attorneys' signatures. This procedure creates a false and misleading impression that the letters come from the attorneys, who did not actually review the appropriateness of the letter for the particular debtor's fact situation. The Seventh Circuit also found the dunning letters to be confusing to debtors, and no matter how efficient they are for the creditor, mass mailings are not allowed if they are false or deceptive.[21]

The subject of proper drafting of collection letters recurred several times in 1997. To the Northern District of Illinois, a letter can violate the FDCPA even if the required notice appears on the back of the letter, if the front of the letter demands quick payment by cashier's check or the customer will be unable to open a bank account or get a check approved by the participating bank. The court found this statement to be confusing, given the consumer's entitlement to at least 30 days to resolve the dispute. (The customer stopped payment on the check, alleging poor quality work by the payee.)[22] This case draws on *Bartlett v. Heibl*[23] which defines overreaching as the creation of a risk of confusion to an unsophisticated debtor who fails to understand the interaction between the threat and the right to contest a debt. Debtors must be informed that collection efforts are suspended when the debtor demands verification of the debt.

According to the Ninth Circuit[24] the FDCPA is not violated by a collection letter that says legal action may ensue unless the debtor telephones the agency within five days, as long as the letter neither demands payment within that time nor conceals the mandatory disclosure of the 30 days to file a written protest.

The FDCPA applies to private guaranty agencies for student loans, because they are private companies with government contracts, not government agencies that can claim a "government actor" exclusion from FDCPA coverage. The federal Higher Education Act preempts any state laws—including collection laws—that are inconsistent with the guaranteed student loan regulations.[25]

The FDCPA has been held to apply to anyone (including a lawyer or a collection agency) who attempts to collect post-due condominium assessments, on the grounds that the assessments relate to home ownership, which is a household purpose.[26] Two recent cases[27] hold that attempts to collect from individuals who write bad checks are subject to the FDCPA, because there is an underlying debt stemming from the payment obligation the checks were supposed to satisfy. In other words, no explicit extension of credit is required for the FDCPA to be triggered. A similar analysis—that only an obligation to pay, and not an extension of credit, is needed for FDCPA applicability—was applied by the Eleventh Circuit to fees (e.g., collision damage waiver) under a car rental agreement.[28]

A California collection agency can attempt to collect a debt from an Idaho resident without getting an Idaho debt collection permit first. The FDCPA is not violated by out-of-state collection efforts as long as they are mild, nonthreatening, not unconscionable, and do not involve false representations.[29]

A statewide, rather than a nationwide, FDCPA class action can properly be certified, even though this might create problems for later class actions elsewhere if the damage cap has already been approached or reached.[30]

15 U.S.C. §1692k makes debt collectors who violate the FDCPA liable for "such additional damages as the court may allow," but according to the Seventh Circuit, this is inherently a common-law tort action with a statutory authorization of punitive damages, so a jury is available, and the jury determines the amount of additional damages.[31]

Another statute with the same acronym, the Federal Debt Collection Procedure Act, 28 U.S.C. §3001 et.seq., was involved in an early 1997 case from the First Circuit.[32] It was held that a restitution order under the Child Support Recovery Act is not a "debt" for purposes of the Federal Debt Collection Procedure Act, because the money goes to the children and not the federal government. Thus, the federal statute cannot be used to enforce the CSRA restitution order.

— **ENDNOTES** —

1. *In re Advisory Committee on Professional Ethics, Docket No. 22-95*, 677 A.2d 1100 (N.J. Sup. 6/13/96).

2. *In re Duke*, 79 F.3d 43 (7th Cir. 3/15/96).

3. *Greenwood Trust Co. v. Smith*, 66 LW 1287 (8th Cir. 10/8/97).

4. *Spellman v. Meridian Bank (Delaware)*, 64 LW 2418 (3rd Cir. 12/29/95). However, *contra Sherman v. Citibank (South Dakota)*, 668 A.2d 1036 (New Jersey Sup. 11/28/95).

5. *Williams v. Direct Cable TV*, 66 LW 1143 (Ala. Circuit Ct. 8/13/97).

6. *Wiley v. Earl's Pawn & Jewelry Inc.*, 65 LW 2491 (S.D. Ala. 1/9/97).

7. *Buckman v. American Bankers Insurance Co. of Florida*, 115 F.3d 892 (11th Cir. 6/20/97).

8. *Purtle v. Eldridge Auto Sales*, 91 F.3d 797 (6th Cir. 8/1/96).

9. *McGee v. Kerr-Hickman Chrysler Plymouth Inc.*, 93 F.3d 380 (7th Cir. 8/19/96).

10. *Gibson v. Bob Watson Chevrolet-Geo Inc.*, 112 F.3d 283 (7th Cir. 4/23/97).

11. *Taylor v. Domestic Remodeling Inc.*, 97 F.3d 96 (5th Cir. 10/14/95).

12. *Silverman v. Eastrich Multiple Investor Fund LP*, 51 F.3d 28 (3rd Cir. 3/28/95).

13. *Roseman v. Premier Financial Services-East LP*, 66 LW 1223 (E.D. Pa. 9/4/97).

14. *Moore v. Department of Agriculture*, 55 F.3d 991 (5th Cir. 6/6/95).

15. See *Cushman v. TransUnion Corp.*, 115 F.3d 220 (3rd Cir. 6/9/97): obligating a consumer reporting agency that is on notice of incorrect information in a consumer report to go beyond its original sources to see if the information is true.

16. *Trans Union Corp. v. FTC*, 81 F.3d 228 (D.C.Cir. 4/19/96).

17. *Greenwood Trust Co. v. Conley*, 65 LW 2802 (Colo.Sup. 6/2/97).

18. *Philbin v. Trans Union Corp.*, 101 F.3d 957 (3rd Cir. 12/6/96).

19. *Heintz v. Jenkins*, #94-367, 115 S.Ct. 1489 (Sup.Ct. 4/18/95).

20. *U.S. v. National Finance Services Inc.*, 98 F.3d 131 (4th Cir. 10/11/96).

21. *Avila v. Rubin*, 84 F.3d 222 (7th Cir. 5/16/96).

22. *Ozkaya v. Telecheck Services Inc.*, 66 LW 1294 (N.D. Ill. 10/23/97).

23. 128 F.3d 497 (7th Cir. 10/8/97).

24. *Terran v. Kaplan*, 109 F.3d 1428 (9th Cir. 3/28/97).

25. *Brannan v. U.S. Student Aid Funds Inc.*, 94 F.3d 1260 (9th Cir. 8/30/96).

26. *Voisenat v. Decker*, 117 F.3d 427 (9th Cir. 7/1/97).

27. *Bass v. Stolper, Koritzinsky, Brewer & Neider SC*, 111 F.3d 1322 (7th Cir. 4/18/97); *Charles v. Lundren & Associates PC*, 119 F.3d 739 (9th Cir. 7/8/97).

28. *Brown v. Budget Rent-a-Car Systems Inc.*, 119 F.3d 922 (11th Cir. 8/15/97).

29. *Wade v. Regional Credit Association,* 87 F.3d 1098 (9th Cir. 7/3/96).

30. *Mace v. Van Ru Credit Corp.,* 109 F.3d 338 (7th Cir. 3/17/97).

31. *Kobs v. Arrow Service Bureau Inc.,* 66 LW 1453 (7th Cir. 1/22/98).

32. *U.S. v. Bongiorno,* 103 F.3d 1027 (1st Cir. 2/7/97).

— FOR FURTHER REFERENCE —

Beckelman, Steven A. and David J. Adler, "Forestalling Apocalypse: Counteracting Defenses to Foreclosure," 113 *Banking Law J.* 53 (January '96).

Buchner, Robert J. and Sara J. Sanders, "Auto Leasing: Let the Dealer Disclose," 70 *Florida Bar J.* 46 (November '96).

Cain, James M., "Proving Fraud in Credit Card Dischargeability Actions: A Permanent State of Flux?" 102 *Commercial L.J.* 233 (Fall '97).

Farley, Andrea Michele, "The Spousal Defense—A Ploy to Escape Payment or Simple Application of the Equal Credit Opportunity Act?" 49 *Vanderbilt L. Rev.* 1287 (October '96).

Fisher, John W. II, "Creditors of a Joint Tenant: Is There a Lien After Death?" 99 *West Virginia L.Rev.* 637 (Summer '97).

Golden, Christopher A., "Fair Debt Collection Practices Act: An Emerging Source of Liability for Attorneys," 69 *New York State Bar J.* 14 (February '97).

Lippman, Steven N., "Proceedings Supplementary and the Uniform Fraudulent Transfer Act," 70 *Florida Bar J.* 22 (January '96).

Lucas, Laurie A. and Alcin C. Harrell, "An Unholy Trilogy: Unresolved Issues Under the Federal Fair Debt Collection Practices Act," 51 *Business Lawyer* 949 (May '96).

Mann, Ronald J., "Searching for Negotiability in Payment and Credit Systems," 44 *U.C.L.A. L.Rev.* 951 (April '97).

Mann, Ronald J., "Strategy and Force in the Liquidation of Bad Debts," 96 *Michigan L.Rev.* 159 (November '97).

Maurer, Virginia G. and Robert E. Thomas, "Getting Credit Where Credit is Due: Proposed Changes in the Fair Credit Reporting Act," 34 *American Business Law J.* 607 (Summer '97).

Ortego, Joseph J., "When Advertising a Foreclosure Sale is Not Enough," 28 *Uniform Commercial Code L. J.* 290 (Winter '96).

Rongeau, Vincent D., "Rediscovering Usury: An Argument for Legal Controls on Credit Card Interest Rates," 67 *U. of Colorado L. Rev.* 1 (Winter '96).

Thomas, Charlotte A., "Defending a Free Standing Equal Credit Opportunity Act Claim," 114 *Banking Law J.* 108 (February '97).

CRIMINAL LAW AND PROCEDURE

[¶1901]   In 1995–1996, perhaps the leading issue in criminal law was forfeiture. When is a forfeiture punitive, thus giving rise to a potential double jeopardy issue? What are the rights of third parties in seized property? In 1997, the focus shifted back to more conventional issues: questions about the death penalty, search and seizure (especially brief on-street stops), and custodial interrogation occupied the courts.

Reference should also be made to the changes in the Federal Rules of Criminal Procedure, effective 12/1/95,[1] affecting Rules 5 (initial appearance before a magistrate judge), 40 (commitment to another district), 43 (presence of the defendant at trial), and 57 (rule-making by the District Courts). Rule 49's provisions for filing of a dangerous offender notice have been abrogated.

The Ninth Circuit decided in 1996 that paying an informant a contingent fee based on the value of drugs seized is not "outrageous" government conduct violating the Constitutional guarantee of due process.[2]

[¶1902] ELEMENTS OF OFFENSES

At the end of 1995, the Supreme Court decided that a conviction under 18 U.S.C. §924 (c)(1)—the "use" of a firearm during or in relation to drug trafficking—requires proof of active employment of the firearm in connection with the predicate offense. Thus, a gun that was in the possession of the defendant, e.g., locked in a car trunk or in the defendant's apartment when the crime was committed somewhere else—will not support a §924(c)(1) conviction.[3] In March, 1997, the Supreme Court decided another case involving the same statute, this time deciding that the §924(c) five-year sentence must run consecutively with all other sentences, state as well as federal.[4]

Earlier in 1995, the Supreme Court had found that false statements in unsworn papers filed in bankruptcy court cannot give rise to an indictment under 18 U.S.C. §1001 (false statements in any matter within the jurisdiction of any "department or agency of the United States"). The rationale is that a federal court is neither a department nor an agency.[5] Early in 1998, the Supreme Court ruled that this statute does not contain an exception for the "exculpatory no"—i.e., a simple denial of wrongdoing can be penalized as a false statement.[6]

In mid-1996, the Supreme Court upheld a Montana law that forbids juries to consider voluntary intoxication in determining the mental state of a homicide defendant (the homicide law penalizes "purposely" or "knowingly" causing a death). The Supreme Court's due process analysis is that defendants do not have an absolute right to have all relevant evidence introduced. Furthermore, a state is justified in continuing to follow the common-law rule that voluntary intoxication is not a defense.[7]

The Constitutionality of two rather dissimilar federal criminal statutes attracted significant attention during the supplement period. One criminalizes carjacking; the other deals with willful failure to pay support to a child who resides in another state. Of course, Commerce Clause issues were paramount in both cases.

In the Third Circuit, it has been held that 18 U.S.C. §2119, which makes it illegal to carjack a car that has been transported, shipped, or received in interstate commerce, is Constitutional, and does not violate Congress' Commerce Clause powers.[8] The Third Circuit decided another carjacking case in 1997, this time ruling that to get a conviction, the prosecution must prove only that the defendant intended to kill or seriously injure any victim who refused to surrender the car. It is not necessary to prove an intent to harm even a compliant victim.[9]

The Child Support Recovery Act of 1992, 18 U.S.C. §228, has been assessed by many courts, to various possible outcomes. Constitutionality has been upheld by District Courts in Kansas and Connecticut.[10] However, initially other courts[11] ruled that Congress exceeded its powers under the Commerce Clause by legislating in an area that is not substantially related to interstate commerce, and where there are already Uniform Laws and state criminal statutes, but eventually a consensus emerged that the statute was valid and enforceable.

As the use of computers in legitimate activities increases, there is an inevitable increase in the use of computers in illicit activities. A First Circuit case declines to apply the federal wire fraud or computer fraud statutes in the case of an IRS employee who gained unauthorized access to confidential file information about various individuals. There was no proof that he disclosed the information to third parties; he didn't gain anything of value by snooping; and he was otherwise an effective employee, so no penalties were imposed.[12]

A defendant can appropriately be charged under a computer crime statute, rather than a fraud statute carrying lesser penalties, where a computer was allegedly used to alter insurance claim forms, because the use of the computer was an additional, more serious, element.[13]

Criminal liability cannot be imposed under Exchange Act §10(b) based on a misappropriation theory, first of all because misappropriation can occur without deception, and second of all because any deception that takes place is not in connection with the purchase or sale of a security.[14]

It has been held that a rapist's knowledge of his HIV-positive status cannot be interpreted as intent to kill rape victims.[15]

A new federal offense was added by P.L. 104-155, the Church Arson Prevention Act (July 3, 1996). The offense, codified at 18 U.S.C. §247, consists of intentional defacement, damage, or destruction of religious real property motivated by the race, color, or ethnicity of persons associated with the place of worship. The penalty for violation can be as high as 40 years imprisonment, if use of fire or explosive results in injury.

[¶1902.6] RICO

"Interstate commerce," for RICO purposes, includes taking money from drug transactions in Arizona and investing it in an Alaskan gold mine: equipment was purchased out of state, workers were hired from out of state, and about 15% of the mine's output was transported out of state.[16]

The Private Securities Litigation Reform (PSLR) Act of 1995 (see ¶3808) eliminates securities fraud as a RICO predicate. However, this portion of the PSLR cannot be applied retroactively in a civil RICO case that was pending on the statute's effective date.[17]

RICO cases continued to be significant in 1997. The District Court for the District of Maryland decided that a law firm can be held liable for participating in a RICO enterprise, if it concealed kickbacks and aided and abetted the predicate acts of mail fraud,thus playing the necessary operational or management role.[18] At mid-year, the Seventh Circuit held that a car company, its subsidiaries, and its dealers carrying out normal business are not a RICO "enterprise" even if the extended warranties on the vehicles are fraudulent. The court declined to apply RICO to every dispute involving multiple parties.[19]

On a related topic, the Second Circuit found that the money laundering statute, 18 U.S.C. §1965(a)(1)(B)(ii) requires proof that the defendant knew that the money derived from illegal activity, but not necessarily that he or she knew the details of the illegal activity.[20]

[¶1902.7] Double Jeopardy

At the end of 1997, the Supreme Court decided a case in which the Office of the Comptroller of the Currency entered into a consent order with bankers under which they agreed to monetary penalties and to stop working in the banking industry unless they receive permission from regulators. This was not a "criminal prosecution" in the Supreme Court's view, and therefore it did not impose a Double Jeopardy bar to criminal charges based on the same conduct. In this reading, a sanction creates jeopardy only upon proof of its criminal nature. A criminal sanction is one that is intended to be punitive, and has historically been viewed as punitive.[21]

When a defendant is charged with two forms of a unitary offense, which are criminalized by different statutory subsections, jeopardy attaches and terminates separately for each. In the case at bar, the jury convicted the defendant of "wanton murder" but were silent on "intentional murder," so jeopardy terminated on the intentional murder count. The conviction of wanton murder was reversed for insufficient evidence, so it would constitute double jeopardy to retry the defendant on the intentional murder count.[22]

In a case of serious prosecutorial misconduct leading to mistrial, the defendant cannot be retried if the prosecutor was aware of the improper conduct and acted in willful disregard of the likelihood of mistrial.[23]

[¶1903] CRIMINAL LIABILITY OF PARTIES TO AN OFFENSE

In late 1994, the Supreme Court ruled that it is not necessary for the prosecution to prove an overt act in order to get a conviction under 21 U.S.C. §846, the drug conspiracy statute.[24] In early 1996, the high court deemed conspiracy to distribute controlled substances to be a lesser included offense of carrying on a continuing criminal enterprise with others (CCE; 21 U.S.C. §848). Therefore, the two counts are the "same offense" and it was improper to sentence the defendant to life imprisonment on each count—notwithstanding the fact that the sentences were concurrent rather than consecutive.[25]

To rebut the defense of entrapment, the prosecution must show predisposition: in other words, that the defendant was in a position to commit the offense and wanted to do so. The query becomes what the defendant would have done without government involvement. The inquiry covers subjects such as the defendant's experience, training, and contacts. Thus, it was held that a minister who desperately needed money for his church, and who became enmeshed in a money laundering sting operation, would not have been used as a money launderer by real drug dealers. He was in no position to commit the crime without government involvement, and therefore was entrapped.[26]

[¶1905] STOPS AND ARRESTS

According to the California Supreme Court, merely running away from a police officer is not enough to create the suspicion that would justify an investigative stop.[27] Similarly, it has been held to be a seizure regulated by the Massachusetts state Constitution (and requiring reasonable suspicion) to pursue an individual in order to question him or her.[28]

Temporary detention, based on reasonable cause to believe that a traffic violation has occurred, does not violate the Fourth Amendment, the Supreme Court found in mid-1996.[29] The temporary detention is allowed even if the detaining police officer had another motive for the detention (such as searching the car for drugs or weapons), and whether or not a hypothetical reasonable police officer would have taken action against the traffic offense if there were no other motivation involved.

Once the stop occurs, Colorado treats as unreasonable (under the Fourth Amendment) continued detention or questioning of the motorist once the police have satisfied the purpose of a valid investigatory stop—i.e., once a valid license and registration have been displayed).[30] A later Colorado case[31] holds that whether "investigative detention," rather than a mere discussion between police and individuals in a parked car, depends on whether the police and police vehicles are positioned in such a way as to prevent the car from driving away—and whether occupants of the car would feel able to tell the police to go away and simply drive off.

127

According to the Pennsylvania Supreme Court, items discarded by an individual fleeing a police officer who had neither probable cause for an arrest nor reasonable suspicion justifying a stop-and-frisk have been "seized." Therefore, the Pennsylvania Constitution requires exclusion of those items from evidence if they turn out to be contraband.[32]

Early in 1997, the U.S. Supreme Court held that, during a traffic stop, the police can legitimately order passengers as well as the driver to leave the car. In this reading, the intrusion on privacy is minimal, and is outweighed by the need to protect the safety of the police officers performing the stop.[33] Building on this decision, a Washington Court of Appeals case equally allows the police to order passengers to remain in the vehicle during a stop. The police have the right to control the circumstances of the stop, even at some compromise to the liberty interest of stoppees.[34]

When a person who was the subject of a traffic stop showed a firearm owner's ID card as identification, it was reasonable for the police to prolong the traffic stop and ask if there was a gun in the car. Even though the driver was outside the car, the passenger was still inside the car, so the police might have been endangered. Therefore, the gun found during the search of the car was admissible.[35]

A police officer who observed that a passenger was wearing a bulletproof vest and appeared to hide something under the seat was justified in searching the car for weapons after the passengers had exited the car and the vest-wearer had been patted down and no weapons were found. The vest and his suspicious movements were deemed by the New York Court of Appeals to provide reasonable suspicion that the car contained a weapon that posed a threat to the police.[36]

To the Eleventh Circuit, police officers who have probable cause to stop a car for a traffic violation can use the traffic operation as a pretext for asking for permission to search the car under a drug interdiction operation. In this reading, roving patrol stops and vehicle stops at fixed locations are impermissible only if stops are made on no suspicion at all.[37] A drug interdiction officer was held to have enough information for reasonable suspicion during a traffic stop, when the persons in the car were nervous and gave inconsistent reasons for travel; a reasonable officer would suspect the rationales given for driving 1300 miles in two days.[38] In contrast, a 1997 Maryland case says that the Fourth Amendment is violated by a pretextual stop used to gain a probable-cause or consent basis to search a vehicle,[39] and a 1997 Ohio case requires reasonable suspicion before the police ask for consent to search a car during a lawful traffic stop.[40]

According to the Fourth Circuit, if a vehicle has heavily tinted windows, police officers doing a stop can open the door to see if occupants of the car are armed. They can therefore seize narcotics that are in plain view when the door is opened. Under this analysis, there is little expectation of privacy in a vehicle (as distinct from a residence), because automotive travel is highly regulated.[41] Yet, according to the Oregon Court of Appeals, the police need reasonable suspicion to "search" a car during a traffic stop, a classification that includes an officer leaning into an open window to hand over and explain the traffic citation.[42]

If, in the course of a traffic stop, the police get the driver's consent to search a car for drugs, that does not give them the right to search a passenger's purse that was left in the car when the driver and passengers were ordered to leave the vehicle.[43] (That is, even if there had been a weapon in the purse, a passenger who was outside the car could not have used it to harm the police officers.)

The standard for appellate review of a trial court's determination of the reasonableness of a stop, or probable cause for a search, is *de novo*, but findings of "historical fact" are reviewed to see if clear error occurred. Nevertheless, the Supreme Court instructed appellate courts to bear in mind the local conditions as assessed by local law enforcement officers and judges.[44]

It has been held that stationing a drug-sniffer dog outside an intercity bus does not operate as a "seizure" of the bus passengers.[45]

It is reasonable to handcuff a suspect before taking him to a porch where a recent rape victim might be able to identify him as her assailant. Handcuffing, although it makes the suspect look more suspicious, is a reasonable safety precaution where the victim reported that the rapist had been armed.[46]

The Pennsylvania Supreme Court ruled that a stop and frisk was not justified by a suspect's resemblance to an unidentified tipster's description of an armed man; articulable facts creating a reasonable suspicion of a crime in progress would be required for a valid stop.[47]

Of course, it is difficult to draw a bright line between legal regulation of stops and legal regulation of searches, because it is common for a stop to result in at least a search, and often an arrest. Also see *U.S. v. Letsinger*,[48] which rules that for Fourth Amendment purposes, a suitcase is seized when the police take actual physical possession of it, not when they announce an intention to take it. In other words, a person can be subject to a stop, but an object cannot.

New Hampshire does not create an exception to the warrant requirements for an "identification search" conducted during an investigative stop; the protective frisk is limited to checking to see if the stopped person is armed.[49]

[¶1906] SEARCH AND SEIZURE

In mid-1995, the Supreme Court held that the common-law "knock and announce" principle is part of the Fourth Amendment inquiry into the reasonableness of police conduct. Nevertheless, there may be circumstances, such as danger to the officers, that make it reasonable to make an unannounced entry. The case was remanded for a factual determination of the reasonableness of police conduct in the case at bar.[50] The Supreme Court returned to "knock and announce" in 1997.[51] The court declined to grant a blanket exception that would allow all drug raids to be made unannounced. However, the reasonableness analysis would continue to apply, based on whether, as of the time of the entry (not the time the magistrate denied an application for a warrant with no-knock provision), the police had a reasonable suspicion that an announced entry would be dangerous or futile, or would impede the investigation.

The Sixth Circuit accepts a neighbor's complaint about loud music coming from a house as an exigent circumstance that will justify a warrantless entry (and thus make admissible the marijuana being grown within the house).[52]

The Fourth Amendment is violated by setting up a real drug interdiction checkpoint with the objective of catching motorists who turn off the road after seeing a sign for a nonexistent drug checkpoint. The appellate court noted that motorists were subjected to excessive stress; the real checkpoint was inadequately supervised; and no empirical evidence of its effectiveness was presented in justification.[53]

A late 1996 Supreme Court ruling permits the police to do a search on consent during a traffic stop, without advising the motorist that he or she is free to go: the totality of the circumstances determines the reasonableness of police conduct.[54] (See above for further discussion of stops.)

Vehicle searches continued to occupy the courts. The sleeping compartment of a tractor-trailer can be searched without a warrant when the driver is arrested, because of the accessibility of that compartment to the arrested driver.[55] However, the Michigan Court of Appeals held that after a driver voluntarily exits a vehicle and is arrested some distance away, the arrest does not justify a search of the vehicle.[56]

The Washington Supreme Court decided that a warrantless investigative search is not authorized merely because an impounded vehicle is seized for forfeiture. In this analysis, the real police objective was finding evidence of other crimes, so they could and should have obtained a warrant for this purpose.[57] In 1997, the Fifth Circuit disapproved warrantless inventory searches when the police officers' subjective intent was to investigate a crime, not to protect themselves or the property of the arrestee.[58]

One of the most significant issues of the supplement period is the extent of police powers when contraband is deemed to be in "plain sight" or "plain touch." A Hawaii case tries to tackle the distinction between "open view" (sighting by the police before any intrusion on privacy occurs) and "plain view" (after the intrusion on privacy, involving materials that are not exposed to the public). In this reading,[59] police who have licit access to an area can seize plain-view evidence with no need to show exigent circumstances. However, exigency is required for warrantless seizure of objects that are exposed to the public in a Constitutionally protected area to which the police have not gained access.

The "inevitable discovery" rule allows introduction of improperly obtained evidence that would definitely have been found even if no Constitutional violation had occurred. According to the Tenth Circuit, the prosecution introducing such evidence need not prove that there was a separate ongoing investigation that would have uncovered the evidence. An investigation commenced after the illegal search can be sufficient for this purpose.[60]

Illinois and Michigan, on one hand, and Connecticut and Indiana on the other, reached opposite conclusions on the "plain touch" question in several cases involving crack cocaine. It has been held that the Illinois Constitution permits warrantless seizure of such contraband when "plain touch" during a pat-down for weapons gives cause for suspicion. But Connecticut treats the power to make a *Terry* stop as the power to search for weapons to protect the safety of the officer. However illicit a vial of crack is, it does not menace the police officer who makes the stop. Michigan permits seizure of drugs in the "groin area" of a suspect's sweatpants under the "plain feel" exception; the Indiana ruling is that the contraband nature of a bulge or bump in a pocket is not apparent to the touch.[61]

The Seventh Circuit permits police engaging in "drug interdiction" activities to touch and feel luggage that bus passengers place on the overhead rack.[62] In this analysis, the luggage was "knowingly exposed to the public" because other passengers had access to the outside of the luggage; therefore, the police activities were not tantamount to a "search." On a related question, the Massachusetts Supreme Judicial Court held that a briefcase was not abandoned when a defendant threw it out a window. The briefcase could properly be seized pursuant to the suspect's arrest, but a warrant was required to search the briefcase.[63]

According to the Fourth Circuit, if grounds exist for a *Terry* stop, a protective search can be done by asking a person detained for a traffic offense to lift his shirt enough to uncover a bulge observed near the waistband.[64] But, according to the Maryland Court of Appeals, *Terry* allows a pat-down of a stoppee, but when the pat-down is negative, the police officer conducting the stop is unjustified in double-checking by lifting the stopped person's shirt.[65]

There are other potential situations in which it must be determined whether a search has occurred—e.g., the Tenth Circuit finds that using a thermal imager to detect "hot spots" indicative of marijuana cultivation on the premises does constitute a search for Fourth Amendment purposes,[66] based on a reasonable expectation of privacy in the "heat signatures." Reasonable expectation of privacy was the gravamen of several 1997 cases. To the Colorado Supreme Court,[67] both the state and federal Constitutions forbid a search of tent, and a backpack contained in the tent, without a warrant on land that, although private, was unimproved, unfenced, and was not posted against trespassing. The court cited a Western tradition of treating a tent as a home.

To the Seventh Circuit, banging on a motel door and window late at night, even after the occupants refused to answer, was a "seizure" requiring reasonable suspicion. Even in conjunction with the suspect's arrest record, the fact that he drove a "target" vehicle (a two-door vehicle with Florida plates) and parked near an airport did not constitute grounds for suspicion of drug trafficking.[68]

Peeking through cracks in a closed window blind, when a police officer stands in a place where neither neighbors nor the general public would be expected to be found, is a search, because it violates the expectation of privacy.[69]

The Fourth Amendment implications of electronic communications will assume greater importance over time. The Washington Supreme Court treated a police scanner (used by a neighbor) as a device "designed to record or transmit." The neighbor used the scanner to intercept cordless telephone conversations, and then relayed this information to the police. The information was excluded under the state privacy statute as an illegally intercepted communication, because the required consent of all parties to the conversation was lacking.[70] In the judgment of the Southern District of New York, warrantless activation of a pager, to retrieve messages, is not classified as interception of an electronic communication as defined by Title I of the Electronic Communications Privacy Act. However, unless a Fourth Amendment exclusion is available, it does violate the Title II prohibition of unauthorized access to stored electronic communications.[71]

There is no reasonable expectation of privacy in chat room communications or e-mails, so persons whose messages dealing with child pornography were seized by federal agents did not have a valid Fourth Amendment claim.[72]

If a computer is an instrumentality of a crime (e.g., used to operate a porno-graphic on-line service), then warrant-based seizure of the computer, including some undelivered e-mail messages, is valid and does not violate the Fourth Amendment or the Electronic Communications Privacy Act. The warrant allows seizure of an entire object that has both licit and illicit purposes, and reasonable reliance on the warrant gives the police a good-faith defense under the Electronic Communications Privacy Act.[73]

A warrantless search incident to an arrest can also include the area within the arrestee's immediate control. The D.C. Circuit interprets this to mean the area that was within the arrestee's control at the moment of arrest, so police can return without a warrant and search a room from which an arrestee has been removed.[74] The Maryland Court of Appeals said that a search is only incident to an arrest if the police intended to take the suspect into custody when they did the search; detention on probable cause doesn't count.[75]

A warrantless search is legitimate if it occurs on consent, but whose consent is required? One recent case says that the police cannot permit the driver to con-sent to the search of a car if they are aware that the owner is present but not oper-ating the vehicle.[76] Another related case says that consent from one roommate per-mits search of an apartment even without consent of another roommate (who hap-pened to be present at the time of the search).[77]

In a 1997 Eighth Circuit case, a suspect consented to a search after the police told her that cooperation would be taken into account—but did not inform her she had already been indicted on drug charges. The deception was ruled not to be egregious enough to vitiate her consent. Asking for cooperation would not neces-sarily lead a reasonable person to believe that no charges would be filed if he or she cooperated.[78]

With all that, it might seem as if searches pursuant to warrants never result-ed in litigation; of course, that's not true. A Sixth Circuit case finds a search war-rant invalid because it covered almost all of a business' records; it should have indicated what the alleged crime was, when the crime was alleged to have occurred, and the location of pertinent documents. The Sixth Circuit deemed the warrant so defective that no reasonable agent could have relied on its validity.[79] In the Tenth Circuit,[80] if the police abuse even a valid warrant and use it to search for any evidence of any crime (rather than for the specific items listed in the war-rant), this abuse requires suppression of all evidence, including the items specifi-cally listed. In contrast, in the Ninth Circuit,[81] an arrest is not considered pretextu-al as long as the police had probable cause to search for anything, and a warrant can be obtained in the hope of finding evidence of another, more serious crime.

California v. Glaser[82] permits police officers executing a search warrant cov-ering drugs to briefly detain persons entering the premises. Occupants can be detained for the duration of the search; other persons must be released absent evi-dence either of a threat to the police or articulable suspicion of connection to the criminal activity for which the warrant was issued.

When executing a search warrant, the police can search the belongings of a visitor to the premises (such as a duffel bag in another room), but not extensions of the visitor's person such as objects worn by or in the personal possession of the visitor.[83]

Several 1997 cases deal with anticipatory search warrants. In the Seventh Circuit's reading, a search warrant can be premised on the occurrence of an event in the future, and the warrant need not describe the event on its face or even in the supporting affidavit, as long as the police and the magistrate are aware of the nature of the event.[84] The Hawaii state Constitution, however, requires additional safeguards for anticipatory search warrants. The police seeking the warrant must swear or affirm the need for the warrant before probable cause occurs. Execution of the warrant must be conditional on occurrence of the event.[85]

The Oklahoma Supreme Court refused to allow a landlord to claim a "taking" in violation of the state Constitution when the police smashed up an apartment in the course of executing a search warrant for drugs allegedly sold by the tenant.[86]

Where the FBI and DEA illegally seize evidence in a criminal investigation, the IRS can use the evidence in a civil tax proceeding without violating the exclusionary rule—unless there was a preexisting agreement that the other federal agencies would convey information to the IRS.[87]

Hawaii permits admission in Hawaii courts of evidence gathered out of state, in a manner valid in that state but not in Hawaii, provided that admission of the evidence would not violate individual privacy, judicial integrity, or the objective of securing proper police conduct. The rationale is that police officers in other states should be permitted to follow their own rules and procedures unless they deliberately flout Hawaii's rules.[88]

To the Third Circuit, an order compelling HIV testing of persons accused or convicted of sexual assault does not violate the Fourth Amendment. An order that satisfies the standards of the Violence Against Women Act (the victim must request the test; confidentiality of test results must be maintained; the defendant must be given an opportunity to contest the results) satisfies the standard of Fourth Amendment reasonableness.[89]

[¶1907] INTERROGATION AND SELF-INCRIMINATION

The Ninth Circuit permits a selective Miranda waiver—i.e., a disclosure of subjects about which a suspect is willing to be questioned.[90]

When a federal court performs habeas review of a state court judgment, the question of whether the suspect was "in custody" and thus entitled to a Miranda warning is a mixed question of law and fact. The U.S. Supreme Court decided in late 1995 that the federal court must resolve the question independently and cannot presume that the state court's judgment as to custody/non-custody was correct.[91]

The California Supreme Court ruled that an interogatee described as a "possible witness" who was asked—not ordered—to accompany the police to the police station, and given a choice of going in either his own car or a police car was not "in custody." Therefore, no Miranda warning was required for brief questioning that was not accusatory—even though the questioning occurred in the jail area of the police station.[92]

However, the California Court of Appeals held that the good-faith exception to the Fourth Amendment exclusionary rule does not cover evidence obtained contrary to the Fifth Amendment right to counsel: protection against self-incrimination is a "mainstay of our adversary system of criminal justice," requiring the police to cease interrogation of a person who has asked for counsel.[93] But what is an invocation of the right to counsel?

According to the Virginia Supreme Court,[94] a suspect's statement, "I'm scared to say anything without talking to a lawyer," is not a clear invocation of the right, and therefore further custodial interrogation is not barred by such a statement. A contrasting Utah formulation is that after a waiver of Miranda rights, questioning can continue until there is an unequivocal assertion of the right to silence. Before a waiver, however, even an equivocal assertion must be probed and clarified by the interrogator.[95] In a late-1997 Massachusetts case,[96] a prisoner asked for an attorney then began to talk to one police officer. An inquiry from another police officer as to why the suspect wanted an attorney was deemed to be a permissible attempt to clear up an ambiguity (a person asserting the right to silence also initiated conversation) rather than impermissible interrogation.

In Michigan, statements deriving from custodial interrogation must be suppressed if the police fail to tell an arrestee that a lawyer has been hired and is reasonably available. The theory behind this ruling is that a waiver of the right to silence cannot be made knowingly and intelligently without data about the actual availability of a lawyer on the premises.[97] In contrast, in Colorado, a waiver of the right to counsel during custodial interrogation is not rendered involuntary by the police failure to inform the suspect that there was already a warrant for his arrest. The rationale is that lies are forbidden, but information can be withheld if the information goes to the advisability, rather than the voluntariness, of the waiver.[98]

The District of Columbia decided two interesting cases in the latter half of 1995. In the first, a "safety" exception was found to the Miranda rule, permitting the police to ask about the location of weapons even after the right to remain silent has been evoked.[99] In the second, words of religious inspiration directed by a police officer to a suspect who he knew belonged to the same church are considered interrogation for Fifth Amendment purposes.[100]

Once a Sixth Amendment right to counsel arises with respect to charged offenses, it is improper to interrogate without counsel present with respect to uncharged offenses that are closely related to the charged offenses.[101] In fact, according to the New York Court of Appeals, once a person is represented by an attorney, it is improper to question the client without the lawyer being present, no matter what offense is the subject of questioning, even if the offense is unrelated, the attorney is not at the site of interrogation to complain, and the suspect does not invoke the right to counsel.[102]

In 1996, the Second Circuit confronted an unusual problem: the excessively voluble arrestee. The Second Circuit decided[103] that a waiver is not involuntary (absent misrepresentation) if the defendant is told he must sign the waiver before talking to the police any further or getting his questions answered. However, it might be coercive for a police officer or other government agent to refuse to answer a suspect's questions before a waiver has been signed.

In Florida, assertion of the right to counsel can only be made when interrogation is imminent or in process. Therefore, a suspect could legitimately be questioned after signing a "claim of rights" form during an information session with a public defender.[104]

A state court, in a case involving fraudulent tax returns used in an insurance scam, can order the defendant to execute IRS Form 8821, authorizing release of tax returns, albeit with certain modifications to prevent self-incrimination. The Massachusetts Supreme Judicial Court found that the form was not really testimonial, if it is not used to assert that the defendants had to file returns or voluntarily consented to disclosure of the returns.[105]

[¶1907.1] Forfeiture and Attorneys' Fees

In early 1996, the Supreme Court decided a somewhat atypical forfeiture case, *Bennis v. Michigan*,[106] in which the forfeited item was a family automobile that had been used by the husband for sexual activity with a prostitute. The court held that the wife was not entitled to an innocent owner defense against the forfeiture.

In the more typical case, items (real estate, cars, and particularly cash) used in drug trafficking are seized, and the question is whether the seizure violates the Unlawful Fines clause of the Eighth Amendment, and especially whether an *in rem* civil forfeiture subjects an individual to double jeopardy if he or she is also prosecuted for the illegal conduct that justified the seizure of the property.

One strand of analysis is that civil forfeiture is not punitive in nature (perhaps unless it is irrational and grossly disproportionate to the alleged offense)—and, therefore, prosecution does not subject the individual to double jeopardy.[107] There are cases to the contrary, holding that the forfeiture itself is punitive, so the same conduct cannot give rise to a criminal prosecution.[108]

In mid-1996, the Supreme Court perhaps left more questions unanswered than it resolved, by ruling that civil *in rem* forfeiture of drug trafficking proceeds, property used in money laundering, and property facilitating drug offenses is not punitive and therefore does not give rise to double jeopardy.[109] The rationale is that the legislature intended these measures to be civil in nature, not punitive, and the measures themselves are not so punitive in form that they defeat the legislative intent.

Some cases (e.g., in the District Courts of Massachusetts and Alabama) focus on whether the defendant concedes the forfeiture. It has been held that concession to civil forfeiture does not bar prosecution in a related criminal proceeding.[110] Yet other cases turn on whether the forfeiture and criminal proceedings are a single, coordinated prosecution; several jurisdictions see no double jeopardy problem if the proceedings are coordinated and simultaneous or close in time.[111]

The Eighth Amendment prohibition of excessive fines applies in the forfeiture context, so the scope of the forfeiture must be proportionate to the seriousness of the offense. According to the Eleventh Circuit, seizure of a lot worth $65,000 was not disproportionate: the property, close to a junior high school, was used in cocaine trafficking, and the owner was found with marijuana, a gun, ammunition, and large amounts of cash.[112]

Proportionality was also at issue in *U.S. v. Wild*,[113] albeit in the context of an *in personam* criminal forfeiture (21 U.S.C. §853(a)(2)) rather than an *in rem* civil forfeiture; the test is whether the value of the allegedly forfeitable property exceeds the seriousness of the offense. In this analysis, *in rem* forfeitures are never excessive in the Constitutional sense (because the property itself is tainted). *In personam* forfeitures—monetary punishment of a culpable individual—is more likely to be constitutionally defective, but even this is described by the court as unlikely.

To the Eleventh Circuit, Due Process requires prior notice and hearing before posting a copy of an arrest warrant that states that the property is subject to federal civil forfeiture, even though law enforcement officers did not take physical control of the property. Although an arrest warrant can issue when a forfeiture complaint is filed, the Eleventh Circuit requires notice and hearing before execution of the warrant.[114]

The mere fact that a criminal defendant fled the country while criminal proceedings were pending did not justify the District Court in striking his pleadings in the civil forfeiture case or granting summary judgment to the prosecution. The Supreme Court found that there was no prejudice to the government in pursuing the forfeiture case in the normal fashion.[115]

A late-1995 Supreme Court ruling requires the court to make a determination (as required by Federal Rules of Criminal Procedure 11[f]) that there is a factual basis for a guilty plea. However, it is not necessary to inquire into the factual basis for a stipulated asset forfeiture that is a component of a plea agreement. The forfeiture is imposed after the guilty plea, and thus is not covered by Rule 11(f). Nor is it necessary for plea agreements to make a specific disclosure of F.R.Crim.P. 31's option of a jury determination of forfeitability. This option is an aspect of sentencing, and purely statutory in origin; it is not covered by the Constitutional right to a jury determination of guilt or innocence of the charges.[116]

According to the Southern District of New York, the Fourth Amendment exclusionary rule is applicable to civil forfeiture proceedings. The upshot was that the government could not retain cash improperly seized in a warrantless search. According to the Ninth Circuit,[117] 18 U.S.C. §984 [civil forfeiture of nontraceable funds found in a bank account used for money laundering] cannot be applied to seizures occurring before the statute's effective date.

Forfeiture problems also arise outside the drug context. It has been held that civil tax penalties are not "punishment" because they are designed to repay the government's cost of enforcement. Therefore, a person convicted of criminal tax offenses can also be charged civil fines.[118] A state statute can be used to evict a public housing tenant based on his or her conviction on drug charges.[119]

Similarly, the judgment in an SEC civil action ordering disgorgement of over $12 million is not punitive (and so cannot constitute double jeopardy) because it was proportionate to the actual damages and costs caused by the defendant, and because funds were returned to defrauded investors. Contempt penalties and a jail sentence for violating an asset freeze were not imposed for the "same offense" as the original securities violation, so there was no double jeopardy problem with those penalties either.[120]

As the title of this section suggests, the rights of third parties in forfeited property are a topic of continuing interest. An attorney who took the deed to real estate as his fee for representing accused cocaine traffickers, and who was aware of the potentially forfeitable acts occurring on the property, has been held by the Eleventh Circuit not to be an "innocent owner" who can block the forfeiture by asserting lack of consent to the criminal use of the property.[121] In this analysis, it is impossible to consent or fail to consent to crimes that have already occurred—the innocent owner defense is limited to those genuinely unaware of the transactions.

However, in the view of the Ninth Circuit, an innocent spouse's interest in community property cannot be seized as "substitute property" of the guilty spouse who has been convicted of a forfeitable offense. The innocent spouse's vested, undivided half interest in the community property is not forfeitable.[122]

Bringing a claim under 21 U.S.C. §853(n) [claim by a third party who has a legal interest in a forfeited property] counts as a "civil action" against the government, even though the actual forfeiture occurs in the course of a criminal proceeding. Therefore, in appropriate cases the prevailing plaintiff can receive an Equal Access to Justice Act attorney's fee award.[123]

[¶1908] TRIAL ISSUES

Although it is presumed (as a result of Riverside County v. McLaughlin, 500 U.S. 44 (Sup. Ct. 1991)) that the Fourth Amendment is violated by a delay of more than 48 hours between a warrantless arrest and a judicial determination of probable cause, evidence obtained during this period (including inculpatory statements) through mere harmless error can be admitted.[124]

The test of whether defendants are similarly situated (when a claim of selective prosecution is made) is whether or not there is a legitimate distinguishing factor that could justify different decisions made by the prosecutor in the various cases.[125]

It is clear that due process is violated if an incompetent defendant is tried. A state violates fundamental fairness if it presumes the defendant is competent unless he or she proves incompetence by clear and convincing evidence. (This is the Oklahoma standard; 46 other states merely require a preponderance of the evidence). In April 1996, the Supreme Court agreed that competence can be presumed[126] but a standard is invalid if it may result in trying persons who, more likely than not, are incompetent to stand trial.

Where a prosecutor knowingly uses perjured testimony, the error is presumed harmless, unless the defense proves (by a preponderance of evidence) that the error contributed to the defendant's conviction or punishment.[127]

The Fifth Circuit says that the defense must be permitted to cross-examine a prosecution witness about the witness' pending federal felony charges in another case.[128] But, in the view of the Maryland Court of Appeals, the confrontation clause is not violated by preventing the defense from raising a witness' criminal or probation charges in other cases: a judge does not abuse discretion by excluding this material on the grounds of limited probative value.[129]

The Supreme Court has held that there is no entitlement to a jury trial when multiple petty offenses are joined for trial—even if the defendant might potentially be sentenced to more than six months as a result of the charges.[130]

Because the Sixth Amendment guarantees the right to a public trial, a specific risk connected to the testimony must be demonstrated in order to close the courtroom while an undercover police officer is testifying.[131] In such a situation, the court is obligated to consider alternatives suggested by the defendant, but need not create its own alternatives sua sponte if closure is limited. (If closure is complete, the court might be obligated to initiate a mechanism.)[132]

[¶1908.1] Jury Selection

Casarez v. Texas[133] permits the use of a peremptory challenge to remove Pentecostal worshippers from a jury. The Texas court permitted religious-based peremptory challenges because religion involves beliefs and attitudes that might affect the hearing of a case. Furthermore, co-religionists (unlike persons of the same race or gender) do not necessarily have anything in common other than their religious beliefs, so excluding them as a group does not involve judgments about a group. (The opinion could have, but did not, stress the voluntary nature of choice of religious affiliation, as opposed to the involuntary nature of racial or gender identity.)

The Ninth Circuit case of *U.S. v. Annigoni*[134] deals with several significant jury issues. The case involved a real estate fraud; an Asian juror was challenged, either because of his race or because he was evasive about his involvement in litigation about the real estate limited partnerships he owned. The Ninth Circuit found that this uncertainty would not support a challenge for cause, but did make the peremptory challenge race-neutral. Thus, the District Court should have permitted the juror to be struck from the panel.

A mid-1997 Texas case does not permit the state to peremptorily challenge persons of the same sex and about the same age as the defendant on the grounds that they are at risk of "potential bias" because of this "common ground." The court deemed such challenges to constitute gender bias, reflecting stereotypes about young males.[135]

A judge can infer bias and dismiss a venireman for cause, if the potential juror has engaged in conduct similar to that the defendant is charged with. The judge is not obligated to question the venireman about his ability to apply the law impartially.[136]

In Virginia, improper denial of a defense peremptory must be analyzed under the harmless error standard, but the conviction is reversed unless the record plainly indicates that granting the peremptory challenge would not have altered the verdict.[137]

The Third Circuit did not deem a defendant in the Virgin Islands to have received ineffective assistance of counsel when his lawyer did not alert the court that a juror had been seen with a newspaper that contained an article derogatory to the defendant. The lawyer said that he did not mention this factor because he wanted to avoid a mistrial.

The jury, in a homicide case where the defendant was white and the victim (like the majority of the Virgin Islands populace) black, contained three white jurors and nine blacks. The lawyer didn't think he could get another jury with that many white jurors. The court ruled that this was a reasonable and legitimate strategic decision (although it didn't work; the case got to the Third Circuit when the defendant appealed his conviction). In this reading, defendants must be given the right to discuss strategy with their lawyers, but lawyers are not obligated to take strategic direction from their clients.[138]

It is Constitutionally permissible to deny a motion by an accused sexual abuser of children to be appointed as his own co-counsel. (The objective was to permit him to cross-examine the allegedly abused children personally.) According to the Fourth Circuit,[139] the state interest in preventing trauma to complaining witnesses outweighs the defendant's dignity interest in being able to control every facet of his defense.

[¶1908.2] Other Jury Issues

Under New Jersey law, prosecutors must present to the Grand Jury any clearly exculpatory evidence (such as an eyewitness' recantation) that directly negates the accused's guilt.[140]

If both sides consent to the jury instructions given by the court, and the instruction was proper at the time it was given but was later ruled unconstitutional, the standard of review is Federal Rules of Criminal Procedure 52(a) (harmlessness), and not 52(b) (plain error). [141]

[¶1909] EVIDENCE

In a capital case, the defendant's conviction was reversed and the Supreme Court remanded his case for a new trial[142] because *Brady* material was not supplied. In this reading, favorable evidence is material, and its suppression is a Constitutional issue, if there is a reasonable probability (not necessarily a preponderance of evidence) that the result of the case would have been different if the material had been disclosed. The prosecution's disclosure burden depends on the cumulative impact of all the material, not an item-by-item analysis of the impact of each.

Two cases from the summer of 1996 deal with evidence of the defendant's prior "bad acts." The D.C. Circuit finds evidence about elements of a crime that the defendant has unequivocally conceded is inadmissible. The only effect of such evidence is to imply that the defendant is an evil person, not to prove the actual allegations facing the defendant in this particular case.[143]

The Wisconsin Court of Appeals says that, wherever possible, the defendant's concessions about prior bad acts should be addressed in a pretrial hearing. The trial judge must then clarify what has been conceded, and the extent to which the bad acts evidence is needed to prove allegations that are not contested. The judge must then perform *voir dire* about the defendant's and lawyer's comprehension of the effect of concessions.[144] If a defendant admits convictions that the prosecutor wants to admit merely to prove elements of those convictions, the admission renders inadmissible both the convictions themselves and the priors elements from the jury's consideration.[145]

Several evidence questions from past years continued to occupy the courts. The decisions were generally favorable to polygraph tests. According to the Fifth Circuit, polygraph evidence cannot be considered presumptively inadmissible, both because of the shift in scientific standards from *Frye* to *Daubert*, and because polygraph technique has improved.

Similarly, the District of New Mexico permits admission of test results performed by a competent polygrapher (and submitted by the defendant, to show that he did not understate his income) because polygraphy has been researched enough to satisfy the *Daubert* test, and the District of Arizona permits the defendant to use the fact that he passed the polygraph test to rebut attacks on his credibility. On the other hand, the Sixth Circuit did not permit another defendant to introduce polygraph evidence without prior agreement as to its admissibility, because of the perceived danger of prejudice outweighing the probative effect.[146]

A Southern District of New York case from July 1995 adds some interesting components to the analysis: for admissibility, the manner of conducting polygraph testing must give the jury genuinely helpful evidence. Questions that merely test the defendant's belief in his own innocence are not sufficiently enlightening.[147]

1995 was a year in which the Supreme Court decided several cases on criminal evidence. Under *Arizona v. Evans*,[148] the exclusionary rule does not require suppression of evidence gained in the course of an arrest, where the arrest was due to an incorrect computer record caused by courthouse clerical errors. The test was who committed the errors: police officers or non-law-enforcement personnel?

F.R.Evidence 410 and F.R.Crim.Pro. 11 exclude statements made by the defendant in the course of plea negotiations that break down, and the rules have no explicit waiver provision. Nevertheless, *U.S. v. Mezzanatto*[149] permits such statements to be admitted if the defendant knowingly and voluntarily waived the protection of those rules. The prosecution cannot introduce statements made by a defendant while undergoing treatment as a sex offender as a condition of probation-even if the defendant does not claim Fifth Amendment immunity.[150]

F.R.Evidence 801(d)(1)(B) says that prior consistent statements are not hearsay if offered to rebut a charge of recent fabrication, improper evidence, or improper motive. Early in 1995, the Supreme Court held that the rule can only be used to introduce a witness' prior out-of-court statement made before the alleged impropriety arose.[151]

Another implication of out-of-court statements was explored by *N.Y. v. Geraci*.[152] Many people were present in a night club where a stabbing occurred; only one person claimed to have seen anything. This witness was later threatened and became uncooperative. The New York Court of Appeals permitted admission of his sworn Grand Jury statement, as an out-of-court statement, based on the prosecution's showing that this "practically unavailable" witness' nonappearance was caused by intimidation from the defendant.

Several recent cases deal with out-of-court statements in cases of alleged sexual abuse of children. The Ninth Circuit permitted admission of statements made by the child's mother to the child's doctor, relating to sex acts she had observed between the defendant and his stepson. The statements were admitted under F.R.Evidence 803, the hearsay exception for statements made during medical diagnosis and treatment. The California Court of Appeals affirmed the conviction of a father for lewd and lascivious conduct, based on accusatory out-of-court statements made by his children and repudiated at trial.[153]

Revived memories are often an important component of trials for sexual abuse of children. According to the Second Circuit, hypnotically produced testimony about buried memories of sexual trauma may or may not be admissible, depending on the circumstances—e.g., any corroboration of the revived memories; the reliability of the procedure; and the qualifications of the hypnotist. The Michigan Supreme Court denies the use of the discovery rule in cases of alleged revived memories; nor is the statute of limitations tolled for infancy in cases where adults allege recently revived memories of childhood sexual abuse.[154]

New Hampshire has devised[155] an eight-factor test for admissibility of testimony on recovered memories of sexual abuse. The plaintiff must show a reasonable likelihood that the recovered memories are as reliable as normal memory. The factors include publication and peer review of literature about recovered memory; acceptance of the phenomenon within the community of psychologists; the possibility of empirically testing reliability; the known or potential rate of false recovered memories; the complainant's age at the time of the alleged incident; the time gap between alleged incident and recovery of memory; any corroboration of the incident; circumstances under which memory was recovered. The court decided not to admit the evidence in the case at bar, deeming recovered memory insufficiently accepted by psychologists.

The Ninth Circuit has held that it does not violate the Fourth Amendment to require a convicted murderer or sex offender to submit a blood sample for the state's DNA database; the state's compelling interest in having this information (to close other cases) outweighs the minimal intrusion on the convicted person.[156]

Apropros of DNA, Oregon permits PCR-based DNA analysis, finding that it does satisfy the state's standard for accepted scientific evidence.[157]

Testimony about microscopic comparison of hair samples was found inadmissible in Indiana, because there was not enough evidence of the acceptance of the technique in the relevant scientific community; in fact, the "relevant scientific community" was not defined.[158]

The rape shield statute prevents introduction of testimony about a male complainant's sexual orientation, in a case alleging rape and assault and where a consensual "rough sex" defense is asserted.[159]

[¶1910] POST-TRIAL ISSUES

The seven-day deadline (measured from the date the jury was discharged) for seeking an order of acquittal despite a federal conviction is absolute. The

Supreme Court would not permit any extension, no matter how brief, and no matter who was responsible for the delay or why.[160]

At the end of 1997, the Supreme Court held that, when a Court of Appeals reviews a District Court's decision on a habeas corpus petition, the Court of Appeals does not have to raise, sua sponte, procedural errors made by the petitioner but not raised by the state.[161]

[¶1910.1] Sentencing Guidelines

On May 1, 1995, the United States Sentencing Commission submitted amendments to Guidelines 5 and 18 for Congressional approval. Approval was denied (P.L. 104-38), so the amendments did not take effect. Congress ordered the Commission to submit new guidelines, this time providing higher sentences for offenses involving crack than for powdered cocaine, and for major traffickers than for minor traffickers.

In mid-1996, the Supreme Court held that an appeals court should review departures from the sentencing guidelines for abuse of discretion; de novo review is not appropriate. Departures are appropriate if they are based, e.g., on victim misconduct, but not on factors that have already been taken into account in setting the guidelines. (The case at bar involved Los Angeles police officers convicted of violating the civil rights of arrestees; the factors were their inevitable loss of employment, and the ban on future law enforcement employment.) If the appeals court finds that the District Court departed from the guideline sentence based on both valid and invalid factors, the case must be remanded–unless the Circuit Court's view is that the sentence would have been the same even if the invalid factors had not been considered.[162]

Money laundering of the proceeds of a drug deal is close enough to conspiracy to engage in drug trafficking to group the two offenses together under §301.2 of the Sentencing Guidelines. They are victimless crimes, but the same social interests are involved, and they are part of the same scheme or plan, so grouping (i.e., a lower sentence) is appropriate.[163]

According to the Eastern District of New York,[164] F.R.Crim.Pro. 11(e) permits a court to accept the sentence evolved under a plea bargain, even if it is lower than the guideline sentence and even if no downward departure factors are present. However, the Fourth Circuit has ruled that an upward departure can be based on activities involved in underlying counts that were dismissed pursuant to a plea bargain.[165]

A defendant's abilities as a computer hacker constitute a "special skill" for which a sentence can be adjusted two levels upward based on the use of a special skill to facilitate a crime.[166] For a sentence to be enhanced due to an abuse of trust, there must be a significant nexus between the defendant's position and commission or concealment of the offense.[167]

"Vocational skills" are not supposed to lead to downward modifications of sentencing. However, if imprisoning the owner of a small business for tax fraud would result in innocent employees losing their jobs, this can be considered in reducing the business owner's sentence.[168]

If a person has to be re-sentenced, post-conviction rehabilitation in prison can be a valid factor in making a downward departure from the Guidelines sentence.[169]

[¶1910.2] Death Penalty

Given the seriousness of the issues, it is understandable that death penalty cases continue to occupy the attention of the Supreme Court. In 1996, it considered issues stemming from habeas corpus petitions.

According to the Supreme Court, habeas can be used to pursue a claim of actual innocence if it can be shown that an innocent defendant was convicted and a Constitutional violation "probably occurred." The habeas petition is not required to show by clear and convincing evidence that, but for the error, no reasonable juror could have convicted him or her.[170]

An April 1996 case involves a situation in which state habeas petitions were filed and dismissed. Almost six years later, shortly before the scheduled execution date, the petitioner filed another state habeas petition. When it, too, was denied, the petitioner filed his first federal petition on an eleventh hour basis. A somewhat exasperated Supreme Court decided that Federal Habeas Corpus Rules Rule 9 does not allow the dismissal of a first federal habeas petition merely because it was filed after an extensive delay; the state must show some prejudice from the delay. The District Court is obligated to issue a stay if it cannot dispose of the federal petition on its merits before the scheduled execution date.[171]

A mid-1997 Supreme Court case[172] deals with a 1984 death sentence (which became final in 1988), based on a determination of the defendant's future dangerousness. The penalty phase introduced evidence of many other crimes. The court refused to give a jury instruction that the defendant could not be paroled if he were sentenced to life imprisonment. The Supreme Court's *Simmons v. South Carolina* decision, 512 U.S. 154 (1994) entitled defendants to an instruction about life without parole if the prosecution argues future dangerousness. However, that 1994 case is a new rule which will not affect the conviction. Under *Teague v. Lane*, 489 U.S. 288 (Sup.Ct. 1989) a final state conviction can be disturbed only if, as of the date the conviction became final, the state court was unreasonable in not doing what the federal court eventually ordered. *Teague* did not compel application of *Simmons* to this conviction.

The Supreme Court's early 1998 decision, *Buchanan v. Angelone*[173] holds that, in the punishment phase of a capital case, the Eighth Amendment's ban on cruel and unusual punishment does not require a jury instruction on the statute's mitigating factors, or even the concept of mitigation in general. Therefore, the conviction did not have to be reversed, even though instructions were given on aggravating but not mitigating factors.

Congress as well as the Supreme Court have weighed in on the issue of habeas. One of the provisions of the Anti-Terrorism and Effective Death Penalty Act of 1996, P.L. 104-132 (AEDPA), enacted April 24, 1996, both limits the number of habeas appeals that can be used to appeal a conviction, and permits a federal court to overturn a state conviction if, and only if, an egregious mistake was made by the state court. The constitutionality of AEDPA Title I was upheld by the Supreme Court in mid-1996. The court found that, because original writs of habeas corpus can still be entertained, the Supreme Court is not deprived of jurisdiction by the AEDPA, and the new rules are not tantamount to a forbidden "suspension" of habeas.[174]

In the Fifth Circuit's reading, a state court decision on a mixed question of law and fact (here, voluntary intoxication at the time of the murder) supports federal habeas relief after the AEDPA if and only if the decision was so clearly incorrect that no reasonable jurist could accept it.[175]

AEDPA's one-year time limit for filing federal habeas petitions is a statute of limitations, not a restriction on the jurisdiction of the federal court. Therefore, to the Ninth Circuit, equitable tolling is possible, given extraordinary circumstances beyond the defendant's control preventing timely filing of the petition.[176] However, the same court has ruled that the time limit is not tolled during evaluation of the defendant's mental competency, because the defense attorney can file a habeas petition even if the client is unable to assist in his own defense.[177]

Discovery (e.g., of FBI files concerning the case) is not available to a death row prisoner before the filing of a habeas petition containing specific allegations.[178]

If a state's death penalty statute requires the judge to consider the advisory jury verdict on penalty level, the Eighth Amendment ban on cruel and unusual punishment does not specify how much weight the judge must give to the verdict.[179]

Cruel and unusual punishment analysis was applied by the Ninth Circuit to ban the use of the gas chamber: California executions must henceforth take place by lethal injection.[180] The Northern District of California ruled in early 1997 that the public and media have a First Amendment right to witness executions from just before the condemned person is strapped to the gurney, until the death sentence has been carried out.[181]

Commerce Clause analysis, discussed above in connection with carjacking and child support, was applied to capital punishment by the Eastern District of Pennsylvania in late 1995.[182] The court upheld 18 U.S.C. §848(e)(1)(A), capital punishment for murder in the furtherance of a continuing criminal enterprise. Under this analysis, Congress can regulate the unlawful interstate traffic in narcotics, provided that the capital sentence is imposed only if the murder furthers the continuing criminal enterprise—not merely if it was committed by a person who was involved in activities other than the underlying criminal enterprise.

Academic testimony about the general success of juries in predicting dangerousness is not relevant and cannot be admitted at the penalty phase of a capital trial. The evidence goes only to the validity of treating dangerousness as an aggravating factor, and this factor has already been upheld as valid.[183]

[¶1910.3] Related Sentencing Issues

The recent trend in sentencing has been more punitive—e.g., indefinite incarceration under appropriate circumstances; post-sentence sanctions such as civil commitment or community notification of the presence of a convicted sex offender.

Kansas allows civil commitment of individuals whose mental abnormality or personality disorder renders them likely to engage in predatory acts of sexual violence. A convicted child molester challenged the statute on substantive Due Process grounds, claiming that commitment requires a finding of "mental illness." The Supreme Court upheld the statute, treating the "mental abnormality" finding as adequate for Due Process purposes. As long as dangerousness is established, detention is proper for individuals who are unable to control their behavior. The commitment system was viewed as civil, not criminal, in nature, because it does not focus on either retribution or deterrence. The Supreme Court did not see double jeopardy issues to be present, because civil commitment is not a second prosecution. The statute was not ex post facto because the Supreme Court sees that as strictly a criminal law doctrine. The statute is not even retroactive in its application because it does not criminalize conduct occurring before its enactment, and it does not remove the defenses available to the accused.[184]

The Western District of Washington has invalidated Washington's Code §71.09 [indefinite post-sentence civil commitment of convicted sexually violent predators],[185] finding a violation of due process because commitment (and indefinite incarceration) can occur without a showing that the committed person is mentally ill.

New Jersey's "Megan's Law" (community notification) has been upheld by the state's Supreme Court, which found that it satisfies due process, does not invade the privacy of committed sex offenders, is not an ex post facto law or cruel and unusual punishment.[186] The District Court for the District of New Jersey ruled that the law could not be applied to individuals who were convicted and sentenced before the effective date of the law, but the Third Circuit reversed, finding that the notification provisions are not punitive in nature and therefore can be applied to an individual convicted before the passage of the statute.[187]

In contrast, the counterpart New York statute has been held to be punitive rather than regulatory in nature, and thus not applicable to offenses committed before enactment of the law.[188]

A federal Megan's Law was enacted in P.L. 104-145 (42 U.S.C. §14071(d), 5/17/96). Under the federal statute, it is permissible to disclose information collected under a state sex-offender registration program, "for any purpose permitted under the laws of the state." State and local law enforcement agencies not only may, but "shall" release any relevant information (except the victim's name) "necessary to protect the public."

Kansas' sex offender notification provision was held to violate the state Constitution's ban on cruel and unusual punishment, where the registrant is not in danger of re-offending, the ten-year notice period greatly exceeds the sentence, and the public is given very broad access to registration information.[189]

Because probation is supposed to be rehabilitative in nature, the Tennessee Supreme Court has found that probation cannot be conditioned on making the defendant put a sign outside his door saying that he's a convicted child molester.[190]

California's "three strikes" law, which significantly increases sentences and reduces prosecutorial and judicial discretion in cases involving repeat offenders has been upheld by the state's Court of Appeals.[191] The court rejected various arguments (that the law violates separation of powers; that it imposes cruel and unusual punishment in violation of the state Constitution), and noted that 75% of voters favored the law, so it does not shock the conscience of a civilized society.

Another California law has been upheld by the U.S. Supreme Court[192]—this time, one permitting parole hearings every two or three years rather than annually in certain circumstances. The circumstances are a conviction of multiple homicides; denial of the initial application by the parole board; and that it would be unreasonable to expect that parole would be granted at a later, annual hearing. Although the defendant committed his crime before the statute was passed, the Supreme Court did not find the law to operate ex post facto because it does not increase the punishment imposed for the crime, it only limits the possibility of mitigation of punishment via parole.

The Supreme Court returned to the subject of parole in early 1997. A "pre-parole" early release program was triggered by prison overcrowding. Because the program had no meaningful differences from ordinary parole, the same formalities are required to re-imprison a "pre-parolee" as to revoke a parole; a pre-parolee could not be summarily re-imprisoned because the governor denied his application for full parole.[193]

Issues that were actually litigated in a criminal case and are needed for the outcome of sentencing qualify for offensive collateral estoppel, and therefore cannot be raised again in a subsequent civil case.[194]

— **ENDNOTES** —

1. The text is reproduced at 63 LW 4379.

2. *U.S. v. Cuellar*, 96 F.3d 1169 (9th Cir. 9/17/96).

3. *Bailey v. U.S.*, #94-7448, 94-7492, 116 S.Ct. 501 (Sup.Ct. 12/6/95); below, 36 F.3d 106 (D.C.Cir. 1994).

4. *U.S. v. Gonzalez*, #95-1605, 65 LW 4157 (Sup. Ct. 3/3/97).

5. *Hubbard v. U.S.*, #94-172, 115 S.Ct. 1754, 131 L.Ed.2d 779 (Sup.Ct. 5/15/95). In another case involving false statements, the Supreme Court decided in early 1997 that the prosecution need not prove the materiality of the falsehood as an element of the 18 U.S.C. §1014 crime of making false statements to a federally insured bank: *U.S. v. Wells*, #95-1228, 65 LW 4146 (Sup.Ct. 2/26/97).

6. *Brogan v. U.S.*, #96-1579, 118 S.Ct. 805 (Sup.Ct. 1/26/98).

7. *Montana v. Egelhoff*, #95-566, 116 S.Ct. 2013 (Sup.Ct. 6/13/96). On November 4, 1996, *California v. Ray*, #95-2025, 65 LW 3338 was remanded for consideration of whether the erroneous jury instructions dealing with intent in a felony murder case represented "harmless error" or reversible error.

8. *U.S. v. Bishop*, 66 F.3d 569 (3rd Cir. 9/7/95). Also see P.L. 104-217, the Carjacking Corrections Act of 1996, amending 18 U.S.C. §2119(2) to clarify

that rape or other sexual assault constitutes "serious bodily injury" sufficient to enhance the penalty under the carjacking statute.

9. *U.S. v. Anderson,* 108 F.3d 478 (3rd Cir. 3/10/97).

10. *U.S. v. Hampshire,* 892 F.Supp. 1327, (D.Kan. 6/14/95), *aff'd* 95 F.3d 999, *cert. denied* 117 S.Ct. 753; *U.S. v. Sage,* 906 F.Supp. 84 (D.Conn. 10/3/95).

11. *U.S. v. Mussari,* 894 F.Supp.1360 (D.Ariz. 7/26/95), *rev'd* 95 F.3d 787 (9th Cir. 9/5/96).

12. *U.S. v. Czubinski,* 106 F.3d 1069 (1st Cir. 2/21/97).

13. *Utah v. Kent,* 65 LW 1223 (Utah App. 9/5/97).

14. *U.S. v. O'Hagan,* 92 F.3d 612 (8th Cir. 8/2/96).

15. *Smallwood v. Maryland,* 680 A.2d 512 (Md.App. 8/1/96). For federal law-making dealing with sexual offenses, see P.L. 104-305, the Drug-Induced Rape Prevention and Punishment Act of 1996, which enhances penalties for cases in which controlled substances were used to drug a victim, to facilitate the perpetrator's commission of rape or another violent crime.

16. *U.S. v. Robertson,* #94-251, 115 S.Ct. 1732, 131 L.Ed.2d 714 (Sup.Ct. 5/1/95).

17. *Matthews v. Kidder, Peabody & Co.,* 947 F.Supp. 180 (W.D. Pa. 9/26/96); *In re Prudential Securities Inc. Limited Partnership Litigation,* 930 F.Supp. 68 (S.D.N.Y. 6/10/96).

18. *In re American Honda Motor Co. Dealerships Relations Litigation,* 969 F.Supp. 716 (D.Md. 3/11/97).

19. *Fitzgerald v. Chrysler Corp.,* 116 F.3d 225 (7th Cir. 6/13/97).

20. *U.S. v. Maher,* 108 F.3d 1513 (2nd Cir. 3/25/97).

21. *Trest v. Cain,* #96-7901, 118 S.Ct. 478 (Sup.Ct. 12/9/97).

22. *Terry v. Potter,* 111 F.3d 454 (6th Cir. 4/15/97).

23. *New Mexico v. Breit,* 65 LW 2464 (N.M.Sup. 12/6/96).

24. *U.S. v. Shabani,* #93-981, 115 S.Ct. 382 (Sup.Ct. 11/1/94).

25. *Rutledge v. U.S.,* #94-8769, 116 S.Ct. 1241 (Sup.Ct. 3/27/96); below, 40 F.3d 879 (7th Cir. 1994).

26. *U.S. v. Knox,* 112 F.3d 802 (5th Cir. 5/1/97).

27. *California v. Souza,* 885 P.2d 982 (Cal.Sup. 12/28/94).

28. *Massachusetts v. Stoute,* 665 N.E.2d 93 (Mass.Sup.Jud.Ct. 5/30/96).

29. *Whren v. U.S.,* #95-5841, 116 S.Ct. 1769 (Sup.Ct. 6/10/96).

30. *Colorado v. Redinger,* 906 P.2d 81 (Colo.Sup. 10/30/95).

31. *Colorado v. Cascio,* 65 LW 2647 (Colo.Sup. 2/24/97).

32. *Pennsylvania v. Matos,* 64 LW 2585 (Pa.Sup. 2/26/96).

33. *Maryland v. Wilson,* #95-1268, 65 LW 4109 (Sup.Ct. 2/17/97).

34. *Washington v. Mendez,* 66 LW 1383 (Wash.App. 11/18/97).

35. *Illinois v. Ross,* 65 LW 2775 (Ill.App. 5/2/97).

36. *New York v. Carvey,* 65 LW 2775 (N.Y.App. 5/1/97).

37. *U.S. v. Holloman,* 65 LW 2831 (11th Cir. 5/22/97).

38. *Louisiana v. Kalie,* 699 So.2d 879 (La.Sup. 9/19/97).

39. *Whitehead v. Maryland,* 698 A.2d 115 (Md.Spec.App. 8/27/97).

40. *Ohio v. Robinette,* 66 LW 1399 (Oh.Sup. 11/12/97).

41. *U.S. v. Stanfield,* 109 F.3d 476 (4th Cir. 3/31/97).

42. *Oregon v. Hendricks,* 66 LW 1399 (Ore.App. 11/19/97).

43. *Illinois v. James,* 645 N.E.2d 195 (Ill.Sup. 12/22/94).

44. *Ornelas v. U.S.,* #95-5257, 116 S.Ct. 1657 (Sup.Ct. 5/28/96).

45. *U.S. v. Jones,* 914 F.Supp. 421 (D.Colo. 2/1/96).

46. *Womack v. U.S.,* 673 A.2d 603 (D.C.App. 3/14/96).

47. *Pennsylvania v. Hawkins,* 65 LW 2759 (Pa.Sup. 4/22/97).

48. 93 F.3d 140 (4th Cir. 8/22/96).

49. *New Hampshire v. Webber,* 65 LW 2748 (N.H.Sup. 5/6/97).

50. *Wilson v. Arkansas,* #94-5707, 115 S.Ct. 1914 (Sup.Ct. 5/22/95).

51. *Richards v. Wisconsin,* #96-5955, 65 LW 4283 (Sup.Ct. 4/28/97).

52. *U.S. v. Rohrig,* 98 F.3d 1506 (6th Cir. 10/31/96).

53. *Missouri v. Damask,* 64 LW 2595 (Mo.App. 2/6/96).

54. *Ohio v. Robinette,* #95-891, 117 S.Ct. 417 (Sup.Ct. 11/18/96).

55. *Washington v. Johnson,* 909 P.2d 293 (Wash.Sup. 1/18/96).

56. *Michigan v. Fernengel,* 549 N.W.2d 361 (Mich.App. 4/26/96).

57. *Washington v. Hindrickson,* 64 LW 2815 (Wash.Sup. 5/9/96).

58. *U.S. v. Castro,* 66 LW 1368 (5th Cir. 11/19/97).

59. *Hawaii v. Meyer,* 63 LW 2732 (Hawaii Sup. 4/11/95).

60. *U.S. v. Larsen,* 66 LW 1280 (10th Cir. 10/21/97).

61. Compare *Illinois v. Mitchell,* 63 LW 2695 (Ill.Sup. 4/20/95) with *Connecticut v. Trine,* 673 A.2d 1098 (Ct.App. 3/19/96); also see *Michigan v. Champion,* 549 N.W.2d 849 (Mich.Sup. 7/2/96); *In re D.D. v. Indiana,* 668 N.E.2d 1250 (Ind.App. 7/8/96). Is that a gun in your pocket, or are you just glad to see me?

62. *U.S. v. McDonald,* 100 F.3d 1320 (7th Cir. 11/21/96).

63. *Massachusetts v. Straw,* 665 N.E.2d 80 (Mass.Sup.Jud.Ct. 5/24/96).

64. *U.S. v. Baker*, 78 F.3d 135 (4th Cir. 3/13/96). Also see *Nebraska v. Williams*, 544 N.W.2d 350 (Neb.Sup. 3/8/96), ruling that a *Terry* stop justifies forcible opening of the suspect's clenched fist. The protective rationale here seems strained—it is likely that a crack vial would fit into a clenched fist, but unlikely that an offensive weapon would do so.

65. *Maryland v. Smith,* 65 LW 2743 (Md.App. 4/15/97).

66. *U.S. v. Cusumano*, 67 F.3d 1497 (10th Cir. 10/4/95). The Montana Supreme Court reached the same conclusion: *Montana v. Siegal,* 65 LW 2679 (Mont.Sup. 3/6/97).

67. *Colorado v. Schafer,* 66 LW 1223 (Colo.Sup. 9/15/97).

68. *U.S. v. Jerez,* 108 F.3d 684 (7th Cir. 2/27/97).

69. *Minnesota v. Carter,* 66 LW 1207 (Minn.Sup. 9/11/97).

70. *Washington v. Faford*, 910 P.2d 447 (Wash.Sup. 2/1/96).

71. *U.S. v. Reyes*, 922 F.Supp. 818 (S.D.N.Y. 1/3/96).

72. *U.S. v. Charbonneau,* 66 LW 1271 (S.D. Ohio 9/30/97).

73. *Davis v. Gracey,* 111 F.3d 1472 (10th Cir. 4/21/97).

74. *U.S. v. Abdul-Saboor*, 85 F.3d 664 (D.C.Cir. 6/7/96).

75. *Evans v. Maryland,* 65 LW 2567 (Md.Spec.App. 1/29/97).

76. *Johnson v. Oklahoma*, 905 P.2d 818 (Okla.Crim.App. 8/15/95).

77. *Colorado v. Sanders*, 904 P.2d 1311 (Colo.Sup. 11/6/95).

78. *U.S. v. Bryson,* 110 F.3d 575 (8th Cir. 4/7/97).

79. *U.S. v. Kow*, 58 F.3d 423 (9th Cir. 6/21/95).

80. *U.S. v. Foster*, 100 F.3d 846 (10th Cir. 11/15/96).

81. *U.S. v. Hudson*, 100 F.3d 1409 (9th Cir. 11/20/96).

82. 11 Cal.4th 354 (Cal.Sup. 10/12/95).

83. *Wisconsin v. Andrews*, 64 LW 2805 (Wis.Sup. 6/4/96).

84. *U.S. v. Dennis,* 115 F.3d 524 (7th Cir. 6/11/97); a similar result was reached in *Massachusetts v. Gauthier*, 65 LW 2798 (Mass. Sup. Jud.Ct. 5/16/97) for the event triggering probable cause.

85. *Hawaii v. Scott,* 65 LW 2799 (Hawaii Int.App. 4/30/97).

86. *Sullivant v. Oklahoma City*, 65 LW 2805 (Okla.Sup. 5/20/97).

87. *Grimes v. Comm'r*, 82 F.3d 286 (9th Cir. 4/17/96).

88. *Hawaii v. Bridges*, 925 P.2d 357 (Haw.Sup. 10/7/96).

89. *U.S. v. Ward,* 66 LW 1343 (3rd Cir. 11/13/97).

90. *U.S. v. Soliz,* 66 LW 1351 (9th Cir. 11/12/97). This builds on earlier cases dealing with the converse situation, allowing a suspect to refuse to discuss certain topics.

91. *Thompson v. Keohane*, #94-6615, 116 S.Ct. 457 (Sup.Ct. 11/29/95); 34 F.3d 1073 (9th Cir. 1994) vacated and remanded.

92. *California v. Stansbury*, 889 P.2d 588 (Cal.Sup. 3/9/95).

93. *California v. Smith*, 37 Cal.Rptr.2d 524 (Cal.App. 1/26/95). Also note that, although California allows a good-faith exception to the exclusionary rule, New Hampshire does not: see *New Hampshire v. Canelo*, 653 A.2d 1097 (N.H.Sup. 2/3/95).

94. *Midkiff v. Virginia*, 462 S.E.2d 112 (Va.Sup. 9/15/95).

95. *Utah v. Leyva*, 66 LW 1175 (Utah Sup. 8/19/97).

96. *Massachusetts v. Nom*, 66 LW 1383 (Mass.Sup.Jud.Ct. 11/18/97).

97. *Michigan v. Bender*, 551 N.W.2d 71 (Mich.Sup. 7/23/96).

98. *Colorado v. Pease*, 65 LW 2694 (Colo.Sup. 4/7/97).

99. *Trice v. U.S.*, 662 A.2d 891 (D.C.App. 7/24/95).

100. *Stewart v. U.S.*, 668 A.2d 857 (D.C.App. 12/21/95).

101. *U.S. v. Arnold*, 106 F.3d 37 (3rd Cir. 2/4/97).

102. *New York v. Burdo*, 66 LW 1310 (New York App. 10/30/97). Also see *New York v. Cohen*, also 66 LW 1310 and (N.Y.App. 10/30/97), voiding a confession made during non-custodial interrogation after the right to counsel had attached (and the attorney told the police not to question the suspect without an attorney present).

103. *U.S. v. Lynch*, 92 F.3d 62 (2nd Cir. 8/8/96).

104. *Sapp v. Florida*, 65 LW 2694 (Fla.Sup. 3/13/97).

105. *Massachusetts v. Burgess*, 66 LW 1390 (Mass.Sup.Jud.Ct. 12/8/97).

106. #94-8729, 116 S.Ct. 994 (Sup.Ct. 3/4/96).

107. See, e.g., *Louisiana v. Johnson*, 667 So.2d 510 (La.Sup. 1/16/96). *U.S. v. Salinas*, 65 F.3d 551 (6th Cir. 9/27/95) treats a civil *in rem* forfeiture of drug proceeds (as distinct from property used to facilitate the narcotics transaction) as remedial rather than punitive, thus permitting a prosecution for the offense.

108. *In re P.S.*, 661 N.E.2d 329 (Ill.Sup. 1/18/96); *U.S. v. Perez*, 70 F.3d 345 (5th Cir. 11/21/95).

109. *U.S. v. Ursery*, consolidated with *U.S. v. $405,089.23*, #95-345, -346, 116 U.S. 2135 (Sup.Ct. 6/24/96).

110. *U.S. v. Smith*, 874 F.Supp. 347 (N.D.Ala. 1/20/95). *U.S. v. Parcel of Land (Altman)*, 63 LW 2403 (D.Mass. 12/2/94) holds that 21 U.S.C. §881(i) requires the court to enter judgment of forfeiture whenever the defendant concedes forfeiture–the court cannot stay the forfeiture, even if the result is that prosecution is rendered impossible by double jeopardy considerations. Also see *U.S. v. Martin*, 38 F.3d 534 (11th Cir. 1994) permitting cumulative punishment for the same conduct under different federal statutes.

111. See, e.g., *U.S. v. Smith*, 75 F.3d 382 (8th Cir. 1/31/96); *U.S. v. One Residence*, 13 F.3d 1493 (11th Cir. 1994); *U.S. v. Millan*, 2 F.3d 17 (2d Cir. 1993).

Also see *U.S. v. Stanwood*, 872 F.Supp. 791 (D.Ore. 12/16/94): jeopardy attaches in a civil forfeiture case when the final judgment of forfeiture is entered, so an individual who pleads guilty to related criminal charges after seizure but before final judgment of forfeiture cannot raise a double jeopardy argument.

112. *U.S. v. One Parcel of Property*, 74 F.3d 1165 (11th Cir. 2/14/96). But see *U.S. v. Chandler*, 36 F.3d 358 (4th Cir. 1994), stating that proportionality is not a factor in determining whether an *in rem* forfeiture is excessive or not.

113. 47 F.3d 669 (4th Cir. 3/2/95).

114. *U.S. v. 408 Peyton Road,* 112 F.3d 1106 (11th Cir. 5/15/97).

115. *Degen v. U.S.*, #95-173, 116 S.Ct. 1777 (Sup.Ct. 6/10/96).

116. *U.S. v. Libretti*, #94-7427, 116 S.Ct. 356 (Sup.Ct. 11/7/95), affirming 38 F.3d 523 (10th Cir.1994). Also see *U.S. $19,047*, 95 F.3d 248.

117. *U.S. v. $814,254.76*, 51 F.3d 207 (9th Cir. 3/29/95).

118. *U.S. v. Alt*, 83 F.3d 779 (6th Cir. 5/15/96), *cert. denied* 117 S.Ct. 188.

119. *Taylor v. Cisneros*, 102 F.3d 1334 (3rd Cir. 12/6/96).

120. *U.S. v. Gartner*, Fed.Sec.L.Rep. ¶99,300 (9th Cir. 8/21/96).

121. *U.S. v. One Parcel of Real Estate*, 41 F.3d 1448 (11th Cir. 1/6/95). However, *U.S. v. One 1973 Rolls Royce*, 43 F.3d 794 (3d Cir. 1994) takes the opposite view.

122. *U.S. v. Lester*, 85 F.3d 1409 (9th Cir. 6/6/96).

123. *U.S. v. Douglas (Lussier)*, 55 F.3d 584 (11th Cir. 6/21/95); *U.S. v. Bachner*, 877 F.Supp. 625 (S.D. Fla. 1/20/95).

124. *Powell v. Nevada*, 65 LW 2477 (Nev.Sup. 1/3/97).

125. *U.S. v. Olvis*, 97 F.3d 739 (4th Cir. 10/11/96). Also see *U.S. v. Armstrong*, #95-157, 116 S.Ct. 1480 (Sup.Ct. 5/13/96): the defendant filed a motion for discovery or dismissal, alleging selective prosecution of blacks in cases involving crack cocaine. The Supreme Court required a threshold showing by the defendant that the government failed to prosecute crack offenders who were not black. In any case, Rule 16 discovery provides material to defend against the government case in chief, and not material needed to prove a pattern of selective prosecution.

126. *Cooper v. Oklahoma*, #95-5207, 116 S.Ct. 1373 (Sup.Ct. 4/16/96); below, 889 P.2d 293.

127. *Ex Parte Fierro*, 934 S.W.2d 370 (Tex.Crim.App. 9/11/96).

128. *U.S. v. Alexius*, 76 F.3d 642 (5th Cir. 2/15/96).

129. *Ebb v. Maryland*, 671 A.2d 974 (Md.App. 2/14/96).

130. *Lewis v. U.S.*, #95-6465, 116 S.Ct. 2163 (Sup.Ct. 6/24/96).

131. *Ayala v. Speckard*, 89 F.3d 91 (2nd Cir. 7/15/96).

132. *Ayala v. Speckard,* 131 F. 3d 62 (2nd Cir. 12/3/97).

133. 64 LW 2421 (Tex.Crim.App. 12/13/95).

134. 57 F.3d 739 (9th Cir. 6/8/95). Also see further proceedings at 96 F.3d 1132 (9th Cir. 9/23/96), finding that improper denial of a defense peremptory challenge is not a harmless error, so the conviction must be reversed.

135. *Fritz v. Texas,* 946 S.W.2d 844 (Tex.Crim.App. 6/11/97). *JEB v. Alabama,* 511 U.S. 127 (Sup.Ct. 1994) holds that sex-based peremptory challenges are a denial of Equal Protection.

136. *U.S. v. Torres,* 66 LW 1287 (2nd Cir. 10/9/97).

137. *Cudjoe v. Virginia,* 473 S.E.2d 821 (Va.App. 9/24/96).

138. *Virgin Islands v. Weatherwax,* 77 F.3d 1425 (3rd Cir. 3/13/96).

139. *Fields v. Murray,* 49 F.3d 1024 (4th Cir. 3/20/95).

140. *New Jersey v. Hogan,* 64 LW 2770 (N.J.Sup. 5/23/96).

141. *U.S. v. Keys,* 95 F.3d 874 (9th Cir. 9/11/96).

142. *Kyles v. Whitley,* #93-7927, 115 S.Ct. 1555 (Sup.Ct. 4/14/95); 5 F.3d 806 (5th Cir. 1993) reversed and remanded.

143. *U.S. v. Crowder,* 87 F.3d 1405 (D.C. Cir. 7/9/96). *Old Chief v. United States,* #95-6556, 117 S.Ct.644 (Sup.Ct. 1/7/97), a prosecution for use of a firearm in commission of a crime by a convicted felon, holds that once the defendant admits his status as a convicted felon, it is improper to introduce evidence of the prior convictions (because the effect would probably be to make the jury believe the defendant is a bad person with a propensity to commit other crimes).

144. *U.S. v. Wallerman,* 552 N.W.2d 128 (Wis.App. 6/26/96).

145. *Wisconsin v. Alexander,* 66 LW 1423 (Wis.Sup. 12/18/97).

146. *U.S. v. Posado,* 57 F.3d 428 (5th Cir. 6/20/95); *U.S. v. Galbreth,* 908 F.Supp. 877 (D.N.M. 10/4/95); *U.S. v. Crumby,* 895 F.Supp. 1354 (D.Ariz. 8/21/95); *U.S. v. Sherlin,* 67 F.3d 1208 (6th Cir. 10/18/95).

147. *U.S. v. Lech,* 895 F.Supp. 582 (S.D.N.Y. 7/26/95).

148. #93-1660, 115 S.Ct. 1185 (Sup.Ct. 3/1/95). Nevertheless, *Florida v. White,* 660 So.2d 664 (Fla.Sup. 7/13/95) finds evidence inadmissible if it was seized under a warrant that was invalid because of the police department's negligent failure to update its computer system to remove outdated information.

149. #93-1340, 115 S.Ct. 797, 130 L.Ed.2d 697 (Sup.Ct. 1/16/95), on remand 54 F.3d 613.

150. *Montana v. Fuller,* 64 LW 2680 (Mont.Sup. 4/16/96).

151. *Tome v. U.S.,* #93-6892, 115 S.Ct. 696 (Sup.Ct. 1/10/95), on remand 61 F.3d 1446.

152. 63 LW 2630 (N.Y.App. 3/28/95).

153. *U.S. v. Yazzie*, 59 F.3d 807 (9th Cir. 6/9/95); *California v. Carey*, 41 Cal.Rptr.2d 715 (Cal.App. 5/22/95).

154. *Borawick v. Shay*, 68 F.3d 597 (2nd Cir. 10/17/95); *Lemmerman v. Fealk*, 534 N.W.2d 695 (Mich.Sup. 7/5/95). Also see *S.V. v. R.V.*, 64 LW 2626 (Tex.Sup. 3/14/96), denying the discovery rule in a recovered-memory incest case, and *Rhode Island v. Quattrocchi*, 681 A.2d 879 (R.I.Sup. 7/31/96) requiring a pretrial hearing about the reliability and appropriateness of recovered-memory evidence of sexual abuse.

155. *New Hampshire v. Hungerford*, 697 A.2d 916 (N.H.Sup. 7/1/97).

156. *Rise v. Oregon*, 59 F.3d 1556 (9th Cir. 7/18/95).

157. *Oregon v. Lyons*, 924 P.2d 802 (Ore.Sup. 10/11/96).

158. *McGrew v. Indiana*, 673 N.E.2d 787 (Ind.App. 11/27/96).

159. *Colorado v. Murphy*, 919 P.2d 191 (Colo.Sup. 6/10/96).

160. *Carlisle v. U.S.*, #94-9247, 116 S.Ct. 1460 (Sup.Ct. 4/29/96).

161. *Hudson v. U.S.*, #96-976, 118 S.Ct. 488 (Sup.Ct. 12/10/97).

162. *Koon v. U.S.*, #94-1664, -8842, 116 S.Ct. 2035 (Sup.Ct. 6/13/96).

163. *U.S. v. Lopez*, 65 LW 2495 (9th Cir. 1/14/97).

164. *U.S. v. Aguilar*, 884 F.Supp. 88 (E.D.N.Y. 5/4/95).

165. *U.S. v. Barber*, 119 F.3d 276 (4th Cir. 7/14/97). Also see *U.S. v Baird*, 109 F.3d 856 (3rd Cir. 3/19/97), if the dismissed counts relate to similar conduct.

166. *U.S. v. Petersen*, 98 F.3d 502 (9th Cir. 10/22/96).

167. *U.S. v. Barakat*, 66 LW 1432 (11th Cir. 12/15/97).

168. *U.S. v. Olbres*, 99 F.3d 28 (1st Cir. 11/1/96).

169. *U.S. v. Core*, 66 LW 1223 (2nd Cir. 9/9/97).

170. *Schlup v. Delo*, #93-7901, 115 S.Ct. 851 (Sup.Ct. 1/23/95). Also see *Illinois v. Washington*, 64 LW 2699 (Ill.Sup. 4/18/96); state Constitutional requirements of substantive due process permit raising a claim of actual innocence as proved by newly discovered evidence, in an action for post-conviction relief.

171. *Lonchar v. Thomas*, #95-5015, 116 S.Ct. 1293 (Sup.Ct. 4/2/96); 58 F.3d 590 (11th Cir.1995) vacated and remanded.

172. *O'Dell v. Netherland*, #96-6867, 117 S.Ct. 1969 (Sup.Ct. 6/19/97). Also see *Lambrix v. Singletary*, #96-5658, 65 LW 4322 (Sup.Ct. 5/12/97 as to the procedure when a "new rule" can be applied retroactively when federal *habeas* relief is sought.

173. #96-8400, 118 S.Ct. 757 (Sup.Ct. 1/21/98).

174. *Felker v. Turpin*, #95-8836(A-890), 116 S.Ct. 2333 (Sup.Ct. 6/28/96). Also see *Lozada v. U.S.*, #96-2887 (2nd Cir. March 1997): appeal of denial of *habeas* relief because of AEDPA goes to the District Court, not the Circuit Court.

175. *Drinkard v. Johnson*, 97 F.3d 751 (5th Cir. 10/7/96).

176. *Calderon v. U.S. District Court for the Central District of California*, 98 F.3d 1102 (9th Cir. 10/22/96).

177. *Calderon v. U.S. District Court for the Central District of California*, 127 F.3d 782 (9th Cir. 9/18/97, [NOTE: These two cases have the same caption but different cites.]

178. *Calderon v. U.S. District Court*, 98 F.3d 1102 (9th Cir. 10/22/96).

179. *Harris v. Alabama*, #93-7659, 115 S.Ct. 1031 (Sup.Ct. 2/22/95).

180. *Fierro v. Gomez*, 77 F.3d 301 (9th Cir. 2/21/96).

181. *California First Amendment Society v. Calderon*, 956 F.Supp. 883 (N.D. Cal. 2/28/97).

182. *U.S. v. Tidwell*, 64 LW 2436 (E.D.Pa. 12/22/95). This statute is also upheld by *U.S. v. Beckford*, 966 F.Supp. 1415 (E.D. Va. 6/3/97), noting that *Beck v. Alabama*, 447 U.S. 625 (Sup.Ct. 1980) requires a "third option," not just a mandatory death sentence or acquittal. However, the court views §848 as acceptable because the verdict on the underlying criminal enterprise provides the required third option.

183. *Rachal v. Texas*, 917 S.W.2d 799 (Tex.App. 1/17/96).

184. *Kansas v. Hendricks*, #95-1649, -9074, 117 S.Ct. 2072 (Sup.Ct. 6/23/97).

185. *Young v. Weston*, 898 F.Supp. 744 (W.D.Wash. 8/25/95).

186. *Doe v. Poritz*, 662 A.2d 367 (N.J.Sup. 7/25/95).

187. *Artway v. New Jersey Attorney General*, 81 F.3d 1235 (3rd Cir. 4/12/96).

188. *Doe v. Pataki*, 919 F.Supp. 691 (S.D.N.Y. 3/21/96).

189. *Kansas v. Scott*, 66 LW 1368 (Kan.App. 11/7/97).

190. *Tennessee v. Burden*, 924 S.W.2d 82 (Tenn.Sup. 5/28/96).

191. *California v. Superior Court, San Diego County*, 37 Cal.Rptr.2d 364 (Cal.App. 1/13/95). See later proceedings, 53 Cal.Rptr.2d 789 (Cal.Sup. 6/20/96) for the proposition that, in a three-strikes case, the court, on its own motion, can strike prior felony conviction allegations in the interests of justice. The consent of the prosecution is not required.

192. *California Department of Corrections v. Morales*, #93-1462, 115 S.Ct. 1597 (Sup.Ct. 4/25/95); on remand 56 F.3d 46.

193. *Young v. Harper*, #95-1598, 65 LW 4197 (Sup.Ct. 3/18/97).

194. *SEC v. Monarch Funding Corp.*, 66 LW 1307 (S.D.N.Y. 10/28/97).

— FOR FURTHER REFERENCE —

Achtenberg, David, "Windfall Analysis: A New Look at Uncharged Conduct Evidence," 27 *Pacific L. J.* 1077 (Spring '96).

Androphy, Joel M., Richard G. Paxton and Keith A. Byers, "General Corporate Criminal Liability," 60 *Texas Bar J.* 121 (February '97).

Berra, Paul Silvio Jr., "Co-Conspirator Liability Under 18 U.S.C. §924(c): Is It Possible to Escape?" 1996 *Wisconsin L. Rev.* 603 (May–June '96).

Carr, Maureen M., "The Effect of Prior Criminal Conduct on the Admission to Practice Law," 66 *The Bar Examiner* 10 (February '97).

Christianson, Scott, "Corrections Law: Federal Death Penalty Protocol—Safeguard or Window Dressing?" 32 *Criminal Law Bulletin* 374 (July–August '96).

Crady, Ann, "Corporate Criminal Liability," 33 *American Criminal Law Rev.* 1053 (Spring '96).

Curriden, Mark, "A New Evidence Tool: First Use of Mitochondrial DNA Test in a U.S. Criminal Trial," 82 *A.B.A.J.* 18 (November '96).

Dietrich, James J., "Problems and Charging Choices in Prosecuting Vehicular Fatalities," 31 *Prosecutor* 32 (January-February '97).

Ellis, Alan and Peter J. Scherr, "Federal Felony Conviction, Collateral Civil Disabilities," 11 *Criminal Justice* 42 (Fall '96).

Fishfader, Vicki L. et.al., "Evidential and Extralegal Factors in Juror Decisions," 20 *Law and Human Behavior* 565 (October '96).

Frank, Jonny J. and Bart M. Schwartz, "Private Eyes: Using Investigators in Criminal Defense Matters," 11 *Criminal Justice* 20 (Fall '96).

Goldsmith, Michael and Chad W. King, "Policing Corporate Crime: The Dilemma of Internal Compliance Programs," 50 *Vanderbilt L.Rev.* 1 (January '97).

Harcourt, Bernard E., "Mature Adjudication: Interpretive Choice in Recent Death Penalty Cases," 9 *Harvard Human Rights J.* 255 (Spring '96).

Harden, Tracey A., "Rethinking Independence: The Lack of an Effective Remedy for Improper For-Cause Removals," 50 *Vanderbilt L.Rev.* 197 (January '97).

Heller, Gerald, "Raising the Joint Defense Privilege," 44 *The Federal Lawyer* 46 (January '97).

Johnston, J. Richard, "Paying the Witness: Why is it OK for the Prosecution, but not for the Defense?" 11 *Criminal Justice* 20 (Winter '97).

Jue, William, "The Continuing Financial Crimes Enterprise and Its Predicate Offenses: A Prosecutor's Two Bites at the Apple," 27 *Pacific L. J.* 1289 (Spring '96).

Kahan, Dan M., "What Do Alternative Sanctions Mean?" 63 *U. of Chicago L. Rev.* 591 (Spring '96).

Kassin, Saul M. and Holly Sukel, "Coerced Confessions and the Jury," 21 *Law and Human Behavior* 27 (February '97).

McMurry, Kelly, "'Three-Strikes' Law Proving More Show Than Go," 33 *Trial* 12 (January '97).

Peake, Jor Elizabeth, "Bound by the Sins of Another: Civil Forfeiture and the Lack of Constitutional Protection for Innocent Owners," 75 *North Carolina L.Rev.* 662 (January '97).

Remshak, Jonathan M., "Truth, Justice and the Media: An Analysis of the Public Criminal Trial," 6 *Seton Hall Constitutional Law J.* 1083 (Summer '96).

Riggsbee, Leslie Shea, "Balanced Blasting for Deadlocked Juries," 74 *North Carolina L. Rev.* 2036 (September '96).

Rudin, Joel B., "Megan's Law: Can It Stop Sexual Predators—And at What Cost to Constitutional Rights?" 11 *Criminal Justice* 2 (Fall '96).

Rueter, Thad, "Why Women Aren't Executed: Gender Bias and the Death Penalty," 23 *Human Rights* 10 (Fall '96).

Schudson, Charles B., "What Children Can't Tell Us and Why: Child Sexual Abuse, Hearsay, and the Rule of Completeness," 19 *Family Advocate* 56 (Summer '96).

Shoop, Julie Gannon, "Whodunit: Courts Ponder Guilt of Defendants with Multiple Personalities," 32 *Trial* 10 (June '96).

Spears, David, "Turning the Tables: Introduction of Similar Act Evidence by a Defendant," *N.Y.L.J.* 2/21/96 p. 1.

Whitney, Cheryl A., "Non-Stranger, Non-Consensual Sexual Assaults," 27 *Rutgers L. J.* 417 (Winter '96).

DRUNK DRIVING CASES

[¶2001] In 1996, the Pennsylvania Supreme Court invalidated the law making it a crime to have a BAC equal to or greater than .10 percent within three hours after driving. The court found this "per se" offense unconstitutional in that it is vague and overbroad, covers both lawful and unlawful conduct, and fails to provide individuals with a reasonable standard for judging their conduct.[1] However, as of early 1998, most of the states had per se limits, with a trend toward the stricter .08 standard replacing .10, and there was a move in Congress to deny federal highway funds to states maintaining a .10 rather than a .08 standard.[2]

A more complex situation was explored in *Wisconsin v. Alexander*[3] where a defendant who did indeed have two prior convictions for drunk driving was charged with violating a statute making it illegal for a person with two priors to drive with a BAC equal to or exceeding 0.08. The defendant admitted the two prior convictions, but the trial court allowed testimony about these convictions. The state Supreme Court ruled that this evidence should not have been admitted. *Old Chief v. United States*, #95–6556, 117 S.Ct. 644 (Sup.Ct. 1/7/97) says that evidence of prior convictions is inadmissable if the jury is likely to rely on it unfairly to show propensity to commit similar crimes.

The Ninth Circuit decided in mid-1995 that the Fourth Amendment does not require that an arrest be made before taking a blood sample without the consent of a person accused of driving while drunk. Certain limitations are imposed. There must be probable cause to suspect DUI; the police officer must have a reasonable belief that there is an emergency that threatens the destruction of evidence; and a reasonable procedure must be used to extract the blood.[4]

The Seventh and Eighth Circuits are in agreement:[5] it does not constitute a violation of the Americans with Disabilities Act to fire or demote an employee who has been arrested for drunk driving (i.e., has committed criminal misconduct). The employer would react the same way to the arrest of a nonalcoholic employee; and it is possible to have the disability of alcoholism without driving while intoxicated, so the employer is not guilty of discrimination.

BAC test results in a hospital record can be admitted in a civil suit under the medical records hearsay exception: neither the chain of custody nor the reliability of BAC testing has to be established.[6]

[¶2002] IMPLIED CONSENT LAWS

To no one's surprise, both Maryland and Hawaii courts ruled that suspending or revoking a license for failing or refusing to take a blood or breath test is not punitive in nature. Since it is not punitive, it cannot constitute double jeopardy. New York joined them in 1996.[7]

Although the administrative license suspension does not violate due process, the Ohio Supreme Court severed the portion of the state law forbidding any court to stay the license suspension pending appeal. The state Supreme Court also found it unconstitutional to impound the car of an innocent owner because of the drunk driving of a third party.[8]

[¶2003]   CHALLENGING THE POLICE CASE

Oregon has joined the states that accept Horizontal Gaze Nystagmus (HGN) testing for intoxication, finding it to be scientifically acceptable and not substantially more prejudicial than probative.[9]

[¶2004]   PLEAS AND ALTERNATIVES

The Second Circuit has decided that the First Amendment ban on establishment of religion is violated by forcing a convicted drunk driver to attend Alcoholics Anonymous meetings as a condition of probation. This is because the AA program requires the invocation of a Higher Power.[10] The county probation department has civil rights liability under 42 U.S.C. §1983. The probation department is not excused merely because the court accepted the probation department's demand, because judges conventionally do listen to probation departments.

New York's Court of Appeals said that the state's probation statute does not authorize a condition of probation that requires a recidivist drunk driver to put a "convicted DWI" sign on his license plate. Probation is supposed to be rehabilitative, not punitive in nature, so public obloquy is not an appropriate condition of probation.[11]

— ENDNOTES —

1. *Pennsylvania v. Barud,* 681 A.2d 162 (Pa.Sup. 7/30/96).

2. See Matthew L. Wald, "Drunken-Driving Standard May Shift," *New York Times* 1/30/98 p. Fl.

3. 571 N.W.2d 662 (Wis.Sup. 12/18/97).

4. *U.S. v. Chapel,* 55 F.3d 1416 (9th Cir. 5/26/95); on remand, 61 F.3d 913. Also see *Fink v. Ryan,* 673 N.E.2d 281 (Ill.Sup. 10/18/96); "special needs" exception to the Fourth Amendment permits blood testing of alcohol and drugs when an arrested driver was involved in a serious accident; chemical testing not deemed a major intrusion on the arrestee, whose movements are already under control.

5. *Maddox v. University of Tennessee,* 62 F.3d 843 (6th Cir. 8/21/95); *Despears v. Milwaukee County,* 63 F.3d 635 (7th Cir. 8/21/95).

6. *Judd v. Louisiana,* 663 So.2d 690 (La.Sup. 11/27/95).

7. *Maryland v. Jones,* 340 Maryland 235 (Md.App. 10/16/96); *Hawaii v. Toyomura,* 904 P.2d 893 (Haw.Sup. 10/11/95); *Matter of Smith, N.Y.L.J.* 11/6/96 p. 25 col. 3 (A.D.3rd Dept.) [license suspension does not constitute double jeopardy].

8. *Ohio v. Hochhausler,* 668 N.E.2d 457 (Ohio Sup. 7/30/96). But see ¶1907.1: the U.S. Supreme Court permits the forfeiture of an innocent wife's interest in the family automobile seized after the husband was arrested for patronizing a prostitute in the automobile.

9. *Oregon v. O'Key,* 899 P.2d 663 (Ore.Sup. 7/7/95).

10. *Warner v. Orange County Department of Probation,* 870 F.Supp. 69 (2nd Cir. 9/9/96); also see *O'Connor v. California,* 855 F.Supp. 303 (C.D. Cal. 1994): constitutionally acceptable to require attendance at either Alcoholics Anonymous or a sobriety program without spiritual content.

11. *New York v. Letterlough,* 86 N.Y.2d 259 (N.Y.App. 6/13/95).

— **FOR FURTHER REFERENCE** —

Hersh, Adam, "Tragedy Behind the Wheel: Understanding Manslaughter by Culpable Negligence, Vehicular Homicide, and DUI Manslaughter," 71 *Florida Bar* J. 46 (December '97).

Honeyman, Michael J. Jr., "Alcoholics Anonymous as a Condition of Drunk Driving Probation: When Does it Amount to Establishment of Religion?" 97 *Columbia L.Rev.* 437 (March '97).

Hugel, David H., "Taking a Closer Look at the Double Jeopardy DWI Defense," 35 *Judges Journal* 16 (Winter '96).

Jean, Joseph D., "Two for the Road: Administrative License Revocation and Multiple Punishments Under the Double Jeopardy Clause," 21 *Vermont L.Rev.* 1259 (Summer '97).

Meaney, Joseph R., "Horizontal Gaze Nystagmus: A Closer Look," 36 *Jurimetrics J.* 383 (Summer '96).

Meyer, Stuart, "Abandoning Judicial Principles in DWI Cases," 68 *New York State Bar J.* 46 (February '96).

Ostrowski, William J., "New York's Drunk Driving Labyrinth-The Maze Flourishes," 30 *Maryland Bar J.* 37 (March–April '97).

Ramsell, Donald J., "A Practical Guide to the DUI Summary Suspension Laws," 85 *Illinois Bar J.* 381 (August '97).

Taheri, Michael S., "Ten Tips for Winning(?) a Refusal Hearing," 69 *N.Y.S. Bar J.* 584 (July–August '97).

EMPLOYER-EMPLOYEE RELATIONS

[¶2101] During the supplement period, the percentage of unionized workers in the economy continued to decline, so it is understandable that discrimination cases reviewed for this supplement outnumbered traditional labor law cases. Within the topic of employment discrimination, the most active issues included sexual harassment and age discrimination. In 1997, one of the most significant issues was the extent to which employers can mandate arbitration of employment-related disputes.

[¶2102] PRIVACY AND DUE PROCESS ISSUES

There is no statutory or general fiduciary duty to disclose the names and addresses of other retirement plan participants on request of a participant.[1]

According to the NLRB, installation and use of security cameras in a unionized workplace is a mandatory bargaining subject, because it is obviously germane to the working environment, and employees detected in wrongdoing would be subject to discipline. The NLRB did not consider installation of the cameras to be a management prerogative "at the core of entrepreneurial control" because it did not affect the way the company did business.[2]

[¶2103] FEDERAL LABOR LAW

In November 1995, the Supreme Court found that a paid union organizer can nevertheless be a protected "employee" under the NLRA. Even under traditional agency principles, it is possible to be the "servant of two masters," and a rank-and-file employee who performs ordinary services for the employer in addition to receiving a union salary comes under the protection of the NLRA.[3] However, it is not an unfair labor practice for a company with a legitimate, non-discriminatory policy against hiring persons with another full-time job to refuse to hire a full-time union organizer.[4]

In April, 1996, the Supreme Court upheld the NLRB's determination that members of "live-haul" crews who transport and process poultry were employees (and thus covered by federal labor laws) rather than exempt agricultural employees.[5]

It violates the NLRA for an employer to implement a managed care program unilaterally, substituting for the existing comprehensive health plan.[6] Bargaining is required for the change because it goes beyond the employer's reserved right to amend or modify the plan. The managed care program is an entirely new delivery system that is not reasonably comprehended within the system already agreed to by the union.

An employee's claim that he was unlawfully discharged in retaliation for filing a Worker's Compensation claim is not removable to federal court, because the claim does not require interpretation of the collective bargaining agreement. Thus, state remedies are not preempted by LMRA §301.[7]

Nor does LMRA §301 preempt state law claims (e.g., fraud, breach of contract, intentional infliction of emotional distress) in a case where employees charge that the employer promised them job security but instead fired them after a union decertification vote. In the Third Circuit's reading, an independent promise of job security, not the collective bargaining agreement, was involved, and CBA interpretation was not required to assess the nature and effect of the employer's promise.[8]

In contrast, the Fifth Circuit has found §301 preemption of claims under state (Texas) law that the employee was not promoted because of his race and in retaliation for his protected labor activity. The Fifth Circuit found the federal system to be the correct locus for the action, because there was a CBA defining the rights of training, promotion, and seniority, and the employer could be expected to defend itself by citing the CBA.

In two recent LMRA §301 cases, employees seemed likely to prevail on claims that the LMRA prevents the employer from terminating retiree health benefits in violation of the CBA.[9] LMRA §301 is itself preempted by the 1987 ERISA amendments that make the employer liable to the PBGC for benefits that are unfunded when a plan terminates. Therefore, according to the Sixth Circuit, the employees and the union cannot bring an LMRA §301 action to recover those nonguaranteed pension benefits.[10]

However, the NLRA does preempt a state statute that makes a successor employer liable under any predecessor's CBA that contains a successor clause, nor does federal labor law require the new employer to hire unwanted employees of the former employer. In this reading, the new employer should not be forced to abide by a CBA it did not bargain for.[11]

On the subject of successor employers, the Seventh Circuit ruled that a food service company clearly intended to retain most of the predecessor's workers under the same terms and conditions of employment. Therefore, the successor had to consult with the incumbent union before cutting wages.[12] The Ninth Circuit agreed with the NLRB: predecessor employees who were not hired by the successor because of their union affiliation were entitled to reinstatement and back pay. The pay rate is the union scale, unless the successor can prove that recognition of, and bargaining with, the predecessor union would have resulted in a wage cut following bargaining to impasse.[13]

The NLRB has the power to order back pay for unfair labor practices committed against undocumented aliens (e.g., firing them for supporting a union organization drive), during the time they worked illegally in the United States.[14] Yet the Second Circuit allowed deportation of an alien union organizer, based on a tip from an anti-union employer. This time, the theory was that companies are not supposed to employ illegal aliens, even if the company has an anti-union animus.[15]

An emergency interim modification of a collective bargaining agreement, under Bankruptcy Code §113(c), does not constitute a rejection of the agreement as defined by Bankruptcy Code §365(g).[16]

Federal labor law preempts a state statute that forbids employment agencies to recruit or refer professional strikebreakers, because management is entitled to have access to a pool of willing workers.[17]

ERISA does not preempt a state law that requires public works contractors to pay the prevailing wages (including prevailing benefits) for the area.[18]

The Supreme Court upheld the Department of Labor's interpretation of the Fair Labor Standards Act (FLSA) as reasonable and entitled to deference: a police department policy that calls for disciplinary reductions in pay (no matter how rarely the policy is invoked) has the effect of turning police officers into non-exempt employees entitled to overtime. The FLSA provides that a worker whose pay can be reduced based on the quality or quantity of work performed is a non-exempt employee.[19]

An employee can bring a Fair Labor Standards Act case in federal court without first arbitrating the wage claim under the CBA.[20] Apropos of arbitration, the Third Circuit upheld an arbitrator who read a CBA provision for discharge "for proper cause" to imply a system of progressive discipline. Therefore, the arbitrator was justified in suspending a driver who caused a rear-end collision rather than firing him immediately.[21] The Sixth Circuit read Federal Arbitration Act §1, excluding contracts of "seamen, railroad employees, or any other class of workers engaged in foreign or interstate commerce" very narrowly, to mean only workers who actively transport goods between states, not all workers whose jobs affect interstate commerce.[22]

The Supreme Court decision in *First Options of Chicago v. Kaplan,* 63 LW 4459 (Sup.Ct. 1995)—that the court must decide the arbitrability of any issue as to which the agreement is silent—does not apply to arbitration of collective bargaining agreements, only to commercial contracts.[23]

In the view of the D.C. Circuit, the arbitrator's authority is limited to what actual parties asked the arbitrator to decide, not the broader interests of the entire bargaining unit. Thus, the arbitrator should have concentrated on the position of employees who brought the grievance, and should not have ordered reinstatement of terminated positions that were no longer wanted by ex-employees.[24]

Both the LMRA and the duty of fair representation are violated when a union hiring hall refers only applicants who are known to the union officials. Referrals must be based on consistent, objective standards.[25] Apropos of hiring halls, a New York State competitive bidding statute can be harmonized with contracts that demand that public contract bidders hire through union hiring halls, follow union rules, and pay into union benefit funds—as long as those contract provisions serve to advance state interests such as efficient and economical completion of projects.[26]

The Ninth Circuit, like the Fourth and Seventh Circuits (but contrary to the D.C.Circuit) holds that the NLRB has the power to issue an investigative subpoena to a third party, such as a newspaper in which an allegedly discriminatory help-wanted ad was placed.[27]

[¶2103.1]   Unfair Labor Practices

To the D.C. Circuit, permanent subcontracting of some bargaining union work during a lockout is not an unfair labor practice without proof of anti-union motivation. Because subcontracting is a mandatory bargaining subject, the employer can act unilaterally after impasse. Furthermore, in this case there was deemed to be too little effect on employee rights for the subcontracting to be "inherently destructive."[28] Similarly, to the Third Circuit, a decision to subcontract certain work was not a term or condition of employment requiring bargaining, because the employer's motivation was to enhance profits and avoid losing sales, not to avoid paying overtime (which would have been an improper objective).[29]

The Sixth Circuit deferred to the NLRB's characterization of a plant council as company-dominated and therefore contrary to the NLRA. The employer created the first council, at about the time of a union organizing drive, to deal with work policy. The council attracted little interest and was discontinued after a year. After the election was held (and the union lost), the council was revived. The NLRB's interpretation, adopted by the court, was that the council dealt with conditions of work; ran on company premises; derived all of its support from the employer; and was created by and could be disbanded by the employer. Thus, it was impermissibly employer-dominated.[30]

NLRA §10(c) does not give the NLRB the authority to order an employer to pay the litigation costs of the union (or the NLRB general counsel) in an unfair labor practices proceeding. The D.C. Circuit held that shifting the fee burden requires clear statutory support, which is not present in this situation.[31]

[¶2103.2]   Union Security/Compulsory Unionism

Individuals who are subject to an agency shop requirement, and who pay representation fees but are not union members, are not parties to the Collective Bargaining Agreement. Therefore, if they wish to dispute the amount of the representation fee, they can sue the union and are not obligated to exhaust the CBA's administrative remedies, because they never agreed to arbitrate under the CBA.[32]

A CBA that required employees to remain union members "in good standing," but does not define that term, is invalid because it implies that full membership is necessary. To the Sixth Circuit, a worker covered by a union security clause has the option of paying only core dues, and not paying any part of the dues allocable to activities that are not related to collective bargaining.[33]

[¶2103.3]   Controls on Strikes

On March 8, 1995, President Clinton issued an executive branch procurement policy forbidding procurement from companies that hire permanent replacements for lawfully striking workers. However, the D.C. Circuit has ruled that the executive order is preempted by the NLRA's permission to replace economic strikers under certain conditions. Furthermore, despite the lower-court ruling that judicial review was inappropriate, the D.C. Circuit viewed judicial review as appropriate in all cases alleging executive branch violation of a statute.[34]

Although the facts of the case are somewhat exotic, a mid-1996 Supreme Court case may nevertheless offer some insights into more everyday labor situations. After negotiations reach an impasse, the Supreme Court says that employers can lawfully group together to implement their last good-faith wage offer. In this case, paying substitute players on NFL teams ("developmental squads") a uniform

$1,000 per week, instead of letting each squad member negotiate individually, does not violate Sherman Act §1.[35]

The D.C. Circuit held that an employer acted reasonably by reinstating strikers but restricting them to well-supervised, nonsensitive positions that limited their movements within the plant. Special factors were present: the reinstated strikers were union activists who returned to work after the union had been decertified with the specific objective of advocating a "union" vote in the rerun election. After the rerun election (which the union lost), the reinstated strikers quit their jobs and went back on strike. The employer was held to have substantial, legitimate business justification for the limitations on the returned workers (and thus did not discriminate against them). There had already been strike-related violence and vandalism; sabotage and product tampering were deemed to be real threats.[36]

The Eighth Circuit has ruled that unfair labor practices occurring during an economic strike are not sufficient to convert the strike into an unfair labor practices strike, except in the limited situation in which the unlawful conduct serves to prolong the strike.[37]

It is an unfair labor practice to lie to workers and tell them that they will be permanently replaced if they go out on strike. However, it is not improper to deliver a truthful warning about replacements who have already been hired.[38]

The past pattern of communications between employer and union determines whether it is reasonable to infer effective communication, and hence whether strikers who fax an unconditional offer to return are entitled to reinstatement.[39]

[¶2103.4] The WARN Act

The Worker Adjustment Retraining and Notice Act (WARN Act, 29 U.S.C. 2101) mandates that employers who have 100 or more full-time employees (or 100 full-timers and part-timers working an aggregate of 4,000 or more hours per week) must give 60 days' notice to workers, unions, and the government before implementing a mass layoff or a plant closing. A plant closing causes employment loss (termination, prolonged layoff, or severe reduction in hours) to 50 or more workers within a 30-day period. A mass layoff is a lesser action involving one-third or more of the work force, or 500 people.[40]

Separate but related facilities can be treated as a single site if they meet all of the three criteria set by the Department of Labor: shared staff and equipment; geographic proximity; and shared purpose, but the workforces cannot be aggregated to determine if 50 workers are affected unless all three tests are met.[41]

The employer's failure to give the proper notice entitles affected employees to receive up to 60 days' back pay and benefits. The employer can also be liable to the federal government for a civil penalty of up to $500 per day for failure to notify. However, the Northern District of Texas has ruled that a company was not obligated to give the notice until it was sure that a major defense contract would be canceled. The cancellation was a business circumstance that was not reasonably foreseeable 60 days before the resulting layoff.[42]

In mid-1996, the Supreme Court upheld the WARN Act's authorization of unions to sue for damages on behalf of union members. The Court found that Congress was within its powers when it gave associations the right to seek relief that normally belongs to association members.[43]

Back pay for a WARN Act violation is calculated based on 60 work days, not calendar days.[44] Various courts have disagreed about the proper statute of limitations for failure to give the mandatory notice; recently, the Eighth Circuit fixed the statute of limitations at five years. This was based on the state statute of limitations for an action on an express or implied contract, rather than state wage and hour or equal pay laws, or on federal Fair Labor Standards Act limitations periods.[45]

In another WARN Act decision, the Eighth Circuit ruled that a secured lender who had some control over the borrower's business, but was not responsible for day-to-day management (or the decision to close the plant), could not be treated as an "employer" obligated to give WARN Act notice.[46]

[¶2104] THE CERTIFICATION PROCESS

In mid-1996, the Supreme Court upheld the NLRB: it is an unfair labor practice for an employer to enter into a contract, then disavow the contract, claiming doubt as to the true majority status of the union. An employer can legitimately use this argument if its doubts are raised after the contract, but not based on information already in its possession at the time of the contract.[47]

An early 1998 Supreme Court decision upholds the NLRB's standard for when an employer can poll employees about their continued support for the union: good-faith reasonable doubt as to continued employee support. This is also the standard used for the employer's unilateral withdrawal of recognition and application for NLRB supervision of an election.[48]

A union that claims that the employer used fraud to get the union's agreement to a CBA can bring a federal court suit under NLRA §301(a). NLRB proceedings are not required. The NLRB has exclusive jurisdiction over claims of bad-faith bargaining, but not over those of fraudulent inducement.[49]

Even though a corporate division was closed eight days before a scheduled representation election that the union would probably have won, the D.C. Circuit reversed the NLRB's finding of anti-union animus, because there was evidence that the division had undergone unstoppable financial decline.[50]

A manufacturer decided to move to a smaller, more automated plant, with the result that many workers were laid off. The Fifth Circuit decided in late 1996 that laid-off workers are not entitled to vote in the election as to whether the union from the old plant will represent the workers at the new plant, given that the laid-off workers had no reasonable expectation of recall.[51]

If the employer relies on an invalid, non-NLRB election to make workplace changes, the Ninth Circuit says that the appropriate remedy is to hold a new election. The NLRB was wrong to enter a bargaining order, because there was no proof that a fair election would have been impossible.[52]

[¶2104.3] Electioneering

The NLRB did not exceed its discretion by holding a representation election by mail, rather than at the employer's various offices—particularly in light of the dispersion of employees during the workday and the inconvenience to the employees if they had been forced to go to the office to vote.[53]

There is no NLRA violation in forbidding union representatives to enter the employer's property in order to distribute handbills telling potential condominium buyers that the employer used underpaid non-union labor. The employer's property rights clearly prevail over the union right of free speech—particularly since union organizing was not involved.[54] Nor is the NLRA violated if the employer refuses to let employees post union materials on the bulletin board used for personal notices—"The employer doesn't have to promote unions by giving them special access to bulletin boards."[55]

The Fourth Circuit found that it was not a violation for the employer to distribute a pre-election flyer containing a mock pink slip predicting closings of unionized stores. This was not deemed to be a threat, and the dispute was concentrated in a single store and was not severe enough to support the bargaining order imposed by the NLRB.[56]

It is a permitted concerted activity for grocery store employees to wear pro-union pins on the sales floor unless the employer can prove that safety, discipline, productivity, or the employer's public image are impaired. The Sixth Circuit deems the right to wear union insignia to be "near absolute."[57]

Where negotiations have reached an impasse, and the employer unilaterally imposes a job flexibility program, employees cannot be forbidden to wear pro-union buttons, T-shirts, or other communications materials. However annoying to management, these displays did not hold the company up to public derogation, and therefore must be permitted.[58]

It is permissible for an employer to forbid union handbilling that asks passers-by to avoid patronizing a non-union establishment, while allowing charitable handbilling that benefits the business by improving its image.[59] It is not discrimination against protected union activity to forbid all non-charitable solicitations, from the union or otherwise.

A union member-plaintiff who wins monetary damages in a case involving union democracy has conferred a "common benefit," justifying an award of attorney's fees. It is not necessary for equitable relief to be ordered, as long as the damages can be expected to have a salutory effect on union governance by rendering union leaders less likely to suppress dissent among the rank-and-file.[60]

[¶2105] PROTECTION OF EMPLOYEES AGAINST DISCRIMINATION

The EEOC has entered into a contract with the Fair Employment Council of Greater Washington and the Legal Assistance Foundation of Chicago for a pilot project on the use of testers to assess employment discrimination, especially in entry-level jobs.[61]

Given the prevalence of temporary employment, the EEOC has issued guidance making employment agencies and employers both generally liable for civil rights violations occurring in the placement of contingent workers. If both entities have control, they are considered joint employers. An employment agency that finds that a company has discriminated against a temporary worker must take immediate and appropriate action, such as refusing to provide other workers until discrimination is ended.[62]

During the supplement period, there were several important Supreme Court cases that dealt with employee discrimination.[63] According to the Fifth Circuit, in order to infer discrimination from a plaintiff's prima facie case and rebuttal of the employer's defense, the trier of fact must decide that there is a conflict in substantial evidence that creates a jury question.[64]

The Third Circuit's reading of the post-*Hicks* burden on the plaintiff, where the defendant submits a defense of nondiscrimination and moves for summary judgment, is to supply a preponderance of the evidence. There are four factors for the court to apply to see if a reasonable finder of fact could agree that the plaintiff submitted the preponderance of the evidence:

➤ Inference of discrimination from the prima facie case

➤ Can discrimination justifiably be inferred from the rejection of the defense's proffered reason?

➤ Strength of the inference that the defense tried to conceal discrimination

➤ Other available evidence.[65]

In a mixed motive case, where the employer company defends itself by claiming a legitimate reason for discharging the plaintiff, the Second Circuit requires the employer to prove not only that it would have fired the employee based on the legitimate reason, but that it would have fired him or her at the actual time of the discharge, not later.[66]

The high court ruled that "after-acquired evidence" (evidence discovered by the employer only after a discharged employee has charged the company with discrimination) does not absolutely bar remedies for the employee.[67] However, if the evidence is sufficiently damning, it means that the employer need not reinstate the employee or provide front pay in lieu of reinstatement. Duration of the back pay period might also be limited.

The Northern District of Iowa reads this to mean that post-discharge misconduct, as opposed to pre-discharge misconduct discovered after the discharge, is irrelevant and prejudicial, and therefore not admissible in the case.[68] The Ninth Circuit says that an employer wishing to use after-acquired evidence to reduce the relief available to the plaintiff must prove, by a preponderance of the evidence, that the employee's misconduct would have caused his or her discharge if the employer had learned about it in time.[69]

According to the Fifth Circuit, Congress designed the EEOC enforcement scheme in separate stages of filing, investigation, conciliation, and enforcement. When private plaintiffs begin a suit, the EEOC investigation is no longer timely, and thus the agency's subpoenas can no longer be enforced.[70]

Affirmative action has not fared well in the courts. A late-1996 District Court case for instance, finds that a state university's affirmative action plan to hire more minority faculty (in order to balance a veterans' preference that advantages white males) violates Title VII, because there was no past discrimination or racial imbalance to redress.[71] In August, 1997, the Department of Labor revised its regulations about retention of records that prove affirmative action compliance by federal contractors. Some large contractors' date to file the EEO-1 form (a breakdown of workforce by job category) is extended from March 31 of each year to September 30, to conform with other EEOC deadlines. The Office of Federal Contract Compliance added new intermediate levels of compliance review, replacing the former possibilities of full-scale review or no review at all. Records must be retained for either one year or two years, depending on the size of the firm and its federal contracts.[72]

A number of cases involving several statutes assessed the potential liability of individual supervisors and employees. The Northern District of Illinois did permit individual liability of supervisors or managers under the Family and Medical Leave Act, finding that the FMLA resembles the Fair Labor Standards Act in contemplating that an individual will deal with multiple "employers," all of whom are potentially liable.[73] However, by and large the result has been that individuals are not considered to be "employers" with a potential Title VII or Americans with Disabilities Act liability.[74]

[¶2105.1]   Title VII

The determination of whether or not a company has 15 employees (and thus is large enough to be subject to Title VII) is made based on the number of persons who are on the payroll because of an employment relationship with the company—not the number of persons receiving compensation on a given work day.[75]

The *prima facie* for a Pregnancy Discrimination Act case is that a nonpregnant employee, similar to the pregnant plaintiff in ability or inability to work, was favored over the pregnant plaintiff.[76]

It's a fact question—in other words, within the ambit of the jury—to determine whether a female manager's job remained open after her maternity leave, or whether the job was eliminated in a reorganization.[77] The Pregnancy Discrimination Act amendment to Title VII makes it unlawful to fire a female employee for either considering or actually having an abortion, because all forms of discrimination based on reproductive capacity are unlawful unless reproductive capacity is somehow relevant to job functions.[78]

In its February 17, 1997 decision in *Robinson v. Shell Oil*, #95-1376, the U.S. Supreme Court held that giving a negative reference to an ex-employee who pressed a claim of racial discrimination could constitute unlawful retaliation. In other words, Title VII §704(a) applies to former as well as active employees.[79] However, for Title VII retaliation to occur, there must be an "ultimate employment decision," not merely a hostile atmosphere or reprimands.[80]

Several important retaliation cases were decided in 1997–1998. The Ninth Circuit decided[81] that a retaliation cause of action can be sustained even if the negative reference given for retaliatory motives was not the reason why the retaliation victim was not hired for the job he or she applied for. In other words, proof of injury is not required in the retaliation case.

Title VII forbids retaliation against an employee who testifies or participates in a Title VII proceeding. The Eleventh Circuit applied this to include an accused sexual harasser who testified at proceedings brought by the person charging sexual harassment—even though the accused harasser testified involuntarily and did not intend to help the harassment claimant.[82]

Attorney-client privilege does not prevent an attorney who once worked for a company as in-house counsel from bringing a Title VII retaliation claim against the company. However, in appropriate cases, the court hearing the claim can protect confidentiality by devices such as sealing orders, protective orders, or even in camera proceedings.[83]

The Fourth Circuit did not permit white male police officers to premise hostile environment and retaliation claims on supervisors' derogatory statements about black and female officers, even if the white officers claim that their work was harmed by the hostile atmosphere.[84]

The *prima facie* for a Title VII racial discrimination case does not require proof that a discharged employee was replaced by someone of a different race—only that racial factors were involved in the discharge.[85]

In late 1995, the Sixth Circuit decided a case involving a class of black employees. The employer entered into a five-year consent decree. One of the employer's several plants was sold. The employees were unsuccessful in having successor liability imposed on the purchaser. Although the decree refers to liability of parties, their agents, and successors, it also allows plant closings. The court accepted the employer's argument that selling the plant to another company is the equivalent of a plant closing.[86]

An alien plaintiff is not required to prove legal work status as part of the Title VII *prima facie*, but the employer can cite the lack of a green card as a valid, nondiscriminatory reason for adverse employment action.[87]

Although some courts do not permit discovery of self-critical analyses performed by federal contractors to assess their equal employment opportunity performance (on the theory that candor should be encouraged), California does permit some discovery for Title VII plaintiffs. The only material that is privileged is that explicitly listed in California's discovery statute: trade secrets, attorney-client privilege, and work product. The self-critical analysis fits into none of these categories, and is written to be divulged to a federal agency. Therefore, the California Court of Appeals finds it to be discoverable.[88]

In mid-1995, the Third Circuit refused to allow four ex-employees who did not file timely EEOC charges to join a suit by five plaintiffs, alleging similar conduct, who did file the timely charges.[89] That Circuit also said that as long as one act within the 300-day period before filing of the charge can be alleged, earlier conduct can be proved to demonstrate a long-standing, persistent, ongoing pattern creating a hostile work environment.[90]

According to the Eleventh Circuit, a race discrimination case should not have been dismissed, even though it was filed prior to the 180-day period, and prior to receipt of a right-to-sue notice. In this reading, the employees were entitled to assume that the EEOC would not be able to complete a timely investigation—even though the EEOC did not certify such inability.[91]

Dismissal of a Title VII action because the charge was untimely is not an adjudication on the merits that would bar an action on an earlier charge that was timely filed.[92]

As noted above, sexual harassment is one of the most active litigation areas within Title VII. (See the Eleventh Edition for developments after the supplement periuod.) One of the most contentious areas is whether or not sexual harassment of one male by another male, or one female by another female, is cognizable.[93] After the supplement period, the Supreme Court established the principle that a male employee can bring a hostile-environment case based on the behavior of other males.[94] Earlier, some cases found that sexually tinged horseplay or innuendo, directed by males against males, is not made "on account of sex" and therefore cannot be treated as sexual harassment,[95] but other cases involving hostile and humiliating, sexually-tinged treatment have deemed the conduct to constitute harassment.[96]

Inaction by the employer is considered ratification of the harasser's conduct, so the employer is still liable for failing to remedy harassment that it incorrectly thought had ended. The employer must take prompt, effective action to end harassment if it wishes to escape liability.[97]

For an example of effective employer action, see *Gary v. Long*,[98] where the employer established, enforced, and advertised effective anti-discrimination measures. In this case, a supervisor raped an employee; but this was clearly outside the scope of his employment, and the employee victim was reassigned following her complaint even though the employer did not find corroborating evidence of the charge.

An issue that attracted significant attention in 1996 was the duration and extent required for offensive conduct to rise to the level of a hostile work environment. Some recent cases find that a single, isolated instance of sexually explicit epithets, or offensive vocal comments over a period of hours, without physical contact or threat, are not sufficient to create a cognizable hostile environment.[99] However, a single very serious incident might qualify: for instance, a suggestion that an employee get paid for becoming the business owner's mistress.[100]

The Eleventh Circuit has ruled[101] that harassment is not actionable if the employee does not perceive the environment to be hostile until *after* the termination of employment. In other words, if the nature of the conduct is not perceived as harassing at the time it occurs, it does not alter the terms and conditions of employment and there is no remedy.

On a related issue of timing, the Seventh Circuit permits claims of continuing harassment violations based on conduct that would be time-barred under the statute of limitations only if the complainant could not reasonably have been expected to bring a timely suit. The plaintiff's duty is to bring suit as soon as the cumulative nature of the conduct in creating a hostile environment is known.[102]

The Ninth Circuit permits introduction of evidence of harassment of other employees in a *quid pro quo* sexual harassment case. The rationale is that it goes to motive and also refutes the employer's contention that the plaintiff was fired for a nondiscriminatory reason.[103] The Tenth Circuit upheld a $200,000 award of emotional distress damages in a sexual harassment case, because the supervisor's comments were made in an open office, where co-workers could overhear, thus exacerbating the severity of the conduct and the embarrassment suffered by the victim.[104]

In 1997, an oft-litigated issue was the role of the employer. After all, since consensus is virtually universal that the employer is the only possible defendant, and in any case the employer has the deepest pockets, the question of the employer's role and potential liability is quite significant. The trend has been to limit the circumstances in which the employer is liable.[105]

What if the fired party was not the alleged victim of harassment, but the accused harasser? The Seventh Circuit defines "gross misconduct" by an employee to include sexual harassment of others. Therefore, it is not arbitrary or capricious to discharge such a person without severance benefits, even if the conduct was not serious enough to support a federal suit.[106]

The Colorado Supreme Court considers state common-law sexual harassment claims to be cumulative with the federal claims. Therefore, a plaintiff is not obligated to exhaust state-law administrative remedies with respect to common-law claims that could have been, but were not, brought under the state anti-discrimination statute.[107]

The Ninth Circuit said that state-court (California) claims for wrongful discharge and intentional interference with contract relations, contrary to the state policy forbidding religious discrimination, could not be removed to federal court.[108] (The employee filed in state court; the defendant employer got the case removed to federal court and was awarded summary judgment by the District Court.) The case neither asserted a federal cause of action nor depended on a federal question. The plaintiff's complaint did mention Title VII, but only to show that the state did have a public policy against religious discrimination. Title VII preemption of state law is not complete; only inconsistent state laws are preempted.

State court remedies are viable, e.g., for employees of companies too small to be covered by the federal statute. The employee can sue for wrongful discharge contrary to state public policy.[109] In Michigan, unemployment benefits serve to reduce damages in a contract action for wrongful discharge.[110]

A company was dissolved before one of its employees brought a Title VII claim. By that time, most of the assets had been distributed to two shareholders. The Northern District of Illinois allowed[111] the plaintiff to seek damages from the shareholders without first getting a judgment against the defunct corporation, allowing a prejudgment collection from a solvent party to resolve claims against an insolvent one.

The Central District of Illinois allows the EEOC to bring a pattern-or-practice suit with respect to *quid pro quo* and hostile environment sexual harassment. The theory is that pattern-or-practice suits are allowed in cases of systemic discrimination, and sexual harassment is clearly viewed as a form of sex discrimination. The criterion is whether an objectively reasonable person would deem the atmosphere to be one of harassment; individual employee perceptions will be reached in the individual relief phase if a hostile environment is found.[112]

[¶2105.2]   Civil Rights Act of 1991

The EEOC filed a suit on behalf of six employees. In late 1997, the District Court for the District of Arizona ruled that each of the six employees can receive the cap amount.[113] In other words, the court refused to treat the case as a single EEOC suit subject to the cap, finding that the provision for multi-party EEOC suits would be frustrated if all the employees had to share a single cap amount.

According to the First Circuit, the $200,000 cap on damages under 42 U.S.C. §1981a(b)(3) means a cap on the total damages (compensatory and punitive) against the employer, and this limit applies to the ADA as well as Title VII and the ADEA.[114] The Sixth Circuit applies the cap to all of one person's claims in a lawsuit, rejecting the EEOC position that the cap applies separately to each claim.[115] The Fourth Circuit says that the CRA '91 bar on the "court" telling the jurors about the statutory caps on compensatory damages equally prohibits the lawyers in the case from mentioning the caps.[116]

The 90-day filing requirement applies to ADEA actions filed after the effective date of CRA '91, referring to discriminatory acts occurring earlier.[117] Furthermore, once the employee receives the right-to-sue notice, the suit must be filed strictly within the 90-day period, which is not tolled by an employee request that the EEOC reconsider its no-reasonable-cause determination.[118] However, where plaintiffs are dismissed from a class action (on the grounds that they are not similarly situated to other plaintiffs), the dismissed plaintiffs' 90-day ADEA statute of limitations is tolled until there has been a final judgment in the underlying class action. This is because the District Court could change its mind or be reversed as to the propriety of the dismissed plaintiffs' membership in the class.[119]

If a named plaintiff made a timely charge in a class action, non-filing complainants are entitled to opt in, but they must file written consent to joining the class before the statute of limitations has expired on the plaintiffs' individual claims. The Fair Labor Standards Act tolling standards, not those of Title VII, apply to ADEA class actions.[120]

CRA '91 §107(b), which limits relief in mixed-motive cases to injunction and declaratory relief, rather than damages, does not apply to Title VII retaliation claims, because the statute does not specifically limit retaliation remedies.[121]

To the D.C. Circuit, the standard for punitive damages for an intentional Title VII violation are the same as for 42 U.S.C. §§1981 or 1983: malice or reckless indifference to federally protected rights. There is no need for a showing of especially egregious conduct. The Second Circuit ruled similarly, and did not require a showing of especially egregious conduct for either punitive damages or award of the full damages allowable under the cap.[122] In a case involving employment discrimination charges under both New York and federal law, the Southern District of New York ruled that the standard for punitive damages is preponderance of the evidence, not clear and convincing evidence.[123]

[¶2105.3] The Equal Pay Act

A job applicant who fails to mention a criminal conviction on a job application is barred from certain remedies, but not an EPA claim that she was paid less than comparable males. The after-acquired evidence of concealment of the conviction does not go to the defendant employer's state of mind (whether it acted in good faith and in the reasonable belief that the EPA was not violated). According to the Eleventh Circuit, the after-acquired evidence counts only if the back pay period ended before the employee was fired.[124]

[¶2105.4] The Age Discrimination in Employment Act

In spring, 1996, the Supreme Court resolved a vexed question by deciding that an ADEA plaintiff need not prove replacement by someone outside the over-40 protected group, as long as the replacement is much younger than the plaintiff.[125] The Eastern District of Pennsylvania has ruled that a retiree has standing to sue the former employer under the ADEA; active employment is not a prerequisite of standing.[126]

At the beginning of 1998, the Supreme Court cleared up an important ADEA problem: whether the employee is required to "tender back" any consideration given for a release before suing to dispute the validity of the release. The ruling is that, if the release is defective under the Older Workers Benefit Protection Act (OWBPA, accepting severance benefits does not ratify the release, so tender back is not a prerequisite of the suit.[127])

In the view of the Eleventh Circuit, a *prima facie* case is made out when a younger employee is transferred or hired to replace an older worker who encountered a Reduction in Force (RIF). In this view, employers do not always have to transfer or rehire older workers, but they do have to consider them for rehiring instead of rejecting them based on their age.[128]

The class of individuals protected by the ADEA against mandatory retirement includes members of corporate Boards of Directors who work full-time as corporate managers or officers and report to the senior board members.[129]

A lateral transfer had only a trivial effect on a salesman's commissions, so it did not operate as a "demotion" for ADEA purposes. The Seventh Circuit remanded the case to determine whether the salesman's post-transfer termination violated the ADEA.[130]

Given the availability of statutory remedies for age discrimination, the Oklahoma Supreme Court has refused to permit an at-will employee to bring an age-based suit in state court for the tort of wrongful termination.[131]

The Tenth Circuit said that there is no such thing as a disparate impact ADEA claim—ADEA plaintiffs must show that they themselves were the victims of disparate treatment.[132] At least in the Sixth Circuit, there *is* such a thing as a hostile work environment ADEA claim, because the ADEA derives from Title VII.[133]

The ADEA allows long-term disability benefits to be offset by the pension benefits for which the claimant is "eligible," a provision that the Ninth Circuit has defined to mean benefits payable at the same time as LTD benefits, not those that the worker would receive if he or she retired.[134]

The Third Circuit said that the standard for jury instructions in an ADEA pre-text case is not whether age was the sole cause of the employer decision, but whether age was a factor that played a determinative role in the employer's decision to discharge or otherwise disadvantage the employee.[135] In a late-1997 Third Circuit case, a company's President told its CFO, four or five months before the CFO was fired, to hire some "young bankers" if he was "getting too old for the job." The court treated this remark as evidence for an inference of age-based animus, but not equivalent to the necessary preponderance of evidence that age was a determinative factor in the CFO's discharge. The president hinted that help was needed, not at future firing.[136]

The Eleventh Amendment precludes employees of a state university from bringing an ADEA claim in federal court, because the state has not waived its immunity.[137]

On another sovereignty issue, several courts came to grips with international implications of the ADEA. According to the Southern District of Florida, foreign corporations are not *pro tanto* exempt from the ADEA; only their operations outside the United States are exempt.[138] The Eastern District of Pennsylvania said that the ADEA is irrelevant to a promotion outside the United States. The relevant worksite is the locus of the position sought by the plaintiff, not where she was working at the time she allegedly underwent age discrimination.[139] The D.C. Circuit reversed the District Court and found that a German employment contract, reflecting German practices, covering employees in Munich and enforceable in German courts, counts as a foreign "law." Therefore, the contract can lawfully reflect the German practice of mandatory retirement at age 65. The Munich Labor Court required mandatory retirement at 65 for the benefit of German workers who might be hired after the compulsory retirement of the American incumbents.[140]

The Eighth Circuit allowed an award of three years' front pay in addition to three years of back pay to an employee who was RIFed because she was 64 years old. Although it is presumed that workers will retire at normal retirement age, the presumption is not absolute. In this case, the plaintiff showed that she had the ability, desire, and need to keep working past 65, so the longer period for damages was proper.[141]

The ADEA is not violated when enhanced severance benefits are offered to everyone who is affected by a reduction in force, regardless of age, in return for their release of all claims. Although people over 40 have an additional claim (under the ADEA), they do not necessarily have accrued claims that make their waiver more valuable than that of younger employees.[142]

There is no bright-line test for how long an employee must be given to ponder whether or not to sign a release, but, absent urgent circumstances, 24 hours is insufficient. For one thing, the employee won't have time to seek legal counsel in so short a time.[143] The EEOC issued regulations about ADEA waivers in March,

1997.[144] If an employer has 20 or more employees, the rule covers waivers offered to a group or class involved in a voluntary or involuntary termination program. The rule deals with the wording of acceptable waivers; consideration; time periods for considering an offer; how to disclose the coverage of the program; and how to use waivers to settle suits and EEOC charges. EEOC guidance released on April, 1997 in a compliance manual for EEOC personnel says that employers cannot legitimately demand in advance that employees waive the right to file charges under any anti-discrimination statute. An agreement that "extracts" such a promise from employees might be treated as retaliation for exercising legal rights.[145]

The terms of the ADEA call for a fee award to the successful plaintiff, but an NASD arbitration panel's failure to make a fee award cannot be disturbed, because there was no "manifest disregard" of the law in the omission.[146]

See ¶2105.2, above, for discussion of the CRA '91 filing requirements. The Second Circuit has held that an ADEA claim is estopped by a laid-off employee's receipt of Social Security Disability Income benefits, on the theory that the benefits were ordered because of the plaintiff's claimed inability to work, so he is estopped from claiming ability to work.[147] For discussion of this issue in the ADA context, see ¶2105.5, below.

[¶2105.5] Handicap/Disability Discrimination

In March, 1995, the EEOC published a guidance memorandum, "Compliance Manual Section 902: Definition of the Term 'Disability.'"[148] According to the memo, personality traits (such as a bad work attitude) are not an impairment, but an actual mental disorder, such as a bipolar mood disorder, is an impairment. Even if an employee is genuinely impaired, the employer can legitimately hold all employees to the same level of performance and conduct.[149]

The memo also defines severe overweight (more than 100 pounds over the individual's normal weight) as an impairment, but being a few pounds overweight is not. In sum, the scope or perceived scope of an individual's condition, without consideration of mitigating measures, determines whether an impairment is present.

Where the employer has specific evidence of an epileptic's inability to work during seizures, and about the danger of the condition (as distinct from generalized beliefs about the abilities of epileptics), there is no violation in firing an epileptic worker who suffers from seizures.[150] Using a similar analysis requiring the employer to consider the individual's medical history and personal capacities, the Eastern District of Michigan ruled that the ADA *is* violated when an employer refuses to hire individuals whose pre-employment drug tests show no drug usage, but elevated blood sugar levels.[151]

In 1996, disability issues generated a high volume of litigation. Late that year, the Eleventh Circuit held that a mixed-motive ADA case can be sustained: in other words, the plaintiff's burden does not include establishing that disability discrimination was the employer's sole motivation for its action.[152] Although, as discussed above, ex-employees can assert Title VII retaliation claims, the Eleventh Circuit limits ADA claims to current rather than former employees.[153] Yet the Eastern

District of California not only permits an ADA retaliation claim, but permits it to be brought against an individual, such as a supervisor, and general and punitive damages as well as equitable relief are available against the individual defendant.[154] In the Third Circuit, a person who charges retaliation under the ADA need not be a qualified individual with a disability.[155]

The Seventh Circuit considered the ADA/labor law interface, and decided that the ADA duty to accommodate disabled employees does not require an employer to "bump" employees who have more seniority under the Collective Bargaining Agreement.[156]

The Southern District of Iowa did not deem procreation to be a "major life activity"—thus, it ruled that neither the ADA, the Pregnancy Discrimination Act, nor Title VII is violated when an employer's health plan excludes infertility treatment.[157] In contrast, the Northern District of Illinois did treat infertility as an ADA disability, deeming it to be a physical impairment affecting the life activity of procreation. Thus, discharging an employee who was frequently absent while seeking fertility treatment did constitute an ADA violation.[158]

A late-1996 Eleventh Circuit case finds for the employer, not the employee, whose side effects of cancer chemotherapy did not constitute a "substantial limitation." The employee's treatments were received only once every three weeks, were well-tolerated, the employee's doctor said he was not disabled, and the employee himself admitted that he was capable of working.[159]

Employers also prevailed in a case where an employee was fired for inability to lift 25 pounds. The Fourth Circuit deemed that such an inability is not a significant restriction in a major life activity.[160]

To the Tenth Circuit, would-be airline pilots with poor uncorrected vision, but 20/20 vision after correction, are not disabled for ADA purposes, because corrected vision does not impair the life activity of seeing. Nor were the applicants disabled in the life activity of working, because they could perform many other jobs.[161]

At the end of 1997, the Seventh Circuit decided a case in which a company implemented a performance-based Reduction in Force. The plaintiff had many absences after a heart attack, and his productivity was low when he was present. The Seventh Circuit considered that his dismissal as part of the RIF was correlated with, but not based on, disability, and therefore the ADA was not violated.[162]

Within the ADA context, perhaps the leading issue of 1996 was the employer's responsibility to offer reasonable accommodation, and determining when this burden has been met. The employer has not violated the ADA as long as it has made a reasonable good-faith effort to communicate with an employee who claims a disability, and has tried to accommodate the individual based on the information in its possession—even if the negotiations break down.[163] The Eleventh Circuit says that the plaintiff has to prove that reasonable accommodations were available—a burden that is not removed by the employer's failure to investigate possible accommodations.[164] A later Eleventh Circuit case[165] gives the ADA plaintiff the burden of production of evidence of accommodations that could be made permitting him or her to do the job, as well as the burden of persuasion that such accommodation is reasonable. Lacking this evidence, there is no case against the employer for failure to offer reasonable accommodation.

The Sixth Circuit divides the responsibilities this way: the plaintiff must prove ability to perform the essential job functions if the proposed accommodation is provided; the employer merely has to show that the accommodation proposed by the plaintiff would impose an undue hardship.[166] A recent District Court case found for the employer, because the employee failed to demonstrate that a voice-activated computer system and split keyboard were reasonable accommodation to a repetitive stress injury. The court agreed with the employer, that the value of split keyboards remains unproven, and the cost of voice-activated systems far exceeds the benefits such systems provide.[167]

In the view of the Fourth Circuit, summary judgment for the employer should not have been granted with respect to the discharge of an HIV-positive salesperson whose work performance was better than that of an HIV-negative employee who was not discharged.[168] However, in later proceedings, the Fourth Circuit ruled that an HIV+ but asymptomatic individual is not an individual with a disability, because such a person is not limited in major life activities.[169] After the supplement period, the Supreme Court rules that asymptomatic HIV+ persons are covered by the ADA.

The Third Circuit and the Eastern District of New York have ruled that claiming disability benefits for AIDS estops the claimant from also asserting that he or she is a "qualified employee" for ADA purposes.[170] Yet, to the D.C. Circuit and Eleventh Circuit, receipt of Social Security Disability Benefits is not necessarily a bar to maintenance of an ADA suit; if double benefits are a risk, the court considered set-off to be more appropriate than denial of a litigation remedy.[171]

The EEOC's position, as expressed in February 12, 1997 guidance to EEOC investigators, is that an ADA claim can legitimately be pursued after an application for disability benefits, even if the benefits claim requires a characterization as totally disabled or unable to work. That characterization is relevant, but not a total bar to maintaining the ADA claim. The ADA presumes ability to work, and disability benefits do not consider the possibility of work given reasonable accommodation.[172]

A nurse who wanted an assignment that did not involve heavy lifting after she suffered a wrist injury was held by the Third Circuit not to be a qualified individual with a disability, because she did not assert that she could perform all requisite job functions without accommodation. The Third Circuit does not require accommodation of a person who is regarded as disabled but really is not disabled.[173]

The Sixth and Seventh Circuits agree that the ADA is not violated when an employer demotes or fires an employee for drunk driving despite the employee's claimed alcoholism disability. The rationale is that the employee was guilty of criminal misconduct for which any employee, irrespective of disability, would have been discharged.[174] The Sixth Circuit also says that it is permissible to fire an employee whose urine test was positive for alcohol (although not at a level connoting intoxication) and even though alcoholism is a disability. In this case[175] employer and employee had signed a "last chance" agreement calling for regular testing and a threat of discharge if positive results were obtained. The court deemed this agreement to be valid because it was voluntarily entered into, and because the employer provided consideration by agreeing not to fire the employee if he lived up to the agreement. The Sixth Circuit did not consider alcohol to be a "drug" falling within the ADA exception for current use of drugs.

Periodic use of illegal drugs during the weeks or months prior to discharge constitutes "current" use of drugs under this exception, so it is lawful to discharge an employee in this category even if he or she was not using drugs and was in a rehab program at the actual time of discharge.[176]

The Sixth and Seventh Circuits disagree about the ADA and long-term disability plans. To the Sixth, maintaining different durations for mental and physical disability in an LTD plan can violate the ADA unless the distinction can be justified by actuarial factors, experience, or bona fide risk classifications.[177] But the Seventh says that placing a two-year limit on benefits for mental disability, with no corresponding limits on periods of physical disability, does not violate the ADA because the requirements were applied equally to all employees. The Seventh Circuit treated the case as essentially a poorly pleaded ERISA claim that the plan should have been drafted to offer parity.[178]

When Delta acquired PanAm, Delta decided whether or not to hire PanAm employees based on various standards, including weight. A New York court upheld such use of "grooming standards" as acceptable business decisionmaking, and not disability, age, or sex discrimination.[179]

ADEA waivers have been discussed above. A 1997 First Circuit case looks at ADA waivers, requiring that they be knowing and voluntary, as determined based on analysis of the totality of circumstances. No special procedures are required. Factors in the analysis include the waiving of employee's education and sophistication, and the clarity or otherwise of the waiver. If the plaintiff claims that depression or another psychiatric disability is involved, the question becomes the plaintiff's capacity to make a knowing and voluntary release of claims.[180]

[¶2105.6] Family and Medical Leave Act (FMLA)

The Family and Medical Leave Act of 1993, 29 U.S.C §2612(c), applies to all companies with 50 or more employees in each working day in 20 or more weeks of a year. Qualifying employees (those who have been employed there for at least 12 months, with at least 1,250 work hours in the preceding 12 months) must be permitted to take up to 12 weeks' unpaid leave per year without penalty, for personal or family health needs. Employees returning after a leave must be reinstated in the old job, or in a position of equivalent responsibilities, working conditions, and compensation. (There is an exception for top executives, who need not be reinstated if their absence has severely impaired corporate operations.)

FMLA leave is available when the employee needs hospitalization or continued medical treatment, or if the employee serves as caregiver for a spouse, child, or parent with a serious health condition. Leave must also be granted for the birth or adoption of a child. The leave can take the form of a reduced schedule or a period of several days at a time—it is not necessary that the employee be absent for an extended period to qualify for leave.

The statute contains a requirement that employees give advance notice of the need for non-emergency leave. Employers can require medical certification of the need for leave.

According to the Western District of Michigan, it is permissible to discharge an employee who was eligible for FMLA leave but failed to satisfy the regulations that require at least verbal notice to alert the employer to the presence of an FMLA claim.[181] However, the Fifth Circuit says that employees are entitled to the protections of the FMLA even if they fail to specifically invoke the statute when they apply for medical leave.[182] In a Pennsylvania case,[183] the employee handbook said that the unpaid parenthood leave could be as long as 16 weeks, but did not mention that the right of reinstatement was forfeited if the leave extended past the FMLA's 12-week protected period. The court treated the inadequate notice as actionable as an interference with FMLA rights, if its effect was to induce employees to extend their leave long enough to forfeit reinstatement.

29 CFR 825.110(d), which says that once an employer confirms the employee's entitlement to leave, it cannot subsequently challenge the employee's eligibility, has been held invalid as contrary to the text of the FMLA itself.[184]

The District of Columbia District Court says that the 1995 FMLA regulations, including the employer's responsibility for notifying employees of eligibility requirements before leave begins, cannot be applied retroactively.[185] Furthermore, "hours of service" for computing eligibility for FMLA leave are hours actually worked, not vacation, holiday, sick leave, or maternity leave hours.

[¶2105.7] Employment Liability Insurance Issues

For various reasons, an employer seeking coverage under its liability policy may find that coverage is unavailable when the employee has claimed discrimination or sexual harassment. For instance, the insurer may refuse to provide coverage on the grounds that the conduct complained of was intentional rather than negligent, and public policy is violated by permitting insurance coverage of known wrongdoing.[186] Yet not all courts do consider it against public policy to maintain insurance against employment torts, or even employment-related intentional torts.[187]

In most jurisdictions, employers can purchase specialized employment liability insurance, which resolves questions about the availability of coverage under a generalized liability policy. Under the CGL, coverage may be unavailable not because of the nature of the employer's conduct, but because it may be deemed that the employee plaintiff has not suffered "bodily injury" or "personal injury" of a type covered by the policy. However, if the employee has had any physical consequences of employment-related stress, the employer may be entitled to CGL coverage.[188]

The Sixth Circuit ruled that an umbrella business liability policy that covered unintentional discrimination but excluded discrimination committed by or at the direction of the insured is ambiguous and must be construed against the insurer. The court's conclusion is that torts cannot be included in a policy's definition of personal injury, yet excluded from the definition of an occurrence.[189]

A further refinement is that the insurer may have a duty to defend (i.e., to provide legal counsel) when allegations of discrimination are made, even if the insurer would not be required to indemnify the employer if the defense is unsuccessful and it is required to pay damages to the plaintiff.

[¶2105.8]   Arbitration of Employment Discrimination Claims

In 1995, the EEOC was granted a preliminary injunction preventing an employer from requiring employees to sign and follow the company's "ADR Policy" instead of litigating claims of Title VII violations. The employer was also enjoined from requiring employees to pay the cost of ADR proceedings, and from interfering with the EEOC charges or Title VII actions.[190] However, if there is already a CBA in place that specifically makes sex and disability claims subject to arbitration, a union member may be unable to litigate Title VII or ADA claims against the employer.[191] Note that an employer's internal grievance procedure is not tantamount to arbitration (because, unlike arbitration, the grievance procedure is not final or binding and does not involve an impartial third-party decisionmaker). Therefore, an employee's agreement to use the grievance procedure does not constitute an agreement to arbitrate claims of wrongful termination on the basis of race and sex in lieu of litigating them.[192]

It is quite common for written employment agreements, whether they are union contracts; the U-4 form used in the securities industry; or individually negotiated contracts to include a clause mandating arbitration rather than litigation of employment-related claims. Employers often prefer to avoid subjecting themselves to litigation, where an employee's claim (whether or not valid) may be judged by an extremely sympathetic jury. It is well-settled law that employment-related claims are suitable subjects for arbitration, but it is a subject of lively controversy whether and when the employer can force arbitration on a claimant who prefers to litigate.

EEOC Chairman Gilbert Casellas issued a statement on July 10, 1997, expressing the agency's continued opposition to compulsory binding arbitration of statutory discrimination claims. He announced that the EEOC will continue to bring suits in cases in which the arbitration agreement appears to have been obtained by coercion, although the EEOC follows the federal policy of supporting voluntary ADR efforts.[193]

Courts differ in the results they reach when the person bringing the discrimination charge is a union member covered by a CBA. At one extreme is the position that the CBA is binding on union members, who therefore must arbitrate rather than litigate claims; at the other extreme is the position that union members had no personal input in the contract negotiations, and did not individually make a knowing waiver of the right to litigate—and therefore cannot be compelled to arbitrate.[194]

For a waiver to be valid, employees must be aware that they are specifically waiving Title VII rights. Therefore, a securities industry employee who signed a U-4 form that referred to possible amendments in securities industry practice, before the NASD code was amended to mandate arbitration of employment-related claims, was able to litigate her claims because she had not made a knowing waiver.[195]

According to the Southern District of New York, if the EEOC brings a pattern-or-practice suit dealing with employees who are subject to the U-4 (securities industry) arbitration clause, the agency cannot seek monetary relief for individual employees. However, if the EEOC seeks relief beyond the immediate litigants, there is sufficient public interest for the case to proceed.[196]

Arbitration agreements cannot require employees to waive attorneys' fees when they bring their discrimination claims to mandatory arbitration, given the public policy that non-affluent individuals should not be dissuaded from bringing meritorious claims.[197]

Courts have also reached varying conclusions about the enforceability of arbitration provisions contained in employee handbooks distributed by an employer. The Eighth Circuit treated a provision which was highlighted, printed as a detachable last page, and used contractual language as an agreement enforceable under the FAA (even though other language in the handbook disclaimed the operation of the handbook as a contract).[198] In contrast, the Ninth Circuit permitted an employee to litigate an ADA claim after signing a form indicating that the handbook (including its arbitration clause) had been read and understood.[199] In this analysis, understanding a provision unilaterally imposed by the employer is not the same as agreeing to the provision.

State (New Jersey) public policy is not violated by an arbitration clause in an individual employment contract, and such a clause can be enforced with respect to anti-discrimination claims under state law.[200]

The D.C. Circuit allows employers to impose a requirement of mandatory arbitration as a condition of employment, but also requires them to pay all the fees of the arbitrator. The arbitrator must be neutral; discovery must be reasonably available; and the arbitration remedies must be comparable to remedies obtainable through the court system.[201]

However, it is overreaching for employers to place an arbitration clause in a job application (as distinct from an employment contract) because the employer doesn't promise anything, including serious consideration of the application, so there has been no consideration.[202]

Once an employment matter does get arbitrated, the standard for judicial review of the arbitrator's decision is exactly the same as for any other issue: whether or not the arbitrator manifestly disregarded the applicable law.[203]

A successor employer that inherits the liabilities of its predecessor can enforce an arbitration agreement that an employee signed with the former employer, thus preventing litigation of the employee's ADA claim.[204]

[¶2106] OTHER LIMITATIONS ON EMPLOYMENT AT WILL

Attorneys with government jobs have a right of intimate association (under the First Amendment). Therefore, a state cannot withdraw a job offer to an attorney, based on her intention to undergo a religious commitment ceremony with her female lover, unless the state can show that refusal to employ the attorney is narrowly tailored to serve a compelling state interest. The Eleventh Circuit could not detect any such compelling state interest in punishing a religious ceremony related to sincere and long-held religious beliefs of both spouses.[205]

In a workplace too small to be covered by state anti-discrimination law, an employee who alleges sexual harassment can nevertheless bring a common-law tort suit for wrongful discharge in violation of public policy.[206]

In a state wrongful discharge case alleging breach of an implied employment contract, unemployment compensation benefits offset the successful plaintiff's damages.[207]

An action alleging religion-based wrongful termination and interference with contractual relations, in violation of state public policy, cannot be removed to federal court, according to the Ninth Circuit.[208] All the claims are state claims (even though presumably Title VII remedies could have been sought), and there is no substantial federal question or cause of action. In this reading, Title VII does not preempt state law completely—only state law that is inconsistent rather than cumulative with Title VII.

California's statute of limitations for breach of contract in the form of constructive discharge begins to run at the actual termination of employment, not the presumably earlier date when conditions became intolerable to a worker of average sensitivity.[209]

— ENDNOTES —

1. *Hughes Action Committee v. Administrator of Hughes Non-Bargaining Retirement Plan,* 72 F.2d 686 (9th Cir. 12/15/95).

2. *Colgate-Palmolive Co.,* 323 NLRB No. 82 (4/23/97).

3. *NLRB v. Town & Country Electric Inc.,* #94-947, 116 S.Ct. 450 (Sup.Ct. 11/28/95), reversing and remanding 34 F.3d 625 (8th Cir.1994).

4. *Architectural Glass & Metal Co. v. NLRB,* 107 F.3d 426 (6th Cir. 2/24/97).

5. *Holly Farms v. NLRB,* #95-210, 116 S.Ct. 4269 (Sup.Ct. 4/22/96).

6. *Loral Defense Systems-Akron,* 320 NLRB #54 (1/31/96). On the obligation to bargain, see *Rock-Tenn Co. v. NLRB,* 101 F.3d 1441 (D.C.Cir. 12/17/96), upholding the NLRB's determination that the employer must bargain over the decision to subcontract work performed by union members. To the D.C. Circuit, the Board made a permissible interpretation of the NLRA, even if the employer's motivation is saving labor costs.

7. *Humphrey v. Sequentia Inc.,* 58 F.3d 1238 (8th Cir. 6/28/95). Also see *Davis v. Bell Atlantic-WV,* 110 F.3d 245 (4th Cir. 4/3/97), finding state claims preempted by §301 in a case where a worker was fired for excessive absence and tardiness. She was reinstated after filing a grievance, on condition that she could be fired summarily if her attendance record continued poor. It did

and she was fired again. She sued for breach of the CBA and the settlement agreement and for wrongful discharge. The Fourth Circuit treated the reinstatement agreement as a rider that supplemented but did not supplant the CBA. Interpreting the rider requires interpretation of underlying CBA concepts of adequate attendance.

8. *Trans Penn Wax Corp. v. McCandless,* 50 F.3d 217 (3rd Cir. 2/28/95).

9. Compare *Golden v. Kelsey-Hayes Co.,* 73 F.3d 648 (6th Cir. 1/18/96); mandatory injunction granted obligating employer to restore benefits, but jury trial denied because money damages only incidental to equitable cause of action, with *Stewart v. KHD Deutz of America Corp.,* 75 F.3d 1522 (11th Cir. 2/28/96) [jury trial available even if LMRA claim is joined with ERISA claim for same monetary relief]. Also see *Exxon Research & Engineering Co. v. NLRB,* 89 F.3d 228 (5th Cir. 7/16/96). Employer is not guilty of unfair labor practice for failure to bargain with the union about benefit plan changes ordered by the plan's trustees, pursuant to their limited authority to make administrative changes.

10. *United Steelworkers of America v. United Engineering Inc.,* 52 F.3d 1386 (6th Cir. 5/2/95).

11. *United Steelworkers of America v. St. Gabriel's Hospital,* 871 F.Supp. 335 (D.Minn. 12/20/94). Query whether the new employer should not be bound by the contract, which it was certainly aware of during the negotiations for the purchase.

12. *Canteen Corp. v. NLRB,* 107 F.3d 1355 (7th Cir. 1/7/97).

13. *New Breed Leasing Corp. v. NLRB,* 111 F.3d 1460 (9th Cir. 4/30/97).

14. *NLRB v. A.P.R.A. Fuel Oil Buyers Group Inc.,* 66 LW 1393 (2nd Cir. 12/5/97).

15. *Montero v. INS,* 124 F.3d 381 (2nd Cir. 8/28/97).

16. *United Food & Commercial Workers v. Almac's Inc.,* 90 F.3d 1 (1st Cir. 7/24/96).

17. *Professional Staff Nurses Ass'n v. Dimensions Health Corp.,* 677 A.2d 87 (Md.App. 6/3/96).

18. *WSB Electric Inc. v. Curry,* 88 F.3d 788 (9th Cir. 7/5/96).

19. *Auer v. Robbins,* #95-897, 65 LW 4136 (Sup.Ct. 2/19/97).

20. *Tran v. Tran,* 54 F.3d 115 (2nd Cir. 5/5/95).

21. *Transportation Union Local 1589 v. Suburban Transit Corp.,* 51 F.3d 376 (3rd Cir. 3/16/95).

22. *Asplundh Tree Expert Co. v. Bates,* 57 F.3d 592 (6th Cir. 12/14/95).

23. *United Brotherhood of Carpenters v. Desert Palace Inc.,* 94 F.3d 1308 (9th Cir. 9/4/96).

24. *Madison Hotel v. Hotel & Restaurant Employees Local 25,* 128 F.3d 1399 (D.C. Cir. 11/7/97).

25. *Plumbers Local 32 v. NLRB,* 50 F.3d 29 (D.C.Cir. 3/28/95).

26. *N.Y.S. Chapter, Associated General Contractors v. N.Y.S. Thruway Authority,* 64 LW 2638 (N.Y.App. 3/28/96).

27. *NLRB v. Bakersfield Californian,* 66 LW 1347 (9th Cir. 11/19/97).

28. *International Paper Co. v. NLRB,* 115 F.3d 1045 (D.C. Cir. 6/27/97).

29. *Dorsey Trailers Inc. v. NLRB,* 134 F.3d 125 (3rd Cir. 1/13/98).

30. *NLRB v. Webcor Packaging Inc.,* 118 F.3d 1115 (6th Cir. 7/11/97).

31. *Unbelievable Inc. v. NLRB,* 118 F.3d 795 (D.C. Cir. 7/18/97).

32. *Miller v. Air Line Pilots Ass'n,* 108 F.3d 1415 (D.C. Cir. 3/14/97).

33. *Buzenius v. NLRB,* 66 LW 1171 (6th Cir. 9/8/97).

34. Original order: see 63 LW 2575. Court decisions: *Chamber of Commerce of the U.S. v. Reich,* 897 F.Supp. 570 (D.D.C. 7/31/95) and 57 F.3d 1099 (D.C.Cir. 2/2/96).

35. *Brown v. Pro Football Inc.,* #95-388, 116 S.Ct. 2116 (Sup.Ct. 6/20/96).

36. *Diamond Walnut Growers Inc. v. NLRB,* 80 F.3d 485 (D.C.Cir. 3/29/96). Also see later proceedings at 65 LW 2769 (D.C. Cir. 5/20/97) reaching a similar conclusion.

37. *F.L. Thorpe & Co. v. NLRB,* 71 F.3d 282 (8th Cir. 12/1/95). Also see *NLRB v. Harding Glass Co.,* 80 F.3d 7 (1st Cir. 3/27/96): the employer wrongfully implemented the wage proposal whose rejection caused the walkout. However, the strike was still an economic strike, not an unfair labor practices strike; the employer motivation had not changed, and the practice merely continued the conduct that had led to the strike.

38. *Noel Foods v. NLRB,* 82 F.3d 1113 (D.C. Cir. 5/3/96).

39. *Clow Water Systems Co. v. NLRB,* 92 F.3d 441 (6th Cir. 8/19/96).

40. *Rifkin v. McDonnell-Douglas Corp.,* 78 F.3d 1277 (8th Cir. 3/6/96) rules that, although a total of 609 workers were laid off, the mass layoff provision was not triggered, because the plants were in different counties and didn't share management or operating activities. Furthermore, in determining whether a mass layoff has occurred, people rehired within six months and people who chose early retirement instead of a layoff should not be counted. Also see *Teamsters Local 413 v. Driver's Inc.,* 101 F.3d 1107 (6th Cir. 12/3/96): eleven facilities in six states can't be considered a "single site" for counting the number of laid-off employees.

41. *Viator v. Delchamps Inc.,* 109 F.3d 1124 (5th Cir. 4/15/97).

42. *Halkias v. General Dynamics,* 65 LW 2664 (N.D. Tex. 3/5/97).

43. *United Food & Commercial Workers v. Brown Group Inc.,* #95-340, 116 S.Ct. 1529 (Sup.Ct. 5/13/96).

44. *Saxion v. Titan-C Mfg. Inc.,* 86 F. 3d 553 (6th Cir. 6/7/96).

45. *Aaron v. Brown Group,* 80 F.3d 1220 (8th Cir. 4/8/96).

46. *Adams v. Westinghouse Credit Corp.*, 65 LW 2080 (8th Cir. 7/1/96).

47. *Auciello Iron Works Inc. v. NLRB*, #95-668, 116 S.Ct. 1754 (Sup.Ct. 6/3/96).

48. *Allentown Mack Sales & Service Inc. v. NLRB*, #96-795, 118 S.Ct. 818 (Sup.Ct. 1/26/98).

49. *United Auto Workers v. Textron Lycoming Reciprocating Engine Division*, 117 F.3d 119 (3rd Cir. 7/7/97).

50. *LCF Inc. v. NLRB*, 66 LW 1384 (D.C. Cir. 11/25/97).

51. *Hughes Christensen Co. v. NLRB*, 101 F.3d 28 (5th Cir. 11/21/96).

52. *Gardner Mechanical Services v. NLRB*, 89 F.3d 586 (9th Cir. 7/10/96).

53. *Kwik Care Ltd. v. NLRB*, 82 F.3d 1122 (D.C. Cir. 5/17/96).

54. *Metropolitan District Council of Philadelphia v. NLRB*, 68 F.3d 71 (3rd Cir. 10/25/95); *United Food and Commercial Workers, Local 880 v. NLRB*, 74 F.3d 292 (D.C.Cir. 1/26/96) is similar for distribution of union literature by non-employees to customers of the employer. With respect to establishments located within a shopping mall, *O'Neil's Markets v. United Food & Commercial Workers*, 95 F.3d 733 (8th Cir. 9/13/96) finds that a store that has only a nonexclusive easement in the mall corridor outside its store cannot bar nonemployee union handbillers. However, *Cleveland Real Estate Partners v. NLRB*, 95 F.3d 457 (6th Cir. 9/13/96) holds that a mall owner does not discriminate against the union by banning non-employee union representatives from soliciting within the mall, even if organizations that are not labor-related are allowed to solicit.

55. *Guardian Industries Corp. v. NLRB*, 49 F.3d 317 (7th Cir. 2/28/95).

56. *Be-Lo Stores v. NLRB*, 66 LW 1186 (4th Cir. 9/16/97).]

57. *Meijer Inc. v. NLRB*, 130 F.3d 1209 (6th Cir. 12/9/97).

58. *NLRB v. Mead Corp.*, 73 F.3d 74 (6th Cir. 1/8/96).

59. *Riesbeck Food Markets Inc. v. NLRB*, 91 F.3d 132 (4th Cir. 7/19/96).

60. *Radonich v. Senshyn*, 52 F.3d 28 (2nd Cir. 4/10/95).

61. See 66 LW 2391.

62. The guidance, part of an EEOC internal compliance manual, can be found at http://www.eeoc.gov/press/12-8-97.html. The guidance also notes that individuals in welfare-to-work programs are covered by federal anti-discrimination laws.

63. Although it is before the supplement period, reference should also be made to *St. Mary's Honor Center v. Hicks*, 509 U.S. 502 (Sup.Ct. 1993), which increases the burden on the plaintiff. Instead of merely having to challenge the defendant's explanation that its conduct was not caused by discriminatory motives, the plaintiff must now prove affirmatively, by preponderance of the evidence, that discriminatory animus motivated the employer's conduct.

64. *Rhodes v. Guiberson Oil Tools,* 82 F.3d 615 (5th Cir. 1/31/96).

65. *Sheridan v. DuPont,* 64 LW 2487 (3rd Cir. 1/31/96); also see later proceedings, 100 F.3d 1061 (3rd Cir. 11/14/96): employer can't get either summary judgment or judgment as a matter of law once the plaintiff establishes a *prima facie* case and produces enough evidence to raise genuine issues of fact about the pretextuality of the employer's explanation of its conduct.

66. *Sagendorf-Teal v. Rensselaer County, New York,* 100 F.3d 270 (2nd Cir. 11/12/96).

67. *McKennon v. Nashville Banner Pub. Co.,* #93-1543, 115 S.Ct. 879 (Sup.Ct. 1/23/95); on remand, 51 F.3d 272. This is an ADEA case, part of the predominance of age cases in employment discrimination litigation.

68. *Carr v. Woodbury County Juvenile Detention Center,* 905 F.Supp. 619 (N.D.Ia. 11/23/95).

69. *O'Day v. McDonnell-Douglas,* 79 F.3d 756 (9th Cir. 3/26/96).

70. *EEOC v. Hearst Corporation,* 65 LW 2508 (5th Cir. 1/22/97).

71. *U.S. v. Board of Trustees, Illinois State University,* 944 F.Supp. 714 (C.D. Ill. 11/1/96).

72. New CFR Part 60-1; see 62 FR 44173 (8/19/97) and 62 FR 66970 (12/22/97).

73. *Freemon v. Foley,* 911 F.Supp. 326 (N.D.Ill. 11/7/95); *Beyer v. Elkay Mfg. Co.,* 66 LW 1200 (N.D. Ill. 9/19/97) reaches the same conclusion, noting that the FMLA provides compensatory and punitive damages, which are typical remedies in suits by one individual against another.

74. *Williams v. Banning,* 72 F.3d 552 (7th Cir. 12/21/95): supervisor, Title VII; *Tomka v. Seiler Corp.,* 66 F.3d 1295 (2nd Cir. 9/27/95): co-employee, hostile work environment sex discrimination]; *Stephens v. Kay Management Co.,* 66 F.3d 41 (E.D.Va. 12/7/95); *Mason v. Stallings,* 82 F.3d 1007 (11th Cir. 5/9/96) [no personal ADA liability for supervisor; *EEOC v. AIC Security Investigations,* 63 LW 2746 (7th Cir. 5/22/95) [supervisors, ADA].

75. *Walters v. Metropolitan Education Enterprises Inc.,* #95-259, 95-779, 117 S.Ct. 660 (Sup.Ct. 1/14/97). Also see *Devine v. Stone, Leyton & Gershman PC,* 100 F.3d 78 (8th Cir. 11/13/96): so-called partners can be counted to determine a law firm's Title VII coverage based on the substance of the working relationship (not just the partner title), but in this case summary judgment for the firm was granted because of the lawyers' policy-making role for the firm, and because the plaintiffs failed to show that their relationship with the firm was more like employment than membership.

76. *Ensley-Gaines v. Runyon,* 100 F.3d 1220 (6th Cir. 11/20/96). Also see *In re Carnegie Center Associates,* 129 F.3d 290 (3rd Cir. 10/31/97): a pregnancy discrimination claim must show that the employee was treated differently from non-pregnant employees on temporary disability. It was not discrimination to fail to offer an employee returning from maternity leave a lower-paying job in which she had never expressed any interest.

77. *Quaratino v. Tiffany,* 71 F.3d 58 (2d Cir. 11/20/95).

78. *Turic v. Holland Hospitality Inc.,* 85 F.3d 1211 (6th Cir. 6/17/96).

79. This conclusion had already been reached by *Veprinsky v. Fluor Daniel Inc.,* 87 F.3d 881 (7th Cir. 6/26/96). Also see *U.S. v. New York Transit Authority,* 97 F.3d 672 (2nd Cir. 10/8/96), finding that the employer was not guilty of retaliation in having a policy of terminating its internal grievance procedure and referring complainants to the legal department, once a complaint became the subject of an agency charge or litigation. The Second Circuit did not believe that sending the file to the company's legal department harmed the employee.

80. *Mattern v. Eastman Kodak Co.,* 104 F.3d 702 (5th Cir. 1/16/97).

81. *Hashimoto v. Dalton,* 118 F.3d 671 (9th Cir. 7/3/97).

82. *Merritt v. Dillard Paper Co.,* 120 F.3d 1181 (11th Cir. 8/29/97).

83. *Kachmar v. Sun Gard Data Systems Inc.,* 109 F.3d 173 (3rd Cir. 3/26/97).

84. *Childress v. Richmond,* 120 F.3d 476 (4th Cir. 1/15/98).

85. *Carson v. Bethlehem Steel Corp.,* 82 F.3d 157 (7th Cir. 4/22/96). The interpretation of the *prima facie* requirement is far from a simple matter. *Fisher v. Vassar College,* 114 F.3d 1332 (2nd Cir. 6/5/97) has five opinions adding up to 140 pages! The majority says that an appellate court has the power to review the trial court's finding of pretextuality for clear error. The finding of pretextuality merely establishes that the employer is hiding something; the underlying finding of discrimination is therefore subject to review.

86. *Huguley v. G.M. Corp.,* 67 F.3d 129 (6th Cir. 10/10/95).

87. *Egbuna v. Time-Life Libraries Inc.,* 95 F.3d 353 (4th Cir. 9/13/96). This case seems designed to turn up on future bar exams: the plaintiff claimed that he was not rehired because the employer retaliated against him for participating in a sexual harassment claim.

88. *Cloud v. Superior Court,* 50 Cal.App.4th 1552 (Cal.App. 11/21/96).

89. *Whalen v. W.R. Grace & Co.,* 56 F.3d 504 (3d Cir. 6/2/95).

90. *West v. Philadelphia Electric Co.,* 45 F.3d 744 (3rd Cir. 1/19/95).

91. *Forehand v. Florida State Hospital,* 89 F.3d 1562 (11th Cir. 8/6/96).

92. *Criales v. American Airlines Inc.,* 105 F.3d 93 (2nd Cir. 1/21/97).

93. For the pre-*Oncale* jurisprudence, see, e.g., Same-sex harassment is not cognizable: *Garcia v. Elf Atochem North America,* 28 F.3d 446 (5th Cir. 1994), *Hopkins v. Baltimore Gas & Electric,* 871 F.Supp. 822 (D.Md. 12/28/94), *Vandeventer v. Wabash National Corp.,* 867 F.Supp. 790 (N.D. Ind. 1994); contra, *Wrightson v. Pizza Hut of America Inc.,* 99 F.3d 138 (4th Cir. 10/31/96); *Tietgen v. Brown's Westminster Motors Inc.,* 921 F.Supp. 1495 (E.D. Va. 4/18/96); *Sardinia v. Dellwood Foods,* 64 LW 2329 (S.D.N.Y. 10/30/95); *King v. M.R. Brown Inc.,* 911 F.Supp. 161 (E.D.Pa. 9/26/95); *EEOC v. Walden Book Co.,* 885 F.Supp. 1100 (M.D.Tenn. 5/4/95).

94. *Oncale v. Sundowner Offshore Services Inc.*, #96-568, 118 S.Ct. 998 (Sup.Ct. 3/4/98).

95. *Hopkins v. Baltimore Gas & Electric Co.*, 77 F.3d 745 (4th Cir. 3/5/96): incidents of innuendo not actionable because they were too few and too widely separated in time to create a hostile environment; *McWilliams v. Fairfax County Board of Supervisors*, 72 F.3d 1191 (4th Cir. 1/1/96): humiliating treatment of one heterosexual male by a group of other heterosexual males; *Fox v. Sierra Development Co.*, 876 F.Supp. 1169 (D.Nev. 1/30/95): pervasive homosexual innuendo in the workplace is not actionable by offended heterosexual male employee; *Johnson v. Hondo Inc.*, 125 F.3d 408 (7th Cir. 8/28/97): repeated references to oral sex, including threat of coercion, made by one heterosexual male to another, were not harassment "because of sex."

96. *Gerd v. UPS*, 934 F.Supp. 357 (D.Colo. 8/19/96); *Quick v. Donaldson Co.*, 80 F.3d 1372 (8th Cir. 7/29/96): triable issue is present re hostile environment where employee claims employer tolerated more than 100 incidents premised on belief that plaintiff was homosexual—even though in fact the plaintiff and the alleged harassers were all heterosexual males; *Fredette v. BVP Management Associates*, 112 F.3d 1503 (11th Cir. 5/22/97): *quid pro quo* harassment of male by a gay male supervisor violates Title VII; *Yeary v. Goodwill Industries-Knoxville*, 107 F.3d 443 (6th Cir. 2/24/97): similar, for harassment by co-worker]; *Doe v. Belleville, Illinois*, 119 F.3d 563 (7th Cir. 7/17/97): sexual preference of harasser is irrelevant; *Cummings v. Koehnen*, 568 N.W.2d 418 (Minn.Sup. 8/28/97): state law eliminates the need to prove that harassment is "because of sex."

97. *Fuller v. Oakland, California*, 47 F.3d 1522 (9th Cir. 2/14/95). Also see *Ellerth v. Burlington Industries Inc.*, 102 F.3d 848 (7th Cir. 11/27/96): employer is liable for *quid pro quo* and hostile environment harassment, although the employer derived no benefit from the harassment, and even though the employee failed to follow the employer's notice procedure, AFF'D 97-569 (Sup.Ct. 6/25/98), and *Varner v. National Super Markets Inc*, 94 F.3d 1209 (8th Cir. 9/9/96); employer is not absolved of liability when harassment victim's fiance, also an employee, reported assaults to the store manager rather than the HR department; an employer policy calling for reporting is inadequate if the information is not relayed to someone who can remedy the harassment.

98. 59 F.3d 1391 (D.C.Cir. 7/28/95).

99. *Jones v. Gatzambide*, 940 F.Supp. 182 (N.D. Ill. 9/16/96): no physical contact; *Galvez v. Means*, 65 LW 2272 (S.D.N.Y. 8/26/96) [isolated instance].

100. *Nadeau v. Rainbow Rugs Inc.*, 64 LW 2727 (Maine Sup.Jud.Ct. 5/7/96).

101. *Faragher v. Boca Raton*, 76 F.3d 1155 (11th Cir. 2/8/96).

102. *Galloway v. General Motors*, 78 F.3d 1164 (7th Cir. 3/5/96).

103. *Heyne v. Caruso*, 69 F.3d 1475 (9th Cir. 11/8/95).

104. *Smith v. Norwest Financial Acceptance Inc.*, 129 F.3d 1408 (10th Cir. 12/3/97).

105. See, e.g., *Davis v. Sioux City*, 115 F.3d 1365 (8th Cir. 6/28/97): employer is not liable for hostile environment harassment by supervisor without actual or constructive knowledge of the harassment; mere agency is not enough; *Faragher v. Boca Raton, Florida*, 111 F.3d 1530 (11th Cir. 4/15/97, *rev'd* 97-282 Sup.Ct. 6/25/98)): supervisors commit harassment for their own benefit, not the employer's, so the employer is not vicariously liable, and will be directly liable only if it had actual knowledge of the harassment, or if the hostile environment was pervasive enough to create constructive knowledge; compare these cases to *Jansen v. Packaging Corp. of America*, 123 F.3d 490 (7th Cir. 8/12/97) employer is strictly liable for *quid pro quo* harassment by supervisor, but is liable for hostile environment created by supervisor only if the employer was negligent in hiring, supervising, or retaining the supervisor, and *Harrison v. Eddy Potash Inc.*, 112 F.3d 1437 (10th Cir. 5/8/97): employer can be liable if harassment was aided by the supervisor's actual or apparent authority to control the victim's working environment, even if the employer did not give the supervisor actual or apparent authority to harass. The Fourth Circuit treated a company president's testimony that the company had no written anti-harassment policy because he was only an employer, in no position to judge right and wrong as sufficient evidence to support the jury's inference of reckless indifference to harassment. Therefore, the punitive damage award was valid: *Harris v. L&L Wings*, 132 F.3d 938 (4th Cir. 12/24/97). Note: After the supplement period, the Supreme Court ruled (in *Faragher and Ellerth*, note 97) that employers can be liable for harrassment by supervisors even if the harassed employee did not suffer adverse job consequences—but that a sound anti-harassment program can indemnify the employer.

106. *Chalmers v. Quaker Oats Co.*, 61 F.3d 1340 (7th Cir. 8/15/95). *Cotran v. Rollings Hudig Hall Int'l*, 57 Cal.Rptr. 2d 129 (Cal.App. 9/26/96) says that an implied contract of termination for good cause only is not breached by terminating an individual based on a reasonable, good-faith belief that the individual was guilty of sexual harassment—whether or not the harassment actually occurred. Also see *Hill v. J.J.B. Hilliard, W.B. Lyons Inc.*, 65 LW 2060 (Ky.App. 6/21/96) re arbitrability of claims that a supervisor in a securities firm committed sexual assault and false imprisonment of a subordinate during a business trip.

107. *Brooke v. Restaurant Services Inc.*, 906 P.2d 66 (Colo.Sup. 9/25/95).

108. *Rains v. Criterion Systems Inc.*, 80 F.3d 339 (9th Cir. 3/26/96).

109. *Molesworth v. Brandon*, 672 A.2d 608 (Md.App. 3/5/96).

110. *Corl v. Huron Casting Inc.*, 544 N.W.2d 278 (Mich.Sup. 3/1/96).

111. *EEOC v. JRG Fox Valley Inc.*, 976 F.Supp. 1161 (N.D. Ill. 9/23/97).

112. *EEOC v. Mitsubishi Motor Mfg. of America Inc.*, 66 LW 1457 (C.D. Ill. 1/20/98).

113. *EEOC v. Moser Foods*, 66 LW 1368 (D.Az. 11/7/97).

114. *Hogan v. Bangor & Aroostook Railroad*, 61 F.3d 1034 (1st Cir. 8/18/95).

115. *Hudson v. Reno,* 130 F.3d 1193 (6th Cir. 12/4/97). Also see *Hall v. Stormont Trice Corp.,* 66 LW 1198 (E.D. Va. 9/11/97) also applying the cap to all counts brought by one plaintiff, noting that juries are not instructed about the cap. They award whatever amount they see fit, and the judge reduces it accordingly.

116. *Sasaki v. Class,* 92 F.3d 232 (4th Cir. 8/12/96). Also see *Rush v. Scott Specialty Gases,* 930 F.Supp. 194 (E.D. Pa. 6/13/96), citing the $300,000 limitation as one of the reasons to reduce $3 million punitive damages in a hostile environment sex discrimination case to $300,000 (the others were the low level of actual damages, the employer's low net income, and the reckless rather than malicious nature of its conduct).

117. *St. Louis v. Texas Workers Compensation Commission,* 65 F.3d 43 (5th Cir. 9/26/95); *Vernon v. Cassadaga Valley Central School District,* 49 F.3d 886 (2nd Cir. 3/8/95).

118. *McCray v. Corry Mfg. Co.,* 61 F.3d 224 (3rd Cir. 8/9/95).

119. *Armstrong v. Martin Marietta Corp.,* 93 F.3d 1505 (11th Cir. 9/11/96).

120. *Grayson v. K Mart Corp.,* 79 F.3d 1086 (11th Cir. 4/9/96).

121. *Tanca v. Nordberg,* 98 F.3d 680 (1st Cir. 20/18/96).

122. *Kolstad v. American Dental Association,* 108 F.3d 1431 (D.C. Cir. 3/21/97); *Luciano v. Olsten Corp.,* 109 F.3d 111 (2nd Cir. 3/21/97).

123. *Greenbaum v. Svenska Handelsbanker NY,* 66 LW 1231 (S.D.N.Y. 9/24/97). This case does not count employees in the parent company in Sweden in determining the applicable CRA '91 cap amount, on the grounds that non-U.S. citizens are not protected by Title VII.

124. *Wallace v. Dunn Construction Co.,* 62 F.3d 374 (11th Cir. 8/30/95).

125. *O'Connor v. Consolidated Coin Caterers Corp.,* #95-354, 116 S.Ct. 1307 (Sup.Ct. 4/1/96), *reversing and remanding* 56 F.3d 542. In fact, the 10th Circuit has said that an ADEA claim can be sustained where the replacement was *older* than the plaintiff, given evidence that the replacement was going to retire soon and was cynically selected to shift the focus away from the age-based termination of the plaintiff: *Greene v. Safeway Stores Inc.,* 98 F.3d 554 (10th Cir. 10/15/96).

126. *McKeever v. Ironworker's District Council,* 65 LW 2608 (E.D. Pa. 3/7/97).

127. *Oubre v. Energy Operations Inc.,* #96-1291, 118 S.Ct. 838 (Sup.Ct. 1/26/98).

128. *Jameson v. Arrow Co.,* 75 F.3d 1528 (11th Cir. 2/28/96).

129. *EEOC v. Johnson & Higgins Inc.,* 91 F.3d 1529 (2nd Cir. 8/8/96).

130. *Williams v. Bristol-Myers Squibb Co.,* 85 F.3d 270 (7th Cir. 5/29/96).

131. *List v. Anchor Paint Mfg. Co.,* 910 P.2d 1011 (Okla.Sup. 1/9/96).

132. *Ellis v. United Airlines,* 73 F.3d 999 (10th Cir. 1/4/96) *cert. denied* 116 S.Ct. 2500. On the question of age claims of persons other than the plaintiff, see *Holt v.*

JTM Industries Inc., 89 F.3d 1224 (5th Cir. 8/7/96): an employee can't assert a claim of retaliation if he or she has not participated in another worker's ADEA claim—even if the other worker is the plaintiff's spouse, and even if the plaintiff suffered adverse job action subsequent to the spouse's ADEA claim.

133. *Crawford v. Medina General Hospital,* 96 F.3d 830 (6th Cir. 9/24/96).

134. *Kalvinskas v. California Institute of Technology,* 96 F.3d 1305 (9th Cir. 9/27/96).

135. *Miller v. Cigna Corp.,* 63 LW 2482 (3rd Cir. 1/23/95).

136. *Keller v. ORIX Credit Alliance Inc.,* 130 F.3d 1101 (3rd Cir. 11/24/97).

137. *MacPhersen v. University of Montevallo,* 938 F.Supp. 785 (N.D.Ala. 9/9/96).

138. *EEOC v. Kloster Cruise Ltd.,* 888 F.Supp. 147 (S.D.Fla. 5/12/95).

139. *Denty v. SmithKline Beecham Corp.,* 907 F.Supp. 879 (E.D.Pa. 11/7/95).

140. *Mahoney v. RFE/RL Inc.,* 47 F.3d 447 (D.C.Cir. 2/28/95).

141. *Curtis v. Electronics & Space Corp.,* 113 F.3d 1498 (8th Cir. 5/28/97).

142. *Di Biase v. SmithKline Beecham Corp.,* 48 F.3d 719 (3d Cir. 2/16/95), reversing the District Court (62 LW 2655).

143. *Puentes v. United Parcel Service,* 86 F.3d 196 (11th Cir. 6/20/96). The case was remanded to the District Court to determine whether the releases were binding: see 65 LW 2060.

144. 62 FR 10878 (3/10/97).

145. See 65 LW 2678.

146. *DiRussa v. Dean Witter Reynolds,* 936 F.Supp. 104 (S.D.N.Y. 7/29/96).

147. *Simon v. Safelite Glass Corp.,* 128 F.3d 68 (2nd Cir. 10/14/97).

148. See 63 LW 2590.

149. Also see *Palmer v. Circuit Court of Cook County,* 117 F.3d 351 (7th Cir. 6/26/97), holding that an employee who engages in, or even threatens, violent acts within the workplace is not considered a qualified employee entitled to accommodation, even if mental illness precipitates the unacceptable behavior. Thus, there is no duty to accommodate potentially or actually violent persons.

150. *EEOC v. Kinney Shoe Corp.,* 917 F.Supp. 419 (W.D.Va. 2/14/96).

151. *EEOC v. Chrysler Corporation,* 917 F.Supp. 1164 (E.D. Mich. 3/6/96). For another aspect of drug testing, see *Loder v. Glendale, California,* 927 P.2d 1200 (Cal. Sup. 1/6/97). urine testing for drugs can be required of applicants who have received conditional job offers, but not from existing employees who are candidates for promotion, because the intrusion on employee privacy would outweigh the employer's interest in testing of all promotion candidates (where there is no reason to suspect drug use).

152. *McNely v. Ocala Star-Banner Corp.,* 99 F.3d 1068 (11th Cir. 11/20/96).

153. *Gonzalez v. Garner Food Service,* 89 F.3d 1523 (11th Cir. 8/2/96): company imposed cap on AIDS benefits before the ADA's effective date, and the alleged discrimination occurred after termination of employment, at a time when the employee was no longer qualified to perform the essential job functions.

154. *Ostrach v. Regents of the University of California,* 957 F.Supp. 196 (E.D. Cal. 3/17/97).

155. *Krouse v. American Sterilizer Co.,* 66 LW 1219 (3rd Cir. 9/26/97).

156. *Eckles v. Consolidated Rail Corp.,* 94 F.3d 1041 (7th Cir. 8/14/96).

157. *Krauel v. Iowa Methodist Medical Center,* 95 F.3d 674 (8th Cir. 9/11/96).

158. *Pacourek v. Inland Steel Co.,* 916 F.Supp. 797 (N.D.Ill. 2/16/96).

159. *Gordon v. Hamm,* 100 F.3d 907 (11th Cir. 12/4/96).

160. *Williams v. Channel Master,* 101 F.3d 346 (4th Cir. 11/27/96).

161. *Sutton v. United Air Lines,* 130 F.3d 893 (10th Cir. 11/26/97).

162. *Matthews v. Commonwealth Edison Co.,* 66 LW 1326 (7th Cir. 11/17/97).

163. *Beck v. University of Wisconsin Board of Regents,* 75 F.3d 1130 (7th Cir. 1/26/96).

164. *Moses v. American Nonwovens Inc.,* 97 F.3d 446 (11th Cir. 9/27/96).

165. *Willis v. Conopco Inc.,* 108 F.3d 282 (11th Cir. 3/25/97).

166. *Monette v. EDS Corp.,* 90 F.3d 1173 (6th Cir. 7/30/96).

167. *Garza v. Abbott Labs,* 940 F.Supp. 1224 (N.D.Ill. 9/12/96).

168. *Runnebaum v. Nationsbank of Maryland,* 95 F.3d 1285 (4th Cir. 9/19/96).

169. *Runnebaum v. NationsBank of Maryland,* 123 F.3d 156 (4th Cir. 8/15/97). This result is questionable in that it seems clear that the ADA statutory formulation of a person "perceived to have a disability" was intended to cover asymptomatic HIV+ individuals, who are at high risk of discrimination. The Supreme Court case is *Bragdon v. Abbott,* #97-156.

170. *McNemar v. Disney Stores,* 91 F.3d 310 (3rd Cir. 7/31/96); *Simon v. Safelite Glass Corp.,* 943 F.Supp. 261 (E.D.N.Y. 10/28/96).

171. *Swanks v. Washington Metro Area Transit Authority,* 116 F.3d 582 (D.C. Cir. 5/5/97); *Talavera v. School Board of Palm Beach County,* 129 F.3d 1214 (11th Cir. 11/24/97). Also see *Labonte v. Hutchins & Wheeler,* 65 LW 2734 (Mass.Sup.Jud.Ct. 5/15/97), holding that a state-law claim of failure to make reasonable accommodations to disability is not precluded by applying for disability benefits after termination, because the key factual inquiry is the plaintiff's ability to have performed essential job functions with accommodation which was not offered, and *Whitbeck v. Vital Signs Inc.,* 116 F.3d 588 (D.C. Cir. 6/20/97).

172. See 65 LW 2549.

173. *Deane v. Pocono Medical Center,* 66 LW 1152 (3rd Cir. 8/25/97).

174. *Maddox v. University of Tennessee,* 62 F.3d 843 (6th Cir. 8/21/95); *Despears v. Milwaukee County,* 63 F.3d 635 (7th Cir. 8/21/95).

175. *Mararri v. WCI Steel Inc.,* 130 F.3d 1180 (6th Cir. 12/2/97).

176. *Shafer v. Preston Memorial Hospital Corp.,* 107 F.3d 274 (4th Cir. 2/26/97).

177. *Parker v. Metropolitan Life Insurance Co.,* 99 F.3d 181 (6th Cir. 10/25/96).

178. *EEOC v. CNA Insurance Co.,* 96 F.3d 1039 (7th Cir. 9/27/96).

179. *Delta Air Lines v. New York Division of Human Rights,* 65 LW 2445 (App.Div. 12/31/96).

180. *Rivera-Flores v. Bristol-Myers Squibb Caribbean,* 112 F.3d 9 (1st Cir. 4/25/97).

181. *Reich v. Midwestern Plastic Engineering Inc.,* 934 F.Supp. 266 (W.D.Mich. 7/22/95), *aff'd* 113 F.3d 1235.

182. *Manuel v. Westlake Polymers Co.,* 66 F.3d 758 (5th Cir. 10/3/95).

183. *Fry v. First Fidelity Bancorporation,* 64 LW 2503 (E.D.Pa. 1/30/96).

184. *Seaman v. Downtown Partnership of Baltimore,* 66 LW 1459 (D.Md. 1/20/98), citing *Wolke v. Dreadnought Marine Inc.,* 954 F.Supp. 1133 (E.D. Va. 1997).

185. *Robbins v. BNA Inc.,* 896 F.Supp. 18 (D.D.C. 8/15/95).

186. See, e.g., *Dopf v. Vigilant Insurance Co.,* 64 LW 2816 (N.Y.Sup. 5/23/96) and *Moore v. Continental Insurance Co.,* 51 Cal.Rptr.2nd 176 (Cal.App. 3/28/96). The test of intentionality is intention to injure, not merely to perform activities, so the insurer does not have to defend against sex discrimination and sexual harassment claims (because these involve intent to injure) but is required to defend supervisors against charges of negligent supervision and retention of harassers, because such an allegation involves poor judgment but not intent to injure: *Sphere Drake Insurance PLC v. Shoney's Inc.,* 923 F.Supp. 1481 (M.D. Ala. 4/18/96).

187. *BlasT (sic) Intermediate Unit 17 v. CNA Insurance Co.,* 674 A.2d 687 (Pa.Sup. 4/18/96) negligent violation of Equal Pay Act is insurable]; *American Management Association v. Atlantic Mutual Insurance Co.,* 64 LW 2660 (N.Y.Sup. 3/29/96): disparate-impact age discrimination is not necessarily intentional, so the insurer has a duty to defend.

188. *Meadowbrook Inc. v. Tower Insurance Co.,* 543 N.W.2d 418 (Minn.App. 1/30/96): employee's claim of neck and back pain alleges "bodily injury"; *General Accident Insurance Co. v. Western American Insurance Co.,* 49 Cal.Rptr.2d 603 (Cal.App. 1/31/96): claim that corporate officer was "ousted" and "ejected" from the company premises alleges "personal injury".

189. *North Bank v. Cincinnati Insurance Cos.,* 66 LW 1220 (6th Cir. 10/1/97).

190. *EEOC v. River Oaks Imaging & Diagnostic,* 63 LW 2733 (S.D.Tex. 4/19/95). Re interference with process, see *EEOC v. Astra USA Inc.,* 94 F.3d 738 (1st Cir. 9/6/96) holding that it violates public policy (and therefore can be enjoined)

for a settlement agreement to forbid current or ex-employees to assist the EEOC in its investigation of charges against the employer, although settling employees can be forbidden to bring charges of their own.

191. *Austin v. Owens-Brockway Glass Container, Inc.,* 78 F.3d 875 (4th Cir. 3/12/96); see note 194.

192. *Cheng-Canindin v. Renaissance Hotel Associates,* 50 Cal.App.4th 676, 57 Cal.Rptr.2d 861 (Cal.App. 10/30/96).

193. The text of the statement appears at http://www.eeoc.gov/docs/mandarb.txt.

194. *Martin v. Dana Corp.,* 65 LW 2824 (3rd Cir. 6/12/97): CBA clause specifically referring to federal statutory claims, where either employer or employee can enforce arbitration, is valid and enforceable; *Almonte v. Coca-Cola Bottling Co. of New York,* 959 F.Supp. 569 (D.Conn. 3/11/97): §1981 race discrimination claims must be arbitrated if the CBA expressly provides for arbitration; *Brisentine v. Stone & Webster Engineering Corp.,* 117 F.3d 519 (11th Cir. 7/21/97): CBA probably does not bar litigation, unless individual agreed to the contract; *Pryner v. Tractor Supply Co.,* 109 F.3d 354 (7th Cir. 3/20/97) CBA cannot compel arbitration of federal statutory discrimination claims.

195. *Renteria v. Prudential Insurance Co.,* 113 F.3d 1104 (9th Cir. 5/20/97).

196. *EEOC v. Kidder, Peabody & Co.,* 66 LW 1252 (S.D.N.Y. 10/6/97). Also see *Ahing v. Lehman Brothers Inc.,* 66 LW 1336 (S.D.N.Y. 10/15/97): participation in a failed mediation effort does not preclude compelling arbitration of a Title VII race claim.

197. *DeGaetano v. Smith Barney,* 66 LW 1315 (S.D.N.Y. 11/6/97).

198. *Patterson v. Tenet Healthcare Inc.,* 113 F.3d 832 (8th Cir. 5/12/97).

199. *Nelson v. Cyprus Bagdad Copper Corp.,* 119 F.3d 756 (9th Cir. 7/10/97).

200. *Great Western Mortgage Corp. v. Peacock,* 110 F.3d 222 (3rd Cir. 4/3/97).

201. *Cole v. Burns International Security Services,* 105 F.3d 1465 (D.C. Cir. 2/11/97).

202. *Brooks v. Circuit City Stores Inc.,* 65 LW 2823 (D.Md. 5/30/97).

203. *Chisholm v. Kidder, Peabody,* 65 LW 2805 (S.D.N.Y. 5/29/97).

204. *Jones v. Tenet Health Network Inc.,* 65 LW 2815 (E.D. La. 4/7/97).

205. *Shahar v. Bowers,* 70 F.3d 1218 (11th Cir. 12/20/95).

206. *Collins v. Rizkana,* 652 N.E.2d 653 (Ohio Sup. 8/16/95). Also see *Molesworth v. Brandon,* 672 A.2d 608 (Md.App. 3/5/96): employer with under 15 employees, and therefore exempt from the state Fair Employment Practices Act, can be sued in state court for tort claims of wrongful discharge contrary to the state's equal employment policy.

207. *Corl v. Huron Castings Inc.,* 544 N.W.2d 278 (Mich.Sup. 3/1/96).

208. *Rains v. Criterion Systems Inc.*, 80 F.3d 339 (9th Cir. 3/26/96).

209. *Mullins v. Rockwell International Corp.*, 65 LW 2793 (Cal.Sup. 5/29/97).

— **FOR FURTHER REFERENCE** —

Cavaliere, Frank J., "In-Site on the Web: Employment Law Sites," 43 *Practical Lawyer 11* (June '97).

Coskey, Susan L., "Vizcaino v. Microsoft Corporation: A Labor and Employment Lawyer's Perspective," *48 Labor Law J.* 91 (February '97).

Dunn, Andrew D., "Insurance Coverage for Wrongful Employment Practices and Sexual Misconduct," 38 *New Hampshire Bar J.* 50 (June '97).

Flanagan, Gary W., "After-Acquired Evidence Defense: Distinguishing Between Tort and Contractual Claims," 26 *Colorado Lawyer* 55 (February '97).

Gonos, George, "The Contest Over 'Employer' Status in the Postwar United States: The Case of Temporary Help Firms," 31 *Law & Society Rev.* (February '97).

Greenlaw, Paul S. and John P. Kohl, "Proving Age Discrimination: The Courts' View," 48 *Labor Law J.* 50 (January '97).

Icenogle, Marjorie L. and Robert A. Shearer, "Emerging Due Process Standards in Arbitration of Employment Discrimination Disputes," 48 *Labor Law J.* 81 (February '97).

Kilberg, William J., "Employment Law and the 105th Congress," 22 *Employee Relations Law J.* 1 (Spring '97).

Levandoski, Dennis, "Proving Punitive Damages in Employment Cases," 33 *Trial* 26 (October '97).

Ryan, Kimberlie K., "Work Zone or War Zone? An Overview of Workplace Violence," 26 *Colorado Lawyer* 19 (November '97).

Schupp, Robert W., "When Is a Union Not a Union? Good-Faith Doubt and Its Limitations in Collective Bargaining," 48 *Labor Law J.* 336 (June '97).

Terrill, Thomas E., "The Americans with Disabilities Act and Labor Arbitration: Some Recent Awards," 48 *Labor Law J.* 3 (January '97).

White, Rebecca Hanner, "Modern Discrimination Theory and the National Labor Relations Act," 39 *William & Mary L.Rev.* 99 (October '97).

Willis, Susan Gaylord, "Stress-Related Disability Claims Under the ADA," 43 *Practical Lawyer* 73 (January '97).

Winterbauer, Steven H., "The Direct Threat Defense: Striking a Balance Between the Duties to Accommodate and to Provide a Safe Workplace," 23 *Employee Relations L.J.* 5 (Summer '97).

ENVIRONMENTAL LAW

[¶2201] On March 31, 1995, the EPA issued an announcement, "Voluntary Environmental Self-Policing and Self-Disclosure Interim Policy Statement."[1] The agency announced that it may refrain from pursuing criminal charges if a company voluntarily corrects and reports its violations. The EPA may also refrain from imposing punitive fines in addition to standard penalties. This announcement falls short of immunity for voluntary reporters; the agency still retains the option of pursuing ultimate penalties in appropriate cases—e.g., where the violations are particularly serious, harmful, or manifest a corporate philosophy of concealment of wrongdoing.

The policy refuses to treat corporate environmental audits as privileged business information (although a number of states have enacted such laws, or have pending bills).

It's clear that a fine or penalty paid to the government is not tax-deductible. Neither is an $8 million contribution to an environmental fund set up to alleviate the toxic effects of the pesticide kepone, in lieu of a criminal fine. (The original fine of $13.2 million was reduced to $5 million because the fund was created.) In the Third Circuit's analysis, the contribution to the fund was at the direction of the government, and hence nondeductible.[2]

The owners of land that abuts the site where a major oil spill occurred must show physical encroachment on their property in order to assert a negligence or private nuisance claim based on fear of future health damages or diminution in the value of their own property.[3]

Unless there is apparent agency or an independent contractor relationship, an oil company is not liable for ground water contamination caused by an independently owned and operated gas station that sells that company's products.[4]

Sale of contaminated property "as is" transfers environmental liability to the buyer only if the deed makes this clear. Requiring transfer of a fee simple, subject to environmental regulations, is not sufficient to shift liability to the buyer.[5] An early 1997 Massachusetts decision[6] says that, in the absence of fiduciary duty, a seller does not have to disclose defects in the property to potential buyers. Therefore, a bank had no duty to warn condominimum purchasers of toxic waste contamination nearby—especially since the condos themselves showed no apparent damage.

As always, see ¶2515.1 for discussion of environment-related insurance issues.

[¶2202]   FEDERAL ENVIRONMENTAL LAWS

To recover from the cleanup fund, claims must be presented under the Oil Pollution Act of 1990 (33 U.S.C. §2713); a claim must also be made before filing a private suit under the OPA.[7]

Also see P.L. 103-311, the Hazardous Materials Transportation Authorization Act, 49 U.S.C. §5101 (8/26/94), under which the DOT is directed to make the National Intelligent Vehicle-Highway Systems Program promote safe transport of hazardous materials, including rules for safely packaging hazmats in fiber drums.

For later lawmaking, see, e.g., P.L. 104-119, the Land Disposal Flexibility Act of 1996, permitting land disposal of solid waste that has been treated to reduce its harmfulness; and P.L. 104-182, the Safe Drinking Water Amendments of 1996, reauthorizing the Safe Drinking Water Act, which is Title XIV of the Public Health Service Act.

1997 was not a very good year for environmental class actions. The Supreme Court upheld the Third Circuit, finding class action certification inappropriate under Rule 23 for settlement of current and future asbestos claims. In this analysis, absentees were not properly represented. There was not enough similarity in the exposure of potential class members to asbestos, and the interests of already injured individuals (who want current compensation) conflict with those of individuals who have been exposed to asbestos but have not manifested injury (who want funds retained for future claims).[8]

A Louisiana court found that a class action should not have been certified against four petroleum companies, because individual issues outweighed common issues of liability and causation. Nor could a class be certified on the basis of a novel theory about the synergistic effect of pollution from the four sources.[9]

[¶2203] SCOPE OF CERCLA

Surprisingly, basic CERCLA issues still occupied the courts in 1996, over a decade after the statute's enactment. The Southern District of Illinois, unsurprisingly, found that statute to be Constitutional, on the grounds that the Congress is empowered by the Commerce Clause to handle interstate commerce issues such as proper waste disposal and site cleanup.[10] Most of the courts that have heard the issue also hold that CERCLA applies retroactively, given Congress' intent to cover acts before the CERCLA effective date.[11]

The Western District of New York requires active human agency in disposing of hazardous materials for CERCLA liability—mere passive release of substances does not subject the landowner to CERCLA §107 liability.[12] The Third Circuit defines "disposal" to exclude spread of contamination from material placed on the site before the current owner became an owner. However, there has been a "disposal" if the current owner performs a soil investigation negligently, with the result that contamination is further spread.[13] A property's current owner has no CERCLA liability if it can prove that the contamination was solely caused by tenants of the former owner—as long as those tenants have never had a contractual relationship with the current owner.[14]

The seller of a building that contains asbestos doesn't become a CERCLA-liable party merely because a subsequent purchaser removes the asbestos. The Seventh Circuit said that the sale was not a disposal of hazardous materials that would make the seller an "arranger." Selling a building cannot be deemed an abnormally hazardous activity, nor can the seller reasonably foresee that the buyer's agents would cause a hazardous condition by mishandling asbestos removal.[15]

CERCLA continues to apply to a corporation after its dissolution (even if state law says that there is no longer any entity with capacity to be sued), so the dissolved corporation has to defend against a suit seeking response costs.[16]

A bankruptcy trustee is considered an appointed officer of the court, not a conventional trustee—and therefore cannot be held personally liable under CERCLA for the debtor's environmental wrongdoing.[17]

A significant CERCLA issue is identification of liable "operators" of contaminated facilities. According to the Sixth Circuit, the parent corporation can be deemed the owner of a facility owned by a subsidiary if, and only if, the corporate veil can be pierced.[18] In a case where the veil can be pierced, the Second Circuit says that a parent corporation that has "owner" liability can also have independent "operator" liability for the subsidiary's facility.[19] Whether or not a limited partner is an "owner" for CERCLA purposes is a function of state partnership law.[20]

An individual employee is not an owner, and therefore escapes CERCLA liability unless he or she falls into another category, such as "operator." The Eighth Circuit says that an employee (whether or not he or she is also an officer, director, or shareholder) must not only *have* the authority, but actually *exercise* the authority to control hazardous waste disposal in order to be liable as an "operator."[21] The Sixth Circuit permits a corporation's sole shareholder to be held liable as an operator, but only in instances in which state law permits the corporate veil to be pierced.[22]

The CERCLA cast of responsible characters also includes "arrangers" and "transporters." To be liable as an arranger, an officer or director of a company must have authority to, and in fact exercise direct or indirect control over, a subsidiary's disposal practices[23]—the same standard as the parent company's liability. To suffer liability as a "transporter," an officer or director must actually participate in the conduct that created the liability. It's not enough to manage the company; one must be aware of the company's substantial participation in choosing disposal facilities and accepting materials for transport.[24]

Under certain circumstances, a party that is liable under CERCLA can look to other parties for contribution. The District Court for the District of Colorado has ruled that proof that a defendant is a Potentially Responsible Party (PRP) under CERCLA §107 is sufficient to make out the *prima facie* case for contribution under CERCLA §113(f).[25] In fact, the federal government's costs of overseeing a cleanup performed by a private party can qualify as response costs under §107.[26]

A company that is responsible for pollution cannot get CERCLA contribution from a company that owned the property at a time when there was neither disposal nor release of hazardous waste.[27] To recover costs, it is not necessary to have a "protectable interest" in the site, only to have encountered costs. Thus, a contractor who cleaned up a site whose owner went broke before paying the costs was entitled to bring a §107 cost recovery action. The contractor was also a PRP because he had delivered hazardous materials to the site, and therefore was also entitled to bring a §113 contribution action.[28]

Private plaintiffs who seek to recover "response costs" under CERCLA must prove a causal link between the defendant's disposal of hazardous materials and the response costs—it is insufficient merely to prove that the disposal occurred.[29] A landowner's failure to provide adequate opportunity for public comment as to its choice of remedies prevents the owner from recovering the cleanup costs— even if there is government supervision of the site cleanup.[30]

Not all courts are in agreement about §107 recovery of cleanup costs by PRPs. The Middle District of Pennsylvania does allow such recovery.[31] On a related issue, the Northern District of California says that only innocent landowners can use the citizen suit provisions of CERCLA to recover their cleanup costs; landfill owners and operators who are aware of hazardous waste release cannot.[32]

The Third Circuit says that a PRP who resolves its liability with a consent decree (even if the consent decree does not admit liability) is not an "innocent party" entitled to §107 cost recovery, although it can get §113 contribution against other PRPs.[33]

The court's discretion to allocate liability in a §113 case is broad enough to permit it to allocate "orphan shares" (that cannot otherwise be assigned) among all the PRPs, including third-party defendants. It would not be fair to require only the named defendants to assume responsibility for the liability shares of defunct or bankrupt PRPs.[34]

According to the Eighth Circuit, a federal consent decree that settles the liability of certain Potentially Responsible Parties (PRPs) and protects them against contribution claims from non-settling PRPs, is serious enough to entitle non-settling PRPs to intervention as of right if they want to challenge the consent decree.[35]

The courts are hopelessly divided on the question of whether state law determines the liability of successor corporations, or whether a federal common law of CERCLA successor liability is required. The First, Sixth, Ninth, and Eleventh Circuits apply state law; the Second, Third, Fourth, and Eighth deem this to be a matter for federal common law.[36]

The six-year statute of limitations under CERCLA §113(g)(2)(B) runs from the start of the cleanup, provided that the §113 contribution place takes place at the same time as the initial §107 recovery action. Otherwise, contribution claims are subject to a three-year statute of limitations.[37]

[¶2204] THE CLEAN WATER ACT

The Ninth Circuit allows a CWA citizen suit to enforce a discharge permit's water quality standard, even if the standard is not expressed as end-of-pipe effluent limitations. In other words, regulations that are qualitative rather than quantitative can still be enforced by citizen suit.[38] However, to the Third Circuit, environmentalist groups and their members do not have standing to sue for violation of a CWA discharge permit unless they can show that they use the waters that are harmed or at serious risk of harm because of the violations of the discharge permit.[39]

To convict a corporate officer under the CWA's criminal provision §309(c)(2), the prosecution must show that the corporate officer knew the nature of his or her acts and performed them intentionally. Because, in 1987, Congress amended the statute to refer to "knowing" rather than "willful" actions, successful prosecution does not require proof that the actor knew that the conduct violated the statute. In this reading, the Congressional intent was to impose more, rather than fewer, criminal penalties.[40] According to the Fifth Circuit, conviction of a CWA felony requires proof that the defendant acted knowingly with respect to *each* element of the offense.[41]

The director of a state transportation agency cannot assert an Eleventh Amendment immunity defense to a CWA citizen suit.[42]

All CWA citizen suit plaintiffs who seek an attorneys' fee award must satisfy the statute's pre-suit notice requirement; one plaintiff can't satisfy the requirement on behalf of all.[43]

[¶2205]   THE CLEAN AIR ACT

The Tenth Amendment is not violated, and state sovereignty is not abridged, when the Clean Air Act imposes sanctions (such as loss of federal highway funds) for failure to comply with the Act's requirements for a state permit program covering stationary sources of pollution.[44]

The Clean Air Act imposes a requirement of prompt notification to the EPA whenever an asbestos-containing structure is renovated. However, it is not clear whether failure to do so is a one-time violation or one that continues until abated, so the Ninth Circuit decided that, absent clear statutory guidance, only the penalty for a single-day violation can be imposed.[45]

Later proceedings in the same case hold that a defendant who had to pay a Clean Air Act judgment, but in an amount lower than its pretrial offer of settlement, cannot recover attorneys' fees as Fed.Rul.Civ.Pro. 68 "costs" unless the government acted unreasonably. However, such a defendant is a prevailing party for EAJA purposes, and can recover costs under the EAJA even if the government did not act unreasonably. In this context, the CAA does not preempt the EAJA or preclude an EAJA award.[46]

[¶2206]   RESOURCE CONSERVATION AND RECOVERY ACT

A current owner cannot bring a RCRA citizen suit against a former owner to recover money that was expended to clean up a site that once was but no longer is imminently hazardous. The Supreme Court decided this in the spring of 1996 because the RCRA citizen suit provision is drafted in terms of "restraining" contamination posing "imminent and substantial endangerment," which no longer exists (because of the cleanup). The Court felt that this distinction between CERCLA and RCRA shared liability concepts indicates an intention to limit the passage of RCRA liability back through the chain of title. This case[47] does not reach the question of whether a party who has properly commenced a citizen suit can get an injunction obligating someone else to pay future cleanup costs for a site that continues to be hazardous—but note that according to the Eighth Circuit, there is no implied private right of action under RCRA §7002 (the citizen suit provision) for recovery of the costs of cleaning up contaminated property.[48] In contrast, the District Court for the District of Kansas does recognize the potential for cleanup orders in citizen suits—but proving the mere presence of petroleum and carcinogens in well water is not sufficient. It is necessary to prove harm to the health of individuals not aware of the contamination, or a threat of future environmental harm.[49] The District of Oregon says that companies can't use RCRA to recover any costs for remedies that were in place, or substantially in place, before the filing of a citizen suit.[50]

The Ninth Circuit has ruled that, under RCRA, states can adopt solid-waste management standards that are more stringent than the federal minimum standards. However, in effect those standards become state law, and will not support a RCRA citizen suit.[51]

Whether the RCRA (and CERCLA) claims of a buyer of contaminated property can be discharged by the seller's bankruptcy depends on whether the cleanup order could be converted into a monetary obligation (a right to payment). If the buyer did not have enough information to impose liability on the seller before bankruptcy was confirmed, the buyer's environmental claims will not be dischargeable.[52]

[¶2206.2] State Regulation of Solid Waste Disposal

The Ninth Circuit saw no Commerce Clause objection to a Washington State statute requiring everyone who collects and transports solid waste within the state to have a certificate of public convenience and necessity—even if they operate in interstate commerce.[53]

The Third Circuit similarly approved of a municipal flow control ordinance that sends solid waste to specific facilities—provided that the process of selecting the facilities is fair and does not discriminate against out-of-state businesses;[54] in 1996, the Second Circuit said much the same thing.[55]

However, the Eighth Circuit found a Commerce Clause violation in a state referendum about putting a large municipal solid waste facility in the state. In this reading, both the purpose and the effect are discriminatory, based on restrictions on bringing out-of-state waste into the state. Because nondiscriminatory alternatives were available, the Court of Appeals did not find the state environmental interest compelling enough to justify the restriction on interstate commerce.[56] The Fourth Circuit invalidated a state restriction on the amount of hazardous waste that could be brought into the state—an interference with interstate commerce that was not justified by the state's desire to preserve its limited disposal capacity.[57]

The Tenth Circuit says that CERCLA preempts municipal zoning ordinances that prohibit maintenance of hazardous waste concentrations in areas zoned for industrial use.[58]

[¶2207]   OTHER FEDERAL ENVIRONMENTAL LAWS

To have standing in a citizen suit against the government for violation of the procedures of the Endangered Species Act, plaintiffs must assert an interest in preserving the species. Thus, ranchers and irrigation districts do not have standing.[59]

The citizen suit provisions of the Emergency Planning and Community Right to Know Act (EPCRA) permit the imposition of penalties on facilities who fail to report the release of toxic substances, even if the reporting violation was cured prior to the institution of the citizen suit.[60]

[¶2208]   ENVIRONMENTAL TAX ISSUES

The Tax Reform Act of 1997 enacted a new rule for qualified brownfields cleanup costs paid or incurred before December 31, 2000. Such costs may qualify for a current deduction if the taxpayer elects to expense them. (If the taxpayer doesn't elect, the costs must be capitalized.) The new tax provision is limited to cleaning up hazardous substances, as defined by CERCLA, at qualified contaminated sites. When such property is sold, gain attributable to the cleanup cost deduction is treated as ordinary income.

For other tax issues, see, e.g., *Norwest Corp. v. Comm'r*[61], holding that if costs of removing asbestos are part of a general plan of rehabilitating a building, the costs must be capitalized. They are not ordinary and necessary business expenses entitled to a current deduction.

The IRS has proposed a procedure for getting an advance ruling on allocation between current deductions and capital expenditures for environmental cleanups to be performed in the future. See Notice 97-7, 1997-1 IRB 8. Announcement 97-22, 1997-12 IRB 47, says that taxpayers can ask for a pre-submission conference before they file for a Private Letter Ruling as to the deductibility of cleanup costs that span both past and future tax years. Also see Revenue Procedure 98-17, 66 LW 2448 (1/16/98). However, Private Letter Rulings will not be issued with respect to completed cleanups.

— ENDNOTES —

1. 60 FR 16875.

2. *Allied-Signal Inc. v. C.I.R.*, 1995 U.S.App. LEXIS 5130 (3rd Cir. 1995).

3. *Adams v. Star Enterprises*, 51 F.3d 417 (4th Cir. 4/6/95).

4. *Bahrle v. Exxon Corp.*, 678 A.2d 225 (N.J.Sup. 7/9/96).

5. *New West Urban Renewal Co. v. Westinghouse Electric Corp.*, 909 F.Supp. 219 (D.N.J. 11/21/95).

6. *Urman v. South Boston Savings Bank*, 424 Mass. 165 (Mass.Sup.Jud.Ct. 1/17/97).

7. *Boca Ciega Hotel Inc. v. Bouchard Transportation Co.*, 51 F.3d 235 (11th Cir. 4/17/95). The statute itself has been upheld against oil industry challenges to its substance and procedures, but the extent to which attorneys' fees are recoverable has been limited by *General Electric v. Commerce Dep't*, 66 LW 1384 (D.C. Cir. 11/18/97).

8. *Amchem Products Inc. v. Windsor*, #96-270, 117 S.Ct. 2231 (Sup.Ct. 6/25/97). The Supreme Court found the "sprawling" putative class unworkable, but declined to state whether exposure-only claimants have standing to sue.

9. *Ford v. Murphy Oil USA Inc.*, 66 LW 1191 (La.Sup. 9/9/97).

10. *U.S. v. NL Industries*, 936 F.Supp. 545 (S.D.Ill. 8/22/96).

11. *Cooper Industries v. Agway Inc.*, 956 F.Supp. 240 (N.D.N.Y. 9/23/96); contra, *U.S. v. Olin Corp.*, 927 F.Supp. 1502 (S.D.Ala. 5/20/96).

12. *Idylwoods Associates v. Mader Capital Inc.*, 915 F.Supp. 1290 (W.D.N.Y. 2/16/96).

13. *U.S. v. CDMG Realty Co.*, 96 F.3d 706 (3rd Cir. 9/27/96).

14. *New York v. Lashins Arcade Co.*, 91 F.3d 353 (2nd Cir. 8/5/96).

15. *G.J. Leasing Co. v. Union Electric Co.*, 54 F.3d 379 (7th Cir. 5/4/95).

16. *New York v. Panex Industries, Inc.*, 860 F.Supp. 977 (W.D.N.Y. 6/24/96).

17. *Tennsco Corp. v. Estey Metal Products Inc.*, 200 B.R. 542 (D.N.J. 9/17/96).

18. *U.S. v. Cordova Chemical Co.*, 59 F.3d 584 (6th Cir. 7/14/95); also see later proceedings at 113 F.3d 572 (6th Cir. 5/13/97).

19. *Schiavone v. Pierce*, 79 F.3d 2603 (2nd Cir. 3/14/96).

20. *Redwing Carriers Inc. v. Saraland Apartments*, 94 F.3d 1489 (11th Cir. 9/12/96).

21. *U.S. v. Gurley*, 43 F.3d 1188 (8th Cir. 12/28/94).

22. *Donahey v. Bogle*, 129 F.3d 838 (6th Cir. 11/17/97).

23. *U.S. v. TIC Investment Corp.*, 68 F.3d 1082 (8th Cir. 10/16/95).

24. *U.S. v. USX Corp.*, 68 F.3d 811 (3rd Cir. 10/23/95).

25. *Farmland Industries Inc. v. Colorado & Eastern Railroad Co.*, 922 F.Supp. 437 (D. Colo. 4/9/96). Also see *Atlantic Richfield Co. v. American Airlines Inc.*, 98 F.3d 564 (10th Cir. 10/10/96): because §107(a) makes PRPs liable for government monitoring costs, those monitoring costs are recoverable in a §113(f) contribution action.

26. *U.S. v. Lowe*, 118 F.3d 399 (5th Cir. 7/31/97).

27. *Joslyn Mfg. Co. v. Koppers Co.*, 40 F.3d 750 (5th Cir. 12/28/94).

28. *OHM Remediation Services v. Evans Cooperage Co.*, 116 F.3d 1574 (5th Cir. 7/22/97).

29. *Acushnet Co. v. Coaters Inc.*, 937 F.Supp. 988 (D.Mass. 7/24/96).

30. *Pierson Sand & Gravel Co. v. Pierson Township*, 89 F.3d 835 (6th Cir. 6/18/96).

31. *Adhesives Research Inc. v. American Inks & Coatings Corp.*, 931 F.Supp. 1231 (M.D. Pa. 7/30/96).

32. *West County Landfill v. Raychem International Corp.*, 64 LW 2563 (N.D.Cal. 2/12/96).

33. *New Castle County v. Halliburton NUS Corp.*, 111 F.3d 1116 (3rd Cir. 5/1/97).

34. *U.S. v. Kramer*, 953 F.Supp. 592 (D.N.J. 1/29/97).

35. *U.S. v. Union Electric Co.*, 64 F.3d 1152 (8th Cir. 8/30/95).

36. See *Atchison, Topeka & Santa Fe Railroad v. Brown & Bryant Inc.*, 66 LW 1425 (9th Cir. 12/30/97).

37. *Sun Co (R&M) v. Browning-Ferris Inc.*, 124 F.3d 1187 (10th Cir. 8/14/97).

38. *Northwest Environmental Advocates v. Portland, Oregon*, 56 F.3d 979 (9th Cir. 6/7/95); follows PUD No. 1 *of Jefferson County v. Washington Department of Ecology*, 114 S.Ct. 1900 (Sup.Ct. 1994).

39. *PIRG of New Jersey v. Magnesium Elektron Inc.*, 123 F.3d 111 (3rd Cir. 8/5/97).

40. *U.S. v. Hopkins*, 53 F.3d 533 (2nd Cir. 4/28/95); *also see U.S. v. Weitzenhoff*, 35 F.3d 1275 (9th Cir. 1994).

41. *U.S. v. Ahmad*, 101 F.3d 386 (5th Cir. 11/27/96).

42. *Natural Resources Defense Counsel v. California Department of Transportation*, 96 F.3d 420 (9th Cir. 9/17/96).

43. *New Mexico Citizens for Clean Air and Water v. Espanola Mercantile Co.*, 72 F.3d 830 (10th Cir. 1/2/96).

44. *General Accident Insurance Co. of America v. New Jersey*, 672 A.2d 1154 (N.J. Sup. 3/26/96).

45. *U.S. v. Trident Seafoods Corp.*, 60 F.3d 556 (9th Cir. 7/12/95).

46. *U.S. v. Trident Seafoods Corp.*, 92 F.3d 855 (9th Cir. 8/7/96).

47. *Meghrig v. KFC Western Inc.*, #95-83, 116 S.Ct. 1251 (Sup.Ct. 3/19/96), *reversing* 49 F.3d 518 (9th Cir. 3/1/95).

48. *Furrer v. Brown*, 62 F.3d 1092 (8th Cir. 8/15/95).

49. *Davies v. National Cooperative Refinery Ass'n*, 963 F.Supp. 990 (D.Kan. 7/12/96).

50. *Express Car Wash Corp. v. Irinaga Brothers Inc.*, 967 F.Supp. 1188 (D.Ore. 6/4/97).

51. *Ashoff v. Ukiah, California*, 130 F.3d 409 (9th Cir. 12/2/97).

52. *AM International Inc. v. Datacard Corp.*, 106 F.3d 1342 (7th Cir. 2/11/97).

53. *Kleenwell Biohazard Waste v. Nelson*, 48 F.3d 391 (9th Cir. 2/9/95).

54. *Harvey & Harvey Inc. v. Chester County, Pennsylvania*, 68 F.3d 788 (3rd Cir. 10/23/95).

55. *Gary D. Peake Excavating Inc. v. Town Board of Hancock, N.Y.,* 93 F.3d 68 (2nd Cir. 8/22/96).

56. *SDDS Inc. v. South Dakota,* 47 F.3d 263 (8th Cir. 2/6/95).

57. *Environmental Technology Council v. Sierra Club,* 98 F.3d 774 (4th Cir. 10/15/96).

58. *U.S. v. Denver, Colorado,* 100 F.3d 1509 (10th Cir. 11/18/96).

59. *Bennett v. Plenert,* 63 F.3d 915 (9th Cir. 8/24/95).

60. *Citizens for a Better Environment v. The Steel Company,* 90 F.3d 1237 (7th Cir. 7/23/96).

61. 108 TC No. 15 (1997).

— FOR FURTHER REFERENCE —

Farber, Daniel A., "Is the Supreme Court Irrelevant? Reflections on the Judicial Role in Environmental Law," 81 *Minnesota L.Rev.* 547 (February '97).

Frohnmayer, Dave, "Environment and Business: Complements Not Opposites in a New Era," 11 *J. of Environmental Law & Litigation* 1 (Spring '97).

Gaines, Sanford and Richard Westin, "Fighting Global Warming With Eco-Taxes," 77 *Tax Notes* 981 (11/24/97).

Kass, Stephen L. and Jean M. McCarroll, "Criminal Sanctions for Marine Pollutions," *N.Y.L.J.* 12/26/97 p. 3.

Lindquist, Ellen C. and Steven E. Chester, "Promoting Environmental Compliance Through Innovative Programs," 76 *Michigan Bar J.* 56 (January '97).

Lininger, Ann M., "The False Claims Act and Environmental Law Enforcement," 16 *Virginia Environmental L.J.* 577 (Summer '97).

Painter, Richard W., "Disclosure of Environmental Legal Proceedings Under the Securities Laws," 11 *J. of Environmental Law and Litigation* 91 (Spring '97).

Powell, Fiona M., "The Public Trust Doctrine: Implications for Property Owners and the Environment," 25 *Real Estate Law J.* 255 (Winter '97).

Reisch, Scott H., "Reaping 'Green' Harvests from 'Brownfields': Avoiding Lender Liability At Contaminated Sites," 26 *Colorado Lawyer* 3 (January '97).

Rodgers, Peter H. and Katherine P. Yarbrough, "EPA's RFG and Anti-Dumping Program," 11 *Natural Resources and Environment* 20 (Winter '97).

Satterfield, James E., "A Funny Thing Happened on the Way to the Revolution: The Environmental Record of the 104th Congress," 27 *Environmental Law Rep.* 10019 (January '97).Silecchia, Lucia Ann, "Judicial Review of CERCLA Cleanup Procedures," 20 *Harvard Environmental L. Rev.* 339 (Summer '96).

Simon, Ron, "Radiation Overexposure Claims: Fighting Defense Tactics Creatively," 32 *Trial* 26 (January '96).

Stone, Douglas S., "Negotiating Environmental Provisions for the Commercial Lease," 42 *Practical Lawyer* 45 (October '96).

ESTATE PLANNING AND ADMINISTRATION

[¶2301] During the supplement period, Congress offered some protection to charities via the Philanthropy Protection Act of 1995, P.L. 104-62 and the Charitable Gift Annuity Antitrust Relief Act of 1995, P.L. 104-63.

The former exempts charitable income pooled funds, such as those set up for charitable remainder trusts, from various securities laws by making it clear that they are not investment companies. Nevertheless, the funds are subject to federal anti-fraud securities laws, and donors are still entitled to disclosure of "material terms of the operation of the fund" within 90 days of making an irrevocable donation. (Funds that accept revocable donations are given three years to restructure.)

The latter makes it clear that it is not an antitrust violation for issuers of charitable gift annuities to use uniform rates, specifically those set by the American Council on Gift Annuities. Further details can be found in P.L. 105-26, the Charitable Donor Antitrust Immunity of 1997, which places charitable remainder trusts and charitable gift annuities outside the purview of the antitrust laws.

As discussed at ¶1202.1, the Small Business Job Protection Act of 1996 (P.L. 104-188) suspends (for the years 1997–1999) the excise tax on excessive payouts from pension plans. However, the 15% excise tax on excessive accumulation within the estate remained in place until the Tax Reform Act of 1997. Therefore, individuals with large pension accounts and potentially taxable estates had an incentive to step up pension consumption during their lifetimes (although this will increase their income tax) to avoid the "double whammy" of having a large estate that is also subject to the excise tax penalty for excessive accumulation. With the elimination of both excise taxes, estate planning decisions can be made with more attention to cash flow consequences and less to taxation.

An early 1997 Virginia case[1] involves an inter vivos trust drafted to require creation of three trusts after the grantor's death, one for each of three beneficiaries. The court ruled that, when any beneficiary requests, the trustees have a duty to disclose information about the entire group of trusts and their corpus, not just the individual beneficiary's separate trust, so that beneficiaries can discover if any improprieties have occurred anywhere within the three trusts.

[¶2301.1]   Tax Relief Act of 1997

The Tax Relief Act of 1997 (TRA '97) had many dramatic effects on financial matters; perhaps the most dramatic effects are within the estate planning area. Congress at last yielded to persuasion and phased in significant increases in the amount that can be sheltered via the unified credit. For 1998, the exempt amount is $625,000 rather than $600,000. For 1999, the amount is $650,000. For 2000 and 2001, the maximum credit shelter is $675,000, versus $700,000 in 2002-2003, $850,000 in 2-4. $950,000 in 2005, and $1 million in 2006.

TRA '97 also applies inflation indexing to the annual gift tax exclusion, the maximum amount to which special use valuation is applicable, and the Generation Skipping Tax exemption.

Because of this legislation, a trust can now take advantage of a rule formerly available only to estates: distributions made within 65 days of the end of a tax year can be treated as if they had been made on the last day of the tax year. For the estates of persons dying after August 5, 1997, transfers made out of a revocable grantor trust within the three years before death will be treated as transfers made directly by the grantor, and thus included or excluded based on the same factors. If it seems worthwhile, however, the trustee and the executor can join in an irrevocable election to treat a qualified revocable trust as part of the estate.

Family farms and other closely held family businesses (including proprietorships, partnerships, and close corporations) can be kept out of the gross estate of individuals who die after December 31, 1997, as long as the value of the unified credit plus the business interest does not exceed $1.3 million. (In other words, as the unified credit phases upward, the amount of family business interest that can be specifically protected phases downward.) The executor must elect such treatment; the business interest must make up at least 50% of the adjusted gross estate; and the business interest must either be transmitted to a family member, or to a non-family employee who worked for the business for at least ten years before the business owner's death. Furthermore, to qualify as a family business, at least 30% of the business must have been owned by the decedent's family. If one family owned the business, at least 50% of the interests in the business must have belonged to that family. If two families owned it, 70% must have belonged to those two families; or 90% if owned by three families. In other words, a qualifying business must not only be non-public, its ownership must be extremely concentrated.

In a community property state, if the spouse who is not a participant in a particular qualified pension plan or IRA dies before the participant-spouse, the decedent's interest in the participant's qualified plan or IRA can become a QTIP.

Also for the estates of individuals dying after August 5, 1997, an estate that is denied the ability to make installment payments of estate taxes is entitled to file with the Tax Court for a declaratory judgment that such relief is available. The filing must be made within 90 days of the mailing date of the adverse IRS determination.

[¶2305]   The Unlimited Marital Deduction

An early 1997 Supreme Court decision finds that it is not necessary to reduce the estate tax marital deduction (or charitable deduction) to account for the share of administration expenses paid out of income earned during the period of estate administration and allocated to the assets bequeathed to the spouse or to charity.[2]

In mid-1997, the Supreme Court ruled that ERISA preempts a state law that allows a non-employee spouse in a community property state to dispose by will of an interest in the employee spouse's undistributed pension benefits. In this analysis, a will cannot be a QDRO and therefore cannot re-direct pension benefits that are not yet in pay status.[3]

No marital deduction was allowed by the Fourth Circuit on trust assets passing to the surviving spouse under a settlement agreement relating to a dispute about the trust's terms. Under the settlement, the survivor received a life estate but no power of appointment. Crucially, the survivor's rights did not pass "from the decedent," and were obtained in her role as litigant rather than that of spouse.[4]

The surviving spouse's interest in QTIP property can be determined at the date of the QTIP election rather than the date of the deceased spouse's death. The surviving spouse, as executor in this case, could also be given discretion to determine the amount of the QTIP election. Once the election was made, the property was placed into a trust that could not be appointed away from the surviving spouse until after her death.[5]

According to the Eleventh Circuit, a trust can be a QTIP even if the surviving spouse receives neither the stub income (income from the last scheduled payment to the survivor's death) nor power of appointment over the stub income. In other words, the stub income can be appointed to someone other than the surviving spouse.[6]

A man and his fiancee entered into an antenuptial agreement stating that, if they were married at the time of his death, she could live in his co-op apartment until her death or remarriage. The fiancee waived the right to alimony and all interest in his estate, including the right of election. The IRS position, upheld by the Tax Court and affirmed by the Second Circuit, is that the value of her interest in the apartment could not be deducted as a claim against the deceased husband's estate. Her interest in the apartment was a non-QTIP terminable interest, and therefore the marital deduction was not available.[7]

Several recent cases have held that, for joint tenancies created before 1977, the entire value of the property can be included in the estate of the first spouse to die—and thus the entire property can get a stepped up basis—if the surviving spouse can prove that he (or usually, she) did not provide any of the consideration for the acquisition of the property.[8]

[¶2307] VALUATION

The IRS issued Final Regulations for income, gift, and estate taxation of annuities, life or term interests, remainders, and reversions. The Final Regulations stipulate situations in which the ordinary IRS §7520 valuation tables cannot be used.[9] The tables cannot be used if the transfer instrument does not give the beneficiary the degree of beneficial enjoyment traditionally applying to that type of property interest as defined by local law.

Nor can the tables be used to value transfers by the terminally ill, defined as persons with a 50 percent likelihood of dying within one year. However, if an individual survives the transfer by 18 months, it is presumed that he or she was not terminally ill at the transfer, unless terminal illness is proved by clear and convincing evidence. Mere age does not make a person terminally ill—unless he or she has one or more illnesses that, separately or together, are life-threatening.

For application of these principles, see, e.g., *Estate of McLendon*,[10] denying use of the valuation tables, even in a pre-1995 situation, where the transferor of a private annuity suffered from cancer so advanced that death was clearly imminent at the time of the transfer.

In late 1996, the Third Circuit ruled on another private annuity situation. An 80-year-old woman transferred a remainder interest in one-half of a close corporation's preferred stock back to the company. She retained her income interest in the shares and received an annuity of approximately $300,000 a year. According to the actuarial tables, the fair market value of the remainder interest and of the annuity were approximately equal (about $1.3 million). When the transferor/annuitant died, she had received $592,000 in annuity payments and $23,500 in dividends. The IRS (upheld by the Tax Court) assessed a deficiency, on the theory that the transfer was essentially testamentary and not made for fair market value. However, the Third Circuit found the transaction to be a bona fide sale for adequate consideration, so the preferred stock was effectively removed from the transferor's estate.[11]

The Fifth Circuit requires the filing of a "recapture agreement," binding all heirs to maintain the special use (and repay tax benefits if it is not) as a condition of electing §2032A special use valuation. The recapture agreement must be enforceable under state law.[12]

The Court of Federal Claims valued "flower bonds" at their par value plus accrued interest on the owner's date of death—a valuation that was affirmed *per curiam* by the Federal Circuit.[13]

[¶2311]   GENERATION-SKIPPING TRANSFER TAX

Final Regulations covering the GST were adopted by T.D. 8644, effective 12/27/95. See 1996-7 IRB 16.

[¶2313]   ADMINISTERING THE ESTATE

Distributions made from a decedent's trust, after his death, to satisfy completed gifts that were enforceable pre-mortem debts are claims against the trust. Therefore, according to the District Court for the District of Massachusetts, they cannot be deducted from the estate as §2053 "claims against the estate." The distributions were mandatory, and therefore the decedent relinquished the power to revoke or amend those distributions within three years of death. The result is that the distributions made within three years of death were included in the trust's fair market value by §2038.[14]

If a custodial parent dies, child support arrears are presumed to be an asset of the deceased's estate—although this presumption can be rebutted if enforcing it would be detrimental to the child(ren).[15]

A man's will specified that the 15 vials of his frozen sperm were to be used to impregnate his girlfriend. The decedent's children contested the will. The will contest was settled, with the girlfriend to receive 20 percent of the estate's residual assets. The probate judge ordered release of three of the 15 vials of sperm. The appeals court held that the frozen sperm was not an estate "asset," or subject to the 20 percent limit; the semen could be used only by the plaintiff, consistent with the decedent's intent.[16]

[¶2316]   TAX DUTIES OF FIDUCIARIES

According to the Eighth Circuit, the IRS could not appeal a District Court order removing a tax lien from a property, because the lien arose at the date of death, and thus had to be appealed within ten years of the date of death.[17] That is, the lien is durational, not limitational. The lien lasts exactly ten years after death; the government does not get ten years to file a claim after discovery of the existence of the claim.

The personal representative of an estate has been held personally liable for the unpaid assessed balance of the estate tax (as well as interest and penalties) because he distributed assets to himself, after receiving notice of the government claim, making the estate insolvent.[18]

If a charitable remainder unitrust (CRUT) receives unrelated business taxable income (UBTI) from a publicly traded limited partnership, all of the income of the trust is taxed under §664(c), not just the UBTI income deriving from the partnership. The trust cannot claim that the partnership income should be treated like corporate dividends (which are not considered UBTI) because Congress could have drafted the Tax Code that way, but chose not to.[19]

[¶2326]   CHECKLIST OF POST-MORTEM TAX PLANNING STEPS

The Tax Court ruled that cash gifts made by a surviving spouse to disclaiming legatees prevented their disclaimers from being valid. Therefore, the estate could not claim the marital deduction for amounts passing to the surviving spouse because of the purported disclaimers—which, in any case, were not freely made because family members would be unlikely to alienate a rich relative. However, the Fifth Circuit reversed in late 1997. The Court of Appeals' analysis was that an implied promise of benefit does not invalidate a disclaimer. The disclaimer becomes invalid only if there has been mutually bargained-for consideration supporting the disclaimer.[20]

— ENDNOTES —

1. *Fletcher v. Fletcher,* 65 LW 2484 (Va.Sup. 1/10/97).

2. *C.I.R. v. Estate of Hubert,* #95-1402, 65 LW 4183 (Sup.Ct. 3/18/97).

3. *Boggs v. Boggs,* #96-79, 117 S.Ct. 1754 (Sup.Ct. 6/2/97).

4. *Estate of Carpenter v. C.I.R.,* 52 F.3d 1266 (4th Cir. 5/9/95).

5. *Estate of Spencer v. C.I.R.,* 43 F.3d 226 (6th Cir. 1/5/95). Although the IRS has litigated the validity of this "wait and see" approach several times, the Fifth and Eighth Circuits also permit "wait and see": *Estate of Clayton v. Comm'r,* 976 F.2d 1486 (5th Cir. 1992); *Estate of Robertson v. Comm'r,* 15 F.3d 779 (8th Cir. 1994).

   The Tax Court allowed contingent QTIPs: *Estate of Clack,* 106 T.C. No. 6 (2/29/96), but only for individuals dying before 3/1/94, applying Reg. §20.2056(b)-7(d)(3) to deny QTIP treatment if placement of assets into the trust is contingent on the executor's election.

   Finally, in early 1997, the IRS conceded and permitted contingent QTIPs for elections made after February 18, 1997: T.D. 8714, Temp.Reg. §20.2044-1(T) et.seq. See CCH Federal Estate & Gift Tax Reporter ¶12,735.

6. *Estate of Shelfer v. Comm'r,* 86 F.3d 1045 (11th Cir. 7/1/96).

7. *Hermann Estate v. Comm'r,* 85 F.3d 1032 (2nd Cir. 6/11/96).

8. *Hahn,* 110 TC No. 14 (3/4/98); *Patten v. C.I.R.,* 97-2 USTC ¶60,279 (6/26/97); *Wilburn v. U.S.,* 97-2 USTC 60,294 (D.Md. 10/14/97), relying on *Gallenstein v. C.I.R.,* 975 F.2d 286 (6th Cir. 1992). See Sidney Kess, "Break for Surviving Spouse of Older Joint Tenancies," *N.Y.L.J.* 4/6/98 p. 3.

9. T.D. 8630, 1996-3 IRB 19 (12/95), finalizing the Regs. proposed in 59 FR 30180 (6/10/94). Also see Rev.Rul. 96-3, 1996-2 IRB 14, pronouncing Rev.Rul. 80-80 (former rules about the valuation tables) obsolete.

10. T.C. Memo 1996-307 (7/8/96).

11. *Estate of D'Ambrosio,* 101 F.3d 309 (3rd Cir. 11/26/96).

12. *Estate of Hudgins v. C.I.R.,* 57 F.3d 1393 (5th Cir. 6/28/95).

13. *Werld v. U.S.,* 55 F.3d 623 (Fed.Cir. 1995).

14. *White v. U.S.,* 906 F.Supp. 24 (D.Mass. 1995).

15. *Costello v. McDonald,* 22 Fam.L.Rep. 1443 (W.Va. 6/14/96).

16. *Hecht v. Los Angeles County Superior Court,* 65 LW 2345 (Cal.App. 11/13/96). In any event, one would hardly expect his children to want the other 80% of the vials.

17. *U.S. v. Davis,* 52 F.3d 781 (8th Cir. 4/21/95).

18. *U.S. v. Estate of Kime,* 97-1 USTC ¶60,256 (D.Neb. 12/13/96).

19. *Leila G. Newhall Unitrust v. C.I.R.,* 65 LW 2502 (9th Cir. 1/21/97).

20. *Estate of Monroe,* 104 T.C. No. 16 (3/27/95) *rev'd* 124 F.3d 399 (5th Cir. 10/9/97).

— FOR FURTHER REFERENCE —

Davis, James C., "Deferral of Estate Taxes: Calculating the Benefit and the Funding," 51 J. *American Society of CLU/ChFC* 58 (January '97).

Dukeminier, Jesse, "Dynasty Trusts: Sheltering Descendents from Transfer Taxes," 23 *Estate Planning* 417 (November '96).

Feinstein, Arnold, "Some Common Estate Planning Mistakes," 2 *Georgia Bar J.* 28 (February '97).

Hudson, Boyd D., "Failure to Make Qualified Disclaimer Can Be Expensive," 28 *The Tax Adviser* 73 (February '97).

Kasner, Jerry A., "Sales of Remainder Interests Don't Work-Or Do They?" 74 *Tax Notes* 203 (1/13/97).

Katzenstein, Andrew M. and Lisa C. McArthur, "Planning for the Family-Owned Business Exclusion Under TRA '97," 24 *Estate Planning* 465 (December '97).

Kiziah, Trent H., "Drafting Wills for the Remarried Spouse," 71 *Florida Bar J.* 34 (January '97).

Miller, Susan L., "Practical Problems and Solutions in Establishing a Qualified Personal Residence Trust," 86 *J. of Taxation* 102 (February '97).

Moore, M. Read, "A Marriage of Convenience: The Credit Shelter Trust and Qualified Plan and IRA Benefits," 24 Estate Planning 83 (February '97).

Schlenger, Jacques T., Robert E. Madden and John P. Edgar, "Reasonable Certainty of Death Prevented Use of Actuarial Tables for Valuation," 24 *Estate Planning* 33 (January '97).

Schneiderman, Gerald, "Including a Health Professional in Will Drafting Aids Transition," 136 *Trusts and Estates* 60 (February '97).

Share, Leslie A., "Planning Impact of New Expatriation and Foreign Trust Tax Rules," 24 *Estate Planning* 51 (February '97).

St.Laurent, Ann, "Estate Planning With Tax-Deferred Annuities: Special Problems Under §72," 13 *Tax Management Financial Planning J.* 3 (1/21/97).

Winslow, William L. and C. John Laugharn, "Estate Planning with Structured Settlements," 50 *J. American Society of CLU/ChFC* 82 (November '96).

Wood, Robert W., "Timing of Charitable Contributions and Intent," 24 *J. of Real Estate Taxation* 323 (Spring '97).

IMMIGRATION

[¶2401] P.L. 104-51 amends §101(b) of the Immigration and Nationality Act (8 U.S.C. §1101(b)) to change the vocabulary used in the Act's definition of "child." Children are now referred to as born "in wedlock" or "out of wedlock" rather than "legitimate" or "illegitimate."

Federal immigration law preempts California's Proposition 187, a 1994 initiative that denies illegal aliens state services or benefits. According to the District Court for the Central District of California, the state law is preempted to the extent that it conflicts with federal law or establishes a state scheme for the inherently federal area of regulation of immigration.[1]

There were three major federal laws passed in 1996, all three quite restrictive in their attitude toward aliens (legal and otherwise). The first of the trilogy is the Antiterrorism and Effective Death Penalty Act (AEDPA), P.L. 104-132. Although most of this statute deals with terrorism and other criminal acts, the AEDPA makes it easier to deport aliens convicted of crimes (even nonviolent crimes) and to deport aliens on grounds of moral turpitude. The AEDPA provides that a final order against an alien convicted of a crime is "not subject to review by any court." AEDPA also limits collateral attack of deportation orders.

Federal limitations on benefits for legal aliens were imposed by the Personal Responsibility and Work Opportunity Act, P.L. 104-193 (8/22/96), with the result that benefit eligibility will be terminated for a number of legal immigrants. P.L. 104-193 denies federal public assistance to immigrants who are not "qualified aliens." (A qualified alien is a refugee, deportee, or alien who has been in the U.S. for less than five years; or a lawful permanent resident who has a work history in the U.S. of at least 40 quarters of work.)

For those who entered the United States legally before August 22, 1996, they will not be eligible for food stamps or Supplemental Security Income (SSI). Each state has the choice whether or not to provide nonemergency Medicaid (health) benefits to legal aliens. (Qualified aliens in the U.S. as of August 22, 1996 who were eligible for Medicaid services continue to be eligible.)

For anyone entering the United States after August 22, 1996 (even if entry is legal), there will be a five-year post-entry period when federal means-tested assistance (including Medicaid) will be denied. Exceptions to this ruling include entrants who are refugees, deportees from other countries, persons entitled to political asylum, and military personnel from other countries. After the end of the five-year period, benefit eligibility will be calculated, including the assets of the immigrant's spouse and sponsor—with the result that many immigrants will be ineligible because these deemed resources will place them over the resource limit.

The final statute of the three is the Illegal Immigration Reform and Immigrant Responsibility Act of 1996, a minor part of the massive Omnibus Appropriations Act, P.L. 104-208 (9/30/96). The immigration provisions of P.L. 104-208 impose more border control, tougher enforcement of laws against alien smuggling, and further limitations on public benefits for aliens. Additional penalties are added for document fraud and employment of undocumented aliens.[2]

(This bill, and its April 1, 1997 deadlines, were the cause of much anxiety among immigrant communities.)

One focus of P.L. 104-208 is to make it harder for immigrants to use their continued presence in the United States, after their visa has expired, to obtain valid immigration status. Neither employment nor marriage to a U.S. citizen will automatically permit permanent U.S. residence. The INS has been given until September 30, 1998 to create an entry/exit control system that indicates when a visa has expired and an immigrant has overstayed his or her authorization.

There is also an emphasis on identifying aliens who attempt to enter the U.S. without adequate documentation, and preventing their entry by subjecting them to summary removal.

This legislation automatically voids nonimmigrant visas as soon as they expire, and the alien will not be issued a new U.S. visa to anywhere except his or her home country, unless the alien proves the existence of extraordinary circumstances.

The INS proposed Regulations, affecting 8 CFr Part 214, on December 30, 1997: see 62 FR 67764. The proposal explains the way INS keeps track of H-1B and H-2B visa applications to keep them within the annual numerical limitations.

At the end of 1997, the District Court for the District of Columbia ruled that it was unlawful to fire a Foreign Service officer who refused to use discriminatory standards based on race, nationality, and appearance when processing applications for visas from Brazil to the United States.[3]

[2401.1] Exclusion and Deportation

P.L. 104-208, discussed above, consolidates exclusion proceedings (for those who have not entered the U.S.) and deportation proceedings (for those who are within the U.S. but whose continued presence is in some way illicit or undesirable) into a single removal proceeding. However, cases involving pre-April 1, 1997 exclusions and deportations will continue to work through the court system for some time. The burden of proof in deportability cases falls on the government (by clear and convincing evidence), but an alien seeking relief from deportation (e.g., on account of seven years' residence and positive factors supporting the application) must prove, by a preponderance of the evidence, that he or she is eligible for such relief.

"Adjustment of status," a procedure permitting aliens to remain within the United States (instead of leaving the country and seeking a green card from outside), is severely restricted effective September 30, 1997. This change will have a particularly severe impact on aliens who have worked in the United States contrary to their visa eligibility.

Many of the cases discussed here relate to pre-Illegal Immigration Reform and Immigrant Responsibility Act immigration law.

A discretionary waiver of deportation can be granted to an otherwise admissible alien who has committed entry fraud—but the Attorney General can consider all acts of fraud in analyzing whether or not the waiver is permissible. A distinction can properly be drawn between a pattern of fraud and an isolated act of misrepresentation.[4]

A U.S. Attorney does not have the authority to promise, in the course of plea negotiations, that the alien will not be deported if he or she pleads guilty to the charges. Therefore, the INS is not bound by any such promise made by the U.S. Attorney's office.[5]

For asylum purposes, a claim of persecution requires proof that the alien left his or her homeland because of race, religion, nationality, social group, or political opinion, and is at risk of prosecution and severe punishment for leaving the homeland without permission, if he or she does not obtain asylum.[6] A further refinement: the Ninth Circuit says that if lawful and peaceful means of dissent are available in the home country, an alien cannot seek asylum in the United States based on fear of prosecution for participation in an attempted coup d'etat.[7]

The BIA turned down an asylum application from a Russian lesbian who did not want to return to Russia because of compulsory "psychiatric" treatment imposed on homosexuals. In the BIA's analysis, the home-country's intention was to "cure" rather than "punish" individuals subjected to these procedures. However, the Ninth Circuit ruled that subjective intent to punish is not a requisite. The test is whether a reasonable asylee would believe that he or she was a victim of persecution inflicted because of his or her characteristics.[8]

Several courts have denied asylum petitions brought by Chinese immigrants who do not want to be subjected to China's policy of coerced abortion or sterilization to limit all families to one child. The asylum petitions are often unsuccessful because the immigrants cannot prove they are at individual risk due to their political opinions; the policy is applied to the population at large.[9] However, a mid-1997 Third Circuit decision involving another Chinese law (requiring informing on colleagues) says that a law of general applicability can still be used as a premise for a claim of asylum.[10]

Other Chinese asylum seekers, who jumped out of a smuggling vessel and swam ashore, did not achieve "entry" sufficient to entitle them to deportation proceedings in lieu of summary exclusion. The Third Circuit said[11] that "entry" requires a lack of official restraint and either admission by immigration officials or an intentional evasion of inspection.

In a recent Ninth Circuit case, the alien was asked at his deportation hearing if he wanted to apply for asylum; he declined. Later, he sought to reopen the deportation proceedings and make an initial application for asylum. The court ruled that he must not only explain why he did not apply initially, but also offer evidence that was not available at the time of the initial deportation hearing.[12]

A "Marielito"—person expelled from Cuba's Mariel prison—had spent about a decade in various U.S. prisons as an excluded alien, because Cuba wouldn't take him back and no other country wished to admit him. The Ninth Circuit said[13] that there is no limitation on the duration of detention where there is no possibility of immediate deportation. Parole is the exception, not the rule; and cases are reviewed at least once a year to see if parole can be granted. In this reading, Congress knew about the potential for lengthy detention, but chose not to eliminate it.

An Eastern District of Virginia case involving another Marielito permits retention of an excludable alien in federal prison after completion of his sentence for an offense committed while on immigration parole.[14]

INA §241(a)(4)(C)(1), which permits the deportation of an alien whose presence could have "serious adverse foreign policy consequences" for the United States, has been held to be void for vagueness and condemned for its failure to provide due process. The District Court also found that it improperly assigns legislative power to the executive branch.[15]

[¶2404]   EXCLUSION AND DEPORTATION PROCEEDINGS

In April 1995, the U.S. Supreme Court held that a motion to reconsider a final deportation order of the Board of Immigration Appeals does not toll the running of the statutory 90-day period for seeking judicial review of the decision.[16]

According to the Tenth Circuit, an immigrant can be deported on the basis of an aggravated felony conviction; a separate showing of dangerousness to the community is not required to support deportation.[17] On the other hand, aliens who have been convicted of federal offenses, which are also deportable offenses, cannot use mandamus to get themselves deported before they finish their prison sentences.[18]

An alien who brings a Constitutional challenge to INA §241(a)(4)(C)(i) (deportation of those whose presence has potentially serious adverse foreign policy consequences) nevertheless has the obligation of exhausting administrative remedies before litigating the Constitutionality of the provision.[19]

A court that sentences an alien to supervised release on condition of deportation is not required to follow INA's procedural regulations.[20]

The Eighth Circuit rejected a Due Process challenge to the 10-day time limit for filing an administrative appeal of a deportation order. The court agreed that potential deportees who live in remote areas can be inconvenienced in satisfying that brief time period, but they don't have to use regular mail; the form can be sent to the INS office by UPS or Federal Express.[21]

The Seventh Circuit found the INS unreasonable in denying suspension of deportation without considering the aliens' community service within the United States, or the hardship to their child.[22]

Under the Anti-Terrorism and Effective Death Penalty Act of 1996, a final order of deportation due to certain crimes is not appealable to any court. In the view of the Seventh Circuit, this statutory provision cannot be applied where deportability was conceded before the AEDPA's effective date, provided that the applicant can assert at least a colorable defense to deportation.[23]

In contrast, according to the Second Circuit, this statute applies to petitioners for review filed before the effective date of the AEDPA, because there is no substantive right to maintain judicial review at its previous level. Furthermore, it is acceptable to oust the jurisdiction of the Court of Appeals, because there is still the possibility of some review through the habeas process.[24]

Once the five-year statute of limitations of INA §246(a) expires, it is too late to rescind the alien's adjustment of status premised on a green-card marriage. It is also too late to deport him based only on conduct that would justify rescission of the adjustment of status, but does not offer independent grounds for deportation.[25]

[¶2405]   EMPLOYER SANCTIONS

Executive Order 12989, 61 FR 6091 of February 13, 1996 debars federal contractors who knowingly hire illegal aliens from getting further federal contracts.

An alien who brings a Title VII employment discrimination action is not obligated to prove possession of a green card as part of the Title VII prima facie case. However, the employer can raise the lack of a green card as a valid nondiscriminatory reason for taking adverse job action against the individual.[26]

In 1997, the Second Circuit decided two cases that seem to reflect contradictory attitudes toward illegal alien workers. In the first, an alien union organizer was deported based on a tip from an anti-union employer. The NLRB issued a complaint against the employer for violating the NLRA, but the court ruled that it is improper to employ illegal aliens, even if an anti-union animus is present in actions taken against those aliens.[27] Yet the later case upholds the NLRB in ordering back pay for unfair labor practices, where the awards were made to undocumented aliens for the time they worked illegally in the United States before they were fired for supporting a union organizing drive. This time, the court found that the NLRB acted within its powers, and not in conflict with IRCA.[28]

— ENDNOTES —

1. *League of United Latin American Citizens v. Wilson,* 908 F.Supp. 755 (C.D.Cal. 11/20/95).

2. As of January 27, 1997, the INS will issue Form I-766, a tamper-resistant card, to aliens who are permitted to work temporarily in the United States. The card satisfies the I-9 identity and work eligibility requirements. A fact sheet about the document is available from INS by calling (800) 870-3676. For discussion of the IIRAIRA, see Michael D. Patrick, "The Diminution of the 'Fleuti' Doctrine," *N.Y.L.J.* 3/23/98 p. 3.

3. *Olsen v. Albright,* 66 LW 1432 (D.D.C. 12/22/97).

4. *INS v. Yang,* #95-938, 117 S.Ct. 350 (Sup.Ct. 11/13/96).

5. *San Pedro v. U.S.,* 79 F.3d 1065 (11th Cir. 4/9/96).

6. *Rodriguez-Roman v. INS,* 98 F.3d 416 (9th Cir. 10/9/96).

7. *Chanco v. INS,* 82 F.3d 298 (9th Cir. 4/19/96). Because peaceful protest was possible, the government (in this case, of the Philippines) could legitimately prosecute someone who attempted to overthrow the ruling regime.

8. *Pitcherskaia v. INS,* 118 F.3d 641 (9th Cir. 6/24/97).

9. *Chen v. Carroll,* 48 F.3d 1331 (4th Cir. 3/6/95); *Zhang v. Slattery,* 55 F.3d 732 (2nd Cir. 5/19/95) and *Chen v. INS,* 95 F.3d 801 (9th Cir. 9/6/96) are similar.

10. *Chang v. INS,* 119 F.3d 1055 (3rd Cir. 7/22/97).

11. *Yang v. Maugans,* 68 F.3d 1540 (3rd Cir. 10/24/95).

12. *Lainez-Ortiz v. INS,* 96 F.3d 393 (9th Cir. 9/16/96).

13. *Barreia-Echavarria v. Rison,* 44 F.3d 1441 (9th Cir. 1/12/95).

14. *Cruz-Elias v. U.S. Attorney General,* 870 F.Supp. 692 (E.D.Va. 12/8/94). The court saw no statutory or Due Process objections, in light of the facts that his status was reviewed at least annually, and that no other country wished to admit him.

15. *Massieu v. Reno,* 915 F.Supp. 681 (D.N.J. 2/18/96).

16. *Stone v. INS,* #93-1199, 115 S.Ct. 1537 (Sup.Ct. 4/19/95).

17. *Al-Salehi v. INS,* 47 F.3d 390 (10th Cir. 2/8/95).

18. *Hernandez-Avalos v. INS,* 50 F.3d 842 (10th Cir. 3/9/95). The Ninth Circuit agrees: *Campos v. INS,* 62 F.3d 311 (9th Cir. 8/4/95).

19. *Massieu v. Reno,* 91 F.3d 416 (3rd Cir. 7/29/96).

20. *U.S. v Oboh,* 92 F.3d 1082 (11th Cir. 8/8/96).

21. *Talamantes-Penalver v. INS,* 51 F.3d 133 (8th Cir. 3/30/95).

22. *Salameda v. INS,* 70 F.3d 447 (7th Cir. 11/9/95).

23. *Reyes-Hernandez v. INS,* 89 F.3d 490 (7th Cir. 7/17/96).

24. *Hincapie-Nieto v. INS,* 92 F.3d 27 (2nd Cir. 8/2/96); *Salazar-Haro v. INS,* 95 F.3d 309 (3rd Cir. 9/13/96) is similar. More recently, *Yesil v. Reno,* 958 F.Supp. 828 (S.D.N.Y. 2/27/97) holds that the AEDPA does not repeal the right to bring a habeas challenge to deportation orders based on certain crimes. But see *Powell v. Jennifer,* 937 F.Supp. 1245 (E.D. Mich. 8/22/96), finding that a District Court cannot exercise habeas jurisdiction to stay a deportation unless the deportation would be a fundamental miscarriage of justice.

25. *Bamidele v. INS,* 99 F.3d 557 (3rd Cir. 11/1/96).

26. *Egbuna v. Time-Life Libraries Inc.,* 95 F.3d 353 (4th Cir. 9/13/96).

27. *Montero v. INS,* 124 F.3d 381 (2nd Cir. 8/28/97).

28. *NLRB v. A.P.R.A. Fuel Oil Buyers Group Inc.,* 66 LW 1393 (2nd Cir. 12/5/97).

— FOR FURTHER REFERENCE —

Chang, Connie, "Immigrants Under the New Welfare Law," 45 *U.C.L.A. L.Rev.* 205 (October '97).

Fallek, Shari B., "Health Care for Illegal Aliens: Why It is a Necessity," 18 *Houston J. of International Law* 951 (Spring '97).

Lamden, Ann L., "Employment Authorization and I-9 Compliance," 96 *Immigration Briefings* 1 (September '96).

Mailman, Stanley, "The Employer as Immigration Inspector," *N.Y.L.J.* 4/22/96 p. 3.

Manning, Colleen, "Deporting the Addicted," 38 *Boston College L.Rev.* 977 (September '97).

McWhirter, Robert James, "The Rings of Immigration Hell: The Immigration Consequences to Aliens Convicted of Crimes," 10 *Georgetown Immigration Law J.* 169 (Winter '96).

Morrison, Trevor, "Removed from the Constitution? Deportable Aliens' Access to Habeas Corpus Under the New Immigration Legislation," 35 *Columbia J. of Transnational Law* 697 (Fall '97).

Murthy, Sheela, "Creative Avenues to Obtain the Green Card," 30 *Maryland Bar J.* 30 (May–June '97).

Palmer, Gary W., "Guarding the Coast: Alien Migrant Interdiction at Sea," 29 *Connecticut L.Rev.* 1565 (Summer '97).

Patrick, Michael D., "Immigration Law: Significant Changes to Take Place in April," *N.Y.L.J.* 3/24/97 p. 3.

Tetzeli, Helena, "Medical and Health-Related Grounds of Exclusion," 97 *Immigration Briefings* 1 (January '97).

Underwood, William C.B., "Unreviewable Discretionary Justice: The New Extreme Hardship in Cancellation of Deportation Cases," 72 *Indiana L.J.* 885 (Summer '97).

INSURANCE

[¶2501] The National Banking Act (12 U.S.C. §92) permits national banks in small towns (population under 5,000) to act as agents for life and property insurance. This somewhat staid statute has given rise to not one, but two Supreme Court cases during the supplement period.

The first, *NationsBank of North Carolina N.A. v. VALIC*[1] upholds the Commissioner of Currency's determination that banks can also sell annuities because this is "within the incidental powers necessary to the business of banking," and furthermore that annuities are investment instruments rather than insurance for this purpose.

The later case holds that a Florida statute forbidding insurance sales by banks is preempted by §92; the federal law does specifically relate to the business of insurance, so it falls within the McCarran-Ferguson Act exemption.[2] The Sixth Circuit found that §92 also preempts a Kentucky statute that prevents bank holding companies from serving as insurance agents. The statute is not entitled to the McCarran-Ferguson exemption because it keeps willing sellers out of the insurance business rather than merely regulating the insurance business.[3]

The Seventh Circuit says that a bank located in a small town has the further right to sell insurance in other, larger towns and cities.[4]

Viatical settlement—the procedure under which a terminally ill person assigns his or her life insurance to a settlement company, in return for a lump sum or continuing payments representing the discounted value of the insurance benefit—was initially held to be an investment contract that is subject to regulation under the Securities Act of 1933 §2(1).[5] In general, insurance is exempt from securities law regulation, but the District Court held that there is no transfer of risk to the insurer and therefore the viatical settlements fall outside the insurance category. In mid-1996, the D.C. Circuit reversed, finding that the profits are dependent on the timing of the viator's death, not on the promoters' efforts, so there is no investment contract that could be subject to securities regulation.

A product sold as a cheaper alternative to title insurance (where the lender waives the requirement of title insurance, but makes the borrower pay a fee for a report in lieu of title) has been held to constitute insurance and therefore be subject to insurance regulation. The bank promoting the plan was ordered to give all affected borrowers a free title insurance policy instead.[6]

An insured who prevails on the issue of the insurer's duty to defend is entitled to an award of attorney's fee award. An insured should be able to enforce the insurance contract, and the insurer's obligations under it, without out-of-pocket expenses.[7]

A Vermont law permitting an arbitration agreement contained in a contract of insurance to be revoked at any time prior to publication of an arbitration award has been struck down. The statute was deemed invalid because it is preempted by the Federal Arbitration Act provisions that make arbitration clauses virtually irrevocable. Therefore, a dispute about uninsured motorist coverage had to be arbitrated and not litigated.[8]

[¶2505.3] Accidental Death and Dismemberment

If an ADD policy covers death caused "solely" by a covered "accident," and excludes "sickness," a death caused by malpractice during surgery for a knee injury is still covered, because the death resulted from the covered injury.[9]

[¶2508] LEGAL ASPECTS OF BENEFICIARY DESIGNATION

A divorcing couple's separation agreement was incorporated into their decree. A clause in the agreement stating that the spouses had no rights in the other's estate "as heirs or otherwise" was not sufficient to terminate the husband's rights as named beneficiary of the wife's insurance. (She never changed the beneficiary designation.) According to the Nevada Supreme Court, specific divestiture in policy rights is required.[10]

[¶2509] LIFE INSURANCE TAXATION

According to the Fifth Circuit, a Qualified Terminable Interest in Property (QTIP) existed, and the Tax Court should not have placed 100 percent of the $650,000 proceeds of term life insurance purchased with community funds into the insured husband's gross estate. (The uninsured wife predeceased him, and the proceeds were payable to his estate). Under Texas community property law, when the husband died, 50 percent of the policy proceeds belonged to the wife's residuary trust. The policy remained community property even though the husband continued to renew the policy after the wife's death—he did not create new, separate policies.[11]

[¶2515] LIABILITY INSURANCE

According to the New Jersey Superior Court, it is contrary to state public policy to allow a company to insure against punitive damages, even if the company's liability is only vicarious.[12] In this analysis, punitive damages are supposed to act as a deterrent, but cannot do so if insurance coverage is available to shift liability. California also forbids indemnification for punitive damages, so the insurer has no duty to settle a claim so that the defendant will not face a jury that imposes punitive damages. Nor can the insurer be accused of bad faith (for failing to settle) and be required to pay the punitive damages through that route.[13]

In a recent Wisconsin case, a child was injured by a meatgrinder. The injured child's family sued the manufacturer, who countersued the child's mother (and the family's homeowner's insurance policy) for negligent supervision. The state's

Supreme Court permitted the enforcement of the family exclusion clause in a third-party contribution claim, because of the serious risk of collusion in intrafamily tort cases.[14]

[¶2515.1]   Liability Insurance and Environmental Claims

Several familiar issues were once again the subject of court decisions. At the end of 1995, the D.C. Circuit ruled that the CGL pollution exclusion clause's reference to "sudden and accidental" events unambiguously excludes coverage for gradual pollution, with the result that the federal government and not the insurer became responsible for a $100 million dioxin clean-up.[15]

Bodily injury caused by inhalation (of sulfur dioxide fumes or paint and glue fumes) has been held to be excluded from coverage by the pollution exclusion.[16] In 1997, it was ruled that the pollution exclusion bars coverage of injuries caused by a release of phenol gas during a workplace accident;[17] that the pollution exclusion does not bar coverage of claims that a leaking furnace caused carbon monoxide poisoning;[18] and that excessive buildup of carbon monoxide in an office building is not so clearly a pollutant to be subject to the pollution exclusion.[19]

The Eleventh Circuit deemed the term "discharge" in the CGL to be susceptible to more than one meaning. As a result, the policyholder was entitled to defense and indemnity when inhalation of a vapor "emission" from an adhesive product caused death, because of the ambiguity as to whether this "emission" was a "discharge."[20] The Second Circuit also found ambiguity in the CGL pollution exclusion—this time, whether the exclusion is limited to environmental pollution or covers the situation in which wrongful death and other injuries resulted from the release of carbon monoxide due to a landlord's negligent maintenance of a heating system.[21] A New Hampshire court has permitted a child to collect for injuries caused by inhalation of lead particles from the parents' work clothes, on the ground that the CGL's exclusion is ambiguous as to whether bringing dust home from the workplace is a "discharge."[22]

Discharge of pollution that is limited within one's own property is likely to be excluded from coverage because of the "own property" exclusion; coverage is more likely if someone else's property is implicated.

However, where a personal injury policy does cover wrongful entry and does not exclude pollution, then the insurer can be made to cover government-mandated cleanup costs.[23] According to the Sixth Circuit, an insured's cleanup costs, incurred after getting a CERCLA "PRP letter" (identifying the insured as a party potentially responsible for cleanup costs) are considered damages sought in a suit. Therefore, they are covered by the CGL. Furthermore, these costs are not subject to the "own property" exclusion, because the state owns the groundwater—the insured property owner does not.[24]

In a case of first impression in the state, the Oklahoma Supreme Court also applied the CGL exclusion to disposal of hazardous waste, on the usual grounds that "sudden" refers to abruptness and immediacy; "accidental" refers to the release itself, not to the result that the release caused pollution.[25]

In mid-1996, the Third Circuit decided that the status of pollution as an occurrence depends on the subjective intent of the policyholder (as to whether the discharge was expected or intended to damage the environment) rather than on objective tests of the effect.[26]

In the Second Circuit, if the insured can prove by a preponderance of the evidence that asbestos-caused disease was triggered continuously throughout the disease process, then coverage will correspondingly be triggered continuously. If several insurance policies are involved, coverage is prorated based on which insurer was liable at each particular time. The policyholder remains liable for the periods in which it was without insurance coverage. With respect to property damage, each time that asbestos-containing material is installed is an occurrence for which another deductible may properly be imposed.[27]

The pollution exclusion prevents coverage of claims of "sick building syndrome" (i.e., pervasive toxicity that causes annoying but hard-to-document symptoms).[28]

[¶2518]   PROPERTY INSURANCE

See Rev.Rul. 95-22, 1995-1 C.B. 145, for circumstances under which gain does not have to be recognized when insurance proceeds are received in connection with a Presidentially proclaimed natural disaster.

[¶2530]   SUPPLEMENTARY BENEFITS UNDER LIABILITY INSURANCE

In a Michigan case, a child sexually coerced another child on two occasions. In the first, the child was six years old; in the second, he was nine years old. The state Supreme Court required the parents' homeowner's insurance to treat these actions as "occurrences" covered by the policy. Although the child intended to obtain sexual gratification by his actions, he did not intend to harm the other child.

Absent proof of subjective intent to harm, he could neither be said to expect nor intend the injuries. Nor could summary judgment be granted based on the characterization of the child's activities as "intentional acts." Although adults are presumed to intend injury when they sexually assault children, no presumption obtains when both the actor and victim are children. Therefore, the jury must decide the fact question of whether a reasonable child of the actor's age would foresee injury resulting from his activities.[29]

A Nebraska homeowner's insurer did not have to cover sexual molestation committed by the policyholder. Although the plaintiff and defendant stipulated that the defendant acted negligently rather than intentionally, the insurer was not involved in the stipulation and was not bound by it.[30] In a Fifth Circuit case from 1997 the insured pleaded guilty to two counts of murder. The heirs of the victims sued for wrongful death, but were not able to collect under the insured's homeowner's insurance policy. A guilty plea is enough litigation to establish the collateral estoppel effect of the plea, and to establish the intentional nature of the insured's actions.[31]

The facts of the case determine whether a single negligent act (of improper supervision of a pedophile priest) will be treated as a single occurrence or multiple occurrences—that is, as multiple independent injuries, not multiple injuries to a single victim.[32]

In a Colorado automobile insurance case, both policies had excess clauses making the other policy primary. This arrangement was deemed to violate public policy because of its effect in denying coverage to policyholders who had paid and reasonably expected to be covered. The court required the loss to be proportioned between the two insurers as co-primaries.[33]

The no-fault automobile policy covering injury to a family member or pedestrian, caused by an object "propelled by or from an automobile" is broad enough to provide PIP benefits in the case of a drive-by shooting.[34]

It has been held that the advertising injury component of a CGL policy covers trademark infringement claims, but not patent infringement claims.[35]

The CGL does not cover intentional acts, so employers may find that they are not insured (for public policy reasons) when they are charged with employment-related torts.[36] However, depending on the jurisdiction and the circumstance, coverage (or at least a defense provided by the insurance company) may be available, especially if the employer's conduct is deemed to be negligent rather than intentionally hurtful and thus morally culpable.[37]

An umbrella business liability policy that covers "discrimination" claims has been held by the Seventh Circuit to be broad enough to cover antitrust claims of price discrimination (as well as the claims of employment discrimination that were probably intended by both parties).[38]

The Sixth Circuit dealt with another umbrella policy. This one covered unintentional discrimination but excluded discrimination committed by or at the direction of the insured. The court found the language to be deliberately ambiguous and accordingly construed it against the insurer. In effect, the Sixth Circuit decided that an insurer cannot include torts in the definition of personal injury while excluding them from the definition of occurrence.[39]

[¶2531]   HEALTH INSURANCE

Because the cost of health care is so high, it is unusual for anyone to pay out-of-pocket for such care. Usually payment is made by a third party—either Medicare or Medicaid (see ¶3903, 3904 in the main volume) or private health insurance. Although some people purchase insurance as individuals, or through affinity groups (such as bar associations), the commonest form of health insurance is through a plan sponsored by the employer. Many ex-employees are entitled to assume individual payment for continuation of their group insurance plans for a period of months or years, as provided by the federal statute COBRA (the Comprehensive Omnibus Budget Reconciliation Act of 1985–86).

The Health Insurance Portability and Accountability Act of 1996 (sometimes called the Kennedy-Kassebaum Act, after its sponsors; P.L. 104-191), as its name suggests, requires EGHPs to make it easier for employees to get benefits under a second plan if they have already participated in another plan. HIPAA restricts the extent to which preexisting condition limitations can be used to deny benefits, although if employees go 63 days without health coverage, they lose all "creditable coverage" for HIPAA purposes.

HIPAA also authorizes a small-scale pilot project to test the viability of Medical Savings Accounts (similar in many ways to IRAs) as a funding mechanism for medical care.

Traditionally, the employer furnished the entire premium for the plan, which either reimbursed employees for their medical expenses or paid on an indemnity basis ($X for a particular service or health condition or per day of hospitalization), subject to a copayment responsibility. The distinction between reimbursement and indemnity is that reimbursement pays back the employee or other insured person for expenses incurred. Indemnity provides the insured with money that can, but need not be, used to pay medical expenses.

Today, however, there is an ever-increasing likelihood that an employer's group health plan (EGHP) will either offer managed care as an option, or require employees to get their care from a managed care entity (see below). Furthermore, employees are required to assume an increasing share of the cost of insurance, both through premiums they pay and through the copayments (deductibles and coinsurance) they are required to assume.

Sometimes employers (especially large companies) will self-insure. That is, instead of purchasing health insurance policies, they will set aside reserves to be used when employees encounter health expenditures of a type covered by the health plan. An insurance company may take a limited role in administering such a plan; it is then called a TPA (third party administrator) or ASO (administrative services only) organization vis-a-vis the employer.

EGHPs are considered welfare benefit plans for ERISA purposes. Therefore, in many instances employees will not have state-law remedies against the insurer or the employer because ERISA preempts the state law—even though ERISA has very little to say on the subject of welfare benefits.

In the spring of 1995, the Supreme Court upheld a New York statute requiring hospitals to collect a surcharge (to be used to pay for the care of the uninsured and destitute) on hospital bills if the patient was covered by a commercial insurer or certain HMOs, but exempting patients covered by Blue Cross/Blue Shield from the surcharge. The Supreme Court rejected the argument that ERISA preempts the state statute, because the surcharges do not "relate to" employee benefit plans, but rather to hospital financing. States can properly regulate hospital costs even if the regulation has an indirect economic effect on benefit plans. The exemption is intended to help out Blue Cross plans in their role as insurer of last resort.[40]

Health insurance policies are generally drafted to exclude "experimental" drugs and procedures. A frequent litigation issue is: when does a treatment become accepted enough to be removed from the experimental class? High-dose chemotherapy for breast cancer has been characterized as nonexperimental by the

Fourth Circuit, ruling that therapy need only be accepted by the scientific community; the person seeking coverage need not demonstrate a statistically significant chance of a cure.[41] However, another case also involving CHAMPUS (the federal agency that finances the medical care of civilian dependents of military personnel) found that CHAMPUS was not arbitrary or capricious when it characterized the high-dose chemotherapy as experimental, and thus denying coverage was not a violation of the Administrative Procedures Act.[42]

Another breast cancer patient succeeded in obtaining a preliminary injunction, given the likelihood of success on her claim that high-dose chemotherapy is an accepted treatment. Thus, her health plan violated the ADA by covering high-dose chemotherapy for certain cancers but denying it for breast cancer.[43]

Also note that a union welfare fund settled a major EEOC case involving discrimination against persons with AIDS by agreeing to pay at least $1 million and extend coverage for PWAs. The settlement applies to the 13 named plaintiffs and to any plan member who responds within 45 days to a mailed notice disclosing the settlement. However, emotional distress damages are limited to $50,000 per person.[44]

On further AIDS issues, note that the Fifth Circuit says that an insurance company has no duty to disclose the results (including HIV+ status) of a medical examination performed to determine insurability, because the insurance applicant was not being treated at the time.[45] The Central District of California permitted the HIV− husband of an HIV+ wife to sue an insurer who denied him coverage, using the Americans with Disabilities Act to challenge a denial of public accommodations.[46]

[¶2531.1] Policy Design

Health insurance policies are usually written as either basic medical insurance or major medical insurance. A basic medical insurance plan covers, e.g., hospital expenses (room and board, drugs, laboratory tests, etc.), surgical fees, and other physician fees. In general, hospital expenses are covered based on a certain amount per day, up to a certain number of days (e.g., 30 days per year; 90 days per year; even 365 days per year). There are two basic payment approaches: reimbursing the insured for the actual cost of hospital care, up to $X per day; or a service benefit, paying whatever the hospital's charge may be for a semi-private room.

Surgical expenses are paid according to a surgical schedule; reasonable and customary fees; or a relative value scale. A surgical schedule sets a "price" for a long list of procedures. The insured receives either what the surgeon actually charges or the amount on the schedule—whichever is less. The reasonable and customary approach pays the full amount of the actual fee, provided that it is comparable to what other surgeons in the same area charge. A relative value scale compares the seriousness of various operations, and compensates more highly for the more serious procedures than for the trivial ones.

Nonsurgical doctor bills (e.g., office visits; care of patients in the hospital who are not undergoing surgery) are usually compensated at a certain amount per visit.

A major medical plan requires the insured person to assume a significant deductible, but offers a very high level of coverage (e.g., up to $1 million in lifetime benefits). A major medical policy can supplement a basic policy; or a person who is very risk-tolerant or very short of cash might purchase a major medical policy as his or her only form of health insurance coverage.

As a general rule, health insurance policies pay only for costs incurred "as a result of injury or sickness," and only for medically necessary services. Thus, elective procedures such as cosmetic surgery are not covered. Nor are experimental procedures that are not scientifically accepted. This is a major litigation area: in many instances, coverage of an expensive procedure will be denied, leading to a charge of bad faith (or wrongful death) by the person seeking coverage or by his or her family or survivors.

Health policies usually contain a preexisting condition waiver—i.e., for a period such as six months or a year after the policy becomes effective, coverage will be denied for conditions for which the insured was already under treatment, or for which a reasonable person would have sought treatment, and which was not disclosed on the application. (Policies are also conventionally written to exclude disclosed preexisting conditions.)

It is unusual for a sick person to collect the full cost of medical care. Usually, payments do not begin until a deductible has been satisfied (for the calendar year or for each sickness or injury), and the insured is usually required to pay a coinsurance amount. Also, to avoid anyone earning a profit on illness, if there are two or more policies that might pay for the care, benefits are coordinated—i.e., there are rules determining the responsibility of each policy, making sure that the insured never collects over 100 percent of the cost of care.

[¶253L.2] Policy Renewals

Health insurance policies may fall into any one of five categories of renewability. A cancelable policy offers the least stability and protection for the insured: it permits the insurer to increase premiums at any time permitted by state regulators, and to terminate the policy at any time by notifying the insured and returning any premiums that were paid in advance.

An optionally renewable policy's premium can be raised for an entire class of insureds, but not for a particular insured who has made large claims. The policy can be terminated on a date set by the contract—typically, the policy anniversary. A conditionally renewable policy can be terminated by the insurer because of conditions named in the contract, such as ceasing to be employed or reaching a triggering age—but not deterioration in health. Here, too, premium increases must be applied to a whole class or not at all.

A guaranteed renewable policy must be renewed until a specific age (typically 65, the age of Medicare eligibility, or age 60) as long as the insured continues to maintain premium payments. Only class-wide premium increases are permitted. Noncancelable health insurance policies are rare. They continue until the insured reaches age 65, and the insurer retains neither the right to terminate the coverage nor to increase the premium.

[¶253L.3]   Managed Care Entities

Managed care developed as a response to continuing double-digit annual increases in the cost of insured medical care. A managed care entity is an organization (typically an insurance company or division of an insurance company) that administers the provision of medical care under terms other than conventional fee-for-service care rendered by any provider of the patient's choice. There are many managed care entities currently operating, many hybrid entities, and the lines of demarcation are not always clear-cut.

Theoretically, managed care entities will lower the cost of health care by "gatekeeper" mechanisms that prevent health care consumers from over-using care, and by removing providers' incentives to over-treat or over-prescribe. The risk of the pure fee-for-service plan is that providers, given an economic incentive to expand the care furnished, will drive up the bill by ordering unnecessary services for purely financial reasons. The risk of the pure managed care plan is that providers, given an economic incentive to restrict treatment, will impair patients' health by withholding necessary services.

At first, managed care entities were absolved of liability on various theories (they did not furnish care, and thus could not commit malpractice, etc.). However, there is an increasing trend to make the managed care entity liable if, for instance, it is negligent in selection or supervision of participating physicians, or if utilization review activities deny access to necessary care, with resulting harm to the would-be patient.

The Health Maintenance Organization, or HMO, might be called the "traditional" mode of managed care. Patients ("lives") who are covered by an HMO are expected to get most or all of their care through the HMO. In exchange for this limitation, they will be insulated from major out-of-pocket expenses: they may receive treatment without explicit cost, or at a small out-of-pocket copayment, within the system.

Depending on the arrangement, patients may be denied reimbursement, or reimbursed at a lower rate, if they seek care outside the HMO's pool of physicians, hospitals, diagnostic facilities, and other resources. However, full reimbursement will typically be available for emergency care outside the network, or if it is agreed that the patient needs a type of specialized care that is not available within the HMO network.

Usually, patients will be required to see a "gatekeeper" family physician before being referred to an HMO specialist. Advance authorization is generally required for surgery; second opinions are usually required before authorization will be granted; and utilization review is generally used to determine if a continued stay in a hospital, nursing facility, or rehabilitation facility continues to be necessary and appropriate.

Typically, HMOs are capitated plans. That is, health care providers receive a fee for each subscriber ("per head") for each month, whether or not a particular subscriber receives health care services in that month. Fees to providers are not dependent on the level or intensity of the services.

In a "staff model" HMO, the physicians, nurses, physical therapists, etc., are salaried employees of the HMO itself. In a "group model" HMO, care is provided by medical groups with diverse specialties, who contract with the HMO.

The "IPA" (Individual Practice Association) model provides services under a contract between the HMO and physicians or medical groups who practice independently. The IPA itself, as an entity, is usually a business corporation with physicians as stockholders and officers.

The general rule is the IPA HMOs do not own hospitals, imaging centers, etc.; usually, they enter into contractual arrangements for the use of existing facilities. However, IPAs often provide utilization management, quality assurance, and retrospective review of services performed by the association members. Vertical integration (direct ownership of facilities) is common among staff and group model HMOs.

A "closed panel" HMO is limited to a certain number of physicians. A rule of thumb is that the key figure is the number of primary care (family) physicians affiliated with the HMO—and that approximately one primary physician is required for every 1,600 HMO members. The panel will have many primary physicians for every specialty physician.

One of the most controversial aspects of the arrangement between HMOs and providers is the frequent use of mechanisms that shift the financial risk to the provider. Depending on the contract, providers may be given incentives (such as payments from a risk pool) if utilization falls below a defined amount—or they may be forced to pay penalties if utilization is higher.

The HMO itself can be organized in many ways. The first HMOs, some of which are still operating (e.g., Kaiser Permanente; Harvard Community Health Plan) are nonprofit organizations, staffed by health care workers (including physicians) who are salaried employees.

The Preferred Provider Organization (PPO) is a business company, generally a conventional for-profit corporation but perhaps a nonprofit or noncorporate proprietary entity, created either by insurers, by providers, or by a coalition. The preferred providers are "members" of the entity, under contract with but not employees of the PPO. The provider contract specifies the rate schedule for provision of services to covered patients.

The general rule is that PPOs do not require licensure as health care facilities, but there may be circumstances under which licensure is mandated. Depending on circumstances, the PPO may be the actual payor for the care, or may merely be an administrative entity that does business with the payors. Patients covered by a PPO usually get to choose their own providers, but receive discounts if they use one of the preferred providers within the network.

An "open-panel" PPO will permit any qualified physician who is willing to accept the plan's fee schedule to join the panel. Some states have passed "any willing provider" laws that obligate PPOs to accept physicians unless there is some valid reason (e.g., professional sanctions; incomplete training) for rejecting them. "Any willing provider" laws protect physicians against the risk of being forced out of practice if most of the patients in an area are covered by managed care plans, and if those plans deny admission to physicians for improper reasons (e.g., racial or sex discrimination).

The Point of Service (POS) plan is a hybrid that has some features of the HMO and some of the PPO. POS plans give patients more choice of provider, with different reimbursement schedules depending on whether the provider selected is within or outside the network. For instance, the patient might pay a 10 percent copayment if a network provider is chosen, but would pay 40 percent for providers outside the network.

A Physician-Hospital Organization (PHO) offers a combination of hospital and medical services, on a risk basis, to HMOs or other managed care entities. PHOs can be set up as for-profit or nonprofit organizations. Usually, the PHO is jointly owned by a hospital and by a group of doctors affiliated with that hospital and providing care there. In turn, the doctors may organize themselves into an IPA or other business entity. PHOs generally do not enter into capitation arrangements, because state law often treats such arrangements as insurance contracts that require licensure (and regulation) as an insurance company.

The Exclusive Provider Organization is an insurance arrangement, under which the employer's plan covers only care that is provided by one of the designated providers, not care from "outsiders" selected by the patient. Although, from the patient's point of view, the EPO and the HMO operate similarly, the two have different legal structures. An HMO is regulated by special state laws covering only HMOs; EPOs are treated as insurance products regulated under the insurance law.

A management services organization is a legal entity, usually a corporation, that owns and operates medical offices, office equipment, diagnostic equipment, and other items needed for a group medical practice. The MSO may also provide support staff and administer managed care contracts. MSOs may be owned by the physicians (free-standing) or by a health care organization (hospital-affiliated or HMO-affiliated). Because the MSO does not furnish medical services, it can be owned and operated by individuals who are not licensed physicians or other health care providers.

Employees who receive employment-related coverage through an MCO may face difficulties in pressing claims of poor medical care or improper denial of coverage. It is very likely that claims brought in state court will be dismissed, on the grounds of ERISA preemption because of the involvement of an employer plan. There may be further difficulties because of the traditional doctrine that corporations can't practice medicine—only people can. Hence, it may be impossible to sue the MCO, and the individual doctor (especially a house staffer with lots of education loans and few assets) may not be a satisfying defendant.

There is an increasing trend toward greater state regulation of MCOs, although not all of these statutes will survive ERISA challenges.A late-1997 Wisconsin case permits subscribers to sue their HMOs for bad faith denial of coverage.[47]

A Sixth Circuit case involved an insurer that denied a pregnancy-related insurance claim because the employee failed to disclose her history of heart ailments on the insurance application. Under the relevant state law (Ohio), a claim can be denied if the policy would not have been issued but for the misrepresentation. However, the Sixth Circuit mandated coverage, because the state law is preempted by ERISA. The insurer was viewed as raising an affirmative defense to the claim for benefits under an ERISA plan. The Ohio law was preempted because it deals with basic fraud principles, not insurance, and because it does not alter the spread of risk among parties.[48]

The Fifth Circuit denied ERISA preemption in a case where a hospital treated a patient in reliance on incorrect information from the insurer that the patient was covered by a health plan. The hospital then sued the insurer for deceptive and unfair trade practices of negligent misrepresentation.[49] ERISA preemption was not found because the hospital is an independent third party with no relation to the employment-related plan.

ERISA preemption was not found (and the insurer lost yet again) in an Eighth Circuit case involving an injured farm employee who charged that the farm bought a policy that the agent described as covering work-related injuries even though it did not. In this analysis, ERISA does not preempt a state tort action for negligent misrepresentation of an insurance policy, because the injured employee doesn't seek anything from the employer's health insurance plan itself, and allowing a recovery will not impair plan administration.[50]

Several states have notice and prejudice laws that do not permit claims to be denied on the basis of late proof of loss unless the delay is actually prejudicial to the insurer. Wisconsin's law has been held not to be preempted by ERISA, because it is insurance regulation.[51] The Ninth Circuit also ruled that such laws are not preempted by ERISA, but additionally ruled that the notice and prejudice rule should not become part of the federal common law of ERISA.[52]

[¶2532]   LONG-TERM CARE INSURANCE

Long term care (LTC) is the provision of services, either at home or in institutions, to aged or disabled individuals who have a continuing need for assistance. The problem requiring assistance may be physical (e.g., paraplegia), cognitive (e.g., Alzheimer's Disease), or both. Some frail elderly people require LTC even though they have no specific acute illness.

Although some health insurance policies have some coverage of home care or physical therapy, usually the coverage can be triggered only if there has been some accident or acute illness. The Medicare system covers acute health care, but not LTC. Since the 1980s, there has been a growing variety of specialized policies covering LTC.

Long-Term Care Insurance (LTCI) policies can be purchased to cover nursing home care; nursing home care plus home care; home care only; or a broad spectrum of LTC services, adding adult day care and innovative housing services to institutional and home care.

Although some companies offer LTCI to their employees (and often their employees' parents as well) as an employee benefit, and there are some other ways of purchasing group LTCI, usually LTCI policies are purchased by individuals.

The general legal requirement is that LTCI policies must be guaranteed renewable–i.e., if the insured person keeps up premium payments, the employer can neither terminate the policy nor refuse to renew it on the basis of deterioration in the insured's health. Furthermore, although the premium can be raised for an entire class of policyholders, insurers are not permitted to raise individual premiums because of health status or claims history. Generally speaking, once the insured selects a policy, the premium for that policy will be based on entry age and will not rise unless a class-wide premium increase has been granted.

At first, LTCI benefits were expressed in dollars per day—e.g., $50 or $100 a day. Often, the home health care benefit was set at 50 percent of the benefit for treatment in a nursing home (e.g., $120/$60 per day). However, it is possible to purchase policies with different ratios, or with equal daily benefits for nursing home and home care. It is also possible to purchase policies with an option to buy increased coverage without proof of insurability, or with an automatic increase to keep pace with the ever-increasing cost of medical care. A more recent trend is for the insurer to adopt disability principles and treat the coverage as a "pot of money"—so benefits that are not used on a particular day after coverage has been triggered can be applied to later needs.

Lifetime LTCI coverage can be purchased. So can coverage for a term of years (two to five years is typical). State law usually imposes a minimum duration (typically one or two years) for policies sold as LTCI policies. Some policies provide benefits as soon as coverage is triggered, but most impose a waiting period. Of course, the shorter the waiting period and/or the longer the duration of the coverage, the higher the premium, because the insurer undertakes more risk.

Eligibility for LTCI benefits depends on "triggering" the coverage. Most policies now on the market use an ADL trigger, a cognitive trigger, or a combination of the two. ADL means "Activities of Daily Living," such as dressing, bathing, eating, or using the toilet. Coverage becomes available under an ADL trigger based on the insured person's need for assistance in these areas. A cognitive trigger makes benefits available based on the presence of Alzheimer's Disease or other condition that impairs mental acuity.

The Health Insurance Portability and Accountability Act of 1996 (P.L. 104-191), discussed above in connection with insurance portability, also contains extensive provisions dealing with long-term care insurance. "Qualified policies" purchased after January 1, 1997 are entitled to favorable tax treatment. (Policies purchased earlier are automatically treated as qualified; or the policy could be exchanged for a new policy tax-free until January 1, 1998.) It is perfectly legal to sell nonqualified policies, but they don't get the favorable tax treatment.

A qualified policy is one that provides necessary medical and personal care services to a chronically ill person. All qualified policies must be triggered both by cognitive impairment and by dependency in either two or three of a standardized list of six Activities of Daily Living.

HIPAA makes it clear that long-term care insurance is treated much like accident and health insurance for tax purposes. That is, if it is offered as an employee benefit, the employer can deduct the cost of the care (as long as it is not part of either a cafeteria plan or flexible spending account), and the employee does not have taxable income because the insurance was provided.

When long-term care insurance benefits are collected, there is no income tax on benefits of up to $175/day. Furthermore, if the policy pays the actual cost of care (rather than a per diem amount), the full benefit can be received tax-free.

Self-employed persons can treat the long-term care insurance premium as a health insurance premium. In 1997, the self-employed can deduct 40 percent of their health insurance premiums; this percentage amount increases over time until it reaches 100 percent.

Persons who buy their own long-term care insurance but are not self-employed can add part of the premium to their potentially deductible medical expenses, but a medical expense deduction is available only to the extent that the aggregate expenses exceed 7.5 percent of adjusted gross income. The amount of long-term care insurance premium that can be treated as a medical deduction varies based on the age of the person seeking the deduction, ranging from $200 per year for a person who has not yet reached age 40, to $2,500 a year for a person over 70.

HIPAA also requires a high measure of consumer protection for purchasers of qualified policies, in areas such as disclosure, and inflation and nonforfeiture protection (both of which must be made available as options, but are not mandatory). Nevertheless, insurers have a lot of flexibility in designing qualified policies, and are not required to offer uniform products.

— ENDNOTES —

1. #93-1612, -1613, 115 S.Ct. 810 (Sup.Ct. 1/18/95); on remand, *VALIC v. Clarke*, 49 F.3d 128.

2. *Barnett Bank of Marion County v. Nelson*, #94-1837, 116 S.Ct. 1103 (Sup.Ct. 3/26/96); 43 F.3d 631 (11th Cir. 1/30/95) reversed.

3. *Owensboro National Bank v. Stephens*, 44 F.3d 388 (6th Cir. 12/29/94).

4. *NBD Bank NA v. Bennett*, 67 F.3d 629 (7th Cir. 10/4/95).

5. *SEC v. Life Partners Inc.*, 898 F.Supp. 14 (D.D.C. 8/30/95), *rev'd* 87 F.3d 536 (D.C.Cir. 7/5/96).

6. *Norwest Corp. v. Nebraska*, 116 F.3d 1227 (Neb.Sup. 12/19/97).

7. *Preferred Mutual Insurance Co. v. Gamache*, 686 N.E.2d 989 (Mass.Sup.Jud.Ct. 11/7/97).

8. *White v. Allstate Insurance Co.*, 66 LW 1243 (Vt.Sup. 10/10/97).

9. *Fegan v. State Mutual Life Assurance Co.*, 945 F.Supp. 396 (D.N.H. 9/30/96).

10. *Ohran v. Sierra Health & Life Ins. Co.*, 63 LW 2788 (Nev.Sup. 5/25/95).

11. *Estate of Cavenaugh*, 51 F.3d 597 (5th Cir. 5/10/95).

12. *Johnson & Johnson v. Aetna Casualty & Surety Co.*, 667 A.2d 1087 (N.J.Super. 12/11/95).

13. *PPG Industries Inc. v. Transamerica Insurance Co.*, 56 Cal.Rptr.2d 889 (Cal.App. 9/26/96).

14. *Whirlpool Corp. v. Ziebert*, 539 N.W.2d 883 (Wis.Sup. 11/16/95).

15. *Charter Oil Co. v. American Employers' Insurance Co.,* 69 F.3d 1160 (D.C.Cir. 11/14/95).

16. *Employers Casualty Co. v. St. Paul Fire & Marine Ins. Co.,* 52 Cal.Rptr.2d 17 (Cal.App. 4/11/96) [sulfur dioxide fumes]; *American States Insurance Co. v. Nethery,* 79 F.3d 473 (5th Cir. 4/9/96).

17. *Certain Underwriters at Lloyds' London v. C.A. Turner Construction Co.,* 112 F.3d 184 (5th Cir. 5/8/97).

18. *American States Insurance Co. v. Koloms,* 687 N.E.2d 72 (Ill.Sup. 10/17/97).

19. *Donaldson v. Urban Land Interest Inc.,* 564 N.W.2d 728 (Wis.Sup. 6/24/97).

20. *Bituminous Casualty Corp. v. Advanced Adhesive Technology,* 73 F.3d 335 (11th Cir. 1/23/96).

21. *Stoney Run Co. v. Prudential-LMI Commercial Insurance Co.,* 47 F.3d 34 (2nd Cir. 1/31/95).

22. *Weaver v. Royal Insurance Co. of America,* 64 LW 2724 (N.H.Sup. 4/17/96).

23. *Martin Marietta Corp. v. Insurance Co. of North America,* 47 Cal.Rptr.2nd 670 (Cal.App. 12/5/95). Also see *Wisconsin Public Service Corp. v. Heritage Mutual Insurance Co.,* 64 LW 2628 (Wis.App. 3/12/96) [Contractor's insurer has to cover contractor's liability to another landowner, where pollutants entered the landowner's property because of the contractor's negligence; the costs were "damages" that are covered by the CGL, not "response costs" that are excluded.] After the land is cleaned up, the policyholder's liability for contribution also counts as "damages": *General Casualty Co. of Wisconsin v. Hills,* also 64 LW 2628 (Wis.App. 3/12/96).

24. *Anderson Development Co. v. Travelers Indemnity Co.,* 49 F.3d 1128 (6th Cir. 3/20/95); also see *Farmland Industries Inc. v. Republic Insurance Co.,* 65 LW 2656 (Mo.Sup. 3/25/97). *American Bumper & Mfg. Co. v. Hartford Fire Insurance Co.,* 550 N.W.2d 475 (Mich.Sup. 7/16/96) says that the costs of performing a remedial investigation and feasibility study, after the EPA identifies the insured as a Potentially Responsible Party under CERCLA, are recoverable under the CGL as a defense cost; they are not an ordinary cost of doing business. This is true even if the study reveals that there was no contamination and there is no need for remediation. *Aerojet-General Corp. v. Transport Indemnity Co.,* 70 Cal Rptr.2d 118 (Cal.Sup. 12/29/97) is similar. A suit by an insured for declaratory judgment that the insurer must indemnify future cleanup costs is an equity suit for specific performance. Therefore, it is triable to the court, not to a jury, even if an ancillary claim for past remediation costs is made: *Ciba-Geigy Corp. v. Liberty Mutual Insurance Co.,* 65 LW 2751 (N.J.Sup. 5/12/97).

25. *Kerr-McGee Corp. v. Admiral Insurance Co.,* 905 P.2d 760 (Okla.Sup. 10/3/95).

26. *Chemical Leaman Tank Lines v. Aetna Casualty and Surety Co.,* 89 F.3d 976 (34d Cir. 6/20/96).

27. *Stonewall Insurance Co. v. Asbestos Claims Management Corp.,* 85 F.3d 49 (2nd Cir. 12/13/95).

28. *West Americans Ins. Co. v. Band & Desenberg,* 925 F.Supp. 758 (M.D. Fla. 5/3/96).

29. *Fire Insurance Exchange v. Diehl,* 545 N.W.2d 602 (Mich.Sup. 3/19/96).

30. *Torrison v. Overman,* 594 N.W.2d 124 (Neb.Sup. 6/7/96).

31. *State Farm Fire and Casualty Co. v. Fullerton,* 118 F.3d 374 (5th Cir. 7/22/97).

32. *Lee v. Interstate Fire & Casualty Co.,* 86 F.3d 101 (7th Cir. 6/11/96).

33. *Allstate Insurance Co. v. Avis Rent-a-Car System Inc.,* 947 P.2d 341 (Colo.Sup. 11/10/97).

34. *Lindstrom v. Hanover Insurance Co.,* 649 A.2d 1272 (N.J.Sup. 12/19/94).

35. *Lebas Fashion Imports of USA v. ITT Hartford Insurance Group,* 44 Cal.App.4th 531, 52 Cal.Rptr.2d 26 (Cal.App. 10/29/96); *Fluoroware Inc. v. Chubb Group of Insurance Companies,* 545 N.W.2d 678 (Minn.App. 4/2/96).

36. See, e.g., *Moore v. Continental Insurance Co.,* 51 Cal.Rptr.2d 176 (Cal.App. 3/28/96): sexual harassment constructive discharge is a noncovered "willful act"; *Dopf v. Vigilant Insurance Co.,* 64 LW 2816 (N.Y.Sup. 5/23/96): sexual harassment claim excluded as intentional; *Sphere Drake Insurance PLC v. Shoney's Inc.,* 923 F.Supp. 1481 (M.D. Ala. 4/18/96) [insurer does not have to cover claims involving intent to injure, such as sex discrimination and sexual harassment, but does have to cover claims of negligent supervision and negligent retention of employees.

37. *BLasT [sic] Intermediate Unit 17 v. CNA Insurance Co.,* 674 A.2d 687 (Pa.Sup. 4/18/96): negligent violation of Equal Pay Act is insurable]; *Meadowbrook Inc. v. Tower Insurance Co.,* 543 N.W.2d 418 (Minn.App. 1/30/96): plaintiff's neck and back pain is coverable "bodily injury" due to hostile environment sexual harassment; *General Accident Insurance Co. v. Western American Insurance Co.,* 49 Cal.Rptr.2d 603 (Cal.App. 1/31/96) [suit by discharged corporate officer who was "ousted" and "ejected" from company premises involves coverable "personal injury"; *American Management Association v. Atlantic Mutual Insurance Co.,* 64 LW 2660 (N.Y.Sup. 3/29/96): disparate-impact age discrimination is not necessarily intentional, so the insurer has a duty to defend.

38. *Federal Insurance Co. v. Stroh Brewing,* 66 LW 1184 (7th Cir. 9/19/97).

39. *North Bank v. Cincinnati Insurance Co.,* 66 LW 1220 (10th Cir. 10/1/97).

40. *New York State Conference of Blue Cross/Blue Shield Plans v. Travelers Insurance Co.,* #93-1408, -1414, -1415, 115 S.Ct. 1671 (Sup.Ct. 4/26/95).

41. *Wilson v. Office of CHAMPUS,* 65 F.3d 361 (4th Cir. 9/15/95).

42. *Smith v. Office of CHAMPUS,* 66 F.3d 905 (7th Cir. 9/26/95).

43. *Henderson v. Bodine Aluminum Inc.*, 70 F.3d 958 (8th Cir. 9/27/95).

44. *EEOC v. Mason Tenders District Council Welfare Fund,* 64 LW 2400 (S.D.N.Y. 12/14/95).

45. *Deramus v. Jackson National Life Ins. Co.*, 92 F.3d 274 (5th Cir. 8/7/96).

46. *Kotev v. First Colony Life Insurance Co.*, 927 F.Supp. 1316 (C.D.Cal. 5/30/96).

47. *McEvoy v. Group Health Cooperative of Eau Claire,* 570 N.W.2d 397 (Wis.Sup. 11/12/97).

48. *Davies v. Centennial Life Insurance Co.*, 128 F.3d 984 (6th Cir. 10/16/97).

49. *Cypress Fairbanks Medical Center Inc. v. PanAmerican Life Insurance Co.*, 110 F.3d 280 (5th Cir. 4/17/97).

50. *Wilson v. Zoellner,* 114 F.3d 713 (8th Cir. 5/21/97).

51. *Bogusewski v. Life Insurance Co. of North America,* 66 LW 1250 (E.D. Wis. 10/10/97).

52. *Cisneros v. UNUM Life Insurance Co.*, 134 F.3d 939 (9th Cir. 1/20/98); the court's earlier opinion, 115 F.3d 669, was withdrawn.

— FOR FURTHER REFERENCE —

Abney, David L., "Insurance Company Assumptions, Consumer Realities and Judicial Rules of Interpretation," 32 *Arizona Attorney* 19 (February '96).

Biscan, Matthew Y., "Coverage for Experimental Treatments," 38 *For the Defense* 16 (August '96).

Christensen, Burke A., "Conditional Receipts for Life Insurance Premiums," 136 *Trusts and Estates* 63 (February '97).

Christopher, A. Mark, "New Law Provides Ways to Reduce Tax Burdens Relating to LTC Expenses," 86 *J. of Taxation* 20 (January '97).

Fleming, Peter D., "Helping Clients Protect Against Risk," 18 *J. of Accountancy* 61 (January '96).

Foggan, Laura A. and John C. Yang, "Tortfeasors' Responsibility for Uninsured Periods," 8 *Environmental Claims J.* 3 (Summer '96).

Gebhart, Timothy M., "A 'Timeless' Interpretation of the 'Sudden and Accidental' Exception to the Pollution Exclusion?" 41 *South Dakota L. Rev.* 375 (Summer '96).

Harris, Jonathan W., "Post-Employment Health Coverage for Executives and Their Families," 24 *Estate Planning* 59 (February '97).

Johnson, Craig N., "Litigating Lost or Missing Insurance Policies," 25 *Colorado Lawyer* 115 (October '96).

Johnson, Karen Imus, "A Step-by-Step Guide to Preparing Insurance Coverage Options," 39 *For the Defense* 21 (January '97).

Mortland, Jean A., "Discrimination Actions Against Landlords: Are They Insurable?" 31 *Real Property, Probate and Trust J.* 55 (Spring '96).

Richmond, Douglas R., "Lost in the Eternal Triangle of Insurance Defense Ethics," 9 *Georgetown J. of Legal Ethics* 475 (Winter '96).

Slavutin, Lee, "Life Insurance and Charitable Giving-Important Tax Rules," 75 *Taxes: The Tax Magazine* 29 (January'97).

Vines, Joan H., "IRS Taxes Cash Surrender Value of Split-Dollar Life Insurance Policy Placed in Trust for Benefit of Executive," 28 *Tax Adviser* 87 (February '97).

INTELLECTUAL PROPERTY

[¶2601] As has been the case for many years, much of the activity in intellectual property in the supplement period involved new technology—particularly computers. However, old-fashioned questions such as trade dress continued to occupy the courts and legislatures.

Congress passed several relevant measures during the supplement period. P.L. 103-349, the Plant Variety Protection Act Amendments of 1994 (10/6/94) conforms United States law to the International Convention for the Protection of New Varieties of Plants.

P.L. 104-41, the Biotechnical Process Patents Act, amends 35 U.S.C. §103 with respect to the conditions under which a biotechnical process will not have to undergo a separate review of non-obviousness. In other words, if it uses or produces a patentable composition of matter, the separate review can be by-passed. The legislation was necessary because, absent the change, patent host cells could be used in offshore manufacturing and then imported into the United States if the process patent were not issued.

P.L. 104-208 amends 35 U.S.C. §287(c) to limit a patent-holder's ability to sue for infringement of a medical process patent. There is a safe harbor under which doctors will be immune from suit for using a patented procedure or diagnostic technique, as long as patented devices and drugs are not involved. The statute contains an exception to the safe harbor for biotechnology, so the courts will have to sort out the scope of the exception.

The Just Compensation: Patents Used by the U.S. Act, P.L. 104-308, permits awards of attorneys' fees and costs to patent owners who prevail when they charge the federal government with unlicensed use of their patents.

The Anticounterfeiting Consumer Protection Act of 1996, P.L. 104-153 (7/2/96), makes it possible for the counterfeiting of trademarks and other intellectual property to constitute a RICO predicate. Counterfeiting movies or computer programs can constitute racketeering. A civil fine can be imposed for aiding and abetting the importation of counterfeit merchandise, and counterfeit goods can be seized and destroyed.

The Economic Espionage Act of 1996, P.L. 104-294, imposes penalties of up to $500,000 and/or 15 years' imprisonment on individuals who steal trade secrets and copy or transmit them (or engage in similar conduct) with the intention of benefiting a foreign government, instrumentality, or agent. Organizations can be fined up to $10 million. The law also penalizes domestic industrial espionage: purely domestic thefts of trade secrets can be punished by a $250,000 fine and/or 10 years' imprisonment, or by criminal forfeiture; organizations can be penalized up to $5 million.

In December 1996, the World Intellectual Property Organization (WIPO), meeting in Geneva, approved two new treaties: one dealing with copyrights in general, one with performances and music recording. At press time, Congress had not yet decided whether to ratify the treaties.

[¶2602] PATENTS

The Patent and Trademark Office rules were altered (see 62 FR 30802, 6/25/97) to increase the time periods for discovery in patent cases. However, it will be more difficult to get an extension once the time period has elapsed. Limits have been placed on the number of interrogatories and other filings allowed in PTO cases. Similarly, the time to file briefs has been extended, but extensions will be limited.

In April 1996, the Supreme Court affirmed a 1995 ruling of the Federal Circuit, holding that construction of a patent claim (determining the meaning and scope of the claims that allegedly were infringed) is a matter of law—in other words, exclusively within the duties of the court. The jury's function is to compare the construed claim to the allegedly infringing device. The Supreme Court said "judges, not juries, are the better suited to find the acquired meaning of patent terms."[1]

The Board of Patent Appeals and Interferences has a duty to render opinions that contain specific findings of fact and conclusions of law sufficient for the appellate court to have a basis of review. In other words, the opinions must meet the same standards applied to District Court opinions.[2] The standard for reviewing the Board's finding of fact is whether the finding is clearly erroneous. The Administrative Procedure Act's substantial evidence and arbitrary and capricious standards do not apply.[3]

Extrinsic evidence (including expert testimony) can be used to construe a patent claim only if the claim remains ambiguous after consulting the specifications and prosecution history.[4] Where the meaning of technical terms is clear and obvious, claim construction is not required to make an obviousness determination.[5]

Under the "doctrine of equivalents," making a trivial change or slight improvement does not prevent a finding of patent infringement. In early 1997, the Supreme Court upheld the doctrine of equivalents in principle. Furthermore, the court said that the doctrine is applied to each element or limitation, not to the patent as a whole. Nevertheless, in many instances, the doctrine will not be applicable because of "file wrapper estoppel": if there is no explanation for a change in claims during the application process, it is rebuttably presumed that the change is based on reasons related to patentability. A major question that the Supreme Court left unresolved is whether it is up to the judge or the jury to apply the doctrine of equivalents.[6]

Section 102(f) subject matter that cannot be patented because someone else invented it can be used in conjunction with other prior art as part of the obviousness determination.[7] Even if it is commercially successful, an over-the-counter combination of well-known decongestant and analgesic ingredients is obvious and hence unpatentable.[8]

The District Court for the District of Massachusetts invalidated a patent for a data processing system that performs accounting calculations for mutual fund investments. In this reading, the system is a mere collection of mathematical operations and thus nonpatentable—or else it was an equally nonpatentable business system. If physical process steps had been involved (for instance, computer control of a cutting machine), the result would have been different.[9]

A company that succeeds in getting a competitor's patent declared invalid is a prevailing party who can recover costs under Federal Rules of Civil Procedure 54(d)(1).[10]

The "on-sale" bar to patentability doesn't apply if an offer is made to sell an invention that is not close to completion and not yet operable.[11]

Infringement of a plant patent means asexual reproduction of the actual patented plant, not merely creating a plant with the same essential characteristics.[12]

[¶2611] ASSIGNMENT VS. LICENSING OF PATENTS

On April 6, 1995, the Department of Justice and the Federal Trade Commission adopted joint guidelines for intellectual property licensing.[13] The transactions will be considered acceptable, and not inhibiting competition, if the licensing entities collectively control 20 percent or less of each relevant market, and the license does not contain restraints that are facially anticompetitive. These guidelines do not apply in circumstances under which the DOJ/FTC merger analysis guidelines apply. A license that does not satisfy the guidelines is not necessarily an antitrust violation, as long as the license does not have anticompetitive effect.

A licensor can get damages for breach of contract with respect to past royalties on a process whose patent was declared invalid. The damages run from the date of the breach to the date of the licensee's initial challenge to the validity of the claims.[14]

One owner of a co-owned patent can license it to a potential defendant, but the second owner can sue the licensee for past infringement. Only a release, not a license, would prevent such a suit. One co-patentee does not have the right to deprive the other of damages for past infringement.[15]

A non-exclusive patent license is a personal license, so it cannot be assumed by a bankruptcy trustee, or assigned by the trustee without the consent of the patentee-licensor.[16] In an early 1997 First Circuit case, the patent holder/licensor objected to a bankrupt licensee's reorganization plan, which called for sale of all of the licensee's stock to a major competitor of the licensor. The First Circuit ruled that Bankruptcy Code §365(c) was not violated, because there was no assignment of executory contract rights without the consent of the patentee. The debtor/licensee continued to be a corporation with a distinct identity, no matter who owned its shares.[17]

Patents held by one spouse are divisible marital property, even if they have no ascertainable current value, so a divorce court was correct to award patents to the husband, subject to the wife's lien on 40 percent of any future net income deriving from the patents.[18]

[¶2613] REMEDIES FOR PATENT INFRINGEMENT

An antitrust allegation (that a patent was obtained fraudulently and used to destroy competition) does not operate as a compulsory counterclaim in an infringement suit involving that patent.[19] The Federal Circuit extended this holding in late 1997, ruling that antitrust liability cannot be asserted on the basis that a patent applicant failed to cite a known prior art reference, and the assignee brought an infringement suit. The Federal Circuit's point was that otherwise, most infringement suits would become antitrust cases.[20]

Whether the mistake was honest or fraudulent, a true inventor who is not named, or who is erroneously named, can bring suit under 35 U.S.C. §256 to get the patent corrected. Although the statute refers to "error," it can be used in a case of fraud rather than mutual mistake.[21]

When a settlement agreement in a patent infringement case is breached, damages are determined under state law and not under 35 U.S.C. §284, because the patent itself was not breached and the case is an ordinary contract matter.[22]

The Patent Act removes state Eleventh Amendment immunity for patent infringements, but the Lanham Act does not abrogate such immunity for false advertising claims. The District Court for the District of New Jersey drew this distinction because false advertising claims do not involve "property"; instead, they protect actors in interstate commerce from unfair competition and protect consumers from falsehood.[23]

A plaintiff's delay in prosecuting a patent case does not give rise to a laches defense in the infringement case.[24]

[¶2614]   DURATION OF PATENT

For drug patents in force on June 8, 1995, term extensions are added to the expiration date prescribed by the Uruguay Round Agreements Act—not the date 17 years from the granting of the initial patent.[25]

[¶2615]   TRADEMARKS AND TRADE NAMES

The Federal Trademark Dilution Act of 1995, P.L. 104-98 (1/16/96) amends Lanham Act §43 (15 U.S.C. §1125) by adding a new sub-section. Once a mark becomes "famous," owners of the mark who demonstrate that it is equitable and reasonable can get an injunction against subsequent commercial use of a mark or trade name that dilutes the famous mark.

Factors in determining which marks qualify include the inherent or acquired distinctiveness of the mark; the duration and extent to which the owner has used and publicized it; the channels of trade in which it is used; the degree of recognition; and the nature and extent of use of similar marks by third parties. If another entity engages in willful dilution of the famous mark (lessening the public ability to distinguish which goods are sold under that mark) Lanham Act §35 and §36 remedies are available. A diluting mark need only be similar to the plaintiff's trademark—it need not be identical.[26] Suits under the Trademark Dilution Act are limited to improper use of trademarks adopted after the statute's effective date, on the theory that otherwise defendants could be penalized for behavior that was legal when it occurred.[27]

To get a jury trial in a dilution case, there must be evidence of the defendant's willful intent to cause harm for which monetary damages can be awarded. When dilution is unintentional, only equitable remedies are available, so of course jury trial is not available.[28]

Even if a mark is incontestable and cannot be canceled, the court can still consider its strength and descriptiveness when assessing the likelihood of confusion.[29]

In early 1995, the Supreme Court settled a vexed question by deciding that color alone can be a registrable trademark (here, a green-gold shade used for dry cleaners' pressing pads) provided that it is nonfunctional and has secondary meaning.[30]

An earlier Supreme Court case[31] allows protection of inherently distinctive trade dress even without proof of secondary meaning. The Eighth Circuit says trade dress is protectable even if it is not "striking in appearance" or "memorable," provided that it is fanciful or arbitrary (not mandated by the nature of the product). Where the trade dress is dictated by the nature of the product, secondary meaning does have to be proved to protect the trade dress.[32]

The Seventh Circuit ruled that if comparison of competing products does not make it clear that consumers are likely to be confused by duplication of a color trademark, the manufacturer who claims that its color trademark is infringed must produce "some" evidence of actual confusion.[33]

Trade dress that is limited to useful product features as defined by Lanham Act §43(a) cannot be protected because useful features are not "nonfunctional" (the key characteristic of a trademark) and are properly covered by a utility patent, not a trademark.[34]

A trade dress case cannot be resolved merely by examining the packages: factors such as strength of trade dress, similarity of trade dress and product, and actual confusion are also relevant.[35]

Eleventh Amendment immunity is not available if a state official violates the Lanham Act by making false and misleading statements about a product in a consumer guide.[36]

Advertising injury coverage under the CGL insurance policy extends to trademark infringement—particularly under a policy which used to have a trademark exclusion, but from which the exclusion was deleted, creating a reasonable expectation of coverage on the part of the insured.[37]

An important issue for 1996 was the trademark status of Internet domain names, and the potential for infringement via domain name. It has been held that a domain name can infringe a trademark.[38] Trademark "greenmail" (the practice of registering someone else's trademark as a domain name, in the hope of payment from the trademark owner) has been held to constitute dilution under the 1995 Trademark Dilution Act.[39] An injunction was granted against the use of planned-parenthood.com as a domain name by an anti-abortion activist, given the likelihood of confusion on the part of Internet users and consequent harm to Planned Parenthood's service mark.[40]

However, perhaps the most vexing source of future Lanham Act issues will be identical or confusingly similar names that are used in good faith by two or more businesses or organizations, each of whom wants to register the name as a domain name. An injunction has been granted to the owner of a federally registered trademark, TeleTech, who alleged dilution when the user of the common-law service mark Tele-Tech registered TeleTech as a domain name. It was held not to be a defense that the defendant was unaware that hyphens could be used in domain names.[41] According to the Northern District of Illinois, merely registering a domain name is not a "use in commerce" for Lanham Act purposes. This court also declined to recognize a suit for trademark misuse, ruling that misuse is a defense rather than a discrete cause of action.[42]

Network Solutions, Inc., the one-time registrar of Internet domain names, is not liable to the owner of a federally registered trademark if it issues a domain name that allegedly infringes the trademark. In this analysis, a domain name does not function as a trademark if it is merely used to find a site on the Internet, and not to sell goods or services, and registering a domain name is not commercial use under the Trademark Dilution Act.[43]

Suing for infringement of a trademark or service mark is basically a tort case, so registrants of domain names identical or similar to the allegedly infringed trademark are joint tortfeasors. These are not indispensable parties under FRCP 19(b) in the trademark infringement action, because the plaintiff has the option of suing less than all of the potential defendants.[44]

Trademark issues can arise on the Internet in other contexts, too. A Web site that contains misrepresentations that injured the plaintiff could become the subject of a Lanham Act passing-off action. A Florida company could be sued in Michigan for maintaining the Web site containing the alleged misrepresentations. Venue for a passing-off action is laid in the district in which confusion about the origin of the products is likely to occur. However, venue in Michigan was not proper for a company that drafted the prospectus containing the alleged misrepresentations.[45]

Apropos of another form of telecommunications, the Sixth Circuit found that there is no Lanham Act violation when a competitor obtains a toll-free telephone number that is frequently dialed mistakenly by callers seeking the plaintiff's vanity number (because the only difference between the two is a zero rather than an O). In this instance, a travel agency used the vanity number H0LIDAY; Holiday Inns used the number HOLIDAY. To the Sixth Circuit, the number 405-4329 is not deceptively similar to the word HOLIDAY, and the defendant did not create the confusion—the confusion was created by individuals who misdialed.[46]

A registration of "Lone Star Café," disclaiming "Café," does not convey exclusive rights to "Lone Star," but only to the full composite mark. Therefore, the defendant's use of "Lone Star Steaks" was not infringing.[47]

An agreement between two clothing companies that assigned trademarks contained an arbitration clause. When one sought to compel arbitration, the Fourth Circuit ruled that the Lanham Act cannot be used as a foundation for federal subject matter jurisdiction, because the dispute was an ordinary contract dispute even if the contract dealt with a trademark.[48]

Lanham Act §35(a) authorizes an attorneys' fee award in exceptional cases, so a losing plaintiff or defendant may be obligated to pay attorneys' fees when guilty of bad faith or malicious conduct. In a recent Ninth Circuit case, no fee award was made because the plaintiff was unsuccessful but nevertheless had a legitimate purpose in bringing suit and raised colorable issues of fact and law.[49]

[¶2632] PROTECTION OF TRADE SECRETS

In the view of the Ninth Circuit, alleged misappropriation of trade secrets does not "arise out of" breach of a licensing agreement, but is a separate tort. Therefore, a tort suit is not barred by the licensing agreement's arbitration clause.[50]

According to the Second Circuit, the concept of novelty applies to analysis of patents, not trade secrets. When infringement of software structure is alleged, the structure of both programs, including unprotectable individual elements, must be compared, because a compilation of unprotectable elements might be copyrightable.[51]

[¶2636] SCOPE OF COPYRIGHT LAW

The No Electronic Theft Act, P.L. 105-147 (12/16/97) imposes penalties for willful copyright infringement, especially in the electronic arena. It removes the requirement that a defendant must have commercial gain from the act of infringement for the infringement to be punishable. The law includes criminal penalties that can range up to six years, depending on the number of works improperly reproduced, their value, and whether it is a first or repeat offense.

A Copyright Office report published August 21, 1997 raised issues about protection of databases, but did not make any recommendations to Congress. The Berne Convention and the Agreement on Trade-Related Aspects of Intellectual Property Rights do accord copyright protection to databases, and the European Union has a database directive, effective January 1, 1998, making the structure of a database copyrightable with some protection for its contents. The Copyright Office report notes that there might be First Amendment problems in making databases protectable, but the problems might be addressed by disclosing that the underlying facts are not copyrighted.[52]

A sculpture incorporated into the structure of a building was created as a work for hire. Thus, the Visual Artists' Rights Act of 1990 did not prevent the building owner from dismantling the artwork.[53]

Copyrighting a collection (e.g., a group of songs) protects individual copyrightable works within the collection, even if they are not listed individually on the copyright registration form.[54]

A party who copies something that is, in turn, an unauthorized copy of primary material is still liable to the copyright owner of the infringed material, even though it was the copy and not the primary material that was directly copied.[55]

[¶2636.1] Copyrightable Subject Matter

Plastic mannequins used to mount animal skins for taxidermy have been held to be copyrightable as sculptural works: the creator used animal skeletons as a model, but did not merely make an impression of the skeletons.[56]

The Central District of California says that mounting and framing prints from an art book infringes the book's copyright (as well as that of the artworks) because the pages are "recast" and "transformed"—but the Northern District of Illinois says that pasting notecards of copyrighted drawings onto ceramic tiles is not the creation of an unauthorized derivative work, because a derivative work would have to be independently copyrightable due to the added material, and the tiles are not.[57]

Recipes consisting of mere lists of ingredients and instructions, with no addition of creative expression, are not copyrightable, although a collection of numerous noncopyrightable recipes may be entitled to a compilation copyright (which will not extend protection to the underlying facts within the compilation).[58]

A taxonomy of dental procedures, that assigns the procedures into numbered groups and gives long and short descriptions of each, has sufficient originality to be copyrighted. Classification can be a protectable creative endeavor, although the taxonomy was not deemed to be a compilation, because the elements within the taxonomy had no independent existence prior to their creation for this specific purpose.[59]

An alphabetical listing of communities that have cable TV, with details on the cable system serving the principal communities, is not copyrightable as a compilation. The Eleventh Circuit found that it was not selective enough. Choosing principal communities did not constitute authorship, because the information was supplied by the cable system.[60]

The command codes used to program long-distance telephone call controllers are not copyrightable. The codes are mainly sequential and were chosen arbitrarily, with no originality or expression that qualifies for copyright.[61]

The codes and formulas used to prepare data about Worker's Compensation insurance are not copyrightable; to the Southern District of Florida, the data is on a par with telephone numbers or accounting systems.[62]

"Star pagination"—the West system of page numbering—has been a controverted copyright issue. According to the District Court for the District of Minnesota, the method of arranging cases in a reporter (including pagination) is a protectable original creative endeavor, and therefore it does not constitute fair use for a competitor to adopt these page breaks in its own product. In this case, the competitor's intent was to reduce West's market share.[63] In contrast, the Southern District of New York says that the copyright on West's case reporters does not protect the page numbers, so a CD-ROM publisher that uses star pagination is undertaking a fair use by giving readers a method of referring to the West reports.[64] The court ruling on the legality of the proposed West-Thompson merger has indicated that upholding a copyright in page numbers would disserve the public interest.[65]

[¶2641]   FAIR USE

The Sixth Circuit initially permitted a copy shop that compiled "coursepacks" of academic articles to assert a fair use/educational use defense unless the copyright holder could show meaningful likelihood of harm to the potential market for the works. The coursepack consists of excerpts adding up to 5-30 percent of the content of the original work; the court did not feel that the "heart" of the work was necessarily contained there. The rationale was that professors would not assign the original work if the coursepack were not available, so the market for the original was not impaired.[66] About nine months later, however, the Sixth Circuit decided that coursepacks are not entitled to the fair use defense, at least if a commercial duplicating operation is involved. In this revised reading, lost permission fees rather than lost sales are relevant.

Use of a phrase from a song lyric, which was a cliché when the song was written, in an advertisement does not violate the song's copyright.[67]

A news station could not claim fair use of the Reginald Denny videotape after a license for its use was denied by the station that had rights to the video. Both stations were competitors in the commercial news business. The defendant news station ran the clip without attribution, precluding the argument that the tape itself became news.[68]

A television show used a copyrighted poster as part of the set. The poster was visible and identifiable, although the show did not focus on it. The Second Circuit ruled this use to be more than *de minimis*, and remanded to see if it constituted fair use.[69]

[¶2643] MUSIC RECORDING RIGHTS

P.L. 104-39, the Digital Performance Right in Sound Recordings Act of 1995 amends 17 U.S.C. §§106 and 114. Because of these amendments, creators and performers do not have a comprehensive right to control public performance. Instead, they are given a "carefully crafted and narrow performance right, applicable only to certain digital transmissions of sound recordings." Thus, copyright owners can control performance of their works as part of an interactive service (e.g., over the Internet). The amendments apply only to digital audio, not conventional analog audio and not digital transmission of an audiovisual work. Congress anticipated that digital transmission ("audio on demand" or "pay per listen") would become a common commercial medium, so a limited performance right is justified. However, conventional, free, advertising-supported radio or similar transmissions are not covered by the amendments.

The Fifth Circuit decided that an ordinary sound recording is not an audiovisual work falling under the work-for-hire rules of Copyright Act §101(2). An audiovisual work must have visible images in addition to sounds; and sound recordings have their own protective provisions.[70]

A karaoke CD that combines video of lyrics and audio of the song itself requires the copyright holder's authorization to display the lyrics; a compulsory license covering a "phonorecord" is not sufficient for this purpose.[71]

A plaintiff owned the copyright to sound recordings, but not the underlying composition. The defendant synchronized the recording into the soundtrack for a television show. The Second Circuit decided[72] that synchronization of previously recorded sounds with an audiovisual work is part of the rights granted under Copyright Act §114(b) to the owner of the rights of the sound recording.

This is true even though it would have been permissible to use the recording in a live broadcast: the synchronization constituted a commercial use, not mere time-shifting. If the work were sufficiently altered, the synchronization might also constitute an unauthorized derivative work. However, the plaintiff did not have an exclusive performance right, so the TV stations who played the broadcast containing the soundtrack were not liable to him.

The licensing organizations ASCAP and BMI have a procedure for using undercover investigators to detect unauthorized public performances of copyrighted music. New York passed a statute requiring landlords to be notified of the investigations within 72 hours of the initial deployment of the investigator. However, the Southern District of New York found that the state statute was preempted by the federal Copyright Act, and granted a preliminary injunction forbidding enforcement of the statute.

The rationale was that Congress established a three-year statute of limitations for copyright infringement suits, so that is the proper time frame for notifying an alleged infringer. The District Court was also troubled by the state statute's potential for "dueling damages," because it permits a damage award if an accused infringer does not receive the 72-hour notice. The court also deemed that the 72-hour notice requirement would prevent ASCAP and BMI from carrying out their enforcement mission.[73]

A swap meet that knows that some of its vendors sell bootleg music recordings is liable to the owner of copyrights and trademarks in those records for contributory infringement. The swap meet's role is not purely passive, in that it provides an environment where bootleg sales can thrive.[74]

[¶2646]   NEW TECHNOLOGY AND COPYRIGHT

Traditionally, the copyright system is concerned with fixation of works of authorship in tangible form, and the physical distribution of those works. However, that paradigm isn't necessarily suitable for digital works that have no physical expression. In November, 1997, the Copyright Office released guidelines for copyright protection of electronic and multi-media works. Such works must be registered using the existing classifications of literary works, pictorial/graphic works, audiovisual materials, and sound recordings. A multi-media work should be registered in conformity with the predominant element. All updates must be separately registered, because blanket registration (e.g., of a Web site as it evolves) is not yet accommodated. The Copyright Office is also experimenting with CORDS, an electronic filing system which can be used for traditional as well as electronic works of authorship.[75]

To make the Quattro spreadsheet compatible with Lotus 1-2-3, Borland International copied the Lotus menu tree but not the underlying code. The First Circuit (reversing the District Court) ruled that a computer program's menu tree (the arrangement of almost 500 commands into more than 50 menus and submenus) is a "method of operation," and consequently not copyrightable subject matter. The First Circuit was affirmed *per curiam* in a 4-4 Supreme Court decision (with one abstention).[76]

Subsequently, the Eleventh Circuit ruled that, although the menu and sub-menu command tree structure are not copyrightable, nonliteral elements are entitled to a compilation copyright if the allegedly infringing work is virtually identical to the allegedly infringed work, or if it reveals bodily appropriation.[77] A company whose United States claims of infringement of its computer program were unsucessful can sue in France charging infringement of the same program in that country. Neither claim nor issue preclusion prevented the French suit. The issues are not identical because various countries define the line between idea and expression differently.[78]

In early 1996, a company that spent a lot of money compiling a CD-ROM phone directory was out of luck when a competitor decided to put the contents of the directory on the Internet. The competitor downloaded the CDs and added its own search engine, then uploaded the directory to the Internet. The Western District of Wisconsin[79] ruled that no copyrightable subject matter existed. Furthermore, the only copying was from the CDs to the hard drive of the competitor's computer, which the court treated as personal use. Although the CDs were sold with the conventional shrink-wrap license, which imposes various draconian rigors on the purchaser, the court found the license unenforceable as a contract of adhesion, imposed contrary to the UCC without adequate notice to the purchaser. Yet, to the Seventh Circuit, the shrink-wrap license was enforceable: there would be no purpose served by smothering the actual product in licensing documents.[80]

The Southern District of New York ruled that newspaper and magazine publishers have a copyright in a collective work (the entire periodical). This copyright gives them rights of reproduction and revision that are broad enough for them to include freelance writers' work in databases and CD-ROMs without paying the freelancers or securing their permission. The court hinted that any change in this area would have to come from Congress.[81]

The Church of Scientology has instituted several cases protesting the unauthorized posting of copyrighted Scientology materials on electronic bulletin boards (BBS) and on the Internet. The District Court for the District of Colorado denied the church a preliminary injunction. It treated posting of the materials on an Internet bulletin board as fair use because it was noncommercial; did not harm the church financially; and occurred in the context of discussion and criticism of Scientology.[82] But, to the Eastern District of Virginia, the fair use defense was not available: the ex-Scientologist who uploaded the documents was not engaged in newsgathering, scholarship, or time-shifting.[83] The Northern District of California found that a BBS or Internet service provider can be contributorily liable for copyright infringement if it was placed on notice that certain posts were infringing, but nevertheless failed to remove them.[84]

Where the operator of a BBS allowed users to download copyrighted software, the federal wire fraud statute could be used to press criminal copyright infringement charges (17 U.S.C. §506(a)). Unlike wire fraud, criminal copyright infringement required proof of personal financial advantage to the infringer. In this case, the infringer did not benefit financially by giving access to the software.[85] But see above: this case has led to amendment of the federal law. It has been held that the Copyright Act preempts a state prosecution for posting copyrighted software to a BBS without authorization, because this is "copying" as defined by the federal act.[86]

An online service that uses a Web site to provide copies of copyrighted adult images is a direct infringer because it had control over the content of the site and the source of images posted there. The defendant online service violated the plaintiff's right of reproduction by putting thumbnails (miniature images) and full images on its Web server, and also violated the right of distribution because users of the defendant's service could download images. Subscribers' ability to see copyrighted images on-line violated the right of display.[87] The Southern District of California issued TROs, directing Internet Service Providers (ISPs) to block access to so-called music archive Web sites charged with distributing unauthorized copies of copyrighted music. The court found a risk of irreparable harm from continued distribution of the music.[88]

[¶2649]   COPYRIGHT LITIGATION AND PROCEDURE

Jury trial is available in a copyright infringement suit for statutory damages,[89] and indeed the parties are always entitled to go to a jury on the amount of statutory damages.[90]

In an infringement suit, a prevailing defendant can receive a fee award if the plaintiff is unsuccessful—whether or not the losing plaintiff is culpable in the sense of bad faith.[91]

An infringer can't avoid imposition of a preliminary injunction merely by stating that money damages are sufficient. This assertion fails to rebut the presumption of irreparable harm.[92]

The Fifth Circuit says that the Copyright Act makes no provision for one co-owner's suit against another for an accounting of royalty income, so any such claim is governed by state law,[93] and a co-owner cannot infringe on the co-owned copyright. However, if a declaration of co-ownership is sought, the Ninth Circuit says that the claim accrues when the claimant is informed explicitly that he, she, or it is *not* a co-owner. That is the time at which the three-year statute of limitations begins to run. The claimant is not entitled to a new accrual each time the allegedly co-owned work is sold.[94]

If there is no dispute about when a transfer of copyright occurred, or the terms of the transfer, an oral transfer of copyright that is confirmed by a later writing can become valid as of the time of the initial oral grant.[95] However, the Southern District of New York has ruled[96] that copyright assignments must be written, although not necessarily negotiated. Thus, the assignment provisions of a work-for-hire agreement were given force.

More complex assignment issues arose in an early 1997 Ninth Circuit case.[97] A composer who had debts coped with them by assigning future song royalties and instructed BMI to make payments directly to the assignees. The IRS asserted a tax lien against his income. The Copyright Act gives priority to the first transfer to be recorded, as long as recording is adequate to give constructive notice. But an assignment of a right to income is not a transfer of copyright ownership, so recordation is not essential to the validity of the transfer. The BMI form created a completed assignment under New York law, leaving nothing for the IRS lien to attach to.

— ENDNOTES —

1. *Markman v. Westview Instruments Inc.*, 52 F.3d 967 (Fed.Cir. 4/5/95), *aff'd* #95-26, 116 S.Ct. 1384 (Sup.Ct. 4/23/96).

2. *Gechter v. Davidson*, 116 F.3d 1454 (Fed.Cir. 6/13/97).

3. *In re Lueders*, 111 F.3d 1569 (Fed.Cir. 4/24/97).

4. *Vitronics Corp. v. Conceptronic Inc.*, 90 F.3d 1576 (Fed.Cir. 7/25/96).

5. *U.S. Surgical Corp. v. Ethicon Inc.*, 103 F.3d 1554 (Fed.Cir. 1/3/97).

6. *Hilton Davis Chemical Co. v. Warner-Jenkinson Co. Inc.*, #95-728, 117 S.Ct. 1040 (Sup.Ct. 3/3/97). Also see *Roton Barrier Inc. v. Stanley Works*, 79 F.3d 1112 (Fed.Cir. 3/4/96): to prove infringement under the doctrine of equivalents, the plaintiff must prove not only the traditional infringement elements under the function/way/result test, but also the insubstantiality of any differences between the products.

7. *OddzOn Products Inc. v. Just Toys Inc.*, 122 F.3d 1396 (Fed.Cir. 8/8/97).

8. *Vicks Inc. v. Upjohn Co.*, 66 LW 1239 (Fed.Cir. 9/26/97).

9. *State Street Bank & Trust v. Signature Financial Group Inc.*, 927 F.Supp. 502 (D.Mass. 3/26/96).

10. *Manildra Milling Corp. v. Ogilvie Mills Inc.*, 76 F.3d 1178 (Fed.Cir. 2/12/96).

11. *Micro Chemical Inc. v. Great Plains Chemical Co.*, 103 F.3d 1538 (Fed.Cir. 1/3/97), *cert. denied* 117 S.Ct. 2576.

12. *Imazio Nursery Inc. v. Dania Greenhouses*, 69 F.3d 1560 (Fed.Cir. 11/3/95).

13. See 63 LW 2654.

14. *Studiengesellschaft Kohle v. Shell Oil Co.*, 112 F.3d 1561 (Fed.Cir. 5/5/97).

15. *Schering Corp. v. Roussel-UCLAF SA*, 104 F.3d 341 (Fed.Cir. 1/8/97).

16. *Everex Systems Inc. v. Cadtrak Corp.*, 89 F.3d 673 (9th Cir. 7/16/96).

17. *Institut Pasteur v. Cambridge Biotech Corp.*, 104 F.3d 489 (1st Cir. 1/17/97), *cert.denied* 117 S.Ct. 2511.

18. *In re Monslow*, 912 P.2d 735 (Kan.Sup. 3/8/96).

19. *Hydranautics v. Film Tec Corp.*, 70 F.3d 533 (9th Cir. 11/15/95).

20. *Nobelpharma AB v. Implant Innovations Inc.*, 66 LW 1384 (Fed.Cir. 11/18/97).

21. *Stark v. Advanced Magnetics Inc.,* 119 F.3d 1551 (Fed.Cir. 7/11/97).

22. *Gjerlov v. Schuyler Laboratories Inc.,* 66 LW 1400 (Fed.Cir. 12/1/97).

23. *College Savings Bank v. Florida Prepaid Postsecondary Education Expense Board,* 919 F.Supp. 756 (D.N.J. 12/13/96).

24. *Advanced Cardiovascular Systems Inc. v. Medtronic Inc.,* 65 LW 2176 (N.D.Cal. 7/24/96).

25. *Merck & Co. v. Kessler,* 903 F.Supp. 964 (E.D.Va. 10/16/95).

26. *Ringling Brothers v. Utah Division of Travel Development,* 935 F.3d 763 (E.D.Va. 9/10/96).

27. *Resorts of Pinehurst Inc. v. Pinehurst National Development Corp.,* 66 LW 1096 (M.D.N.C. 6/24/97).

28. *Ringling Brothers v. Utah Division of Travel Development,* 935 F.Supp. 763 (E.D. Va. 2/21/97).

29. *Petro Stopping Centers LP v. James River Petroleum Inc.,* 66 LW 1384 (4th Cir. 11/26/97).

30. *Qualitex Co. v. Jacobsen Products Co.,* #93-1577, 115 S.Ct. 1300 (Sup.Ct. 3/28/95).

31. *Two Pesos Inc. v. Taco Cabana Inc.,* 503 U.S. 957 (Sup.Ct. 1992).

32. *Stuart Hall Co. v. Ampad Corp.,* 51 F.3d 780 (8th Cir. 4/7/95).

33. *Libman Co. v. Vining Industries, Inc.,* 69 F.3d 1360 (7th Cir. 11/16/95).

34. *Elmer v. ICC Fabrication Inc.,* 67 F.3d 1571 (Fed.Cir. 10/10/95). *Vornado Air Circulation Systems Inc. v. Duracraft Corp.,* 58 F.3d 1498 (10th Cir. 7/5/95) denies protection to the spiral shape of the grill of a household fan because it is a nonfunctional product configuration that was a significant inventive component of an invention for which a utility patent was issued.

35. *Insty*Bit Inc. v. Poly-Tech Industries Inc.,* 95 F.3d 663 (8th Cir. 9/10/96).

36. *Sofamor Danek Group Inc. v. Brown,* 66 LW 1190 (9th Cir. 9/15/97).]

37. *Lebas Fashion Imports of USA v. ITT Hartford Insurance Group,* 44 Cal.App.4th 531, 52 Cal.Rptr.2nd 26 (Cal.App. 10/29/96).

38. *Comp Examiner Agency v. Juris Inc.,* 64 LW 2724 (C.D.Cal. 4/26/96): preliminary injunction granted against "advertising, operation or maintenance" of Internet site or BBS called juris.com, because of the likelihood of infringement of the Juris trademark. Also see *Heroes Inc. v. Heroes Foundation,* 65 LW 2486 (D.D.C. 12/19/96): publishing an advertisement in a newspaper, in conjunction with operating a Web site in the forum, is sufficient to give long-arm jurisdiction over an out-of-state defendant charged with trademark infringement and unfair competition.

39. *Panavision Int'l LP v. Toeppen,* 938 F.Supp. 616 (C.D.Cal. 11/2/96).

40. *Planned Parenthood Federation of America Inc. v. Bucci,* 65 LW 2662 (S.D.N.Y. 3/19/97).

41. *TeleTech Customer Care Management v. Tele-Tech Co.,* 65 LW 2832 (C.D. Cal. 5/9/97). Sometimes you can't tell the players even with a scorecard.

42. *Juno Online Services, LP v. Juno Lighting Inc.,* 66 LW 1253 (N.D. Ill. 9/29/97).

43. *Lockheed Martin Corp. v. Network Solutions Inc.,* 66 LW 1350 (C.D. Cal. 11/17/97).

44. *Lockheed Martin Corp. v. Network Solutions Inc.,* 65 LW 2744 (C.D. Cal. 3/19/97).

45. *IA Inc. v. Thermacell Technologies Inc.,* 66 LW 1400 (E.D. Mich. 11/10/97).

46. *Holiday Inns Inc. v. 800 Reservation Inc.,* 86 F.3d 619 (6th Cir. 6/24/96).

47. *Lone Star Steakhouse v. Longhorn Steaks Inc.,* 106 F.3d 355 (11th Cir. 2/23/97).

48. *Gibraltar P.R. Inc. v. Otoki Group Inc.,* 104 F.3d 616 (4th Cir. 1/13/97).

49. *Stephen W. Boney Inc. v. Boney Services Inc.,* 127 F.3d 821 (9th Cir. 9/30/97).

50. *Tracer Research Corp. v. National Env. Services Co.,* 42 F.3d 1292 (9th Cir. 12/19/94).

51. *Softel Inc. v. Dragon Medical and Scientific Communications, Inc.,* 118 F.3d 955 (2nd Cir. 7/9/97).

52. The report can be accessed at http://lcweb.loc.gov/copyright/more.htlm#rpt. (There is no www in the URL.)

53. *Carter v. Helmsley-Spear Inc.,* 71 F.3d 77 (2nd Cir. 12/1/95).

54. *Szabo v. Errisson,* 68 F.3d 940 (5th Cir. 11/20/95).

55. *Lipton v. Nature Co.,* 71 F.3d 464 (2nd Cir. 11/28/95).

56. *Superior Form Builders Inc. v. Dan Chase Taxidermy Supply Co.,* 74 F.3d 488 (4th Cir. 1/29/96).

57. Compare *Greenwich Workshop Inc. v. Timber Creations Inc.,* 932 F.Supp. 1210 (C.D.Cal. 5/20/96) with *Lee v. Deck the Walls Inc.,* 925 F.Supp. 576 (N.D.Ill. 5/1/96). *Lee v. A.R.T. Co.,* 66 LW 1181 (7th Cir. 9/18/97) does not consider a notecard glued to a tile to be a derivative work, because the artwork is not altered by gluing it to the tile, so the copyright holder's exclusive right to create derivative works is not usurped.

58. *Publications Int'l Ltd. v. Meredith Corp.,* 88 F.3d 473 (7th Cir. 7/8/96).

59. *American Dental Association v. Delta Dental Plans Association,* 66 LW 1214 (7th Cir. 9/30/97). *Practice Management Information Corp. v. American Medical Association,* 66 LW 1099 (9th Cir. 8/6/97) upholds the AMA's copyright on a catalogue of medical procedures, albeit on different grounds.

60. *Warren Publishing Inc. v. Microdos Data Corp.,* 115 F.3d 1509 (11th Cir. 6/10/97).

61. *Mitel v. Iqtel Inc.,* 124 F.3d 1366 (10th Cir. 9/22/97).

62. *National Council on Compensation Insurance Inc. v. Insurance Data Resources Inc.*, 65 LW 2272 (S.D.Fla. 10/3/96).

63. *Oasis Publishing Co. v. West Publishing Co.*, 924 F.Supp. 918 (D.Minn. 5/17/96).

64. *Bender v. West*, 551 N.W.2d 71 (S.D.N.Y. 11/22/96); another case with the same caption, 65 LW 2747 (S.D.N.Y. 5/19/97) reaches a similar result.

65. *U.S. v. Thomson*, 65 LW 2455 (D.D.C. 12/23/96).

66. *Princeton University Press v. Michigan Document Services*, 74 F.3d 1512 (6th Cir. 2/12/96); 99 F.3d 1381 (6th Cir. 11/8/96) *cert. denied* 117 S.Ct. 1336.

67. *Acuff-Rose Music Inc. v. Jostens Inc.*, 66 LW 1388 (S.D.N.Y. 12/11/97).

68. *Los Angeles News Service v. KCAL-TV*, 108 F.3d 1119 (9th Cir. 3/11/97).

69. *Ringgold v. Black Entertainment Television Inc.*, 66 LW 1182 (2nd Cir. 9/16/97).

70. *Lulirama Ltd. v. Axcess Broadcasting Services Inc.*, 66 LW 1368 (5th Cir. 11/10/97).

71. *ABKCO Music Inc. v. Stellar Records Inc.*, 96 F.3d 60 (2nd Cir. 9/19/96).

72. *Agee v. Paramount Communications Inc.*, 59 F.3d 317 (2nd Cir. 6/26/95).

73. *ASCAP v. Pataki*, 930 F.Supp. 873 (S.D.N.Y. 3/20/96).

74. *Fonovisa Inc. v. Cherry Auction Inc.*, 76 F.3d 259 (9th Cir. 1/25/96).

75. Copyright Registration for Online Works, part of the Copyright Office's fax on demand service accessible at (202) 707-2600. See Robert J. Bernstein and Robert W. Clarida, "New Policies and Procedures for the Digital Age," *N.Y.L.J.* 1/16/98 p. 3.

76. *Lotus Development Corp. v. Borland International*, 49 F.3d 807 (1st Cir. 3/9/95), *aff'd per curiam* #94-2003, 116 S.Ct. 1062 (Sup.Ct. 1/16/96).

77. *MiTek Holdings v. Arce Engineering Co.*, 89 F.3d 1548 (11th Cir. 8/5/96).

78. *Computer Associates International Inc. v. Altai Inc.*, 66 LW 1197 (2nd Cir. 9/25/97).

79. *Pro CD Inc. v. Zeidenberg*, 908 F.Supp. 640 (W.D.Wis. 1/4/96).

80. 86 F.3d 1447 (7th Cir. 6/20/96).

81. *Tasini v. New York Times Corp.*, 972 F.Supp. 804 (S.D.N.Y. 8/13/97).

82. *Religious Technology Center v. FACTNET Inc.*, 901 F.Supp. 1519 (D.Colo. 9/15/95).

83. *Religious Technology Center v. Lerma*, 908 F.Supp. 1362 (E.D.Va. 10/4/96).

84. *Religious Technology Center v. Netcom*, 907 F.Supp. 1361 (N.D.Cal. 11/21/95).

85. *U.S. v. LaMacchia*, 871 F.Supp. 535 (D.Mass. 12/28/94).

86. *Ohio v. Perry*, 65 LW 2571 (Ohio App. 2/12/97).

87. *Playboy Enterprises Inc. v. Webbworld Inc.*, 66 LW 1463 (N.D. Tex. 12/11/97). *Playboy Enterprises Inc. v. Russen Hardenburgh Inc.*, 66 LW 1431 (N.D. Ohio

11/25/97 is similar, finding both direct and contributory infringement based on the BBS encouragement of uploading of copyrighted files.

88. *Sony Music Entertainment Inc. v. Internet Sites,* 66 LW 1016 (S.D. Cal. 6/10/97).

89. *Cass Country Music Co. v. C.H.L.R. Inc.,* 88 F.3d 635 (8th Cir. 7/8/96).

90. *Feltner v. Columbia Pictures Television,* #96-1978, 66 LW 4245 (Sup.Ct. 3/31/98).

91. *Fantasy Inc. v. Fogerty,* 94 F.3d 553 (9th Cir. 8/26/96).

92. *Cadence Design Systems Inc. v. Avant! Corporation,* 66 LW 1196 (9th Cir. 9/23/97).

93. *Goodman v. Lee,* 78 F.3d 1007 (5th Cir. 4/1/96).

94. *Zuill v. Shanahan,* 80 F.3d 1366 (9th Cir. 4/10/96).

95. *Magnuson v. Video Yesteryear,* 85 F.3d 1424 (9th Cir. 6/11/96).

96. *Zyware Inc. v. Middlegate Inc.,* 66 LW 1351 (S.D.N.Y. 11/3/97).

97. *BMI Inc. v. Hersch,* 104 F.3d 1163 (9th Cir. 1/15/97).

— FOR FURTHER REFERENCE —

Berkowitz, Leslie G., "The Economic Espionage Act of 1996: An Experiment in Unintended Consequences?" 26 *Colorado Lawyer* 47 (December '97).

Bernstein, Hiram H. and Robert W. Bahr, "Major Changes to Patent Rules," 79 *J. of the Patent and Trademark Office Society* 677 (October '97).

Chon, Margaret, "New Wine Bursting from Old Bottles: Collaborative Internet Art, Joint Works, and Entrepreneurship," 75 *Oregon L. Rev.* 257 (Spring '96).

Cohen, Barbara, "A Proposed Regime for Copyright Protection on the Internet," 22 *Brooklyn J. of International Law* 401 (December '96).

Dinwoodie, Graeme B., "Reconceptualizing the Inherent Distinctiveness of Product Design Trade Dress," 75 *North Carolina L.Rev.* 471 (January '97).

Dornbas, William A., "Structuring, Financing, and Preserving Security Interests in Intellectual Property," 113 *Banking Law J.* 656 (July–August '96).

Ferron, William O. Jr., Christopher J. Daley-Watson and Michael J. Kiklis, "On-Line Copyright Issues," 14 *The Computer Lawyer* 7 (January '97).

Finch, Andrew Corydon, "When Imitation is the Sincerest Form of Flattery," 63 *U. of Chicago L. Rev.* 1243 (Summer '96).

Hansmann, Henry and Marina Santile, "Authors' and Artists' Moral Rights: A Comparative Legal and Economic Analysis," 26 *J. of Legal Studies* 95 (January '97).

Hartnick, Alan J., "Copyright and Trademark on the Internet—and Where to Sue,"

N.Y.L.J. 2/21/97 p. 5.

Hein, Clinton, "Confused About Federal Trademark Dilution?" 87 *Trademark Reporter* 370 (July–August '97).

Hoffman, Gary M. and Eric Oliver, "Closing Arguments in Patent Cases: Knowing Your Theory," 13 *Computer Lawyer* 12 (September '96).

Lichtman, Douglas Gary, "The Economics of Innovation: Protecting Unpatentable Goods," 81 *Minnesota L.Rev.* 693 (February '97).

Lunney, Glynn S. Jr., "Reexamining Copyright's Incentives-Access Paradigm," 49 *Vanderbilt L. Rev.* 483 (April '96).

Masson, Douglas J., "Fixation on Fixation: Why Imposing Old Copyright Law on New Technology Will Not Work," 71 *Indiana L. J.* 1049 (Fall '96).

Melone, Wendy M., "Contributory Liability for Access Providers: Solving the Conundrum Digitization Has Placed on Copyright Laws," 49 *Federal Communications Law J.* 491 (February '97).

Reichman, J.H. and Pamela Samuelson, "Intellectual Property Rights in Data?" 50 *Vanderbilt L.Rev.* 49 (January '97).

Sartori, Michael A., "Tax Ramifications of Recent Changes in the Patent Laws," 49 *Tax Lawyer* 981 (Summer '96).

VerSteeg, Russ, "Defining 'Author' for Purposes of Copyright," 45 *American U. L. Rev.* 1323 (June '96).

Willhite, John M., "Denial of Copyright and Trademark Protection for Interactive Games," 16 *Loyola of Los Angeles Entertainment Law J.* 789 (Spring '96).

Yen, Alfred C., "Entrepreneurship, Copyright, and Personal Home Pages," 73 *Oregon L. Rev.* 331 (Spring '96).

Youn, Monica, "Neither Intellectual Nor Property," 107 *Yale L.J.* 267 (October '97).

Young, Jessica W. and Jerry R. Selinger, "Suing an Infringing Competitor's Customers: Or Life Under the Single Recovery Rule," 31 *John Marshall Law Rev.* 19 (Fall '97).

MATRIMONIAL MATTERS

[¶2901] During the supplement period, issues involving both traditional and nontraditional families were assayed—although not necessarily resolved; simple questions such as the Constitutionality of federal law about interstate child support received conflicting answers.

This supplement adds discussion of adoption, an increasingly active area of litigation. Many of these cases involve the same-sex partners of biological parents. On the related issue of whether same-sex couples can marry, the District of Columbia Court of Appeals found no Constitutional barrier to limiting the issuance of marriage licenses to male-female couples.[1]

Advocates both of gay marriage and of traditional families paid profound attention to Hawaii. Although Hawaii has a state statute requiring marriage partners to be of opposite sexes, three gay couples challenged the statute. An injunction against enforcement of the law was granted (on equal protection grounds), but the injunction was immediately stayed pending appeal to the state Supreme Court.[2] In the meantime, however, Congress had passed the Defense of Marriage Act, H.R. 3396, 28 U.S.C. §1738C (9/21/96), which says that states do not have to give full faith and credit to same-sex marriages performed in other states. Atlanta's municipal ordinance providing health and other employee benefits to the domestic partners of city employees has been upheld because its definition of "dependent" was consistent with that of other statutes.[3]

According to the D.C. Circuit, there is no private right of action under 42 U.S.C. §1983 (civil rights law) to enforce the state's obligation under the federal Child Abuse Prevention and Treatment Act to investigate and act on child abuse reports. The Act has no mandatory method or schedule for investigation and intervention that the states must satisfy,[4] and therefore no penalties can be imposed for dilatory investigation.

Effective August 15, 1997, Louisiana created a new form of marriage, the "covenant" marriage (Covenant Marriage Act, House Bill 756). Applicants for a marriage license choose between conventional and covenant marriage; the latter requires premarital counseling and is subject to statutory restrictions on divorce. Only the party who has not breached the covenant of marriage can seek a divorce, and only if a complete breach of the marital covenant commitment has occurred. An existing marriage can be made subject to the covenant restrictions by declaration. A covenant marriage can be dissolved only on the grounds of adultery, felony conviction, abandonment for one year, sexual abuse of the petitioner or a child of the marriage; or a two-year separation. Divorce can also be granted one year after a divorce from bed and board.

[¶2902] ANTENUPTIAL AGREEMENTS

In 1995, the Louisiana Supreme Court found that a premarital waiver of the right to permanent alimony will not be enforceable, on the theory that the state has an interest in preventing divorced persons from becoming public charges;[5] in 1996, however, the court reversed itself, finding that there is no valid distinction between premarital and post-separation waivers of permanent alimony, so an otherwise valid prenuptial agreement can waive alimony.

A Montana case[6] makes waiver of the right of election in the future spouse's estate enforceable as long as general information about the future spouse's net worth is disclosed, and as long as the antenuptial agreement includes a general statement that fair disclosure was made. It is not necessary for the proponent of the antenuptial agreement to show that specific asset-by-asset disclosure was made.

However, a prenuptial agreement that was conscionable at the time of making can become unconscionable and hence unenforceable by a change in circumstances, such as the waiving spouse's poor health and need for support.[7]

At least in Florida, an Islamic *saddaq,* an arrangement for return of the dowry to the wife in case of divorce, is enforceable as an antenuptial agreement to the extent that it complies with contract law. The marriage is consideration for the wife's side of the bargain.[8]

[¶2907]   INCOME TAX CONSEQUENCES

U.S. v. Williams[9] is doubly unusual: It is both a Supreme Court income tax case, and a Supreme Court domestic relations case. When the Williamses divorced, Mrs. Williams was awarded the family home. Nevertheless, the IRS imposed a lien on all of Mr. Williams' property. Mrs. Williams, under protest, paid the tax to get the IRS lien removed from the house. The Supreme Court gave her standing, under 28 U.S.C. §1346, to bring suit in federal District Court for recovery of tax alleged to have been assessed or collected erroneously or illegally. The court rejected the IRS' contention that only the person against whom the tax was assessed has standing in this situation.

Another tax-deficient ex-husband had a Code §6321 lien imposed on all his property. However, the one-time family home did not fall into this category, because it had been awarded entirely to the ex-wife under the divorce decree. Even though the decree was not recorded until after the lien attached, the house was nevertheless not the property of the ex-husband and thus was not subject to the lien.[10]

The Supreme Court decided another matrimonial issue in early 1998, striking down a New York law that allows an alimony deduction on resident, but not non-resident, state tax returns. The Court found no substantial justification that would support this violation of the Privileges and Immunities clause of the Constitution.[11]

Where a couple had a premarital agreement specifying that each spouse's employment income would remain separate property (a Texas procedure for partitioning future earnings and opting out of community property), the IRS was powerless to levy on the wife's salary to collect the husband's premarital tax debts.[12]

No alimony deduction is available for amounts paid pursuant to a written proposal to pay submitted to the payee spouse's attorney. Such a proposal is neither a court decree nor a written separation agreement, so no deduction is available for what are deemed to be purely voluntary payments.[13]

Where the parties did not intend payments to terminate at the recipient wife's death, payments described as "alimony as division of equity" that must be "paid in full" constitute property settlements, not alimony. Consequently, such amounts are neither deductible by the payor nor gross income to the payee.[14]

Although no gain or loss is recognized (for tax purposes) when property is transferred incident to a divorce, the Tax Court has ruled that if the transfer is supposed to be carried out over a period of years, with a provision for interest payments, the interest is taxable to its recipient.[15]

A couple's separation agreement severed the joint tenancy in the house and conveyed a life estate to the wife. When the IRS foreclosed on a tax lien against the husband, it could not reach the wife's interest in the residence—even though she did not record the separation agreement.[16]

As for another housing issue, the Ninth Circuit has decided that a spouse who makes a permanent move out of the family home incident to a divorce, with no intent to return, is ineligible to use Code §1034 to defer taxation on proceeds of the eventual sale of the residence.[17]

According to the Tax Court, a distribution made to the wife's IRA prior to a divorce decree did not constitute a tax-free rollover.[18]

[¶2907.1] Liability for Tax on a Joint Return

Two other Tax Court cases deal with interesting joint-return questions. *Shackelford*[19] finds that an annulment does not relate back to the beginning of the marriage for tax purposes. Therefore, a person who held himself or herself out as married in a particular year cannot file a return as a single person for that year, even if the marriage was later annulled.

An ex-wife who received a property distribution in excess of normal support was held to have benefited by her ex-husband's tax shelter investments, even though tax shelter limited partnership interests per se were not distributed to her. Because of the benefit she received, she was not permitted to claim innocent spouse status when the shelters were disallowed.[20] In contrast, the Second Circuit did permit innocent spouse characterization of a spouse who was aware of tax shelter transactions, because the spouse's limited education and financial experience precluded imputation of knowledge that tax liability had been substantially understated. In this reading, the innocent spouse reasonably relied on the common perception that legitimate tax shelters were available, as well as the assurances of her husband and recommendations from an accountant and tax shelter expert.[21]

The Ninth Circuit allows the IRS to consult a couple's prenuptial agreement to trace and allocate an overpayment of tax to see if it is attributable to community or separate property, and thus determine which spouse's tax liability can be reduced by the overpayment after divorce.[22]

[¶2913.1] Interspousal Torts

Even prior to finalization of the divorce, breaking into the home of an estranged spouse constitutes burglary and criminal trespass.[23]

It is not mandatory that tort claims between spouses be raised in the divorce action. For instance, one divorced spouse can sue the other for alleged fraud occurring during the marriage. The divorce action has no *res judicata* effect on the tort issue.[24]

[¶2926] FACTORS INFLUENCING ALIMONY AWARD

Given societal changes and changing attitudes toward permanent alimony, it is understandable that several cases in the supplement period deal with rehabilitative alimony. Mississippi permits a divorce court to specify a time-limited period for periodic rehabilitative alimony, even though ordinarily periodic alimony is indefinite and vests as it becomes due; rehabilitative periodic alimony is for a limited period of time and vests as it accrues.[25]

A Florida case holds that, absent an agreement to the contrary, remarriage is merely a factor in determining whether there has been a change of circumstances justifying termination of rehabilitative alimony—termination upon remarriage is not automatic.[26] The Arizona Court of Appeals held that spousal support cannot be terminated simply by characterizing cohabitation as a *de facto* marriage; the trial court must examine the economic effect of the live-in relationship.[27] However, a 1996 North Carolina case finds that a woman who concededly had a sexual relationship with another man subsequent to granting of a divorce from "bed and board" was guilty of adultery (because the marriage had not yet been dissolved) and therefore was not entitled to permanent alimony.[28]

Illinois considers smoking and weight to be inappropriate issues for consideration as to the extension of rehabilitative maintenance.[29]

Even if a divorcing wife does not require maintenance at the time of divorce, the Wisconsin Court of Appeals says that the court can keep the issue open in case her chronic kidney condition creates a need for maintenance in the future.[30]

An ex-wife had a judgment for post-due alimony when the former husband, who had remarried, retired. The court granted a Qualified Domestic Relations Order (QDRO) to the first wife and made her payee of his death benefits. However, the Fourth Circuit ruled in early 1997 that when an employee retires, his or her survivor benefits vest, and can no longer be re-allocated with a QDRO.[31]

[¶2927] COMMUNITY PROPERTY

The innocent spouse's interest in community property cannot be characterized as "substitute property" and seized when the guilty spouse is convicted of a forfeitable offense. The Ninth Circuit said[32] that the innocent spouse's vested undivided half interest in the property is not forfeitable.

In California, post-separation disability benefits are not community property, even if the insurance policy paying the benefits was purchased with community funds, and even if the intention was to safeguard the community's financial position.[33]

Community-property-like principles have been applied to a cohabiting couple in a long-term, stable, quasi-marital relationship. Thus, there is a rebuttable presumption that property acquired during the relationship is jointly owned, irrespective of title. (The presumption can be overcome by showing acquisition with funds that would have been separate if the couple had been married.)[34]

[¶2928]   EQUITABLE DISTRIBUTION OF PROPERTY

For many couples, the family home and the potential pension rights of one or both spouses are the most significant assets—if not the only significant assets—to be divided. Thus, the continuing presence of these issues in court is to be expected.

The Fifth Circuit ruled that ERISA does not preempt a state community property law that vests each spouse equally as soon as a benefit vests. The theory was that domestic relations law is a traditional concern of the states—and that the disposition of benefits that are in pay status is really a dispute between family members, not between a plan administrator and a beneficiary (which probably would invoke ERISA preemption). But the Supreme Court reversed in mid-1997, and did find ERISA preemption, particularly since the first wife's will could not be accepted as a QDRO, because there was no court involvement.[35]

During the supplement period, the Fourth Circuit permitted a separation agreement, which was incorporated into the divorce decree, to waive the non-employee spouse's interest in ERISA pension plan proceeds.[36] In contrast, a provision in an incorporated decree waiving all rights to the ex-spouse's estate, as heir or otherwise, has been held insufficiently explicit to waive an interest in the pension plan.[37]

A Massachusetts state court took the position that Congress wanted to prevent "assignment" or "alienation" of plan benefits (i.e., transfer of rights) but not to prevent a "waiver" (outright surrender of rights). This means that a nonemployee spouse's waiver of interest in the employee spouse's retirement benefits, incorporated into a divorce decree, prevails over the wife's designation as plan beneficiary—even though the waiver was not incorporated into a QDRO.[38]

A settlement incorporated into a divorce decree gave the wife the sum of $1 million from the husband's pension. The 10th Circuit treated this as a QDRO, with the result that the wife (as alternate payee) was liable for the taxes on the funds.[39]

Both state and federal courts have concurrent jurisdiction to determine if an order is really a QDRO. A mid-1997 California case finds that the purported QDRO did not qualify as such because it was rendered before the employee spouse's retirement, and ordered payments of "Rule of 75" early retirement benefits without actuarial reduction. (The Rule of 75 allows a full benefit to be paid to employees who retire at 55 or over, when their age and years of service equal or exceed 75.) The court treated the Rule of 75 benefit as an employer subsidy which could not be paid to the non-employee spouse without a reduction.[40]

A nonvested pension was valued, and the nonemployee spouse given a sum equal to her interest right away, rather than waiting for the interest to vest in 1996. The rationale is that the nonemployee spouse has the option of accepting the risk of nonvesting. The Alaska Supreme Court's methodology for valuing anticipated pension benefits is reduction to present value, with upward adjustment for inflation and discount using the market interest rate.[41]

However, the Eighth Circuit found the obligation to pay a set amount to the spouse, in settlement of the pension interest, is dischargeable in bankruptcy if embodied in a pre-petition divorce decree—even if installment payments are supposed to continue after the bankruptcy filing.[42] In this analysis, the obligation was not a QDRO (because it was not directed to the plan administrator) and was not linked to the retirement income actually to be earned by the employee spouse. Instead, the nonemployee spouse's interest was reduced to an amount certain to be paid from the bankruptcy debtor's assets. Therefore, it was a simple and dischargeable pre-petition debt rather than nondischargeable support or maintenance.

On the other hand, the Sixth Circuit said in 1996 that pension benefits awarded to the ex-wife before the husband's bankruptcy filing never entered the bankruptcy estate (even though monthly payments were supposed to continue past the filing) and thus were not dischargeable.[43]

Where the employee spouse acquired a retirement fund prior to the marriage, the enhancement in the fund's value during the marriage is divisible marital property only to the extent that it derives from employer contributions, labor of the spouses, or funds of the spouses. The portion deriving from investment appreciation, inflation, or management by others is separate property of the employee spouse.[44]

For a spouse serving in the military, post-divorce promotions do not increase the marital portion of the nonvested pension—although passive appreciation, such as Cost of Living Increases, does serve to increase the marital share.[45] Future Social Security benefits can be considered in setting alimony, but not in distributing marital property; Iowa says that the Social Security Act preempts state law in this context. Therefore, the property settlement should not be adjusted to reflect the comparative size of the Social Security benefit each spouse can expect.[46]

Indiana and Washington State disagree about unvested options in the stock of a spouse's employer. Indiana says that unvested options that can be exercised only contingent on working for the employer when they vest are not marital property, because of their contingent nature.[47] Washington says that unvested options acquired during marriage but vesting post-separation are part community property, part separate property. Vested stock options are acquired when granted (either before or after the marriage), and the time of acquisition determines their community status.[48]

A QDRO can require the plan administrator to pay part of the monthly benefit to satisfy alimony obligations (as distinct from equitably distributing the pension interest). This has been deemed to constitute enforcement of the court's alimony award rather than an unlawful modification of the property award.[49]

QDROs can be issued in connection with a welfare plan, not just a pension plan—e.g., an agreement to maintain the children of the marriage as beneficiaries of group insurance invalidates the later designation of the second wife as beneficiary.[50] A divorce decree in which the wife waives her interest in the husband's life insurance prevails over plan documents that continue to name her as beneficiary.[51] According to the Eighth Circuit, federal common law, rather than the ERISA anti-alienation provision (here read to apply only to pension benefits, not welfare benefit plans) applies to an ex-wife's claim to the life insurance policy of which she was named as irrevocable beneficiary in the divorce decree.[52]

Another viewpoint is that ERISA lacks a definition of a valid waiver of benefits by an ex-spouse beneficiary—with the result that federal common law applies, and a waiver incident to divorce must specifically mention each plan in which benefits are waived. A broad-based global waiver is not specific enough.[53]

Yet another perpetual question is the correct treatment of divorcing spouses' business interests and professional practices. Late in 1995 New York's highest court altered its policy and permitted a professional license to be assigned independent value as a marital asset—it is no longer deemed to merge into the professional practice.[54] In Oklahoma, the goodwill of a professional practice is divisible, if it is marketable as distinct from the professional reputation of the practitioner.[55]

Illinois drew a distinction between "personal" and "enterprise" goodwill in the division of a car dealership conducted as a partnership. Enterprise goodwill is divisible, but personal goodwill is not, because it duplicates other elements used in allocating property.[56]

An attorney undergoing a divorce has separate property in the part of a contingent fee that relates to work done on the case after the spouses separated. It is not necessary to apply a legal fiction that the lawyer resigned from his law firm on the date of the separation.[57]

New York treats stock options received during marriage to be divisible marital property, even if exercise is contingent on future employment that continues after the divorce. New York uses a four-step process to calculate each spouse's appropriate share, including allocating between amounts due to past and future service. The share attributable to past service is marital to the extent that the grantee spouse was married at the time of the grant (i.e., if 50% of the options are allocable to work done before the marriage, only 50% is divisible). The portion assigned to future services is partially divisible, using a ratio between the time between the date of separation and the date of the option grant divided by the difference between the exercise date and the date of grant. Finally, the marital portion of the options is equitably distributed between grantee and non-grantee spouse.[58]

Patents held by one spouse are divisible marital property, even if they have no ascertainable current value—so, for instance, the inventor-spouse can be awarded the patents subject to the non-inventor spouse's lien on a percentage of any future income produced by the patents.[59]

In a civil RICO case alleging fraudulent concealment of marital assets, the First Circuit permitted the federal court to defer its RICO decision on abstention grounds (although it could not dismiss the RICO claim) until the state court allocated the couple's property.[60]

A commercial fisherman's award of punitive damages, received in connection with the Exxon Valdez oil spill, is divisible marital property, because the underlying compensatory damages are marital property.[61]

An action for divorce abates when either party dies, and an equitable distribution claim does not survive the claimant's death.[62]

[¶2928.1] Attorneys' Fees

According to the District Court for the Central District of California, ERISA preempts a state domestic relations law that requires pension plans to pay attorneys' fees in connection with QDROs.[63]

Some recent cases treat the obligation to pay fees to one's ex-spouse's attorney as being in the nature of maintenance—and therefore not dischargeable in bankruptcy.[64] Fees paid to health professionals, and Guardian ad Litem fees for representing the child in a custody case, are not dischargeable in the Ninth Circuit, because they are not directly owed to the child or the former spouse.[65]

The conduct of divorce attorneys also received some attention. According to the West Virginia Supreme Court, sexual relations with a divorce client is not by itself a breach of professional responsibility—but the attorney can be disqualified from further representation of the client if ethical rules, such as those respecting conflict of interest, are violated.[66]

A divorce lawyer can be sued for malpractice for failure to advise clients on well-established principles of law, such as the substantive law about termination of the alimony obligation upon remarriage of the alimony recipient.[67]

[¶2928.2] Bankruptcy Issues in Divorce

A bankruptcy court (which is a federal court, of course) has discretion to lift the automatic stay so that the nondebtor spouse's equitable distribution action against the debtor spouse can proceed in state court.[68]

Nor does the automatic stay prevent distribution of 50 percent of the debtor's pension, under a decree granted before the Chapter 13 bankruptcy petition, because the pension funds have become the nonemployee spouse's sole and separate property and not a claim on the debtor's estate. However, spousal support payments come from the debtor's income, which is property of the bankruptcy estate. Thus, the bankruptcy trustee cannot make support payments without getting relief from the automatic stay.[6]

According to the Northern District of Illinois, post-divorce obligations created by an antenuptial agreement are non-dischargeable because they stem from a property settlement agreement. In this reading, ex-spouses should not lose agreed-upon support merely because the agreement preceded the marriage instead of being made as part of its dissolution.[70]

In a 1996 Fourth Circuit case, the debtor was divorced while her bankruptcy petition was pending; she was awarded the house. The court found that the divorce severed the tenancy by the entireties, with the result that the marital exemption was lost and the house became part of her bankruptcy estate.[71]

A frequent bankruptcy issue is the extent to which divorce-related obligations are dischargeable. For instance, an Illinois settlement required the husband to reimburse the wife for her loss in the sale of the marital home. But the wife was much more affluent than the husband, so, deeming the benefit of discharge to the husband to outweigh the detriment to the wife, the bankruptcy court permitted discharge of the obligation to reimburse.[72]

A bankruptcy court can order homestead or other property that is exempt under Bankruptcy Code §522 to be conveyed to an ex-spouse who seeks to enforce a pre-bankruptcy divorce judgment and property settlement.[73]

A bankruptcy debtor's obligation to assume the mortgage payments on the ex-wife's home, incorporated into the divorce decree, was treated as a non-dischargeable maintenance obligation by the Eighth Circuit, even though the underlying marital settlement agreement described the obligation as non-dischargeable.[74]

Similarly, whether "equalization" payments—lump sums that one spouse is supposed to pay to the other to create parity in the distribution of property and debts—are dischargeable depends on whether the benefit of discharge to the potential payor exceeds the detriment to the potential payee.[75]

An award of half of the husband's pension benefits, made to the wife in a pre-petition divorce decree, is not dischargeable. The Ninth Circuit treated the wife's claim as one against the pension plan, not a personal liability of the husband's that he could discharge in bankruptcy.[76]

A Chapter 7 debtor was awarded a judgment equalling her contribution to her own retirement and that of her former domestic partner. However, because it was a property settlement rather than an employment-related retirement plan, the money was not exempt from execution.[77]

A North Dakota husband was not allowed to discharge a cash property settlement to his wife, because he practiced "willful and malicious injury to another's property" by giving away farmland to his parents (while continuing to farm the land rent-free), demonstrating intent to deprive the wife of the court-ordered amount.[78]

To the First Circuit, attorneys' fees for enforcing family support obligations are just as non-dischargeable as the obligations themselves.[79]

It should also be noted that if an equitable distribution award is discharged in bankruptcy, that may be deemed a change in circumstances that warrants an upward adjustment in the amount of spousal support.[80]

[¶2929] PAYMENTS FOR SUPPORT OF MINOR CHILDREN

During the supplement period, there were two items of federal legislation involving child support. P.L. 103-383, the Full Faith and Credit for Child Support

Orders Act, 28 U.S.C. §1 denies a state court the power to modify the order of another state court that requires the payment of child support, unless either of two conditions is met. First, the recipient of the payments can reside in the state where the modification is sought; second, the recipient can consent to the modification being heard in the courts of the first state.

P.L. 104-35, the Child Support Retrieval Systems Act, 42 U.S.C. §654(24) gives states an extra two years (to 1997) to implement electronic data processing and information retrieval systems within state plans for assuring that spousal and child support are paid (thus preventing the designated payees from becoming public charges).

An earlier piece of federal legislation, 1992's Child Support Recovery Act, 18 U.S.C. §228, was litigated in several District Courts and six Circuits. Virtually without exception, the courts found that the measure, which makes it a criminal offense willfully to fail to pay past-due obligations to support a child who lives in another jurisdiction, was Constitutional.[81]

There is no Constitutional bar to bringing a CSRA prosecution in the district where the children (rather than the obligor parent) live. For federal venue purposes, non-support is a continuing offense that can be prosecuted in any place where it was begun, continued, or completed.[82]

At the death of a custodial parent, there is a presumption that child support arrears are an asset of the estate, although the presumption can be rebutted if upholding it would be detrimental to the child or children whose support is involved.[83]

Arrears of child support assigned by the intended recipient to a nongovernmental collection agency cannot be discharged in the intended payor's bankruptcy—because the transfer was merely an assignment for collection, not a true assignment that would be nondischargeable.[84]

A high-income parent (here, a sports figure) can be required to pay child support in accordance with the statutory guidelines, even if the result is that the payment exceeds the child's actual needs.[85] In other words, the child is entitled to benefit from the parent's affluence, even if the child would not be needy if a lower support payment were ordered. Social Security benefits received by a child after the parent's retirement can be considered as a factor in the judge's decision about deviating from the support guidelines, but are not an automatic offset to the support obligation.[86]

States are not permitted to contradict the Federal Child Support and Establishment of Paternity Act by imposing a $25 per month minimum support award that is irrebuttable. Federal law requires a chance for low-income obligors to rebut the minimum award.[87]

A personal injury settlement is not necessarily "income" that can be used to calculate the child support obligation, because part of the award is the counterpart of a "return of capital" that serves to make the victim whole. Only the portion that replaces lost earnings is cognizable for child support purposes.[88]

The Constitutionality of a South Dakota law forbidding issuance or renewal of a driver's license to persons who have over $1,000 in child support arrears was upheld.[89] The court was persuaded by the state's argument that depriving a nonpayor of a driver's license makes it harder to change jobs or move to avoid detection.

Pennsylvania has a statute permitting a court order obligating divorcing parents to contribute to the cost of their children's college education. In February of 1995, the Superior Court upheld this statute (even though married parents are not obligated to support "children" over 18); in October, the state Supreme Court found it unconstitutional.[90] In the interim, the Superior Court held that actual education expenses, not counting personal expenses of the college student, should be used to calculate the obligation—not the Child Support Guidelines.[91]

[¶2931]   UNIFORM RECIPROCAL ENFORCEMENT OF SUPPORT ACT

A custodial parent cannot use URESA to increase a foreign support order as long as the out-of-state parent is current in payments under a valid foreign order.[92]

[¶2932]   CHILD CUSTODY

At the end of 1996, the Supreme Court decided that indigent parents must be allowed to appeal the termination of their parental rights, even if they cannot afford to pay fees for the preparation of the record of the termination hearing.[93]

A man who was led to believe that he was the father of a child born to his wife in wedlock is an "equitable parent" who is entitled to seek custody of the child, even if in fact he was not the father of the child.[94] This stress on relationship rather than genetics was also applied in a Pennsylvania case in which the "best interests of the child" standard was applied in a custody battle between parents and the grandparents who actually took care of the children. Parenthood was viewed as a significant factor, but the court refused to presume that parents are the best individuals to receive custody.[95]

Proposed child care arrangements (a paid child care center vs. a grandparent) are relevant to the custody determination, but the child's best interests remain paramount.[96]

A divorcing wife was given "custody" of in vitro pre-embryos; it was held that her soon-to-be ex-husband does not have a right to prevent the use of his sperm for procreation,[97] but later proceedings held the couple to the terms of their divorce agreement, and to the agreement they made with the vitro fertilization program, so that if they could not agree on the disposition of frozen embryos, the IVF program would be allowed to keep them.[98]

New York's highest court established a new principle in March 1996, ruling that the focus in an application for relocation of custodial parent and child to another state must be the child's best interests—not whether or not the noncustodial parent will be deprived of meaningful access to the child.[99]

267

The California view is that a parent seeking initial custody is not required to prove that a relocation is necessary. Once custody is granted, a custodial parent need not prove the necessity of a move. However, the court can restrain a move that is prejudicial to the rights or welfare of the child (not the convenience of the noncustodial parent).[100] The Tennessee standard is that the custodial parent can relocate unless the noncustodial parent can prove a vindictive motivation to disrupt visitation.[101]

According to the California Court of Appeals, a promise made before marriage to raise children of the marriage in the Jewish faith is not legally enforceable after the parents' divorce. Unless there is a showing of harm to the child, the parent retains religious freedom to practice other religions.[102] In contrast, an Arkansas appellate case[103] requires a noncustodial father to continue to send children to church and Sunday school during visitation. Although the decree does not impose this requirement, the custodial parent maintained consistent church attendance for the children. In this reading, the noncustodial parent's religious freedom is not impugned, because he is not required to attend the services personally, only to make sure that the children continue their religious practice.

A 1997 Second Circuit case upholds the International Parental Kidnapping Crime Act of 1993, which bars parents from removing or keeping children outside the United States with intent to obstruct the other parent's right to physical custody. The court did not permit use of the affirmative defenses in the Hague Convention on Child Abduction, because the federal statute contains its own defenses.[104]

Under the International-Hague Convention, the definition of "exercising" custody rights includes retaining or seeking to retain contact with a child (including a parent who has custody rights in the country where the child lives), and "grave risk" means imminent danger or serious abuse the country of current residence cannot protect against. The definition of grave risk does not include adjustment problems caused by returning a parentally kidnapped child to the other parent's country of residence.[105]

A father who has joint custody can be guilty of custodial interference if he secretly removes and hides his daughter: violating the other joint custodial parent's right to physical custody is a criminal act.[106]

In light of the extremely low risk of infection posed by casual contact, the Kentucky Court of Appeals decided[107] that the custodial parent's cohabitation with an HIV+ stepparent is not, taken by itself, grounds for modifying custody in favor of the noncustodial parent.

Once again, there were numerous cases dealing with lesbian mothers, e.g., the South Dakota Supreme Court's determination that it was not an abuse of discretion to grant custody to a mother living with a female life partner, in that cohabitation was not per se contrary to the best interests of the children.[108] To the Virginia Supreme Court, a lesbian mother is not per se unfit, but custody was nevertheless granted to the child's grandmother because the mother, for reasons including "active lesbianism" that could subject the child to social condemnation, offered a home less suitable than the grandmother's.[109]

In contrast, the New York Family Court awarded custody to the lesbian partner of a deceased mother, in preference to the child's grandmother and the deceased mother's ex-husband: the mother died shortly after the child's birth, and her life partner had provided a home for the child for four years.[110]

The best interests of the child may call for custody by a non-parent, even in situations in which the parent's conduct is not bad enough to justify termination of parental rights. Therefore, where a mother voluntarily surrendered custody to her ex-cohabitant, the parental preference would not automatically bar an award of custody to the ex-cohabitant, although whether the surrender was intended to be temporary or permanent would be an important factor.[111]

[¶2932.1] Surrogate Motherhood

In a case where a sister served as the gestational surrogate for the implanted egg of her sister (who had suffered a hysterectomy), fertilized with the sperm of the sister's husband, the married couple were ruled the natural and legal parents of a legitimate child. They were deemed to be the parents of the child (notwithstanding the sister's gestation of the embryo) because they are the genetic parents who have not waived their rights and who intend to raise the child as their own.[112]

An Arizona statute has been voided on Equal Protection grounds. The law permitted the biological father, but not the biological mother, of a child born pursuant to a surrogate parenting contract to rebut the presumption that the husband of the surrogate mother is the legal father of the child. Instead, the would-be adoptive mother must be given access to a "maternity" proceeding just as a sperm donor can assert his paternity in court. (The case arose because the potential adopters under the surrogacy contract got a divorce.).[113]

[¶2932.2] Visitation

Two cases upheld laws (from Wyoming and New Mexico) that give grandparents visitation rights. Although the parents have the primary role in determining whom their children will associate with, the best interests of the child may give the children a right of association with their grandparents.[114]

Similarly, a mother's former lesbian partner, who took a step-parental role, can petition for visitation, according to the Wisconsin Supreme Court.[115] The court has equitable authority to hear the case and decide if visitation is so strongly in the child's best interest that it overrides the mother's right to control association with the child. However, a 1997 Vermont decision finds that trial courts lack jurisdiction over such disputes, until and unless legislation is passed.[116]

The Maryland Court of Special Appeals ruled that it is not per se harmful for a child to meet his father's male lover or gay friends, so it is improper to rule out overnight visitation when individuals with "homosexual tendencies" were present.[117]

[¶2932.3] Establishment of Paternity

In a paternity proceeding, the state's role as Guardian ad Litem for the child is adequately satisfied by presenting overwhelming evidence of the defendant's paternity. It is not necessary to locate and join all potential fathers. Proof by physical resemblance and genetic testing has been deemed sufficient to establish paternity.[118]

The Tennessee Court of Appeals was tougher on those seeking to establish paternity. The court found that putative fathers are deprived of due process by a statute that makes the presumption of paternity conclusive when the DNA test shows a probability of paternity equal to or over 99%. Making the presumption irrebuttable deprives some putative fathers of the opportunity to be heard on an issue that can have important consequences (i.e., a child support order continuing for many years).[119]

[¶2933] UNIFORM CHILD CUSTODY JURISDICTION ACT

According to the Utah Court of Appeals, the UCCJA does not apply to proceedings for termination of parental rights.[120]

Where the mother and child are in Virginia, and the father and his parents are in North Carolina, North Carolina is considered a convenient forum for Uniform Child Custody Jurisdiction Act purposes, because North Carolina does not have to relinquish jurisdiction to modify the custody and visitation provisions of its own divorce decree.[121]

Japan is a "state" as defined by the Uniform Child Custody Jurisdiction Act (UCCJA), so an Oregon court could hear an American mother's custody petition at a time when the father's petition was before a court in Japan (where the children were born).[122]

Under the UCCJA, the order of a Muslim religious court in the Philippines can only be enforced in Washington if the mother is first given a meaningful opportunity to contest the order. Showing that the foreign court used rules of law, evidence, or procedure repugnant to Washington State's law or public policy would prevent enforcement of the order.[123]

[¶2934] SUPPORT AGREEMENTS BETWEEN UNMARRIED COHABITANTS

A breach of contract claim accrued when a man, who allegedly offered to support his female cohabitant for life, stopped making the payments. The California Court of Appeals refused to accept his theory that the cause of action accrued nine years earlier, when he terminated the cohabitation relationship and married someone else.[124]

[¶2935] ADOPTION

Adoption is the creation of a parent-child relationship. Once adopted, a child has the same status as a child born into the family: he or she becomes a distributee of relatives who *die intestate*, for example. Adoptions occur in several legal postures. In some cases, the biological parents of an infant surrender custody of the infant—to an adoption agency, or directly to potential adoptive parents. The adoption is then finalized by a court order approving the validity of the surrender and the suitability of the adoptive parents.

Children may become available for adoption if the parental rights of their biological parents are terminated, e.g., in cases of severe abuse. There is a strong presumption of parental fitness; parental rights can be terminated only on clear and convincing evidence (although unfitness—unlike criminal assault charges— need not be proved beyond a reasonable doubt).[125]

More than half of adoptions in the U.S. are stepparent adoptions: the new spouse of a natural parent assumes legal parenthood of the children. If the other natural parent is still alive, he or she must surrender parental rights for the adoption to proceed. In general, a stepparent adoption terminates the biological parent's child support obligation, but does not extinguish the obligation to satisfy arrears of support.[126]

A 1997 federal law, the Adoption and Safe Families Act of 1997, P.L. 105-89, 11/19/97, strives to coordinate foster placement with termination of parental rights, with a view toward promoting adoption of children by their foster parents. The statute provides for grants to states so they can offer adoption incentives and Medicaid health benefits for special-needs children, easing the burden of their adoptive parents.

Most adoptions are of infants or young children, but it is generally legally possible for one adult to adopt another. A number of cases authorize adult adoption for estate planning purposes.[127] Adoption of an adult requires consent by the adoptee, adopter, and adopter's spouse. State law may require consent of the biological parent whose rights are terminated, or proof that the adoption creates a genuine parent-child relationship rather than giving legal sanction to a non-marital liaison.

However, an Idaho case from early 1995 denies a stepparent adoption of an 18-year-old. The stepchild was willing to be adopted, but his biological father objected. Idaho has no specific procedure for adult adoptions, and the court was unwilling to overcome the objections of the biological father.[128]

In a sense, adoption traditionally was analyzed more like a property transaction than as a matter of family law. For instance, parental rights cannot be surrendered in the abstract: either rights must be surrendered to an adoption agency, or directly to a stepparent or other potential adoptive parent.[129]

A child cannot have more than two legal parents, so it is not possible for, e.g., a stepfather to adopt his wife's child without the biological father surrendering his rights. This argument has also been used to deny adoption to some lesbian couples, on the grounds that the biological mother would have to surrender her parental rights for her life partner to be able to adopt the baby.[130]

However, there is a trend to reject this "exclusivity theory" and to permit the biological mother's life partner to adopt as a step parent.[131] Another possibility is joint adoption by the couple (or by unmarried couples, whether male or heterosexual), where one partner has already given birth to or adopted a child. Here again, the rights of the biological mother are not forfeited by the adoption.[132]

If the adoptee is handicapped or has other special needs, agreements for assistance must be entered into before entry of the final decree of adoption.

Employers can provide financial assistance to employees who adopt, and such assistance can be received tax-free (within limits). See IRS Notice 97-9, 1997-2 IRB 35, and Announcement 97-64, 1997-26 IRB 9, for reporting and administration of employment-related adoption assistance.

[¶2935.1] The Placement Process

Traditionally, the adoption process was controlled by adoption agencies. When nonmarital births were shrouded in shame and secrecy, the agency played an important role as an intermediary between women surrendering babies for adoption and prospective adoptive parents. Both parties usually preferred not to be aware of the identity of the other.

Today, there is much greater acceptance of single parenthood (biological or adoptive), and in many cases the potential adoptive parents prefer to deal directly with pregnant women seeking to place infants for adoptions. All of the states except Colorado, Connecticut, Delaware, and Massachusetts allow "direct placement" adoptions that do not involve agency intervention.

State laws set strict limits on what payments can be made and to whom, in connection with an adoption. It is permissible for prospective adopters to pay maternity expenses, legal expenses, and living expenses incident to the mother's pregnancy, delivery, and the adoption itself. However, it is illegal for payment of expenses to be made contingent on the mother consenting to the adoption and surrendering her parental rights.

There are also statutory and ethical constraints imposed on the activities of "intermediaries" or "facilitators" (including attorneys) who are involved in the adoption process but who are not a licensed adoption agency. It is unethical for an attorney to receive a fee for procuring a child for adoption (as distinct from getting a fee for performing legal services in connection with the adoption).[133]

Some states criminalize deliberate fraud (accepting money with no intention of surrendering the infant for adoption), but potential adoptive parents are at risk and cannot recover payments they made to a pregnant woman who experiences a genuine change of heart about the advisability of adoption.

If it is proved that improprieties occurred (such as excessive or inappropriate payments), but the adoption is nevertheless in the best interests of the child, the adoption will probably be allowed to proceed, with other sanctions imposed on the guilty parties as necessary.[134] However, the Ninth Circuit has held that there is no due process right enforceable under 42 U.S.C. §1983 in the society of one's grandchildren. Thus, grandparents had no protectable liberty interest in preventing their daughter from surrendering her children for adoption by a third party.[135]

A number of states consider "wrongful adoption"—e.g., negligent material misrepresentation of fact about the infant's heritage or medical history—to be a tort for which compensatory damages may be recovered.[136]

In many instances, the birth mother is a minor. The adoption court may, on its own motion, develop evidence about the validity of her consent, or appoint a *Guardian ad Litem* to safeguard her interests.[137] A number of cases[138] require appointment of counsel for indigent biological parents in adoption cases, on the same terms as counsel would be appointed in an abuse-based proceeding to terminate parental rights.

An adoption is a legal proceeding, and the court's approval for the adoption will not be given unless a home study has been performed by a court-appointed investigator to determine the suitability of potential adopters. This requirement is waived for stepparent adoptions. Adoptions are not finalized for a period such as three months, six months, or a year. The court retains ongoing jurisdiction to protect the adoptee. In cases where an adoption agency is involved, the proceeding for termination of the biological parents' parental rights may be distinct from the adoption proceeding. The two proceedings are usually joined in direct placement cases.

There is an increasing trend to permit "open adoptions," where the biological mother and the adopters are aware of each other's identity. In some cases, the birth mother is given the option of visiting the child, and the child is aware of her identity.[139]

In most states, an adopted child will be able to get some health and genetic information about his or her birth parents, with identifying data removed. A number of states maintain registries that adoptees and people who surrendered children for adoption can contact to find out if the other is interested in meeting or providing information. The Sixth Circuit ruled against a privacy-based challenge to a state law permitting adoptees to get access to adoption records once they reach age 21. The statute allows birth parents to veto contact with the adoptee, but not to prevent disclosure of their names. The court found that the need to know the identity of one's parents outweighs the parents' right to prevent disclosure.[140]

Generally speaking, a birth mother will not be permitted to consent to adoption until after the baby's birth, although some states do permit consent before the birth (which does not become effective unless confirmed after the birth). A valid consent must be written and witnessed, or made orally before a judge or court-appointed referee.

The National Conference on Commissioners of Uniform State Law's Uniform Adoption Act §2-406 requires that consent for direct placement or relinquishment of a child to an agency must evidence, in plain language, consent to transfer of legal and physical custody and extinguishment of parental rights. It must be made in the parent's native language.

The document must specify that consent is generally final and irrevocable except under the circumstances specified in the document itself—and cannot, for example, be set aside if a visitation agreement is violated. The Uniform Act provides a 192-hour period after birth, during which consents given before the infant's birth can be revoked.

If the biological father of the baby is known, he will generally be entitled to notice of the adoption proceeding, and to participate in it, although he will probably not be given outright veto power over the adoption.[141] Some states (e.g., Arizona, Indiana, Iowa, New York, Oregon) maintain Putative Father Registries; in order to contest an adoption, the father must sign the registry and admit paternity (thus making himself potentially responsible for support of the child).

The biological father's right to re-open an adoption that has already occurred will probably depend on his actions vis-a-vis the child. A father who never provided support or took an interest in a child is unlikely to be permitted to overturn an adoption.[142]

[¶2935.2] Interstate and Choice of Law Issues

The federal Adoption Assistance and Child Welfare Act of 1980, 42 U.S.C. §§620-628, 670-676 requires, as a condition of receiving federal AFDC funding, that states must make assistance payments to persons who adopt special-needs children who would not be adoptable absent such a subsidy.

The Multiethnic Placement Act, 42 U.S.C. §5115a, inspired by the controversy over placing children for adoption in homes where the parents are of a different race than the children, imposes limits on racial matching policies in adoption or foster care on agencies that are publicly funded.[143]

By the late 1980s, all of the states had adopted the Interstate Compact on Placement of Children (ICPC), to protect children placed across state lines. The "sending agency" has to transmit the Form ICPC-100A, Interstate Compact Placement Request, to the welfare department official designated as Compact Administrator in the receiving state. (The transmission may have to be routed through the Compact Administrator in the sending state as well.) A social and case history of the child, and a home study of the potential adopters, is attached to the form. Placements of children with relatives in other states is exempt from the ICPC process. However, several appellate cases hold that the Uniform Child Custody Jurisdiction Act and/or Parental Kidnapping Prevention Act prevail over the ICPC.[144]

In early 1995, a Colorado court used the Uniform Dissolution of Marriage Act to determine that a child should remain with adoptive parents rather than being returned to the birth mother, who wanted the child returned about six months after a private placement. The court said the UDMA was applicable because the adoptive parents had physical custody for more than six months, and furthermore that UDMA custody did not terminate parental rights, so there was no requirement of determining unfitness of the birth mother.[145]

— ENDNOTES —

1. *Dean v. District of Columbia*, 635 A.2d 307 (D.C.App. 1/19/95).

2. *Baehr v. Miike*, 23 Fam.Law Rep. 1063 (Hawaii Circuit Ct. 12/3/96; stay granted 12/4/96—see 65 LW 2399).

3. *Atlanta v. Morgan*, 66 LW 1320 (Ga.Sup. 11/3/97).

4. *Doe v. D.C.*, 93 F.3d 861 (D.C. Cir. 8/27/96).

5. *McAlpine v. McAlpine*, 650 So.2d 1142 (La.Sup. 2/9/95), *rev'd* 22 Fam.Law Rep. 1524 (La.Sup. 9/5/96). Also see *Cary v. Cary*, 22 Fam.Law Rep. 1403 (Tenn.Sup. 6/3/96): Antenuptial contract can waive or limit alimony, unless the lack of alimony would render the spouse a public charge.

6. *Thies v. Lowe*, 903 P.2d 186 (Mont.Sup. 9/21/95).

7. *Rider v. Rider*, 22 Fam.Law Rep. 1454 (Ind.Sup. 7/26/96).

8. *Akileb v. Elchalal*, 666 So.2d 246 (Fla.App. 1/12/96). On a somewhat comparable religious issue, see *Alfalo v. Alfalo*, 65 LW 2439 (N.J.Super. 2/29/96), finding that a court order mandating that a husband give his wife a *get* (Orthodox Jewish divorce papers) is a violation of the husband's freedom of religion. The Superior Court did not find that the husband was withholding the *get* as a tactic to secure an unfair advantage in divorce-related negotiations; in fact, he wanted to reconcile with his wife.

9. #94-395, 115 S.Ct. 1611 (Sup.Ct. 4/25/95).

10. *Thomson v. U.S.*, 66 F.3d 160 (8th Cir. 9/19/95).

11. *Lunding v. New York Tax Appeals Tribunal*, #96-1462, 118 S.Ct. 766 (Sup.Ct. 1/21/98).

12. *Calmes v. U.S.*, 22 Fam.Law Rep. 1360 (N.D. Tex. 5/21/96).

13. *Keegan v. Comm'r*, TC Memo 1997-359 (8/5/97).

14. *Hoover v. C.I.R.*, T.C. Memo 1995-183, 4/20/95, *aff'd* 102 F.3d 842 (6th Cir. 12/18/96).

15. *Gibbs v. Comm'r*, TC Memo 1997-196 (4/29/97).

16. *Gibbons v. Comm'r*, 71 F.3d 1496 (10th Cir. 12/1/95).

17. *Perry v. Comm'r*, 91 F.3d 82 (9th Cir. 7/31/96).

18. *Rodoni v. C.I.R.*, 105 T.C. No. 3 (Tax Ct. 7/24/95).

19. T.C. Memo 1995-484 (1995).

20. *Stiteler*, T.C. Memo 1995-279 (6/21/95).

21. *Friedman v. C.I.R.*, 53 F.3d 523 (2nd Cir. 4/26/95).

22. *U.S. v. Elam*, 112 F.3d 1036 (9th Cir. 5/2/97).

23. *Colorado v. Johnson*, 906 P.2d 122 (Colo.Sup. 11/14/95).

24. *Delahunty v. Mass. Mutual Life Ins.*, 236 Conn. 582 (Sup. 4/9/96).

25. *Hubbard v. Hubbard*, 63 LW 2803 (Miss.Sup. 6/1/95).

26. *Vaccato (Pustizzi) v. Pustizzi*, 648 So.2d 1206 (Fla.App. 1/11/95).

27. *Van Dyke (Steinle) v. Steinle*, 21 Fam.Law Rep. 1262 (Ariz.App. 3/28/95).

28. *Coombs v. Coombs*, 468 S.E.2d 807 (N.C.App. 3/5/96).

29. *In re Offer*, 657 N.E.2d 694 (Ill.App. 10/31/95).

30. *Grace v. Grace*, 63 LW 2803 (Wis.App. 6/1/95).

31. *Hopkins v. AT&T Global Information Solutions Co.*, 105 F.3d 153 (4th Cir. 1/24/97).

32. *U.S. v. Lester*, 85 F.3d 1409 (9th Cir. 6/6/96).

33. *In re Elfmont*, 891 P.2d 136 (Cal.Sup. 4/10/95).

34. *Connell v. Francisco*, 127 Wash.2d 339, 898 P.2d 831 (Wash.Sup. 7/20/95).

35. *Boggs v. Boggs*, 82 F.3d 90 (5th Cir. 4/17/96), *rev'd* #96-79, 65 LW 4418 (Sup.Ct. 6/2/97).

36. *Estate of Altobelli v. IBM*, 77 F.3d 2573 (4th Cir. 2/28/96).

37. *Ohran v. Sierra Health & Life Insurance Co.*, 895 P.2d 1321 (Nev.Sup. 5/25/95).

38. *Wennett v. Capone*, 22 Fam.Law Rep. 1320 (Mass.Super. 3/7/96).

39. *Hawkins v. Comm'r*, 86 F.3d 982 (10th Cir. 6/14/96).

40. *Oddino v. Oddino*, 16 Cal.4th 67, 65 Cal.Rptr.2d 566, 939 P.2d 1266 (Cal.Sup. 7/28/97).

41. *Wainwright v. Wainwright*, 888 P.2d 762 (Alaska Sup. 1/13/95).

42. *In re Ellis*, 72 F.3d 628 (8th Cir. 2/18/95).

43. *McCafferty v. McCafferty*, 96 F.3d 192 (6th Cir. 9/18/96).

44. *Thielenhaus v. Thielenhaus*, 21 Fam.Law Rep. 1176 (Okla.Sup. 1/31/95).

45. *In re Hunt*, 63 LW 2788 (Colo.Sup. 5/15/95).

46. *In re Boyer*, 63 LW 2671 (Ia.App. 3/30/95).

47. *Hann v. Hann*, 655 N.E.2d 566 (Ind.App. 9/20/95).

48. *In re Short*, 125 Wash.2d 865, 890 P.2d 12 (Wash.Sup. 2/23/95).

49. *Bruns v. Iowa District Court for Linn County*, 21 Fam.Law Rep. 1396 (Ia.App. 5/30/95).

50. *Metropolitan Life Ins. Co. v. Wheaton*, 42 F.3d 1080 (7th Cir. 12/14/94); *Metropolitan Life Inc. Co. v. Fowler*, 22 Fam.Law Rep. 1308 (E.D. Mich. 4/15/96).

51. *Metropolitan Life Ins. Co. v. Barlow*, 884 F.Supp. 1118 (E.D.Mich. 4/18/95).

52. *Equitable Life Insurance Society v. Crysler*, 66 F.3d 944 (8th Cir. 9/29/95).

53. *Trustees of Iron Workers Local 451 Annuity Fund v. O'Brien*, 22 Fam.Law Rep. 1515 (D.Del. 8/2/96).

54. *McSparron v. McSparron*, 662 N.E.2d 745 (N.Y.App. 12/7/95). It's interesting to note that here, each spouse had a professional license (one doctor, one lawyer), so the net effect was limited. But see *Becker v. Perkins-Becker*, 669 A.2d 524 (R.I.Sup. 1/12/96), holding that an advanced degree acquired during marriage is not a marital asset, notwithstanding its potential impact on earning capacity.

55. *Traczyk v. Traczyk,* 896 P.2d 1277 (Okla.Sup. 3/21/95).

56. *In re Talty,* 652 N.E.2d 330 (Ill.Sup. 6/22/95); *In re Head,* 652 N.E.2d 1246 (Ill.App. 6/30/95) uses the "enterprise goodwill" concept in the valuation of a professional practice. Also see *Endres v. Endres,* 532 N.W.2d 65 (S.D.Sup. 5/17/95), treating the goodwill of a business as marital property.

57. *White v. Williamson,* 453 S.E.2d 666 (W.Va.Sup. 12/21/94). The divorcing wife in this case, also an attorney, was awarded rehabilitative alimony for the time she spent raising the couple's children rather than practicing law.

58. *DeJesus v. DeJesus,* 66 LW 1298 (N.Y.App. 10/30/97). *In re Marriage of Triller,* 915 P.2d 1314 (Colo.Sup. 1996) also treats options as divisible marital property.

59. *In re Monslow,* 912 P.2d 735 (Kan.Sup. 3/8/96).

60. *De Mauro v. De Mauro,* 115 F.3d 94 (1st Cir. 6/11/97).

61. *Lundquist v. Lundquist,* 22 Fam.Law Rep. 1487 (Alaska Sup. 8/16/96).

62. *Thorson v. Thorson,* 541 N.W.2nd 692 (N.D.Sup. 1/3/96).

63. *AT&T Management Pension Plan v. Tucker,* 64 LW 2224 (C.D.Cal. 8/17/95).

64. *Holliday v. Kline,* 65 F.3d 749 (8th Cir. 9/12/95); *In re Miller,* 55 F.3d 1487 (10th Cir. 5/19/95); *Brown v. Brown,* 21 Fam.Law Rep. 1148 (Bank. M.D.Fla. 11/22/94). However, the Sixth Circuit disagrees: *In re Perlin,* 30 F.3d 39 (6th Cir. 1994).

65. *Chang v. Beaupied,* 66 LW 1127 (9th Cir. 7/18/97).

66. *Musick v. Musick,* 453 S.E.2d 361 (W.Va.Sup. 1/25/95).

67. *McMahon v. Shea,* 657 A.2d 938 (Pa.Super. 2/23/95). By the way, a jury trial is available in a legal malpractice suit, even though it was not available in the underlying matrimonial litigation: *Ceriale v. L.A. Superior Court,* 22 Fam. Law Rep. 1518 (Cal.App. 8/19/96).

68. *Roberge v. Roberge,* 188 B.R. 366 (E.D.Va. 11/7/95).

69. *Debolt v. Comerical Bank,* 177 B.R. 31 (Bank. W.D. Pa. 12/23/94).

70. *Sparks v. Sparks,* 206 B.R. 481 (N.D. Ill. 3/24/97).

71. *Cordova v. Mayer,* 73 F.3d 38 (4th Cir. 1/9/96). Similar results were reached in *Massie v. Yamrose,* 169 B.R. 585 (W.D.Va. 1994) and *In re Alderton,* 179 B.R. 63 (Bank. E.D. Mich. 1995).

72. *Taylor v. Taylor,* 191 B.R. 760 (Bank. N.D. Ill. 1/23/96).

73. *In re Davis,* 65 LW 2540 (5th Cir. 2/5/97).

74. *In re Tatge,* 66 LW 1286 (8th Cir. 10/8/97).

75. Compare *Bodily v. Morris,* 193 B.R. 949 (Bank. S.D.Cal. 4/3/96): Equalization payment dischargeable if benefit exceeds detriment with *Samayoa (Jodoin) v. Jodoin,* 22 Fam.Law Rep. 1371 (Bank. E.D. Cal. 5/26/96): Equalization payment, much of which represents unpaid family support, is not dischargeable, given husband's greater assets and higher standard of living than potential payee-wife.

76. *Gendreau v. Gendreau,* 122 F.3d 815 (9th Cir. 8/15/97).

77. *Sticka v. Wilbur,* 126 F.3d 1218 (9th Cir. 10/6/97).

78. *Straub v. Straub,* 192 B.R. 522 (Bank. D.N.D. 2/22/96).

79. *Macy v. Macy,* 114 F.3d 1 (1st Cir. 5/23/97).

80. *Dickson v. Dickson,* 22 Fam.Law Rep. 1475 (Va.App. 8/20/96).

81. *U.S. v. Sage,* 906 F.Supp. 84 (D.Conn. 10/3/95), *aff'd* 22 Fam.Law Rep. 1463 (2nd Cir. 8/12/96); *U.S. v. Mussari/U.S. v. Schroeder,* 95 F.3d 787 (9th Cir. 9/5/96); *U.S. v. Hampshire,* 892 F.Supp. 1327 (D.Kan. 6/14/95), *aff'd* 95 F.3d 999 (10th Cir. 9/11/96); *U.S. v. Collins,* 921 F.Supp. 1026 (W.D.N.Y. 4/16/96); *U.S. v. Parker,* 65 LW 2632 (3rd Cir. 3/7/97). *U.S. v. Johnson,* 65 LW 2832 (4th Cir. 5/30/97) upholds the statute and additionally holds that the government does not have the burden of proving paternity in a CSRA prosecution. *U.S. v. Bongiorno,* 65 LW 2557 (1st Cir. 2/7/97) upholds the statute and also says that a CSRA restitution order is not a debt as defined by the Federal Debt Collection Procedure Act, 28 U.S.C. 3001-3008 because it goes to the children rather than the federal government, and hence the FeDCPA cannot be used for this purpose. The Uniform Interstate Family Support Act has been adopted in Arizona, Arkansas, Colorado, Delaware, Idaho, Illinois, Kansas, Maine, Massachusetts, Minnesota, Montana, Nebraska, New Mexico, North Dakota, Oklahoma, Oregon, South Carolina, South Dakota, Texas, Virginia, Washington, Wisconsin, and Wyoming.

82. *U.S. v. Crawford,* 115 F.3d 1397 (8th Cir. 6/23/97).

83. *Costello v. McDonald,* 22 Fam.Law Rep. 1443 (W.Va. 6/14/96).

84. *Smith v. Child Support Enforcement,* 21 Fam.Law Rep. 1287 (D.Utah 4/13/95).

85. *Mary L.O. v. Tommy R.B.,* 544 N.W.2d 417 (Wis.Sup. 2/15/96).

86. *Anderson v. Anderson,* 66 LW 1288 (Md.Spec.App. 9/29/97).

87. *Gilbert v. Gilbert,* 66 LW 1320 (Wash.App. 10/13/97).

88. *Villanueva (Garcia) v. O'Gara,* 22 Fam.Law Rep. 1500 (Ill.App. 8/5/96).

89. *Thompson v. Ellenbecker,* 21 Fam.Law Rep. 1571 (D.S.D. 9/18/95).

90. *Byrnes v.Caldwell,* 654 A.2d 1125 (Pa.Super. 2/9/95); *Curtis v. Kline,* 21 Fam.Law Rep. 1583 (Pa.Sup. 10/10/95).

91. *Bolton v. Bolton,* 657 A.2d 1270 (Pa.Super. 4/25/95).

92. *Alabama ex.rel. Robertson v. Robertson,* 21 Fam.Law Rep. 1183 (Ala.Civ.App. 2/10/95).

93. *M.L.B. v. S.L.J.,* #95-853, 117 S.Ct. 555 (Sup.Ct. 12/16/96).

94. *In re Gallagher,* 539 N.W.2d 479 (Ia.Sup. 10/25/95).

95. *Rowles v. Rowles,* 668 A.2d 126 (Pa.Sup. 22/19/95).

96. *Ireland v. Smith,* 64 LW 2784 (Mich.Sup. 5/21/96).

97. *Kass v. Kass,* 21 Fam.Law Rep. 1172 (N.Y.Sup. 1/23/95). Contra, *Davis v. Davis,* 842 S.W.2d 588 (Tenn.Sup. 1992).

98. *Kass v. Kass,* 66 LW 1223 (N.Y.A.D. 9/8/97).

99. *Tropea v. Tropea,* 64 LW 2619 (N.Y.App. 3/26/96).

100. *Burgess v. Burgess,* 51 Cal.Rptr.2d 444, 913 P.2d 473 (Cal.Sup. 4/15/96).

101. *Aaby v. Strange,* 22 Fam.Law Rep. 1319 (Tenn.Sup. 4/22/96).

102. *In re Weiss,* 44 Cal.Rptr.2d 339, 42 Cal.App.4th 106 (Cal.App. 1/31/96).

103. *Johns v. Johns,* 53 Ark.App. 90, 918 S.W.2d 728 (Ark.App. 4/3/96).

104. *U.S. v. Amer,* 110 F.3d 873 (2nd Cir. 3/26/97).

105. *Friedrich v. Friedrich,* 78 F.3d 1060 (6th Cir. 3/13/96).

106. *Strother v. Alaska,* 891 P.2d 214 (Ala.App. 3/3/95). *Oregon v. Fitouri,* 133 Ore.App. 672, 893 P.2d 556 (Ore.App. 4/12/95) reaches a similar conclusion even where the custody order was not granted until after the father removed the child outside the United States.

107. *Newton v. Riley,* 899 S.W.2d 509 (Ky.App. 6/9/95).

108. *Van Driel v. Van Driel,* 525 N.W.2d 37 (S.D.Sup. 12/7/94). Similarly, a divorced father's cohabitation with a male partner was not considered a substantial change in circumstances that would warrant a change of custody to the mother, given that there was no evidence that the relationship had a deleterious effect on the children: *Pulliam v. Smith,* 476 S.E.2nd 446 (N.C.App. 10/15/96).

109. *Bottoms v. Bottoms,* 63 LW 2704 (Va.Sup. 4/21/95).

110. *In re Astonn H.,* 64 LW 2351 (N.Y.Fam.Ct. 11/1/95).

111. *Price v. Howard,* 65 LW 2799 (N.C.Supp. 5/9/97).

112. *Belsito v. Clark,* 67 Oh.Misc.2d 54 (Ohio Comm.Pleas 11/14/94).

113. *Soos v. Maricopa County Superior Court,* 63 LW 2390 (Ariz.App. 12/8/94).

114. *Michael v. Hertzler,* 900 P.2d 1144 (N.M.App. 6/2/95); *Ridenour v. Ridenour,* 901 P.2d 770 (Wyo.Sup. 8/4/95).

115. *Holtzman v. Knott,* 533 N.E.2d 419 (Wis.Sup. 6/13/95).

116. *Titchenal v. Dexter,* 65 LW 2648 (Vt.Sup. 2/28/97).

117. *Boswell v. Boswell,* 66 LW 1320 (Md.Spec.App. 10/29/97).

118. *Washington ex rel McMichael v. Fox,* 132 Wash.2d 346, 937 P.2d 1075 (Wash.Sup. 6/5/97).

119. *Tennessee DHS v. Hooper,* 65 LW 2712 (Tenn.App. 2/28/97).

120. *T.B. v. M.M.J.,* 908 P.2d 345 (Utah App. 11/22/95).

121. *Wilson (Slomanski) v. Wilson,* 465 S.E.2nd 44 (N.C.App. 1/2/96).

122. *Horiba v. Horiba,* 66 LW 1400 (Ore.App. 12/3/97). *Ivaldi v. Ivaldi,* 685 A.2d 1319 (N.J.Sup. 12/23/96) also treats a non-U.S. country, this time Morocco, as a UCCJA state.

123. *Noordin v. Abdulla,* 66 LW 1325 (Wash.App. 11/14/97).

124. *Cochran v. Cochran,* 66 Cal.Rptr.2d 337 (Cal.App. 7/14/97).

125. *Santosky v. Kramer,* 455 U.S. 745 (1982).

126. *In re Marriage of Ramirez,* 840 P.2d 311 (Az.App. 1992); *Michels v. Weingartner,* 848 P.2d 1010 (Kan.App. 1993). The recipient parent's agreement to forgive the arrears in exchange for the delinquent payor's consent to the stepparent adoption is probably illegal as against public policy: *Stambaugh v. Child Support Enforcement Administration,* 17 Fam.Law Rep. 1447 (Maryland App. 1991).

    On a related issue, see *Shasta County ex.rel. Caruthers v. Caruthers,* 38 Cal.Rptr. 18 (Cal.App. 2/3/95), finding that a child—who is not a party to the paternity action—is not barred by the mother's settlement with the biological father. The mother has no right to terminate the child's right to a relationship with—or support from—the father unilaterally.

127. *In re Fortney's Estate,* 611 P.2d 599 (Kan.App. 1980); *In re Adoption of Swanson,* 623 A.2d 1095 (Del. 1993).

128. *In re Adoption of Chaney,* 887 P.2d 1061 (Ida.Sup. 1/5/95).

129. See, e.g., *Green v. Sollenberger,* 338 Md. 118, 656 A.2d 773 (1995). *Peregood v. Cosmides,* 663 So.2d 665 (Fla.App. 10/27/95) gives a child, even a young minor, standing to challenge a sham adoption in which the mother surrendered and then adopted her child in order to terminate the father's parental rights. The rationale is that a purported adoption that forfeits support from the father, and places the child in economic jeopardy, is not in the child's best interests.

130. *In re Angel Lace M.,* 516 N.W.2d 678 (Wis.Sup. 1994); *In re Adoption Petition of Bruce M.,* 20 Fam.Law Rep. 1307 (D.C.Super. 1994); *In re Dana (G.M.),* 624 N.Y.S.2d 635 (A.D.2d Dept. 4/3/95); *In re Adoption of T.K.J.,* 22 Fam.Law Rep. 1379 (Colo.App. 6/13/96).

131. *In re Jacob,* 660 N.E.2d 397 (N.Y.App. 11/2/95); whether unmarried couple is heterosexual or homosexual; *In re Adoption Petition of K.H. and R.Z.,* 21 Fam.Law Rep. 1535 (Colo.Dist.Ct. 7/26/95); *In re Petition of D.L.G.,* 22 Fam.Law Rep. 1488 (Md. Circuit Ct. 6/27/96).

132. *In re M.M.D.,* 662 A.2d 837 (D.C.App.6/30/95); *In re Adoption of Minor Child,* 21 Fam.Law Rep. 1332 (D.C.Super. 5/4/95); *In re Petition of K.M. and D.M.,* 653 N.E.2d 888 (Ill.App. 7/18/95); *In re Adoption by H.N.R.,* 666 A.2d 535 (N.J.Super. 10/27/95).

133. Also see *Rushing v. Bosse,* 652 So.2d 869 (Fla.App. 3/8/95) granting standing to a child to sue the lawyers for the adoptive parents for malpractice and malicious prosecution. (One of the lawyers also served as intermediary.) The adoptive parents falsified Florida residence, with the result that the child was

removed from her grandmother and unlawfully adopted out of state. The court found the child to be the intended beneficiary of the client's actions, thus able to sue the attorney for malpractice despite the lack of privity (particularly in light of an attorney-intermediary's obligation to act in the best interests of the child). The malicious prosecution cause of action could proceed because legal machinery was misused for an unlawful purpose. However, the intentional infliction of emotional distress claim was dismissed; the mother's transportation of the child for adoption purposes was not deemed to be reckless or an outrageous violation of the standards of a civilized community.

134. *In re Anonymous,* 16 Fam.Law Rep. 1165 (N.Y. Surr. 1990); *Yopp v. Bate,* 237 Neb. 779, 467 N.W.2d 868 (1991).

135. *Mullins v. Oregon,* 57 F.3d 789 (9th Cir. 6/12/95). In this instance, the grandparents had not established a custodial or quasi-parental relationship with the grandchildren; in fact, they seldom saw them.

136. See, e.g., *Mohr v. Massachusetts,* 421 Mass. 147 (Mass Sup.Jud.Ct. 8/14/95); *Mallette v. Children's Friend & Services,* 21 Fam.Law Rep. 1433 (R.I.Sup. 1995); *Juman v. Louise Wise Services,* 620 N.Y.S.2d 371 (N.Y.A.D. 1995): intentional tort only; *Gibbs v.Ernst,* 647 A.2d 881 (Pa. Sup. 1994).

137. *Adoption of Thomas,* 408 Mass. 446, 559 N.E.2d 1230 (1990).

138. *In re Adoption of Taylor,* 570 N.E.2d 1333 (Ind.App. 1991); *In re Adoption of Fanning,* 310 Ore. 514, 800 P.2d 773 (1990); *Appellate Defenders, Inc. v. Cheri S.,* 35 Cal.App.4th 1819, 42 Cal.Rptr.2d 195 (1995).

139. See, e.g., *South Dakota ex.rel. S.A.H.,* 21 Fam.Law Rep. 1517 (S.D.Sup. 8/16/95), permitting the trial court to order an open adoption, with visitation by the birth mother, where this is found to be in the best interests of the child. Factors in the determination include the child's need to know his or her background, whether open adoptions would render adoption more or less attractive overall, and how openness would affect the adoptee's integration into the new, adoptive family.

140. *Doe v. Sundquist,* 106 F.3d 702 (6th Cir. 2/11/97).

141. The adoption agency is a quasi-state actor in the adoption process, so its activities vis-a-vis the biological father are subject to Constitutional scrutiny: *Swayne v. LDS Social Services,* 795 P.2d 637 (Utah 1990); *In re Adoption of Doe,* 572 So.2d 986 (Fla. 1990); *In re Adoption of BBC,* 831 P.2d 197 (Wyoming 1992).

140. *In re Dearing,* 98 Oh.App.3d 197, 648 N.E.2d 57 (1994).

143. Also see HHS' "Policy Guidance: Race, Color, or National Origin as Considerations in Adoption and Foster Care Placements," 60 FR 20272 (4/25/95).

144. See, e.g., *In re Zachariah K.,* 6 Cal.App.4th 1025, 8 Cal.Rptr.2d 423 (1992); *JDS v. Franks,* 893 P.2d 732 (Ariz. 1994); *In re Adoption by TWC,* 270 N.J.Super. 225, 636 A.2d 1083 (1994).

145. *C.R.S. v. T.A.M.,* 21 Fam.Law Rep. 1173 (Colo.Sup. 1/30/95).

— FOR FURTHER REFERENCE —

Dickinson, Kelvin H., "Divorce and Life Insurance: Post Mortem Remedies for Breach of a Duty to Maintain a Policy for a Designated Beneficiary," 61 *Missouri L. Rev.* 533 (Summer '96).

Dyer, Adair, "The Internationalization of Family Law," 30 U.C. *Davis L.Rev.* 625 (Spring '97).

Fitzgerald, Robert G., "Interest Income on Transfer of Property Subject to a Divorce," 53 *J. of the Missouri Bar* 385 (November–December '97).

Giovannucci, Marilou T., "Understanding the Role of the Mediator in Child Protection Proceedings," 35 *Family and Conciliation Courts Review* 143 (April '97).

Johnson, Meredith, "At the Intersection of Bankruptcy and Divorce," 97 *Columbia L.Rev.* 91 (January '97).

Kiziah, Trent S., "Drafting Wills for the Remarried Spouse," 71 *Florida Bar J.* 34 (January '97).

Kozol, George B., "Providing for Children from a Prior Marriage: An Estate Planning Entry Point," 51 *J. American Society CLU/ChFC* 52 (January '97).

McCoy, James M., "Reunification-Who Knows the Child's Best Interests?" 53 *J. of the Missouri Bar* 40 (January–February '97).

Pianko, Howard and Dean L. Silverberg, "Domestic Partner Benefits on the Rise," *National L.J.* 11/17/97 p. 53.

Raby, Burgess and William L. Raby, "Alimony Requires 'Death Do Us Part,'" 74 *Tax Notes* 79 (1/6/97).

Richman, Bruce L., "Taxpayer Relief Act of 1997: A Summary of Provisions Affecting the Divorce Practitioner," 11 *Am.J. of Family Law* 213 (Winter '97).

Rothenberg, Sandra I. and Anne W. Gill, "Appealable Orders in Family Law," 26 *Colorado Lawyer* 43 (December '97).

Sandweiss, Kathi Mann, "An Adoptive Child's Right to Inherit," 33 *Arizona Attorney* 27 (March '97).

Smith, Rita and Pamela Coukos, "Fairness and Accuracy in Evaluations of Domestic Violence and Child Abuse in Custody Determinations," 36 *Judges J.* 38 (Fall '97).

Yavitz, David B., "Divorce Databases," 19 *Family Advocate* 26 (Winter '97).

PERSONAL INJURY AND NO-FAULT

[¶3201] During the supplement period, some of the most heavily litigated issues were related to AIDS—issues of liability for infected blood products, and for incorrect reporting of HIV test results. Medical issues relating to products liability for medical devices were also prominent.

In mid-1996, the Supreme Court ruled that punitive damages must not be grossly excessive—the reprehensibility of the defendant's conduct is an important decisional factor, as is the ratio between punitive damages and actual harm suffered. Also considered are the penalties exacted in other contexts for similar criminal or tortious conduct.[1]

In late 1995, Arizona abolished parental tort immunity. The new test is whether the parent acted reasonably and prudently, but the child was nevertheless injured.[2]

The Supreme Court decided two important personal injury cases in 1997. The first deals with "junk science" by setting an abuse of discretion standard for reviewing a lower court's determination of admissibility (including expert testimony subject to *Daubert*). The standard does not change merely because evidence was excluded rather than admitted—or even if the decision determined the outcome of the case.[3]

The Supreme Court also ruled that, when a state court hears a personal injury case, it is not obligated by the Full Faith and Credit clause to enforce another state's gag order forbidding employees of the defendant to testify in personal injury suits.[4]

[¶3202] INTENTIONAL TORTS

The Eighth Circuit says that, in a libel case brought by a private person, as long as the trier of fact's decision as to the truth or falsity of a news report is supported by substantial evidence, the judge must accept it. The determination is not subject to independent judicial review.[5]

A California plaintiff who alleges intentional interference with prospective economic relations must prove that the defendant's conduct was wrongful in some way other than its inconvenience to the plaintiff; disruption of an existing, bargained-for contract is treated more seriously than prevention of a potential contract.[6]

In Michigan, unemployment compensation benefits offset the damages awarded in a state suit for wrongful discharge.[7]

New Jersey permits a suit for malpractice against a clergy member who allegedly misused his counseling role to seduce a parishioner. In this view, the court does not become impermissibly entangled with religion: it is not necessary to interpret church doctrine to conclude that the church is opposed to sexual relationships between clergy and persons receiving counseling. On appeal, the court clarified that there is no separate tort of clergy malpractice, but improper sexual conduct by clergymembers involving vulnerable parishioners can constitute breach of fiduciary duty.[8]

In contrast, a similar Wisconsin case, also involving alleged seduction of a person being counseled, rules that the Establishment Clause prevents a suit against a Catholic diocese for negligent supervision of the hospital chaplain. In this analysis, permitting the suit would require interpretation of canon law and church policy and the development of a "reasonable cleric" standard of care. The Catholic priest's vow of celibacy does not create a civil duty, and it would be excessive entanglement with religion to attempt to determine if the vow was violated.[9]

An Oklahoma wife was permitted to sue her husband's mistress for infecting him with herpes (which was then transmitted to his wife), but only if the mistress failed to tell the husband about her infectious status, thus breaching her duty of due care.[10]

[¶3202.3] Intentional Infliction of Mental Distress (or Anguish)

In Montana, negligent infliction of emotional distress can be a separate tort provided that the defendant's negligent act or omission reasonably could be foreseen to result in serious emotional distress to the plaintiff. The distress must be so severe that a reasonable person could not be expected to endure it. The same standard is used for intentional infliction of mental distress, but intentional conduct can subject the tortfeasor to punitive damages.[11]

In Alaska, negligent infliction of emotional distress (where there is no physical injury) is cognizable only if there is a pre-existing contract or fiduciary duty that obligates the actor not to disrupt the plaintiff's life. If there is no such duty, only intentional infliction of emotional distress is actionable.[12]

This case involved an incorrect HIV+ diagnosis. In Florida, the impact rule applies, so an HIV misdiagnosis does not entitle the plaintiff to emotional distress damages unless some physical injury results. However, unnecessary medical treatment with serious side effects would qualify as physical injury.[13]

The California Court of Appeals denied emotional distress damages to homeowners who live near power lines. The homeowner plaintiffs failed to submit adequate scientific evidence that electric and magnetic fields generated by the power lines are "more likely than not" to cause cancer. Fear, without scientific justification, is not actionable. In this reading, property damage claims that rely on public perception of danger should be raised before the state public utility commission, not in court.[14]

A three-year statute of limitations, and not the discovery rule, was applied in a Wisconsin case in which the plaintiff knew that a coercive sexual relationship with a priest was coercive when it occurred (27 years earlier) but did not perceive the emotional damage caused by the relationship until 1992.[15]

[¶3202.4] Defamation

The Communications Decency Act gives Internet Service Providers (ISPs) immunity for negligent facilitation of defamatory statements that are posted to the ISPs' Internet sites. The Eastern District of Virginia ruled that this preempts state-law causes of action against an ISP for negligently permitting online dissemination of defamatory statements. On appeal, the Fourth Circuit added that immunity is available in suits filed after the enactment of the CDA, even if the defamatory statement was posted earlier.[16]

[¶3203] NEGLIGENCE

Mandamus issued in the Seventh Circuit to decertify a nationwide class of HIV+ hemophiliacs who alleged negligence by a manufacturer of blood products. The writ was granted because the court deemed the manufacturer to be at risk of irreparable harm because of intense pressure to settle the case.[17]

In another AIDS-related blood product case, the Third Circuit permitted a suit against the American Red Cross alleging negligence in connection with a blood transfusion. The Red Cross is not entitled to sovereign immunity.[18]

Florida applies the "economic loss" rule (which says that no damages are available when the malfunction of a defective product causes economic loss, but no other damages) to bar negligence claims. This is true even if economic loss is the plaintiff's only claim, so the suit must be dismissed. The court considers economic loss a contract concept, not one properly raised in a tort suit.[19]

In California, although state law imposes safety duties on skiers, the assumption of risk doctrine applies so that there is no liability for inadvertent injury to another skier (who has assumed the risk of undertaking a dangerous activity).[20]

[¶3203.3] Medical Malpractice

Once plaintiffs receive the cap limit against the hospital under EMTALA (the statute banning "patient dumping"—discharge of patients who are too sick to leave the hospital), they are not permitted to receive the cap limit again in a malpractice suit involving the same injuries against a hospital physician.[21]

If the result of malpractice is the loss of the patient's chance of surviving, it is not necessary for the surviving plaintiffs to prove that the patient's odds of recovery or even survival were greater than even. The effect of malpractice in diminishing the odds of survival affects the damages available in the action.[22]

[¶3203.4] Other Tort Reform Statutes

The Tenth Circuit has upheld Kansas' $250,000 cap on non-economic loss in personal injury cases. The Tenth Circuit found that the limitation does not violate Equal Protection or the Americans with Disabilities Act.[23]

[¶3205] PRODUCTS LIABILITY

The Third Circuit has held,[24] in a case involving implanted heart valves, that the federal Medical Device Amendments of 1976 preempt state-law claims for negligent design, negligent manufacture, strict products liability, breach of implied warranty of merchantability, and fraud on the FDA. However, certain state law claims were not preempted: those involving breach of express warranty and advertising fraud. According to the Ninth Circuit, the Medical Device Amendments prempt state-law failure to warn claims involving tampons whose label complies with federal regulations.[25]

However, where the device enters the market through the "pre-market notification" process of §510(k) of the Medical Device Amendments, the manufacturer of a Class III medical device can be sued in state court for common-law claims involving negligent design, negligent manufacture, and failure to warn: the Supreme Court has found that such claims are not preempted by the federal law.[26]

In a Ninth Circuit case, a woman who developed the auto-immune disorder lupus sued the manufacturer of the collagen implants for negligence, battery, breach of warranty, strict liability, and other claims. The manufacturer's position was that the implants are Class III medical devices pre-approved by the FDA, and thus the claims are preempted by the Medical Device Amendments. The Ninth Circuit was not persuaded, finding that state common-law claims of general applicability are not preempted; the approval process is not a "specific requirement applicable to a particular device" that would preempt state-law regulation. Furthermore, Congress would not want to replace state common law's role in compensating the injured.[27] The Seventh Circuit reached a different result in 1997, finding that the pre-market approval process for collagen-based products preempts state common-claims dealing with strict liability, negligence, fraud, mislabeling, misbranding, or implied warranty when the state requirements are different from, or in addition to, their federal counterparts.[28]

The Medical Device Act Amendments preempt state tort claims based on a manufacturer's failure to comply with the amendments themselves.[29]

The FDA has proposed regulations to deal with some of these problems: see 62 FR 65384 (12/12/97). The FDA says that state common law claims about faulty medical devices are generally not preempted, because neither FDA pre-market approval nor Investigative New Drug exemption from approval creates federal requirements specific to the device. Therefore, preemption under the Medical Device Amendments would usually be unavailable under this proposal.

Federal jurisdiction issues were also involved in a breast implant case. The Northern District of Texas decided that a co-defendant could not get the case removed from Texas state court to federal court merely because of the bankruptcy of co-defendant Dow Corning.[30]

Nor can a bankruptcy court enjoin a personal injury suit against the purchaser of all of a manufacturer/Chapter 11 debtor's assets, where retailers and wholesalers of the firearms manufactured by the debtor did not have notice of the transfer and had no opportunity to comment on the reorganization plan.[31]

A hospital doctor who implants a medical device (in this case a jaw prosthesis) is not "selling" the device and thus cannot be held strictly liable for defects in the device.[32]

To the Ninth Circuit, federal law and regulations preempt state claims against auto manufacturers for failure to install air bags.[33] However, the District Court for the District of Puerto Rico has held that neither the Federal Motor Vehicle Traffic

Safety Act nor the federal air bag regulations preempt claims of defective design of air bags.[34] In this reading, the federal rules deal only with warning labels, not design criteria. When federal law leaves design decisions open, state claims can be pursued as to defects in the chosen designs.

Wisconsin does not allow evidence of comparisons between the defendant's product (in this case, a three-wheeled All Terrain Vehicle) and dissimilar products such as minibikes, trailbikes, and snowmobiles. Nor may the risks of using an ATV be compared to hazards of other recreational activities (e.g., swimming, scuba, horseback riding) because the comparisons are not relevant enough and are too likely to confuse the jury.[35] California law does not require a separate warning that riding in the cargo bed of a pickup truck is dangerous, in light of the absolute obviousness of the hazard.[36]

Under Michigan law, a manufacturer does have a duty to warn if it detects a manufacturing defect that was not discoverable at the time of manufacture. The duty is satisfied by the mere warning—though there is no duty to recall or repair the products.[37]

California's requirement that dental amalgam carry warnings as a chemical known to cause cancer or reproductive toxicity is not preempted by the federal Food, Drug and Chemical Act or by the Medical Device Amendment.[38] California manufacturers of prescription drugs can be held strictly liable for failure to warn about risks either actually known or scientifically ascertainable when the drugs were distributed.[39]

In contrast, pharmacists in Florida have no duty to warn about potential adverse drug effects; their sole duty is to fill the prescription correctly.[40]

Manufacturers of nicotine patches must warn the users directly; the manufacturers cannot rely on warnings to be provided by the learned intermediaries who prescribe the patches.[41]

A keyboard manufacturer has no duty to warn users of the risk of carpal tunnel syndrome, because a keyboard is in the same category as office furniture: it is not inherently dangerous. The risk derives from the physiology of the user and the way the device is used.[42] Another RSI case precludes a postal worker with RSI from suing the manufacturer of a letter-sorting machine. The machine satisfied Post Office specifications, and therefore qualified for a government contractor defense (which is available to civilian as well as military contractors).[43]

A Connecticut plaintiff who charges defective design does not have to prove the existence of a reasonable alternative design—only that the actual design failed to meet the reasonable safety expectations of an ordinary consumer.[44]

The family of a child injured by a meat grinder sued the manufacturer. The manufacturer countersued the child's mother (i.e., the family's homeowner's insurance carrier) for negligent supervision. The Wisconsin Supreme Court permitted enforcement of the family exclusion clause in a third party contribution claim, because of the serious risk of collusion in family claims.[45]

The Federal Cigarette Labeling and Advertising Act doesn't preempt state-law tort claims brought against a cigarette manufacturer by a non-smoker alleging injuries by second-hand smoke. To the Southern District of Florida, preemption relates to dangers of "smoking" rather than those of contacting someone else's cigarette smoke. This court reads Congress' failure to mention second-hand smoke as a lack of intention to preempt such claims.[46]

The Fifth Circuit permits certification of a non-opt-out settlement class of all future claimants against an asbestos manufacturer. Absent class certification, the manufacturer could become insolvent in the course of paying claims, thus substantially impairing the interests of the class.[47]

The Ninth Circuit agreed that a nationwide prescription drug class action is a theoretical possibility. However, it disapproved the proposed class (all users of the drug before a certain date) and subclass (victims of aplastic anemia or liver failure). The proposed class and subclass were deemed not to be typical of potential plaintiffs; notice and representation were inadequate; and the tests of predominance and superiority were not met. The Ninth Circuit did not find the class action to be a superior form of litigation in this case, because there were few claims of liver failure or aplastic anemia, and the percentage of drug users allegedly injured by the drug was small, making it difficult to determine who should receive notification.[48]

A class action was intended to settle the current and future claims with respect to exposure to asbestos, with and without manifestation of injury. In its mid-1997 decision, the Supreme Court did not clarify whether or not exposure-only claimants have standing to sue. It did, however, find the "sprawling" class to be unsuitable for certification, because it was too diverse to meet the predominance requirement. Absentees were not properly represented, and the interests of currently injured persons are adverse to those who were only exposed, and who require the segregation of a large fund for future claims rather than large current payments.[49]

In 1997, several other intended mass-tort classes were denied certification or decertified. The Eastern District of Pennsylvania decertified a class of Pennsylvania cigarette smokers alleging that manufacturers concealed the addictive qualities of nicotine, and seeking a mandatory injunction to establish a medical monitoring program, in light of a developing record showing factual and legal issues requiring individualized determination.[50] However, a class of cigarette smokers was certified as to injunctive and declaratory relief only, for the medical monitoring claim.[51]

The Southern District of West Virginia found a group of claimants to Liggett Group Inc.'s settlement fund, comprising smokers, relatives of smokers, persons exposed to environmental tobacco smoke, and government agencies, to be too large and too diverse to be certified as a class.[52] The District of New Jersey refused to certify a class with respect to charges of a defective ignition switch in Ford cars. The court ruled that too many issues required individual resolution, and a determination of defectiveness would require inquiries varying by model year and type. The purported class did not have a plan for handling state-by-state variations, and the court found that claims of fraudulent concealment and breach of implied warranty involve reliance, privity, and other issues unsuitable for class resolution.[53]

[¶3205.1] Warranty Aspects of Products Liability

The test for breach of implied warranty is whether the product satisfies minimal safety standards for the product's intended purpose—that is, whether or not the manufacturer behaved reasonably. This test can be satisfied even if the plaintiff cannot prove strict product liability (which requires proof that a reasonable manufacturer would have decided that the danger outweighed the utility of the product).[54]

[¶3205.2] Statute of Limitations Problems

The civil RICO statute of limitations is four years. The petitioners in a mid-1997 Supreme Court case brought suit in August, 1993, claiming injuries beginning in 1974, when they purchased a silo that they claim causes feed to rot and injures cattle. They claim that the defendants continued to defraud them with false representations until 1991, thus preventing them from investigating. Although the Third Circuit's position was that civil RICO claims accrue with the last predicate act (when the plaintiff knew or should have known of the last injury or the last predicate act in the pattern, even if the plaintiff was not injured by the last act), the Supreme Court disagreed,[55] refusing to extend the RICO limitations period based on an indefinite series of predicate acts. The Court also refused to apply fraudulent concealment analysis for the benefit of plaintiffs who were not diligent enough in investigating.

The District of Columbia Court of Appeals did not permit the use of market share liability principles to charge 14 petroleum companies with the leukemia deaths of two mechanics who were exposed to petroleum products of uncertain brand. The exposure took place over a 20- to 30-year period; it was not proven that all the petroleum brands used the same formula; and leukemia is not necessarily caused by exposure to benzene.[56]

Two recent New York cases about Repetitive Stress Injury (RSI) caused by keyboard use agree that the statute of limitations is three years. However, one starts the clock running with the first RSI injury, on the theory that no one can allege a tort before injury has occurred. The other starts with either the last use of the keyboard or the onset of RSI symptoms, whichever comes first. In this reading, the discovery standard is inappropriate to RSIs because it applies only to toxic torts.[57]

Another New York case involves a DES daughter who was treated for a precancerous uterine condition in 1978-9, and had surgery in 1988. She heard about DES in March of 1988, but didn't pursue the issue until she overhead (in late 1989) a doctor describing her condition as classic DES symptoms. She brought suit in August, 1992 but was time-barred because the statute of limitations is three years from discovery of the injury (i.e., discovery of her uterine condition in 1988, not discovery of the true causation of her injury).[58]

[¶3206] THE WRONGFUL DEATH ACTION

Under the Warsaw Convention, compensation for airline accidents is limited to harms cognizable under the forum's choice of law rules. The U.S. rule is that a crash over water is governed by the Death on High Seas Act, which provides compensation only for pecuniary loss. Therefore, the Supreme Court has ruled that damages are unavailable for survivors' loss of society of the crash victims.[59]

The Northern District of Illinois did not permit expert testimony on the hedonic value of life in a wrongful death case. The purported expert testimony did not use scientific methods or procedures. In any event, the jury's burden is to value a specific decedent's life, not the average value of life. The testimony is not "helpful" to the jury and thus cannot be admitted under F.R.Evidence 702.[60]

There is no independent cause of action in New Mexico for the wrongful death of a *nonviable* fetus occurring when a pregnant woman is involved in an accident.[61]

[¶3207]   PREMISES LIABILITY

A range of liability issues affecting owners and tenants of property has been identified as the legal topic of "premises liability." Liability may arise in many contexts:

➤ Presence of hazardous substances on the premises

➤ Discharge, escape, or transportation of hazardous substances away from the premises, to areas owned by potential plaintiffs or where potential plaintiffs are affected (e.g., being poisoned by toxic fumes)

➤ Personal injury to a person employed on the premises (involving occupational safety and Workers' Compensation issues)

➤ Personal injury to a user of the premises (e.g., "slip and fall")

➤ Lack of adequate security on the premises, rendering users of the premises vulnerable to crime

➤ Failure to comply with the Americans with Disabilities Act (ADA)—which can lead to private suits or administrative enforcement

➤ Violation of a zoning regulation

➤ Improper use of the premises—e.g., sale of alcoholic beverages to minors; perpetrating or even tolerating the sale of illegal drugs

Depending on the severity of the incident and who is involved, consequences may range from a small fine to a multimillion-dollar judgment. Property used in connection with illegal activities is subject to forfeiture—even if the owner is not the perpetrator of the crime.

Premises liability risk is frequently shifted through the purchase of insurance. However, as discussed in ¶2515.1, it is likely that environmental premises liability will not be covered by the conventional business insurance policy, although it may be covered by special (and expensive) environmental risks insurance.

[¶3207.1]   Environmental Premises Liability

The use or generation of solid waste on the premises may give rise to liability under several federal statutes. Under CERCLA (the "Superfund" law; see ¶2203), business owners have an obligation to report the use of hazardous substances on the premises. As that paragraph discusses, quite a few current or past parties in the chain of ownership or use of the premises may have liability under CERCLA, either directly or by contribution.

In a limited number of cases, an innocent landowner may be exempt from CERCLA liability, if a buyer or seller of contaminated property had no actual knowledge of the contamination, and furthermore if the contamination was not discoverable by a reasonable party exercising due diligence.

Since 1986, CERCLA has contained a Title III, Emergency Planning and Community Right to Know Act (EPCRA). Owners of premises on which potentially hazardous substances are used must notify local agencies (and must respond to queries from the interested public) about the substances that are used there and the amount of toxic substances routinely emitted each year in a controlled fashion (e.g., vapors exiting a smokestack). The facilities must also develop an emergency plan for coping with unplanned releases. There is a notification procedure in case of such an emergency release.

As discussed in ¶2206, RCRA regulates the on-premises storage of solid waste as well as the transportation of such substances off the premises and their storage or disposal elsewhere. Many nonhazardous substances are covered by RCRA; its reach is not limited to substances conventionally considered polluting or toxic.

Depending on the use of the premises, it may be necessary to obtain a permit for the discharge of pollutants into the air or water. This is, of course, more likely if the premises are used for manufacturing than if they are offices or retail stores. However, almost any type of older building may contain asbestos, because this material was commonly used for insulation and fire protection. As a general rule, the mere fact that asbestos is in place on the premises does not give rise to liability (although concealing the presence of asbestos may give the buyer a cause of action against the nondisclosing seller).

It is probably safe to leave intact asbestos in place, although continued monitoring by a qualified asbestos removal firm is a good idea.

Removing asbestos is an extremely hazardous practice, because asbestos fibers are released into the air and persons on the premises are endangered by breathing these fibers. Asbestos removal must always be done by EPA-certified firms that are bonded and have adequate insurance. Most of the states license asbestos firms and certify workers who handle removal.

It is usually necessary to get a special local building permit to remove asbestos or to undertake any demolition or alteration which has the effect of exposing asbestos. On the federal level, the National Emission Standard for Asbestos program (NESAP) requires a notification to be filed with the nearest EPA Regional Office at least 10 days before the start of any building work that will expose asbestos.

In general, workers who suffer illness because of asbestos exposure are barred from suing the employer because of Workers' Compensation exclusivity. However, if the allegation is one of emotional rather than physical injury, if the employer was guilty of outrageous conduct, or perhaps guilty of negligence, the injured worker will be permitted to sue. In some cases, Workers' Compensation will prevent a damage award to the employee, but will require the employer to pay for continuing medical monitoring of the employee's condition. Of course, Workers' Compensation exclusivity does not bar a suit against the non-employer owner of the property where the allegedly harmful asbestos exposure occurred.

A number of suits have been brought—although few have succeeded—alleging the existence of an actionable "sick building syndrome." The theory is that some buildings contain building materials that off-load toxic vapors, and that the building's ventilation system is inadequate to clear these vapors. The tenant of a "sick building" may be able to sue the landlord for breach of the lease's covenant of quiet enjoyment. Fraud damages may be available if there was misrepresentation as to the condition of the premises. The landlord also might be liable for latent defects in the premises, provided that the landlord knew or should have known about the latent defect, failed to inform the tenant, and the tenant had no reasonable means of discovering or protecting against the risk.

[¶3207.2] Occupational Safety and Premises Liability

The federal Occupational Safety and Health Act (OSHA), administered by the Occupational Safety and Health Administration—also called OSHA—obligates employers to make routine annual reports of their safety records. If a workplace illness or injury does occur, a report to OSHA must be made within a short time after the incident. However, employers with fewer than 10 employees, and retail, service, and financial industries (deemed nonhazardous) are exempt from OSHA's record-keeping requirements.

Under OSHA's general duty clause, there is an obligation to maintain a safe workplace, where the risk of injury or occupational disease is reduced as much as possible. The CFR contains both general industry standards and special standards for the construction industry. OSHA also includes provisions about the use of Material Safety Data Sheets (MSDS) to inform workers about the presence of toxic materials on the premises, and how to handle these materials safely. Employees must be given training in working with toxic materials without endangering themselves or accidentally releasing the substances into the outside environment.

[¶3207.3] Premises Liability for Accidents, Crimes

Although strict liability is imposed in unavoidably dangerous situations (e.g., the use of explosives; much construction work; some uses of electricity), in general the liability standard is the negligence of the owner or operator of the premises. A premises owner or tenant may be liable for incidents occurring near but not on the premises—e.g., the sidewalk or parking lot. The owner or tenant may also be liable for public or private nuisance—for instance, if vapors are transmitted to nearby areas; or if patrons of a bar or restaurant are noisy or disruptive to the public.

In the conventional "slip and fall" accident scenario, there will be liability only if the premises were defective, and the defendant furthermore had both actual or constructive notice of the defect and a reasonable chance to remedy it. For instance, a patron who slips in a pool of water on a store floor can prevail by proving that the water was there for an hour—but not if the spill occurred three seconds before the accident.

If an employee, customer, or other person on or near the premises becomes a crime victim, the business owner or landlord may have liability. If the perpetrator is an employee, then the employer may be liable either if the crime is in the scope of the employee's employment (a very unlikely scenario!) or if the employer was negligent in hiring or supervision of the criminal. If the crime was committed by a third party, premises liability depends on whether or not the crime was foreseeable, and on whether there were reasonable precautions that could have been taken to prevent the crime. Foreseeability, in turn, depends on local conditions—a carjacking is far more predictable in Los Angeles than in Peoria.

Several 1997 cases deal with premises liability for crime. To the New Jersey Supreme Court, the business' responsibility depends on the totality of circumstances. Similar criminal acts committed nearby in the past are relevant, but not a pre-requisite to premises liability.[62] Another New Jersey court found that a robbery was reasonably foreseeable (based on an increasing number of robberies in the area; lack of video camera or alarms on premise; and availability of escape routes for robbers), so a convenience store in which a clerk was murdered had a duty to take reasonable security measures. A corporation that owned but did not operate the store was an appropriate defendant, because it was the parent corporation of an operating subsidiary.[63]

To the Washington Supreme Court, a mall's common-law duty to protect its invitees against foreseeable criminal conduct does not extend to an outright obligation to provide security guards. Imposing such an obligation would shift the responsibility for policing from the public to the private sector.[64]

In contrast, the Arizona Supreme Court treated a condominium association as analogous to a landowner, with the same duty to protect guests from foreseeable dangers. (In the case at bar, a guest of a condo unit owner was shot in the parking lot by a gang member.) The court treated the relevant relationship as not the one between the condominium association and the shooting victim (who, arguably, had no connection with the association) but between the association and the land on which the units were built. In this reading, landowners have a duty of reasonable care to forestall crime, including employing enough guards.[65]

— ENDNOTES —

1. *BMW of North America Inc. v. Gore,* #94-896, 116 S.Ct. 1589 (Sup.Ct. 5/20/96).

2. *Broadbent v. Broadbent,* 907 P.2d 43 (Ariz.Sup. 11/14/95).

3. *G.E. v. Joiner*, #96-188, 118 S.Ct. 512 (Sup.Ct. 12/15/97). Also see *McKendall v. Crown Control Corp.*, 66 LW 1103 (9th Cir. 8/8/97): expert testimony based on a witness' experience in personal injury cases is admissible under Federal Rules of Evidence 702 as long as it's relevant and helpful; the testimony need not satisfy the *Daubert* standard.

4. *Baker v. G.M. Corp.*, #96-653, 117 S.Ct. 1310 (Sup.Ct. 1/13/97).

5. *Lundell Mfg. Co. v. ABC*, 98 F.3d 351 (8th Cir. 10/15/96).

6. *Della Penna v. Toyota Motor Sales U.S.A.*, 11 Cal.4th 376 (Cal.Sup. 10/12/95).

7. *Corl v. Huron Castings Inc.*, 544 N.W.2d 278 (Mich.Sup. 3/1/96).

8. *F.G. v. MacDonnell*, 677 A.2d 258 (N.J. Super. 6/14/96); later proceedings, 150 N.J. 550, 696 A.2d 697 (N.J. Sup. 7/22/97).

9. *L.L.N. v. Clauder*, 65 LW 2774 (Wis.Sup. 5/23/97).

10. *Lockhart v. Loosen*, 66 LW 1112 (Okla.Sup. 7/15/97).

11. *Sacco v. High Country Independent Press Inc.*, 63 LW 2768 (Mont.Sup. 5/19/95).

12. *Chizmar v. Mackie*, 63 LW 2767 (Alaska Sup. 5/19/95).

13. *R.J. v. Humana of Florida, Inc.*, 652 So.2d 360 (Fla.Sup. 3/2/95). Also see *Heiner v. Moretuzzo*, 652 N.E.2d 664 (Ohio Sup. 8/16/96) denying a cause of action for negligent infliction of emotional distress in a false-positive HIV case where there is no physical "peril." Physical injury is not required, but the plaintiff must either be imperiled or observe someone else's peril. In New Jersey, the standard for negligent infliction of emotional distress in an AIDS-phobia case is whether the tortfeasor's negligence proximately caused a level of genuine and substantial emotional distress that would be experienced by a reasonable person whose knowledge about AIDS transmission was equivalent to that of the general public. It is not necessary to prove actual exposure to HIV: *Williamson v. Waldman*, 150 N.J. 232, 696 A.2d 14 (N.J.Sup. 7/21/97).

14. *San Diego Gas & Electric Co. v. Superior Court of Orange County*, 38 Cal.Rptr.2d 811 (Cal.App. 2/28/95).

15. *Pritzlaff v. Archdiocese of Milwaukee*, 533 N.W.2d 780 (Wis.Sup. 6/27/95).

16. *Zeran v. America Online*, 958 F.Sup. 1124 (E.D.Va. 3/21/97) and 66 LW 1317 (4th Cir. 11/12/97).

17. *In re Rhone-Poulenc Rorer Inc.*, (7th Cir. 3/16/95) *cert. denied* 116 S.Ct. 184.

18. *Marcella v. Brandywine Hospital*, 47 F.3d 618 (3rd Cir. 2/15/95).

19. *Airport Rent-a-Car Inc. v. Prevost Car Inc.*, 650 So.2d 628 (Fla.Sup. 6/15/95).

20. *Cheong v. Antablin*, 66 LW 1366 (Cal.Sup. 11/24/97).

21. *Power v. Alexandria Physician's Group Ltd.*, 887 F.Supp. 945 (E.D.Va. 5/18/95), *aff'd* 91F.3d 132, *cert. denied* 1175 S.Ct. 514. EMTALA is not violated by a failure to order x-rays of an injured patient, because doctors must give equal treatment to patients whose condition they perceive to be equal;

inaccurate diagnosis is negligence, not an EMTALA violation: *Summers v. Baptist Medical Center,* 91 F.3d 1132 (8th Cir. 8/5/96).

22. *Roberts v. Ohio Permanente Medical Group Inc.,* 76 Oh.St.3d 483, 668 N.E.2d 480 (Ohio Sup. 8/28/96). Also see *Holton v. Memorial Hospital,* 65 LW 2686 (Ill.Sup. 4/17/97), also permitting a loss of chance suit in a case where the patient's chance of recovery was below 50%, as long as there is a reasonable degree of medical certainty that the malpractice increased the risk of harm or decreased the effectiveness of the treatment.

23. *Patton v. TIC United Corp.,* 77 F.3d 1235 (10th Cir. 2/16/96).

24. *Michael v. Shiley Inc.,* 46 F.3d 1316 (3rd Cir. 2/7/95).

25. *Papike v. Tambrands Inc.,* 107 F.3d 737 (9th Cir. 2/20/97).

26. *Medtronic Inc. v. Lohr,* #95-754, -886, 116 S.Ct. 2240 (Sup.Ct. 6/26/96). 1997 saw a number of post-*Lohr* cases about Class III devices. *Martin v. Telectronics Pacing Systems Inc.,* 105 F.3d 1090 (6th Cir. 1/31/97) holds that the Medical Device Amendments preempt claims of manufacturing or design defects or inadequate warnings in investigative medical devices (IMDs). However, *Chambers v. Osteonics Corp.,* 109 F.3d 1243 (7th Cir. 4/3/97) finds that the Medical Device Amendments preempt state requirements that are greater or different, but a state-law claim of negligent manufacturing, alleging that the manufacturer failed to comply with FDA rules, is not preempted. *Niehoff v. Surgidev Corp.,* 66 LW 1042 (Ky.Sup. 6/19/97) allows state strict liability and negligence claims involving an IMD (an implanted lens used in cataract operations). In the Fifth Circuit view (see *Reeves v. AcroMed Corp.,* 103 F.3d 442 (5th Cir. 1/20/97), the FDA premarket approval process merely tests that a device is substantially equivalent to an existing device, not that its design is safe or effective. Therefore, such approval does not rule out state law claims that the device is unreasonably dangerous per se.

27. *Kennedy v. Collagen Corp.,* 67 F.3d 1153 (9th Cir. 10/17/95). For preemption analysis relating to another statute (the Federal Flammable Fabrics Act), see *Wilson v. Bradlees of New England, Inc.,* 96 F.3d 552 (1st Cir. 9/25/96): the federal law prevents states from establishing their own flammability standards, but does not preempt state common-law claims for negligence, strict liability, failure to warn, or breach of implied warranty. For preemption analysis under FIFRA (the Federal Insecticide, Fungicide, and Rodenticide Act), see, e.g., *Romah v. Hygienic Sanitation Co.,* 66 LW 1368 (Pa.Super. 11/12/97): FIFRA preempts failure-to-warn claims, but not claims that the manufacturer was negligent in designing, manufacturing, or testing a pesticide; and *Lyall v. Leslie's Poolmart,* 66 LW 1314 (E.D. Mich. 10/31/97): FIFRA does not preempt state tort claims dealing with negligent design and manufacture of containers for chemicals, where FIFRA lacks specific standards for adequately manufactured containers.

28. *Mitchell v. Collagen Corp.,* 66 LW 1203 (7th Cir. 9/23/97).

29. *Talbott v. C.R. Bard Inc.,* 63 F.3d 25 (1st Cir. 8/14/95). Compare *Berish v.*

Richards Medical Co., 937 F.Supp. 181 (N.D.N.Y. 8/22/96) [state negligent design and strict liability claims are preempted if the device received pre-market approval] with *Connelly v. Iolab Corp.*, 927 S.W.2d 848 (Mo.Sup. 8/20/96) [state claims are not preempted because manufacturer could comply with both state and federal requirements by disclosing complications to doctors].

30. *McCratic v. Bristol-Myers Squibb & Co.*, 183 B.R. 113 (N.D.Tex. 6/14/95).

31. *Western Auto Supply Co. v. Savage Arms Inc.*, 43 F.3d 714 (1st Cir. 12/14/94).

32. *Cafazzo v. Central Medical Health Services Inc.*, 668 A.2d 521 (Pa.Sup. 11/28/95).

33. *Harris v. Ford Motor Co.*, 65 LW 2675 (9th Cir. 4/8/97).

34. *Collazo-Santiago v. Toyota Motor Corp.*, 957 F.Supp. 349 (D.P.R. 1/31/97).

35. *Bittner v. American Honda Motor Co.*, 533 N.W.2d 476 (Wis.Sup. 6/21/95).

36. *Maneely v. GM Corp.*, 108 F.3d 1176 (9th Cir. 3/13/97).

37. *Gregory v. Cincinnati Inc.*, 450 Mich.1 (Mich.Sup. 8/15/95).

38. *Committee of Dental Amalgam Manufacturers v. Stratton*, 92 F.3d 807 (9th Cir. 8/5/96).

39. *Carlin v. Sutter County Superior Court*, 56 Cal.Rptr.2d 162, 13 Cal.4th 1104 (Cal.Sup. 8/30/96).

40. *Johnson v. Walgreen Co.*, 675 So.2d 1036 (Fla.App. 7/3/96).

41. *Edwards v. Basel Pharmaceuticals*, 65 LW 2680 (Okla.Sup. 3/5/97).

42. *Reiff v. Convergent Technologies*, 957 F.Supp. 573 (D.N.J. 2/28/97).

43. *Yeroshefsky v. Unisys Corp.*, 962 F.Supp. 710 (D.Md. 4/24/97).

44. *Potter v. Chicago Pneumatic Tool Co.*, 241 Conn. 199 (Conn.Sup. 5/27/97).

45. *Whirlpool Corp. v. Ziebert*, 539 N.W.2d 883 (Wis.Sup. 11/16/95).

46. *Wolpin v. Philip Morris Inc.*, 66 LW 1158 (S.D. Fla. 8/18/97).

47. *In re Asbestos Litigation (Flanagan v. Ahearn)*, 90 F.3d 963 (5th Cir. 7/25/96).

48. *Valentino v. Carter-Wallace Inc.*, 97 F.3d 1227 (9th Cir. 10/7/96).

49. *Amchem Products v. Windsor*, #96-270. Below, *Georgine v. Amchem Products Inc.*, 83 F.3d 610 (3rd Cir.6/27/96). 118 S.Ct. 2231 (Sup. Ct. 6/25/97). Below, *Georgine v. Amchem Products Inc.*, 83 F.3d 610 (3rd Cir.6/27/96).

50. *Barnes v. American Tobacco Co.*, 66 LW 1260 (E.D. Pa. 10/17/97).

51. *Arch v. American Tobacco Co.*, 66 LW 1150 (E.D. Pa. 8/25/97).

52. *Walker v. Liggett Group Inc.*, 66 LW 1116 (S.D.W.V. 8/5/97).

53. *Wilks v. Ford Motor Co.*, 66 LW 1151 (D.N.J. 8/28/97).

54. *Denny v. Ford Motor Co.*, 662 N.E.2d 750 (N.Y.App. 12/5/95).

55. *Klehr v. A.O. Smith Corp.*, #96-663, 117 S.Ct. 1984 (Sup.Ct. 6/19/97).

56. *Bly v. Tri-Continental Industries Inc.*, 663 A.2d 1232 (D.C.App. 8/21/95).

57. Compare *Blanco v. AT&T*, 66 LW 1347 (N.Y. App. 11/25/97): last use of keyboard or onset of RSI, whichever comes first; *Dorsey v. Apple Computers Inc.*, 936 F.Supp. 89 (E.D.N.Y. 9/25/96) [initial injury].

58. *Wetherill v. Lilly*, 65 LW 2546 (N.Y.App. 2/11/97).

59. *Zicherman v. Korean Air Lines Co.*, #94-1361, -1477, 116 S.Ct. 629 (Sup.Ct. 1/16/96).

60. *Ayers v. Robinson*, 887 F.Supp. 1049 (N.D.Ill. 5/23/95).

61. *Miller v. Kirk*, 905 P.2d 194 (N.M.Sup. 10/17/95).

62. *Clohesy v. Food Circus Supermarkets Inc.*, 149 N.J. 496, 694 A.2d 1017 (N.J.Sup. 6/26/97).

63. *Morris v. Krauszer's Food Stores*, 65 LW 2800 (N.J. Super. 5/9/97).

64. *Nivens v. 7-11 Hoagy's Corner*, 943 P.2d 286 (Wash.Sup. 9/11/97).

65. *Martinez v. Woodmar IV Condominium Association Inc.*, 941 P.2d 218 (Ariz.Sup. 6/24/97).

— FOR FURTHER REFERENCE —

DeCarlo, Kean J., "Tilting at Windmills": Defamation and the Private Person in Cyberspace," 13 *Georgia State U. L.Rev.* 547 (February '97).

Goldberg, Neil A., Dennis R. McCoy and John P. Freedenberg, "Finding the Facts in Products Liability Litigation," 38 *For the Defense* 19 (October '96).

Grell, Jeffrey E., "Restatement (Third) of Torts, Section 8(D): Back to the Future of the Learned Intermediary Doctrine," 19 *Hamline L. Rev.* 349 (Spring '96).

Haig, Robert L. and Steven P. Caley, "Successfully Defending Product Liability Cases," 19 *Trial Diplomacy J.* 27 (January–February '96).

Intyre, Nancy G., "Exclusion Limitation on Personal Injury Awards," 75 *Y. of Detroit Mercy L.Rev.* 219 (Fall '97).

Nader, Ralph and Joseph A. Page, "Automobile-Design Liability and Compliance With Federal Standards," 64 *George Washington L. Rev.* 415 (March '96).

Nolan, Virginia E. and Edmund Ursin, "Enterprise Liability and the Economic Analysis of Tort Law," 57 *Ohio State L. J.* 835 (June '96).

Seidelson, David E., "The Rescue Doctrine in Medical Malpractice and Product Liability Actions," 17 *Miss.Coll. L.Rev.* 325 (Spring '97).

Smith, Janet H., "Increasing Fear of Future Injury Claims," 64 *Defense Counsel J.* 547 (October '97).

Taylor, Meredith L., "North Carolina's Recognition of Tort Liability for the Intentional Infliction of Emotional Distress During Marriage," 32 *Wake Forest L.Rev.* 1261 (Winter '97).

Wiechmann, Eric Watt, Rosanne C. Baxter and John P. McKinney, "Mass Tort Class Actions: Is the Tide Turning?" 64 *Defense Counsel Journal* 67 (January '97).

Zabel, Steven P. and Jeffrey A. Eyres, "Conflict of Law Issues in Multistate Product Liability Class Actions," 19 *Hamline L. Rev.* 429 (Spring '96).

REMEDIES AND DAMAGES

[¶3401] In recent years, two issues have dominated the jurisprudence of remedies: the availability and appropriate dimensions of punitive damages, and the scope of the Code §104 exclusion from taxable income of damages received for "personal injuries."

[¶3401.1]   Taxation of Damages

Under the Internal Revenue Code, contract damages are clearly includible in the recipient's gross income. On the other hand, damages for "personal injuries" are excludable. Thus, the inquiry becomes whether a particular cause of action is sufficiently tort-like to generate personal injury damages.

At the end of 1996, the Supreme Court held that even in what is unmistakably a tort suit, punitive damages are not compensatory in nature. Thus, they are not received "on account of" the underlying personal injury, and they do represent taxable income to the recipient.[1]

More guidance is available from the Small Business Job Protection Act of 1996, P.L. 104-188, which says that gross income includes personal injury damages unless they were awarded for a physical injury or physical sickness. However, compensatory damages that flow from an injury or sickness (such as loss of consortium) do not have to be included in gross income. Furthermore, punitive damages from state wrongful death actions are not includible. Emotional distress by itself does not constitute physical injury, but emotional distress damages are excludible up to the amount of medical bills incurred to treat the emotional distress.

According to the Fifth Circuit, settlement proceeds in an age discrimination wrongful discharge case are taxable, because the plaintiff has not suffered personal injury.[2] The Fourth Circuit held in August, 1997 that an ERISA settlement is taxable income because it is covered by an "expansive" definition of wages and is not sufficiently similar to a tort cause of action to be excluded.[3]

The Ninth Circuit has found a suit against a union for breach of the duty of fair representation to involve personal injury.[4] Corporations are not "persons" to the extent that they can suffer "personal injuries," even if the corporation has only one shareholder, and even if the corporation receives damages for breach of contract, malicious prosecution, interference with business relationships, fraud, and violations of fiduciary duty.[5]

The status of prejudgment interest is also problematic. The Tenth Circuit says that statutory prejudgment interest must be included in gross income, because it is not received "on account of personal injuries."[6]

A similar analysis was used in a more complex fact situation in the First Circuit.[7] In a personal injury action, the jury awarded $175,000. Statutory prejudgment interest of $112,000 was added. While the appeal was pending, the parties settled for $250,000. The settlement agreement failed to mention interest at all. The stipulation of dismissal said there would be no interest and no costs—but didn't clarify whether prejudgment or post-judgment interest was ruled out. The First Circuit agreed with the Tax Court, that whatever portion of the $250,000 represents prejudgment interest must be included in gross income, because the interest was not an element of damages under state law. Because the taxpayers failed to prove that a lesser amount was attributable to the interest, the First Circuit required inclusion in income of 39 percent of the $250,000 (i.e., the same ratio as $112,000/$175,000 + $112,000). The First Circuit opinion says that whether statutory prejudgment interest can ever be excluded from gross income for tax purposes is "an important question left for another day."

The IRS has responded to the case law and the SBJPA by promulgating Rev.Rul. 96-65, 1996-53 IRB 5, which says in effect that back pay is taxable, but damages for emotional distress are excludible if and only if the distress has manifested in physical phenomena requiring medical care.

[¶3406]   TORT DAMAGES

Survivors of plane crash victims are not entitled to damages for loss of society. The Supreme Court reached this conclusion in early 1996 because the Warsaw Convention calls for compensation only of harms cognizable under the choice-of-law rules of the forum. Crashes over water are governed by the Death on High Seas Act, which compensates "pecuniary loss" and nothing else.[8]

Another Supreme Court damages case involves a New York statute that permits appellate courts to review jury verdicts and order a new trial if the verdict materially deviates from reasonable compensation. The statute was upheld: the Seventh Amendment right to a jury trial is not violated, as long as the federal trial judge observes the "material deviation" standard. Furthermore, the Circuit Court's review of the trial court's determination is limited to whether or not the District Court abused its discretion; *de novo* review is inappropriate.[9]

Opposite conclusions were reached in California's state and federal courts about the constitutionality of a state law denying damages for pain and suffering and hedonic damages to survivors (on the grounds that these causes of action are not survivable).[10]

A state tort reform statute, capping non-economic personal injury damages at $250,000 has been upheld by the Tenth Circuit, which did not see any problems with either Equal Protection or the Americans with Disabilities Act in sustaining the statute.[11]

The Tenth Circuit has upheld a $200,000 award of emotional distress damages in a sexual harassment case. The harassing comments were made in a non-private office, where co-workers could overhear the comments. This increased the victim's humiliation and exacerbated the severity of the conduct.[12]

[¶3406.1] Employment Litigation Damages

For many reasons, including the difficulties of interpreting the Civil Rights Act of 1991 (see ¶2105.2), employment litigation damages have been the focus of many cases. The Eighth Circuit permitted an award of three years of front pay in addition to three years of back pay, for a woman who lost her job when she was 64. Although employees are presumed to retire at the plan's normal retirement age, the presumption can be rebutted (as here where the plaintiff was healthy, continued to seek employment, and had a financial need to continue working until age 70).[13]

In late 1997, the first Circuit Court of Appeals to decide the issue (although there had been several District Court cases) decided that the CRA '91 cap applies to all of one person's claims in an employment suit, it does not apply individually to each claim of alleged discrimination. The Sixth Circuit thus disagreed with the EEOC's position that the cap should be applied on a per-claim basis (the EEOC position would result in much larger recoveries for plaintiffs).[14]

Where the EEOC files suit on behalf of several employees, the District Court for the District of Arizona has allowed each employee to recover the cap amount.[15] In other words, the case is not treated as a single EEOC suit with a single recovery limited by the cap.

In the Second Circuit, it is not necessary to prove extraordinarily egregious conduct by the employer in order to recover the full cap amount—or to receive punitive damages under 42 U.S.C. §1981a (intentional violation of Title VII).[16] The D.C. Circuit has ruled that the standard for punitive damages under §1981a is the same as under 42 U.S.C. §1981 or 1983—i.e., malice or reckless indifference to federally protected rights. In this reading, showing of extraordinarily egregious conduct is not required.[17]

A corporation president testified that he was just an employer, not a judge who could define right and wrong—so there was no written corporate anti-harassment policy. This testimony was deemed sufficient to support the jury's inference of reckless indifference to the possibility of workplace sexual harassment, and thus to support the jury's punitive damage award.[18]

[¶3407] PUNITIVE DAMAGES

In mid-1996, the Supreme Court ruled that punitive damages must not be grossly excessive. The test of gross excessiveness involves the degree to which the defendant's conduct was reprehensible, and the civil and criminal penalties assessed for similar conduct. A litigant in one state is not permitted to introduce lawful conduct performed outside the state that did not harm any residents of the state.[19]

How much is excessive? Several recent cases explore that question. A $500,000 punitive damage award was overturned in Alabama.[20] Although a pilot was blinded in a plane crash, there was no evidence that the manufacturer of the shoulder harness wantonly produced a defective product (e.g., by knowingly selling it with inadequate stitching, or routinely selling products that fail to conform to company standards). Because there was no conscious culpability, the $2.5 million compensatory damage award was sustained, but punitive damages were not available.

The Second Circuit (examining awards in comparable police misconduct cases, not the ratio between compensatory and punitive damages) determined that $200,000 in punitive damages was excessive in a malicious prosecution civil rights action against a police officer; the award of actual damages was only the symbolic $1.[21]

The Tenth Circuit found $30 million in punitive damages to be excessive when an intentional economic tort caused an actual and potential loss of between $1 million and $2 million.[22] Although reduced to $6 million, the punitive award was not eliminated. The court's theory was that the $6 million award would reward the plaintiffs for their persistence and discourage the defendant from future misconduct.

In March, 1998, after the close of the supplement period, the Supreme Court ruled in *Cohen v. De La Cruz*, 66 LW 4209 (3/24/98) that neither punitive nor compensatory fraud damages are dischargeable in bankruptcy.

Virtually all the states require that punitive damages must be proved by clear and convincing evidence. Proof by a preponderance of the evidence is insufficient, because punitive damages are so harsh that they should be imposed sparingly.[23] However, according to the Seventh Circuit, a plaintiff who seeks punitive damages does not have an obligation to provide the jury with evidence of the defendant's net worth.[24]

The Fourth Circuit's late 1996 ruling is that the standard of review for punitive damages is whether the jury's award represents a miscarriage of justice.[25]

For another aspect of punitive damages, see *Lundquist v. Lundquist*:[26] because the underlying compensatory damages were divisible marital property, the punitive damages received by a commercial fisherman in connection with the Exxon Valdez oil spill were also marital assets.

— ENDNOTES —

1. *O'Gilvie v. U.S.*, #95-966, -977, 117 S.Ct. 452 (Sup.Ct. 12/10/96); 66 F.3d 1550 *aff'd.*

2. *McKay, Jr. v. Comm'r*, 96-1 USTC ¶50,279 (5th Cir. 4/10/96). But see the same Circuit's ruling in *Dotson v. Comm'r*, 87 F.3d 682 (5th Cir. 6/27/96), that settlement proceeds in an ERISA wrongful termination suit could be excluded from gross income; the trial court should not have relied on cases decided after the settlement and limiting ERISA compensatory damages; the settlement proceeds reflected personal injury to the extent they were received for emotional distress and other nonpecuniary losses.

3. *Hemelt v. U.S.*, 97-2 USTC ¶50,596 (4th Cir. 8/7/97).

4. *Banks v. U.S.*, 81 F.3d 874 (9th Cir. 4/16/96).

5. *P&X Markets, Inc. v. Comm'r*, 106 T.C. No. 26 (6/13/96).

6. *Brabson v. U.S.*, 73 F.3d 1040 (10th Cir. 1/11/96).

7. *Delaney v. Comm'r,* 99 F.3d 20 (1st Cir. 11/1/96).

8. *Zicherman v. Korean Airlines Co.,* #94-1361, -1477, 116 S.Ct. 629 (Sup.Ct. 1/16/96).

9. *Gasperini v. Center for Humanities Inc.,* #95-719, 116 S.Ct. 2211 (Sup.Ct. 6/24/96).

10. Compare *Garcia v. Superior Court,* 49 Cal.Rptr. 580 (Cal.App. 1/31/96): statute is constitutional; damages unavailable to survivors in 42 U.S.C. §1983 action alleging wrongful death in police custody; with *Williams v. Oakland,* 915 F.Supp. 1074 (N.D.Cal. 1/29/96): pain and suffering and hedonic damages available to survivors.

11. *Patton v. TIC United Corp.,* 77 F.3d 1235 (10th Cir. 2/16/96).

12. *Smith v. Norwest Financial Acceptance Inc.,* 129 F.3d 1408 (10th Cir. 12/3/97).

13. *Curtis v. Electronics & Space Corp.,* 113 F.3d 1498 (8th Cir. 5/28/97).

14. *Hudson v. Reno,* 130 F.3d 1193 (6th Cir. 12/4/97). This was also the conclusion of *Hall v. Stormont Trice Corp.,* 66 LW 1198 (E.D. Va. 9/11/97).

15. *EEOC v. Moser Foods,* 66 LW 1368 (D.Ariz. 11/7/97).

16. *Luciano v. Olsten Corp.,* 110 F.3d 210 (2nd Cir. 3/21/97).

17. *Kolstad v. American Dental Ass'n,* 108 F.3d 1431 (D.C. Cir. 3/21/97).

18. *Harris v. L&L Wings,* 132 F.3d 978 (4th Cir. 12/24/97).

19. *BMW of North America, Inc. v. Gore,* #94-896, 116 S.Ct. 1589 (Sup.Ct. 5/20/96). On remand, 65 LW 2800 (Ala.Sup. 5/9/97), the $2 million damages were reduced to $50,000, and the plaintiff was given a choice between accepting the $50,000 or getting a new trial.

20. *Cessna Aircraft Co. v. Trzcinski,* 682 So.2d 17 (Ala.Sup. 7/12/96).

21. *Lee v. Edwards,* 101 F.3d 805 (2nd Cir. 10/31/96).

22. *Continental Trend Resources Inc. v. OXY U.S.A. Inc.,* 101 F.3d 634 (10th Cir. 11/26/96).

23. See, e.g., *Rodriguez v. Suzuki Motor Corp.,* 65 LW 2504 (Mo.Sup. 12/17/96). However, *Greenbaum v. Svenska Handelsbanker,* 66 LW 1231 (S.D.N.Y. 9/24/97) does permit punitive damages to be awarded based on a preponderance of evidence. This employment discrimination case does not count employees in the employer's parent company in Sweden for purposes of setting the CRA '91 cap, because non-U.S. citizens are not covered by Title VII.

24. *Kemezy v. Peters,* 79 F.3d 33 (7th Cir. 3/8/96).

25. *Atlas Food Systems v. Crane Nat'l Vendors Inc.,* 99 F.3d 587 (4th Cir. 10/30/96).

26. 22 Fam.Law Rep. 1487 (Alaska Sup. 8/16/96).

— FOR FURTHER REFERENCE —

Barton, Denise M., "The Evolution of Punitive Damage Awards in Securities Arbitration," 70 *Tulane L. Rev.* 1537 (May '96).

Charlton, Michael B., "Criminal Law and Punitive Damages: A Guide to the Penal Code for Civil Attorneys," 59 *Texas Bar J.* 854 (October '96).

Doerhoff, Dale C., "Raising the Bar for Punitive Damages and Other Recent Developments," 53 *J. of the Missouri Bar* 5 (January–February '97).

Feldman, Heidi Li, "Harm and Money: Against the Insurance Theory of Tort Compensation," 75 *Texas L.Rev.* 1567 (June '97).

Nicholson, Brent B., "Recent Developments Concerning the Taxation of Damages Under Section 104(a)(2) of the Internal Revenue Code," 61 *Albany L.Rev.* 215 (Fall '97).

Partlett, David F., "Punitive Damages: Legal Hot Zones," 56 *Louisiana L. Rev.* 781 (Summer '96).

Royall, M. Sean, "Disaggregation of Antitrust Damages," 65 *Antitrust L.J.* 311 (Winter '97).

Waddams, S.M., "Profits Derived from Breach of Contract: Damages or Restitution," 11 *J. of Contract Law* 115 (March '97).

Wells, Michael, "Punitive Damages for Constitutional Torts," 56 *Louisiana L. Rev.* 841 (Summer '96).

Willis, Christopher J., "Aggregation of Punitive Damages in Diversity Class Actions," 30 *Loyola of Los Angeles L.Rev.* 779 (January '97).

Wood, Robert W., "Will Courts Import Punitive Characterization?" 74 *Tax Notes* 1200 (3/3/97).

SECURITIES REGULATION

[¶3801] The supplement period has not been a happy one for would-be securities plaintiffs. The trend (both in Congress and in the courts) has been to deny the existence of private rights of action and in general to restrict access to litigation.

P.L. 104-62 and -63 were enacted in 1995 to offer a safe harbor for certain charitable annuities used in estate planning. Charitable income pooled funds, such as those used in connection with charitable remainder trusts, are held not to be investment companies. Donors are still entitled to disclosure of material terms of the operation of the fund within 90 days of making a donation. Such funds are exempt from all securities provisions (except anti-fraud) of the '33 and '34 Acts.

P.L. 104-290, the National Securities Markets Improvement Act of 1996, adds a new category of private investment companies that do not require registration. The objective is to give venture capital firms better access to money that can be used to fund start-up companies. This statute also authorizes the SEC to create standards for the mutual fund industry as a single national marketplace. On the other hand, regulation of investment advisers is divided between the states and the SEC: the states handle small-scale operations, the SEC handles the larger ones. There is also an "Investor Hotline" to find out if a particular individual has been implicated in improprieties.

Also see the changes announced by the SEC in May 1996, based on the recommendations of the Task Force on Disclosure Simplification. Four forms and 44 rules were eliminated. Form D must still be completed and retained by the issuer, but it no longer has to be filed with the SEC. Form SR, a report on the use of IPO proceeds, is no longer required, but comparable information must be included in the periodic reports under the Exchange Act.[1]

[¶3801.1]   Securities Litigation and Settlement

An early 1996 Supreme Court decision requires a federal court to give full faith and credit to a Delaware court release of class-action '34 Act claims, with respect to parties who failed to either object or opt out.[2]

The Supreme Court returned to securities issues in mid-1997, ruling that trading for personal profit, with information misappropriated in breach of fiduciary duty (e.g., a partner in a law firm that was involved in merger negotiations), violates 10(b) and Rule 10b-5.[3] Misappropriation theory can be applied in this context because the trader is guilty of deceptive conduct in connection with a securities transaction. Transaction participants have exclusive property rights in confidential information about securities transactions. Persons in a fiduciary role have an obligation to disclose their trades, and failure to do so is deceptive.[4]

According to the Second Circuit, you cannot get benefit-of-the-bargain damages under Securities Act §11, but you can get such damages under Exchange Act §10 if the damages can be established with reasonable certainty.[5]

An allegation that a company's directors set its initial public offering (IPO) price far too low (thus enhancing the profit opportunities of those receiving stock in the concurrent private offering) is really a challenge to the terms of the private placement—and therefore individuals who bought IPO shares (necessarily after the IPO price was set) lack standing to challenge the price-setting activities.[6]

In the view of the Ninth Circuit, the judgment in an SEC civil action ordering the defendant to disgorge more than $12 million is not punitive (and therefore cannot constitute double jeopardy when criminal charges are brought). In this reading, the disgorgement order was proportional to the actual harm caused by the defendant, and fraud victims got their money back. Nor were there double jeopardy issues involved in imposing contempt penalties or jailing the defendant for violating the freeze imposed on his assets, because these punishments were not imposed for the "same offense" as the securities fraud.[7]

The bankruptcy automatic stay does not bar SEC fraud enforcement actions that seek injunction and disgorgement of improper profits. Such actions fall under the "police power" exemption from the automatic stay.[8]

A securities class action can have multiple lead plaintiffs, and the lead plaintiffs can have more than one law firm, although sanctions will be ordered if the various attorneys "unreasonably and vexatiously" expand the scope of litigation.[9]

The Eastern District of Pennsylvania has authorized the use of the percentage of recovery method to set the attorneys' fees in a securities fraud class action at 25% of the settlement fund. In most cases, it will be necessary to cross-check the award against the lodestar, but in this case, neither detailed time sheets nor information about prevailing fees in the community were available, so the lodestar could not be used.[10]

It should be noted that the Seventh Circuit affirmed Rule 11 sanctions imposed on a plaintiff and plaintiff's attorney based on an unsuccessful fraud class action brought after a stock price tumbled. According to the court, neither of the two theories in the complaint was supported with specific factual allegations, and the complaint was not reasonably grounded in fact or law.[11]

The Supreme Court declined to hear a case (and thus upheld the Fifth Circuit) in which an investor sued a commodities broker when his account balance became negative.[12] He said he was a forced or defrauded seller of commodities entitled to damages; the court said he was merely suing for conversion and had no specific securities law claim.

[¶3802] THE SECURITIES ACT OF 1933

The first cautious steps are being taken for the use of the Internet (especially its World Wide Web component) in the issuance and sale of securities. Rules are evolving for making initial public offerings in electronic form; for delivering prospectuses electronically instead of on paper; and for creating a small-scale "securities exchange" for very small stocks that are not available on other exchanges. Although it might seem impossible to have an "intrastate" offering on an electronic system that is accessible throughout the world, nevertheless in some circumstances, registration exemptions are available.[13]

[¶3805] THE SECURITIES EXCHANGE ACT

In 1994, the Supreme Court made it clear that there is no private remedy for "aiding and abetting" a §10(b) violation.[14] Because Connecticut's Uniform Securities Act is based on §10(b) and Uniform Securities Act §101, there is no state-law cause of action for aiding and abetting either.[15] Nevertheless, *respondeat superior* is still a workable theory where a defendant, acting as agent of a corporation, wrongfully induced plaintiffs to tender their stock to the corporation, with the effect of preventing dilution of the defendant's ownership interest in the corporation.[16] In the view of the Ninth Circuit, a class action can be brought claiming that a computer firm and its directors and officers misled securities analysts with falsely optimistic statements, which would then be transmitted to the markets. The Ninth Circuit deemed this to be a case of blaming a company for its own misstatements, not an aiding and abetting case.[17]

Early in 1995, the Supreme Court limited the application of §12(2) of the Exchange Act (material misrepresentation or omission of fact in a prospectus or oral communication) to public offerings made by an issuer or controlling shareholder. A private secondary sale of substantially all of a close corporation's stock was not covered. Statements in the contract of sale—whether true or false—do not constitute a "prospectus."[18]

In mid-1995, the Supreme Court struck down[19] §27A of the '34 Act (which, in turn, was enacted to revive suits barred under the 1991 *Lampf Pleva* decision).[20] The Supreme Court, which could hardly have been expected to like Congress' attempt to overturn its ruling, held that the statute violates the separation of powers doctrine because it makes the federal courts re-open final judgments that were entered before the enactment of §27A.

Early in 1996, the Second Circuit ruled that 10b-5's disclosure requirement was satisfied by a statement that market share was an important consideration in business strategy. The issuing corporation did not omit material fact by not disclosing that it intended to cut prices (a departure from its usual price-hike strategy).[21]

The Fourth Circuit did not permit use of the misappropriation theory (improper use of material nonpublic information secured by breach of fiduciary duty) in a 10(b) action. The rationale is that a 10(b) action is premised on deception of a market participant. Although misappropriation involves deception, it seldom involves misrepresentation or nondisclosure.[22]

The Ninth Circuit holds that a §10(b) claim for primary fraud liability in connection with the purchase or sale of a stock can be stated by alleging that an outside CPA firm issued a false and misleading opinion to be included in a 10-K filing. Primary 10(b) liability can exist without trading securities, as long as there is a connection between trading and the fraud. The introduction of fraudulent information into the securities market damages the public, and therefore can be penalized by the legal system.[23]

The Ninth Circuit also says that the cause of action for contribution under 10(b) and Rule 10b-5 accrues when the defendant pays the judgment. The statute of limitations for contribution actions is one year after the discovery of facts and three years after the violation.[24]

On another 10b-5 issue, an attorney, hired by a corporation to draft an opinion letter about a private placement, was not liable for failure to disclose to investors that the private placement financing would operate as a default under the corporation's bank loans. To the Sixth Circuit, the attorney's engagement did not include preparing an offering circular or discussing terms of corporate loans. In this reading, an attorney's silence can only be a securities law violation if there is a duty to speak.[25]

A lender who finances a leveraged buyout (LBO) but does not control everyday operations or management policies is not an Exchange Act §20(a) "controlling person," and thus is not liable under 10b-5 if the LBO borrower is guilty of fraud.[26]

The Eleventh Circuit's mid-1996 ruling in *Brown v. Enstar Group Inc.*[27] establishes a new three-prong test for liability of a "controlling person" under §20(a) of the Exchange Act. To be liable, the defendant must actually have committed a securities law violation; must have had power to control the entity's general affairs at the time of the infraction; and must have had control over the particular corporate policy from which the primary liability stems.

Dealers and investors who couldn't buy IPO shares that appreciated significantly in value before the company's collapse do not have standing under 10(b). The plaintiffs charged concealment of insiders' superior access to IPO shares. However, the Ninth Circuit noted that the prospectus reserved the right to cancel the issue and reject subscriptions. Would-be purchasers therefore did not have an enforceable contract or rights against the issuer.[28]

In 1995–1996, courts ruled on numerous questions about the enforceability of various securities rules by private parties. In each case, the private parties were sent away, on the grounds that private rights of action do not lie under their chosen provision.

There is no private right of action for injunctive relief under §13(a) of the '34 Act, so a shareholder cannot use this provision to sue to compel a corporation and its officers to file quarterly and annual reports.[29]

There is no private right of action under the '34 Act's provisions about membership in self-regulatory organizations (e.g., the American Stock Exchange), so it is not possible to use these provisions to sue an SRO for money damages based on an allegation that a membership application was wrongfully denied.[30]

Nor is there a private right of action under §10(a), illegal short sales, so an issuer that made a secondary public offering of some of its shares cannot sue the short sellers who allegedly depressed the price of the shares. The Southern District of New York held open the prospect of a private action under Rule 10b-21 (the ban on covering short positions with stock purchased in a secondary public offering), but noted that scienter must be proved.[31]

Angry brokerage customers do not have a private right of action under Rule 10b-10(a)(7)(i), which imposes a duty to comply with a written request to disclose the identity of the buyer of the customer's former shareholdings.[32]

The statute of limitations for an SEC administrative proceeding under §15(b) of the '34 Act, for censure or suspension of a securities industry supervisor, is five years. According to the D.C. Circuit, the proceeding operates for enforcement of a civil fine, penalty, or forfeiture, so 28 U.S.C. §2462 governs.[33]

Cumulative convertible preferred Class B stock is a separate "class" of stock, because it has characteristics different from other securities with the same voting rights. Therefore, individuals owning more than 10 percent of the B shares can be compelled to disgorge their short-swing profits under §16(b).[34]

[¶3805.1] Regulation of Broker-Dealers

Transactions in foreign currency options that occur "over the counter" (and not on a regulated exchange or board of trade) are exempt from the Commodity Exchange Act and are not subject to regulation by the CFTC.[35]

Defining the scope of securities arbitration remained a vital question during the supplement period.

Punitive damages can be awarded under an arbitration agreement that incorporates an SRO's rules by reference, provided the rules permit punitive damages. The Supreme Court held this to be true even in situations where the arbitration agreement also contains a choice of law provision calling for submission to the law of a state which does not permit arbitral punitive damages.[36]

Speaking of choice of law, Federal Arbitration Act (FAA) §4 allows a petition to compel arbitration in any district, with arbitration to be held in that district. However, according to the Seventh Circuit, §4 does not overrule the arbitration agreement's forum selection clause. Nor may the District Court where the petition was filed enjoin arbitration in the district which is proper under the arbitration agreement.[37] In the view of the Second Circuit, federal courts lack federal question jurisdiction over actions to stay arbitration, even if the underlying claims stem from the Exchange Act.[38]

The majority view is that it is up to the federal courts to decide when arbitration is timely under NASD Arbitration Code §15.[39] The minority view is that the arbitrator, and not a federal court, determines if an investor's claims against a securities brokerage are timely.[40] The Fifth Circuit's rationale is that this is a question of procedural arbitrability and not a substantive eligibility requirement that a court must determine before the brokerage must submit to arbitration. According to the Eleventh Circuit, the six-year statute of limitations begins to run with the last event that would permit the plaintiff's claim to survive an FRCP 12(b)(6) motion to dismiss. Therefore, a plaintiff might allege multiple occurrences and multiple claims, some of which would be timely and some time-barred.[41]

Securities firm employees who sign the U-4, the standard employment agreement, cannot be compelled to arbitrate their Title VII claims instead of litigating them. The U-4's arbitration clause requires arbitration of disputes that are arbitrable under Self-Regulatory Organization rules, but the SRO (in this case, the NASD) did not specifically mandate arbitration of employment discrimination claims; so employees did not make a knowing waiver of the right to bring discrimination suits.[42]

NASD is entitled to "arbitral immunity" (similar to judicial immunity) and thus cannot be sued for appointing an arbitrator who was partial (even if the result was that the award was vacated based on this partiality).[43]

Class arbitration cannot be ordered unless the underlying agreement specifically permits it; FAA §4 calls for enforcement of the arbitration agreement in accordance with its terms.[44] Nor can expedited arbitration be compelled under either state law or the FAA unless expedited arbitration is specifically mentioned in the arbitration agreement.[45]

On another arbitration issue, the Florida Supreme Court decided that it constitutes unauthorized practice of law for non-lawyers to receive pay for representing investors in securities arbitrations.[46] The court reached this result even though the Securities Industry Association's manual allows non-attorney representation. The Florida court was concerned about harm caused by unregulated non-attorneys who are not subject to any form of sanction if they perform poorly.

A brokerage customer can demand arbitration of a claim that one firm misrepresented a stock in which it was a market maker (causing the stock to be overvalued)—even though the plaintiff purchased the security from another firm.[47]

In April, 1997, the Southern District of New York decided that institutional investors can be included as class members and class representatives in a class action charging leading NASDAQ market makers with conspiring to secure excessive profits by inflating the spread. (The allegation was that they refused to quote prices in terms of "odd eighths," but insisted on rounding up the price.) [48] The institutional investors were permitted to be added to the individual investors already bringing suit, on the grounds that their trading patterns were similar, and that both groups had suffered similar injury by having to pay too much to purchase securities. Furthermore, the institutional investors were much heavier traders and therefore had greater incentive to pursue the claims vigorously.

There is no affirmative duty to disclose the common practices used by the securities industry to execute orders. Therefore, there is no 10(b)/10b-5 violation if brokers fail to disclose that the NASDAQ price quotes for OTC execution did not always provide the best price. (Practices have since been reformed.)[49]

State court suits for breach of contract or on agency grounds are not available to investors who want to force brokers to disgorge "order flow" payments that they received for placing the customers' orders. The Illinois Supreme Court ruled that the '34 Act preempts the state causes of action, given Rule 10b-10's coverage of disclosure of order flow payments.[50]

A tip from a neighbor, who was a consultant to the acquiring corporation, confirmed rumors that a merger would take place. The tip extended the publicly available information, so trading on it violated rule 14e-3.[51]

Where a stockbroker is sanctioned by the NASD, can the SEC base a separate proceeding on the same conduct? The Fourth Circuit treated the SEC action as a public proceeding to preserve market integrity, and its sanctions as remedial rather than punitive. Therefore, no double jeopardy argument could be sustained.[52] In contrast, the Southern District of New York deemed SEC sanctions in excess of the government's cost of prosecution to be punitive. Therefore, subsequent criminal charges based on the same conduct had to be dismissed.[53]

[¶3805.2] Regulation of the Proxy Process

The Second Circuit permits an attorneys' fee award to shareholders who win a Rule 14a-8 action and mandate inclusion of their proposal in the proxy statement—even if, when the vote is held, the proposal is defeated overwhelmingly. The court found that a common benefit was created because the shareholders at least got the chance to exercise their franchise by considering (and rejecting) the proposal.[54]

If a proxy statement includes discussion of the history of a merger at all, it is incomplete if it fails to disclose that a bid even higher than the accepted bid was made earlier but rejected by the Board of Directors.[55]

A press release about a material corporate development taking place within the issuer of a security is a solicitation covered by the proxy rules, if the press release describes the transactions "in a manner objectively likely to predispose security holders toward or against it."[56]

[¶3805.3] Williams Act Disclosure (Tender Offers)

Section 14(d)(7) of the '34 Act requires a bidder who raises a bid to pay the increased amount to all shareholders who tender. The Ninth Circuit says that tendering shareholders who do not get the increased amount have an implied private right of action.[57]

[¶3808] PRIVATE SECURITIES LITIGATION REFORM ACT OF 1995

This statute, P.L. 104-67, was vetoed by President Clinton on December 19, 1995, but re-passed over his veto on December 22, 1995. The PSLR adds a new §27, "Private Securities Litigation," to 15 U.S.C. §77a *et seq.* (the Securities Act of 1933) and also amends §21 of the Exchange Act of 1934. The legislation's objective is to discourage frivolous securities litigation and to provide a safe harbor for "forward-looking statements" such as earnings projections that do not pan out.[58]

The bulk of the statute deals with securities class actions. (These provisions are effective for actions commenced on or after December 22, 1995.[59]) The party with the greatest financial interest in the proposed relief is rebuttably presumed to be the "most adequate plaintiff" who must lead the class action.[60] The court hearing the class action must approve the most adequate plaintiff's selection of counsel for the class.

Within 20 days of the filing of the complaint, the plaintiff who files the complaint must notify class members using a wire service or "widely circulated business publication." The legislative history shows that electronic means, such as e-mail, are acceptable forms of notice. The court then designates the most adequate plaintiff within 90 days of the publication of this notice.

Liability of multiple defendants is proportionate, not joint and several; Congress was concerned about the pressure on defendants with no or minimal culpability to settle strike suits to avoid the specter of being liable for the full amount of a massive judgment.

The PSLR Act states that there is no express private right of action against those who aid or abet securities law violations; this complements the 1994

Supreme Court decision in *Central Bank of Denver v. First Interstate Bank,* discussed above, that there is no implied private right of action under 10b-5 for aiding and abetting. Nor can securities fraud serve as a predicate offense for civil RICO claims; and no one—even the SEC—can bring a conspiracy case against a trader who allegedly participated in a market manipulation scheme.[61]

The 1995 legislation resolves the question of "loss causation" by requiring plaintiffs to demonstrate that the misstatements or omissions alleged in the complaint—and not market conditions—caused their damages.

New pleading requirements are imposed. Fraud plaintiffs must specify each statement alleged to be misleading, give reasons why it is misleading, and also provide facts giving rise to a strong inference that the defendant acted with the requisite state of mind to constitute fraud.[62]

Unless exceptional circumstances are present (e.g., terminal illness of a vital witness), discovery will be stayed[63] pending the ruling on a motion to dismiss. Of course, a motion to dismiss will be filed in nearly every case, so plaintiffs' ability to achieve discovery during the interim period is eliminated.

The PSLR Act retains the one-year/three-year statute of limitations provided by *Lampf Pleva.*

If the court deems a securities suit to be abusive, the plaintiff class can be ordered to pay reasonable attorneys' fees of the defendant(s). In a securities class action, the plaintiff class—or their attorneys—can be required to provide undertakings for payment of these attorneys' fees. On the other hand, fees to be recovered by attorneys for prevailing plaintiffs are limited to a reasonable percentage of the damages and prejudgment interest actually paid to the plaintiffs. Funds disgorged in an SEC suit or administrative action are not considered part of the fund generated by the private suit, and therefore do not affect the plaintiffs' attorneys' fees.

In a July 22, 1996 statement,[64] SEC General Counsel Richard Walker stated that the PSLR greatly reduced the number of federal class actions: there were only about 40 of them as compared to 150 in a comparable pre-PSLR period. However, state litigation seemed to continue apace.

Several courts wrestled with interpretation of the PSLR in 1997. The Northern District of Illinois interpreted the mission of the PSLR as adopting the Second Circuit's standard, but nothing stricter–so the plaintiff must plead motive and opportunity to commit fraud or circumstantial evidence of conscious misbehavior or recklessness.[65]

To the Southern District of New York, recklessness can constitute scienter under the PSLR, but no strong inference of scienter can be derived from mere pleading of motive and opportunity.[66]

The Tenth Circuit found the particularity requirement to be satisfied by incorporation by reference in a pleading of all the statements of the prospectus, then specifying various paragraphs and expressly linking the violations to press releases, prospectuses, and reports. The plaintiff's complaint was timely because it was filed within one year of the issuance of the relevant Form 10Q, because the report was what would put a reasonable investor on notice that the company was misrepresenting the value of a distribution deal.[67]

[¶3808.1] Safe Harbor

There is a safe harbor for oral or written forward-looking statements. Such statements are not actionable unless they are material (bearing in mind that plaintiffs must show loss causation to prevail). Nor are statements actionable if they are accompanied by "meaningful cautionary statements" about the factors that could prevent the predictions from coming true. Finally, there is no liability unless the plaintiff can prove that the maker of the statement had actual knowledge that it was false or misleading. If the statement was made by a corporation or other entity, the standard is whether the statement was made by or with the approval of an executive officer of the entity who knew the statement to be false or misleading.

In 1997, both the Eighth and Tenth Circuits decided "bespeaks caution" cases. The Eighth Circuit treated alleged misrepresentations as immaterial because the prospectus gave adequate disclosure of the risky nature of the enterprise. Alleged misrepresentations about the duty to pay sales tax to various states were not actionable, because the prospectus cautioned about potential state tax liability. A $6.8 million overstatement of assets was not material, because that was only 2% of the corporation's assets, and would not affect a reasonable investor's decision to make or reject a high-risk investment.[68]

The Tenth Circuit held that a statement is not material (and therefore not a potential source of liability) if investors have access to other documents that suggest caution: e.g., warnings in the registration statement can "detoxify" statements in a press release.[69]

— ENDNOTES —

1. See 28 Sec.Reg.L.Rep. 696.

2. *Matsushita Electric Industrial Co. v. Epstein,* #94-1809, 116 S.Ct. 873, *reversing and remanding* 50 F.3d 644.

3. *U.S. v. O'Hagan,* #96-842, 117 S.Ct. 2199 (Sup.Ct. 6/25/97).

4. However, an aiding and abetting theory is unavailable: see note 14.

5. *McMahan & Co. v. Wherehouse Entertainment,* 65 F.3d 1044 (2nd Cir. 9/13/95).

6. *7547 Partners v. Beck,* 682 A.2nd 160 (Del.Sup. 8/19/96).

7. *U.S. v. Gartner,* 93 F.3d 633 (9th Cir. 8/21/96), *cert. denied* 117 S.Ct 624.

8. *SEC v. Towers Financial Corp.,* FSLR ¶99,418 (S.D.N.Y. 1/22/97).

9. *Zuckerman v. Foxmeyer Health Corp.,* FSLR ¶99,443 (N.D. Tex. 3/28/97).

10. *Pozzi v. Smith,* 952 F.Supp. 218 (E.D. Pa. 1/24/97).

11. *Katz v. Household International Inc.,* 91 F.3d 1036 (7th Cir. 8/6/96).

12. *Ragan v. Conti Commodity Services Inc.,* 63 F.3d 438 (5th Cir.9/12/95), *cert. denied* #95-1147, 116 S.Ct. 1318, (3/25/96).

13. See Bradford P. Weirick, "Securities Law," *Nat. L. J.* 5/6/96 p. B5; Michael Selz, "Small Stock Issuers Find a New Market on the Internet," *Wall St. J.* 5/14/96 p. B2.

    Spring Street Brewing Co. was permitted to resume operation of its Wit-Trade on-line trading system on condition that Spring Street surrendered control over investor funds, added a third-party bank or escrow agent to hold funds, and enhanced disclosure, especially of information of particular use to novice investors: see the SEC Staff Letter reproduced at 28 Sec.Reg.L.Rep. 437.

    An organization called IPONET was granted '33 Act relief by the SEC's Division of Corporate Finance, so IPONET can offer private placement securities to accredited investors who register with the company's Internet site, which includes red herrings and tombstone ads: see 28 Sec.Reg.L.Rep. 990.

    The Commodity Futures Trading Commission launched a six-month pilot project in August, 1996 to test electronic filing of disclosure documents; in the meantime, commodity pool operators and trading advisors who use the Internet are subject to all normal regulatory requirements. See 28 Sec.Reg.L.Rep. 983. A company can make a market in its own stock on the Internet: SEC staff letter re Real Goods Trading Corp., 28 Sec.Reg.L.Rep. 850 (6/25/96).

    The SEC's Division of Corporate Finance announced in September, 1997 that roadshows about public offerings can be transmitted over the Internet without violating the '33 Act's prospectus delivery requirements, as long as the roadshow is presented after the filing of the registration statement. Roadshows can be made available on-line to qualified investors who contact an institutional salesperson to get an access code. A log must be kept of who gets the access code, and each qualified investor can view the roadshow for only one day and must be denied the ability to download, copy, or distribute it. See 66 LW 2175. The SEC's Division of Enforcement can be contacted about securities fraud through the "Internet Enforcement Complaint Center" at http://www.sec.gov/enforce/comctr.htm, launched July 14, 1996.

14. *Central Bank of Denver v. First Interstate Bank of Denver,* #92-854, 114 S.Ct. 1439 (Sup. Ct. 1994); *on remand, First Interstate Bank of Denver v. DBLKM Inc.,* 28 F.3d 112.

15. *Connecticut National Bank v. Giacomi,* 233 Conn. 304 659 A.2d 1166 (Sup. 5/30/95).

16. *Seolas v. Bilzerian,* 951 F.Supp. 978 (D.Utah 1/28/97).

17. *Cooper v. Pickett,* 122 F.3d 1186 (9th Cir. 8/8/97). Also see *Weiner v. Quaker Oats Co.,* 129 F.3d 310 (3rd Cir. 11/6/97): a 10(b) claim is stated by charging a company with failing to update its debt:capitalization ratio to reflect a projected tripling of corporate debt pursuant to a planned acquisition of another company.

18. *Gustafson v. Alloyd Co.,* #94-404, 115 S.Ct. 1061 (Sup.Ct. 2/28/95), *on remand* 53 F.3d 333.

19. *Plaut v. Spendthrift Farm*, #93-1121, 115 S.Ct. 1447 (Sup.Ct. 4/18/95). Also see *Raven v. Oppenheimer & Co.*, 74 F.3d 329 (11th Cir. 1/22/96): §27A applies to 10(b) claims that were pending on the 12/19/91 date the statute was enacted.

20. *Lampf Pleva Lipkind Prupis & Petigrow v. Gilbertson*, 501 U.S. 350 (1991).

21. *San Leandro Emergency Medical Group Profit Sharing Plan v. Philip Morris Co.*, 75 F.3d 801 (2nd Cir. 1/25/96). Maybe it serves them right for investing in a cigarette company anyway. A company that made an Initial Public Offering in the fourth quarter had no duty to disclose intra-quarter results unless the issuer had non-public information showing an extreme departure in the fourth quarter from the range of earnings already disclosed: *Steckman v. Hart Brewing, Inc.*, FSLR ¶99,420 (S.D. Cal. 12/24/96). However, in a stock-for-stock exchange undertaken to complete a merger, the registrant had a duty to disclose many items of "bad news" about both companies in the registration statement. Disclosing some of the information within months of the merger would not be sufficient: *Freedman v. Value Health, Inc.*, 958 F.Supp. 745 (D.Conn. 3/3/97). The court analyzed the transaction using insider-trading standards, because the company was trading its own stock. However, pure forward-looking information did not have to be disclosed, and it is general knowledge that business financial data fluctuates, so only extreme departures from normal require disclosure.

22. *U.S. v. Bryan*, 58 F.3d 933 (4th Cir. 6/27/95).

23. *McGann v. Ernst & Young*, 95 F.3d 821 (9th Cir. 9/9/96).

24. *Asdar Group v. Pillsbury, Madison and Sutro*, 99 F.3d 289 (9th Cir. 10/16/96).

25. *Rubin v. Schottenstein, Zox & Dunn*, 110 F.3d 1247 (6th Cir. 4/15/97).

26. *Paracor Finance Inc. v. G.E. Capital Corp.*, 79 F.3d 878 (9th Cir. 3/13/96).

27. 84 F.3d 393 (11th Cir. 5/31/96), *cert.denied* 117 S.Ct. 950. (11th Cir. 5/31/96).

28. *In re Stratosphere Corp.*, 115 F.3d 695 (9th Cir. 6/6/97).

29. *Gray v. Furia Organization Inc.*, 896 F.Supp. 144 (S.D.N.Y. 8/22/95).

30. *Feins v. American Stock Exchange Inc.*, 81 F.3d 1215 (2nd Cir. 4/24/96).

31. *Advanced Magnetics Inc. v. Bayfront Partners Inc.*, 64 LW 2528 (S.D.N.Y. 1/16/96) vacated and remanded in part on other grounds, 106 F.3d 11.

32. *Arst v. Stifel, Nicolaus & Co. Inc.*, 86 F.3d 973 (10th Cir. 6/11/96).

33. *Johnson v. SEC*, 87 F.3d 484 (D.C. Cir. 6/21/96).

34. *Morales v. New Valley Corp.*, 936 F.Supp. 119 (S.D.N.Y. 7/31/96). On §16(b), also see May 30, 1996 SEC amendments simplifying the short-swing profit recovery rule (Rule 16b-3), expanding the range of circumstances under which transactions between officers and directors and the issuer (including its employee benefit plans) can be legitimate: 28 Sec.Reg.L.Rep. 695.

35. *Dunn v. CFTC*, #95-1181, 117 S.Ct. 913 (Sup.Ct. 2/25/97).

36. *Mastrobuono v. Shearson Lehman Hutton Inc.,* #94-18, 115 S.Ct. 1212 (Sup.Ct. 3/6/95), *on remand* 54 F.3d 779. For a case in which it was applied, see, e.g., *Roubek v. Merrill Lynch,* 28 Sec.Reg.L.Rep. 640 (Ill.App. 5/1/96).

37. *Merrill Lynch v. Lauer,* 49 F.3d 323 (7th Cir. 3/1/95).

38. *Westmoreland Capital Corp. v. Findlay,* 100 F.3d 263 (2nd Cir. 11/7/96).

39. *Cogswell v. Merrill Lynch,* 78 F.3d 474 (10th Cir. 2/26/96); *Paine Webber v. Hoffmann,* 984 F.2d 1372 (3rd Cir. 1993); *Dean Witter Reynolds v. McCoy,* 995 F.2d 649 (6th Cir. 1993); *Smith Barney v. Schell,* 53 F.3d 807 (7th Cir. 1995); *Merrill Lynch v. Cohen,* 62 F.3d 381 (11th Cir. 1995).

40. *Smith Barney v. Boone,* 47 F.3d 750 (5th Cir. 3/20/95); *FSC Securities Corp. v. Freel,* 14 F.3d 1310 (8th Cir. 1994). This position has also been taken by the New York Court of Appeals: *Smith Barney Shearson Inc. v. Sacharow,* 66 LW 1381 (N.Y.App. 12/4/97). Also see *Paine Webber Inc. v. Bybyk,* 81 F.3d 1193 (2nd Cir. 4/19/96): if the agreement makes all controversies about construction of the agreement arbitrable, then questions of arbitrability and timeliness under New York law are, indeed, arbitrable.

41. *Kidder, Peabody & Co. v. Brandt,* 131 F.3d 1001 (11th Cir. 12/22/97).

42. *Prudential Insurance Co. v. Lai,* 42 F.3d 1299 (9th Cir. 12/20/94). But see *Thomas James Associates Inc. v. Jameson,* 102 F.3d 60 (2nd Cir. 12/12/96): a broker who signed the U-4 also signed an employment agreement with the firm waiving all right to arbitration. The waiver of the right to arbitrate is void as against public policy, because in 1987 the NASD adopted a resolution forbidding its members to force their employees to waive arbitration. See ¶2105.8 for more on arbitration of discrimination claims.

43. *Olson v. NASD,* 85 F.3d 381 (8th Cir. 6/27/96).

44. *Champ v. Siegel Trading Co.,* 55 F.3d 269 (7th Cir. 5/18/95).

45. *Salvano v. Merrill Lynch,* 647 N.E.2d 1298 (N.Y.App. 2/21/95).

46. *Florida Bar Re: Advisory Opinion on Nonlawyer Representation in Securities Arbitration,* 696 So.2d 1178 (Fla.Sup. 7/3/97).

47. *Lehman Brothers Inc. v. Certified Reporting Co.,* 939 F.Supp. 1333 (N.D.Ill. 9/5/96).

48. *In re NASDAQ Market Makers Antitrust Litigation,* 938 F.Supp. 232 (S.D.N.Y. 4/14/97).

49. *Newton v. Merrill Lynch,* 115 F.3d 1127 (3rd Cir. 6/19/97).

50. *Orman v. Charles Schwab & Co.,* 66 LW 1349 (Ill.Sup. 11/20/97).

51. *SEC v. Mayhew,* 66 LW 1128 (2nd Cir. 7/29/97).

52. *Jones v. SEC,* 115 F.3d 1173 (4th Cir. 6/16/97).

53. *U.S. v. Morse,* FSLR ¶99,488 (S.D.N.Y. 4/11/97). Also see *SEC v. Monarch Funding Corp.,* 66 LW 1307 (S.D.N.Y. 10/28/97): when the criminal case is pursued first, issues that were actually litigated and were needed for the out-

come of sentencing qualify for offensive collateral estoppel and cannot be re-litigated in a subsequent civil case.

54. *Amalgamated Clothing and Textile Workers Union v. Wal-Mart Stores,* 54 F.3d 69 (2nd Cir. 4/20/95).

55. *Arnold v. Society for Savings Bancorp Inc.,* 650 A.2d 1270 (Del.Sup. 12/28/94).

56. *Capital Realty Investors Tax Exempt Fund United Partnership v. Schwartzberg,* 929 F.Supp. 105 (S.D.N.Y. 4/23/96).

57. *Epstein v. MCA Inc.,* 50 F.3d 644 (9th Cir. 2/27/95).

58. See, e.g., *Gross v. Summa Four, Inc.,* 93 F.3d 987 (1st Cir. 8/12/96): an investor who bought before a company stated it had "strong financial per-formance" could not have been influenced by that statement. Furthermore, a company is not liable if it makes a true statement about past events (such as having secured many orders for its products) and does not disclose current problems filling those orders.

59. PSLR §104, which permits the SEC to seek injunctions against aiding and abet-ting 10(b) and 15(d) violations, applies to cases pending as of the PSLR's effective date, dealing with earlier conduct: *SEC v. Fehn,* 97 F.3d 1276 (9th Cir. 10/9/96). However, the PSLR provision that eliminates securities fraud as a RICO predicate cannot be applied retroactively in a civil RICO action: *Mathews v. Kidder, Peabody & Co.,* 947 F.Supp. 180 (W.D. Pa. 9/26/96); *In re Prudential Securities Inc. Limited Partnership Litigation,* 930 F.Supp. 68 (S.D.N.Y. 6/10/96) says that the PSLR lacks the "clear expression" that would allow civil RICO defendants to take advantage of retroactivity.

60. See *Cephalon Securities Litigation,* CCH Fed.Sec.L.Rep. ¶99,313 (E.D. Pa. 8/27/96), permitting appointment of more than one lead in a PSLR class action, given that PSLR §27(a)(3)(B)(i) refers to the "member or members" best able to represent the purported class.

61. *SEC v. U.S. Environmental Inc.,* 897 F.Supp. 117 (S.D.N.Y. 8/24/95).

62. Compare *Warshaw v. Xoma Corp.,* 74 F.3d 955 (9th Cir. 1/25/96): complaint charging biotech company with making false optimistic statements, e.g., about imminent FDA approval, about a new drug's prospects, is adequately pleaded; and *Marksman Partners LP v. Chantal Pharmaceutical Corp.,* 927 F.Supp. 1297 (5/21/96): PSLR scienter requirement can be satisfied by show-ing factors such as lack of corporate revenues and eroding capital to demon-strate the defendant's motive and opportunity to commit fraud, with *Zeid v. Kimberley,* 930 F.Supp. 431 (N.D.Cal. 6/6/96): complaint dismissed, albeit with leave to replead, for failure to specify each misleading statement about a company's expansion plans, why each was misleading, and what facts jus-tify a strong inference that scienter was present. Also see *Silicon Graphics, Inc. Securities Litigation,* Fed.Sec.L.Rep. ¶99,325 (N.D.Cal. 9/25/96): the safe harbor for forward-looking statements is limited to statements that are not subject to material dispute. To plead scienter, the plaintiff must produce cir-

cumstantial evidence raising a strong inference of either actual knowledge of fraud or conscious misbehavior. The mere fact that a company makes optimistic statements while it is aware of negative factors is not sufficient. Later proceedings in the same case, at 65 LW 2816 (N.D.Cal. 5/23/97), "deliberate recklessness" satisfies the PSLR pleading standard. Motive, opportunity, and non-deliberate recklessness can be evidence of wrongdoing, but do not constitute scienter unless the totality of the circumstances gives strong evidence of fraud. This case also holds that, in order to be "contemporaneous" with the plaintiff's trading, a defendant's alleged insider trading must occur within six days of the plaintiff's trade (computed as the maximum three days allowed for settlement, plus a three-day weekend).

63. In the view of *Medhekar v. U.S. District Court for the Northern District of California*, 99 F.3d 325 (9th Cir. 10/31/96), the stay is broad enough to encompass initial, informal disclosure under F.R.C.P. 26 (a)(1).

64. See 28 Sec.Reg.L.Rep. 914.

65. *Rehm v. Eagle Finance Corp.*, 954 F.Supp. 1246 (N.D. Ill. 1/27/97). The court considered allegations that the corporation's losses were vastly understated when compared with GAAP to be adequately pleaded.

66. *In re Baesa Securities Litigation*, 969 F.Supp. 238 (S.D.N.Y. 7/9/97). In this analysis, a corporation's mere knowledge of mismanagement at a subsidiary does not create an inference that the subsidiary's financial statements were false. Thus, the corporate parent's acceptance of the statements at face value does not subject the parent, its president, or its principal owner to liability.

67. *Schwartz v. Celestial Seasonings Inc.*, FSLR ¶99,538 (10th Cir. 9/5/97). On statute of limitations questions, also see *Law v. Medco Research*, 113 F.3d 781 (7th Cir. 5/15/97): the one-year statute of limitations begins when the plaintiff knows or would have known with reasonable diligence that the defendant knowingly made a false representation; and *Bernstein v. Misk*, 948 F.Supp. 228 (E.D.N.Y. 1/28/97): fraud action was time-barred because the promoter's evasiveness and breach of contract raised "red flags" that would have impelled a reasonable investor to investigate.

68. *Parnes v. Gateway 2000 Inc.*, 122 F.3d 539 (8th Cir. 8/8/97).

69. *Grossman v. Novell Inc.*, 120 F.3d 1112 (10th Cir. 8/8/97).

— FOR FURTHER REFERENCE —

Beach, Mary E.T., "Developments in Securities Registration and Prospectus Delivery," 21 ALI-ABA *Course Materials J.* 5 (February '97).

Benston, George J., "Regulation of Stock Trading: Private Exchanges vs. Government Agencies," 83 *Virginia L.Rev.* 1501 (October '97).

Bertram, K. Robert, "Offers and Sales of Securities On the Internet," 42 *Practical Lawyer* 23 (October '96).

Bloomenthal, Harold S., "The Private Securities Litigation Reform Act: How Safe is the Safe Harbor?" 18 *Securities and Federal Corporate Law Report* 89 (January '96).

Calderon, Jeanne and Rachel Kowal, "Safe Harbors: Historical and Current Approaches to Future Forecasting," 22 *J. of Corporation Law* 661 (Summer '97).

Carleton, Willard T., Michael S. Weisbach and Elliott J. Weiss, "Securities Class Action Lawsuits," 38 *Arizona L. Rev.* 491 (Summer '96).

Friedman, Howard M., "On Being Rich, Accredited, and Undiversified: The Lacunae in Contemporary Securities Regulation," 28 *Securities Law Rev.* 249 (1996).

Griff, Tracy, "Offering and Trading Securities on the Internet," 16 *Preventive L.Rep.* 18 (Fall '97).

Gwyn, William B. Jr. and W. Christopher Matton, "The Duty to Update the Forecasts, Predictions, and Projections of Public Companies," 24 *Sec.Reg. L.J.* 366 (Winter '97).

Krawiec, Kimberly D., "Fiduciaries, Misappropriators and the Murky Outlines of the Den of Thieves," 33 *Tulsa L.J.* 163 (Fall '97).

Langevoort, Donald C., "The Reform of Joint and Several Liability Under the Private Securities Law Reform Act of 1995," 57 *Business Lawyer* 1157 (August '96).

Mendales, Richard E., "Looking Under the Rock: Disclosure of Bankruptcy Issues Under the Securities Laws," 57 *Ohio State L. J.* 731 (June '96).

Merwin, Jay G. Jr., "Misappropriation Theory Liability Awaits Clear Signal," 51 *Business Lawyer* 803 (May '96).

Olson, John F. and D. Jarrett Arp, "What Makes a Company a Good Candidate for Going Public?" 21 ALI-ABA *Course Materials J.* 23 (February '97).

Painter, Richard W., "Disclosure of Environmental Legal Proceedings Under the Securities Laws," 11 *J. of Environmental Law & Litigation* 91 (Spring '97).

Simkin, Morris N., "MD&A: When to Include Forward-Looking Statements," *N.Y.L.J.* 5/16/96 p. 5.

Steinberg, Marc I., "Securities Litigation Developments: The 'Bespeaks Caution' Doctrine and Related Defenses," 23 *Securities Regulation L. J.* 447 (Winter '96).

Thompson, Robert B., "Securities Regulation in an Electronic Age: The Impact of Cognitive Psychology," 75 *Washington U. L.Q.* 779 (Summer '97).

SOCIAL SECURITY, MEDICARE, AND MEDICAID

[¶3901] The supplement period was a time of great concern about federal entitlement programs. Some people felt that these programs were unfairly generous to pre-Baby Boom senior citizens. Others felt that the fiscal soundness of important programs was at risk. The concept of privatizing Social Security attracted interest, but no such legislation passed during the supplement period.

In general, the Congressional mood during the supplement period could be described as restrictive, with attempts to prevent abuses and limit payments, both fraudulent and some previously considered legitimate.

[¶3902]   OASDI RETIREMENT BENEFITS

For tables of covered compensation (covered compensation for individuals born 1907–1964; rounded covered compensation for individuals born 1932–1958), see Rev.Rul. 96-53, 1996-47 IRB 4. In 1997, there was no change in the OASDI or Medicare tax rates. The Cost of Living Adjustment for the year was a mild 2.1%. Maximum earnings subject to FICA tax went to $68,400.

The Senior Citizens Right to Work Act (a somewhat Orwellian name) is Title I of the Contract with America Act, P.L. 104-121, signed March 29, 1996. As a result of this law, the amount that senior citizens are permitted to earn without losing a portion of their Social Security benefit is increased gradually, reaching $2,500 per month when fully phased-in in the year 2003.

Also see P.L. 104-115 (3/12/96), the Timely Payment of Social Security Benefits Act, authorizing the Secretary of the Treasury to issue to federal funds enough money to pay Social Security benefits without interruption.

The Social Security benefits received by a child after a parent's retirement can be considered as to whether the judge should deviate from the child support guidelines. However, the benefits are not an automatic offset against the support obligation.[1]

[¶3903]   MEDICARE

Medicare beneficiaries have the option of choosing HMO membership instead of the regular fee-for-service Medicare delivery system. Usually, this choice will appear to be cost-free, because the federal government pays the HMO premium (via deductions from the senior citizen's Social Security check). The Balanced Budget Act of 1997, P.L. 105-33, strives to encourage Medicare managed care by adding a new Medicare Part C, containing the rules and safeguards for the "Medicare + Choice" managed care program. The Tax Reform Act of 1997 sets up a four-year pilot project to test another managed care form, the Medicare Managed

Savings Account. MSAs are IRA-like accounts that can be used to save money for later use in paying for care.

The Balanced Budget Act also allows doctors to enter into private-pay contracts with senior citizen patients, outside the Medicare system (and therefore outside the limits that Medicare imposes on physician charges). However, doctors who "go private" will have to opt out of the Medicare system entirely, and will not be re-admitted for two years.

Concerns have been raised about the adequacy of HMO care of senior citizens, and expecially about their procedural rights. A district court has found that the notice, hearing, and appeals procedures when HMOs deny services are grossly inadequate. The court ordered processing of claims denials to be expedited, and listed ten rights that HCFA must guarantee to Medicare HMO enrollees.[2]

A state (Ohio) law restricting "balance billing" (charging more than the Medicare rate for services to a Medicare beneficiary) has been sustained by the Sixth Circuit.[3] Although the general federal rule is that nonparticipating physicians may not balance bill more than 15%, states have the option of imposing their own, stricter limits.

The Health Care Financing Authority (HCFA) sent a memo to its Medicare contractors demanding Year 2000 compliance by December 31, 1998. Failure to meet the deadline could mean denial of a new Medicare contract or future HCFA contracts.[4]

A doctor can maintain a *qui tam* action based on allegations that other providers falsely certified their compliance with Medicare's anti-kickback rules in their cost reports. Because Medicare payment is contingent on the certification, a falsified certificate is a federal false claim that can become the subject of a *qui tam* action.[5]

Many senior citizens are "dual eligibles"–that is, eligible for both Medicare (because of age) and Medicaid (because of medical indigence). Traditionally, dual eligibles were treated as primarily Medicare beneficiaries, so health care providers could get reimbursed at the higher Medicare rate rather than being restricted to the lower Medicaid rate when treating these patients. However, the Balanced Budget Act of 1997 changed the characterization. State Medicaid systems now have the option of paying the full Medicare rate for treatment of dual eligibles, but they are not required to do so. The statute has been upheld by the Ninth Circuit.[6] The court treated the Balanced Budget Act provision as a mere clarification, not a change, and therefore it can be applied retroactively.

[¶3904] MEDICAID

The Health Insurance Portability and Accountability Act of 1996, P.L. 104-191, contains a lengthy provision aimed at limiting Medicare fraud, especially fraud by health care providers. However, HIPAA §217 criminalizes (as a misdemeanor punishable by a fine of up to $10,000 and/or a year's imprisonment) any Medicaid-oriented transfer (by trust or otherwise) that gives rise to a penalty period. Therefore, transfers that do not give rise to a penalty period are not criminalized, including interspousal transfers or transfers of a homestead to the permitted class of transferees. Also exempt are transfers made before the statute's January 1, 1997 effective date.

This unpopular statute was nicknamed the "Granny Goes to Jail" bill. It was modified by the Balanced Budget Act into a "Granny's Lawyer Goes to Jail" bill. That is, the misdemeanor penalty was repealed for Medicaid applicants, but transferred to attorneys and others who, for a fee, advise clients to transfer assets. This statute was, of course, even more unpopular with the legal community. However, in April, 1998, Attorney General Reno made a public announcement that the Justice Department would not bring any prosecutions against attorneys and other advisors.[7]

Although 42 CFR §440.70(a)(1) defines Medicaid home health services as services furnished at the recipient's place of residence, the Second Circuit viewed this as an unreasonable interpretation of the Social Security Act, which requires but does not define home health services. The court pointed out that disabled people need to leave home, and the cost of providing a nurse in a community setting (such as a disabled child's school) is no greater than the cost of providing a nurse in a home setting.[8]

A number of states have brought suit against tobacco companies, seeking reimbursement for Medicaid costs incurred to treat smokers. One such statute, Florida's, has been upheld as constitutional on its face—although the state was required to name individual Medicaid recipients harmed by tobacco, and was forbidden to combine the intellectually inconsistent liability theories of market share and joint and several liability.[9]

[¶3905]   SUPPLEMENTAL SECURITY INCOME (SSI)

As a result of the Personal Responsibility and Work Opportunity Act, P.L. 104-193 (8/22/96), most individuals who entered the United States as legal immigrants before the statute's enactment date will not be eligible for SSI. Existing SSI cases will be closed after a review. Although the general rule is that losing SSI eligibility also means loss of Medicaid coverage, states have the option of continuing Medicaid services for these legal immigrants.

If a person enters the U.S. as a legal immigrant subsequent to August 22, 1996, that person will not be eligible for public benefits for the first five years he or she is in this country. (Refugees and people entitled to political asylum are exempt from this bar.) Even after the five-year period has elapsed, Medicaid eligibility will be tested based on the resources of the immigrant's sponsor and sponsor's spouse as well as the immigrant's and immigrant's spouse's resources.

The Contract with America Act, P.L. 104-121, noted above, also provides (at §105 of the statute) that SSI disability benefits cannot be paid for any disability to which alcoholism or drug addiction is a material contributing factor. According to the Eastern District of Pennsylvania, this provision applies only to claims for disability accruing after the statute's effective date.[10]

In February, 1997, regulations under the Personal Responsibility and Work Opportunity Reconciliation Act, P.L. 104-193, raised the standard for childrens' SSI disability claims from a disability seriously limiting the ability to perform the activities normal for the child's age, to a standard requiring marked and severe functional limitations. About 45,000 children were potentially affected. However, on December 17, 1997, Social Security Commissioner Kenneth Apfel announced that the cases would be reexamined, and parents of potentially affected children would be given an additional chance to appeal. A toll-free number was established for information about *pro bono* legal assistance. Commissioner Apfel stated that all cases involving retarded children would be reopened, or at least reviewed.[11]

— ENDNOTES—

1. *Anderson v. Anderson,* 66 LW 1288 (Md.App. 9/29/97).

2. *Grijalva v. Shalala,* 946 F.Supp. 747 (D.Ariz. 10/17/96).

3. *Downhour v. Somani,* 85 F.3d 261 (6th Cir. 6/7/96), *cert. denied* 117 S.Ct. 389.

4. See 66 LW 2397 (11/19/97).

5. *U.S. ex.rel. Thompson v. Columbia/HCA Healthcare Corp.,* 66 LW 1271 (5th Cir. 10/23/97).

6. *Beverly Community Hospital Ass'n v. Belshe,* 66 LW 2376 (9th Cir. 12/2/97).

7. See Gary Spencer, "Medicaid Advice Law Abandoned," *N.Y.L.J.* 4/7/98 p. 1. The article discusses the suit filed to challenge the ban on client counseling, *New York State Bar Ass'n v. Reno,* 97-CV-1768 (N.D.N.Y.).

8. *Skubel v. Fuoroli,* 113 F.3d 320 (2nd Cir. 5/13/97).

9. *Agency for Health Care Administration v. Associated Industries of Florida Inc.,* 65 LW 2034 (Fla.Sup. 6/27/96).

10. *Teitelbaum v. Chater,* 949 F.Supp. 1206 (E.D. Pa. 12/18/96). Also see *Torres v. Chater,* 66 LW 1188 (3rd Cir. 9/18/97): the denial of disability benefits for alcoholism or drug-related disabilities applies to claims that were not finally adjudicated as of March 29, 1996 (the effective date of the amendment), irrespective of the time the disability arose.

11. See Ruth Singleton, "Disabled Kids Win Back Their SSI Benefits," *National L.J.* 1/12/98 p. B7.

— FOR FURTHER REFERENCE —

Boone, Nicola Jaye, "Increasing the Community Spouse Income Allowance Through the Judicial Process: What Standard Applies?" 71 *Florida Bar J.* 58 (January '97).

Bove, Alexander H. Jr., "A Creative Strategy for Protecting the Home for Medicaid Purposes," 24 *Estate Planning* 22 (January '97).

Brienza, Julie, "Change in Medicaid Criminalizes Asset Transfers," 33 *Trial 14* (January '97).

Clark, Elizabeth G., "Substituted Judgment: Medical and Financial Decisions by Guardians," 24 *Estate Planning* 66 (February '97).

Dauster, William G., "Protecting Social Security and Medicare," 33 *Harvard J. on Legislation* 461 (Summer '96).

Feldstein, Martin S., "Social Security and Saving: New Time Series Evidence," 49 *National Tax J.* 151 (June '96).

Hubbard, Kenneth, "The Medicaid Cost Crisis," 43 *Cleveland State L. Rev.* 627 (January '97).

Kruger, Robert, "Paying a Medicaid Lien After *Cricchov v. Pennisi*," 69 *N.Y.S. Bar J.* 58 (December '97).

Myers, Robert J., "Privatization of Social Security: A Good Idea?" 50 *J. American Society of CLU/ChFC* 20 (July '96).

Note, "Home Care, Nursing Spending Adding to Trust Fund Woes," 12 *Tax Management Financial Planning J.* 279 (12/17/96).

Reske, Henry J., "A Wider Medicaid Fraud Net," 83 *A.B.A.J.* 26 (January '97).

Weissert, William G. et al., "Cost Savings from Home and Community-Based Services: Arizona's Capitated Medicaid Long Term Care Program," 22 *J. of Health Politics, Policy & Law* 1329 (December '97).

TAX ENFORCEMENT

[¶4101] Although the impact of the Tax Reform Act of 1997 is concentrated in the tax planning area, there are some enforcement provisions. The underpayment penalty will be waived if tax liability, less withholding and estimated tax payments, does not exceed $1,000. The IRS has a new policy of accepting tax payments by any "commercially acceptable means," such as credit or debit cards, if the means are deemed appropriate by the Secretary of the Treasury and authorized by Regulations. Also see T.D. 8703, permitting individuals to obtain the four-month automatic extension without paying the full tax (although an estimate of the amount due must be provided). This T.D. also allows the Form 4868 request for an extension to be filed electronically.

The adage "if you can't be good, be careful" was reinforced by a Spring, 1996 Fourth Circuit decision,[1] which permits the IRS to use information in a civil tax proceeding that was illegally obtained by the FBI and DEA in the course of a criminal investigation. However, the exclusionary rule would forbid use of the material if the other agencies had operated under a pre-existing agreement to supply tax information to the IRS.

According to the Ninth Circuit, a District Court can't enforce an IRS summons conditionally (subject to conditions suggested by the defendant, such as a requirement of prior notice before the IRS turns documents over to the U.S. Attorney's office). A summons for testimony or production of documents must either be enforced as drafted, or denied.[2]

A late-1997 Massachusetts case permits a state court, in a case involving false income tax returns used in an insurance fraud scheme, to order the defendant to execute IRS Form 8821 (authorizing release of tax returns). The court did not consider the form to be truly testimonial if it was not used to assert that the defendants either had an obligation to file returns, or voluntarily consented to disclosure of the returns. However, certain modifications were made in the form to cope with self-incrimination concerns.[3]

The materiality of false matter within a return (IRC §7206) is an issue of law, to be decided by the court, not by a jury. Even small falsehoods (in this case, fraudulent charitable deductions claimed by a return preparer on his own initiative) are material because they cause the return to be inaccurate.[4]

In 1995, the IRS announced[5] that nonbinding mediation could be used to assist the settlement of issues in some cases within the Appeals administrative process, as long as the case had not been docketed in any court. The procedure is optional; the mediator's role is to facilitate settlement between the taxpayer and the IRS Appeals personnel.

However, taxpayer rights suffered a blow in the Fifth Circuit.[6] This case holds that a Federal Tort Claims Act suit cannot be brought against the IRS for releasing confidential taxpayer information about the plaintiff in violation of Code §6103. The rationale is that the IRS' press releases about the taxpayer's conviction for filing a fraudulent tax return were not actionable under Texas tort law as either invasion of privacy or negligence per se. Later, taxpayers got some protection under P.L. 105-35, the Taxpayer Browsing Protection Act, which penalizes unauthorized inspection of tax returns and tax return information.

Although the IRS is not supposed to disclose "return information" except under limited and controlled circumstances, Field Service Advice (FSAs) memoranda (taxpayer-specific answers to queries, sent to revenue agents, field attorneys, and appeals officers by lawyers in the IRS Office of Chief counsel) can be obtained through a FOIA request. (The IRS will black out information that could be used to identify the taxpayer.) The D.C. Circuit allowed FOIA requests because the FSAs are quite similar to Taxpayer Advice Memoranda, which are already available. The FSA is an objective discussion of IRS policy, so attorney-client privilege is not involved. However, some portions of FSAs prepared in contemplation of specific litigation might be covered by work product privilege.[7]

The Fifth Circuit said that although the FTCA does waive sovereign immunity, it does so only if a private person would be liable for the same conduct under state law. Texas does have a tort of disclosure of embarrassing private information, but the facts disclosed in this case, to the extent they were nonpublic, were not deemed embarrassing by the court.

In the supplement period, the Ninth, Tenth, and Eleventh Circuits examined the position of the "responsible person" who is accused (under Code §6672) of failure to collect and remit employment tax. The "responsible person" penalty has been held to be penal in nature, rather than a revenue measure. Thus, the payor cannot deduct it, whether as a nonbusiness bad debt or under any other theory.[8] The standard as to whether nonpayment was "willful" is reckless disregard for the obligation to pay the tax.[9] In this context, use of a jury instruction drawn from an instruction on gross negligence is acceptable, because gross negligence is more serious than simple negligence and therefore does not permit the jury to convict on too low a showing. The Tenth Circuit weighed in in August, 1997, disagreeing with the Ninth Circuit. To the Tenth Circuit, a responsible person does not act willfully if reasonable efforts to protect funds for payment are frustrated by circumstances beyond the control of the responsible person. The role of the jury in this view is to decide if scienter is present.[10]

In the Sixth Circuit's view, civil tax penalties are designed to repay the government's cost of enforcement, and are not "punishment"—so there is no double jeopardy problem in charging both civil fines and criminal tax penalties against the same convicted tax violator.[11]

The distinction between punitive and revenue measures arose in another context: civil fraud penalties assessed on unreported narcotics income. According to the Fourth Circuit, this addition to tax is imposed to secure revenue, not as punishment, and therefore imposing the civil fraud penalty is not an excessive fine forbidden by the Eighth Amendment, nor does criminal prosecution for the narcotics offense constitute double jeopardy.[12]

At the end of 1996, the personal representative of an estate was held personally liable for the unpaid assessed balance of the estate tax, interest, and penalties. The personal representative distributed assets to himself, although he was aware of the government claim, and the estate was thus rendered insolvent.[13] In mid-1997, the Second Circuit treated the taxpayer's duty to file timely returns as personal and non-delegable. The upshot was that the taxpayer had to pay the §6651(a)(1) late filing penalty despite reliance on an attorney to get an extension, and the attorney's representation that the mandatory extension had been applied for.[14]

Interest imposed on an income tax deficiency is a nondeductible personal expense; a business expense deduction is unavailable.[15]

Even though the tax shelter limited partnerships in question were not distributed to a divorced woman, she was held not to qualify for innocent spouse relief, because she benefited from her ex-husband's tax shelters by receiving property in excess of normal support she would otherwise have received[16]—but innocent spouse relief was allowed in another tax shelter case, based on reliance on the spouse who purchased the tax shelters, engaged the accountant, and consulted the financial adviser.[17] An early 1996 Fourth Circuit case says that overstating the cost of goods sold on a tax return can be "grossly erroneous" (and thus sufficient for the nonseller spouse to be considered an innocent spouse) even if the statement does not lack basis in fact or law.[18]

The IRS' own internal procedure manual obligates the agency to do a computer search to find a taxpayer's new address once correspondence is returned as undeliverable—even if the taxpayer has failed to report the new address. Therefore, a deficiency notice mailed to an address on the most recent return is invalid, if the IRS knows that the address is incorrect, and the taxpayer can succeed in a motion to dismiss.[19]

The IRS is not obligated to follow its "John Doe" summons procedure (requiring court authorization) where the lawyer, rather than the clients, is the target of investigation. Thus, the IRS can serve the lawyer with a summons to learn the names of clients that were omitted from Form 8300 (reporting of large cash transactions). The identity of clients, and the nature of their fee agreements, is not generally privileged.[20]

The IRS' investigative powers are broad enough to require a corporation being audited to turn over the tax preparation software used to compile its returns. Under the §7602 summons power, the software is a "record" or "other data" subject to subpoena.[21]

[¶4101.1] Bankruptcy and Tax Enforcement

The 10 percent tax on failure to make the required annual funding contribution to the pension plan under IRC §4971(a) is punitive, said the Supreme Court in 1996. So if the penalty is imposed on a bankrupt company, it does not constitute an "excise tax" that takes priority over other claims. It is merely a regular unsecured claim.[22] It should be noted that the Internal Revenue Code §4980 15 percent excise tax on pension overfunding that reverts to the employer has the priority granted by Bankruptcy Code §507(a)(7); it is not an ordinary unsecured claim.[23]

Another 1996 Supreme Court case finds that Bankruptcy Code §510(c) gives bankruptcy courts the power of equitable subordination, but the power does not allow the court to subordinate categories of claims contrary to the priority system set up by the Bankruptcy Code. Therefore, a post-petition tax penalty retains its first priority as an administrative expense.[24]

An aspect of the §6672 penalty on the "responsible person" was explored by *Bronson v. U.S.*,[25] which treats imposing the penalty contrary to the automatic stay as merely voidable, not void. Thus, the taxpayer must pay unless action is taken within the bankruptcy proceeding to void the assessment.

A couple's Chapter 11 plan called for them to continue living in their residence, which was subject to a tax lien reflecting their debt to the IRS. Because there was no plan for foreclosure, the Ninth Circuit held that the creditor's security interest equals the fair market value of the property—not its (lower) foreclosure value.[26]

The Tenth Circuit says that *res judicata* will not be applied to keep the IRS from presenting additional claims for taxes in a year in which the bankruptcy court has already determined an amount of taxes. Although this might seem to impair the debtor's chance at a fresh start, that's the way the court reads the rules.

The taxpayer was not entitled to equitable estoppel, because the IRS did not affirmatively mislead him (the court considers the possibility of estoppel against the federal government to be an open question in any event). In this reading, the IRS was not guilty of misconduct in failing to inform the debtor that further claims might be made; a reasonable debtor would assume that collection of all nondischargeable taxes would be sought.[27]

Under Bankruptcy Code §523(a)(1)(C), willful attempts to evade or defeat claims such as taxes, are not dischargeable. However, evasion is worse than simple nonpayment (nonpayment would include a situation in which limited funds are used to pay other debts). The mere fact that the taxpayer knew that the taxes were not paid is not enough to constitute willful evasion.[28] In contrast, if the taxpayer has hidden income or assets, or failed to file a return, the mere fact that simple nonpayment of taxes is not a felony will not make the tax debt dischargeable in bankruptcy.[29] What does constitute willful evasion of tax as defined by Code §7201? According to the Ninth Circuit, filing a sham bankruptcy petition to release an IRS levy on wages falls into this category.[30]

The personal property of a Chapter 13 debtor is immune from administrative levies under Code §6334, but is not thereby exempt from federal tax liens imposed under §6321 for neglect or refusal to pay income tax after a demand has been made.[31]

A bankruptcy trustee can become personally liable for amounts collectable by IRS levy if, after notice of levy, the trustee turned over the proceeds of a property sale to the taxpayer rather than to the IRS.[32] The trustee's status as hypothetical bona fide purchaser does not justify an exception under Code §6323 from enforcement of a federal tax lien; Congressional policy favors enforcement of such liens.[33]

Both federal and state taxes on income that the debtor earned or accrued pre-petition, but that were payable after the petition, are treated as "allowed unsecured claims" (with seventh priority in bankruptcy). They do not qualify for first priority as administrative expenses.[34]

A bankruptcy court is a "court of the United States" permitted to make an IRC §7430 award of attorneys' fees to a prevailing party and against the IRS.[35]

A Ninth Circuit case involves a composer who coped with his debts by assigning future song royalties, instructing BMI to make payments of the royalties directly to his assignees. The IRS asserted a tax lien against his income. The Copyright Act provides that the first transfer recorded will prevail, as long as recording is adequate to give constructive notice. However, assignment of a right to income is not the same as transfer of copyright ownership. Thus, it is not necessary to record an income assignment to make it valid. The BMI form created a complete assignment under New York state law. The result was that there was nothing for the IRS' lien to attach to.[36]

[¶4104.3] Statute of Limitations Questions

In early 1996, the U.S. Supreme Court denied the taxpayers a refund of over-withheld taxes because they did not file a return for the year in question. If no return is filed, there is no three-year lookback period to determine the earliest year for which a refund is available, and thus the default period of two years from the date of the mailing of the deficiency notice applies.[37]

The statute of limitations prescribed by Code §7426 (nine months for wrongful levy) is the only statute of limitations available to a surety or other non-party whose property is levied on. The Ninth Circuit says that the six-year statute of limitations in a 28 U.S.C. §2410 action to quiet title is not available to the non-party.[38]

In the view of the Third Circuit, an IRS tax claim gets priority, even though the bankruptcy petition was filed more than three years after the tax returns were due. The IRS is entitled to a full three years to collect, and the automatic stay tolls the three-year period during which unpaid taxes are nondischargeable.[39]

The automatic stay does not apply to partners, guarantors, sureties, and insurers of the bankruptcy debtor,[40] but Code §6503(h), which suspends the statute of limitations during the taxpayer's bankruptcy, also suspends running of the statute of limitations against such derivatively liable parties, such as partners of a bankrupt partnership. Derivative parties who could take advantage of the statute of limitations when suit against the primary party is time-barred remain liable if the main suit can be revived.[41]

Several cases[42] permit the IRS to assert its priority claim in a Chapter 7 case, even if the assertion is untimely. In early 1995, the Sixth Circuit refused to extend this permission to Chapter 13 cases, finding that only timely-filed IRS claims can be allowed. The rationale is that Chapter 7 is a liquidating process, where creditors must wait for payment of claims, including late-filed claims. In contrast, the Chapter 13 debtor retains his or her assets and makes periodic payments to creditors.[43]

IRS' Form 872-A, the extension of time to assess tax, is a waiver of the statute of limitations, not a contract that terminates automatically 60 days after the taxpayer's bankruptcy filing.[44]

[¶4113] THE REFUND ROUTE

If the IRS seizes a third party's property to satisfy someone else's tax debt (e.g., if the property belongs to a creditor of a taxpayer who fails to pay payroll taxes), the third party is entitled to make both a refund claim and a wrongful levy claim. However, in a mid-1995 Ninth Circuit case, the plaintiff creditor failed to file the wrongful levy suit on time (the statute of limitations is nine months, which can be extended to 12 months). The request for release of levy must be sent to the IRS office that imposed the levy—not to the office where the third party pays its taxes.[45] A trust that taxpayers used to avoid paying taxes is not an independent third party qualified to bring a wrongful levy action.[46]

Webb v. U.S.[47] refuses equitable tolling of the §6511 statute of limitations. Thus, taxpayers whose financial adviser stole their money and compounded insult with injury by paying gift tax on this "gift" to himself with the taxpayers' money were unable to get a refund for gift tax paid more than two years before the filing of the refund claim. In contrast, the Ninth Circuit did allow equitable tolling (for mental incapacity) under §6511 in a case where a "senile" taxpayer sent the IRS a check for $7,000 instead of the appropriate $700 but the Supreme Court reversed, finding that equitable tolling is not available under §6511, no matter what the taxpayer's mental condition.[48]

Although in general the IRS will comply with directions from a taxpayer, Code §6402(a) nonetheless gives the agency discretion to apply an overpayment to "any liability" of the taxpayer, including tax liability for a year other than that designated by the taxpayer.[49] If there are both underpayments and overpayments, each bearing a different interest rate, the two payments will only be netted if the IRS chooses to exercise its discretion under §6402(a) to credit the taxpayer's overpayment against the outstanding liability.[50]

[¶4119] TAX LIENS

In mid-1995, the Supreme Court decided that a party who makes a payment under protest of tax assessed against someone else (for the purpose of removing a tax lien from the property) can sue in federal District Court under 28 U.S.C. §1346(a)(1)—a civil action for the recovery of tax allegedly erroneously or illegally assessed or collected.[51] (The plaintiff was an ex-wife who received the family home in conjunction with a divorce; the lien covered all of the husband's property for taxes the wife was not liable on.)

The Supreme Court read the statute to give standing to any taxpayer, not merely the person against whom the tax was assessed (the IRS interpretation). As the Supreme Court pointed out, it is unlikely that the IRS will be assailed by hordes of volunteers who pay other people's taxes and then bedevil the IRS for removal of liens.

On a related issue, the Eighth Circuit decided that a house awarded entirely to a divorcing wife no longer belonged to the husband and thus could not be subject to IRS' §6321 lien on all his property.[52]

The IRS can put a tax lien on a debtor's home, even though Worker's Compensation proceeds were used to purchase the home. (Although a lien is permitted in this situation, a levy would not be.[53])

In an early 1997 Pennsylvania case, an estate had many debts and only one asset: a piece of real estate subject to both a judgment lien and a subsequent tax lien. The estate administrator petitioned to transfer the real estate to the judgment creditor; the IRS objected. Code §6323(a) says that a federal tax lien is not valid as against other liens without notice, but 31 U.S.C. §3713 gives the tax lien absolute first priority in an insolvent estate. The Pennsylvania Supreme Court applied the rule of "first in time, first in right," rather than the absolute priority of the tax lien, citing interests of commercial stability. A business cannot prepare for federal liens that might arise, only those of which it has notice.[54]

A tax lien survives the taxpayer's death, and the IRS can execute the lien against half of the fair market value of property jointly owned by the deceased taxpayer. FMV is measured as of the date of foreclosure, not the date of death.[55]

The IRS has to win a suit alleging that a refund was erroneous before placing a tax lien; merely filing the refund suit will not justify the imposition of a lien.[56]

When an attorney is notified of a tax lien against a client's property, the attorney can be dismissed from the case by bringing an interpleader action and depositing funds from the client trust account in the court registry; the attorney does not have to remit the funds to the U.S. government.[57]

The Second Circuit permitted the IRS to levy on the bank accounts of a hospital's general partners when the hospital's payroll taxes went unpaid—even though the IRS did not provide written notice of seizure. The agency did send notice of levy which, when read in conjunction with the hospital's monthly bank statements, should have apprised the partners of the levy on the account.[58]

The IRS is supposed to send copies of notices and other written communications to the representative designated by the taxpayer (unless the taxpayer asks that copies not be sent). However, a Notice Levy remains valid even if the copies are not sent, because this is clearly expressed in the IRS' Statement of Procedural Rules.[59]

In 1996, the IRS announced that some parts of the Taxpayer Bill of Rights II initiative (which were included in the Revenue Reconciliation Act of 1995 that failed to pass) will nevertheless be implemented by the agency. For instance, the taxpayer ombudsman has the power to order the IRS to make an immediate hardship refund. Congress did its part in P.L. 104-168, the Taxpayer Bill of Rights II (7/30/96), setting up a Taxpayer Advocate office within the IRS, expanding conditions under which interest and penalties can be abated, and increasing the amount of fees and civil damages that taxpayers can collect when they are victimized by unauthorized collection activities.

Effective April 1, 1996, taxpayers who are the target of proposed IRS liens, levies, or seizures will be issued copies of Publication 1660 explaining their appeal rights. The IRS can notify each spouse of collection activities against the other spouse (balancing a potential loss of privacy against protecting the rights of a possibly innocent spouse).[60]

Certain property was seized and put up for tax sale because of a deficiency. The IRS' advertisement for the sale included the taxpayers' names, description of the property, and the reason for the seizure. The taxpayers filed suit, charging that their tax return information had been improperly disclosed. They lost. The Sixth Circuit said that the information was already disclosed when the tax lien was filed, and tax lien information is designed to be part of the public domain, not confidential.[61]

ERISA contains an anti-alienation provision that generally prevents anticipation of a pension. However, a Sixth Circuit case from early 1996 permits garnishment of a vested plan interest to meet an IRS judgment. The anti-alienation provision contains language exempting federal tax levies and judgments, and the paramount federal interest in tax compliance means that the garnishment rules cannot be deemed arbitrary or capricious.[62]

— ENDNOTES —

1. *Grimes v. Comm'r,* 82 F.3d 286 (9th Cir. 4/17/96).

2. *U.S. v. Jose,* 131 F.3d 1325 (9th Cir. 12/19/97).

3. *Massachusetts v. Burgess,* 66 LW 1390 (Mass.Sup.Jud.Ct. 12/8/97).

4. *U.S. v. Klausner,* 80 F.3d 55 (2nd Cir. 3/27/96).

5. Announcement 95-86, 1995-44 IRB 27.

6. *Johnson v. Sawyer,* 47 F.3d 716 (5th Cir. 3/16/95).

7. *Tax Analysts v. IRS,* 117 F.3d 607 (D.C. Cir. 7/8/97).

8. *Duncan v. C.I.R.,* 68 F.3d 315 (9th Cir. 10/12/95).

9. *Phillips v. IRS,* 73 F.3d 939 (9th Cir. 1/10/96).

10. *Finley v. U.S.,* 82 F.3d 966 (10th Cir. 8/20/97).

11. *U.S. v. Alt,* 64 LW 2736 (6th Cir. 5/15/96).

12. *Thomas v. C.I.R.,* 62 F.3d 97 (4th Cir. 8/14/95).

13. *U.S. v. Estate of Kime,* 97-1 USTC ¶60,256 (D.Neb. 12/13/96).

14. *McMahan v. C.I.R.,* 114 F.3d 366 (2nd Cir. 5/12/97).

15. *Miller v. C.I.R.,* 65 F.3d 687 (9th Cir. 9/7/95).

16. *Stiteler,* T.C. Memo 1995-279 (6/21/95).

17. *Friedman v. C.I.R.,* 53 F.3d 523 (2nd Cir. 1995). Also see *Reser v. C.I.R.,* 112 F.3d 1258 (5th Cir. 5/12/97): a person who knows or has reason to know that a deduction will create substantial understatement of tax liability cannot be an innocent spouse. Improper deductions, unlike omission of taxable

income, are visible on the face of the return, so the test is whether a reasonable spouse would have had reason to question the deductions.

18. *Lilly v. IRS*, 76 F.3d 568 (4th Cir. 2/20/96).

19. *Crawford v. C.I.R.*, T.C. Memo 1996-460 (10/10/96).

20. *U.S. v. Blackman*, 72 F.3d 1418 (9th Cir. 12/29/95).

21. *U.S. v. Norwest Corp.*, 116 F.3d 1227 (8th Cir. 6/26/97).

22. *Reorganized CF&I Fabricators of Utah, Inc.*, 116 S.Ct. 2106 (Sup.Ct. 6/20/96).

23. *U.S. v. Juvenile Shoe Corp. of America*, 99 F.3d 898 (8th Cir. 11/7/96).

24. *U.S. v. Noland*, #95-323, 116 S.Ct. 1524 (Sup.Ct. 5/13/96).

25. 46 F.3d 1573 (Fed.Cir. 1/26/95).

26. *Taffi v. U.S.*, 96 F.3d 1190 (9th Cir. 9/17/96).

27. *De Paolo v. U.S.*, 45 F.3d 373 (10th Cir. 1/9/95).

28. *Haas v. IRS*, 48 F.3d 1153 (11th Cir. 3/30/95).

29. *Bruner v. U.S.*, 55 F.3d 195 (5th Cir. 6/21/95).

30. *U.S. v. Huebner*, 48 F.3d 376 (9th Cir. 12/16/94).

31. *In re Voelker*, 42 F.3d 1050 (7th Cir. 12/12/94).

32. *U.S. v. Ruff*, 99 F.3d 1559 (11th Cir. 11/21/96).

33. *Battley v. U.S.*, 121 F.3d 535 (9th Cir. 8/14/97).

34. *Towers v. IRS*, 64 F.3d 1292 (9th Cir. 8/23/95): federal; *Missouri Dep't of Revenue v. L.J. O'Neill Shoe Co.*, 64 F.3d 1146 (8th Cir. 8/30/95): state.

35. *U.S. v. Yochum*, 89 F.3d 661 (9th Cir. 7/16/96).

36. *Broadcast Music Inc. v. Hirsch*, 104 F.3d 1163 (9th Cir. 1/15/97).

37. *Lundy v. C.I.R.*, #94-1785, 116 S.Ct. 647 (S.Ct. 1/17/96), *reversing* 45 F.3d 856 (4th Cir. 1995).

38. *Fidelity & Deposit Co. v. Adelanto, California*, 87 F.3d 334 (9th Cir. 6/21/96).

39. *In re Taylor*, 81 F.3d 20 (3rd Cir. 4/3/96).

40. *National Tax Credit Partners v. Havlik*, 20 F.3d 705 (7th Cir. 1994).

41. *U.S. v. Wright*, 57 F.3d 561 (7th Cir. 6/14/95).

42. *See, e.g., In re Vecchio*, 20 F.3d 555 (2nd Cir. 1994); *In re Pacific Atlantic Trading Co.*, 33 F.3d 1064 (9th Cir. 1994).

43. *U.S. v. Chavis*, 47 F.3d 818 (6th Cir. 2/23/95).

44. *Bilski v. C.I.R.*, 69 F.3d 64 (5th Cir. 11/20/95).

45. *WWSM Investors v. U.S.*, 64 F.3d 456 (9th Cir. 5/31/95).

46. *Juris Trust Co. Ltd.*, 97-1 USTC ¶50,147 (D.Cal 7/17/96).

47. 66 F.3d 691 (4th Cir. 10/2/95).

48. *Brockamp v. U.S.,* 67 F.3d 260 (9th Cir. 10/5/95), *rev'd* #95-1225, 117 S.Ct. 849 (Sup.Ct. 2/18/97).

49. *U.S. v. Ryan,* 64 F.3d 1516 (11th Cir. 9/26/95).

50. *Northern States Power Co. v. U.S.,* 73 F.3d 764 (8th Cir. 1/2/96). *Also see* Rev.Proc. 95-17, 1995-1 C.B. 556, new uniform interest tables for overpayments and underpayments. The tables apply to calculations made after 12/31/94.

51. *U.S. v. Williams,* #94-395, 115 S.Ct. 1611 (Sup.Ct. 4/25/95).

52. *Thomson v. U.S.,* 66 F.3d 160 (8th Cir. 9/19/95).

53. *Sills v. U.S.,* 82 F.3d 111 (5th Cir. 5/3/96).

54. *In re Estate of Romani,* 65 LW 2501 (Pa.Sup. 1/17/97).

55. *U.S. v. Librizzi,* 108 F.3d 136 (7th Cir. 3/5/97).

56. *Bilzerian v. Comm'r,* 96-2 USTC ¶50,356 (11th Cir. 7/1/96).

57. *Kurland v. U.S.,* 919 F.Supp. 419 (M.D.Fla. 3/6/96).

58. *Kaggen v. IRS,* 57 F.3d 163 (2nd Cir. 11/29/95).

59. *Swann v. Alameda County Retirement Ass'n,* 97-2 USTC ¶50,676 (9th Cir. 9/2/97).

60. IRS Announcement 96-5, 1996-4 IRB 99. Also see Notice 97-50, 1997-37 IRB 21, naming four carriers (Federal Express, UPS, Airborne Express, and DHL Worldwide Express) as designated private delivery services that can be used, pursuant to Taxpayer Bill of Rights II, to satisfy the "timely mailed, timely filed" rule. The list of carriers will be updated annually. At the end of the year, the IRS required its agents to get approval from the District Director before seizing rental properties. Taxpayers can apply to the taxpayer advocate to avoid property seizures that would cause hardship. See Jacob M. Schlesinger, "IRS Unveils New Taxpayer Protections to Limit Agents' Ability to Seize Assets," *Wall Street Journal* 12/15/97 p. A6.

61. *Rowley v. U.S.,* 76 F.3d 796 (6th Cir. 2/27/96).

62. *U.S. v. Sawaf,* 74 F.3d 119 (6th Cir. 1/26/96).

— FOR FURTHER REFERENCE —

Brager, Dennis N., "IRS Guidelines for Installment Payment Agreements," 19 *Los Angeles Lawyer* 15 (March '96).

Bucy, Pamela H., "Criminal Tax Fraud: The Downfall of Murderers, Madams and Thieves," 29 *Arizona State L.J.* 639 (Fall '97).

Dellinger, Kip, "A Substitution for Shifting the Burden in Ordinary Tax Disputes," 77 *Tax Notes* 1281 (12/15/97).

Ely, Mark, "IRS Has Expanded Examination Settlement Authority," 27 *Tax Adviser* 439 (July '96).

Goodman, George R., "Tax Return Compliance," 76 *Tax Notes* 1201 (9/1/97).

Herskovitz, Donald L., "Managing an IRS Audit: Practical Insights and Techniques," 49 *Tax Executive* 376 (September–October '97).

Hollingsworth, Tracy, "Qualified Plans and Self-Correction," 183 *J. of Accountancy* 28 (May '97).

Lindley, Susan and Ron J. Jong, "Your Client Got a Notice From the IRS! Where Do You Start?" 13 *Compleat Lawyer* 34 (Summer '96).

Lipton, Richard M., "Tax Administration in the 90s: The New 'Reign of Terror'," 74 *Taxes: The Tax Magazine* 227 (April '96).

Lucero, Tessa C., "Abatement of Interest and Penalties on Payroll Taxes," 28 *The Tax Adviser* 630 (October '97).

Lynch, Michael, "Late Filing Penalties," 181 *J. of Accountancy* 29 (March '96).

Margaroli, Richard, "Federal and State Governments Wrestle with Cybertaxes," 28 *Tax Adviser* 632 (October '97).

Oliva, Robert R., "When Will Reliance on a Tax Adviser Avoid an Accuracy-Related Penalty?" 28 *Tax Adviser* 772 (December '97).

Raby, William M. and Burgess J.W., "Proper Mailing of IRS Notices," 70 *Tax Notes* 995 (2/19/96).

Rettig, Charles P., "Financial Status Audits: The Internal Revenue Service Returns to Basic Investigative Techniques," 43 *Federal Lawyer* 26 (August '96).

Sansing, Richard, "Voluntary Binding Arbitration as an Alternative to Tax Court Litigation," 50 *National Tax J.* 279 (June '97).

Susswein, Donald B., "Can a 'Return-Free' Tax System Be 'Employer-Friendly'?" 78 *Tax Notes* 211 (1/12/98).

Urban, Michael A. and Janice M. Flood, "The Failure-to-File Penalty: Nuances Every Tax Practitioner Should Know," 28 *Tax Adviser* 420 (July '97).

TAX PLANNING

[¶4201] The figures announced by the IRS for use in tax compliance in 1998 are as follows:

➤ Standard deduction: $4,250 for a single person, $6,250 for a head of household, $7,100 for a joint return, $3,550 for a married person filing separately.

➤ The personal exemption starts to phase out at $124,500 for a single person, $186,800 for a joint return, $155,650 for a head of household, and $90,900 for a married person filing separately.

➤ The personal exemption is $2,700.

The taxpayer must obtain an IRS Statement of Value (for which a user fee is imposed) before filing a tax return claiming a charitable deduction for a donation of art appraised at more than $50,000.[1]

In mid-1995, the Supreme Court ruled that damages awarded under the Age Discrimination in Employment Act constitute taxable income, because they are not awarded for personal injury, nor are they sufficiently similar to tort damages to be excluded from income.[2]

Similarly, the Fifth Circuit decided that punitive damages received in a state-law malicious prosecution case are includable in gross income because they are imposed to punish the defendant rather than to make the plaintiff whole. Thus, they are not really damages for "personal injury."[3] In late 1996, the Supreme Court held that punitive damages in a wrongful death tort suit were not received "on account of personal injury," and thus are taxable.[4]

On a related issue, the Tenth Circuit also decided that a statutory grant of prejudgment interest does not represent personal injury damages, and thus the interest must be included in taxable income.[5]

Several 1996 cases deal with the tax status of damages in employment-related cases. A suit against a union for breach of the duty of fair representation has been held by the Ninth Circuit to be a personal injury suit, and thus the settlement proceeds are excludable.[6] The Fifth Circuit held that the trial court should not have relied on cases decided after the settlement of an ERISA suit (for wrongful termination) to limit ERISA compensatory damages. The amounts representing emotional distress and other nonpecuniary losses can be excluded from gross income; awards for back pay and future lost wages are not subject to employment taxes.[7] On the other hand, an employer's settlement of claims relating to its scheme to avoid paying mandated ERISA pensions has been held to generate gross income to recipient employees.[8]

According to the Tax Court, corporations are not "people" to the extent that they can receive a personal injury settlement (e.g., for breach of contract, malicious prosecution, fraud, violation of fiduciary duty, interference with business relationships) that is excludable from gross income. This is true even if the corporation has only one sole shareholder; electing the corporate form involves certain tradeoffs.[9]

Some of the confusion will be ameliorated by the Small Business Job Protection Act of 1996, P.L. 104-188, which amends IRC §104(a) to provide that gross income includes damages for personal injury unless the injury constitutes physical injury or physical sickness. Compensatory damages that flow from an injury or sickness (such as the spouse's loss of consortium) are not included in gross income. Punitive damages from a state wrongful death action are also excluded from gross income. Emotional distress per se is not considered a physical injury, but damages can be excluded up to the amount of the medical bills incurred to treat the emotional distress.

As for the attorneys in a personal injury case, if their fees are payable in future years under a structured settlement, and if the defendant purchases annuities to cover the payment to the attorneys, the purchase of the annuities does not trigger income for the attorneys. If the settlement agreement is unfunded and unsecured, the attorneys do not constructively receive the funds paid for the annuity, because they have no immediate right to the principal sum, only to the annuity benefits each year.[10]

The so-called "mailbox rule"—the rebuttable presumption that materials placed in a mailbox with proper address and stamp must have been delivered—has been held by the Sixth Circuit not to apply to regular mail sent to the IRS. In order to establish a date on which delivery can be presumed, the taxpayer must use registered mail.[11]

In 1995–1997, the IRS issued numerous rulings about electronic tax filing—even though the agency itself experienced continual difficulties with its computer system, and was unable to process certain electronic returns. It should be noted that anyone who must issue 250 or more W-2 forms is obligated to make the filing on magnetic media, unless a waiver for undue hardship is obtained. The IRS ruled on the correct method of filing various forms electronically (1040 series; 940, 941, 945) and via on-line services, as well as the requirements for developing substitutes for conventional paper tax forms and getting them approved for filing.[12]

[¶420L1]   TRA '97

The Taxpayer Relief Act of 1997, P.L. 105-34, is an extremely significant statute that makes tremendous changes in many areas. Although neither the income tax brackets nor the estate tax brackets have changed, there are major developments in the figures subject to these brackets.

Perhaps the most significant TRA '97 change is its impact on capital gains taxation. The holding period for long-term capital gains has increased, from 12 to 18 months (for assets sold or exchanged after 7/28/97). However, at press time, a return to the 12-month holding period was very likely. The maximum capital gains rate on 18-month assets is 20% (even if they are held by a trust or estate). Furthermore, individuals in the 15% bracket need pay only 10% tax on capital gains on assets sold or exchanged after 5/6/97. For mid-term assets (owned more than 12, but less than 18 months prior to being sold or exchanged after 7/28/97), ordinary income tax rates apply, subject to a maximum of 28%. For sales and exchanges after 12/31/2000, there is a separate ultra-low capital gains tax rate for assets held five years or more. The base rate is 18%, reduced to 8% for individuals in the lowest tax bracket (e.g., asset-rich but income-poor senior citizens).

TRA '97 also alters the taxation of capital gains on home sales. Under prior law, there were two separate provisions (which could, in appropriate circumstances, be combined): a one-time exclusion of gains for persons over 55, and a repeatable "rollover" of gain when the taxpayer purchased a more expensive home after selling a principal residence. In effect, TRA '97 merges these two provisions into one. An individual of any age who sells a principal residence is entitled to exclude from taxation up to $250,000 in capital gains (or $500,000, for a couple filing a joint tax return). The process can be repeated once every two years (pre-5/7/97 sales are disregarded). A principal residence is one lived in for two out of the five years before the sale (one year out of five, for persons confined to nursing homes). If the durational test is not met, but the sale or exchange was due to health or employment factors or unforeseen circumstances, the exclusion can be prorated.[13]

Apropos of taxpayers' homes, a home office deduction is available whenever the taxpayer uses the home as the sole fixed location for substantial administrative or management activity for the trade or business.

Two new IRA options have been created: the Education IRA, and the Roth IRA. The education IRA can receive deposits of up to $500 per child per year. Distributions from an Education IRA are tax-exempt up to the taxpayer's qualified higher education expenses for the year. Distributions in excess of education expenses are not only taxable income, but are subject to a 10% excise tax.

The "back-loaded" Roth IRA does not give rise to a current deduction, but funds can be withdrawn from the IRA without being subject to income tax (as long as the funds were not entitled to a deduction in the first place). This qualification is necessary, because it is also possible to roll over funds from a conventional to a Roth IRA. Thus, some taxpayers will eventually have Roth IRA accounts containing both types of funds. Qualified first-time homebuyers can withdraw funds from the Roth IRA without paying income tax on the funds (subject to limits). The Roth IRA is also useful in estate planning, because individuals who want to pass along their IRA balance rather than spending it during lifetime can leave funds in the Roth IRA. (The rollover is a taxable event, although in 1998 the tax impact can be spread over four years.) Unlike a conventional IRA, it is not subject to a requirement that distributions begin the year after attainment of age 70 1/2. In fact, persons over 70 1/2 can continue to contribute to a Roth (but not to a conventional) IRA.

Nor are conventional IRAs ignored by TRA '97. The law increases the Adjusted Gross Income (AGI) level at which taxpayers who are qualified plan participants will also be permitted to make deductible contributions to their IRAs. One spouse's participation in a qualified plan will no longer be attributed to the other spouse in determining the non-participant spouse's entitlement to an IRA deduction. The 10% excise tax (although not the income tax) is waived on distributions that would otherwise be premature, but that are used by first-time homebuyers or for qualified higher education expenses. Unlike most consumer interest, qualified interest on education loans is deductible: up to $1,000 in 1998, phasing up to $2,500 in 2001 and later years.

In addition to deductions, TRA '97 increases the tax credits available to individual taxpayers. A child tax credit of $400 per qualifying child (increasing to $500 in 1999 and later years) is available, although the credit diminishes based on income and phases out for high-income taxpayers. Complex rules are added for the HOPE scholarship credit and lifetime learning credit, two education credits with differing eligibility requirements.

The most dramatic estate tax change is the adoption of a more generous new unified credit schedule. The maximum amount that could be sheltered goes from $600,000 to $625,000 in 1998. The exclusion is scheduled to reach $1 million in 2006. Inflation indexing has been adopted for the annual exclusion, the maximum amount subject to special use valuation, and the Generation Skipping Tax exempt amount.

The treatment of Net Operating Losses (NOLs) has been changed. The carryback period is reduced from three to two years—but NOLs can be carried forward 20 rather than 15 years.(The three-year carryback period will still be permitted for individual taxpayers' casualty and theft losses, and disaster losses of farms or small businesses.) The research tax credit and work opportunity credit have been extended, and a new welfare to work tax credit is added for hiring in and after 1998.

There is a new income forecast method of depreciating assets to be used for film, videotape, sound recordings, copyrights, books, and patents, to be used only if the property is not depreciable under §197, and only if the income stream is uneven or unpredictable and the passage of time does not really reflect economic depreciation of the asset.

Certain expenses paid or incurred before 12/31/2000 to clean up environmentally contaminated "brownfields" will qualify for current deduction. However, if the taxpayer fails to make an election to expense these costs, they will have to be capitalized.[14]

[¶4202.3] Employment-Related Taxes

In P.L. 104-7, the Deduction for Health Insurance Costs of Self-Employed Individuals Act (4/11/95), Code §162(l)(1) has been amended to make the health insurance deduction permanent (for tax years beginning after 12/31/93). For taxable years beginning after 12/31/94, the deduction is increased from 25 percent phasing up to 80 percent of the amount paid by the self-employed to purchase their own health insurance. Another consequence of TRA '97 is that the health insurance deduction for the self-employed increases: the deductible amount for 1998 and 1999 is 45%, reaching 100% in 2007.

In some instances, the cost of paying taxes and providing benefits to full-time permanent employees is prohibitive. Therefore, companies have an incentive to treat certain individuals as independent contractors. In October, 1996 the Ninth Circuit decided a significant case on characterization of employees.[15] The court held that all Microsoft common-law employees, including individuals described as freelancers, were eligible for plan participation, whether they were paid by the personnel department or the accounts payable department; the three-judge panel was upheld by the full court in July, 1997.

Leased employees can be excluded from a pension plan without violating the Tax Code's minimum participation and coverage rules for qualified plans. But, because the leased employees had a colorable claim to coverage, the Fifth Circuit ruled that the leased employees were "participants" for ERISA purposes and entitled to receive plan information from the administrator; the administrator's refusal to provide the information could give rise to statutory penalties.[16]

A used car dealer qualified for relief from penalties (and refund of employment taxes already paid) because it was reasonable to follow industry practice and treat salespersons as independent contractors rather than employees.[17]

IR-96-44, "Independent Contractor or Employee"[18] permits relief from federal employment tax requirements if a business consistently files information returns with the IRS, and has a reasonable basis for characterizing certain workers as contractors rather than employees (e.g., consistent treatment of similarly situated individuals).

Defined-benefit plan actuaries are entitled to use conservative actuarial assumptions, thus requiring the corporation to contribute more to the plan but also increasing the tax deduction. In the Ninth Circuit's reading, actuaries have a greater duty to prevent plan underfunding (which could imperil payment of plan benefits) than to restrict the corporation's tax deduction.[19]

Compensation paid to a small business' founder (and 95 percent owner) was not reasonable and therefore not fully deductible by the corporation, for numerous reasons identified by the Second Circuit.[20] For one thing, the president was in a position to set his own compensation. An excessive share of the compensation was in the form of a bonus, not salary—suggesting dividend equivalence. Preincorporation papers included a system for calculating bonuses, but the system was ignored. Even the corporation's own expert witness estimated that reasonable compensation was far lower than the actual amount paid.

Although, as noted above, TRA '97 makes it easier for plan participants to make deductible IRA contributions, a Tax Court case using prior law denies an IRA deduction to a person who earned more than $35,000, even though she was a plan participant for less than one month in the year in question, and did not contribute to the qualified plan.[21]

For a question-and-answer discussion of how to establish and use a Medical Savings Account, see Notice 96-53, 1991-51 IRB 5. Notice 97-9, 1997-2 IRB 35, provides guidance on implementing the Small Business Job Protection Act's tax credit for adoption assistance and qualified adoption expenses. Announcement 97-64, 1997-26 IRB 9, clarifies the way in which adoption benefits provided by the employer should be reflected on the W-2 form.

The Small Business Job Protection Act also altered the requirement that rank-and-file employees draw their first qualified pension payment no later than April

1 of the year after the year in which they reach age 70 1/2. See Announcement 97-24, 1997-11 IRB 24, for guidance in applying the new rule before the plan has been amended to comply with the SBJPA; and Notice 97-45, 1997-33 IRB 7, for guidance in applying the SBJPA's simplified definition of "highly compensated employee." Temporary and Proposed Regulations at 62 FR 60195 and 60196 (11/7/97) give employers added leeway in changing cafeteria plan elections, when an employee's status or family status changes.

[¶4204] TAX FEATURES OF PARTNERSHIP OPERATION

Final Regulations under §1.704-3 have been promulgated for allocating built-in gain and loss on property contributed to partnerships,[22] and anti-abuse regulations allow the IRS to recast transactions involving a partnership to prevent abusive tax planning.[23]

The Tenth Circuit permitted a law firm partner a §162 deduction for litigation costs (e.g., filing fees, travel expenses, fees of medical consultants) that the firm paid under its "gross fee" contingency arrangements with clients. Local bar rule (but not local statute) bars firms from paying these costs rather than merely advancing them for future repayment. The court said that unethical, but not illegal, expenses can qualify for a deduction.[24]

Form 8832, the Entity Classification Election form, can be used by businesses that do not want to accept the normal characterization as partnerships or corporations (based on their continuity and mode of operation), or that want to change a previous characterization. See Announcement 97-5, 1997-3 IRB 15 for details.

[¶4207] TAX FEATURES OF S CORPORATIONS

The Small Business Job Protection Act also made significant changes in the treatment of S corporations for tax years beginning after 12/31/96:

➤ An S corporation can have 75 shareholders (not just 35).

➤ An "electing small business trust" can hold S corporation stock without causing the corporation to lose its qualification. However, the trust will be taxed at the highest trust rates, so this strategy may not be desirable.

➤ A qualified retirement plan trust or 501(c)(3) nonprofit organization can also own S corporation stock.

➤ S corporations have been granted the power to own 80 percent or more of a C corporation; an S corporation can also have a qualified S corporation subsidiary.

➤ The IRS can treat a late Sub-chapter S election as timely if the corporation can show that reasonable cause existed for the delay.

➤ Because the SBJPA changes the tax treatment of S corporations so dramatically, corporations that converted from Sub S to Sub C during the five years before the SBJPA's enactment get a chance to re-elect Sub S status.

According to the Ninth Circuit, pass-through income received from an S Corporation does not constitute "net earnings from self-employment" that can be used to calculate a Keogh plan deduction.[25]

IRS Notice 97-12, 1997-3 IRB 11, explains the method for the trustee of an Electing Small Business Trust to become an S Corporation shareholder. Announcement 97-4, 1997-3 IRB 14 is the IRS' relief procedure for waiving defects in an invalid election, or the untimeliness of the election itself. Also see IR 97-34, Rev.Proc. 97-40, 1997-33 IRB 50 allowing relief for late filing of the S Corporation election as long as the due date (including extensions) for filing the return for the first year in intended S Corporation status has not passed.

[¶4207.9]   Built-In Gains

At the end of 1994, Final §1374 Regulations were promulgated for calculating the built-in gain when a C Corporation is converted to S Corporation status.[26]

[¶4211]   LIMITED LIABILITY COMPANIES

In general, neither gain nor loss is recognized to the partners if a general partnership is converted to an LLC; a parallel is drawn between conversion to an LLC and conversion to a limited partnership, which is also generally a tax-free event.[27]

[¶4212]   CUSHIONING PERSONAL AND BUSINESS LOSSES

It is no longer necessary to attach an information statement to the tax return to claim a loss on §1244 stock.[28]

A married couple was permitted by the Tax Court to deduct interest paid on a tax deficiency arising out of accounting errors in their proprietorship business; these sums were not considered to constitute nondeductible personal interest.[29]

The Third Circuit ruled out one attempt to cushion a loss. A corporation was fined $13.2 million because of inappropriate disposition of the toxic pesticide kepone. The corporation contributed $8 million to an environmental fund to reduce the environmental impact of the pesticide, with the result that the fine was reduced to $5 million. The Third Circuit denied a deduction, because

§162(f) makes fines and penalties paid to the government nondeductible—and, by extension, amounts paid at the direction of the government are likewise nondeductible.[30]

Another unsuccessful attempt was parried by the Tax Court, when a lawyer who misappropriated client funds but made restitution before charges were filed attempted to treat the misappropriations as loans. Instead, he was required to report income for the year of the misappropriation, balanced by a miscellaneous itemized deduction, not used in calculating AMT, in the year of repayment.[31]

The Ninth Circuit has permitted taxpayers to claim a capital loss for worthless, canceled shares in a bankrupt corporation, even if the same taxpayers had to make an unrelated capital investment for shares in the corporation's post-bankruptcy reorganized incarnation.[32]

[¶4212.1] Tax Planning for Bankruptcy

Net Operating Losses pass to the bankruptcy estate, and therefore cannot be used by the debtor to reduce income for the year of the bankruptcy filing.[33]

A bankruptcy trustee cannot claim the §1034 one-time exclusion (under prior law) for sale of a principal residence, even though the residence was in the bankruptcy estate. The §1034 exclusion was available only to individuals. Nor can the bankruptcy estate get a stepped-up basis in residences that enter the estate.[34]

If the bankruptcy petition is filed in the middle of the debtor's tax year, tax on post-petition income is entitled to first priority as an administrative expense. However, tax on the pre-petition portion of the income is only entitled to seventh priority.[35]

Two recent cases deal with dischargeability of tax liability in bankruptcy. If there is a knowing and voluntary failure to file returns and make payments, the tax liabilities are non-dischargeable (willful attempts to evade or defeat taxation, as defined by Bankruptcy Code §523(a)(1)(C)). There is no requirement that the debtor intend to commit fraud as such.[36] Tax liabilities stemming from fraud are non-dischargeable, but liabilities due to negligence are dischargeable. The bankruptcy court is bound by the Tax Court's allocation of liabilities between the two.[37]

[¶4213] ACCOUNTING METHODS AND TAXABLE YEARS

Final Regulations have been issued under §1.446-1, permitting the IRS to impose a cut-off method when a taxpayer changes accounting methods.[38]

Also see T.D. 8666, 1996-26 IRB 4, providing Final Regulations for handling reimbursements or advances for business meals. These amounts are not subject to withholding, even though the employer is entitled to deduct only 50 percent of such amounts. This T.D. also details the treatment of employees' club memberships and the travel expenses of employees' spouses who accompany employees on business trips.

[¶4222] PLANT AND EQUIPMENT

Starting Jan. 1, 1997, the amount that can be expensed under §179 has been raised by the Small Business Job Protection Act from $17,500 to $25,000 per year.

[¶4224] PLANNING FOR CAPITAL TRANSACTIONS

A mid-1995 Tax Court case compels capitalization of defense costs of a class action brought by minority shareholders alleging that a merger breached the board's fiduciary duty.[39] The Seventh Circuit, reversing the Tax Court, permitted fees paid to investment bankers for an unsuccessful defense against a takeover bid to be deducted rather than capitalized.[40] The Court of Federal Claims permitted a current deduction of ongoing retainer fees paid to a law firm even though the actual legal work in a particular year involved a capital acquisition.[41]

Money paid to defer the closing date of a merger-oriented stock purchase agreement is deductible, under Code §153(a), as interest.[42]

Fees to raise capital for a leveraged buyout, allocable to the noninterest portion of the debt generated by a merger, can be amortized over the term of the indebtedness; the Small Business Job Protection Act rules that such expenses are not disallowed for tax purposes.[43]

Spare parts used to repair computers in compliance with service contracts were not inventory, because they were not held primarily for sale to customers. Therefore, according to the Federal Circuit, they could be treated as a depreciable capital asset.[44]

A professional musician's precious 17th century instrument, placed in service during the period 1980–1987, qualifies for ACRS depreciation under §168, whether or not it has a determinable useful life, and even if its value is actually increasing. Property is depreciable merely if it is subject to wear, tear, and exhaustion, even if it is not consumed within the foreseeable future.[45]

[¶4227] SHIFTING INCOME IN THE FAMILY

For wages paid after Dec. 31, 1994, FICA and FUTA tax and income tax withholding can be done for "nannies" and other household employees on a calendar year rather than a quarterly basis, but W-2 forms must still be compiled and submitted to the employee and to the IRS.[46]

[¶4227.1] Tax Planning for Divorce

It violates the Constitution's Privileges and Immunities clause for a state to allow alimony deductions on resident income tax returns while denying the deduction on non-resident returns.[47]

The Tax Court denies an alimony deduction for amounts paid pursuant to a written proposal to pay submitted to the recipient spouse's attorney, on the gruonds that the proposal is neither a divorce decree nor a written separation agreement.[48]

Neither gain nor loss is recognized on a property transfer incident to divorce. However, if property is supposed to be transferred over a period of years, with provision for interest payments, the interest payments are taxable income to their recipient.[49]

According to the Ninth Circuit, a couple's pre-nuptial agreement can be consulted to determine whether a tax overpayment is attributable to community or separate property (which determines which spouse can use the overpayment to reduce tax liability now that they are in the process of divorcing). Property is presumed community, but can be transmuted by a pre-nuptial agreement.[50]

— ENDNOTES —

1. Rev.Proc. 96-15, 1996-3 IRB 41.

2. *C.I.R. v. Schleier,* #94-500, 115 S.Ct. 2159 (Sup.Ct. 6/14/95). *McKay, Jr.,* 96-1 USTC ¶50,279 (5th Cir. 4/10/96) reads *Schleier* to mean that the settlement proceeds in an age discrimination wrongful discharge case are included in gross income, because they are not received for personal injury.

3. *Estate of Moore v. C.I.R.,* 53 F.3d 712 (5th Cir. 6/2/95). *Also see Wesson v. U.S.,* 48 F.3d 894 (5th Cir. 3/30/95), *C.I.R. v. Miller,* 914 F.2d 586 (4th Cir. 1990), *Reese v. U.S.,* 24 F.3d 228 (Fed.Cir. 1994), and *Hawkins v. U.S.,* 30 F.3d 1077 (9th Cir. 1994), all of which include punitive damages in gross income. On the other hand, *Horton v. C.I.R.,* 33 F.3d 625 (6th Cir. 1994) excludes punitive damages from gross income, but the case involves Kentucky law, which deems punitive damages to be a hybrid between compensatory and punitive motivations. Also see Rev.Rul. 96-65, 1996-53 IRB 5, to the effect that back pay received in an employment discrimination case is taxable income; emotional distress damages are excludable to the extent that they compensate physical injuries with medical consequences.

4. *O'Gilvie v. U.S.,* 66 F.3d 1550 (10th Cir. 9/19/95), *aff'd* #95-955, -977, 117 S.Ct. 452 (Sup.Ct. 12/10/96).

5. *Brabson v. U.S.,* 73 F.3d 1040 (10th Cir. 1/11/96).

6. *Banks v. U.S.,* 81 F.3d 874 (9th Cir. 4/9/96).

7. *Dotson v. C.I.R.,* 87 F.3d 682 (5th Cir. 6/27/96).

8. *Hemelt v. U.S.,* 97-2 U.S.T.C. ¶50,596 (4th Cir. 8/7/97).

9. *P&X Markets, Inc.,* 106 T.C. No. 26 (6/13/96).

10. *Childs v. Comm'r,* 96-2 USTC ¶50,504 (11th Cir. 6/11/96).

11. *Carroll v. C.I.R.,* 71 F.3d 1228 (6th Cir. 12/26/95).

12. Rev.Proc. 95-49, 1995-50 IRB 5; Rev.Proc. 95-16, -17, -18, -20 1995-1 C.B. 525, 556, 657, 668; T.D. 8683, 1996-44 IRB 9; Rev.Proc. 96-17, 1996-4 IRB 69; 96-18, 1996-4 IRB 73, Rev.Proc. 96-20, 1994-4 IRB 88; Rev.Proc. 96-48, 1996-39 IRB 10; Rev. Proc. 97-34, 1997-30 IRB 14. IR-97-5 sets out a procedure under which an online service sends returns to the IRS, which notifies the taxpayer if the return has been accepted or, if it is not acceptable, what corrective steps are required. IR-96-6 covers the TeleFile paperless telephone filing for individuals who would otherwise use the paper 1040EZ form. T.D. 8661 governs deposit of federal taxes by Electronic Funds Transfer.

13. Under prior law, see *Snowa v. C.I.R.,* 123 F.3d 190 (4th Cir. 8/19/97): §1034 did not include a "same spouse" requirement, so amounts contributed by the former spouse can be included in the cost of the new principal residence even if the sale takes place when the taxpayer is married to a new spouse.

14. See Notice 97-7, 1997-1 IRB 8 for the proposed procedure for getting an advance ruling on allocation between current deductions and capital expenditures for environmental cleanups that will be performed in the future (as distinct from sorting out the tax consequences of cleanups already performed). Announcement 97-22, 1997-12 IRB 47 allows taxpayers to request a pre-submission conference with the IRS before filing for a Private Letter Ruling on the deductibility of cleanup costs that span both past and future tax years; on this point, also see Revenue Procedure 98-17, 66 LW 2448 (1/16/98). However, PLRs will not be issued with respect to completed cleanups. Also see *Norwest Corp. v. Comm'r,* 108 T.C. No. 15 (4/28/97): if the costs of removing asbestos are part of a general plan of rehabilitating a building, they must be capitalized and not currently deducted.

15. *Vizcaino v. Microsoft Corp.,* 97 F.3d 1187 (9th Cir. 10/3/96), *aff'd* 97-2 U.S.T.C. ¶50,566 (9th Cir. 7/24/97).

16. *Abraham v. Exxon Corp.,* 64 LW 2811 (5th Cir. 6/10/96).

17. *Springfield v. Comm'r,* 88 F.3d 750 (7/3/96).

18. Available at CCH Standard Federal Tax Reporter ¶46,548.

19. *Citrus Valley Estates Inc. v. C.I.R.,* 49 F.3d 1410 (9th Cir. 3/8/95).

20. *Rapco Inc. v. Comm'r,* 85 F.3d 950 (2nd Cir. 6/4/96).

21. *Henry v. C.I.R.,* 66 LW 1224 (Tax Court 9/22/97).

22. T.D. 8585, 1995-1 C.B. 120 (12/27/94).

23. T.D. 8588, 1995-1 C.B. 109 (12/29/94).

24. *Boccardo v. C.I.R.,* 56 F.3d 1016 (9th Cir. 5/26/95).

25. *Durando v. U.S.,* 70 F.3d 548 (9th Cir. 11/6/95).

26. T.D. 8579, 1995-1 C.B. 170 (12/29/94).

27. Rev.Rul. 95-37, 1995-1 CB 130.

28. T.D. 8594, 1995-1 C.B. 146 (4/27/95).

29. *Redlark v. C.I.R.,* 106 T.C. No. 2 (1/11/96).

30. *Allied-Signal Inc. v. C.I.R.,* 1995 U.S.App. LEXIS 5130 (3rd Cir. 1995).

31. *James O'Hagan,* T.C. Memo 1995-409 (8/22/95).

32. *Delk v. C.I.R.,* 113 F.3d 984 (9th Cir. 5/7/97).

33. *Kahle v. Comm'r,* TC Memo 1997-91 (2/20/97).

34. *In re Barden,* 97-1 U.S.T.C. ¶50,244 (2nd Cir. 1/29/97).

35. *U.S. v. Hillsborough Holding Corp.,* 116 F.3d 1391 (11th Cir. 7/10/97).

36. *U.S. v. Fegeley,* 118 F.3d 979 (3rd Cir. 7/8/97).

37. *In re Palmer,* 97-1 U.S.T.C. ¶50,228 (D.Mont. 12/13/96).

38. T.D. 8608, 1995-36 IRB 10.

39. *Berry Petroleum Co.,* 104 T.C. No. 30 (5/22/95).

40. *A.E. Staley Manufacturing Co. v. C.I.R.,* 119 F.3d 482 (7th Cir. 7/2/97).

41. *Dana Corp. v. IRS,* 66 LW 1091 (Ct. Fedl. Claims 7/15/97).

42. *Halle v. Comm'r,* 83 F.3d 649 (4th Cir. 5/6/96).

43. *Fort Howard Corp. v. Comm'r,* 107 T.C. No. 12 (10/22/96).

44. *Hewlett-Packard Co. v. U.S.,* 71 F.3d 398 (Fed.Cir. 12/7/95). Also see *Norwest Corp. v. C.I.R.,* 65 LW 2776 (Tax Court 4/30/97): software acquired by a company for use in its business is tangible personal property that qualifies for the investment tax credit, if acquired under a license allowing non-transferable, non-exclusive use, with no assignment of underlying intellectual property rights.

45. *Liddle v. C.I.R.,* 65 F.3d 329 (3rd Cir. 9/8/95).

46. Social Security Domestic Employment Reform Act of 1994, P.L. 103-387, as implemented by IRS Notice 95-18, 1995-1 C.B. 300.

47. *Lunding v. New York Tax Appeals tribunal,* #96-1462, 118 S.Ct. 766 (Sup.Ct. 1/21/98).

48. *Keegan v. Comm'r,* T.C. Memo 1997-359 (8/5/97).

49. *Gibbs v. Comm'r,* TC Memo 1997-196 (4/29/97).

50. *U.S. v. Elam,* 112 F.3d 1036 (9th Cir. 5/2/97).

— FOR FURTHER REFERENCE —

Anderson, Kim, "Amortizing §197 Intangibles Using a §754 Election," 28 *The Tax Adviser* 70 (February '97).

Barker, Thomas G. Jr., "Environmental Issues: An Overview of Tax Policy," 27 *Tax Adviser* 602 (October '96).

Barron, Michael S., "When Will the Tax Court Allow a Discount for Lack of Marketability?" 86 *J. of Taxation* 46 (January '97).

Bortnick, Jeffrey S. and Philip S. Gross, "Tax Advantages of the §83(b) Election Can be Significant," 86 *J. of Taxation* 39 (January '97).

Conjura, Carol, "Changing an Accounting Method Now Easier but Barriers Remain for Taxpayers Under Examination," 87 *J. Taxation* 5 (July '97).

Dance, Glenn E. and William T. Carman, "Final Regulations Define Publicly Traded Status for Partnerships," 27 *Tax Adviser* 669 (November '96).

Dondershine, Scott A. and Ginger McGuffie, "Avoid The Employment Tax Delinquency Trap," 182 *J. of Accountancy* 43 (October '96).

Ellentuck, Albert B., "Tax Planning for the Sole Proprietor," 28 *Tax Adviser* 732 (November '97).

Ely, Mark, "Internal IRS Guidelines on Requests for Field Service Advice and Technical Advice," 27 *Tax Adviser* 638 (October '96).

Godfrey, John, "Tax Credits for Computers and the Slow Death of Tax Reform," 74 *Tax Notes* 992 (2/24/97).

Green, Franklin L., "The Folly of Long-Term Tax Planning: Comments on the Instability of the Tax Law," 74 *Tax Notes* 481 (1/27/97).

Hansen, Kenneth A., "Maximizing the Deferral of IRA Required Minimum Distributions," 74 *Taxes: The Tax Magazine* 622 (October '96).

Herskowitz, Donald L. and Edward Sair, "Federal Tax Advantages for Qualified State Tuition Programs," 28 *Tax Adviser* 149 (March '97).

Hollingsworth, Tracy, "Taxation and Electronic Commerce," 183 *J. of Accountancy* 29 (March '97).

Howe, Victoria M., "Automatic Revenue Procedure Allows Businesses to Recoup Missed Depreciation Deductions," 24 *J. of Real Estate Taxation* 189 (Winter '97).

Katzenstein, Andrew M. and Lisa C. McArthur, "Planning for the Family-Owned Business Exclusion Under TRA '97," 24 *Estate Planning* 465 (December '97).

Nolan, Leo F. II, "Can the Cash Method of Accounting Clearly Reflect Income?" 74 *Tax Notes* 1063, 1175; 2/24/97 and 3/3/97.

Silverman, Mark J. and Andrew J. Weinstein, "INDOPCO and the Tax Treatment of Reorganization Costs," 47 *Tax Executive* 31 (January–February '97).

Singer, Robert M., "TRA '97: Relief for Some; More Aggravation for Others," 28 *Tax Adviser* 767 (December '97).

Trier, Dana L. et al., "Post Reorganization Continuity of Interest," 73 *Tax Notes* 481 (10/28/96).

Wechsler, David A. and Lisa Weinstein, "Gifting the House to Save the Home: Qualified Personal Residence Trusts," 12 *Washington Lawyer* 30 (November–December '97).

TRUSTS

[¶4301] Special rules are in place for the situation in which a U.S. citizen is survived by a noncitizen spouse. A Qualified Domestic Trust, or QDOT, can be used to minimize the extent to which tax treatment of noncitizen survivors is less favorable than that of citizen surviving spouses. Final Regulations governing QDOTs for decedents dying and gifts made after August 22, 1995 have been promulgated, as have Temporary Regulations to assure that that Code §2056A QDOT estate tax actually gets collected.[1]

An early 1997 Virginia case involves an *inter vivos* trust that calls for setting up three trusts after the grantor's death. The Virginia Supreme Court held that, on request of any beneficiary, the trustees have a duty to disclose information about the entire trust corpus and all the trusts, not just about that beneficiary's individual trust. Without the more general information, beneficiaries would be unable to determine if fiduciaries have committed any misconduct.[2]

[¶4306] ESTATE AND GIFT TAXATION OF TRUSTS

The Tax Reform Act of 1997 affects trusts in several ways. The Generation-Skipping Trust (GST) exemption will be indexed for inflation. Distributions made within 65 days of the end of a tax year can be treated as made on the last day of the tax year. (This was the rule under Code §663 for estates; TRA '97 makes the rule equally applicable to trusts.) TRA '97 also treats transfers out of a revocable grantor trust in the three years before the grantor's death as made directly by the grantor, not the trust itself. However, the executor can also make an irrevocable election (with the consent of the trustee) to treat a qualified revocable trust as part of the estate.

Another 1997 statute, the Charitable Donor Antitrust Immunity Act of 1997, P.L. 105-26 (7/3/97) exempts charitable remainder trusts and charitable gift annuities from antitrust regulation.

The IRS has announced (in Rev.Proc. 97-23, 1997-17 IRB 7) that neither advance rulings nor determination letters will be issued as to the qualification of a charitable remainder trust whose grantor, trustee, or beneficiary can control the timing of the trust's receipt of income from a partnership or deferred annuity contract. This announcement is part of the IRS' continuing effort to wipe out abusive trusts. See also Notice 97-24, 1997-16 IRB 6, a reminder that civil and criminal penalties can be imposed for use of improper trusts that profess to reduce taxes impermissibly, with no meaningful change in control or application of income.

If a charitable remainder unitrust (CRUT) gets unrelated business taxable income (UBTI) from publicly traded limited partnerships, the Ninth Circuit has decided that Code §664(c) mandates taxation of all of the trust's income, not just the portion stemming from the partnerships.[3]

The Sixth Circuit has joined the Fifth and Eighth Circuit in permitting a "wait and see" power that permits the executor to determine which property will be subject to the QTIP election at the time of the election itself. The IRS position at the time of the litigation was that property must satisfy the QTIP definition at the time of the first spouse's death; but the courts say that the election would degenerate into a mere formality if executors were not permitted to select the qualifying property at the time of the election.[4] (Eventually, however, the IRS gave in and permitted contingent QTIP elections to be made after February 18, 1997.)[5]

According to the Eleventh Circuit, a trust can be a QTIP even if the surviving spouse receives neither the stub income (income from the last scheduled payment to the survivor's death) nor power of appointment over the stub income. In other words, the stub income can be appointed to someone other than the surviving spouse.[6]

In a recent Seventh Circuit case, the wife was the beneficiary of two trusts—the Marital Trust and the Family Trust. Her share of the Family Trust was limited to 5 percent in any year, and only if the Marital Trust had already been exhausted. The court ruled that the wife had enough dominion to be construed to have a general power of appointment over both trusts. Thus, both trusts were included in her estate to some extent, but just 5 percent of the Family Trust was included.[7]

The Fifth Circuit allowed a QTIP, and criticized the Tax Court for including 100 percent of the proceeds of term life insurance, purchased with community funds, in the insured husband's gross estate. (The uninsured wife predeceased him.) Under Texas community property law, when the husband died, 50 percent of the proceeds belonged to his wife's residuary trust. The policy (payable to his estate) remained community property even though the husband renewed it after the wife's death; he did not create new, separate policies but only renewed the community property policy.[8]

Thanks to TRA '97, in a community property state only, if the nonparticipant spouse dies first, his or her community interest in the surviving participant spouse's qualified plan or IRA can qualify for QTIP treatment.

The marital deduction was not available for trust assets going to the surviving spouse under a settlement agreement that resolved a dispute over the terms of the trust. The agreement gave the surviving spouse a life estate but no power of appointment. Furthermore, the surviving spouse's rights derived from the settlement, and not from a bona fide recognition of her spousal rights; nor did they pass from the decedent. All these factors determined the absence of a qualified terminable interest that would support the marital deduction.[9]

[¶4306.2] Transfers Taking Effect at Death

Distributions made from a decedent's trust after his death, for completed gifts that are enforceable pre-mortem debts, constitute claims against the trust. As such, they cannot be deducted under §2053 as claims against the decedent's estate. Furthermore, the distributions were includable in the fair market value of the trust under §2038 because the distributions were mandatory, and therefore the decedent relinquished the power to revoke or amend the distributions within three years of death.[10]

[¶4309] TERMINATION OF THE TRUST

In late 1996, the Kansas Supreme Court decided[11] that any will that is supposed to revoke an existing trust must include an express statement of trust revocation.

— ENDNOTES —

1. T.D. 8612, 8613, 1995-2 C.B. 192, 216.

2. *Fletcher v. Fletcher,* 65 LW 2484 (Va.Sup. 1/10/97).

3. *Leila G. Newhall Unitrust v. C.I.R.,* 105 F.3d 482 (9th Cir. 1/21/97).

4. *Estate of Spencer v. C.I.R.,* 43 F.3d 226 (6th Cir. 1/5/95); *Estate of Robertson v. Comm'r,* 15 F.3d 779 (8th Cir. 1994); *Estate of Clayton v. Comm'r,* 976 F.2d 1486 (5th Cir. 1992).

5. T.D. 8714, Temp. Regs. §20.2044-1(T) et.seq.; see CCH Fed'l Estate & Gift Tax Reporter ¶12,735.

6. *Estate of Shelfer v. Comm'r,* 86 F.3d 1045 (11th Cir. 7/1/96).

7. *Estate of Kurz v. C.I.R.,* 68 F.3d 1027 (7th Cir. 10/30/95).

8. *Estate of Cavenaugh v. C.I.R.,* 51 F.3d 597 (5th Cir. 1995).

9. *Estate of Carpenter v. C.I.R.,* 52 F.3d 1266 (4th Cir. 1995).

10. *White v. U.S.,* 906 F.Supp. 24 (D.Mass. 1995).

11. *In re Estate of Sanders,* 1996 WESTLAW 714034 (Kan.Sup. 12/13/96).

— FOR FURTHER REFERENCE —

Brophy, Peter M., "QPRT Requirements: New Proposed Regs Raise Questions," 27 *Tax Adviser* 597 (October '96).

Bryant, Jeffrey J. and Cherie Warchuck, "Steps to Take to Preserve Deductions for Beneficiaries at the Termination of a Trust or Estate," 86 *J. of Taxation* 51 (January '97).]

Commito, Thomas F., "Retirement Distribution Planning With Trusts," 50 *J. American Society of CLU/ChFC* 10 (November '96).

Engelbrecht, Ted D., Bob Burgoon and Govind Iyer, "Grantors Should Beware When Borrowing from a Trust," 135 *Trusts and Estates* 48 (October '96).

Feldman, Henry A. Jr., "Attorneys as Professional Trustees: Another Way to Build Your Practice," 23 *Law Practice Management* 44 (January–February '97).

Flynn, Maura P., "Using Administrative Powers to Create Income Tax Defective Trust," 27 *Tax Adviser* 463 (August '96).

Horwich, Alan, "Bank Fiduciaries With Material Inside Information: Responsibilities and Risks," 113 *Banking Law J.* 4 (January '96).

Last, Jennifer I., "Is It a Grantor Charitable Lead Trust or Not?" 30 *John Marshall L.Rev.* 1023 (Summer '97).

Margolin, Stephen M. and Andrew M. Curtis, "The Flexible Irrevocable Trust," 50 *J.American Society of CLU & ChFC* 44 (January '96).

Miller, Michael D. and David L. Koche, "The Qualified Domestic Trust Regulations," 70 *Florida Bar J.* 48 (July–August '96).

Neser, Arlin P., "Trust Accounting for Lawyers," 6 *Law Office Computing* 40 (August–September '96).

Note, "1996 Trust Software Update," 135 *Trusts and Estates* 29 (November '96).

Schwab, Eileen Caulfield, "Requirements for QDOTs Liberalized in New Regulations," 23 *Estate Planning* 11 (January '96).

Valente, Peter C. and Joann T. Palumbo, "Equitable Deviation from Terms of Trust Instrument," *N.Y.L.J.* 4/30/96 p. 3.

Wechsler, David A. and Lisa Weinstein, "Gifting the House to Save the Home: Qualified Personal Residence Trusts," 12 *Washington Lawyer* 30 (November–December '97).

White, Richard S., "Trust Professionals Can Excel in a Period of Significant Change," 136 Trusts & Estates 50 (March '97).

INDEX

370